MORE PRAISE FROM ACROSS THE NATION
FOR THE JOBBANK SERIES...

"If you are looking for a job, you need to know which industries are hiring. Then you need to know which employers fall within those industries. *The Houston JobBank* tells you this and much more."
-Joel C. Wagher, Labor Market Analyst
Texas Workforce Commission

"*JobBank* books are all devoted to specific job markets. This is helpful if you are thinking about working in cities like San Antonio, Washington, Boston, or states such as Tennessee or the Carolinas. You can use them for research, and a particularly useful feature is the inclusion of the type of positions that are commonly offered at the companies listed."
-Karen Ronald, Library Director
Wilton Library, Wilton, CT

"Help on the job hunt ... Anyone who is job-hunting in the New York area can find a lot of useful ideas in a new paperback called *The Metropolitan New York JobBank* ..."
-Angela Taylor, *New York Times*

"For those graduates whose parents are pacing the floor, conspicuously placing circled want ads around the house and typing up resumes, [*The Carolina JobBank*] answers job-search questions."
-*Greensboro News and Record*

"A timely book for Chicago job hunters follows books from the same publisher that were well received in New York and Boston ... [*The Chicago JobBank* is] a fine tool for job hunters ..."
-Clarence Peterson, *Chicago Tribune*

"Job-hunting is never fun, but this book can ease the ordeal ... [*The Los Angeles JobBank*] will help allay fears, build confidence, and avoid wheel-spinning."
-Robert W. Ross, *Los Angeles Times*

"Job hunters can't afford to waste time. *The Minneapolis-St. Paul JobBank* contains information that used to require hours of research in the library."
-Carmella Zagone
Minneapolis-based Human Resources Administrator

"A superior series of job-hunt directories."
-Cornell University Career Center's *Where to Start*

"*The Florida JobBank* is an invaluable job-search reference tool. It provides the most up-to-date information and contact names available for companies in Florida. I should know -- it worked for me!"
-Rhonda Cody, Human Resources Consultant
Aetna Life and Casualty

"*The Boston JobBank* provides a handy map of employment possibilities in greater Boston. This book can help in the initial steps of a job search by locating major employers, describing their business activities, and for most firms, by naming the contact person and listing typical professional positions. For recent college graduates, as well as experienced professionals, *The Boston JobBank* is an excellent place to begin a job search."
-Juliet F. Brudney, Career Columnist
Boston Globe

"No longer can jobseekers feel secure about finding employment just through want ads. With the tough competition in the job market, particularly in the Boston area, they need much more help. For this reason, *The Boston JobBank* will have a wide and appreciative audience of new graduates, job changers, and people relocating to Boston. It provides a good place to start a search for entry-level professional positions."
-Journal of College Placement

"If you are looking for a job ... before you go to the newspapers and the help-wanted ads, listen to Bob Adams, publisher of *The Metropolitan New York JobBank*."
-Tom Brokaw, *NBC*

"Because our listing is seen by people across the nation, it generates lots of resumes for us. We encourage unsolicited resumes. We'll always be listed [in *The Chicago JobBank*] as long as I'm in this career."
-Tom Fitzpatrick, Director of Human Resources
Merchandise Mart Properties, Inc.

"*The Phoenix JobBank* is a first-class publication. The information provided is useful and current."
-Lyndon Denton
Director of Human Resources and Materials Management
Apache Nitrogen Products, Inc.

"*The Seattle JobBank* is an essential resource for job hunters."
-Gil Lopez, Staffing Team Manager
Battelle Pacific Northwest Laboratories

"*The San Francisco Bay Area JobBank* ... is a highly useful guide, with plenty of how-to's ranging from resume tips to interview dress codes and research shortcuts."
-A.S. Ross, *San Francisco Examiner*

What makes the
JobBank series
the nation's premier
line of employment guides?

With vital employment information on thousands of employers across the nation, the JobBank series is the most comprehensive and authoritative set of career directories available today.

Each book in the series provides information on **dozens of different industries** in a given city or area, with the primary employer listings providing contact information, telephone and fax numbers, addresses, Websites, a summary of the firm's business, and in many cases descriptions of the firm's typical professional job categories, the principal educational backgrounds sought, internships, and the fringe benefits offered.

In addition to the **detailed primary employer listings,** JobBank books give telephone numbers and addresses for **thousands of additional employers,** as well as information about executive search firms, placement agencies, and professional associations.

All of the reference information in the JobBank series is as up-to-date and accurate as possible. Every year, the entire database is thoroughly researched and verified by mail and by telephone. Adams Media Corporation publishes **more local employment guides more often** than any other publisher of career directories.

In addition, the JobBank series features current information about the local job scene -- **forecasts on which industries are the hottest** and **lists of regional professional associations,** so you can get your job hunt started off right.

The JobBank series offers **32 regional titles,** from Minneapolis to Houston, and from Boston to San Francisco. All of the information is organized geographically, because most people look for jobs in specific areas of the country.

A condensed, but thorough, review of the entire job search process is presented in the chapter **The Basics of Job Winning**, a feature which has received many compliments from career counselors. In addition, each JobBank directory includes a section on **resumes and cover letters** the *New York Times* has acclaimed as "excellent."

The JobBank series gives job hunters the most comprehensive, timely, and accurate career information, organized and indexed to facilitate the job search. An entire career reference library, JobBank books are the consummate employment guides.

Top career publications from Adams Media Corporation

1999
THE Dallas–
Fort Worth
JobBank

<table>
<tr><td>*Managing Editor:*</td><td>Steven Graber</td></tr>
<tr><td>*Assistant Managing Editor:*</td><td>Jennifer J. Pfalzgraf</td></tr>
<tr><td>*Senior Editor:*</td><td>Marcie DiPietro</td></tr>
<tr><td>*Senior Associate Editors:*</td><td>Michelle Roy Kelly
Heidi E. Sampson</td></tr>
<tr><td>*Editorial Assistants:*</td><td>Michelle Forcier Anderson
Jayna S. Stafford
Heather Vinhateiro</td></tr>
</table>

Adams Media Corporation
HOLBROOK, MASSACHUSETTS

Published by Adams Media Corporation
260 Center Street, Holbrook, MA 02343

Manufactured in the United States of America.

Because addresses and telephone numbers of smaller companies change rapidly, we recommend you call each company and verify the information before mailing to the employers listed in this book. Mass mailings are not recommended.

While the publisher has made every reasonable effort to obtain and verify accurate information, occasional errors are inevitable due to the magnitude of the database. Should you discover an error, or if a company is missing, please write the editors at the above address so that we may update future editions.

"This publication is designed to provide accurate and authoritative information with regard to the subject matter covered. It is sold with the understanding that the publisher is not engaged in rendering legal, accounting, or other professional advice. If legal advice or other expert assistance is required, the services of a competent professional person should be sought."
--From a *Declaration of Principles* jointly adopted by a Committee of the American Bar Association and a Committee of Publishers and Associations

The appearance of a listing in the book does not constitute an endorsement from the publisher.

ISBN: 1-58062-086-8
ISSN: 1069-5435

This book is available at quantity discounts for bulk purchases.
For information, call 800/872-5627.

Visit our exciting job and career site at http://www.careercity.com

TABLE OF CONTENTS

INTRODUCTION

HOW TO USE THIS BOOK

Right now, you hold in your hands one of the most effective job-hunting tools available anywhere. In *The Dallas-Fort Worth JobBank*, you will find a wide array of valuable information to help you launch or continue a rewarding career. But before you open to the book's employer listings and start calling about current job openings, take a few minutes to learn how best to use the resources presented in *The Dallas-Fort Worth JobBank*.

The Dallas-Fort Worth JobBank will help you to stand out from other jobseekers. While many people looking for a new job rely solely on newspaper help-wanted ads, this book offers you a much more effective job-search method -- direct contact. The direct contact method has been proven twice as effective as scanning the help-wanted ads. Instead of waiting for employers to come looking for you, you'll be far more effective going to them. While many of your competitors will use trial and error methods in trying to set up interviews, you'll learn not only how to get interviews, but what to expect once you've got them.

In the next few pages, we'll take you through each section of the book so you'll be prepared to get a jump-start on your competition.

Basics of Job Winning

Preparation. Strategy. Time-management. These are three of the most important elements of a successful job search. *Basics of Job Winning* helps you address these and all the other elements needed to find the right job.

One of your first priorities should be to define your personal career objectives. What qualities make a job desirable to you? Creativity? High pay? Prestige? Use *Basics of Job Winning* to weigh these questions. Then use the rest of the chapter to design a strategy to find a job that matches your criteria.

In *Basics of Job Winning*, you'll learn which job-hunting techniques work, and which don't. We've reviewed the pros and cons of mass mailings, help-wanted ads, and direct contact. We'll show you how to develop and approach contacts in your field; how to research a prospective employer; and how to use that information to get an interview and the job.

Also included in *Basics of Job Winning*: interview dress code and etiquette, the "do's and don'ts" of interviewing, sample interview questions, and more. We also deal with some of the unique problems faced by those jobseekers who are currently employed, those who have lost a job, and college students conducting their first job search.

Resumes and Cover Letters

The approach you take to writing your resume and cover letter can often mean the difference between getting an interview and never being noticed. In this section, we discuss different formats, as well as what to put on (and what to leave off) your resume. We review the benefits and drawbacks of professional resume writers, and the importance of a follow-up letter. Also included in this section are sample resumes and cover letters which you can use as models.

CD-ROM Job Search

Jobseekers who are looking for an edge against the competition may want to check out these CD-ROM products.

The Employer Listings

Employers are listed alphabetically by industry, and within each industry, by company names. When a company does business under a person's name, like "John Smith & Co.," the company is usually listed by the surname's spelling (in this case "S"). Exceptions occur when a company's name is widely recognized, like "JCPenney" or "Howard Johnson Motor Lodge." In those cases, the company's first name is the key ("J" and "H" respectively).

The Dallas-Fort Worth JobBank covers a very wide range of industries. Each company profile is assigned to one of the industry chapters listed below.

Accounting and Management Consulting
Advertising, Marketing, and Public
   Relations
Aerospace
Apparel and Textiles
Architecture, Construction, and
   Engineering
Arts and Entertainment/Recreation
Automotive
Banking/Savings and Loans
Biotechnology, Pharmaceuticals, and
   Scientific R&D
Business Services and Non-Scientific
   Research
Charities and Social Services
Chemicals/Rubber and Plastics
Communications: Telecommunications
   and Broadcasting
Computer Hardware, Software, and
   Services
Educational Services
Electronic/Industrial Electrical
   Equipment

Environmental and Waste Management
   Services
Fabricated/Primary Metals and Products
Financial Services
Food and Beverages/Agriculture
Government
Health Care: Services, Equipment, and
   Products
Hotels and Restaurants
Insurance
Legal Services
Manufacturing: Miscellaneous Consumer
Manufacturing: Miscellaneous Industrial
Mining/Gas/Petroleum/Energy Related
Paper and Wood Products
Printing and Publishing
Real Estate
Retail
Stone, Clay, Glass, and Concrete
   Products
Transportation/Travel
Utilities: Electric/Gas/Water
Miscellaneous Wholesaling

Many of the company listings offer detailed company profiles. In addition to company names, addresses, and phone numbers, these listings also include contact names or hiring departments, and descriptions of each company's products and/or services. Many of these listings also feature a variety of additional information including:

Common positions - A list of job titles that the company commonly fills when it is hiring, organized in alphabetical order from Accountant to X-ray Technician. Note: Keep in mind that *The Dallas-Fort Worth JobBank* is a directory of major employers in the area, not a directory of openings currently available. Many of the companies listed will be hiring, others will not.

However, since most professional job openings are filled without the placement of help-wanted ads, contacting the employers in this book directly is still a more effective method than browsing the Sunday papers.

Educational backgrounds sought - A list of educational backgrounds that companies seek when hiring.

Benefits - What kind of benefits packages are available from these employers? Here you'll find a broad range of benefits, from the relatively common (medical insurance) to those that are much more rare (health club membership; child daycare assistance).

Special programs - Does the company offer training programs, internships, or apprenticeships? These programs can be important to first time jobseekers and college students looking for practical work experience. Many employer profiles will include information on these programs.

Parent company - If an employer is a subsidiary of a larger company, the name of that parent company will often be listed here. Use this information to supplement your company research before contacting the employer.

Number of employees - The number of workers a company employs.

Company listings may also include information on other U.S. locations and any stock exchanges the firm may be listed on.

Because so many job openings are with small and mid-sized employers, we've also included the addresses and phone numbers of such employers. While none of these listings include any additional hiring information, many of them do offer rewarding career opportunities. These companies are found under each industry heading. Within each industry, they are organized by the type of product or service offered.

A note on all employer listings that appear in *The Dallas-Fort Worth JobBank*: This book is intended as a starting point. It is not intended to replace any effort that you, the jobseeker, should devote to your job hunt. Keep in mind that while a great deal of effort has been put into collecting and verifying the company profiles provided in this book, addresses and contact names change regularly. Inevitably, some contact names listed herein have changed even before you read this. We recommend you contact a company before mailing your resume to ensure nothing has changed.

At the end of each industry section, we have included a directory of other industry-specific resources to help you in your job search. These include: professional and industrial associations, many of which can provide employment advice and job-search help; magazines that cover the industry; and additional directories that may supplement the employer listings in this book.

Employment Services

Immediately following the employer listings section of this book are listings of local employment services firms. Many jobseekers supplement their own efforts by contracting "temp" services, headhunters, and other employment search firms to generate potential job opportunities.

This section is a comprehensive listing of such firms, arranged alphabetically under the headings Temporary Employment Agencies, Permanent Employment Agencies, and Executive Search Firms. Each listing includes the firm's name, address, telephone number, and contact person. Most listings also include the industries the firm specializes in, the type of positions commonly filled, and the number of jobs filled annually.

Index

The Dallas-Fort Worth JobBank index is a straight alphabetical listing.

THE JOB SEARCH

THE BASICS OF JOB WINNING:
A CONDENSED REVIEW

This chapter is divided into four sections. The first section explains the fundamentals that every jobseeker should know, especially first-time jobseekers. The following three sections deal with special situations faced by specific types of jobseekers: those who are currently employed, those who have lost a job, and college students.

THE BASICS:
Things Everyone Needs to Know

Career Planning   The first step to finding your ideal job is to clearly define your objectives. This is better known as career planning (or life planning if you wish to emphasize the importance of combining the two). Career planning has become a field of study in and of itself.

If you are thinking of choosing or switching careers, we particularly emphasize two things. First, choose a career where you will enjoy most of the day-to-day tasks. This sounds obvious, but most of us have at one point or another been attracted by a glamour industry or a prestigious job title without thinking of the most important consideration: Would we enjoy performing the everyday tasks the position entails?

The second key consideration is that you are not merely choosing a career, but also a lifestyle. Career counselors indicate that one of the most common problems people encounter in job-seeking is that they fail to consider how well-suited they are for a particular position or career. For example, some people, attracted to management consulting by good salaries, early responsibility, and high-level corporate exposure, do not adapt well to the long hours, heavy travel demands, and constant pressure to produce. Be sure to ask yourself how you might adapt to not only the day-to-day duties and working environment that a specific position entails, but also how you might adapt to the demands of that career or industry choice as a whole.

Choosing Your Strategy   Assuming that you've established your career objectives, the next step of the job search is to develop a strategy. If you don't take the time to develop a strategy and lay out a plan, you may find yourself going in circles after several weeks of randomly searching for opportunities that always seem just beyond your reach.

The most common job-seeking techniques are:

- following up on help-wanted advertisements
- using employment services
- relying on personal contacts
- contacting employers directly (the Direct Contact method)

Many professionals have been successful in finding better jobs using each one of these approaches. However, the Direct Contact method boasts twice the success rate of the others. So unless you have specific reasons to believe that other strategies would work best for you, Direct Contact should form the foundation of your job search.

If you prefer to use other methods as well, try to expend at least half your effort on Direct Contact, spending the rest on all of the other methods combined. Millions of other jobseekers have already proven that Direct Contact has been twice as effective in obtaining employment, so why not benefit from their experience?

With your strategy in mind, the next step is to work out the details of **Setting** your search. The most important detail is setting up a schedule. Of course, **Your** since job searches aren't something most people do regularly, it may be **Schedule** hard to estimate how long each step will take. Nonetheless, it is important to have a plan so that you can monitor your progress.

When outlining your job search schedule, have a realistic time frame in mind. If you will be job-searching full-time, your search could take at least two months or more. If you can only devote part-time effort, it will probably take at least four months.

You probably know a few currently employed people who seem to spend their whole lives searching for a better job in their spare time. Don't be one of them. If you are presently working and don't feel like devoting a lot of energy to job-seeking right now, then wait. Focus on enjoying your present position,

> **The first step in beginning your job search is to clearly define your objectives.**

performing your best on the job, and storing up energy for when you are really ready to begin your job search.

Those of you who are currently unemployed should remember that job-hunting is tough work physically and emotionally. It is also intellectually demanding work that requires you to be at your best. So don't tire yourself out by working on your job campaign around the clock. At the same time, be sure to discipline yourself. The most logical way to manage your time while looking for a job is to keep your regular working hours.

If you are searching full-time and have decided to choose several different contact methods, we recommend that you divide up each week, designating some time for each method. By trying several approaches at once, you can evaluate how promising each seems and alter your schedule accordingly. But be careful -- don't judge the success of a particular technique just by the sheer number of interviews you obtain. Positions advertised in the newspaper, for instance, are likely to generate many more interviews per opening than positions that are filled without being advertised.

If you are searching part-time and decide to try several different contact methods, we recommend that you try them sequentially. You simply won't have enough time to put a meaningful amount of effort into more than one method at once. Estimate the length of your job search, and then allocate so many weeks or months for each contact method, beginning with Direct Contact.

And remember that all schedules are meant to be broken. The purpose of setting a schedule is not to rush you to your goal but to help you periodically evaluate how you're progressing.

The Direct Contact Method

Once you have scheduled your time, you are ready to begin your search in earnest. If you decide to begin with the Direct Contact method, the first step is to develop a checklist for categorizing the types of firms for which you'd like to work. You might categorize firms by product line, size, customer type (such as industrial or consumer), growth prospects, or geographical location. Your list of important criteria might be very short. If it is, good! The shorter it is, the easier it will be to locate a company that is right for you.

Now you will want to use this *JobBank* book to assemble your list of potential employers. Choose firms where *you* are most likely to be able to find a job. Try matching your skills with those that a specific job demands. Consider where your skills might be in demand, the degree of competition for employment, and the employment outlook at each company.

Separate your prospect list into three groups. The first 25 percent will be your primary target group, the next 25 percent will be your secondary group, and the remaining names you can keep in reserve.

After you form your prospect list, begin work on your resume. Refer to the Resumes and Cover Letters section following this chapter to get ideas.

Once your resume is complete, begin researching your first batch of prospective employers. You will want to determine whether you would be happy working at the firms you are researching and to get a better idea of what their employment needs might be. You also need to obtain enough information to sound highly informed about the company during phone conversations and in mail correspondence. But don't go all out on your research yet! You probably won't be able to arrange interviews with some of these firms, so save your big research effort until you start to arrange interviews. Nevertheless, you should plan to spend several hours researching each firm. Do your research in batches to save time and energy. Start with

> **The more you know about a company, the more likely you are to catch an interviewer's eye. (You'll also face fewer surprises once you get the job!)**

this book, and find out what you can about each of the firms in your primary target group. Contact any pertinent professional associations that may be able to help you learn more about an employer. Read industry publications looking for articles on the firm. (Addresses of associations and names of important publications are listed after each industrial section of employer listings in this book.) Then try additional resources at your local library. Keep organized, and maintain a folder on each firm.

If you discover something that really disturbs you about the firm (they are about to close their only local office), or if you discover that your chances of getting a job there are practically nil (they have just instituted a hiring freeze), then cross them off your prospect list. If possible,

---

DEVELOPING YOUR CONTACTS: NETWORKING

Some career counselors feel that the best route to a better job is through somebody you already know or through somebody to whom you can be introduced. These counselors recommend that you build your contact base beyond your current acquaintances by asking each one to introduce you, or refer you, to additional people in your field of interest.

The theory goes like this: You might start with 15 personal contacts, each of whom introduces you to three additional people, for a total of 45 additional contacts. Then each of these people introduces you to three additional people, which adds 135 additional contacts. Theoretically, you will soon know every person in the industry.

Of course, developing your personal contacts does not work quite as smoothly as the theory suggests because some people will not be able to introduce you to anyone. The further you stray from your initial contact base, the weaker your references may be. So, if you do try developing your own contacts, try to begin with as many people that you know personally as you can. Dig into your personal phone book and your holiday greeting card list and locate old classmates from school. Be particularly sure to approach people who perform your personal business such as your lawyer, accountant, banker, doctor, stockbroker, and insurance agent. These people develop a very broad contact base due to the nature of their professions.

---

supplement your research efforts by contacting individuals who know the firm well. Ideally you should make an informal contact with someone at that particular firm, but often a direct competitor, or a major supplier or customer, will be able to supply you with just as much information. At the very least, try to obtain whatever printed information the company has available -- not just annual reports, but product brochures and any other printed materials that the firm may have to offer, either about its operations or about career opportunities.

142041

Getting the Interview

Now it is time to arrange an interview, time to make the Direct Contact. If you have read many books on job-searching, you may have noticed that most of these books tell you to avoid the personnel office like the plague. It is said that the personnel office never hires people; they screen candidates. Unfortunately, this is often the case. If you can identify the appropriate manager with the authority to hire you, you should try to contact that person directly. However, this will take a lot of time in each case, and often you'll be bounced back to personnel despite your efforts. So we suggest that initially you begin your Direct Contact campaign through personnel offices. If it seems that the firms on your prospect list do little hiring through personnel, you might consider some alternative courses of action.

The three obvious means of initiating Direct Contact are:

- Showing up unannounced
- Mail (postal or electronic)
- Phone calls

Cross out the first one right away. You should never show up to seek a professional position without an appointment. Even if you are somehow lucky enough to obtain an interview, you will appear so unprofessional that you will not be seriously considered.

Mail contact seems to be a good choice if you have not been in the job market for a while. You can take your time to prepare a letter, say exactly what you want, and of course include your resume. Remember that employers receive many resumes every day. Don't be surprised if you do not get a response to your inquiry, and don't spend weeks waiting for responses that may never come. If you do send a letter, follow it up (or precede it) with a phone call. This will increase your impact, and because of the initial research you did, will underscore both your familiarity with and your interest in the firm.

Another alternative is to make a "cover call." Your cover call should be just like your cover letter: concise. Your first statement should interest the employer in you. Then try to subtly mention your familiarity with the firm. Don't be overbearing; keep your introduction to three sentences or less. Be pleasant, self-confident, and relaxed. This will greatly increase the chances of the person at the other end of the line developing the conversation. But don't press. If you are asked to follow up with "something in the mail," this signals the conversation's natural end. Don't try to prolong the conversation once it has ended, and don't ask what they want to receive in the mail. Always send your resume and a highly personalized follow-up letter, reminding the addressee of the phone conversation. *Always* include a cover letter if you are asked to send a resume.

> **Always include a cover letter if you are asked to send a resume.**

Unless you are in telephone sales, making smooth and relaxed cover calls will probably not come easily. Practice them on your own, and then with your friends or relatives.

If you obtain an interview as a result of a telephone conversation, be sure to send a thank-you note reiterating the points you made during the

DON'T BOTHER WITH MASS MAILINGS OR BARRAGES OF PHONE CALLS

Direct Contact does not mean burying every firm within a hundred miles with mail and phone calls. Mass mailings rarely work in the job hunt. This also applies to those letters that are personalized -- but dehumanized -- on an automatic typewriter or computer. Don't waste your time or money on such a project; you will fool no one but yourself.

The worst part of sending out mass mailings, or making unplanned phone calls to companies you have not researched, is that you are likely to be remembered as someone with little genuine interest in the firm, who lacks sincerity -- somebody that nobody wants to hire.

HELP WANTED ADVERTISEMENTS

Only a small fraction of professional job openings are advertised. Yet the majority of jobseekers -- and quite a few people not in the job market -- spend a lot of time studying the help wanted ads. As a result, the competition for advertised openings is often very severe.

A moderate-sized employer told us about their experience advertising in the help wanted section of a major Sunday newspaper:

It was a disaster. We had over 500 responses from this relatively small ad in just one week. We have only two phone lines in this office and one was totally knocked out. We'll never advertise for professional help again.

If you insist on following up on help wanted ads, then research a firm before you reply to an ad. Preliminary research might help to separate you from all of the other professionals responding to that ad, many of whom will have only a passing interest in the opportunity. It will also give you insight about a particular firm, to help you determine if it is potentially a good match. That said, your chances of obtaining a job through the want ads are still much smaller than they are with the Direct Contact method.

conversation. You will appear more professional and increase your impact. However, unless specifically requested, don't mail your resume once an interview has been arranged. Take it with you to the interview instead.

Preparing for the Interview   Once the interview has been arranged, begin your in-depth research. You should arrive at an interview knowing the company upside-down and inside-out. You need to know the company's products, types of customers, subsidiaries, parent company, principal locations, rank in the industry, sales and profit trends, type of ownership, size, current plans, and much more. By this time you have probably narrowed your job search to one industry. Even if you haven't, you should still be familiar with the trends in the firm's industry, the firm's principal competitors and their relative performance, and the direction in which the industry leaders are headed.

Dig into every resource you can! Read the company literature, the trade press, the business press, and if the company is public, call your stockbroker (if you have one) and ask for additional information. If possible, speak to someone at the firm before the interview, or if not, speak to someone at a competing firm. The more time you spend, the better. Even if you feel extremely pressed for time, you should set aside several hours for pre-interview research.

> You should arrive at an interview knowing the company upside-down and inside-out.

If you have been out of the job market for some time, don't be surprised if you find yourself tense during your first few interviews. It will probably happen every time you re-enter the market, not just when you seek your first job after getting out of school.

Tension is natural during an interview, but knowing you have done a thorough research job should put you more at ease. Make a list of questions that you think might be asked in each interview. Think out your answers carefully and practice them with a friend. Tape record your responses to the problem questions. If you feel particularly unsure of your interviewing skills, arrange your first interviews at firms you are not as interested in. (But remember it is common courtesy to seem enthusiastic about the possibility of working for any firm at which you interview.) Practice again on your own after these first few interviews. Go over the difficult questions that you were asked.

Interview Attire   How important is the proper dress for a job interview? Buying a complete wardrobe of Brooks Brothers pinstripes or Donna Karan suits, donning new wing tips or pumps, and having your hair styled every morning are not enough to guarantee you a career position as an investment banker. But on the other hand, if you can't find a clean, conservative suit or won't take the time to wash your hair, then you are just wasting your time by interviewing at all.

Top personal grooming is as important as finding appropriate clothes for a job interview. Careful grooming indicates both a sense of thoroughness and self-confidence. This is not the time to make a statement -- take out the extra earrings and avoid any garish hair colors not found in nature. Women should not wear excessive makeup, and both men and women should refrain from wearing any perfume or cologne (it only takes a small spritz to leave an allergic interviewer with a fit of sneezing and a bad impression of your meeting). Men should be freshly shaven, even if the interview is late in the day, and men with long hair should have it pulled back and neat.

Men applying for any professional position should wear a suit, preferably in a conservative color such as navy or charcoal gray. It is easy to get away with wearing the same dark suit to consecutive interviews at the same company; just be sure to wear a different shirt and tie for each interview.

Women should also wear a businesslike suit. Professionalism still dictates a suit with a skirt, rather than slacks, as proper interview garb for women. This is usually true even at companies where pants are acceptable attire for female employees. As much as you may disagree with this guideline, the more prudent time to fight this standard is after you land the job.

SKIRT VS. PANTS:
An Interview Dilemma

For those women who are still convinced that pants are acceptable interview attire, listen to the words of one career counselor from a prestigious New England college:

I had a student who told me that since she knew women in her industry often wore pants to work, she was going to wear pants to her interviews. Almost every recruiter commented that her pants were "too casual," and even referred to her as "the one with the pants." The funny thing was that one of the recruiters who commented on her pants had been wearing jeans!

The final selection of candidates for a job opening won't be determined by dress, of course. However, inappropriate dress can quickly eliminate a first-round candidate. So while you shouldn't spend a fortune on a new wardrobe, you should be sure that your clothes are adequate. The key is to dress at least as formally or slightly more formally and more conservatively than the position would suggest.

What to Bring   Be complete. Everyone needs a watch, a pen, and a notepad. Finally, a briefcase or a leather-bound folder (containing extra, *unfolded*, copies of your resume) will help complete the look of professionalism.

Sometimes the interviewer will be running behind schedule. Don't be upset, be sympathetic. There is often pressure to interview a lot of candidates and to quickly fill a demanding position. So be sure to come to your interview with good reading material to keep yourself occupied and relaxed.

The Interview   The very beginning of the interview is the most important part because it determines the tone for the rest of it. Those first few moments are especially crucial. Do you smile when you meet? Do you establish enough eye contact, but not too much? Do you walk into the office with a self-assured and confident stride? Do you shake hands firmly? Do you

---

BE PREPARED:
Some Common Interview Questions

Tell me about yourself...

Why did you leave your last job?

What excites you in your current job?

Where would you like to be in five years?

How much overtime are you willing to work?

What would your previous/present employer tell me about you?

Tell me about a difficult situation that you
faced at your previous/present job.

What are your greatest strengths?

What are your greatest weaknesses?

Describe a work situation where you took initiative
and went beyond your normal responsibilities.

Why do you wish to work for this firm?

Why should we hire you?

make small talk easily without being garrulous? It is human nature to judge people by that first impression, so make sure it is a good one. But most of all, try to be yourself.

Often the interviewer will begin, after the small talk, by telling you about the company, the division, the department, or perhaps, the position. Because of your detailed research, the information about the company should be repetitive for you, and the interviewer would probably like nothing better than to avoid this regurgitation of the company biography. So if you can do so tactfully, indicate to the interviewer that you are very familiar with the firm. If he or she seems intent on providing you with background information, despite your hints, then acquiesce.

But be sure to remain attentive. If you can manage to generate a brief discussion of the company or the industry at this point, without being forceful, great. It will help to further build rapport, underscore your interest, and increase your impact.

Soon (if it didn't begin that way) the interviewer will begin the questions, many of which you will have already practiced. This period of the interview usually falls into one of two categories (or somewhere in between): either a structured interview, where the interviewer has a prescribed set of questions to ask; or an unstructured interview, where the interviewer will ask only leading questions to get you to talk about

> **The interviewer's job is to find a reason to turn you down; your job is to not provide that reason.**
>
> -John L. LaFevre, author,
> *How You Really Get Hired*
>
> Reprinted from the 1989/90 *CPC Annual,* with permission of the National Association of Colleges and Employers (formerly College Placement Council, Inc.), copyright holder.

yourself, your experiences, and your goals. Try to sense as quickly as possible in which direction the interviewer wishes to proceed. This will make the interviewer feel more relaxed and in control of the situation.

Remember to keep attuned to the interviewer and make the length of your answers appropriate to the situation. If you are really unsure as to how detailed a response the interviewer is seeking, then ask.

As the interview progresses, the interviewer will probably mention some of the most important responsibilities of the position. If applicable, draw parallels between your experience and the demands of the position as detailed by the interviewer. Describe your past experience in the same manner that you do on your resume: emphasizing results and achievements and not merely describing activities. But don't exaggerate. Be on the level about your abilities.

The first interview is often the toughest, where many candidates are screened out. If you are interviewing for a very competitive position, you will have to make an impression that will last. Focus on a few of your greatest strengths that are relevant to the position. Develop these points carefully, state them again in different words, and then try to summarize them briefly at the end of the interview.

Often the interviewer will pause toward the end and ask if you have any questions. Particularly in a structured interview, this might be the one chance to really show your knowledge of and interest in the firm. Have a list prepared of specific questions that are of real interest to you. Let your questions subtly show your research and your knowledge of the firm's activities. It is wise to have an extensive list of questions, as several of them may be answered during the interview.

> **Getting a job offer is a lot like getting a marriage proposal. Someone is not going to offer it unless they're pretty sure you're going to accept it.**
>
> -Marilyn Hill,
> Associate Director,
> Career Center,
> Carleton College

Do not turn your opportunity to ask questions into an interrogation. Avoid reading directly from your list of questions, and ask questions that you are fairly certain the interviewer can answer (remember how you feel when you cannot answer a question during an interview).

Even if you are unable to determine the salary range beforehand, do not ask about it during the first interview. You can always ask about it later. Above all, don't ask about fringe benefits until you have been offered a position. (Then be sure to get all the details.)

Try not to be negative about anything during the interview (particularly any past employer or any previous job). Be cheerful. Everyone likes to work with someone who seems to be happy.

Don't let a tough question throw you off base. If you don't know the answer to a question, simply say so -- do not apologize. Just smile. Nobody can answer every question -- particularly some of the questions that are asked in job interviews.

Before your first interview, you may be able to determine how many rounds of interviews there usually are for positions at your level. (Of course it may differ quite a bit even within the different levels of one firm.) Usually you can count on attending at least two or three interviews, although some firms are known to give a minimum of six interviews for all professional positions. While you should be more relaxed as you return for subsequent interviews, the pressure will be on. The more prepared you are, the better.

Depending on what information you are able to obtain, you might want to vary your strategy quite a bit from interview to interview. For instance, if the first interview is a screening interview, then be sure a few of your strengths really stand out. On the other hand, if later interviews are primarily with people who are in a position to veto your hiring, but not to push it forward, then you should primarily focus on building rapport as opposed to reiterating and developing your key strengths.

If it looks as though your skills and background do not match the position the interviewer was hoping to fill, ask him or her if there is another division or subsidiary that perhaps could profit from your talents.

Write a follow-up letter immediately after the interview, while it is still fresh in the interviewer's mind (see the sample follow-up letter format found in the Resumes and Cover Letters chapter). Then, if you haven't heard from the interviewer within a week, call to stress your continued interest in the firm, and the position, and request a second interview. **After the Interview**

THE BALANCING ACT:
Looking for a New Job While Currently Employed

For those of you who are still employed, job-searching will be particularly tiring because it must be done in addition to your normal work responsibilities. So don't overwork yourself to the point where you show up to interviews looking exhausted and start to slip behind at your current job. On the other hand, don't be tempted to quit your present job! The long hours are worth it. Searching for a job while you have one puts you in a position of strength.

If you're expected to be in your office during the business day, then you have additional problems to deal with. How can you work interviews into the business day? And if you work in an open office, how can you even call to set up interviews? As much as possible you should keep up the effort and the appearances on your present job. So maximize your use of the lunch hour, early mornings, and late afternoons for calling. If you keep trying, you'll be surprised how often you will be able to reach the executive you are trying to contact during your out-of-office hours. You can catch people as early as 8 a.m. and as late as 6 p.m. on frequent occasions. **Making Contact**

Your inability to interview at any time other than lunch just might work to your advantage. If you can, try to set up as many interviews as possible for your lunch hour. This will go a long way to creating a relaxed atmosphere. But be sure the interviews don't stray too far from the agenda on hand. **Scheduling Interviews**

Lunchtime interviews are much easier to obtain if you have substantial career experience. People with less experience will often find no alternative to taking time off for interviews. If you have to take time off, you have to take time off. But try to do this as little as possible. Try to take the whole day off in order to avoid being blatantly obvious about your job search, and try to schedule two to three interviews for the same day. (It is very difficult to maintain an optimum level of energy at more than three interviews in one day.) Explain to the interviewer why you might have to juggle your interview schedule -- he/she should honor the respect you're

> **Try calling as early as 8 a.m. and as late as 6 p.m. You'll be surprised how often you will be able to reach the executive you want during these times of the day.**

showing your current employer by minimizing your days off and will probably appreciate the fact that another prospective employer is interested in you.

References What do you tell an interviewer who asks for references? Just say that while you are happy to have your former employers contacted, you are trying to keep your job search confidential and would rather that your current employer not be contacted until you have been given a firm offer.

IF YOU'RE FIRED OR LAID OFF:
Picking Yourself Up and Dusting Yourself Off

If you've been fired or laid off, you are not the first and will not be the last to go through this traumatic experience. In today's changing economy, thousands of professionals lose their jobs every year. Even if you were terminated with just cause, do not lose heart. Remember, being fired is not a reflection on you as a person. It is usually a reflection of your company's staffing needs and its perception of your recent job performance and attitude. And if you were not performing up to par or enjoying your work, then you will probably be better off at another company anyway.

> **Be prepared for the question "Why were you fired?" during job interviews.**

A thorough job search could take months, so be sure to negotiate a reasonable severance package, if possible, and determine what benefits, such as health insurance, you are still legally entitled to. Also, register for unemployment compensation immediately. Don't be surprised to find other professionals collecting unemployment compensation -- it is for everyone who has lost their job.

Don't start your job search with a flurry of unplanned activity. Start by choosing a strategy and working out a plan. Now is not the time for major changes in your life. If possible, remain in the same career and in the same geographical location, at least until you have been working again for a while. On the other hand, if the only industry for which you are trained is leaving, or is severely depressed in your area, then you should give prompt consideration to moving or switching careers.

Avoid mentioning you were fired when arranging interviews, but be prepared for the question "Why were you fired?" during an interview. If you were laid off as a result of downsizing, briefly explain, being sure to reinforce that your job loss was not due to performance. If you were in fact fired, be honest, but try to detail the reason as favorably as possible and portray what you have learned from your mistakes. If you are confident one of your past managers will give you a good reference, tell the interviewer to contact that person. Do not to speak negatively of your past employer and try not to sound particularly worried about your status of being temporarily unemployed.

Finally, don't spend too much time reflecting on why you were let go or how you might have avoided it. Think positively, look to the future, and be sure to follow a careful plan during your job search.

THE COLLEGE STUDENT:
How to Conduct Your First Job Search

While you will be able to apply many of the basics covered earlier in this chapter to your job search, there are some situations unique to the college student's job search.

Gaining Experience

Perhaps the biggest problem college students face is lack of experience. Many schools have internship programs designed to give students exposure to the field of their choice, as well as the opportunity to make valuable contacts. Check out your school's career services department to see what internships are available. If your school does not have a formal internship program, or if there are no available internships that appeal to you, try contacting local businesses and offering your services -- often, businesses will be more than willing to have any extra pair of hands (especially if those hands are unpaid!) for a day or two each week. Or try contacting school alumni to see if you can "shadow" them for a few days, and see what their day-to-day duties are like. Either way, try to begin building experience as early as possible in your college career.

THE GPA QUESTION

You are interviewing for the job of your dreams. Everything is going well: You've established a good rapport, the interviewer seems impressed with your qualifications, and you're almost positive the job is yours. Then you're asked about your GPA, which is pitifully low. Do you tell the truth and watch your dream job fly out the window?

Never lie about your GPA (they may request your transcript, and no company will hire a liar). You can, however, explain if there is a reason you don't feel your grades reflect your abilities, and mention any other impressive statistics. For example, if you have a high GPA in your major, or in the last few semesters (as opposed to your cumulative college career), you can use that fact to your advantage.

What do you do if, for whatever reason, you weren't able to get experience directly related to your desired career? First, look at your previous jobs and see if there's anything you can highlight. Did you supervise or train other employees? Did you reorganize the accounting system, or boost productivity in some way? Accomplishments like these demonstrate leadership, responsibility, and innovation -- qualities that most companies look for in employees. And don't forget volunteer activities and school clubs, which can also showcase these traits.

On-Campus Recruiting

Companies will often send recruiters to interview on-site at various colleges. This gives students a chance to get interviews at companies that may not have interviewed them otherwise, particularly if the company schedules "open" interviews, in which the only screening process is who is first in line at the sign-ups. Of course, since many more applicants gain interviews in this format, this also means that many more people are rejected. The on-campus interview is generally a screening interview, to see if it is worth the company's time to invite you in for a second interview. So do everything possible to make yourself stand out from the crowd.

The first step, of course, is to check out any and all information your school's career center has on the company. If the information seems out of date, call the company's headquarters and ask to be sent the latest annual report, or any other printed information.

Many companies will host an informational meeting for interviewees, often the evening before interviews are scheduled to take place. DO NOT MISS THIS MEETING. The recruiter will almost certainly ask if you attended. Make an effort to stay after the meeting and talk with the company's representatives. Not only does this give you an opportunity to find out more information about both the company and the position, it also makes you stand out in the recruiter's mind. If there's a particular company that you had your heart set on, but you weren't able to get an interview with them, attend the information session anyway. You may be able to convince the recruiter to squeeze you into the schedule. (Or you may discover that the company really isn't suited for you after all.)

Try to check out the interview site beforehand. Some colleges may conduct "mock" interviews that take place in one of the standard interview rooms. Or you may be able to convince a career counselor (or even a custodian) to let you sneak a peek during off-hours. Either way, having an idea of the room's setup will help you to mentally prepare.

Be sure to be at least 15 minutes early to the interview. The recruiter may be running ahead of schedule, and might like to take you early. But don't be surprised if previous interviews have run over, resulting in your 30-minute slot being reduced to 20 minutes (or less). Don't complain; just use whatever time you do have as efficiently as possible to showcase the reasons *you* are the ideal candidate.

LAST WORDS

A parting word of advice. Again and again during your job search you will be rejected. You will be rejected when you apply for interviews. You will be rejected after interviews. For every job offer you finally receive, you probably will have been rejected a multitude of times. Don't let rejections slow you down. Keep reminding yourself that the sooner you go out and get started on your job search, and get those rejections flowing in, the closer you will be to obtaining the job you want.

RESUMES AND COVER LETTERS

When filling a position, a recruiter will often have 100-plus applicants, but time to interview only a handful of the most promising ones. As a result, he or she will reject most applicants after only briefly skimming their resumes.

Unless you have phoned and talked to the recruiter -- which you should do whenever you can -- you will be chosen or rejected for an interview entirely on the basis of your resume and cover letter. Your cover letter must catch the recruiter's attention, and your resume must hold it. (But remember -- a resume is no substitute for a job search campaign. *You* must seek a job. Your resume is only one tool.)

RESUME FORMAT:
Mechanics of a First Impression

The Basics

Recruiters dislike long resumes, so unless you have an unusually strong background with many years of experience and a diversity of outstanding achievements, keep your resume length to one page. If you must squeeze in more information than would otherwise fit, try using a smaller typeface or changing the margins.

Keep your resume on standard 8-1/2" x 11" paper. Since recruiters often get resumes in batches of hundreds, a smaller-sized resume may get lost in the pile. Oversized resumes are likely to get crumpled at the edges, and won't fit easily in their files.

First impressions matter, so make sure the recruiter's first impression of your resume is a good one. Print your resume on quality paper that has weight and texture, in a conservative color such as white, ivory, or pale gray. Use matching paper and envelopes for both your resume and cover letter.

Getting it on Paper

Modern photocomposition typesetting gives you the clearest, sharpest image, a wide variety of type styles, and effects such as italics, bold-facing, and book-like justified margins. It is also much too expensive for many jobseekers. And improvements in laser printers mean that a computer-generated resume can look just as impressive as one that has been professionally typeset.

A computer or word processor is the most flexible way to type your resume. This will allow you to make changes almost instantly and to store different drafts on disk. Word processing and desktop publishing systems also offer many different fonts to choose from, each taking up different amounts of space. (It is generally best to stay between 9-point and 12-point font size.) Many other options are also available, such as bold-facing for emphasis, justified margins, and the ability to change and manipulate spacing.

The end result, however, will be largely determined by the quality of the printer you use. You need at least "letter quality" type for your resume. Do not use a "near letter quality" or dot matrix printer. Laser printers will generally provide the best quality.

Household typewriters and office typewriters with nylon or other cloth ribbons are *not* good enough for typing your resume. If you don't have access to a quality word processor, hire a professional who can prepare your resume with a word processor or typesetting machine.

Don't make your copies on an office photocopier. Only the personnel office may see the resume you mail. Everyone else may see only a copy of it, and copies of copies quickly become unreadable. Either print out each copy individually, or take your resume to a professional copy shop, which will generally offer professionally-maintained, extra-high-quality photocopiers and charge fairly reasonable prices.

Proof with Care Whether you typed it yourself or paid to have it produced professionally, mistakes on resumes are not only embarrassing, but will usually remove you from further consideration (particularly if something obvious such as your name is misspelled). No matter how much you paid someone else to type, write, or typeset your resume, *you* lose if there is a mistake. So proofread it as carefully as possible. Get a friend to help you. Read your draft aloud as your friend checks the proof copy. Then have your friend read aloud while you check. Next, read it letter by letter to check spelling and punctuation.

> **The one piece of advice I give to everyone about their resume is: Show it to people, show it to people, show it to people. Before you ever send out a resume, show it to at least a dozen people.**
>
> -Cate Talbot Ashton,
> Associate Director,
> Career Services,
> Colby College

If you are having it typed or typeset by a resume service or a printer, and you can't bring a friend or take the time during the day to proof it, pay for it and take it home. Proof it there and bring it back later to get it corrected and printed.

If you wrote your resume on a word processing program, also use that program's built-in spell checker to double-check for spelling errors. But keep in mind that a spell checker will not find errors such as "to" for "two" or "wok" for "work." It's important that you still proofread your resume, even after it has been spell-checked.

Types of Resumes The two most common resume formats are the functional resume and the chronological resume (examples of both types can be found at the end of this chapter). A functional resume focuses on skills and de-emphasizes job titles, employers, etc. A functional resume is best if you have been out of the work force for a long time and/or if you want to highlight specific skills and strengths that your most recent jobs don't necessarily reflect.

Choose a chronological format if you are currently working or were working recently, and if your most recent experiences relate to your desired field. Use reverse chronological order. To a recruiter your last job and your latest schooling are the most important, so put the last first and list the rest going back in time.

Organization

Your name, phone number, and a complete address should be at the top of your resume. Try to make your name stand out by using a slightly larger font size or all capital letters. Be sure to spell out everything -- never abbreviate St. for Street or Rd. for Road. If you are a college student, you should also put your home address and phone number at the top.

Next, list your experience, then your education. If you are a recent graduate, list your education first, unless your experience is more important than your education. (For example, if you have just graduated from a teaching school, have some business experience, and are applying for a job in business, you would list your business experience first.)

Keep everything easy to find. Put the dates of your employment and education on the left of the page. Put the names of the companies you worked for and the schools you attended a few spaces to the right of the dates. Put the city and state, or the city and country, where you studied or worked to the right of the page.

This is just one suggestion that may work for you. The important thing is simply to break up the text in some way that makes your resume visually attractive and easy to scan, so experiment to see which layout works best for your resume. However you set it up, stay consistent. Inconsistencies in fonts, spacing, or tenses will make your resume look sloppy. Also, be sure to use tabs to keep your information vertically lined up, rather than the less precise space bar.

RESUME CONTENT:
Say it with Style

Sell Yourself

You are selling your skills and accomplishments in your resume, so it is important to inventory yourself and know yourself. If you have achieved something, say so. Put it in the best possible light. But avoid subjective statements, such as "I am a hard worker" or "I get along well with my coworkers." Just stick to the facts.

While you shouldn't hold back or be modest, don't exaggerate your achievements to the point of misrepresentation. Be honest. Many companies will immediately drop an applicant from consideration (or fire a current employee) if inaccurate information is discovered on a resume or other application material.

Keep it Brief   Write down the important (and pertinent) things you have done, but do it in as few words as possible. Your resume will be scanned, not read, and short, concise phrases are much more effective than long-winded sentences. Avoid the use of "I" when emphasizing your accomplishments. Instead, use brief phrases beginning with action verbs.

While some technical terms will be unavoidable, you should try to avoid excessive "technicalese." Keep in mind that the first person to see your resume may be a human resources person who won't necessarily know all the jargon -- and how can they be impressed by something they don't understand?

Also, try to keep your paragraphs at six lines or shorter. If you have more than six lines of information about one job or school, put it in two or more paragraphs. The shorter your resume is, the more carefully it will be examined. Remember: Your resume usually has between eight and 45 seconds to catch an employer's eye. So make every second count.

Job Objective   A functional resume may require a job objective to give it focus. One or two sentences describing the job you are seeking can clarify in what capacity your skills will be best put to use.

Examples: An entry-level position in the publishing industry.
A challenging position requiring analytical thought
and excellent writing skills.

Don't include a job objective in a chronological resume. Even if you are certain of exactly what type of job you desire, the presence of a job objective might eliminate you from consideration for other positions that a recruiter feels are a better match for your qualifications. But even though you may not put an objective on paper, having a career goal in mind as you write can help give your resume a sense of direction.

Work Experience   Some jobseekers may choose to include both "Relevant Experience" and "Additional Experience" sections. This can be useful, as it allows the jobseeker to place more emphasis on certain experiences and to de-emphasize others.

Emphasize continued experience in a particular job area or continued interest in a particular industry. De-emphasize irrelevant positions. Delete positions that you held for less than four months (unless you are a very recent college grad or still in school). Stress your results, elaborating on how you contributed in your previous jobs. Did you increase sales, reduce costs, improve a product, implement a new program? Were you promoted? Use specific numbers (i.e., quantities, percentages, dollar amounts) whenever possible.

Mention all relevant responsibilities. Be specific, and slant your past accomplishments toward the position that you hope to obtain. For example, do you hope to supervise people? If so, then state how many people, performing what function, you have supervised.

Keep it brief if you have more than two years of career experience. **Education** Elaborate more if you have less experience. If you are a recent grad with two or more years of college, you may choose to include any high school activities that are directly relevant to your career. If you've been out of school for awhile, list post-secondary education only.

Mention degrees received and any honors or special awards. Note individual courses or research projects you participated in that might be relevant for employers. For example, if you are an English major applying for a position as a business writer, be sure to mention any business or economics courses.

USE ACTION VERBS

How you write your resume is just as important as *what* you write. The strongest resumes use short phrases beginning with action verbs. Below are a few action verbs you may want to use. (This list is not all-inclusive.)

achieved	developed	integrated	purchased
administered	devised	interpreted	reduced
advised	directed	interviewed	regulated
analyzed	discovered	invented	reorganized
arranged	distributed	launched	represented
assembled	eliminated	maintained	researched
assisted	established	managed	resolved
attained	evaluated	marketed	restored
budgeted	examined	mediated	restructured
built	executed	monitored	revised
calculated	expanded	negotiated	scheduled
collaborated	expedited	obtained	selected
collected	facilitated	operated	served
compiled	formulated	ordered	sold
completed	founded	organized	solved
computed	generated	participated	streamlined
conducted	headed	performed	studied
consolidated	identified	planned	supervised
constructed	implemented	prepared	supplied
consulted	improved	presented	supported
controlled	increased	processed	tested
coordinated	initiated	produced	trained
created	installed	proposed	updated
designed	instituted	provided	upgraded
determined	instructed	published	wrote

Highlight Impressive Skills   Be sure to mention any computer skills you may have. You may wish to include a section entitled "Additional Skills" or "Computer Skills," in which you list any software programs you know. An additional skills section is also an ideal place to mention fluency in a foreign language.

Personal Data   This section is optional, but if you choose to include it, keep it very brief (two lines maximum). A one-word mention of hobbies such as fishing, chess, baseball, cooking, etc., can give the person who will interview you a good way to open up the conversation. It doesn't hurt to include activities that are unusual (fencing, bungee jumping, snake-charming) or that somehow relate to the position or the company you're applying to (for instance, if you are a member of a professional organization in your industry). Never include information about your age, health, physical characteristics, marital status, or religious affiliation.

References   The most that is needed is the sentence, "References available upon request," at the bottom of your resume. If you choose to leave it out, that's fine.

HIRING A RESUME WRITER:
Is it the Right Choice for You?

If you write reasonably well, it is to your advantage to write your own resume. Writing your resume forces you to review your experience and figure out how to explain your accomplishments in clear, brief phrases. This will help you when you explain your work to interviewers.

If you write your resume, everything will be in your own words -- it will sound like you. It will say what you want it to say. If you are a good writer, know yourself well, and have a good idea of which parts of your background employers are looking for, you should be able to write your own resume better than

> **Those things [marital status, church affiliations, etc.] have no place on a resume. Those are illegal questions, so why even put that information on your resume?**
>
> -Becky Hayes, Career Counselor
> Career Services, Rice University

anyone else can. If you decide to write your resume yourself, have as many people review and proofread it as possible. Welcome objective opinions and other perspectives.

When to Get Help   If you have difficulty writing in "resume style" (which is quite unlike normal written language), if you are unsure of which parts of your background you should emphasize, or if you think your resume would make your case better if it did not follow one of the standard forms outlined either here or in a book on resumes, then you should consider having it professionally written.

There are two reasons even some professional resume writers we know have had their resumes written with the help of fellow professionals. First, they may need the help of someone who can be objective about their background, and second, they may want an experienced sounding board to help focus their thoughts.

The best way to choose a writer is by reputation -- the **If You Hire** recommendation of a friend, a personnel director, your school placement **a Pro** officer, or someone else knowledgeable in the field.

Important questions:
- "How long have you been writing resumes?"
- "If I'm not satisfied with what you write, will you go over it with me and change it?"
- "Do you charge by the hour or a flat rate?"

There is no sure relation between price and quality, except that you are unlikely to get a good writer for less than $50 for an uncomplicated resume and you shouldn't have to pay more than $300 unless your experience is very extensive or complicated. There will be additional charges for printing.

Few resume services will give you a firm price over the phone, simply because some resumes are too complicated and take too long to do for a predetermined price. Some services will quote you a price that applies to almost all of their customers. Once you decide to use a specific writer, you should insist on a firm price quote before engaging their services. Also, find out how expensive minor changes will be.

COVER LETTERS:
Quick, Clear, and Concise

Always mail a cover letter with your resume. In a cover letter you can show an interest in the company that you can't show in a resume. You can also point out one or two skills or accomplishments the company can put to good use.

The more personal you can get, the better. If someone known to the **Make it** person you are writing has recommended that you contact the company, **Personal** get permission to include his/her name in the letter. If you have the name of a person to send the letter to, address it directly to that person (after first calling the company to verify the spelling of the person's name, correct title, and mailing address). Be sure to put the person's name and title on both the letter and the envelope. This will ensure that your letter will get through to the proper person, even if a new person now occupies this position. But even if you don't have a contact name and are simply addressing it to the "Personnel Director" or the "Hiring Partner," definitely send a letter.

Type cover letters in full. Don't try the cheap and easy ways, like using a computer mail merge program, or photocopying the body of your letter and typing in the inside address and salutation. You will give the impression that you are mailing to a host of companies and have no particular interest in any one.

Cover letter do's and don'ts

- *Do* keep your cover letter brief and to the point.
- *Do* be sure it is error-free.
- *Don't* just repeat information verbatim from your resume.
- *Don't* overuse the personal pronoun "I."
- *Don't* send a generic cover letter -- show your personal knowledge of and interest in that particular company.
- *Do* accentuate what you can offer the company, not what you hope to gain from them.

FUNCTIONAL RESUME

(Prepared on a word processor
and laser printed.)

ELIZABETH HELEN LaFRANCE
129 Shoreline Drive
Harbor Point OH 45822
419/555-6652

Objective

A position as a graphic designer commensurate with my acquired skills and expertise.

Summary

Extensive experience in plate making, separations, color matching, background definition, printing, mechanicals, color corrections, and personnel supervision. A highly motivated manager and effective communicator. Proven ability to:

- **Create Commercial Graphics**
- **Produce Embossed Drawings**
- **Color Separate**
- **Control Quality**
- **Resolve Printing Problems**
- **Analyze Customer Satisfaction**

Qualifications

Printing:
Knowledgeable in black and white as well as color printing. Excellent judgment in determining acceptability of color reproduction through comparison with original. Proficient at producing four- or five-color corrections on all media, as well as restyling previously reproduced four-color artwork.

Customer Relations:
Routinely work closely with customers to ensure specifications are met. Capable of striking a balance between technical printing capabilities and need for customer satisfaction through entire production process.

Specialties:
Practiced at creating silk screen overlays for a multitude of processes including velo bind, GBC bind, and perfect bind. Creative design and timely preparation of posters, flyers, and personalized stationery.

Personnel Supervision:
Skillful at fostering atmosphere that encourages highly talented artists to balance high-level creativity with maximum production. Consistently meet or beat production deadlines. Instruct new employees, apprentices, and students in both artistry and technical operations.

Experience

Graphic Arts Professor, Ohio State University, Columbus OH (1987-1993).
Manager, Design Graphics, Lima OH (1993-present).

Education

Massachusetts Conservatory of Art, Ph.D. 1987
University of Massachusetts, B.A. 1984

CHRONOLOGICAL RESUME
(Prepared on a word processor
and laser printed.)

RANDALL ELLIS
557 Pine Street
Seattle, WA 98404
(206) 555-6584

EXPERIENCE

THE CENTER COMPANY   Seattle, WA
Systems Programmer   1993-present
- Develop and maintain over 100 assembler modules.
- Create screen manager programs, using Assembler and Natural languages, to trace input and output to the VTAM buffer.
- Install and customize Omegamon 695 and 700 on IBM mainframes.
- Develop programs to monitor complete security control blocks, using Assembler and Natural.
- Produce stand-alone IPLs and create backrests on IBM 3380 DASD.

INFO TECH, INC.   Seattle, WA
Technical Manager   1991-1993
- Designed and managed the implementation of a network providing the legal community with a direct line to Supreme Court cases, using Clipper on IBM 386s.
- Developed a system which catalogued entire library inventory, using Turbo Pascal on IBM AT.
- Used C to create a registration system for university registrar on IBM AT.

EDUCATION

SALEM STATE UNIVERSITY   Salem, OR
    B.S. in Computer Science.   1989
    M.S. in Computer Science.   1991

COMPUTER SKILLS

- Programming Languages: C, C++, Assembler, COBOL, Natural, Turbo Pascal, dBASE III+, and Clipper.
- Software: VTAM, Complete, TSO, JES 2, ACF 2, Omegamon 695 and 700, and Adabas.
- Operating Systems: MVS/XA, MVS/SP, MS-DOS, and VMS.

FUNCTIONAL RESUME
(Prepared on an office-quality typewriter.)

MEAGHAN O'LEARY
703 Mulberry Avenue
Chicago, IL 60601
(312) 555-8841

OBJECTIVE:
To contribute over eight years of experience in promotion, communications, and administration to an entry-level position in advertising.

SUMMARY OF QUALIFICATIONS:
- Performed advertising duties for small business.
- Experience in business writing and communications skills.
- General knowledge of office management.
- Demonstrated ability to work well with others, in both supervisory and support staff roles.
- Type 75 words per minute.

SELECTED ACHIEVEMENTS AND RESULTS:
Promotion:
Composing, editing, and proofreading correspondence and PR materials for own catering service. Large-scale mailings.

Communication:
Instruction; curriculum and lesson planning; student evaluation; parent-teacher conferences; development of educational materials. Training and supervising clerks.

Computer Skills:
Proficient in MS Word, Lotus 1-2-3, Excel, and Filemaker Pro.

Administration:
Record-keeping and file maintenance. Data processing and computer operations, accounts receivable, accounts payable, inventory control, and customer relations. Scheduling, office management, and telephone reception.

WORK HISTORY:
Teacher; Self-Employed (owner of catering service); Floor Manager; Administrative Assistant; Accounting Clerk.

EDUCATION:
Beloit College, Beloit, WI, BA in Education, 1987

CHRONOLOGICAL RESUME
(Prepared on a word processor
and laser printed.)

PAUL K. NORTON
16 Charles Street
Marlborough CT 06447
203/555-9641

EDUCATION

Keene State College, Keene NH
Bachelor of Arts in Elementary Education, 1995
- Graduated *magna cum laude*
- English minor
- Kappa Delta Pi member, inducted 1993

EXPERIENCE
September 1995-
Present

Elmer T. Thienes Elementary School, Marlborough CT
Part-time Kindergarten Teacher
- Instruct kindergartners in reading, spelling, language arts, and music.
- Participate in the selection of textbooks and learning aids.
- Organize and supervise class field trips and coordinate in-class presentations.

Summers
1993-1995

Keene YMCA, Youth Division, Keene NH
Child-care Counselor
- Oversaw summer program for low-income youth.
- Budgeted and coordinated special events and field trips, working with Program Director to initiate variations in the program.
- Served as Youth Advocate in cooperation with social worker to address the social needs and problems of participants.

Spring 1995

Wheelock Elementary School, Keene NH
Student Teacher
- Taught third-grade class in all elementary subjects.
- Designed and implemented a two-week unit on Native Americans.
- Assisted in revision of third-grade curriculum.

Fall 1994

Child Development Center, Keene NH
Daycare Worker
- Supervised preschool children on the playground and during art activities.
- Created a "Wishbone Corner," where children could quietly look at books or take a voluntary "time-out."

ADDITIONAL INTERESTS
Martial arts, skiing, politics, reading, writing.

GENERAL MODEL
FOR A COVER LETTER

Your mailing address
Date

Contact's name
Contact's title
Company
Company's mailing address

Dear Mr./Ms. _____:

Immediately explain why your background makes you the best candidate for the position that you are applying for. Describe what prompted you to write (want ad, article you read about the company, networking contact, etc.). Keep the first paragraph short and hard-hitting.

Detail what you could contribute to this company. Show how your qualifications will benefit this firm. Describe your interest in the corporation. Subtly emphasizing your knowledge about this firm and your familiarity with the industry will set you apart from other candidates. Remember to keep this letter short; few recruiters will read a cover letter longer than half a page.

If possible, your closing paragraph should request specific action on the part of the reader. Include your phone number and the hours when you can be reached. Mention that if you do not hear from the reader by a specific date, you will follow up with a phone call. Lastly, thank the reader for their time, consideration, etc.

Sincerely,

(signature)

Your full name (typed)

Enclosure (use this if there are other materials, such as your resume, that are included in the same envelope)

SAMPLE COVER LETTER

16 Charles Street
Marlborough CT 06447
March 16, 1998

Ms. Lia Marcusson
Assistant Principal
Jonathon Daniels Elementary School
43 Mayflower Drive
Keene NH 03431

Dear Ms. Marcusson:

Janet Newell recently informed me of a possible opening for a third grade teacher at Jonathon Daniels Elementary School. With my experience instructing third-graders, both in schools and in summer programs, I feel I would be an ideal candidate for the position. Please accept this letter and the enclosed resume as my application.

Jonathon Daniels' educational philosophy that every child can learn and succeed interests me, since it mirrors my own. My current position at Elmer T. Thienes Elementary has reinforced this philosophy, heightening my awareness of the different styles and paces of learning and increasing my sensitivity toward special needs children. Furthermore, as a direct result of my student teaching experience at Wheelock Elementary School, I am comfortable, confident, and knowledgeable working with third-graders.

I look forward to discussing the position and my qualifications for it in more detail. I can be reached at 203/555-9641 evenings or 203/555-0248 weekdays. If I do not hear from you before Tuesday of next week, I will call to see if we can schedule a time to meet. Thank you for your time and consideration.

Sincerely,

PK Norton

Paul K. Norton

Enclosure

GENERAL MODEL FOR A
FOLLOW-UP LETTER

Your mailing address
Date

Contact's name
Contact's title
Company
Company's mailing address

Dear Mr./Ms._____:

Remind the interviewer of the reason (i.e., a specific opening, an informational interview, etc.) you were interviewed, as well as the date. Thank him/her for the interview, and try to personalize your thanks by mentioning some specific aspect of the interview.

Confirm your interest in the organization (and in the opening, if you were interviewing for a particular position). Use specifics to re-emphasize that you have researched the firm in detail and have considered how you would fit into the company and the position. This is a good time to say anything you wish you had said in the initial meeting. Be sure to keep this letter brief; a half-page is plenty.

If appropriate, close with a suggestion for further action, such as a desire to have an additional interview, if possible. Mention your phone number and the hours that you can be reached. Alternatively, you may prefer to mention that you will follow up with a phone call in several days. Once again, thank the person for meeting with you, and state that you would be happy to provide any additional information about your qualifications.

Sincerely,

(signature)

Your full name (typed)

CD-ROM JOB SEARCH

Jobseekers who are looking for any edge they can find may want to check out the following selected CD-ROM products. Since most of these databases cost upwards of $500, and are designed for use by other businesses or libraries, don't expect to find these at your local software store. Of course, not all libraries will have all of these resources. Depending on how technologically advanced your library is, you may find only one or two of these electronic databases. Call your library to find out what electronic resources it has available. Many of these databases can also be found in the offices of career counselors or outplacement specialists, and are used as part of your service.

ADAMS JOBBANK FASTRESUME SUITE
260 Center Street
Holbrook MA 02343
800/872-5627
The CD-ROM version of the best-selling *JobBank* series contains almost 20,000 detailed profiles of companies in all industries, 1,800 executive search firms, and 1,100 employment agencies. For most companies, you will find the name, address, company description, and key contact name. The database also lists common professional positions and information on benefits for most companies. You can search the database by company name, state, industry, and job title. Calling itself a "total job search package," the CD-ROM also creates personalized resumes and cover letters and offers advice on job interviews, including over 100 sample interview questions and answers. *Adams JobBank FastResume Suite* CD-ROM is for Windows® and Windows®95.

AMERICAN BIG BUSINESS DIRECTORY
5711 South 86th Circle
P.O. Box 27347
Omaha NE 68127
800/555-5211
American Big Business Directory has profiles of 160,000 privately and publicly held companies employing more than 100 people. The CD-ROM contains company descriptions which include company type, industry, products, and sales information. Also included are multiple contact names for each company, with a total of more than 340,000. You can search the database by industry, SIC code, sales volume, employee size, or zip code.

AMERICAN MANUFACTURER'S DIRECTORY
5711 South 86th Circle
P.O. Box 27347
Omaha NE 68127
800/555-5211
Made by the same company that created *American Big Business Directory*, *American Manufacturer's Directory* lists over 531,000 manufacturing

companies of all sizes and industries. The directory contains product and sales information, company size, and a key contact name for each company. The user can search by region, SIC code, sales volume, employee size, or zip code.

BUSINESS U.S.A.

5711 South 86th Circle
P.O. Box 27347
Omaha NE 68127
800/555-5211

Also from the makers of *American Big Business Directory* and *American Manufacturer's Directory*, this CD-ROM contains information on 10 million U.S. companies. The profiles provide contact information, industry type, number of employees, and sales volume. Each listing also indicates whether the company is public or private, as well as providing information about the company's products. There are a number of different search methods available, including key words, SIC code, geographic location, and number of employees.

CAREER SEARCH - INTEGRATED RESOURCE SYSTEM

21 Highland Circle
Needham MA 02194-3075
617/449-0312

Career Search is a database which contains listings for over 490,000 privately and publicly held companies. It has contact information, including names of human resources professionals or other executives, for companies of virtually all sizes, types, and industries. The database can be searched by industry, company size, or region. This product is updated monthly.

COMPANIES INTERNATIONAL

835 Penobscot Building
645 Griswald Street
Detroit MI 48226
800/877-GALE

Produced by Gale Research Inc., this CD-ROM is compiled from *Ward's Business Directory* and the *World's Business Directory*, and contains information on more than 300,000 companies worldwide. You can find industry information, contact names, and number of employees. Also included is information on the company's products and revenues. The database can be searched by industry, company products, or geographic location.

CORPTECH DIRECTORY

12 Alfred Street, Suite 200
Woburn MA 01801-1915
800/333-8036

The *CorpTech Directory* on CD-ROM contains detailed descriptions of over 45,000 technology companies. It also lists the names and titles of nearly 155,000 executives -- CEOs, sales managers, R&D managers, and human resource professionals. World Wide Web and e-mail addresses are also available. In addition to contact information, you can find detailed information about each company's products or services and annual revenues. The *CorpTech Directory* also lists both the number of current employees, and the number of employees one year ago. Some companies also list the number of employees they project having in one year. You can search the database by type of company, geographic location, or sales revenue. This product is updated quarterly.

DISCOVERING CAREERS & JOBS
835 Penobscot Building
645 Griswald Street
Detroit MI 48226
800/877-GALE
Provides overviews on 1,200 careers, 1,000 articles from trade publications, and contact information for professional associations. This CD-ROM also contains self-assessment tests, college profiles, and financial aid data.

DISCOVERING CAREERS & JOBS PLUS
835 Penobscot Building
645 Griswald Street
Detroit MI 48226
800/877-GALE
This CD-ROM gives users contact information on more than 45,000 companies, with 15,000 in-depth profiles and 1,000 company history essays. In addition, the product also provides profiles and application procedures for all major two- and four-year U.S. colleges and universities.

DUN & BRADSTREET MILLION DOLLAR DISC PLUS
3 Sylvan Way
Parsippany NJ 07054
800/526-0651
This CD-ROM provides information on over 400,000 companies in virtually every industry. About 90 percent of the companies listed are privately held, and all have at least $3 million in annual sales or at least 50 employees. Each company's listing includes the number of employees, sales volume, name of the parent company, and corporate headquarters or branch locations. The *Million Dollar Disc Plus* also provides the names and titles of top executives, as well as biographical information on those executives, including education and career background. Searches can be done by location, industry, SIC code, executive names, or key words in the executive biographies. This directory is updated quarterly.

ENCYCLOPEDIA OF ASSOCIATIONS:
NATIONAL ORGANIZATIONS OF THE U.S.
835 Penobscot Building
645 Griswald Street
Detroit MI 48226
800/877-GALE

Contains descriptions and contact information for nearly 23,000 national organizations. You can search by association name, geographic location, and key words. This CD-ROM is available in both single- and multi-user formats.

GALE BUSINESS RESOURCES CD-ROM
835 Penobscot Building
645 Griswald Street
Detroit MI 48226
800/877-GALE
This two CD-ROM set contains detailed profiles on certain industries and covers the major companies in each industry, with statistics on over 200,000 businesses nationwide. You can search by company name, industry type, products, and more. This product is available in both single- and multi-user formats.

HARRIS INFOSOURCE INTERNATIONAL
2057 East Aurora Road
Twinsburg OH 44087
800/888-5900
This directory of manufacturers profiles thousands of companies. Although the majority of the companies listed are located in the United States, there are also listings for some businesses overseas. The listings include the number of employees, plant size, and sales revenue, as well as the names and titles of top executives. This CD-ROM is updated annually and can be purchased in smaller regional or state editions.

HOOVER'S COMPANY AND INDUSTRY DATABASE ON CD-ROM
1033 La Posada Drive
Suite 250
Austin TX 78752
512/454-7778
This CD-ROM contains *Hoover's Handbook of American Businesses, Hoover's Handbook of World Businesses,* and *Hoover's Handbook of Emerging Businesses,* as well as listings of various computer companies, media companies, and more. *Hoover's Company and Industry Database* contains 2,500 company profiles in 450 industries. This CD-ROM has three quarterly updates and is available in both single- and multi-user formats.

MOODY'S COMPANY DATA
99 Church Street
New York NY 10007
800/342-5647
Moody's Company Data is a CD-ROM which has detailed listings for over 10,000 publicly traded companies. In addition to information such as industry, company address, and phone and fax numbers, each listing includes the names and titles of its top officers, including the CEO, president, and vice president; company size; number of shareholders; corporate history; subsidiaries; and

financial statements. Users can conduct searches by region, SIC codes, industry, or earnings. This CD-ROM is updated monthly.

STANDARD & POOR'S REGISTER
65 Broadway
8th Floor
New York NY 10004
800/221-5277
The CD-ROM version of this three-volume desk reference provides the same information as its printed companion. The database lists over 55,000 companies, including more than 12,000 public companies. In addition to contact information, which includes the names and titles of over 500,000 executives, you can find out about each company's primary and secondary sources of business, annual revenues, number of employees, parent company, and subsidiaries. When available, the *Standard & Poor's Register* also lists the names of banks, accounting firms, and law firms used by each company. Also, the directory provides biographies of more than 70,000 top executives, which include information such as directorships held and schools attended. There are 55 different search modes available on the database. You can search geographically, by zip code, industry, SIC code, or stock symbol. You can also limit your search to only private or only public companies. This directory is updated quarterly.

WALKER'S CORPORATE DIRECTORY OF U.S. PUBLIC COMPANIES
835 Penobscot Building
645 Griswald Street
Detroit MI 48226
800/877-GALE
A directory of 9,500 publicly held U.S. corporations. The user can access each company's income, earnings per share, assets, stock exchange symbol, and more. Searches on business information include classifications by company, SIC code, and stock exchange. This CD-ROM also allows the user to print company reports and labels.

PRIMARY EMPLOYERS

ACCOUNTING AND MANAGEMENT CONSULTING

 Accounting and management consulting firms are facing more competitive pressures than ever, coupled with declining profits. Competition is forcing accounting firms to redesign the services they offer, cut costs significantly, and upgrade their recruiting efforts to attract more highly-skilled accountants. Fortunately, innovations in tax software and other technologies have made accounting practices more efficient.

The nation's largest and most dominant accounting firms, known as the Big Six, are focusing more on management consulting, and revenues in the consulting arena have grown significantly. The split of Arthur Andersen into a separate division, Andersen Consulting, reflects a trend that will continue to transform the larger accounting firms and push some business customers toward these smaller divisions or toward private firms.

The Big Six are continuing to create partnerships worldwide, and some of the smaller firms are following suit. The majority of the mid-sized accounting firms, however, concentrate on maintaining strong regional client relationships. According to Inc. magazine, while some accounting firms will be forced out of business due to competition, many have responded by specializing in a particular area.

ARTHUR ANDERSEN & COMPANY
901 Main Street, Suite 5600, Dallas TX 75202. **Contact:** Personnel. **Description:** One of the largest certified public accounting firms in the world. Arthur Andersen's four key practice areas include Audit and Business Advisory, Tax and Business Advisory, Business Consulting, and Economic and Financial Consulting. Arthur Andersen is a segment of the Arthur Andersen Worldwide Organization, one of the leading providers of professional services throughout the world. With over 380 worldwide locations, the global practice of its member firms is conducted through two business units: Arthur Andersen and Andersen Consulting, which provides global management and technology consulting. **NOTE:** This firm does not accept unsolicited resumes. Please respond to advertised openings only.

BOOZ-ALLEN & HAMILTON, INC.
901 Main Street, Suite 6500, Dallas TX 75202. 214/746-6500. **Contact:** Personnel Administrator. **World Wide Web address:** http://www.bah.com. **Description:** A diversified, international management consulting organization offering services in both the commercial and public sectors. Areas of expertise include technology, strategy, and planning, as well as social research and many other technical fields. Specific services include corporate strategy and long-range planning; organization design; human resources management; financial management and control; acquisitions and divestiture; information systems and automation; manufacturing; inventory and distribution control; qualitative and quantitative market research; attitudinal and demographic trend research; marketing strategy and positioning; venture management; transportation and environmental systems; technology research; new products and process development; government programs; and regulatory compliance. Booz-Allen & Hamilton operates 15 regional offices in the United States and eight in Europe, North Africa, and Latin America, all offering a full range of services. **Common positions include:** Biomedical Engineer; Chemical Engineer; Computer Programmer; Electrical/Electronics Engineer; Financial Analyst; Industrial Engineer; Industrial Production Manager; Marketing Specialist; Petroleum Engineer; Statistician; Systems Analyst. **Educational backgrounds include:** Accounting; Business Administration; Computer Science;

Economics; Engineering; Finance; Marketing; Mathematics. **Benefits:** Dental Insurance; Disability Coverage; Life Insurance; Medical Insurance; Pension Plan; Profit Sharing; Savings Plan; Tuition Assistance. **Special programs:** Internships. **Corporate headquarters location:** McLean VA. **Operations at this facility include:** Administration; Manufacturing; Research and Development. **Number of employees at this location:** 65.

CHESHIER AND FULLER, L.L.P.

14175 Proton Road, Dallas TX 75244-3604. 972/387-4300. **Contact:** Firm Administrator. **Description:** Cheshier and Fuller offers accounting, tax, audit, management advisory, business valuation, and litigation support services. **Common positions include:** Accountant/Auditor. **Educational backgrounds include:** Accounting. **Benefits:** 401(k); Cafeteria; Disability Coverage; Life Insurance; Medical Insurance. **Listed on:** Privately held. **Number of employees at this location:** 35.

COOPERS & LYBRAND

1999 Bryan Street, Suite 3000, Dallas TX 75201. 214/754-5000. **Contact:** Director of Personnel. **World Wide Web address:** http://www.colybrand.com. **Description:** One of the largest certified public accounting and management consulting firms, Coopers & Lybrand offers a wide range of services, including accounting, auditing, tax, management consulting, emerging business services, and actuarial consulting services. **Common positions include:** Accountant/Auditor. **Educational backgrounds include:** Accounting. **Benefits:** 401(k); Dental Insurance; Disability Coverage; Life Insurance; Medical Insurance; Savings Plan. **Special programs:** Internships. **Corporate headquarters location:** New York NY. **Operations at this facility include:** Regional Headquarters. **Number of employees at this location:** 600. **Number of employees nationwide:** 66,000.

DELOITTE & TOUCHE

2200 Ross Avenue, Suite 1600, Dallas TX 75201. 214/777-7000. **Contact:** Steve Gass, Human Resources Director. **World Wide Web address:** http://www.dttus.com. **Description:** Deloitte & Touche is an international firm of certified public accountants, providing professional accounting, auditing, tax, and management consulting services to widely diversified clients. Deloitte & Touche has a specialized program consisting of some 25 national industry groups and 50 functional (technical) groups that cross industry lines. Groups are involved in various disciplines, including accounting, auditing, taxation management advisory services, small and growing businesses, mergers and acquisitions, and computer applications. Deloitte & Touche has international facilities with more than 500 offices throughout the world. **Common positions include:** Accountant/Auditor; Actuary. **Educational backgrounds include:** Accounting. **Benefits:** Dental Insurance; Disability Coverage; Life Insurance; Medical Insurance; Savings Plan. **Special programs:** Internships. **Corporate headquarters location:** Wilton CT. **Operations at this facility include:** Regional Headquarters. **Number of employees at this location:** 450. **Number of employees nationwide:** 16,000.

ERNST & YOUNG

2121 San Jacinto, Suite 1500, Dallas TX 75201. 214/969-8000. **Fax:** 214/969-8587. **Contact:** Pamela Tomberlin, Director of Human Resources. **World Wide Web address:** http://www.ey.com. **Description:** A certified public accounting firm that also provides its clients with management consulting services. Ernst & Young operates more than 300 offices in 70 countries worldwide. The consulting staff is involved in such fields as data processing, financial modeling, financial feasibility studies, production planning and inventory management, management sciences, health care planning, human resources, and cost accounting and budgeting systems. The company provides services to numerous industries, including health care, financial institutions, insurance, manufacturing, retailing, government, utilities, and transportation. **Corporate headquarters location:** New York NY. **Listed on:** Privately held. **Number of employees nationwide:** 8,500. **Number of employees worldwide:** 16,000.

FARROW AND FARROW

P.O. Box 180309, Dallas TX 75218. 214/328-4615. **Contact:** Human Resources. **Description:** An accounting, auditing, and bookkeeping service.

GRANT THORNTON LLP

1445 Ross Avenue, Suite 3600, Dallas TX 75202. 214/855-7300. **Fax:** 214/855-7370. **Contact:** Human Resources. **World Wide Web address:** http://www.grantthornton.com. **Description:** An international certified public accounting organization offering consulting and accounting services as well as strategic and tactical planning assistance to a diverse clientele. **NOTE:** Entry-level positions are offered. **Common positions include:** Accountant/Auditor; Management Analyst/Consultant; Market Research Analyst; Software Engineer; Systems Analyst; Tax Specialist; Typist/Word Processor. **Educational backgrounds include:** Accounting; Business Administration; Computer Science; Engineering; M.I.S. **Benefits:** 401(k); Dental Insurance; Disability Coverage; Employee Discounts; Leave Time; Life Insurance; Mass Transit Available; Medical Insurance; Telecommuting; Tuition Assistance. **Special programs:** Internships; Training. **Corporate headquarters location:** Chicago IL. **Other U.S. locations:** Nationwide. **Operations at this facility include:** Administration; Regional Headquarters; Sales; Service. **Listed on:** Privately held. **Annual sales/revenues:** More than $100 million. **Number of employees at this location:** 125. **Number of employees nationwide:** 2,700. **Number of employees worldwide:** 23,000.

H&R BLOCK

3701 West NW Highway, Suite 210, Dallas TX 75220. 214/358-4560. **Fax:** 214/357-2826. **Contact:** Dieter Krause, District Manager. **World Wide Web address:** http://www.hrblock.com. **Description:** Primarily engaged in consumer tax preparation, operating more than 9,500 United States offices, and preparing more than 10 million tax returns each year. The company also operates more than 800 offices in Canada. H&R Block has established offices in over 750 Sears stores in both the United States and Canada. H&R Block Inc. is also engaged in a number of other tax-related activities, including Group Tax Programs, Executive Tax Service, Tax Training Schools, and Real Estate Tax Awareness Seminars. **Corporate headquarters location:** Kansas City MO. **Listed on:** New York Stock Exchange. **Number of employees nationwide:** 80,000.

I.T. PARTNERS, INC.

2735 Villa Creek Drive, Suite 175, Dallas TX 75234. 972/484-5300. **Fax:** 972/484-5605. **Contact:** Human Resources. **World Wide Web address:** http://www.itpartners.net. **Description:** Provides management consulting and information systems consulting services.

KPMG PEAT MARWICK

200 Crescent Court, Suite 300, Dallas TX 75201. 214/754-2000. **Contact:** Personnel Department. **World Wide Web address:** http://www.kpmg.com. **Description:** A certified public accounting firm providing auditing, assurance, management consulting, and tax services. KPMG Peat Marwick operates approximately 135 offices in the United States, and approximately 1,100 offices in 131 countries.

WILLIAM M. MERCER, INC.

3500 Chase Tower, 2200 Ross Avenue, Dallas TX 75201. 214/855-5222. **Contact:** Human Resources. **World Wide Web address:** http://www.mercer.com. **Description:** One of the world's largest actuarial and human resources management consulting firms, providing advice to organizations on all aspects of employee/management relationships. Services include retirement, health and welfare, performance and rewards, communication, investment, human resources administration, risk, finance and insurance, and health care provider consulting. **Corporate headquarters location:** New York NY.

PRICE WATERHOUSE

2001 Ross Avenue, Suite 1800, Dallas TX 75201-2997. 214/754-7900. **Contact:** Ms. Nancy Maurice, Human Resources Coordinator. **World Wide Web address:** http://www.pw.com. **Description:** One of the country's six largest certified public accounting firms, with offices in 90 cities in the United States, and more than 300 other offices in approximately 90 foreign countries. **Corporate headquarters location:** New York NY. **Other U.S. locations:** Nationwide.

REAL ESTATE TAX SERVICES

5550 Lyndon B. Johnson Freeway, Suite 700, Dallas TX 75240. 972/776-6000. **Contact:** Office Manager. **Description:** An accounting firm involved in property taxation.

REAL ESTATE TAX SERVICES
P.O. Box 771, Abilene TX 79601. 915/677-8155. **Contact:** Office Manager. **Description:** An accounting firm involved in property taxation.

Note: Because addresses and telephone numbers of smaller companies can change rapidly, we recommend you call each company to verify the information below before inquiring about job opportunities. Mass mailings are not recommended.

Additional small employers:

ACCOUNTING, AUDITING, AND BOOKKEEPING SERVICES

Arthur Andersen
777 Main St, Ste 1100, Fort Worth TX 76102-5315. 817/870-3000.

BDO Seidman
2323 Bryan Street, Ste 1800, Dallas TX 75201-2645. 214/880-3700.

BDO Seidman
2400 Plaza of The Americas, Dallas TX 75201. 214/220-3131.

Coopers & Lybrand
301 Commerce Street, Fort Worth TX 76102-4140. 817/332-2243.

Coopers & Lybrand
14800 Landmark Blvd, Dallas TX 75240-7565. 972/448-5000.

Dallas County Auditor
509 Main St, Ste 407, Dallas TX 75202-3557. 214/653-6472.

Deloitte & Touche
301 Commerce St, Ste 2950, Fort Worth TX 76102-4129. 817/336-2531.

Deloitte & Touche
2001 S Barnett Ave, Dallas TX 75211-8871. 214/220-8000.

Ernst & Young
104 Decker Ct, Irving TX 75062-2705. 214/665-5000.

Ernst & Young
500 Throckmorton Street, Fort Worth TX 76102-3708. 817/335-1900.

KPMG Peat Marwick LLP
301 Commerce St, Ste 2500, Fort Worth TX 76102-4125. 817/335-2655.

Lane Gorman Trubitt LLP
1909 Woodall Rodgers Fwy, Dallas TX 75201-2286. 214/871-7500.

Lexington Companies
2120 West Walnut Hill Lane, Irving TX 75038-4418. 972/714-0585.

McBee Systems Inc.
635 N Jupiter Rd #11325, Richardson TX 75081-3242. 972/231-8428.

Price Waterhouse LLP
1700 City Center Tower II, Fort Worth TX 76102. 817/870-5500.

SRF Personnel Inc.
8615 Freeport Parkway, Suite 200, Irving TX 75063. 972/929-4880.

Travis Wolff & Co. LLP
5580 LBJ Freeway, Suite 400, Dallas TX 75240-6265. 972/661-1843.

Viastar Service Inc.
PO Box 1090, Ennis TX 75120-1090. 972/875-3824.

Weaver and Tidwell LLP
307 W 7th St, Fort Worth TX 76102-5100. 817/332-7905.

Weaver and Tidwell LLP
12221 Merit Drive, Ste 1700, Dallas TX 75251-2252. 972/490-1970.

BUSINESS CONSULTING SERVICES

Ajilon Services Inc.
3625 North Hall St, Ste 800, Dallas TX 75219-5119. 972/263-8450.

American Express Financial Advisors
801 E Campbell Rd, Ste 250,
Richardson TX 75081-1866. 972/437-9311.

American Express Financial Advisors
14800 Landmark Blvd, Dallas TX 75240-7565. 972/392-1788.

American Transtech Inc.
702 N Twin Creek Dr, Killeen TX 76543-4235. 254/680-6200.

Andersen Consulting
5215 North O'Connor Blvd, Irving TX 75039-3713. 972/402-7800.

Bell Northern Research
PO Box 833871, Richardson TX 75083-3871. 972/684-8000.

Blackmarr Consulting
2515 McKinney Avenue, Dallas TX 75201-1978. 214/922-9030.

Chapdelaine & Associates
PO Box 612226, Dallas TX 75261-2226. 817/282-5707.

Com 2000+
3630 North Josey Lane, Carrollton TX 75007-3144. 972/395-2000.

Consumer Credit Counseling
1320 South University Dr, Fort Worth TX 76107-5764. 817/732-2227.

Corphealth Inc.
1300 Summit Ave, Ste 600, Fort Worth TX 76102-4420. 817/332-2519.

Corporate Systems Inc.
PO Box 31780, Amarillo TX 79120-1780. 806/376-4223.

Cura Inc.
2735 Villa Creek Dr, Dallas TX 75234-7454. 972/620-7117.

Dallas Fan Fares Inc.
5485 Belt Line Rd, Ste 270,
Dallas TX 75240-7656. 972/239-
9969.

Dallas Hospitality Services
2711 North Haskell Avenue,
Dallas TX 75204-2923. 214/841-
6791.

DHC
PO Box 460036, Garland TX
75046-0036. 972/238-9231.

**Electronic Commerce
Resources**
2000 S Loop 256, Ste 11,
Palestine TX 75801-5918.
903/729-4440.

Equicor Inc.
600 Las Colinas Boulevard East,
Irving TX 75039-5616. 972/770-
4151.

ETC Transit Services
2900 Bataan St, Dallas TX
75212-5409. 214/747-7102.

George Group Inc.
13355 Noel Road, Ste 1100,
Dallas TX 75240-6643. 972/661-
8066.

HCL America Inc.
1700 Alma Dr, Plano TX 75075-
6937. 972/509-9000.

Inacom Professional Service
15280 Addison Road #100,
Dallas TX 75248-4509. 972/376-
8300.

**JF Jaynes Certified Financial
Planners**
3701 West Waco Drive, Waco
TX 76710-5346. 254/750-8119.

Kuhler & Associates Inc.
5430 LBJ Freeway, Ste 1120,
Dallas TX 75240-2632. 972/991-
8100.

M/A/R/C Inc.
1700 Wilshire St, Denton TX
76201-6572. 940/566-6668.

Marvin F. Poer and Company
5430 Lyndon B. Johnson Fwy,
Dallas TX 75240-2601. 972/770-
1100.

Metro Networks Inc.
12300 Ford Rd, Ste 360, Dallas
TX 75234-7274. 972/488-1166.

Mobile Systems International
1755 North Collins Blvd,
Richardson TX 75080-3562.
972/644-6886.

Origin Technology In Business
5000 S Bowen Rd, Arlington TX
76017-2616. 817/264-8200.

Paladin Consulting Inc.
8131 LBJ Freeway, Suite 210,
Dallas TX 75251. 972/783-1995.

Physicians Resource Group
5430 LBJ Freeway, Ste 1540,
Dallas TX 75240-2601. 972/982-
8200.

Price Waterhouse LLP
15301 Dallas Pkwy, Ste 300,
Dallas TX 75248-4669. 972/386-
9922.

Prioris Inc.
5205 North O'Connor Boulevard,
Irving TX 75039. 972/831-5190.

Regency Communications Inc.
3301 Airport Fwy, Ste 300,
Bedford TX 76021-6035.
817/283-9292.

Renzenberger
123 N Vine St, Euless TX 76040-
3811. 817/222-1196.

Safari Associates
2008 E Randol Mill Rd,
Arlington TX 76011-8205.
817/543-0007.

**Safety & Loss Control
Consulting**
16479 Dallas Pkwy, Ste 700,
Dallas TX 75248-2621. 972/380-
2898.

Techlaw Inc.
750 North Saint Paul Street,
Dallas TX 75201-7105. 214/953-
0045.

Techsource Services Inc.
6908 Wellesley Dr, Plano TX
75024-6300. 972/618-5341.

Telecom Technologies Inc.
1701 North Collins Blvd,
Richardson TX 75080-3564.
972/918-0202.

The Amend Group Inc.
8150 N Central Expy, Dallas TX
75206-1815. 214/696-6900.

Total Dealers Solutions
165 W Main St, Lewisville TX
75057-3973. 972/219-0748.

VHA Inc.
PO Box 140909, Irving TX
75014-0909. 972/830-0050.

Watson Wyatt Worldwide
2121 San Jacinto St, Dallas TX
75201-2739. 214/978-3400.

MANAGEMENT SERVICES

**American Staff Resources
Company**
13155 Noel Road, Ste 1501,
Dallas TX 75240-5029. 972/980-
1990.

AMR Investment Services Inc.
4333 Amon Carter Blvd, Fort
Worth TX 76155-2605. 817/967-
1529.

Blankinship Enterprises
PO Box 8248, Amarillo TX
79114-8248. 806/355-9936.

**Foundation Management
Services**
2220 San Jacinto Boulevard,
Denton TX 76205-7589. 940/243-
5858.

Human Resource Solutions
1333 Corporate Dr, Ste 117,
Irving TX 75038-2516. 972/550-
1413.

Impel Management Services
9003 Airport Fwy, Ste 300, Fort
Worth TX 76180-7771. 817/514-
5200.

JPI Partners Inc.
600 Las Colinas Boulevard East,
Irving TX 75039-5616. 972/556-
1700.

Massimos
2931 Irving Boulevard, Ste 105,
Dallas TX 75247-6200. 214/637-
6881.

Phycor IPA Management
3811 Turtle Creek Boulevard,
Dallas TX 75219-4461. 214/523-
6300.

**Rosewood Corporate
Administration Inc.**
100 Crescent Court, Ste 500,
Dallas TX 75201-1869. 214/871-
5750.

Smith-Laurin Group Inc.
3250 W Pleasant Run Rd,
Lancaster TX 75146-1050.
972/274-2000.

Tascor Inc.
1501 Lyndon B. Johnson Fwy,
Dallas TX 75234-6029. 972/406-7855.

Thomas Group Inc.
5215 North O'Connor Boulevard,
Irving TX 75039. 972/869-3400.

Sunbelt Management Services
500 Terminal Rd, Fort Worth TX
76106-1923. 817/624-7253.

TCA Management Company
PO Box 130489, Tyler TX
75713-0489. 903/595-3701.

For more information on career opportunities in accounting and management consulting:

Associations

AMERICAN ACCOUNTING ASSOCIATION
5717 Bessie Drive, Sarasota FL 34233. 941/921-7747.
World Wide Web address: http://www.aaa-edu.org.
An academically-oriented accounting association that
offers two quarterly journals, a semi-annual journal, a
newsletter, and a wide variety of continuing education
programs.

**AMERICAN INSTITUTE OF CERTIFIED
PUBLIC ACCOUNTANTS**
1211 Avenue of the Americas, New York NY 10036.
212/596-6200. World Wide Web address: http://www.
aicpa.org. A national professional organization for all
CPAs. AICPA offers a comprehensive career package
to students.

AMERICAN MANAGEMENT ASSOCIATION
1601 Broadway, New York NY 10019. 212/586-8100.
Provides a variety of publications, training videos, and
courses, as well as an Information Resource Center,
which provides management information, and a
library service.

**ASSOCIATION OF GOVERNMENT
ACCOUNTANTS**
2200 Mount Vernon Avenue, Alexandria VA 22301.
703/684-6931. World Wide Web address: http://www.
aga.org. Serves financial management professionals
and offers continuing education workshops.

**ASSOCIATION OF MANAGEMENT
CONSULTING FIRMS**
521 Fifth Avenue, 35th Floor, New York NY 10175.
212/697-9693. World Wide Web address:
http://www.amcf.org.

INSTITUTE OF INTERNAL AUDITORS
249 Maitland Avenue, Altamonte Springs FL 32701.
407/830-7600. World Wide Web address: http://www.
theiia.org. Publishes magazines and newsletters.
Provides information on current issues, a network of
more than 50,000 members in 100 countries, and
professional development and research services. Also
offers continuing education seminars.

**INSTITUTE OF MANAGEMENT
ACCOUNTANTS**
10 Paragon Drive, Montvale NJ 07645. 201/573-9000.
World Wide Web address: http://www.rutgers.edu/
accounting/raw/ima. Offers a Certified Management
Accountant Program, periodicals, seminars,
educational programs, a research program, a financial
management network, and networking services. The

association has about 80,000 members and 300 local
chapters.

**INSTITUTE OF MANAGEMENT
CONSULTANTS**
521 Fifth Avenue, 35th Floor, New York NY 10175.
212/697-8262. World Wide Web address: http://www.
imcusa.org. Offers certification programs,
professional development, and a directory of
members.

**NATIONAL ASSOCIATION OF TAX
PRACTITIONERS**
720 Association Drive, Appleton WI 54914-1483.
414/749-1040. World Wide Web address: http://www.
natptax.com. Offers seminars, research, newsletters,
preparer worksheets, state chapters, insurance, and
other tax-related services.

**NATIONAL SOCIETY OF PUBLIC
ACCOUNTANTS**
1010 North Fairfax Street, Alexandria VA 22314.
703/549-6400. World Wide Web address: http://www.
nsacct.org. Offers professional development services,
government representation, a variety of publications,
practice aids, low-cost group insurance, annual
seminars, and updates for members on new tax laws.

Magazines

CPA JOURNAL
The New York State Society, 530 Fifth Avenue, 5th
Floor, New York NY 10036. 212/719-8300. Monthly.

CPA LETTER
American Institute of Certified Public Accountants,
1211 Avenue of the Americas, New York NY 10036.
212/596-6200.

**THE FINANCE AND ACCOUNTING JOBS
REPORT**
Career Advancement Publications, Jamestown NY.
World Wide Web address: http://www.madbbs.com/
careers/finance.htm. This publication is dedicated to
finance and accounting professionals who are looking
for a job. Each issue includes several hundred job
openings in the United States and abroad. This report
also offers subscribers networking opportunities
through its contact and referral program.

JOURNAL OF ACCOUNTANCY
American Institute of Certified Public Accountants,
1211 Avenue of the Americas, New York NY 10036.
212/596-6200.

MANAGEMENT ACCOUNTING
Institute of Management Accountants, 10 Paragon Drive, Montvale NJ 07645. 201/573-9000.

Online Services

ACCOUNTANTS FORUM
Go: Aicpa. A CompuServe forum sponsored by the American Institute of Certified Public Accountants.

FINANCIAL/ACCOUNTING/INSURANCE JOBS PAGE
http://www.nationjob.com/financial. This Website provides a list of financial, accounting, and insurance job openings.

JOBS IN ACCOUNTING
http://www.cob.ohio-state.edu/dept/fin/jobs/account.htm#Link7. Provides information on the accounting profession, including salaries, trends, and resources.

MANAGEMENT CONSULTING JOBS ONLINE
http://www.cob.ohio-state.edu/dept/fin/jobs/mco/mco.html. Provides information and resources for jobseekers looking to work in the field of management consulting.

ADVERTISING, MARKETING, AND PUBLIC RELATIONS

Professionals in advertising, marketing, and public relations face an industry that is constantly changing and extremely competitive due to the high salaries it commands. Growth is forecast for all areas of advertising through 2000; and the public relations sector is projected to be one of the fastest growing through 2005.

Advertising executives are reporting that certain trends are dictating the industry's direction. Perhaps the most prominent is a renewed emphasis on corporate branding and the strategy of advertising products to individual consumers rather than larger groups or corporations. Business Week *cites growing consumer spending as a positive factor creating a boom in the advertising market.*

Publishers Information Bureau reports that although ad receipts were up by 8 percent in 1996, ad pages were down. Even so, magazines and newspapers continue to be the popular source of advertising and should continue to prosper well into the next decade. Although the cost of television ad time has not increased significantly over the last few years, networks are subtly trying to crowd more ads into programming. In 1998, the networks are expected to collect $14 billion in ad sales, 5.5 percent above 1997.

The latest trend in advertising is on the Internet. Companies are investing in "pop-up ads" that are linked to Websites related to the types of products and services they offer. This method of advertising is popular because it allows companies to target wider audiences and it provides consumers with easy access to information about specific advertisers. Online advertisers are also using well known search engines as springboards to their sites, but at great expense. It costs millions of dollars for companies to have their logos displayed on these high-traffic areas of the Web.

Direct mail is another successful area of the industry. According to U.S. News and World Report, *in 1997 consumers spent $244 billion in response to direct mail advertisers, including $48 billion on catalog merchandise. The growth in this sector is fueled by newer, more precise data-collection databases and the volume of "junk mail" is expected to triple in the next decade.*

ACKERMAN McQUEEN, INC.
545 East John Carpenter Freeway, Suite 600, Irving TX 75062. 972/444-9000. **Fax:** 972/869-4363. **Contact:** Melissa Evinger, Account Executive. **World Wide Web address:** http://www.am.com. **Description:** A full-service advertising agency. Founded in 1939. **Common positions include:** Account Manager; Account Representative; Administrative Assistant; Advertising Account Executive; Broadcast Technician; Buyer; Human Resources Manager; Market Research Analyst; Marketing Specialist; Technical Writer/Editor; Telecommunications Manager; Transportation/Traffic Specialist. **Educational backgrounds include:** Business Administration; Communications; Marketing; Public Relations. **Benefits:** Dental Insurance; Life Insurance; Medical Insurance. **Special programs:** Internships. **Internship information:** Unpaid internships are offered during the fall, spring, and summer for college credit. **Corporate headquarters location:** Oklahoma City OK.

BERRY * BROWN ADVERTISING
3100 McKinnon Street, Suite 1100, Dallas TX 75201-1046. 214/871-1001. **Fax:** 214/871-1137. **Contact:** Ms. Virdie Horton, Personnel Manager. **Description:** An advertising agency. **Common positions include:** Accountant/Auditor; Administrative Manager; Clerical Supervisor; Commercial Artist; Computer Operator; Marketing Manager; Media Specialist; Payroll Clerk; Receptionist; Secretary; Typist/Word Processor. **Educational backgrounds include:** Accounting; Art/Design; Business Administration; Communications; Liberal Arts; Marketing. **Benefits:** Dental Insurance; Disability Coverage; Life Insurance; Medical Insurance; Pension Plan; Profit Sharing; Savings Plan; Tuition Assistance. **Special programs:** Internships. **Corporate headquarters location:** This Location. **Number of employees at this location:** 55.

BURK ADVERTISING & MARKETING, INC.
2906 McKinney Avenue, Suite 100, Dallas TX 75204. 214/953-0494. **Contact:** Personnel. **World Wide Web address:** http://www.wambam.com. **Description:** An advertising and marketing agency offering print and multimedia services.

DDB NEEDHAM
200 Crescent Court, Suite 7A, Dallas TX 75201. 214/969-9000. **Contact:** Human Resources Department. **Description:** An advertising agency.

THE DOZIER COMPANY
3232 McKinney Avenue, Suite 300, Dallas TX 75204. 214/953-3900. **Contact:** Dianne Dozier, Human Resources. **Description:** An advertising agency. **Common positions include:** Advertising Account Executive; Advertising Clerk; Marketing Specialist. **Educational backgrounds include:** Art/Design; Marketing. **Benefits:** Life Insurance; Medical Insurance. **Special programs:** Internships. **Corporate headquarters location:** This Location.

BERNARD HODES ADVERTISING
7502 Greenville Avenue, Suite 630, Dallas TX 75231. 214/361-9986. **Contact:** Branch Manager. **World Wide Web address:** http://www.hodes.com. **Description:** An advertising agency specializing in recruitment and employee communications. **Corporate headquarters location:** New York NY. **Other U.S. locations:** Phoenix AZ; Chicago IL; Cambridge MA. **Parent company:** Omnicom.

JOINER, ROWLAND, SERIO
2305 Cedar Springs Road, Suite 400, Dallas TX 75201. 214/871-2305. **Contact:** Jay Serio, President. **Description:** A full-service advertising agency.

THE MARC GROUP
7850 North Beltline Road, Irving TX 75063. 972/506-3400. **Contact:** Human Resources. **World Wide Web address:** http://www.marcgroup.com. **Description:** A public relations firm.

MONEYHUN ADVERTISING INC.
3000 Carlisle Street, Suite 109, Dallas TX 75204. 214/871-2525. **Contact:** Media Director. **Description:** An advertising agency.

PROFORMA WATSONRISE BUSINESS SYSTEMS
501 Duncan Perry Road, Arlington TX 76011-5414. 817/640-1184. **Contact:** Human Resources. **Description:** An advertising agency.

PUBLICIS/BLOOM
3500 Maple Avenue, Suite 450, Dallas TX 75219. 214/443-9900. **Contact:** Personnel Director. **World Wide Web address:** http://www.publicis-bloom.com. **Description:** An advertising agency. Founded in 1952. **Number of employees nationwide:** 300.

RICHARDS GROUP, INC.
8750 North Central Expressway, Suite 1200, Dallas TX 75231-6437. 214/891-5700. **Contact:** Human Resources. **Description:** An advertising agency. **Listed on:** Privately held.

WITHERSPOON & ASSOCIATES

1000 West Weatherford, Fort Worth TX 76102. 817/335-1373. **Contact:** Mike Wilie, Senior Vice President. **Description:** An advertising agency. **Common positions include:** Graphic Artist. **Educational backgrounds include:** Art/Design; Business Administration; Marketing. **Benefits:** Life Insurance; Medical Insurance. **Corporate headquarters location:** This Location. **Operations at this facility include:** Service. **Number of employees at this location:** 35.

Note: Because addresses and telephone numbers of smaller companies can change rapidly, we recommend you call each company to verify the information below before inquiring about job opportunities. Mass mailings are not recommended.

Additional small employers:

DIRECT MAIL ADVERTISING SERVICES

ADVO Inc.
10155 Technology Blvd East, Dallas TX 75220. 214/630-7404.

Epsilon
2410 Gateway Dr, Irving TX 75063-2727. 972/582-9600.

Lee Data Mail Services
PO Box 226837, Dallas TX 75222-6837. 214/630-6941.

Mail Box Inc.
PO Box 226776, Dallas TX 75222-6776. 214/688-0331.

National Presort Services
921 W Commerce St, Dallas TX 75208-1742. 214/745-8870.

Republic Mailing & Fulfillment
2527 Willowbrook Rd, Dallas TX 75220-4420. 214/638-6505.

Tacito Direct Marketing
14165 Proton Rd, Dallas TX 75244-3604. 972/458-2026.

Texas Direct
PO Box 161097, Fort Worth TX 76161-1097. 817/234-9000.

MISC. ADVERTISING SERVICES

Cable Adnet
8150 Brookriver Dr, Dallas TX 75247-4068. 214/637-7744.

Eller Outdoor Advertising Co.
3700 E Randol Mill Rd, Arlington TX 76011-5435. 817/640-4550.

Evans Advertising & Public Relations
3100 Monticello Ave, Dallas TX 75205-3442. 214/520-1200.

Hadeler Sullivan & Law
5430 LBJ Fwy, Ste 1100, Dallas TX 75240. 972/776-8000.

LMS/Marc Advertising LP
2501 Cedar Springs Rd, Dallas TX 75201-1472. 214/979-5000.

Moroch & Associates Inc.
3625 N Hall St, Ste 1200, Dallas TX 75219-5123. 214/520-9700.

Regian Wilson Advertising & Public Relations
219 S Main St, Fort Worth TX 76104-1224. 817/870-1128.

Sports Promotion Network
1924 Baird Farm Road, Arlington TX 76006-6502. 817/795-5656.

Spotplus
200 Crescent Court, Ste 700, Dallas TX 75201-1827. 214/855-2200.

Temerlin McClain Inc.
PO Box 619200, Dallas TX 75261-9200. 972/556-1100.

The Focus Agency
200 Crescent Court, 9th Floor, Dallas TX 75201-1875. 214/855-2900.

PUBLIC RELATIONS SERVICES

Levenson Public Relations
PO Box 219051, Dallas TX 75221-9051. 214/880-0200.

Scurlock Permian Corporation
PO Box 10, Spearman TX 79081-0010. 806/659-2571.

TLP Inc.
200 Crescent Court, Ste 900, Dallas TX 75201-1875. 214/871-5600.

For more information on career opportunities in advertising, marketing, and public relations:

Associations

ADVERTISING RESEARCH FOUNDATION
641 Lexington Avenue, 11th Floor, New York NY 10174. 212/751-5656. Fax: 212/319-5265. E-mail address: email@arfsite.org. World Wide Web address: http://www.arfsite.org/arf. A nonprofit organization comprised of advertising, marketing, and media research companies. For institutions only.

AMERICAN ASSOCIATION OF ADVERTISING AGENCIES
405 Lexington Avenue, 18th Floor, New York NY 10174. 212/682-2500. World Wide Web address:

http://www.commercepark.com/aaaa. Offers educational and enrichment benefits such as publications, videos, and conferences.

AMERICAN MARKETING ASSOCIATION
250 South Wacker Drive, Suite 200, Chicago IL 60606. 312/648-0536. World Wide Web address: http://www.ama.org. An association with nearly 45,000 members worldwide. Offers a reference center, 25 annual conferences, and eight publications for marketing professionals and students.

DIRECT MARKETING ASSOCIATION
1120 Avenue of Americas, New York NY 10036-

6700. 212/768-7277. World Wide Web address: http://www.the-dma.org. This association offers monthly newsletters, seminars, and an annual telephone marketing conference.

INTERNATIONAL ADVERTISING ASSOCIATION
521 Fifth Avenue, Suite 1807, New York NY 10175. 212/557-1133. Fax: 212/983-0455. E-mail address: iaa@ibnet.com. World Wide Web address: http://www.iaaglobal.com. Over 3,600 members in 89 countries. Membership includes publications; professional development; congresses, symposia, and conferences; annual report and membership directory; and worldwide involvement with governments and other associations. Overall, the organization looks to promote free speech and the self-regulation of advertising.

LEAGUE OF ADVERTISING AGENCIES
2 South End Avenue #4C, New York NY 10280. 212/945-4991. Seminars available for agency principals.

MARKETING RESEARCH ASSOCIATION
1344 Silas Deane Highway, Suite 306, Rocky Hill CT 06067. 860/257-4008. World Wide Web address: http://www.mra-net.org. Publishes several magazines and newsletters.

PUBLIC RELATIONS SOCIETY OF AMERICA
33 Irving Place, New York NY 10003-2376. 212/995-2230. World Wide Web address: http://www.prsa.org. Publishes three magazines for public relations professionals.

Directories

AAAA ROSTER AND ORGANIZATION
American Association of Advertising Agencies, 405 Lexington Avenue, 18th Floor, New York NY 10147. 212/682-2500.

DIRECTORY OF MINORITY PUBLIC RELATIONS PROFESSIONALS
Public Relations Society of America, 33 Irving Place, New York NY 10003-2376. 212/995-2230.

O'DWYER'S DIRECTORY OF PUBLIC RELATIONS FIRMS
J. R. O'Dwyer Company, 271 Madison Avenue, Room 600, New York NY 10016. 212/679-2471.

PUBLIC RELATIONS CONSULTANTS DIRECTORY
American Business Directories, Division of American Business Lists, 5711 South 86th Circle, Omaha NE 68127. 402/593-4500. World Wide Web address: http://www.salesleadsusa.com.

STANDARD DIRECTORY OF ADVERTISING AGENCIES
Reed Reference Publishing Company, P.O. Box 31, New Providence NJ 07974. Toll-free phone: 800/521-8110.

Magazines

ADVERTISING AGE
Crain Communications, 740 North Rush Street, Chicago IL 60611. 312/649-5200. World Wide Web address: http://www.crainchicagobusiness.com.

ADWEEK
BPI, 1515 Broadway, 12th Floor, New York NY 10036-8986. 212/536-5336. World Wide Web address: http://www.adweek.com.

BUSINESS MARKETING
Crain Communications, 740 North Rush Street, Chicago IL 60611. 312/649-5200. World Wide Web address: http://www.crainchicagobusiness.com.

JOURNAL OF MARKETING
American Marketing Association, 250 South Wacker Drive, Suite 200, Chicago IL 60606. 312/648-0536.

THE MARKETING NEWS
American Marketing Association, 250 South Wacker Drive, Suite 200, Chicago IL 60606. 312/648-0536. A biweekly magazine offering new ideas and developments in marketing.

PR REPORTER
PR Publishing Company, P.O. Box 600, Exeter NH 03833. 603/778-0514. World Wide Web address: http://www.prpublishing.com.

PUBLIC RELATIONS NEWS
Phillips Publishing Inc., 1201 Seven Locks Road, Suite 300, Potomac MD 20854. 301/340-1520. Fax: 301/424-4297. World Wide Web address: http://www.phillips.com.

Newsletters

PUBLIC RELATIONS CAREER OPPORTUNITIES
1575 I Street NW, Suite 1190, Washington DC 20005. 202/408-7904. Fax: 202/408-7907. World Wide Web address: http://www.entremkt.com/ceo. Contact: James J. Zaniello, Managing Director. Newsletter listing public relations, public affairs, special events, and investor positions nationwide compensating above $35,000 annually. Available on a subscription basis, published 24 times a year on behalf of the Public Relations Society of America. Company also publishes other newsletters, including *CEO Job Opportunities Update* and *ASAE Career Opportunities* (for the American Society of Association Executives).

Online Services

ADVERTISING & MEDIA JOBS PAGE
http://www.nationjob.com/media. This Website offers advertising and media job openings that can be searched by a variety of criteria including location, type of position, and salary. This site also offers a service that will perform the search for you.

DIRECT MARKETING WORLD'S JOB CENTER
http://www.dmworld.com. Posts professional job openings for the direct marketing industry. This site also provides a career reference library, a list of direct marketing professionals, and a list of events within the industry.

MARKETING CLASSIFIEDS ON THE INTERNET
http://www.marketingjobs.com. Offers job listings by state, resume posting, discussions with other marketing professionals, links to other career sites, and company home pages.

AEROSPACE

Strong growth is predicted for the aerospace industry, where demand for commercial planes is high and suppliers are scrambling to keep up. The Aerospace Industries Association projected that profit margins would get a significant boost in 1998. Commercial aircraft shipments will be primarily responsible, and healthy growth is also expected for space launch vehicles, large transport aircraft, small business jets, and helicopters.

ASSOCIATED AIRCRAFT SUPPLY
6020 Cedar Springs Road, Dallas TX 75235. 214/331-4381. **Contact:** Ellen Hines, Personnel. **Description:** A distributor of aircraft parts and machinery.

BELL HELICOPTER TEXTRON
P.O. Box 482, Fort Worth TX 76101. 817/280-2011. **Contact:** Employment Department. **World Wide Web address:** http://www.bellhelicopter.textron.com. **Description:** Bell Helicopter Textron manufactures a variety of commercial and civilian helicopters and also conducts extensive research and development activities. **Corporate headquarters location:** This Location.

THE BOEING COMPANY
P.O. Box 9577, Dyess Air Force Base TX 79607. 915/695-3740. **Contact:** Personnel. **World Wide Web address:** http://www.boeing.com. **Description:** This location manufactures electrical and hydraulic components for repair work on aircraft. Overall, The Boeing Company is one of the largest aerospace firms in the United States, one of the nation's top exporters, and one of the world's leading manufacturers of commercial jet transports. The company is a major U.S. government contractor, with capabilities in missile and space, electronic systems, military aircraft, helicopters, and information systems management.

BOEING DEFENSE & SPACE
IRVING COMPANY
P.O. Box 152707, Irving TX 75015-2707. 972/659-2600. **Contact:** Human Resources Department. **World Wide Web address:** http://www.boeing.com. **Description:** Manufactures electrical components for aircraft. **Common positions include:** Buyer; Computer Programmer; Electrical/Electronics Engineer; Industrial Engineer; Software Engineer; Systems Analyst. **Educational backgrounds include:** Accounting; Business Administration; Chemistry; Computer Science; Engineering. **Benefits:** 401(k); Daycare Assistance; Dental Insurance; Disability Coverage; Fitness Program; Life Insurance; Medical Insurance; Tuition Assistance. **Corporate headquarters location:** Seattle WA. **Other U.S. locations:** Wichita KS; Philadelphia PA; Oakridge TN; Corinth TX. **Parent company:** The Boeing Company. **Operations at this facility include:** Manufacturing. **Number of employees at this location:** 1,150.

COLTEC INDUSTRIES, INC.
MENASCO AEROSYSTEMS DIVISION
4000 South Highway 157, Euless TX 76040. 817/283-4471. **Contact:** Kathy Johnson, Human Resources. **Description:** Manufactures aircraft landing gear. The company's primary customers are major airframe manufacturers and the U.S. Department of Defense. **Common positions include:** Accountant; Blue-Collar Worker Supervisor; Buyer; Computer Programmer; Department Manager; General Manager; Human Resources Manager; Machinist; Mechanical Engineer; Metallurgical Engineer; Operations/Production Manager; Quality Control Supervisor. **Educational backgrounds include:** Accounting; Business Administration; Computer Science; Engineering; Finance; Marketing. **Benefits:** Dental Insurance; Disability Coverage; Life Insurance; Medical Insurance; Pension Plan; Savings Plan; Tuition Assistance. **Corporate headquarters location:** Charlotte NC. **Operations at this facility include:** Administration; Divisional Headquarters; Manufacturing;

Research and Development. **Listed on:** New York Stock Exchange. **Number of employees nationwide:** 575.

W. PAT CROW FORGINGS
200 Luxton Street, Fort Worth TX 76104. 817/536-2861. **Contact:** Personnel. **Description:** Manufactures aircraft parts.

FOSTER-EDWARDS AIRCRAFT COMPANY INC.
P.O. Box 574, Addison TX 75001-0574. 972/931-0933. **Contact:** Human Resources. **Description:** Designs and manufactures aircraft interiors.

FOXTRONICS INC.
BATTERY DIVISION
3448 West Mockingbird Lane, Dallas TX 75235. 214/358-2490. **Contact:** Human Resources. **World Wide Web address:** http://www.foxtronics.com. **Description:** Engaged in the service and sale of aircraft batteries.

HELI-DYNE SYSTEMS INC.
P.O. Box 966, Hurst TX 76053. 817/282-9804. **Contact:** Human Resources. **Description:** A helicopter completion company.

KC AVIATION INC.
P.O. Box 7145, Dallas TX 75209. 214/902-7500. **Fax:** 214/630-9107. **Contact:** Eric Pate, Personnel Director. **Description:** Refurbishes and performs completion work on corporate aircraft.

LOCKHEED MARTIN SUPPORT SYSTEMS INC.
1600 East Pioneer Parkway, Suite 440, Arlington TX 76010-6563. 817/261-0295. **Contact:** Human Resources. **Description:** This location provides technical support for aircraft technicians. **NOTE:** In March 1998, Lockheed Martin was discussing merger plans with Northrop Grumman. Please contact this location for more information. **Parent company:** Lockheed Martin Corporation is a diversified defense contractor with businesses in engineering contracting, civil space programs, government services, commercial electronics, aeronautical systems, avionics, aerodynamics, and materials. Subsidiaries include a missiles and space systems group; an aeronautical systems group; a technology services group; an electronic systems group; and Lockheed Financial Corporation.

LOCKHEED MARTIN TACTICAL AIRCRAFT SYSTEMS
P.O. Box 748, Fort Worth TX 76101-0748. 817/777-2000. **Recorded jobline:** 817/777-1000. **Contact:** Human Resources. **World Wide Web address:** http://www.lmtas.com. **Description:** Engaged in the development and production of tactical aircraft. **NOTE:** In March 1998, Lockheed Martin was discussing merger plans with Northrop Grumman. Please contact this location for more information. **Common positions include:** Aerospace Engineer; Electrical/Electronics Engineer; Materials Engineer; Mechanical Engineer; Software Engineer; Systems Analyst. **Benefits:** 401(k); Dental Insurance; Disability Coverage; Life Insurance; Medical Insurance; Pension Plan; Savings Plan. **Corporate headquarters location:** Bethesda MD. **Other U.S. locations:** Nationwide. **Parent company:** Lockheed Martin Corporation operates in five major areas: Space Systems (develops space technology systems such as rocket systems, Space Shuttle support technology, and other products); Missile Systems (produces fleet ballistic missiles for military applications); Advanced Systems (operates as the research and development organization exploring military, commercial, and scientific needs); information processing (develops comprehensive database systems to process the specific needs of other company divisions); and the Austin Division (Austin TX -- responsible for designing and producing military tactical support systems). **Operations at this facility include:** Administration; Manufacturing; Research and Development. **Listed on:** New York Stock Exchange. **Number of employees at this location:** 12,000. **Number of employees nationwide:** 170,000.

LOCKHEED MARTIN VOUGHT SYSTEMS
P.O. Box 650003, Mail Stop LHR-PE, Dallas TX 75265-0003. 972/603-1000. **Contact:** Personnel. **Description:** Manufactures advanced tactical missiles, rockets, and space systems. **NOTE:** In March 1998, Lockheed Martin was discussing merger plans with Northrop Grumman. Please

contact this location for more information. **Common positions include:** Accountant/Auditor; Administrator; Aerospace Engineer; Attorney; Buyer; Ceramics Engineer; Computer Programmer; Department Manager; Electrical/Electronics Engineer; Financial Analyst; General Manager; Human Resources Manager; Industrial Engineer; Mechanical Engineer; Metallurgical Engineer; Physicist; Purchasing Agent/Manager; Systems Analyst. **Educational backgrounds include:** Accounting; Business Administration; Computer Science; Engineering; Finance; Marketing; Physics. **Benefits:** Dental Insurance; Disability Coverage; Employee Discounts; Life Insurance; Medical Insurance; Profit Sharing; Tuition Assistance. **Corporate headquarters location:** This Location. **Parent company:** Lockheed Martin Corporation is a diversified defense contractor with businesses in engineering contracting, civil space programs, government services, commercial electronics, aeronautical systems, avionics, aerodynamics, and materials. Subsidiaries include a missiles and space systems group; an aeronautical systems group; a technology services group; an electronic systems group; and Lockheed Financial Corporation. **Operations at this facility include:** Administration; Divisional Headquarters; Manufacturing; Research and Development. **Listed on:** New York Stock Exchange. **Number of employees at this location:** 2,800. **Number of employees nationwide:** 170,000.

LUMINATOR
1200 East Plano Parkway, Plano TX 75074. 972/424-6511. **Contact:** Denise Boyd, Human Resource Manager. **World Wide Web address:** http://www.luminatorusa.com. **Description:** Manufactures aircraft parts.

MARATHON POWER TECHNOLOGIES COMPANY
P.O. Box 8233, Waco TX 76714-8233. 254/776-0650. **Fax:** 254/776-1309. **Contact:** Jeff Oliver, Personnel Manager. **Description:** Manufactures nickel-cadmium aircraft batteries and electronic assemblies. **Common positions include:** Accountant/Auditor; Blue-Collar Worker Supervisor; Buyer; Chemical Engineer; Chemist; Clinical Lab Technician; Computer Programmer; Draftsperson; Electrical/Electronics Engineer; Electrician; General Manager; Human Resources Manager; Industrial Engineer; Industrial Production Manager; Mechanical Engineer; Purchasing Agent/Manager; Quality Control Supervisor; Services Sales Representative. **Educational backgrounds include:** Accounting; Business Administration; Chemistry; Engineering; Liberal Arts; Marketing. **Benefits:** 401(k); Dental Insurance; Disability Coverage; Life Insurance; Medical Insurance; Tuition Assistance. **Corporate headquarters location:** This Location. **Parent company:** Metapoint Partners. **Operations at this facility include:** Administration; Manufacturing; Research and Development; Sales; Service. **Number of employees at this location:** 190.

NORTHROP GRUMMAN CORPORATION
P.O. Box 655907, Mail Stop 49-ER, Dallas TX 75265-5907. 972/266-4238. **Contact:** Human Resources. **World Wide Web address:** http://www.northgrum.com. **Description:** An aircraft specialty manufacturer, producing structural subassemblies for military and commercial airplanes and helicopters. **NOTE:** In March 1998, Lockheed Martin was discussing merger plans with Northrop Grumman. Please contact this location for more information. **Common positions include:** Accountant/Auditor; Aerospace Engineer; Buyer; Human Resources Manager; Industrial Engineer; Mechanical Engineer; Metallurgical Engineer. **Educational backgrounds include:** Computer Science; Engineering. **Benefits:** Dental Insurance; Disability Coverage; Employee Discounts; Life Insurance; Medical Insurance; Pension Plan; Profit Sharing; Savings Plan; Tuition Assistance. **Corporate headquarters location:** This Location. **Operations at this facility include:** Administration; Manufacturing; Research and Development. **Listed on:** Privately held. **Number of employees at this location:** 5,200.

PRECISION AVIATION
5240 South Collins Street, Suite 100, Arlington TX 76018. 817/465-0908. **Contact:** Personnel. **Description:** An aircraft maintenance company that works primarily on small passenger planes.

SPINKS INDUSTRIES INC.
P.O. Box 821, Fort Worth TX 76101. 817/293-2140. **Contact:** Personnel Department. **World Wide Web address:** http://www.skyline-usa.com. **Description:** A manufacturer of aircraft parts.

STEARNS AIRPORT EQUIPMENT COMPANY, INC.

2300 West Risinger Road, Fort Worth TX 76134. 817/294-2020. **Fax:** 817/294-9206. **Contact:** Human Resources. **Description:** Manufactures passenger boarding bridges and conveyor systems for airports. **Common positions include:** Blue-Collar Worker Supervisor; Buyer; Cost Estimator; Customer Service Representative; Electrical/Electronics Engineer; Electrician; General Manager; Human Resources Manager; Industrial Production Manager; Mechanical Engineer; Operations/Production Manager; Purchasing Agent/Manager; Quality Control Supervisor; Services Sales Representative. **Educational backgrounds include:** Business Administration; Engineering; Marketing. **Benefits:** 401(k); Dental Insurance; Disability Coverage; Employee Discounts; Life Insurance; Medical Insurance; Pension Plan; Profit Sharing; Tuition Assistance. **Corporate headquarters location:** Dallas TX. **Parent company:** Trinity Industries, Inc. **Operations at this facility include:** Administration; Manufacturing; Sales. **Listed on:** New York Stock Exchange. **Number of employees at this location:** 150.

UNISHIPPERS ASSOCIATION

800 West Airport Freeway, Suite 611, Lock Box 6065, Irving TX 75062. 972/445-0088. **Contact:** Human Resources. **Description:** An authorized reseller of airplanes for air freight companies.

WHITEHALL CORPORATION

2659 Nova Drive, Dallas TX 75229. 972/247-8747. **Contact:** Michael Brinkley, Vice President, Controller. **Description:** Through subsidiaries, Whitehall Corporation modifies and maintains military and commercial aircraft, designs and manufactures marine sensor systems, and manufactures electronic components. **Common positions include:** Accountant/Auditor; Computer Programmer; Draftsperson; Electrical/Electronics Engineer. **Educational backgrounds include:** Accounting; Business Administration; Computer Science; Engineering. **Benefits:** Medical Insurance; Stock Option; Tuition Assistance. **Corporate headquarters location:** This Location. **Operations at this facility include:** Manufacturing; Service. **Listed on:** New York Stock Exchange. **Number of employees at this location:** 520.

Note: Because addresses and telephone numbers of smaller companies can change rapidly, we recommend you call each company to verify the information below before inquiring about job opportunities. Mass mailings are not recommended.

Additional small employers:

AIRCRAFT

American Eurocopter Corp.
2701 Forum Dr, Grand Prairie TX 75052-7027. 972/641-0000.

Premier Aviation Inc.
2621 Aviation Pkwy, Grand Prairie TX 75052-7608. 972/988-6181.

AIRCRAFT EQUIPMENT AND PARTS

Aerobotics Industries Inc.
1400 Westpark Way, Euless TX 76040-6734. 817/868-1707.

Aerospace Optics Inc.
3201 Sandy Lane, Fort Worth TX 76112-7203. 817/451-1141.

Hac Corporation
PO Box 531166, Grand Prairie TX 75053-1166. 972/263-4387.

Intercontinental Manufacturing
PO Box 461148, Garland TX 75046-1148. 972/276-5131.

Pratt & Whitney
PO Box 2425, Wichita Falls TX 76307-2425. 940/855-8401.

For more information on career opportunities in aerospace:

Associations

AMERICAN INSTITUTE OF AERONAUTICS AND ASTRONAUTICS
1801 Alexander Bell Drive, Reston VA 20191. World Wide Web address: http://www.aiaa.org. Membership required. Publishes six journals and books.

NATIONAL AERONAUTIC ASSOCIATION OF USA
1815 North Fort Myer Drive, Suite 700, Arlington VA 22209. 703/527-0226. World Wide Web address: http://www.naa.ycg.org. Publishes a magazine. Membership required.

PROFESSIONAL AVIATION MAINTENANCE ASSOCIATION
636 I Street, Suite 300, Washington DC 20001-3736. World Wide Web address: http://www.pama.org. Members' resumes are distributed to companies who advise the organization of employment opportunities. Many local chapters also provide job referrals.

Members have access to the Worldwide Membership Directory.

Online Services

AIAA CAREER ENHANCEMENT
http://www.lmsc.lockheed.com/aiaa/sf/career.html.

Resource center for aerospace professionals. AIAA Career Enhancement offers employment opportunities, an online resume service, consultants, aerospace news, career placement services, continuing education resources, and networking opportunities.

APPAREL AND TEXTILES

Employment in the apparel and textiles industry has been hurt by advances in labor-saving technology. Machinery such as computer-controlled cutters, semi-automatic sewing machines, and automated material handling systems continues to reduce the need for apparel workers.

Increased overseas production of apparel and textiles has also decreased the need for domestic workers who perform sewing functions. In fact, the U.S. Department of Commerce projected that imports would grow by about 9.2 percent in 1998. The industry has responded by attempting to develop niche markets, strong brand names, and faster customer response systems, according to Monthly Labor Review. *Despite these efforts, over 1 million U.S. textile and apparel jobs were eliminated between 1973 and 1997, and the U.S. Department of Labor expects employment to decline steadily through the year 2000.*

AMERICAN COTTON GROWERS
P.O. Box 430, Littlefield TX 79339-0430. 806/385-6401. **Contact:** Martha Rose, Personnel Manager. **Description:** Manufactures and wholesales denim. The company's primary customer is Levi-Strauss, a manufacturer of denim jeans. **Parent company:** Plains Cotton Cooperative Association (Lubbock TX). **Operations at this facility include:** Manufacturing.

BONHAM MANUFACTURING
2525 North Center Street, Bonham TX 75418. 903/583-9595. **Contact:** Human Resources. **Description:** Bonham Manufacturing is a producer of men's Western apparel.

COLESCE COUTURE INC.
9004 Ambassador Row, Dallas TX 75247. 214/631-4860. **Contact:** Human Resources. **Description:** A manufacturer and wholesaler of misses' and women's apparel.

DE LONG SPORTSWEAR
P.O. Box 299, Crowell TX 79227. 940/684-1561. **Contact:** Human Resources. **Description:** De Long Sportswear is a manufacturer of baseball caps.

FIBERITE INC.
4300 Jackson Street, Greenville TX 75402. 903/454-2004. **Contact:** Human Resources. **Description:** Manufactures silk and man-made broadwoven fabrics.

FOCUS APPAREL GROUP
8319 Chancellor Row, Dallas TX 75247-5515. 214/951-7356. **Contact:** Human Resources. **Description:** Focus Apparel Group is a manufacturer and wholesaler of misses' and women's clothing.

HAGGAR CLOTHING COMPANY
6113 Lemmon Avenue, Dallas TX 75209. 214/956-4235. **Fax:** 214/956-4419. **Contact:** Human Resources. **Description:** An apparel manufacturing company. **Common positions include:** Accountant/Auditor; Blue-Collar Worker Supervisor; Computer Programmer; Industrial Engineer; Management Trainee; Operations/Production Manager; Systems Analyst. **Educational backgrounds include:** Accounting; Business Administration; Communications; Computer Science; Engineering; Marketing. **Benefits:** 401(k); Daycare Assistance; Dental Insurance; Disability Coverage; Employee Discounts; Life Insurance; Medical Insurance; Profit Sharing; Tuition Assistance. **Special programs:** Internships. **Corporate headquarters location:** This

Location. **Operations at this facility include:** Administration; Research and Development; Service. **Listed on:** NASDAQ. **Number of employees at this location:** 800.

HATCO
601 Marion Drive, Garland TX 75042. 972/494-0511. **Contact:** Personnel Manager. **Description:** Manufactures a variety of men's weather-resistant hats and headgear. **Corporate headquarters location:** This Location.

JLN, INC.
111 North Main Street, Ferris TX 75125. 972/544-2271. **Contact:** Human Resources. **Description:** Manufactures leather bags and belts.

JUSTIN BOOT COMPANY
610 West Dagget Street, Fort Worth TX 76104. 817/332-4385. **Contact:** Personnel Director. **Description:** Manufactures cowboy boots, leather belts, handbags, and billfolds.

LEVI STRAUSS & COMPANY
2720 Market Street, Wichita Falls TX 76303. 940/767-1441. **Contact:** Human Resources. **World Wide Web address:** http://www.levi.com. **Description:** This location of Levi Strauss & Company manufactures jeans. Overall, the company designs, manufactures, and markets a diversified line of apparel for both sexes and all ages, including jeans, pants, skirts, tops, shirts, jackets, belts, accessories, activewear, and skiwear. Levi Strauss & Company's apparel is marketed principally under the Levis trademark in the United States and in numerous foreign countries. The company sells to retailers (primarily department stores) and to specialty stores. Levi Strauss & Company has over 120 locations nationwide. **Corporate headquarters location:** San Francisco CA.

PILLOWTEX CORPORATION
4111 Mint Way, Dallas TX 75237. 214/333-3225x114. **Fax:** 214/337-8398. **Contact:** Personnel Director. **World Wide Web address:** http://www.pillowtex.com. **Description:** A manufacturer of bed pillows, comforters, and mattress pads. **Common positions include:** Manufacturer's/Wholesaler's Sales Rep. **Benefits:** Dental Insurance; Disability Coverage; Employee Discounts; Life Insurance; Medical Insurance; Pension Plan; Tuition Assistance. **Corporate headquarters location:** This Location. **Other U.S. locations:** Monroe NC; Lando SC. **Operations at this facility include:** Administration.

PINDLER & PINDLER
1444 Oak Lawn Avenue, Oak Lawn Plaza, Suite 116, Dallas TX 75207. 214/939-9116. **Contact:** Human Resources. **World Wide Web address:** http://www.pindler.com. **Description:** A distributor of fabrics to wholesalers.

RC SEWING
200 Metro Park, Ennis TX 75119. 972/878-7453. **Contact:** Human Resources. **Description:** RC Sewing is a manufacturer of ladies sportswear.

RED KAP INDUSTRIES
P.O. Box 1409, Clarksville TX 75426. 903/427-3888. **Contact:** Human Resources. **Description:** This location manufactures men's jeans. Overall, Red Kap Industries manufactures occupational apparel as a division of VF Corporation, an international apparel company. Other specialties of Red Kap Industries include safety and flame resistant products, including high-visibility and reflective trim garments, as well as fluid-resistant apparel and other types of protective apparel. The company's brand names of work utility wear include Big Ben and WorkWear.

RUSSELL-NEWMAN MANUFACTURING COMPANY
Route 4, Box 6, Cisco TX 76437. 254/442-2005. **Contact:** Human Resources. **Description:** Russell-Newman Manufacturing Company is a manufacturer of women's lingerie and daywear.

SCOTT GROUP
5495 Belt Line Road, Suite 290, Dallas TX 75240-7658. 972/991-4919. **Contact:** Human Resources. **Description:** Scott Group is a manufacturer of hand-woven carpets.

SIDRAN INC.
2875 Merrell Road, Dallas TX 75229. 214/352-7979. **Contact:** Human Resources. **Description:** Sidran Inc. is a manufacturer and wholesaler of men's Western apparel.

SUNNY SOUTH FASHIONS
7777 Hines Place, Dallas TX 75235. 214/637-4333. **Contact:** Human Resources. **Description:** A manufacturer and wholesaler of women's and misses' clothing.

TANDY BRANDS ACCESSORIES
690 East Lamar Boulevard, Suite 200, Arlington TX 76011. 817/548-0090. **Contact:** Human Resources. **World Wide Web address:** http://www.tandybrands.com. **Description:** Tandy Brands Accessories manufactures belts, ties, suspenders, and other leather products.

UNICO CARPET COMPANY
5051 Sharp Street, Dallas TX 75247. 214/630-7875. **Contact:** Human Resources. **Description:** A manufacturer and distributor of floor coverings and carpets.

WALLS INDUSTRIES, INC.
1905 North Main Street, Cleburne TX 76031. 817/645-4366. **Contact:** Human Resources. **Description:** A manufacturer of outerwear for men, women, and children. **Corporate headquarters location:** This Location.

WALLS INDUSTRIES, INC.
P.O. Box 196, Sweetwater TX 79556-0196. 915/235-5455. **Fax:** 915/235-8512. **Contact:** Personnel Director. **World Wide Web address:** http://www.wallsoutdoors.com. **Description:** A manufacturer of men's and women's jackets. **Corporate headquarters location:** Gatesville TX. **Number of employees at this location:** 210.

WALLS INDUSTRIES, INC.
P.O. Box 18, Gatesville TX 76528. 254/865-7215. **Physical address:** 1501 West Main, Gatesville TX 76528. **Contact:** Human Resources. **World Wide Web address:** http://www.wallsoutdoors.com. **Description:** A manufacturer of outerwear for men, women, and children. **Corporate headquarters location:** This Location.

WILLIAMSON-DICKIE MANUFACTURING COMPANY
P.O. Box 1779, Fort Worth TX 76101. 817/336-7201. **Contact:** Estelle Lewis, Director of Human Resources. **Description:** Manufactures apparel for men and boys. The company's primary products are casual slacks and work pants. **Corporate headquarters location:** This Location.

HOWARD B. WOLF INC.
3809 Parry Avenue, Dallas TX 75226. 214/823-9941. **Fax:** 214/828-0631. **Contact:** Eugene K. Friesen, Senior Vice President. **E-mail address:** gene@hbwolf.com. **World Wide Web address:** http://www.hbwolf.com. **Description:** An apparel company specializing in the manufacture of women's fashions. **Benefits:** Employee Discounts; Life Insurance; Mass Transit Available; Medical Insurance; Profit Sharing. **Operations at this facility include:** Administration; Manufacturing; Research and Development; Sales. **Annual sales/revenues:** $11 - $20 million.

Note: Because addresses and telephone numbers of smaller companies can change rapidly, we recommend you call each company to verify the information below before inquiring about job opportunities. Mass mailings are not recommended.

Additional small employers:

APPAREL WHOLESALE

Polo Ralph Lauren LP
2800 Routh St, Ste 260, Dallas TX 75201-1448. 214/954-4343.

BROADWOVEN FABRIC MILLS

Eastlander Designs
202 N College Ave, Eastland TX 76448-1606. 254/629-2514.

Hobbs Industries
PO Box 640, Groesbeck TX 76642-0640. 254/729-3223.

FOOTWEAR

Justin Boot Company
PO Box 548, Fort Worth TX
76101-0548. 817/348-2841.

Nocona Boot Company
PO Box 599, Nocona TX 76255-
0599. 940/825-3321.

KNITTING MILLS

Haggar Clothing Co.
11990 Shiloh Rd, Dallas TX
75228-1503. 972/270-7493.

LEATHER TANNING AND FINISHING

Bronco Products
PO Box 8008, McKinney TX
75070-8008. 972/542-0055.

MEN'S AND BOYS' CLOTHING

Angelica Image Apparel
2201 S Harwood St, Dallas TX
75215-1324. 214/428-4995.

Capital Industries
332 S Hampton Rd, De Soto TX
75115-5746. 972/223-8440.

Reebok Team Uniforms
PO Box 326, Waco TX 76703-
0326. 254/752-2511.

Walls Industries
PO Box 339, Merkel TX 79536-
0339. 915/928-4761.

Wolf Manufacturing Company
PO Box 3100, Waco TX 76707-
0100. 254/753-7301.

NONWOVEN FABRICS

Hobbs Bonded Fiber
PO Box 2521, Waco TX 76702-
2521. 254/741-0040.

TEXTILES

Levi Strauss & Co.
4724 NE 24th Ave, Amarillo TX
79107-5802. 806/381-2323.

Rose Tree
7900 Ambassador Row, Dallas
TX 75247-4814. 214/637-6900.

WOMEN'S AND MISSES' CLOTHING

Watters & Watters
4320 Spring Valley Rd, Dallas
TX 75244-3701. 972/991-6994.

For more information on career opportunities in the apparel and textiles industries:

Associations

AMERICAN APPAREL MANUFACTURERS ASSOCIATION
2500 Wilson Boulevard, Suite 301, Arlington VA
22201. 703/524-1864. World Wide Web address:
http://www.americanapparel.org. Publishes numerous
magazines, newsletters, and bulletins for the benefit of
employees in the apparel manufacturing industry.

AMERICAN TEXTILE MANUFACTURERS INSTITUTE
Office of the Chief Economist, 1130 Connecticut
Avenue, Suite 1200, Washington DC 20036. 202/862-
0500. Fax: 202/862-0570. World Wide Web address:
http://www.atmi.org. The national trade association
for the domestic textile industry. Members are
corporations only.

THE FASHION GROUP
597 Fifth Avenue, 8th Floor, New York NY 10017.
212/593-1715. World Wide Web address: http://www.
fgi.org. A nonprofit organization for professional
women in the fashion industries (apparel, accessories,
beauty, and home). Offers career counseling
workshops 18 times per year.

INTERNATIONAL ASSOCIATION OF CLOTHING DESIGNERS
475 Park Avenue South, 9th Floor, New York NY
10016. 212/685-6602. Fax: 212/545-1709.

Directories

AAMA DIRECTORY
American Apparel Manufacturers Association, 2500
Wilson Boulevard, Suite 301, Arlington VA 22201.
703/524-1864. A directory of publications distributed
by the American Apparel Manufacturers Association.

APPAREL TRADES BOOK
Dun & Bradstreet Inc., One Diamond Hill Road,
Murray Hill NJ 07974. 908/665-5000.

FAIRCHILD'S MARKET DIRECTORY OF WOMEN'S AND CHILDREN'S APPAREL
Fairchild Publications, 7 West 34th Street, New York
NY 10001. 212/630-4000.

Magazines

ACCESSORIES
Business Journals, 50 Day Street, P.O. Box 5550,
Norwalk CT 06856. 203/853-6015.

AMERICA'S TEXTILES
Billiam Publishing, 555 North Pleasant Bark Drive,
Suite 132, Greenville SC 29607. 864/242-5300.

APPAREL INDUSTRY MAGAZINE
Shore Verone Inc., 6255 Barfield Road, Suite 200,
Atlanta GA 30328-4300. 404/252-8831. World Wide
Web address: http://www.svi-atl.com.

BOBBIN MAGAZINE
Bobbin Publishing Group, P.O. Box 1986, 1110 Shop
Road, Columbia SC 29202. 803/771-7500.

TEXTILE HILIGHTS
American Textile Manufacturers Institute, Office of
the Chief Economist, 1801 K Street NW, Suite 900,
Washington DC 20006. A quarterly publication.
Subscriptions: $125.00 per year (domestic); $200.00
per year (international).

WOMEN'S WEAR DAILY (WWD)
Fairchild Publications, 7 West 34th Street, New York
NY 10001. 212/630-4000. World Wide Web address:
http://www.wwd.com.

Online Services

THE INTERNET FASHION EXCHANGE
http://www.fashionexch.com. An excellent site for those industry professionals interested in apparel and retail. The extensive search engine allows you to search by job title, location, salary, product line, industry, and whether you want a permanent, temporary, or freelance position. The Internet Fashion Exchange also offers career services such as recruiting and outplacement firms that place fashion and retail professionals.

ARCHITECTURE, CONSTRUCTION, AND ENGINEERING

Building on its success in the mid-'90s, the construction industry is flourishing. Approximately 7.1 million workers were employed in the industry in 1997, a record year according to U.S. Industry and Trade Outlook 1998. *While the nation's booming economy has encouraged new construction projects across the country, the Associated Builders and Contractors Association is predicting a shortage of 250,000 workers each year into the next decade.*

For jobseekers who choose construction, the best opportunities will be in projects at electric utilities, educational facilities, and water supply facilities. In 1998, housing starts are expected to total 1.41 million, a 1 percent increase over 1997. Construction is likely to remain strongest in the Midwest and the South. Building trade workers such as architects, bricklayers, concrete masons, and sheet metal workers will see only average growth in their industries through 2005.

In engineering, the best opportunities through 2005 are in the civil, industrial, and electrical sectors. Aerospace engineers will continue to face fierce competition and chemical engineers will have more opportunities with companies that focus on developing specialty chemicals.

ANDERSON INDUSTRIES, INC.
5440 Harvest Hill Road, Dallas TX 75230. 972/233-1805. **Contact:** Personnel Department. **Description:** A producer of pre-fabricated building materials. **Corporate headquarters location:** This Location.

APAC TEXAS, INC.
P.O. Box 224048, Dallas TX 75222-4048. 214/741-3531. **Contact:** Personnel. **Description:** A general contracting company specializing in concrete and asphalt paving work.

AUSTIN COMMERCIAL INC.
P.O. Box 2879, Dallas TX 75221. 214/443-5700. **Contact:** Human Resources Department. **World Wide Web address:** http://www.austin-ind.com. **Description:** A special trade construction contracting company.

JOHN F. BEASLEY CONSTRUCTION
4001 Jaffee Street, Dallas TX 75216. 214/376-3000. **Contact:** Personnel Department. **Description:** A general contracting firm.

BUELL DOOR COMPANY
5200 East Grand Avenue, Dallas TX 75223. 214/827-9260. **Contact:** Personnel Department. **Description:** A manufacturer of architectural doors and hardware.

THOMAS S. BYRNE INC.
900 Summit Avenue, Fort Worth TX 76102. 817/335-3394. **Contact:** Personnel. **Description:** A general construction company.

CAVALIER HOMES, INC.
P.O. Box 5003, Wichita Falls TX 76307. 940/723-5523. **Physical address:** 719 Scott Street, Suite 600, Wichita Falls TX 76301. **Contact:** Human Resources. **E-mail address:**

cavhomes@cyberstation.net. **Description:** This location houses administrative offices. Overall, Cavalier Homes, Inc. designs and manufactures a wide range of homes and markets them through approximately 500 independent dealers located in 32 states, with approximately 625 sale centers. Through its wholly-owned subsidiary, Cavalier Acceptance Corporation, the company makes installment sale financing available to qualifying retail customers of these exclusive dealers. **Corporate headquarters location:** Addison AL. **Other U.S. locations:** GA; NC; PA.

CENTEX CONSTRUCTION COMPANY, INC.
P.O. Box 299009, Dallas TX 75229-9009. 214/357-1891. **Fax:** 214/902-6391. **Contact:** David Preston, Vice President of Administration. **World Wide Web address:** http://www.centex-construction.com. **Description:** A commercial general contractor providing pre-construction, construction, management, and general contracting services. **Common positions include:** Civil Engineer; Construction Contractor; Cost Estimator; Project Manager; Purchasing Agent/Manager; Quality Control Supervisor. **Educational backgrounds include:** Construction. **Benefits:** 401(k); Dental Insurance; Disability Coverage; Life Insurance; Medical Insurance; Profit Sharing. **Corporate headquarters location:** This Location. **Other U.S. locations:** Fairfax VA. **Subsidiaries include:** Centex Landis (New Orleans LA). **Parent company:** Centex Corporation. **Operations at this facility include:** Regional Headquarters. **Listed on:** New York Stock Exchange. **Number of employees at this location:** 65. **Number of employees nationwide:** 260.

CENTEX CORPORATION
P.O. Box 199000, Dallas TX 75219. 214/981-5000. **Contact:** Human Resources. **World Wide Web address:** http://www.centex.com. **Description:** Provides home building, mortgage banking, contracting, and construction products and services. **Corporate headquarters location:** This Location. **Subsidiaries include:** Centex Homes is one of America's largest home builders; CTX Mortgage Company is among the top retail originators of single-family home mortgages; Centex Construction Company, Inc. is one of the largest general building contractors in the U.S., as well as one of the largest constructors of health care facilities; Centex Construction Products, Inc., which manufactures and distributes cement, ready-mix concrete, aggregates, and gypsum wallboard, is one of the largest U.S.-owned cement producers; Centex Development Company, LP conducts real estate development activities. **Listed on:** New York Stock Exchange.

CULLUM CONSTRUCTION COMPANY
2814 Industrial Lane, Garland TX 75041. 214/987-9191. **Contact:** Personnel. **Description:** A contractor specializing in heavy utility construction.

DeMOSS COMPANY
4205 Stadium Drive, Suite 100, Fort Worth TX 76133. 817/920-9990. **Contact:** Ms. Renee Wallis, Personnel. **Description:** A general construction contractor.

ELCOR CORPORATION
14643 Dallas Parkway, Suite 1000, Dallas TX 75240-8871. 972/851-0500. **Contact:** Human Resources. **World Wide Web address:** http://www.elcor.com. **Description:** Manufactures roofing products including fiberglass asphalt shingles.

ELJER INDUSTRIES INC./ZURN INDUSTRIES, INC.
P.O. Box 709001, Dallas TX 75370-9998. 972/560-2000. **Physical address:** 14801 Quorum Drive, Dallas TX. **Fax:** 972/560-2279. **Contact:** Human Resources. **World Wide Web address:** http://www.zurn.com. **Description:** A leading manufacturer of building products for residential construction, commercial construction, and repair and remodeling markets. Eljer Industries Inc. manufactures and markets plumbing, heating, ventilating, and air conditioning products in North America and Europe. The company markets its products through wholesale distribution channels and, in North America, directly to building products retailers. **Corporate headquarters location:** This Location. **Number of employees at this location:** 4,800.

ELK CORPORATION OF TEXAS
202 Cedar Drive, Ennis TX 75119. 972/875-9611. **Fax:** 972/872-2392. **Contact:** Human Resources. **World Wide Web address:** http://www.elcor.com. **Description:** Manufactures residential roofing products and fiberglass mats. **Common positions include:** Accountant/Auditor;

Blue-Collar Worker Supervisor; Chemical Engineer; Clerical Supervisor; Designer; Electrical/Electronics Engineer; Human Resources Manager; Manufacturer's/Wholesaler's Sales Rep.; Mechanical Engineer. **Educational backgrounds include:** Accounting; Engineering; Marketing. **Benefits:** 401(k); Disability Coverage; Life Insurance; Medical Insurance; Profit Sharing; Savings Plan; Tuition Assistance. **Corporate headquarters location:** Dallas TX. **Other U.S. locations:** Tuscaloosa AL; Shafter CA. **Parent company:** Elcor Corporation. **Operations at this facility include:** Administration; Manufacturing; Sales. **Listed on:** New York Stock Exchange.

FACTORY MUTUAL ENGINEERING
12222 Merit Drive, Suite 1800, Dallas TX 75251. 972/661-9202. **Fax:** 972/661-1402. **Contact:** Jean Stouffer, Administrative Manager. **World Wide Web address:** http://www.factorymutual. com. **Description:** A loss control services organization with 17 district offices strategically located throughout the United States and Canada. Factory Mutual Engineering helps owner company policyholders to protect their properties and occupancies from damage caused by fire, wind, flood, and explosion; boiler, pressure vessel, and machinery accidents; and many other insured hazards. **Common positions include:** Chemical Engineer; Civil Engineer; Electrical/Electronics Engineer; Fire Science/Protection Engineer; Mechanical Engineer. **Educational backgrounds include:** Engineering. **Benefits:** Dental Insurance; Disability Coverage; Employee Discounts; Life Insurance; Medical Insurance; Pension Plan; Savings Plan; Tuition Assistance. **Corporate headquarters location:** Norwood MA.

FISHBACH & MOORE INC.
2525 Walnut Hill Lane, Suite 201, Dallas TX 75229. 972/241-4282. **Contact:** Human Resources Department. **Description:** Fishbach & Moore Inc. is an electrical contracting firm.

GAF MATERIALS CORPORATION
2600 Singleton Boulevard, Dallas TX 75212. 214/637-1060. **Contact:** Human Resources Department. **World Wide Web address:** http://www.ispcorp.com. **Description:** GAF Materials Corporation is a multiproduct manufacturer with sales in both consumer and industrial markets. The company's product line includes building, roofing, and insulation materials for the construction trades; specialty chemicals and plastics; and reprographic products. **Common positions include:** Accountant/Auditor; Blue-Collar Worker Supervisor; Customer Service Representative; Electrical/Electronics Engineer; Industrial Engineer; Manufacturer's/Wholesaler's Sales Rep.; Operations/Production Manager; Production Worker; Purchasing Agent/Manager; Quality Control Supervisor. **Educational backgrounds include:** Accounting; Business Administration; Engineering; Manufacturing Management. **Benefits:** 401(k); Dental Insurance; Disability Coverage; Life Insurance; Medical Insurance; Pension Plan; Tuition Assistance. **Corporate headquarters location:** Wayne NJ. **Other U.S. locations:** Nationwide. **Operations at this facility include:** Manufacturing; Sales. **Listed on:** Privately held. **Number of employees at this location:** 235.

GENERAL ALUMINUM CORPORATION
1001 West Crosby Road, Carrollton TX 75006. 972/242-5271. **Contact:** Personnel Department. **Description:** Manufactures aluminum doors and windows, partition screens, sliding glass doors, and related products.

HNTB CORPORATION
14114 Dallas Parkway, Suite 630, Dallas TX 75240. 972/661-5626. **Fax:** 972/661-5614. **Contact:** Claire Caldwell, Manager of Administration. **World Wide Web address:** http://www.hntb.com. **Description:** Offers architectural, engineering, and planning services to public agencies and private industry. **NOTE:** Entry-level positions are offered. Interested jobseekers should check the company's employment page on the World Wide Web and fax a resume. **Common positions include:** Civil Engineer; Construction and Building Inspector; Construction Contractor; Cost Estimator; Design Engineer; Designer; Draftsperson; Environmental Engineer; Structural Engineer; Technical Writer/Editor; Transportation/Traffic Specialist; Typist/Word Processor; Urban/Regional Planner. **Educational backgrounds include:** Engineering. **Benefits:** 401(k); Dental Insurance;

Disability Coverage; Life Insurance; Medical Insurance; Profit Sharing; Tuition Assistance. **Special programs:** Training. **Corporate headquarters location:** Kansas City MO. **Other U.S. locations:** Nationwide. **Subsidiaries include:** Alcyone Group, Inc.; Infrastructure Management Group; Thomas K. Dyer, Inc. **Operations at this facility include:** Sales. **Listed on:** Privately held. **Annual sales/revenues:** $5 - $10 million. **Number of employees at this location:** 30. **Number of employees nationwide:** 1,880.

HENNINGSON, DURHAM & RICHARDSON, INC.
12700 Hillcrest Road, Suite 125, Dallas TX 75230. 972/960-4000. **Fax:** 972/960-4185. **Contact:** Human Resources. **Description:** Offers architectural and engineering design services, in addition to construction consulting and interior design services. The company's three main business sectors are health care, justice, and science and industry. Founded in 1917. **Common positions include:** Administrative Assistant; Administrative Manager; Architect; Architectural Engineer; Controller; Draftsperson; Electrical/Electronics Engineer; Marketing Specialist; Mechanical Engineer; Project Manager; Systems Analyst. **Educational backgrounds include:** Art/Design; Engineering; Health Care; Marketing. **Special programs:** Internships. **Corporate headquarters location:** Omaha NE. **Other U.S. locations:** Alexandria VA. **Operations at this facility include:** Administration; Marketing; Regional Headquarters; Service. **Listed on:** Privately held. **Number of employees at this location:** 85. **Number of employees nationwide:** 1,600.

D.R. HORTON, INC.
1901 Ascension Boulevard, Suite 100, Arlington TX 76006. 817/856-8200. **Fax:** 817/856-8249. **Contact:** Human Resources. **Description:** D.R. Horton, Inc. and its operating subsidiaries are engaged primarily in the construction and sale of single-family homes, designed principally for the entry-level and move-up market segments. **Number of employees nationwide:** 400.

HOWE-BAKER ENGINEERS, INC.
P.O. Box 956, Tyler TX 75710. 903/597-0311. **Physical address:** 3102 East Fifth Street, Tyler TX 75701. **Contact:** Human Resources. **Description:** An engineering services company.

INSITUFORM TEXARK, INC.
3001 Roy Orr Boulevard, Grand Prairie TX 75050. 972/228-8888. **Contact:** Human Resources. **Description:** This location conducts pipeline rehabilitation. Overall, Insituform Texark, Inc. uses various trenchless technologies for rehabilitation, new construction, and improvements of pipeline systems, including sewers, gas lines, industrial waste lines, water lines, and oil field, mining, and industrial process pipelines. **Parent company:** Insituform Mid-America, Inc. provides a wide variety of technologies including Insituform, PALTEM, Tite Liner, and tunneling.

LAUREN ENGINEERS & CONSTRUCTORS
901 South First Street, Abilene TX 79602. 915/670-9660. **Contact:** Paula Eaves, Personnel. **World Wide Web address:** http://www.laurenec.com. **Description:** Designs and builds power plants, refineries, and related large-scale projects.

LENNOX INTERNATIONAL, INC.
P.O. Box 799900, Dallas TX 75379-9900. 972/497-5000. **Physical address:** 2100 Lake Park Boulevard, Dallas TX. **Fax:** 972/497-5476. **Contact:** Human Resources. **Description:** Produces Lennox brand heating and air conditioning equipment. **Common positions include:** Accountant/Auditor; Buyer; Computer Programmer; Customer Service Representative; Manufacturing Engineer; Mechanical Engineer; Sales Representative; Systems Analyst. **Educational backgrounds include:** Accounting; Business Administration; Computer Science; Engineering; Finance; Liberal Arts; Marketing. **Benefits:** 401(k); Dental Insurance; Disability Coverage; Employee Discounts; Life Insurance; Medical Insurance; Pension Plan; Profit Sharing; Tuition Assistance. **Special programs:** Internships. **Corporate headquarters location:** This Location. **Subsidiaries include:** Armstrong; Heatcraft Inc.; Lennox Industries. **Operations at this facility include:** Administration. **Listed on:** Privately held. **Annual sales/revenues:** More than $100 million. **Number of employees at this location:** 1,000. **Number of employees nationwide:** 9,000. **Number of employees worldwide:** 10,000.

MANUFACTURING GROUP INTERNATIONAL
2841 Pierce Street, Dallas TX 75233. 214/467-4444. **Contact:** Human Resources. **Description:** Manufactures kitchen cabinets and bathroom vanities.

MASTER SHIELD INC.
1202 North Bowie Drive, Weatherford TX 76086-1539. 817/596-7090. **Contact:** Human Resources. **Description:** A manufacturer of vinyl siding for homes and other buildings.

MORGAN BUILDING & SPAS, INC.
P.O. Box 660280, Dallas TX 75266-0280. 972/840-1200. **Physical address:** 2800 McCree Road, Garland TX 75041. **Fax:** 972/864-7304. **Contact:** Leslie McLoad, Personnel Coordinator. **World Wide Web address:** http://www.morgandallastx.com. **Description:** Manufactures, transports, and retails relocatable buildings of all sizes and uses, as well as spas, recreational vehicles, swimming pools, and decks to consumers, businesses, government buyers, and institutional buyers. The firm has four manufacturing facilities in the United States, 25 company-owned stores, and 40 dealer outlets. **Common positions include:** Accountant/Auditor; Advertising Clerk; Architect; Attorney; Blue-Collar Worker Supervisor; Branch Manager; Budget Analyst; Buyer; Clerical Supervisor; Computer Programmer; Cost Estimator; Draftsperson; Financial Analyst; Human Resources Manager; Management Trainee; Manufacturer's/Wholesaler's Sales Rep.; Operations/Production Manager; Paralegal; Purchasing Agent/Manager; Quality Control Supervisor; Structural Engineer; Systems Analyst; Wholesale and Retail Buyer. **Educational backgrounds include:** Accounting; Art/Design; Business Administration; Computer Science; Engineering; Mathematics. **Benefits:** Dental Insurance; Disability Coverage; Employee Discounts; Life Insurance; Medical Insurance; Tuition Assistance. **Corporate headquarters location:** This Location. **Other U.S. locations:** AL; AR; CO; GA; LA; MO; MS; NM; OK; TN. **Operations at this facility include:** Administration; Divisional Headquarters. **Listed on:** Privately held. **Number of employees at this location:** 120. **Number of employees nationwide:** 800.

MORRISON SUPPLY COMPANY
P.O. Box 70, Fort Worth TX 76101. 817/336-0451. **Contact:** Charles Allen, Personnel Manager. **Description:** A wholesaler of plumbing and heating equipment, tools, and supplies.

NATURALITE INC.
P.O. Box 629, Terrell TX 75160. 972/551-6400. **Contact:** Human Resources. **Description:** A special trade construction contracting company.

O'HAIR SHUTTERS
P.O. Box 2764, Lubbock TX 79408. 806/765-5791. **Contact:** Hiring Manager. **Description:** Manufactures outdoor shutters for homes. **Corporate headquarters location:** This Location.

OVERHEAD DOOR CORPORATION OF TEXAS
6750 LBJ Freeway, Suite 1200, Dallas TX 75240. 972/233-6611. **Contact:** Renee Carrico, Director of Human Resources. **Description:** Manufactures aluminum, steel, fiberglass, and wooden overhead doors, rolling steel fire doors, grilles, and metal insulated entrance doors. Products are distributed through a network of more than 400 authorized distributors in the United States and Canada. The company also manufactures truck and trailer doors. **Corporate headquarters location:** This Location. **Other U.S. locations:** Dallas TX; Carrollton TX; Corpus Christi TX; Fort Worth TX; Houston TX; Mount Pleasant TX; Richardson TX. **Listed on:** New York Stock Exchange.

QUALITY CABINETS
515 Big Stone Gap Road, Duncanville TX 75137. 972/298-6101. **Contact:** Human Resources. **World Wide Web address:** http://www.qualitycabinets.com. **Description:** A special trade construction contracting company.

R.E. SWEENEY COMPANY INC.
3700 Noble Avenue, Fort Worth TX 76111. 817/834-7191. **Contact:** Ron Belota, Controller. **Description:** A wholesaler of building materials.

TD INDUSTRIES, INC.
P.O. Box 819060, Dallas TX 75381-9060. 972/888-9505. **Physical address:** 13850 Diplomat Drive, Dallas TX 75234. **Fax:** 972/888-9507. **Contact:** Ms. Jessie McCain, Vice President of Administration. **World Wide Web address:** http://www.tdindustries.com. **Description:** An employee-owned, national construction and service company that designs, installs, and repairs HVAC, plumbing, high-purity process piping, and energy management systems in commercial and industrial markets. Founded in 1946. **Common positions include:** Design Engineer; Mechanical Engineer. **Educational backgrounds include:** Engineering. **Benefits:** 401(k); Dental Insurance; Disability Coverage; Employee Discounts; Financial Planning Assistance; Life Insurance; Medical Insurance; Pension Plan; Profit Sharing; Savings Plan; Tuition Assistance. **Corporate headquarters location:** This Location. **Other U.S. locations:** Houston TX; San Antonio TX. **Annual sales/revenues:** More than $100 million. **Number of employees at this location:** 800. **Number of employees nationwide:** 1,000.

WING INDUSTRIES INC.
6202 Industrial Drive, Greenville TX 75402. 903/455-1200. **Contact:** Human Resources. **Description:** Manufactures wooden doors.

H.B. ZACHRY COMPANY
P.O. Box 531558, Grand Prairie TX 75053-1558. 972/262-8898. **Contact:** Human Resources. **Description:** This location is a field district office. Overall, H.B. Zachry is a construction management company operating through the following seven divisions: Process, Power, Heavy, Maintenance & Service, Commercial, International, and Pipeline. The company primarily builds power plants, highways, and pipelines in the southern United States as well as in foreign countries. H.B. Zachry Company does not handle residential construction contracts.

H.B. ZACHRY COMPANY
P.O. Box 7309, Longview TX 75607-7309. 903/643-2253. **Fax:** 903/643-9103. **Contact:** Human Resources. **Description:** A construction management company operating through the following seven divisions: Process, Power, Heavy, Maintenance & Service, Commercial, International, and Pipeline. The company primarily builds power plants, highways, and pipelines in the southern United States as well as in foreign countries. H.B. Zachry Company does not handle residential construction contracts.

Note: Because addresses and telephone numbers of smaller companies can change rapidly, we recommend you call each company to verify the information below before inquiring about job opportunities. Mass mailings are not recommended.

Additional small employers:

ARCHITECTURAL SERVICES

Aguirre Inc.
12700 Park Central Dr, Dallas TX 75251-1500. 972/788-1508.

Corgan Associates Inc.
PO Box 155369, Fort Worth TX 76155-0369. 817/963-1734.

Corgan Associates Inc.
501 Elm St, Ste 500, Dallas TX 75202-3339. 214/748-2000.

FDS International
8615 Freeport Parkway, Irving TX 75063-2586. 972/915-3004.

HED
2625 Elm St, Ste 212, Dallas TX 75226-1497. 214/820-2872.

HKS Inc.
700 N Pearl St, Ste 1100, Dallas TX 75201-2814. 214/969-5599.

PSP
3500 Maple Ave, Ste 700, Dallas TX 75219-3902. 214/522-3900.

RTKL Associates Inc.
2828 Routh St, Ste 200, Dallas TX 75201-1435. 214/871-8877.

SHW Group Inc.
4101 McEwen Rd, Ste 300, Dallas TX 75244-5128. 972/701-0700.

Wilson & Associates
3811 Turtle Creek Blvd, Dallas TX 75219-4461. 214/521-6753.

BRIDGE, TUNNEL, AND HIGHWAY CONSTRUCTION

SA Healy Company
4405 Worcola St, Dallas TX 75206-5013. 214/823-8123.

CONCRETE WORK

Cortez Group Inc.
1401 Cates St, Ste 201, Bridgeport TX 76426-3117. 940/683-3273.

Don Jr. Concrete Construction
Drawer 50 Box 5050, Lewisville TX 75067. 972/221-8499.

JPS Construction Inc.
528 S Coppell Rd, Coppell TX
75019-3903. 972/471-1972.

JRJ Paving Inc.
PO Box 59934, Dallas TX 75229-
1934. 972/869-2971.

**Mobley-Speed Cement
Contractors**
PO Box 35148, Dallas TX 75235-
0148. 214/637-3270.

Potter Concrete Co. Inc.
5601 Bridge St, Fort Worth TX
76112-2384. 817/429-7919.

Site Concrete Inc.
PO Box 140096, Irving TX
75014-0096. 972/313-0733.

Striland Construction Inc.
10860 Switzer Ave, Ste 109,
Dallas TX 75238-5302. 214/340-
1811.

**CONSTRUCTION
MATERIALS WHOLESALE**

ACI Distribution
PO Box 815547, Dallas TX
75381-5547. 972/484-3691.

Fashion Glass & Mirror
585 S Beckley Ave, De Soto TX
75115-6402. 972/223-8936.

ELECTRICAL WORK

Accucom Technical Services
990 N Bowser Rd, Ste 840,
Richardson TX 75081-2859.
972/238-7502.

Alman Electric Inc.
7677 Hunnicut Rd, Dallas TX
75228-6947. 214/388-1800.

Cactus Service Co.
PO Box 11357, Lubbock TX
79408-7357. 806/744-4240.

Clark Electrical Construction
PO Box 2049, Fort Worth TX
76113-2049. 817/831-0678.

Design Electric
2650 Andjon Dr, Dallas TX
75220-1310. 214/357-5697.

E-MC Electrical Contractors
2900 E Randol Mill Rd,
Arlington TX 76011-6726.
817/695-1313.

Gentzler Electrical Contractors
10520 Plano Rd, Ste 112, Dallas
TX 75238-1356. 214/503-0302.

Humphrey & Associates Inc.
PO Box 59247, Dallas TX 75229-
1247. 972/620-1075.

**Lanehart Electrical
Contractors**
2411 River Hill Rd, Irving TX
75061-8909. 972/721-1004.

Mills Electrical Contractor
PO Box 59186, Dallas TX 75229-
1186. 214/357-4300.

Pro Tec Installations Inc.
3727 Dilido Rd, Ste 154, Dallas
TX 75228-5531. 214/324-0265.

Raines Electric Co. Inc.
PO Box 460031, Garland TX
75046-0031. 972/272-5595.

Regional Electrical Systems
13350 Euless St, Euless TX
76040-7225. 817/267-2231.

Smith Alarm Systems
7777 Carpenter Fwy, Dallas TX
75247. 214/634-3434.

TIC
997 Hampshire Ln, Richardson
TX 75080-5192. 972/699-1111.

Walker Engineering Inc.
10999 Petal St, Dallas TX 75238-
2488. 214/349-5900.

ENGINEERING SERVICES

Alpha Testing Inc.
2209 Wisconsin St, Ste 100,
Dallas TX 75229-2060. 972/620-
8911.

ATC Associates
11356 Mathis Ave, Dallas TX
75229-3157. 972/556-2204.

Brockette Davis Drake Inc.
4144 N Central Expressway,
Dallas TX 75204-3140. 214/824-
3647.

Carter & Burgess Inc.
PO Box 985006, Fort Worth TX
76185-5006. 817/735-6000.

Chromalloy Dallas
13880 Harry Hines Blvd, Dallas
TX 75234-3402. 972/241-7283.

Dikita Engineering
1420 W Mockingbird Lane,
Dallas TX 75247-4931. 214/634-
8844.

EXE Technologies Inc.
12740 Hillcrest Rd, Dallas TX
75230-2038. 972/233-3761.

Food Plant Engineering Inc.
1600 Airport Freeway, Ste 502,
Bedford TX 76022-6882.
817/545-1515.

Freese & Nichols Inc.
4055 Intl Plaza, Ste 200, Fort
Worth TX 76109. 817/735-7300.

**Hicks & Ragland Engineering
Co. Inc.**
PO Box 65700, Lubbock TX
79464-5700. 806/791-7700.

Huitt-Zollars Inc.
3131 McKinney Ave, Ste 600,
Dallas TX 75204-2456. 214/871-
3311.

Huitt-Zollars Inc.
512 Main St, Ste 1500, Fort
Worth TX 76102-3922. 817/335-
3000.

Kimley-Horn and Associates
12660 Coit Rd, Ste 300, Dallas
TX 75251-1702. 972/386-7007.

Kinro Inc.
500 Airport Dr, Mansfield TX
76063-2216. 817/473-4421.

Landis & Gyr Powers Inc.
1311 Regal Row, Dallas TX
75247-3615. 214/631-5280.

**Law Engineering &
Environmental Services**
7616 LBJ Freeway, Suite 600,
Dallas TX 75251. 972/934-0800.

Lockwood Greene Engineers
4201 Spring Ave, Dallas TX
75210-1620. 972/991-5505.

Maxim Technologies Inc.
8235 Douglas Ave, Ste 700,
Dallas TX 75225-6007. 972/247-
7576.

**Nathan D. Maier Consulting
Engineers**
8080 Park Ln, Ste 600, Dallas TX
75231-5911. 214/739-4741.

Parkhill Smith & Cooper Inc.
4010 Avenue R, Lubbock TX
79412-1603. 806/747-0161.

Pelton Marsh Kinsella
1420 West Mockingbird Ln,
Dallas TX 75247-4931. 214/638-
0145.

Post Buckley Schuh & Jerniga
5999 Summerside Dr, Dallas TX
75252-5222. 972/380-2605.

Sewell Netherland & Associates
1601 Elm St, Ste 4500, Dallas TX
75201-7206. 214/969-5401.

Shermco Industries Inc.
PO Box 540545, Dallas TX
75354-0545. 214/358-4271.

Tippett & Gee Inc.
502 N Willis St, Abilene TX
79603-6910. 915/673-8291.

TPA Inc.
PO Box 951219, Dallas TX
75395-1219. 972/773-2156.

Transystems Corp.
500 W 7th St, Ste 600, Fort
Worth TX 76102-4703. 817/339-
8950.

Trinity Consultants Inc.
12801 N Central Expy, Dallas TX
75243-1716. 972/661-8100.

Turner Engineers Inc.
5327 North Central Expressway,
Dallas TX 75205-3361. 214/521-
4100.

GENERAL CONTRACTORS

Babcock & Wilcox Company
PO Box 9090, Paris TX 75461-
9090. 903/784-2571.

**Capitol Painting &
Construction Inc.**
811 S Central Expressway,
Richardson TX 75080-7415.
972/644-6046.

Centex Homes
9229 LBJ Freeway, Bldg 1,
Dallas TX 75243-3405. 972/437-
6319.

Gulf Lake Contracting Inc.
15851 Dallas Pkwy, Ste 100,
Dallas TX 75248-3330. 972/490-
3255.

Highland Homes of Dallas
12850 Hillcrest Rd, Dallas TX
75230-1509. 972/387-7905.

Ralph Goble & Associates
4125 North Central Expressway,
Dallas TX 75204-2126. 214/526-
1041.

Ryland Homes
10908 Brandenberg Drive, Frisco
TX 75035-2909. 972/335-1756.

The Drees Company
1405 Rollins Dr, Allen TX
75013-2930. 972/727-9002.

Twin Cities Contracting Inc.
PO Box 3805, Arlington TX
76007-3805. 817/261-5622.

Weekley Homes Inc.
1310 Lake Dr, Southlake TX
76092-2951. 817/329-8882.

**GENERAL INDUSTRIAL
CONTRACTORS**

AL Helmcamp Inc.
PO Box 456, Buffalo TX 75831-
0456. 903/626-5911.

Architectural Utilities Inc.
PO Box 11586, Fort Worth TX
76110-0586. 817/926-4377.

**BFW Construction Company
Inc.**
PO Box 628, Temple TX 76503-
0628. 254/778-8941.

Casey Industrial Inc.
820 Sparks Dr, Cleburne TX
76031-0347. 817/556-2822.

Clark Construction Group
13760 Noel Road, Ste 1030,
Dallas TX 75240-4397. 972/490-
9390.

Clark Contractors
5949 Sherry Lane, Ste 650,
Dallas TX 75225-8002. 214/636-
6063.

**Dal-Mac Construction
Company**
PO Box 830160, Richardson TX
75083-0160. 972/238-0401.

HC Beck Ltd.
1700 Pacific Ave, Ste 3800,
Dallas TX 75201-4691. 214/965-
1100.

Horn Construction Co.
819 Penn St, Fort Worth TX
76102-3413. 817/737-6163.

Manhattan Construction Co.
3890 W Northwest Hwy, Dallas
TX 75220-8108. 214/357-7400.

McFadden & Miller Inc.
PO Box 59882, Dallas TX 75229-
1882. 972/401-2356.

Medco Construction
2625 Elm St, Ste 216, Dallas TX
75226-1497. 214/820-2492.

Omega Contracting Inc.
2818 Ruder St, Dallas TX 75212-
4217. 214/689-3815.

Performance Contracting Inc.
PO Box 166497, Irving TX
75016-6497. 972/550-0563.

Rogers-O'Brien Construction
11145 Morrison Ln, Dallas TX
75229-5608. 972/243-1335.

Waco Construction Inc.
PO Box 3216, Waco TX 76707-
0216. 254/772-3660.

Walker Building Corporation
PO Box 820217, Fort Worth TX
76182-0217. 817/595-1121.

HEAVY CONSTRUCTION

Driver Pipeline Company Inc.
2019 Ruder St, Dallas TX 75212-
5542. 214/638-7131.

Electrical Construction Service
PO Box 1261, Amarillo TX
79170-0001. 806/378-4164.

Enerpipe Corporation
PO Box 2329, Amarillo TX
79105-2329. 806/371-8851.

Flowers Construction Company
PO Box 1207, Hillsboro TX
76645-1207. 254/582-2501.

Larry H. Jackson Construction
5112 Sun Valley Dr, Fort Worth
TX 76119-6410. 817/572-3303.

SM&P Utility Resources
2211 E Division St, Arlington TX
76011-6621. 817/633-4085.

Tri Dal Ltd.
540 Commerce St, Southlake TX
76092-9113. 817/481-2886.

MASONRY, STONEWORK, AND PLASTERING

FD Hamilton Masonry
305 N Briery Rd, Ste 305, Irving TX 75061-6329. 972/253-7186.

Metro Masonry Construction
3900 Split Trail Rd, Plano TX 75074-2105. 972/881-8100.

P&S Masonry
PO Box 649, Hamilton TX 76531-0649. 254/386-8975.

Ray Boyd Plaster & Tile Inc.
PO Box 461523, Garland TX 75046-1523. 972/272-1548.

Texas Stone & Tile Inc.
PO Box 540755, Dallas TX 75354-0755. 214/358-4621.

MISC. SPECIAL TRADE CONTRACTORS

Dover Elevator Company
PO Box 569330, Dallas TX 75356-9330. 214/631-7600.

Lundy Services Inc.
4050 Black Gold Dr, Dallas TX 75247-6304. 214/951-8181.

Montgomery Kone Inc.
2101 Couch Dr, McKinney TX 75069-7314. 972/542-0351.

Orval Hall Excavating Co. Inc.
201 NE 29th St, Fort Worth TX 76106-5901. 817/624-7207.

Rodman Excavation Inc.
PO Box 957, Frisco TX 75034-0957. 972/335-4510.

Shea Services Inc.
PO Box 59934, Dallas TX 75229-1934. 972/247-9682.

Southland Contracting Inc.
PO Box 40664, Fort Worth TX 76140-0664. 817/293-4263.

Weir Bros. Inc.
PO Box 541793, Dallas TX 75354-1793. 972/556-9696.

OPERATIVE BUILDERS

Centex Homes
1660 S Stemmons Freeway, Lewisville TX 75067-6398. 972/221-8266.

Weekley Homes LP
3010 LBJ Fwy, Ste 1420, Dallas TX 75234. 972/243-8414.

PLUMBING, HEATING, AND A/C

Axon Inc.
PO Box 45028, Dallas TX 75245-0028. 214/634-3515.

Brandt Engineering Company
PO Box 29559, Dallas TX 75229-0559. 972/241-9411.

Buckner Blvd Plumbing Co. Inc.
4030 Gus Thomasson Rd, Mesquite TX 75150-2224. 972/681-2425.

Ceramic Cooling Tower Co.
1100 Northway Dr, Fort Worth TX 76131-1425. 817/232-4661.

Dallas Plumbing
PO Box 551648, Dallas TX 75355-1648. 214/741-7611.

Dyna Ten Corp.
7415 Whitehall St, Ste 101, Fort Worth TX 76118-6427. 817/595-1391.

Frymire Services
PO Box 29197, Dallas TX 75229-0197. 972/620-3500.

Grinnell Fire Protection Systems
PO Box 1361, Lubbock TX 79408-1361. 806/765-6691.

Grinnell Fire Protection Systems
11590 Emerald St, Dallas TX 75229-2010. 972/488-1060.

Ivey Mechanical Company
8225 Bent Branch Dr, Irving TX 75063-6028. 972/401-0601.

K&N Plumbing & Mechanical
2706 West Pioneer Pkwy, Arlington TX 76013-5906. 817/261-2117.

Mechanical Contractors Inc.
PO Box 29509, Dallas TX 75229-0509. 214/241-8503.

Specialized Mechanical Services
325 Shawnee Trl, Keller TX 76248-4935. 817/293-4488.

United Mechanical
PO Box 551206, Dallas TX 75355-1206. 214/341-2042.

PLUMBING, HEATING, AND A/C EQUIPMENT WHOLESALE

Chem Aqua
PO Box 152170, Irving TX 75015-2170. 972/438-0232.

Ferguson Enterprises
PO Box 698, Euless TX 76039-0698. 817/540-1888.

Fields & Company
PO Box 2160, Lubbock TX 79408-2160. 806/762-0241.

Mansfield Plumbing Products
PO Box 472, Kilgore TX 75663-0472. 903/984-3525.

NIBCO
4050 Cooperate, Ste 100, Grapevine TX 76051. 817/416-2003.

Titus
990 Security Row, Richardson TX 75081-6101. 972/699-1030.

ROAD CONSTRUCTION

AK Gillis & Sons Inc.
PO Box 576, Sulphur Springs TX 75483-0576. 903/885-3124.

Austin Bridge & Road
11143 Goodnight Lane, Dallas TX 75229-4412. 972/484-8863.

Champagne-Webber Inc. Texas
2000 Interstate Highway 45 South, Palmer TX 75152. 972/449-3240.

Edwards Construction
193 Industrial Boulevard, McKinney TX 75069-7220. 972/562-6522.

Gilbert Texas Construction
PO Box 50368, Amarillo TX 79159-0368. 806/467-0138.

Gilvin-Terrill Inc.
PO Box 9027, Amarillo TX 79105-9027. 806/374-0932.

Glenn Thurman Inc.
PO Box 850842, Mesquite TX 75185-0842. 972/286-6333.

Granite Construction Company
PO Box 1099, Rowlett TX
75030-1099. 972/412-0373.

J. Lee Milligan Inc.
PO Box 30188, Amarillo TX
79120-0188. 806/373-4386.

JD Abrams Inc.
PO Box 540425, Dallas TX
75354-0425. 214/688-0525.

JH Strain & Sons Inc.
PO Box 277, Tye TX 79563-
0277. 915/692-0067.

LH Lacy Company
PO Box 541297, Dallas TX
75354-1297. 214/357-0146.

Rosiek Construction Co. Inc.
2000 E Lamar Blvd, Ste 410,
Arlington TX 76006-7338.
817/277-4342.

Statewide Paving Inc.
9090 Skillman St, Dallas TX
75243-8259. 972/226-9066.

**Williams & Peters Construction
Co.**
PO Box 3907, Lubbock TX
79452-3907. 806/745-4171.

**ROOFING, SIDING, AND
SHEET METAL WORK**

Empire Roofing Inc.
5301 Sun Valley Dr, Fort Worth
TX 76119-6568. 817/572-2250.

Johnson Roofing Inc.
PO Box 11009, Waco TX 76716-
1009. 254/662-5571.

Lon Smith Roofing
904 E Waggoman St, Fort Worth
TX 76110-5723. 817/926-8400.

Panel Constructors Inc.
2321 E Pioneer Dr, Irving TX
75061-8807. 972/721-1825.

Seyforth Roofing Co. Inc.
PO Box 550576, Dallas TX
75355-0576. 972/864-8591.

Supreme Roofing
1355 N Walton Walker Blvd,
Dallas TX 75211-1042. 214/330-
8913.

Williams Insulation Co.
11111 Plano Rd, Dallas TX
75238-1309. 214/341-0668.

Wind River Roofing Inc.
3200 Handley Ederville Rd, Fort
Worth TX 76118-5813. 817/284-
1361.

For more information on career opportunities in architecture, construction, and engineering:

Associations

**AACE INTERNATIONAL: THE ASSOCIATION
FOR TOTAL COST MANAGEMENT**
209 Prairie Avenue, Suite 100, Morgantown WV
26505. 304/296-8444. Toll-free phone: 800/858-2678.
Fax: 304/291-5728. World Wide Web address:
http://www.aacei.org. A membership organization
which offers *Cost Engineering*, a monthly magazine;
employment referral services; technical reference
information and assistance; insurance; and a
certification program accredited by the Council of
Engineering Specialty Boards. Toll-free number
provides information on scholarships for
undergraduates.

**AMERICAN ASSOCIATION OF
ENGINEERING SOCIETIES**
1111 19th Street NW, Suite 403, Washington DC
20036-3690. 202/296-2237. World Wide Web
address: http://www.aaes.org. A multidisciplinary
organization of professional engineering societies.
Publishes reference works, including *Who's Who in
Engineering*, *International Directory of Engineering
Societies*, and the *Thesaurus of Engineering and
Scientific Terms*, as well as statistical reports from
studies conducted by the Engineering Workforce
Commission.

**AMERICAN CONSULTING ENGINEERS
COUNCIL**
1015 15th Street NW, Suite 802, Washington DC
20005. 202/347-7474. Fax: 202/898-0068. World
Wide Web address: http://www.acec.org. A national
organization of more than 5,000 member firms. Offers
Last Word, a weekly newsletter; *American Consulting
Engineer* magazine; life and health insurance
programs; books, manuals, video- and audiotapes, and
contract documents; conferences and seminars; and
voluntary peer reviews.

AMERICAN INSTITUTE OF ARCHITECTS
1735 New York Avenue NW, Washington DC 20006.
202/626-7300. Toll-free phone: 800/365-2724. World
Wide Web address: http://www.aia.org. Contact toll-
free number for brochures.

AMERICAN INSTITUTE OF CONSTRUCTORS
466 94th Avenue North, St. Petersburg FL 33702.
813/578-0317. World Wide Web address: http://www.
aicnet.org.

**AMERICAN SOCIETY FOR ENGINEERING
EDUCATION**
1818 N Street NW, Suite 600, Washington DC 20036.
202/331-3500. World Wide Web address: http://www.
asee.org. Publishes monthly magazines.

AMERICAN SOCIETY OF CIVIL ENGINEERS
1801 Alexander Bell Drive, Reston VA 20191-4400.
Toll-free phone: 800/548-2723. World Wide Web
address: http://www.asce.org. A membership
organization which offers subscriptions to *Civil
Engineering* magazine and *ASCE News,* discounts on
various other publications, seminars, video- and
audiotapes, specialty conferences, an annual
convention, group insurance programs, and pension
plans.

**AMERICAN SOCIETY OF HEATING,
REFRIGERATING AND AIR CONDITIONING
ENGINEERS**
1791 Tullie Circle NE, Atlanta GA 30329. 404/636-
8400. Fax: 404/321-5478. World Wide Web address:
http://www.ashrae.org. A society of 50,000 members
which offers handbooks, a monthly journal, a monthly
newspaper, discounts on other publications, group
insurance, continuing education, and registration
discounts for meetings, conferences, seminars, and
expositions.

AMERICAN SOCIETY OF LANDSCAPE ARCHITECTS
636 I Street NW, Washington DC 20001. 202/686-2752. World Wide Web address: http://www.asla.org. Check out the Website's Joblink for listings of employment opportunities.

AMERICAN SOCIETY OF MECHANICAL ENGINEERS
345 East 47th Street, New York NY 10017. 212/705-7722. World Wide Web address: http://www.asme. org. Handles educational materials for certified engineers, as well as scholarships.

AMERICAN SOCIETY OF NAVAL ENGINEERS
1452 Duke Street, Alexandria VA 22314. 703/836-6727. World Wide Web address: http://www.jhvapl. edu/asne. Holds symposiums based on technical papers. Publishes a journal and newsletter bimonthly.

AMERICAN SOCIETY OF PLUMBING ENGINEERS
3617 Thousand Oaks Boulevard, Suite 210, Westlake CA 91362-3649. 805/495-7120. Provides technical and educational information.

AMERICAN SOCIETY OF SAFETY ENGINEERS
1800 East Oakton Street, Des Plaines IL 60018-2187. 847/699-2929. Jobline service available at ext. 243. Fax: 847/296-3769. World Wide Web address: http://www.asse.org. A membership organization offering *Professional Safety*, a monthly journal; educational seminars; an annual professional development conference and exposition; technical publications; certification preparation programs; career placement services; and group and liability insurance programs.

ASSOCIATED BUILDERS AND CONTRACTORS
1300 North 17th Street, 8th Floor, Arlington VA 22209. 703/812-2000. World Wide Web address: http://www.abc.org. Sponsors annual career fair.

ASSOCIATED GENERAL CONTRACTORS OF AMERICA, INC.
1957 E Street NW, Washington DC 20006. 202/393-2040. World Wide Web address: http://www.agc.org. A full-service construction association of subcontractors, specialty contractors, suppliers, equipment manufacturers, and professional firms. Services include government relations, education and training, jobsite services, legal services, and information services.

THE ENGINEERING CENTER (TEC)
One Walnut Street, Boston MA 02108-3616. 617/227-5551. Contact: Abbie Goodman. World Wide Web address: http://www.engineers.org. An association that provides services for many engineering membership organizations.

ILLUMINATING ENGINEERING SOCIETY OF NORTH AMERICA
120 Wall Street, 17th Floor, New York NY 10005-

4001. 212/248-5000. World Wide Web address: http://www.iesna.org. An organization for industry professionals involved in the manufacturing, design, specification, and maintenance of lighting systems. Conference held annually. Offers a Technical Knowledge Examination.

JUNIOR ENGINEERING TECHNICAL SOCIETY
1420 King Street, Suite 405, Alexandria VA 22314-2794. 703/548-JETS. Fax: 703/548-0769. E-mail address: jets@nae.edu. World Wide Web address: http://www.asee.org/jets. A nonprofit, educational society promoting interest in engineering, technology, mathematics, and science. Provides information to high school students and teachers regarding careers in engineering and technology.

NATIONAL ACTION COUNCIL FOR MINORITIES IN ENGINEERING
350 Fifth Avenue, New York NY 10118. 212/279-2626. Offers scholarship programs for students.

NATIONAL ASSOCIATION OF HOME BUILDERS
1201 15th Street NW, Washington DC 20005. 202/822-0200. World Wide Web address: http://www. nahb.com. A trade association promoting safe and affordable housing. Provides management services and education for members.

NATIONAL ASSOCIATION OF MINORITY ENGINEERING
1133 West Morse Boulevard, Suite 201, Winter Park FL 32789. 407/647-8839.

NATIONAL ELECTRICAL CONTRACTORS ASSOCIATION
http://www.necanet.org. Provides information on the hiring and trade shows. The association also publishes a magazine called *Electrical Contractor*.

NATIONAL SOCIETY OF BLACK ENGINEERS
1454 Duke Street, Alexandria VA 22314. 703/549-2207. World Wide Web address: http://www.nsbe.org. A nonprofit organization run by college students. Offers scholarships, editorials, and magazines.

NATIONAL SOCIETY OF PROFESSIONAL ENGINEERS
1420 King Street, Alexandria VA 22314-2794. 703/684-2800. Call 703/684-2830 for scholarship information for students. Fax: 703/836-4875. World Wide Web address: http://www.nspe.org. A society of over 73,000 engineers. Membership includes the monthly magazine *Engineering Times;* continuing education; scholarships and fellowships; discounts on publications; and health and life insurance programs.

SOCIETY OF AMERICAN REGISTERED ARCHITECTS
303 South Broadway, Suite 322, Tarrytown NY 10591. 914/631-3600. Fax: 914/631-1319.

SOCIETY OF FIRE PROTECTION ENGINEERS
7315 Wisconsin Avenue, Bethesda MD 20814. 301/718-2910. Fax: 301/718-2242. A professional

society which offers members reports, newsletters, *Journal of Fire Protecting Engineering,* insurance programs, short courses, symposiums, tutorials, an annual meeting, and engineering seminars.

Directories

DIRECTORY OF ENGINEERING SOCIETIES
American Association of Engineering Societies, 1111 19th Street NW, Suite 403, Washington DC 20036. 202/296-2237. $185.00. Lists other engineering association members, publications, and convention exhibits.

DIRECTORY OF ENGINEERS IN PRIVATE PRACTICE
National Society of Professional Engineers, 1420 King Street, Alexandria VA 22314-2794. 703/684-2800. $50.00. Lists members and companies.

Magazines

THE CAREER ENGINEER
National Society of Black Engineers, 1454 Duke Street, Alexandria VA 22314. 703/549-2207.

CHEMICAL & ENGINEERING NEWS
American Chemical Society, 1155 16th Street NW, Washington DC 20036. 202/872-4600. World Wide Web address: http://www.acs.org.

COMPUTER-AIDED ENGINEERING
Penton Publishing, 1100 Superior Avenue, Cleveland OH 44114. 216/696-7000.

EDN CAREER NEWS
Cahners Publishing Company, 275 Washington Street,

Newton MA 02158. 617/964-3030. World Wide Web address: http://www.cahners.com.

ENGINEERING TIMES
National Society of Professional Engineers, 1420 King Street, Alexandria VA 22314. 703/684-2800.

NAVAL ENGINEERS JOURNAL
American Society of Naval Engineers, 1452 Duke Street, Alexandria VA 22314. 703/836-6727. Subscription: $48.00.

Online Services

ARCHITECTURE AND BUILDING FORUM
Go: Arch. A CompuServe discussion group for architectural professionals.

ARCHITECTURE AND LANDSCAPE ARCHITECTURE JOBS
http://www.clr.toronto.edu/virtuallib/jobs.html. This Website provides job openings for architects and landscape architects, as well as links to other related sites.

HOT JOBS! - CONSTRUCTION
http://www.kbic.com/construction.htm. Provides construction employment opportunities organized by job title.

P.L.A.C.E.S. FORUM
Keyword: places. A discussion group available to America Online subscribers who are professionals in the fields of architecture, construction, and engineering.

ARTS AND ENTERTAINMENT/RECREATION

Diversity is the trend in the entertainment industry. Recently, Business Week *reported that media corporations and entertainment powerhouses are trying to gain revenue by creating new divisions. These companies have originated record labels, online services, movie studios, theme parks, and cable networks. As a result, the market is oversaturated and profits are falling.*

A recent study predicted that the average television viewer will gain almost 1,000 channel choices by the time that digital compression of television is complete and the linking of TVs to the Internet becomes an option. With the creation of new channels comes more competition and as a result, programming costs have hit the roof. In an attempt to ease the sting of losing Seinfeld, NBC *reportedly agreed to pay close to $900 million to renew* ER *(its highest-rated show) for three years. Look for movie makers to create more distinct products that attract consumers in all areas. Fox and Paramount struck a golden iceberg with* Titanic, *which has spawned book tie-ins, a best-selling soundtrack, and a $30 million sale to NBC for the television rights.*

Broadway completed its most successful season ever in June 1997, with ticket sales slightly over $1 billion. Prosperity on The Great White Way is a direct result of focused industrywide ad campaigns and easier ticket accessibility. Productions are linking with larger corporations like Continental Airlines to promote themselves and the strategy is working.

Fans of professional sports continue to spend money on their teams and 1998 should be no exception. The National Football League has closed a highly profitable television contract. Major League Baseball has expanded by two more teams and is climbing back from its slump of the mid-'90s with the help of interleague play. The National Hockey League also has plans to expand, with four new teams possible by the year 2000. On the other hand, National Basketball Association officials reported that 13 of the 29 teams in the league lost money in 1997, in part due to an inefficient salary cap and escalating demands for franchise players.

All this adds up to survival of the fittest for jobseekers in the entertainment field. Across much of the industry costs are being cut and joint ventures continue. Those with business savvy and a flair for marketing may find some solid opportunities.

ALLIED DIGITAL TECHNOLOGIES CORPORATION
6305 North O'Connor Road, Suite 111, Building Four, Irving TX 75039. 972/869-0100. **Contact:** Human Resources. **World Wide Web address:** http://www.allied-digital.com. **Description:** Offers CD-audio and CD-ROM mastering and replication, videocassette and audiocassette duplication, laser video disc recording, off-line and online video editing, motion picture film processing, film-to-tape and tape-to-film transfers and complete finishing, packaging, and fulfillment services.

ALLIED PERCIVAL INTERNATIONAL (API)
500 Main Street, Suite 400, Fort Worth TX 76102. 817/870-0300. **Contact:** Human Resources. **World Wide Web address:** http://www.apitc.com. **Description:** An operator/promoter of worldwide tours.

DALLAS MUSEUM OF ART
1717 North Harwood, Dallas TX 75201. 214/922-1200. **Contact:** Scott Gensemer, Director of Personnel. **Description:** Offers a wide range of exhibits in all art media. **NOTE:** All candidates for positions listed should have Master's or Ph.D. degrees. **Common positions include:** Administrator; Curatorial Specialist; Financial Analyst. **Educational backgrounds include:** Art/Design.

DALLAS MUSEUM OF NATURAL HISTORY
P.O. Box 150349, Dallas TX 75315-0349. 214/421-3466. **Contact:** Robert B. Townsend, Interim Director. **World Wide Web address:** http://www.dallasdino.org. **Description:** Operates a natural history museum offering a full range of exhibits and presentations.

DISCOVERY ZONE INC.
15240 Dallas Parkway, Dallas TX 75248. 972/392-4386. **Contact:** Human Resources. **Description:** An operator of indoor fitness centers for small children and their families. Discovery Zone Inc. offers activities for children accompanied by an adult including tubes, tunnels, turbo slides, and obstacle courses. The facilities also house private party rooms for birthdays, and provide special events on a daily and monthly basis. **Corporate headquarters location:** Chicago IL.

DISCTRONICS
2800 Summit Avenue, Plano TX 75074. 972/881-8800. **Contact:** Human Resources. **Description:** Disctronics manufactures CDs and CD-ROMS.

GENERAL CINEMA CORPORATION
12377 Merit Drive, Suite 220, Dallas TX 75251. 972/934-7700. **Contact:** Human Resources. **Description:** Operates movie theaters. **Corporate headquarters location:** Boston MA. **Operations at this facility include:** Regional Headquarters.

NEST ENTERTAINMENT
6100 Colwell Boulevard, Irving TX 75039. 972/402-7100. **Contact:** Human Resources. **World Wide Web address:** http://www.nest-ent.com. **Description:** Develops animated educational VHS videotapes for children. Founded in 1988.

PRIORITY ONE PUBLISHING
555 Republic Drive, Suite 510, Plano TX 75074. 972/423-3800. **Contact:** Employment. **World Wide Web address:** http://www.total.tv.com. **Description:** Produces Christian videos. **NOTE:** Interested jobseekers must apply in person.

Q THE SPORTS CLUB
4600 West Park Boulevard, Plano TX 75093. 972/612-6960. **Contact:** Ms. Dana Wood, Manager. **World Wide Web address:** http://www.qclub.com. **Description:** A sports and fitness facility.

TEXAS STADIUM
2401 East Airport Freeway, Irving TX 75062. 972/438-7676. **Contact:** Human Resources Department. **Description:** A sporting arena. Texas Stadium is the home field of the Dallas Cowboys professional football team.

Note: Because addresses and telephone numbers of smaller companies can change rapidly, we recommend you call each company to verify the information below before inquiring about job opportunities. Mass mailings are not recommended.

Additional small employers:

AMUSEMENT AND RECREATION SERVICES

Billy Bob's
2520 Rodeo Plaza, Fort Worth TX 76106-8208. 817/624-7117.

Discovery Zone
1118 W Arbrook Blvd, Arlington TX 76015-4205. 817/472-9973.

Discovery Zone
3301 WAirport Freeway, Irving TX 75062-5937. 972/256-1900.

Fort Worth Parks & Recreation Dept.
4200 South Freeway, Ste 2200, Fort Worth TX 76115-1415. 817/871-8700.

Southfork Ranch
3700 Hogge Dr, Allen TX 75002-6734. 972/442-7800.

Surf & Swim
440 Oates Dr, Garland TX 75043. 972/205-2757.

Ticketmaster
4849 Greenville Ave, Dallas TX 75206-4130. 214/750-7400.

ENTERTAINERS AND ENTERTAINMENT GROUPS

Dallas Symphony Orchestra
2301 Flora St, Ste 300, Dallas TX 75201-2413. 214/871-4000.

Fort Worth Symphony Orchestra
4401 Trail Lake Dr, Fort Worth TX 76109-5201. 817/921-2676.

MOTION PICTURE AND VIDEO TAPE PRODUCTION AND DISTRIBUTION

Lyons Group
2435 North Central Expy, Richardson TX 75080-2753. 972/390-6300.

Victor Duncan Inc.
6305 N O'Connor Blvd, Irving TX 75039-3538. 972/869-0200.

Video Post and Transfer Inc.
2727 Inwood Rd, Dallas TX 75235-7446. 214/350-2676.

MUSEUMS AND ART GALLERIES

Fort Worth Museum of Science
1501 Montgomery St, Fort Worth TX 76107-3017. 817/732-1631.

PHYSICAL FITNESS FACILITIES

Baylor Fitness Center
411 N Washington Ave, Dallas TX 75246-1713. 214/820-7870.

Brookhaven Country Club
3333 Golfing Green Dr, Dallas TX 75234-3705. 972/484-6585.

Cooper Fitness Center
12200 Preston Rd, Dallas TX 75230-2223. 972/233-4832.

Golds Gym Aerobics & Fitness
4502 Buffalo Gap Rd, Abilene TX 79606-2704. 915/695-8900.

Greenhouse Spa Inc.
PO Box 1144, Arlington TX 76004-1144. 817/640-4000.

Q The Sports Club
1375 E Campbell Rd, Richardson TX 75081-1938. 972/644-4888.

Spa at the Crescent Inc.
400 Crescent Ct, Dallas TX 75201-1838. 214/871-3232.

University Club of Dallas
13350 Dallas Pkwy, Dallas TX 75240-6670. 972/239-0050.

PROFESSIONAL SPORTS CLUBS AND PROMOTERS

Dallas Cowboys Football Club
1 Cowboys Parkway, Irving TX 75063-4945. 972/556-9900.

Streetball Partners LP
4006 Beltline Rd, Ste 220, Dallas TX 75244. 972/392-5700.

Texas Rangers
PO Box 90111, Arlington TX 76004-3111. 817/273-5222.

THEATRICAL PRODUCERS AND SERVICES

ABC Radio Network Inc.
13725 Montfort Dr, Dallas TX 75240-4455. 972/991-9200.

SOA Productions Inc.
PO Box 29904, Dallas TX 75229-0904. 214/821-7621.

Vari-Lite International Inc.
201 Regal Row, Dallas TX 75247-5201. 214/630-1963.

For more information on career opportunities in arts, entertainment, and recreation:

Associations

AMERICAN ASSOCIATION OF MUSEUMS
1575 I Street NW, Suite 400, Washington DC 20005. 202/289-1818. Fax: 202/289-6578. World Wide Web address: http://www.aam-us.org. Publishes *AVISO*, a monthly newsletter containing employment listings for the entire country.

AMERICAN CRAFTS COUNCIL
72 Spring Street, New York NY 10012-4019. 212/274-0630. Operates a research library. Publishes *American Crafts* magazine.

AMERICAN DANCE GUILD
31 West 21st Street, New York NY 10010. 212/627-3790. Holds an annual conference with panels, performances, and workshops. Operates a job listings service (available at a discount to members).

AMERICAN FEDERATION OF MUSICIANS
1501 Broadway, Suite 600, New York NY 10036. 212/869-1330. World Wide Web address: http://www.afm.org.

AMERICAN FILM INSTITUTE
2021 North Western Avenue, Los Angeles CA 90027. 213/856-7706. Toll-free phone: 800/774-4AFI. World Wide Web address: http://www.afionline.org. Membership is required, and includes a newsletter; members-only discounts on events, seminars, workshops, and exhibits; and two free tickets and discounts at the AFI Theater in Washington DC.

AMERICAN MUSIC CENTER
30 West 26th Street, Suite 1001, New York NY 10010-2011. 212/366-5260. Fax: 212/366-5265. World Wide Web address: http://www.amc.net. A nonprofit research and information center for contemporary music and jazz. Provides information services and grant programs.

AMERICAN SOCIETY OF COMPOSERS, AUTHORS, AND PUBLISHERS (ASCAP)
One Lincoln Plaza, New York NY 10023. 212/621-6000. World Wide Web address: http://www.ascap.com. A membership association which licenses members' work and pays members' royalties. Offers showcases and educational seminars and workshops. The society also has an events hotline: 212/621-6485. Many events listed are free.

AMERICAN SYMPHONY ORCHESTRA LEAGUE
1156 15th Street NW, Suite 800, Washington DC 20005. 202/776-0212.

AMERICAN ZOO AND AQUARIUM ASSOCIATION
Oglebay Park, Wheeling WV 26003. 304/242-2160. E-mail address: azaoms@aol.com. World Wide Web address: http://www.aza.org. Publishes a monthly newspaper with employment opportunities for members.

AMERICANS FOR THE ARTS
One East 53rd Street, 2nd Floor, New York NY 10022. 212/223-2787. World Wide Web address: http://www.artsusa.org. A nonprofit organization for the literary, visual, and performing arts. Supports K-12 education and promotes public policy through meetings, forums, and seminars.

ASSOCIATION OF INDEPENDENT VIDEO AND FILMMAKERS
625 Broadway, 9th Floor, New York NY 10012. 212/807-1400. World Wide Web address: http://www.virtualfilm.com/aivf.

NATIONAL ARTISTS' EQUITY ASSOCIATION
P.O. Box 28068, Central Station, Washington DC 20038-8068. 202/628-9633. A national, nonprofit organization dedicated to improving economic, health, and legal conditions for visual artists.

NATIONAL ENDOWMENT FOR THE ARTS
1100 Pennsylvania Avenue NW, Washington DC 20506. 202/682-5400. World Wide Web address: http://www.arts.endow.gov.

NATIONAL RECREATION AND PARK ASSOCIATION
22377 Belmont Ridge Road, Ashburn VA 20148. 703/858-0784. Fax: 703/8580794. World Wide Web address: http://www.nrpa.org. A national, nonprofit service organization. Offers professional development and training opportunities in recreation, parks, and leisure services. Publishes a newsletter and magazine that offer employment opportunities for members only.

PRODUCERS GUILD OF AMERICA
400 South Beverly Drive, Suite 211, Beverly Hills CA 90212. 310/557-0807. Fax: 310/557-0436. Membership is required, and includes credit union access; subscription to *P.O.V. Magazine* and the association newsletter; attendance at the annual Golden Laurel Awards and other events; and special screenings of motion pictures.

Directories

ARTIST'S MARKET
Writer's Digest Books, 1507 Dana Avenue, Cincinnati OH 45207. 513/531-2222.

BLACK BOOK ILLUSTRATION
The Black Book, 10 Astor Place, 6th Floor, New York NY 10003. 212/539-9800. World Wide Web address: http://www.blackbook.com.

BLACK BOOK PHOTOGRAPHY
The Black Book, 10 Astor Place, 6th Floor, New York NY 10003. 212/539-9800. World Wide Web address: http://www.blackbook.com.

PLAYERS GUIDE
165 West 46th Street, New York NY 10036. 212/869-3570.

ROSS REPORTS TELEVISION
Billboard Publications, Inc., 1515 Broadway, New York NY 10036-8986. 212/764-7300.

Magazines

AMERICAN CINEMATOGRAPHER
American Society of Cinematographers, 1782 North Orange Drive, Hollywood CA 90028. 213/969-4333. World Wide Web address: http://www.cinematographer.com.

ARTFORUM
65 Bleecker Street, New York NY 10012. 212/475-4000. World Wide Web address: http://www.artforum.com.

AVISO
American Association of Museums, 1575 I Street NW, Suite 400, Washington DC 20005. 202/289-1818.

BACK STAGE
Billboard Publications, Inc., 1515 Broadway, New York NY 10036-8986. 212/764-7300. World Wide Web address: http://www.backstage.com.

BILLBOARD
Billboard Publications, Inc., 1515 Broadway, New York NY 10036-8986. 212/764-7300. World Wide Web address: http://www.billboard.com.

CRAFTS REPORT
300 Water Street, Wilmington DE 19801. 302/656-2209. World Wide Web address: http://www.craftsreport.com.

DRAMA-LOGUE
P.O. Box 38771, Los Angeles CA 90038. 213/464-5079.

HOLLYWOOD REPORTER
5055 Wilshire Boulevard, 6th Floor, Los Angeles CA 90036. 213/525-2000. World Wide Web address: http://www.hollywoodreporter.com.

VARIETY
245 West 17th Street, 5th Floor, New York NY 10011. 212/337-7001. Toll-free phone: 800/323-4345.

WOMEN ARTIST NEWS
300 Riverside Drive, New York NY 10025. 212/666-6990.

<u>Online Services</u>

AMERICAN CAMPING ASSOCIATION
http://www.aca-camps.org/. This Website allows
jobseekers to search for outdoor summer jobs by
position and by geographic location.

ARTJOB
Gopher://gopher.tmn.com/11/Artswire/artjob.
Provides information on jobs, internships, and
conferences in theater, dance, opera, and museums.
This site is only accessible through America Online.

COOLWORKS
http://www.coolworks.com/. Provides links to 22,000
job openings in national parks, summer camps, ski
areas, river areas, ranches, fishing areas, cruise ships,
and resorts. This site also includes information on
volunteer openings.

VISUAL NATION ARTS JOBS LINKS
http://fly.hiwaay.net/%7Edrewyor/art_job.html.
Provides links to other sites that post arts and
academic job openings and information.

AUTOMOTIVE

 *In the face of fierce competition both in the U.S. and abroad, automotive manufacturers have been forced to lower car prices, grant low interest-rate financing, and offer better deals on leasing. With consumer confidence at a dramatic high, this presents a strong buyer's market, but according to* Business Week, *auto consumers are also more discriminating than ever.*

In fact, J.D. Power & Associates forecasted a 2 percent drop in 1998 automotive prices, even though the "Big Three" -- General Motors Corporation, Chrysler Corporation, and Ford Motor Corporation -- had made significant price cuts in 1997. Used car prices are also projected to decline further, and leasing remains a popular alternative to traditional car purchasing.

ATCO PRODUCTS, INC.
P.O. Box 430, Ferris TX 75125. 972/544-3653. **Fax:** 972/544-2164. **Contact:** Human Resources. **Description:** Manufactures automotive air conditioning fittings, dryers, accumulators, and hoses. **Common positions include:** Accountant/Auditor; Customer Service Representative; Draftsperson; Industrial Engineer; Manufacturer's/Wholesaler's Sales Rep.; Purchasing Agent/Manager; Quality Control Supervisor. **Educational backgrounds include:** Business Administration; Engineering. **Benefits:** Dental Insurance; Life Insurance; Medical Insurance. **Corporate headquarters location:** This Location. **Operations at this facility include:** Administration; Manufacturing; Sales. **Listed on:** Privately held. **Number of employees at this location:** 225.

CHRYSLER CORPORATION
P.O. Box 110370, Carrollton TX 75011. 972/418-4600. **Contact:** Human Resources. **World Wide Web address:** http://www.chrysler.com. **Description:** Manufactures cars, trucks, minivans, and sport-utility vehicles for customers in more than 100 countries. In North America, the company markets vehicles through three divisions: Chrysler/Plymouth, Dodge/Dodge Truck, and Jeep/Eagle. Founded in 1924. **NOTE:** In May 1998, Chrysler Corporation and Daimler-Benz (Germany) announced plans to merge. The two will combine to form a new company called DaimlerChrysler. **Corporate headquarters location:** Highland Park MI. **Subsidiaries include:** Chrysler Financial Corporation provides financing for Chrysler's dealers and customers; Pentastar Transportation Group, Inc. includes Thrifty Rent-A-Car System, Inc., and Dollar Systems, Inc.; Chrysler Technologies Corporation manufactures high-technology electronic products.

HILITE INDUSTRIES, INC.
P.O. Box 814649, Dallas TX 75381. 972/242-2116. **Contact:** Personnel Department. **Description:** Designs, manufactures, and sells automotive components, including brake proportioning valves, electromagnetic clutches and machined components, springs, stampings, and assemblies.

PETERBILT MOTORS COMPANY
P.O. Box 550, Denton TX 76202. 940/566-7100. **Contact:** Human Resources Manager. **Description:** Designs and markets custom heavy-duty trucks. **Common positions include:** Accountant/Auditor; Electrical/Electronics Engineer; Mechanical Engineer; Systems Analyst. **Educational backgrounds include:** Accounting; Computer Science; Engineering; Marketing. **Operations at this facility include:** Divisional Headquarters.

SCS-FRIGETTE CORPORATION
P.O. Box 40557, Fort Worth TX 76140. 817/293-5313. **Contact:** Jane Turner, Human Resources. **Description:** A manufacturer of automobile air conditioning and heating systems, cruise controls, security systems, and accessories. **Common positions include:** Accountant/Auditor; Buyer; Clerical Supervisor; Credit Manager; Customer Service Representative; Designer; Draftsperson; Electrical/Electronics Engineer; Manufacturer's/Wholesaler's Sales Rep.; Materials Engineer; Mechanical Engineer; Purchasing Agent/Manager; Quality Control Supervisor; Services Sales

Representative. **Educational backgrounds include:** Accounting; Art/Design; Business Administration; Engineering; Finance; Marketing. **Benefits:** 401(k); Dental Insurance; Life Insurance; Medical Insurance; Savings Plan. **Corporate headquarters location:** This Location. **Operations at this facility include:** Administration; Manufacturing; Regional Headquarters; Research and Development; Sales; Service. **Listed on:** Privately held.

SST TRUCK COMPANY
4030 Forest Lane, Garland TX 75042. 972/276-5121. **Contact:** Human Resources. **Description:** Manufactures trucks for Navistar. **Corporate headquarters location:** This Location. **Listed on:** Privately held.

Note: Because addresses and telephone numbers of smaller companies can change rapidly, we recommend you call each company to verify the information below before inquiring about job opportunities. Mass mailings are not recommended.

Additional small employers:

AUTOMOTIVE REPAIR SHOPS

City Motor Supply Inc.
11670 Harry Hines Blvd, Dallas TX 75229-2295. 972/484-2611.

DC Bumper
3044 Morrell Ave, Dallas TX 75203-4053. 214/942-8444.

ITM Automotive Parts
1011 Regal Row, Dallas TX 75247-4404. 214/630-5100.

Luxury Conversions
PO Box 970, Grandview TX 76050-0970. 817/866-2901.

Wes-T-Go Truck Stop
PO Box 305, Tye TX 79563-0305. 915/692-8736.

INDUSTRIAL VEHICLES AND MOVING EQUIPMENT

K-D Manitou Inc.
PO Box 154009, Waco TX 76715-4009. 254/799-0232.

Serco
1612 Hutton Dr, Ste 140, Carrollton TX 75006-6696. 972/466-0707.

Standard Manufacturing Company
PO Box 210300, Dallas TX 75211-0300. 214/337-8911.

MOTOR VEHICLE EQUIPMENT WHOLESALE

Adesa Dallas
PO Box 270159, Dallas TX 75227-0159. 972/288-7585.

Chrome Specialties Inc.
4200 Diplomacy Rd, Fort Worth TX 76155-2634. 817/868-2000.

Cosmos International Inc.
501 Industrial Dr, Ste 101, Richardson TX 75081-2811. 972/699-1683.

Dallas Auto Auction Inc.
PO Box 210488, Dallas TX 75211-0488. 214/330-1800.

Dallas Freightliner
PO Box 560505, Dallas TX 75356-0505. 214/819-2500.

Dealers Auto Auction of Dallas
2717 E Main St, Grand Prairie TX 75050-6214. 972/642-3900.

Dick Smith Auto Supply
PO Box 163529, Fort Worth TX 76161-3529. 817/625-2525.

Ford Motor Company
PO Box 110037, Carrollton TX 75011-0037. 972/417-6100.

Fort Worth Auto Auction
2245 Jacksboro Hwy, Fort Worth TX 76114-2319. 817/626-5494.

General Motors Service Parts
PO Box 40370, Fort Worth TX 76140-0370. 817/551-3546.

Interstate Battery System
12770 Merit Dr, Ste 400, Dallas TX 75251-1212. 972/991-1444.

Mercedes-Benz
15050 Frye Rd, Fort Worth TX 76155-2700. 817/685-5200.

Nissan Motor Corp.
PO Box 167728, Irving TX 75016-7728. 972/929-2600.

Regency Conversions
2800 Golden Triangle Blvd, Fort Worth TX 76177-7016. 817/847-7171.

Western Auto Distribution
PO Box 6120, Temple TX 76503-6120. 254/771-8100.

MOTOR VEHICLES AND EQUIPMENT

AER Manufacturing Inc.
PO Box 979, Carrollton TX 75011. 972/418-6499.

Allen Group Inc.
PO Box 35908, Dallas TX 75235-0908. 214/637-6740.

Astro Air Inc.
PO Box 1988, Jacksonville TX 75766-1988. 903/586-3691.

Dayco Products
PO Box 2508, Fort Worth TX 76113-2508. 817/831-7100.

DSR Automotive Inc.
7537 Jack Newell Blvd N, Fort Worth TX 76118-7111. 817/284-4564.

General Motors
2525 E Abram St, Arlington TX 76010-1346. 817/652-2222.

Kalyn Siebert Inc.
PO Box 758, Gatesville TX 76528-0758. 254/865-7235.

LW Ledwell & Son Enterprises
PO Box 1106, Texarkana TX
75504-1106. 903/838-6531.

Metro Electric Co.
PO Box 1856, Amarillo TX
79105-1856. 806/376-5603.

Prior Remanufacturing Inc.
PO Box 462167, Garland TX
75046-2167. 972/494-4254.

RA Phillips Industries
3101 Marquis Dr, Ste 300,
Garland TX 75042-7740.
972/205-0733.

Rayloc
PO Box 908, Stephenville TX
76401-0908. 254/965-5075.

Sanden International
601 Sanden Blvd, Wylie TX
75098-4923. 972/442-8400.

Supreme Corporation of Texas
PO Box 2828, Cleburne TX
76033-2828. 817/641-6282.

Trailmaster Corporation
PO Box 161759, Fort Worth TX
76161-1759. 817/232-0900.

Tymco Inc.
PO Box 2368, Waco TX 76703-
2368. 254/799-5546.

US Bus Manufacturing Inc.
PO Box 2232, Pampa TX 79066-
2232. 806/665-0646.

US Liberty Trailer
PO Box 759, Mansfield TX
76063-0759. 817/477-1734.

**Watson & Chalin
Manufacturing Inc.**
2060 Couch Dr, McKinney TX
75069-7313. 972/547-6020.

For more information on career opportunities in the automotive industry:

Associations

**AMERICAN AUTOMOBILE
MANUFACTURERS ASSOCIATION**
1401 H Street NW, Suite 900, Washington DC 20005.
202/326-5500. Fax: 202/326-5567. World Wide Web
address: http://www.aama.org. A trade association
consisting of the Big Three U.S. automakers:
Chrysler, Ford, and General Motors. Sponsors
research projects, distributes publications, and reviews
social and public policies pertaining to the motor
vehicle industry and its customers.

**ASSOCIATION OF INTERNATIONAL
AUTOMOBILE MANUFACTURERS**
1001 North 19th Street, Suite 1200, Arlington VA
22209. 703/525-7788. World Wide Web address:
http://www.aiam.org.

AUTOMOTIVE SERVICE ASSOCIATION
1901 Airport Freeway, Suite 100, P.O. Box 929,
Bedford TX 76095. 817/283-6205. World Wide Web
address: http://www.asashop.org. Works with shops to
find workers. Publishes a monthly magazine with
classified advertisements.

**AUTOMOTIVE SERVICE INDUSTRY
ASSOCIATION**
25 Northwest Point Boulevard, Suite 425, Elk Grove
Village IL 60007-1035. 847/228-1310. World Wide
Web address: http://www.aftmkt.com. Members are
manufacturers and distributors of automobile

replacement parts. Sponsors a trade show. Publishes
educational guidebooks and training manuals.

Directories

AUTOMOTIVE NEWS MARKET DATA BOOK
Crain Communications, Automotive News, 1400
Woodbridge Avenue, Detroit MI 48207-3187.
313/446-6000.

WARD'S AUTOMOTIVE YEARBOOK
Ward's Communications, Inc., 3000 Town Center,
Suite 2750, Southville MI 48075. 248/357-0800.
http://www.wardsauto.com.

Magazines

AUTOMOTIVE INDUSTRIES
Chilton Book Company, 201 King of Prussia Road,
Radnor PA 19089. Toll-free phone: 800/695-1214.

AUTOMOTIVE NEWS
Crain Communications, 1400 Woodbridge Avenue,
Detroit MI 48207-3187. 313/446-6000.

**WARD'S AUTO WORLD
WARD'S AUTOMOTIVE REPORTS**
Ward's Communications, Inc., 3000 Town Center,
Suite 2750, Southville MI 48075. 248/357-0800.
World Wide Web address: http://www.wardsauto.
com.

BANKING/SAVINGS AND LOANS

The banking industry is still plagued by uncertainty heading into 2000. Mergers and acquisitions continue to be the norm, the Asian crisis looms abroad, and the Year 2000 computer glitch is causing concerns for many banks. Although most banks remain unscathed and continue to prosper, some are still losing ground to security houses and financial divisions of large corporations.

According to the Federal Deposit Insurance Corporation, 156 new bank charters were granted in 1996, 165 in 1997, and 89 applications were still pending at the end of December 1997. More and more consumers are choosing to take their money out of banking conglomerates and are giving their business to smaller, more personalized community banks. In fact, Business Week reports that even analysts in the field are beginning to lose faith in the promised efficiency of the mega-mergers of 1997.

A successful banking trend is automation. Automated teller machines will begin to offer more services like check cashing and printouts of account information. Jobseekers will find less opportunities for bank tellers and more opportunities for call center customer service representatives. The Bureau of Labor Statistics expects bank tellers to lose 152,000 jobs by 2005 and projects numerous layoffs for bank office workers and managers.

AMARILLO NATIONAL BANK
P.O. Box 1, Amarillo TX 79178. 806/378-8000. **Contact:** Human Resources. **World Wide Web address:** http://www.anb.com. **Description:** A full-service bank.

BANK OF AMERICA TEXAS
1925 West John Carpenter Freeway, Irving TX 75063. 972/444-5700. **Recorded jobline:** 972/444-6970. **Contact:** Human Resources Department. **Description:** A full-service bank. Founded in 1904. **NOTE:** Entry-level positions as well as second and third shifts are offered. In April 1998, BankAmerica Corporation and NationsBank Corporation announced plans to merge in the year's final quarter. The two companies will retain the name BankAmerica Corporation. **Common positions include:** Bank Officer/Manager; Branch Manager; Customer Service Representative; Sales Representative. **Educational backgrounds include:** Business Administration; Finance. **Benefits:** 401(k); Dental Insurance; Disability Coverage; Employee Discounts; Financial Planning Assistance; Flexible Schedule; Job Sharing; Life Insurance; Mass Transit Available; Medical Insurance; On-Site Daycare; Pension Plan; Tuition Assistance. **Parent company:** BankAmerica Corporation. **Listed on:** New York Stock Exchange. **Annual sales/revenues:** More than $100 million. **Number of employees worldwide:** 90,000.

BANK ONE TEXAS
500 Throckmorton Street, Fort Worth TX 76102. 817/884-4000. **Contact:** Human Resources. **Description:** A full-service commercial bank. **Common positions include:** Accountant/Auditor; Bank Officer/Manager. **Educational backgrounds include:** Accounting; Finance. **Benefits:** Dental Insurance; Disability Coverage; Employee Discounts; Life Insurance; Medical Insurance; Pension Plan; Profit Sharing; Savings Plan; Tuition Assistance. **Corporate headquarters location:** Columbus OH. **Other U.S. locations:** AZ; CO; IL; IN; KY; MI; OH; OK; UT; WI; WV. **Parent company:** Banc One Corporation. **Listed on:** New York Stock Exchange. **Number of employees nationwide:** 89,000.

CHASE BANK OF TEXAS
2200 Ross Avenue, Suite 720, Dallas TX 75201. 214/922-2421. **Contact:** Human Resources. **Description:** An $11 billion banking organization, operating through a network of 40 member banks in Texas (including 17 in Houston and 11 in Dallas-Fort Worth), and offices in Denver, New York, and eight foreign countries. Banking operations include energy banking, commercial banking, real estate banking, and international banking. **Corporate headquarters location:** Houston TX.

CHASE BANK OF TEXAS
P.O. Box 250, Arlington TX 76004-0250. 817/856-3277. **Contact:** Human Resources. **Description:** An $11 billion banking organization, operating through a network of 40 member banks in Texas (including 17 in Houston and 11 in Dallas-Fort Worth), and offices in Denver, New York, and eight foreign countries. Banking operations include energy banking, commercial banking, real estate banking, and international banking. **Corporate headquarters location:** Houston TX.

FEDERAL RESERVE BANK OF DALLAS
P.O. Box 655906, Dallas TX 75265-5906. 214/922-6000. **Physical address:** 2200 North Pearl Street, Dallas TX 75201. **Recorded jobline:** 214/922-6166. **Contact:** Employment. **World Wide Web address:** http://www.dallasfed.org. **Description:** One of 12 regional Federal Reserve banks that, along with the Federal Reserve Board of Governors in Washington DC, and the Federal Open Market Committee, comprise the Federal Reserve System. As the nation's central bank, the Federal Reserve is charged with three major responsibilities: monetary policy, banking supervision and regulation, and processing payments. **Common positions include:** Accountant/Auditor; Attorney; Computer Programmer; Economist; Financial Analyst. **Educational backgrounds include:** Accounting; Business Administration; Computer Science; Economics; Finance. **Benefits:** 401(k); Dental Insurance; Mass Transit Available; Medical Insurance. **Special programs:** Internships. **Other U.S. locations:** San Francisco CA; Washington DC; Atlanta GA; Chicago IL; Boston MA; Minneapolis MN; Kansas City MO; New York NY; Cleveland OH; Philadelphia PA; Richmond VA.

FIRST NATIONAL BANK OF ABILENE
P.O. Box 701, Abilene TX 79604. 915/627-7000. **Contact:** Pam Mann, Director of Human Resources. **World Wide Web address:** http://www.fnbabilene.com. **Description:** A full-service bank.

INDEPENDENT BANKSHARES, INC.
P.O. Box 3296, Abilene TX 79604. 915/677-5550. **Fax:** 915/677-5943. **Contact:** Human Resources. **Description:** A bank holding company. Founded in 1981. **Common positions include:** Accountant/Auditor; Administrative Assistant; Bank Officer/Manager; Chief Financial Officer; Controller; Operations/Production Manager; Secretary. **Educational backgrounds include:** Accounting; Business Administration; Finance. **Benefits:** 401(k); Dental Insurance; Disability Coverage; Employee Discounts; ESOP; Life Insurance; Medical Insurance. **Corporate headquarters location:** This Location. **Subsidiaries include:** Independent Financial Corporation (Abilene TX) owns First State Bank, N.A. **Listed on:** American Stock Exchange. **Stock exchange symbol:** IBK. **Annual sales/revenues:** $11 - $20 million. **Number of employees at this location:** 20. **Number of employees nationwide:** 125.

NATIONSBANK
P.O. Box 831000, Dallas TX 75283-1000. 214/508-6262. **Contact:** Personnel Department. **World Wide Web address:** http://www.nationsbank.com. **Description:** In addition to a complete selection of financial accounts, NationsBank offers a wide variety of banking services. **NOTE:** In April 1998, NationsBank Corporation and BankAmerica Corporation announced plans to merge in the year's final quarter. The two companies will operate under the name BankAmerica Corporation.

NORWEST BANK
P.O. Box 1241, Lubbock TX 79408-1241. 806/765-8861. **Contact:** Human Resources. **World Wide Web address:** http://www.norwest.com. **Description:** A full-service banking institution

including personal services such as savings, checking, loans, and trust and commercial lending departments.

WELLS FARGO BANK

800 West Airport Freeway, Suite 200, Irving TX 75062. 972/445-8499. **Fax:** 972/554-7485. **Contact:** Human Resources Recruiter. **World Wide Web address:** http://www.wellsfargo.com. **Description:** A full-service commercial bank. **NOTE:** This company offers entry-level positions and second and third shifts. **Common positions include:** Bank Officer/Manager; Bank Teller; Branch Manager; Customer Service Representative. **Educational backgrounds include:** Accounting; Business Administration; Finance. **Benefits:** 401(k); Dental Insurance; Disability Coverage; Life Insurance; Medical Insurance; Profit Sharing; Tuition Assistance. **Corporate headquarters location:** San Francisco CA. **Operations at this facility include:** Regional Headquarters; Service. **Number of employees nationwide:** 33,500.

Note: Because addresses and telephone numbers of smaller companies can change rapidly, we recommend you call each company to verify the information below before inquiring about job opportunities. Mass mailings are not recommended.

Additional small employers:

COMMERCIAL BANKS

American Bank of Texas
2011 Texoma Parkway, Sherman TX 75090-2688. 903/892-2181.

Bank One Texas
PO Box 540, Wichita Falls TX 76307-0540. 940/689-6505.

Chase Bank of Texas
100 North Central Expressway, Richardson TX 75080-5332. 972/497-1801.

First National Bank
PO Box 6101, Temple TX 76503-6101. 254/773-2115.

First National Bank
PO Drawer 937, Killeen TX 76540-0937. 254/634-2161.

First National Bank
PO Box 1000, Grapevine TX 76099-1000. 817/481-2531.

First State Bank
PO Box 100, Denton TX 76202-0100. 940/382-5421.

First State Bank
PO Box 100, Rio Vista TX 76093-0100. 817/373-2944.

First Texas Bank Inc.
PO Box 609, Killeen TX 76540-0609. 254/634-2132.

Longview Bank & Trust Company
PO Box 3188, Longview TX 75606-3188. 903/237-5500.

NationsBank of Texas NA
411 N Akard St, Fl 7, Dallas TX 75201-3307. 214/871-2600.

NationsBank of Texas NA
500 West Seventh Street, Fort Worth TX 76102-4700. 817/390-6161.

North Dallas Bank & Trust
PO Box 679001, Dallas TX 75367-9001. 972/387-1300.

Norwest Bank Texas NA
PO Box 2626, Waco TX 76702-2626. 254/754-5431.

Overton Bank & Trust NA
PO Box 16509, Fort Worth TX 76162-0509. 817/731-0101.

Plains National Bank of West Texas
PO Box 271, Lubbock TX 79408-0271. 806/795-7131.

Southside Bank
PO Box 1079, Tyler TX 75710-1079. 903/531-7236.

Texas Bank
PO Box 760, Weatherford TX 76086-0760. 817/594-8721.

Texas Independent Bank
PO Box 560528, Dallas TX 75356-0528. 972/650-6000.

Town North National Bank
PO Box 814810, Dallas TX 75381-4810. 972/391-6800.

Tyler Bank and Trust NA
PO Box 2020, Tyler TX 75710-2020. 903/595-1941.

Wells Fargo Bank NA
9 Village Cir, Roanoke TX 76262-5917. 817/258-5080.

Wells Fargo Corporate Services
1445 Ross Ave, Ste 300, Dallas TX 75202-2740. 214/740-0099.

CREDIT UNIONS

Dallas Teachers Credit Union
PO Box 517028, Dallas TX 75251-7028. 972/301-1800.

Omni American Federal Credit Union
PO Box 150099, Fort Worth TX 76108-0099. 817/246-0111.

Southwest Corp. Federal Credit Union
7920 Beltline Rd #109, Dallas TX 75240. 972/861-3000.

SAVINGS INSTITUTIONS

Bank One Texas
PO Box 12000, Dallas TX 75225-1000. 214/360-4330.

Beal Bank
15770 Dallas Parkway, Dallas TX 75248. 972/404-4000.

Guaranty Federal Bank FSB
8333 Douglas Avenue, Dallas TX 75225-5845. 214/360-3360.

For more information on career opportunities in the banking/savings and loans industry:

Associations

AMERICA'S COMMUNITY BANKERS
900 19th Street NW, Suite 400, Washington DC
20006. 202/857-3100. World Wide Web address:
http://www.acbankers.org. A trade association
representing the expanded thrift industry. Membership
is limited to institutions.

AMERICAN BANKERS ASSOCIATION
1120 Connecticut Avenue NW, Washington DC
20036. 202/663-5221. World Wide Web address:
http://www.aba.com/aba. Provides banking education
and training services, sponsors industry programs and
conventions, and publishes articles, newsletters, and
the *ABA Service Member Directory*.

Directories

AMERICAN BANK DIRECTORY
Thomson Financial Publications, 1770 Breckenridge
Parkway, Suite 500, Duluth GA 30136. 770/381-2511.

AMERICAN SAVINGS DIRECTORY
Thomson Financial Publications, 1770 Breckenridge
Parkway, Suite 500, Duluth GA 30136. 770/381-2511.

MOODY'S BANK AND FINANCE MANUAL
Moody's Investors Service, Inc., 99 Church Street, 1st
Floor, New York NY 10007-2701. 212/553-0300.
World Wide Web address: http://www.moodys.com.

RANKING THE BANKS/THE TOP NUMBERS
American Banker, Inc., One State Street Plaza, New
York NY 10004. 212/803-6700. World Wide Web
address: http://www.americanbanker.com.

Magazines

ABA BANKING JOURNAL
American Bankers Association, 1120 Connecticut

Avenue NW, Washington DC 20036. 202/663-5221.
World Wide Web address: http://www.aba.com.

BANK ADMINISTRATION
One North Franklin, Suite 1000, Chicago IL 60606.
Toll-free phone: 800/323-8552. World Wide Web
address: http://www.bai.org.

BANKERS MAGAZINE
Warren, Gorham & Lamont, Park Square Building, 31
St. James Avenue, Boston MA 02116-4112. 617/423-
2020.

**JOURNAL OF COMMERCIAL BANK
LENDING**
Robert Morris Associates, 1650 Market Street, Suite
2300, Philadelphia PA 19103. 215/446-4000.

Online Services

JOBS FOR BANKERS!
http://www.bankjobs.com. This site provides access to
a database of over 6,000 banking-related job
openings. Jobs for Bankers! is run by Careers Inc.
This Website also includes a resume database.

JOBS IN COMMERCIAL BANKING
http://www.cob.ohio-
state.edu/dept/fin/jobs/commbank.htm. Provides
information and resources for jobseekers looking to
work in the field of commercial banking.

**NATIONAL BANKING NETWORK:
RECRUITING FOR BANKING AND FINANCE**
http://www.banking-financejobs.com/. Offers a
searchable database of job openings in banking and
financial services. The database is searchable by
region, keyword, and job specialty.

BIOTECHNOLOGY, PHARMACEUTICALS, AND SCIENTIFIC R&D

The forecast is bright for the biotechnology industry, with the advent of new technologies in drug research and a heightened demand for prescription drugs of all types. Analysts from Cowen & Company predict a healthy sales increase of about 12 percent in 1998, up from 8 percent in 1997. In effect, marketing costs are also expected to rise.

Large drug companies are preparing to release a plethora of new products and continue to face competition from generic drug makers. Advances in genetic research offer promising new developments, but capitalizing on them requires significant investment. Therefore, those companies with bigger research budgets currently dominate. However, a trend is developing whereby large drug companies form partnerships with smaller biotechnology firms that provide them with research services. Often, these partnerships allow a drug to move through the trial process faster, therefore gaining FDA approval much sooner.

Among the industry leaders in breakthrough drug development is Merck & Company, Inc., which plans to introduce new painkillers; antidepressants; and drugs for asthma, arthritis, and male pattern baldness. Other drug manufacturers anticipate new drugs for hepatitis-B as well as new AIDS drug combinations. In addition, drug-delivery companies are working to improve the ways in which drugs are absorbed by the body.

ADS ENVIRONMENTAL SERVICES INC.
10715 Plano Road, Suite 200, Dallas TX 75238. 214/340-5696. **Contact:** Human Resources Department. **World Wide Web address:** http://www.adsenv.com. **Description:** A research and development laboratory.

ABBOTT DIAGNOSTICS
P.O. Box 152020, Irving TX 75015-2020. 972/518-6000. **Contact:** Personnel Department. **World Wide Web address:** http://www.abbott.com. **Description:** Designs, develops, and manufactures automated laboratory instruments, primarily used in the fields of clinical chemistry, microbiology, and therapeutic drug monitoring. **Corporate headquarters location:** Abbott Park IL. **Parent company:** Abbott Laboratories is an international manufacturer of a wide range of health care products, including pharmaceuticals, hospital products, diagnostic products, chemical products, and nutritional products.

ALLERGAN, INC.
P.O. Box 2675, Waco TX 76702. 254/666-3331. **Contact:** Human Resources. **Description:** Develops, manufactures, and distributes prescription and non-prescription pharmaceutical products in the specialty fields of ophthalmology and dermatology.

APPLIED EARTH SCIENCES
2833 Trinity Square, Suite 149, Carrollton TX 75006. 972/416-7171. **Contact:** Human Resources. **Description:** A research and development laboratory.

CARRINGTON LABORATORIES
P.O. Box 168128, Irving TX 75016-8128. 972/518-1300. **Contact:** Human Resources. **World Wide Web address:** http://www.carringtonlabs.com. **Description:** Develops, manufactures, and

markets a number of wound care, pharmaceutical, and veterinary products, all of which are based on complex carbohydrates derived from aloe vera. Products include Carrasyn Hydrogel Wound Dressing; CarraSorb H Calcium Alginate Wound Dressing; CarraFilm Transparent Film Dressing; CarraSorb M Freeze-Dried Gel; DiaB, a line of wound care products for diabetics; and RadiaCare, a line of products to treat radiation dermatitis. **Corporate headquarters location:** This Location. **Subsidiaries include:** Caraloe, Inc. manufactures and markets nutritional aloe drinks.

LTC MEDICAL LABORATORIES, INC.
4747 Irving Boulevard, Suite 245, Dallas TX 75247. 214/630-5227. **Contact:** Human Resources. **Description:** A full-service medical laboratory that provides comprehensive clinical laboratory services, such as tests and bloodwork, for long-term care facilities and for people in home health care. **Parent company:** Horizon/CMS Healthcare Corporation acquires and operates long-term care facilities throughout the United States; provides health care services, such as nursing care, rehabilitation, and other therapies; provides institutional pharmacy services; provides specialty care to Alzheimer's patients; and offers subacute care.

LABORATORY CORPORATION OF AMERICA (LABCORP)
7777 Forest Lane, Building C, Suite 350, Dallas TX 75230. 972/566-3353. **Toll-free phone:** 800/788-9892. **Fax:** 972/991-0381. **Recorded jobline:** 800/645-5680x3070. **Contact:** Kelli Elmore, Assistant Human Resources Manager. **World Wide Web address:** http://www.labcorp.com. **Description:** LabCorp is one of the nation's leading clinical laboratory companies, providing services primarily to physicians, as well as hospitals, clinics, nursing homes, and other clinical labs nationwide. LabCorp performs tests on blood, urine, and other body fluids and tissue, aiding the diagnosis of disease. **Common positions include:** Account Representative; Customer Service Representative; Data Entry Clerk; Medical Technologist. **Educational backgrounds include:** Biology; Chemistry. **Benefits:** 401(k); Credit Union; Dental Insurance; Disability Coverage; Life Insurance; Mass Transit Available; Medical Insurance; Pension Plan; Profit Sharing; Savings Plan; Tuition Assistance. **Office hours:** Monday - Friday, 7:30 a.m. - 5:30 p.m. **Corporate headquarters location:** Burlington NC. **Other U.S. locations:** Nationwide. **Listed on:** American Stock Exchange; NASDAQ; New York Stock Exchange. **Co-CEO:** Dr. Larry Leonard. **Number of employees at this location:** 2,000.

MEDICAL LABORATORIES
31 Windmill Circle, Suite D, Abilene TX 79606. 915/691-5377. **Contact:** Manager. **Description:** A phlebotomy laboratory. **Corporate headquarters location:** Denton TX.

NATIONAL INSTITUTIONAL PHARMACY SERVICES, INC. (NIPSI)
4747 Irving Boulevard, Suite 214, Dallas TX 75247. 214/630-1985. **Contact:** Human Resources. **Description:** Through an established network of 22 pharmacies in nine states, NIPSI provides a full range of prescription drugs, enteral and perenteral nutritional therapy products, and infusion therapy products, such as antibiotic therapy, pain management, and chemotherapy services to over 520 facilities operated by its parent company and third parties. **Parent company:** Horizon/CMS Healthcare Corporation acquires and operates long-term care facilities throughout the United States; provides health care services, such as nursing care, rehabilitation, and other therapies; provides institutional pharmacy services; provides specialty care to Alzheimer's patients; and offers subacute care.

SMITHKLINE BEECHAM CLINICAL LABORATORIES
8000 Sovereign Row, Dallas TX 75247. 214/638-1301. **Contact:** Human Resources. **World Wide Web address:** http://www.sb.com. **Description:** One of the largest clinical laboratories in North America, providing a broad range of clinical laboratory services to more than 50,000 health care and industry clients. The company offers and performs 1,500 tests on blood, urine, and other bodily fluids and tissues to provide information for health and well-being. SmithKline Beecham Clinical Laboratories was among the first to receive certification from the U.S. government's National Institute on Drug Abuse. The company operates 24 laboratories throughout the U.S., as well as an additional 300 testing sites and specimen collection centers to support these labs. Labs are staffed by certified technologists, including more than 200 physicians and Ph.D.s. The company performs more than 56 million tests a year. Clients include physicians, hospitals, clinics, dialysis centers, pharmaceutical companies, and corporations. **Parent company:** SmithKline Beecham Corporation

is a health care company engaged in the research, development, manufacture, and marketing of ethical pharmaceuticals, animal health products, ethical and proprietary medicines, and eye care products. In addition to SmithKline Beecham Clinical Laboratories, the company's principal divisions include SmithKline Beecham Pharmaceuticals, SmithKline Beecham Animal Health, and SmithKline Beecham Consumer Healthcare. The company is also engaged in many other aspects of the health care field, including the production of medical and electronic instruments. The company manufactures proprietary medicines through its subsidiary, Menley & James Laboratories, including such nationally known products as Contac Cold Capsules, Sine-Off sinus medicine, Love cosmetics, and Sea & Ski outdoor products.

TEXAS DRUG COMPANY
5235 Rufe Snow, Fort Worth TX 76180. 817/498-6059. **Contact:** Harold Pinker, President. **Description:** A wholesale distributor of prescription drugs.

TEXAS VETERINARY MEDICAL DIAGNOSTIC LABORATORY
P.O. Box 3200, Amarillo TX 79116. 806/353-7478. **Physical address:** 6610 Amarillo Boulevard West, Amarillo TX. **Toll-free phone:** 888/646-5624. **Fax:** 806/359-0636. **Contact:** Robert W. Sprowls, Associate Agency Director. **Description:** This location is a diagnostic laboratory that performs medical testing on animals to assist veterinarians with diagnosis and prognosis. The test fields include chemistry, hematology, urology, toxicology, serology, histology, bacteriology, and necropsies. **Common positions include:** Chemist; Clinical Lab Technician; Computer Operator; Human Resources Manager; Medical Records Technician; Microbiologist; Pathologist; Secretary; Toxicologist. **Educational backgrounds include:** Chemistry; Veterinary Medicine. **Benefits:** 401(k); Dental Insurance; Life Insurance; Medical Insurance; Pension Plan. **Office hours:** Monday - Friday, 8:00 a.m. - 5:00 p.m., and Saturday, 8:00 a.m. - 12:00 p.m. **Other U.S. locations:** College Station TX. **Executive Director:** A. Konrad Eugster.

For more information on career opportunities in biotechnology, pharmaceuticals, and scientific R&D:

Associations

AMERICAN ASSOCIATION FOR CLINICAL CHEMISTRY
2101 L Street NW, Suite 202, Washington DC 20037-1526. 202/857-0717. Toll-free phone: 800/892-1400. World Wide Web address: http://www.aacc.org. International scientific/medical society of individuals involved with clinical chemistry and other clinical lab science-related disciplines.

AMERICAN ASSOCIATION OF COLLEGES OF PHARMACY
1426 Prince Street, Alexandria VA 22314-2841. 703/739-2330. World Wide Web address: http://www.aacp.org. An organization composed of all U.S. pharmacy colleges and over 2,000 school administrators and faculty members. Career publications include *Shall I Study Pharmacy?*, *Pharmacy: A Caring Profession*, and *A Graduate Degree in the Pharmaceutical Sciences: An Option For You?*

AMERICAN ASSOCIATION OF PHARMACEUTICAL SCIENTISTS
1650 King Street, Suite 200, Alexandria VA 22314-2747. 703/548-3000. World Wide Web address: http://www.aaps.org.

AMERICAN COLLEGE OF CLINICAL PHARMACY (ACCP)
3101 Broadway, Suite 380, Kansas City MO 64111.

816/531-2177. Operates ClinNet jobline at 412/648-7893 for members only.

AMERICAN PHARMACEUTICAL ASSOCIATION
2215 Constitution Avenue NW, Washington DC 20037-2985. 202/628-4410. World Wide Web address: http://www.aphanet.org.

AMERICAN SOCIETY FOR BIOCHEMISTRY AND MOLECULAR BIOLOGY
9650 Rockville Pike, Bethesda MD 20814-3996. 301/530-7145. Fax: 301/571-1824. World Wide Web address: http://www.asbmb.org. A nonprofit scientific and educational organization whose primary scientific activities are in the publication of the *Journal of Biological Chemistry* and holding an annual scientific meeting. Also publishes a career brochure entitled *Unlocking Life's Secrets: Biochemistry and Molecular Biology.*

AMERICAN SOCIETY OF HEALTH SYSTEM PHARMACISTS
7272 Wisconsin Avenue, Bethesda MD 20814. 301/657-3000. World Wide Web address: http://www.ashp.com/pub/ashp/index.html. Provides pharmaceutical education. Updates pharmacies on current medical developments. Offers a service for jobseekers for a fee.

BIOMEDICAL RESEARCH INSTITUTE
355 K Street, Chula Vista CA 91911-1209. 619/793-

2750. Fax: 619/427-2634. A nonprofit organization which promotes scientific research and education and provides annual scholarships to students. Maintains a national Institutional Review Board.

BIOTECHNOLOGY INDUSTRY ORGANIZATION (BIO)

1625 K Street NW, Suite 1100, Washington DC 20006-1604. 202/857-0244. Fax: 202/857-0237. World Wide Web address: http://www.bio.org. Represents agriculture, biomedical, diagnostic, food, energy, and environmental companies. Publishes an informative profile of the U.S. Biotechnology Industry.

NATIONAL PHARMACEUTICAL COUNCIL

1894 Preston White Drive, Reston VA 20191. 703/620-6390. Fax: 703/476-0904. An organization of research-based pharmaceutical companies. Fax requests to the attention of Pat Adams, Vice President of Finance and Administration.

Directories

DRUG TOPICS RED BOOK

Medical Economics Company, 5 Paragon Drive, Montvale NJ 07645. 201/358-7200.

Magazines

DRUG TOPICS

Medical Economics Company, 5 Paragon Drive, Montvale NJ 07645. 201/358-7200.

PHARMACEUTICAL ENGINEERING

International Society of Pharmaceutical Engineers, 3816 West Linebaugh Avenue, Suite 412, Tampa FL 33624. 813/960-2105. World Wide Web address: http://www.ispe.org.

Online Services

MEDZILLA

E-mail address: info@medzilla.com. World Wide Web address: http://www.medzilla.com. Lists job openings for professionals in the fields of biotechnology, health care, medicine, and science related industries.

SCI.MED.PHARMACY

A networking discussion group focusing on the pharmaceutical field.

SCI.RESEARCH.CAREERS

A networking group discussing various careers relating to scientific research.

BUSINESS SERVICES AND NON-SCIENTIFIC RESEARCH

 Standard & Poor's *forecasts 7.5 percent growth across the board for the business services industry in 1998. This sector covers a broad range of services, from adjustment and collection to data processing. While the outlook varies depending on the service, in general, the business services sector is among the fastest-growing in the nation. Increasingly, companies are outsourcing functions like data processing to outside firms.*

Steady consolidation across many industries will continue to result in a greater need for services in 1998, from temporary help to consulting and engineering services. Security firms also expect a significant boost in employment through the year 2005, due to increased concern about crime and vandalism, and the surge in commercial use of sophisticated computer equipment and guards trained to operate such equipment.

ACE AMERICA'S CASH EXPRESS INC.
1231 Greenway Drive, Irving TX 75038. 972/550-5000. **Contact:** Human Resources. **Description:** One of the largest check cashing companies in the United States, offering check cashing services for government and payroll checks. Ace America's Cash Express Inc. operates over 450 stores across the country.

AFFILIATED COMPUTER SERVICES, INC. (ACS)
2828 North Haskell Avenue, Dallas TX 75243. 214/841-6111. **Contact:** Personnel. **World Wide Web address:** http://www.acs-inc.com. **Description:** A full-service provider of data processing services, computer outsourcing, facilities management, electronic transaction processing, and telecommunications services. The firm owns several data centers across the United States, and a telecommunications network that encompasses leading edge technologies. The company uses many different computer platforms, including IBM, Amdahl, Hewlett-Packard, Tandem, and UNIX-based systems. **Common positions include:** Accountant/Auditor; Computer Programmer; Computer Scientist; Project Manager; Software Developer; Software Engineer.

AUTOMATIC DATA PROCESSING (ADP)
2735 Stemmons Freeway, Dallas TX 75207. 214/630-9311. **Toll-free phone:** 800/829-2775. **Fax:** 214/905-2828. **Contact:** Tamara Trummer, Human Resources Director. **World Wide Web address:** http://www.adp.com. **Description:** Provides computerized transaction processing, recordkeeping, data communications, and information services. ADP helps more than 300,000 clients improve their business performance by providing services such as payroll, payroll tax, and human resource information management; brokerage industry market data, back office, and proxy services; industry-specific services to auto and truck dealers; and computerized auto repair and replacement estimating for auto insurance companies and body repair shops. Employer Services, Brokerage Services, Dealer Services, and Claims Services are the company's four largest businesses. Together, they represent over 95 percent of ADP's revenues. **Common positions include:** Account Representative; Administrative Assistant; Customer Service Representative; Sales Manager; Sales Representative; Secretary; Typist/Word Processor. **Educational backgrounds include:** Accounting; Business Administration. **Benefits:** 401(k); Daycare Assistance; Dental Insurance; Disability Coverage; Life Insurance; Medical Insurance; Pension Plan; Savings Plan; Stock Purchase; Tuition Assistance. **Corporate headquarters location:** Roseland NJ. **Other U.S. locations:** Nationwide. **Listed on:** New York Stock Exchange. **Annual sales/revenues:** More than $100 million. **Number of employees at this location:** 500. **Number of employees nationwide:** 29,000.

BMS ENTERPRISES INC.
308 Arthur Street, Fort Worth TX 76107. 817/810-9200. **Fax:** 817/810-9226. **Contact:** Human Resources. **Description:** A high-tech restoration and cleaning firm with affiliate companies involved in providing environmental services. BMS Enterprises Inc. has specific technical expertise with electronics and wet document recovery. The company provides disaster restoration services following fire and water catastrophes. BMS Enterprises Inc. is also involved in providing HVAC services to improve indoor air quality. **Common positions include:** Accountant/Auditor; Advertising Clerk; Attorney; Biological Scientist; Budget Analyst; Chemical Engineer; Chemist; Computer Programmer; Cost Estimator; Emergency Medical Technician; Financial Analyst; Geologist/Geophysicist; Human Resources Manager; Public Relations Specialist; Services Sales Representative. **Educational backgrounds include:** Accounting; Biology; Business Administration; Chemistry; Computer Science; Engineering; Finance; Geology. **Benefits:** 401(k); Dental Insurance; Life Insurance; Medical Insurance. **Corporate headquarters location:** This Location. **Operations at this facility include:** Administration; Research and Development; Sales; Service. **Listed on:** Privately held. **Number of employees at this location:** 200. **Number of employees nationwide:** 600.

BUSINESS RECORDS CORPORATION (BRC)
1111 West Mockingbird Lane, Suite 1400, Dallas TX 75247. 214/688-1800. **Fax:** 214/905-2398. **Contact:** Nancy Schuerr, Director of Human Resources. **World Wide Web address:** http://www.brcp.com. **Description:** Provides information management and data processing products and services that can be classified into four major categories: Technology Outsourcing Services, Election Products and Services, Governmental Records Management, and Other Products and Services. **Common positions include:** Accountant/Auditor; Computer Programmer; Systems Analyst. **Educational backgrounds include:** Accounting; Business Administration; Computer Science; Marketing. **Benefits:** 401(k); Dental Insurance; Disability Coverage; Life Insurance; Medical Insurance. **Special programs:** Internships. **Corporate headquarters location:** This Location. **Other U.S. locations:** Birmingham AL; St. Cloud MN; Washington MO; Syracuse NY. **Listed on:** NASDAQ. **Number of employees nationwide:** 1,200.

COMPUTER LANGUAGE RESEARCH, INC. (CLR)
2395 Midway Road, Carrollton TX 75006. 972/250-7430. **Fax:** 972/250-7763. **Recorded jobline:** 800/FAST-TAX. **Contact:** Tom Parson, Technical Recruiting Manager. **World Wide Web address:** http://www.clr.com. **Description:** Engages in the computation and printing of tax returns for CPA firms distributed under the name Fast-Tax. Fast-Tax services include high-speed laser printing of tax-returns, online processing, in-house laser printing, CD-ROM software delivery, and electronic linking tax compliance to tax research. Other products are developed and marketed under the trade names Rent Roll, On-Site, and Credit Interfaces which provide real estate software and services for property managers and developers. In addition to tax-related and real estate services, CLR addresses the government market and provides consulting services. **Common positions include:** Accountant/Auditor; Software Engineer; Technical Writer/Editor. **Educational backgrounds include:** Accounting; Computer Science; Engineering; Finance. **Benefits:** 401(k); Dental Insurance; Disability Coverage; Employee Discounts; Life Insurance; Medical Insurance; Tuition Assistance. **Corporate headquarters location:** This Location. **Operations at this facility include:** Divisional Headquarters; Regional Headquarters; Research and Development. **Listed on:** NASDAQ. **Number of employees at this location:** 900. **Number of employees nationwide:** 1,100.

DWYER GROUP INC.
1010 North University Parks Drive, Waco TX 76707. 254/745-2444. **Contact:** Human Resources. **Description:** An international provider of specialty services through a group of service-based franchisers. **Subsidiaries include:** Rainbow International Carpet Dyeing & Cleaning Company has 487 franchises in the U.S., 30 franchises in Canada, and 121 franchise operations in 16 foreign countries. The company specializes in indoor restoration and cleaning services including upholstery and drapery cleaning, carpet dying and cleaning, ceiling cleaning, deodorization, and comprehensive fire and water damage restoration and cleanup. Mr. Rooter Corporation is a complete residential and commercial plumbing service company, with a total of 240 franchises in the U.S. and five foreign countries. General Business Services, Inc. (GBS) and E.K. Williams & Company, established in 1962 and 1938 respectively, provide small business owners with business

counseling, tax planning, tax research, tax return preparation, recordkeeping systems, computer services, and financial management planning. GBS has a total of 320 franchises in the U.S. and Canada. E.K. Williams has a total of 186 franchises located throughout the U.S. Aire Serv Heating & Air Conditioning, Inc. is a franchiser of heating, ventilation, and air conditioning maintenance and repair services. The primary client base for its franchisees includes residential and light commercial applications. Aire Serv has 39 U.S. franchises. Mr. Electric, an electrical contracting service franchise has one U.S. franchise.

MBNA INFORMATION SERVICES
16001 North Dallas Parkway, Dallas TX 75380. 972/233-7101. **Toll-free phone:** 800/527-3890. **Contact:** Human Resources Department. **Description:** MBNA Information Services, a subsidiary of MBNA American Bank, is an information processing company serving financial institutions and merchant plans nationwide. MBNA Information Services also provides printing, data processing, and mailing services to businesses in a number of industries. **Corporate headquarters location:** This Location. **Parent company:** MBNA Corporation (Newark DE) is one of the world's leaders in issuing the Gold MasterCard cards, and one of the largest lenders through bank credit cards in the world. MBNA is also a leading issuer of affinity credit cards. Other operations of the company include home equity and personal loans, and accepting deposits. Other subsidiaries of MBNA Corporation include MBNA American Bank, N.A., a national bank, and MBNA Marketing Systems.

MEDAPHIS PHYSICIAN SERVICES
9441 LBJ Freeway, Suite 400, Dallas TX 75243. 972/664-6900. **Contact:** Human Resources. **Description:** Medaphis Physician Services, formerly Advacare Inc., provides physicians with full practice management services. The company's services include billing and accounts receivable management.

PINKERTON SECURITY COMPANY
7610 Stemmons Freeway, Suite 140, Dallas TX 75247. 214/631-5934. **Contact:** Personnel Administrator. **World Wide Web address:** http://www.pinkerton.com. **Description:** Pinkerton Security Company is one of the oldest and largest non-governmental security services organizations in the world. The company's principal business is providing security, investigative, and consulting services to a multitude of commercial, industrial, institutional, governmental, and residential clients. The company operates from 129 offices in the United States, Canada, and Great Britain. Major services include industrial and nuclear plant security, institutional security, commercial and residential building security, retail security, construction security, patrol and inspection services, community security, sports and special events services, K-9 patrol services, courier services, inventory services, investigation services, security consultation, and equipment evaluation. **Common positions include:** Security Officer. **Educational backgrounds include:** College Degree; High School Diploma/GED. **Benefits:** Life Insurance. **Corporate headquarters location:** Van Nuys CA. **Operations at this facility include:** Administration; Service. **Number of employees worldwide:** 35,000.

RENTERS CHOICE, INC.
13800 Montfort Drive, Suite 300, Dallas TX 75240. 972/701-0489. **Contact:** Human Resources. **Description:** A lease-to-own company dealing primarily in the areas of furniture, electronics, and appliances.

WARRANTECH CORPORATION
150 Westpark Way, Suite 200, Euless TX 76040. 817/283-7267. **Contact:** Human Resources. **World Wide Web address:** http://www.warrantech.com. **Description:** Provides marketing and administrative services to retailers, distributors, and manufacturers of automobiles, recreational vehicles, automotive components, home appliances, home entertainment products, computers and peripherals, and office and communications equipment. Administrative services pertain primarily to extended service contracts and limited warranties, issued by the retailer, distributor, or manufacturer to the purchaser of the consumer product. **Benefits:** Incentive Plan; Profit Sharing; Stock Option. **Corporate headquarters location:** This Location. **Other U.S. locations:** Stamford CT. **Listed on:** NASDAQ. **Number of employees nationwide:** 240.

Note: Because addresses and telephone numbers of smaller companies can change rapidly, we recommend you call each company to verify the information below before inquiring about job opportunities. Mass mailings are not recommended.

Additional small employers:

ADJUSTMENT AND COLLECTION SERVICES

Commercial Recovery Systems
PO Box 28989, Dallas TX 75228-0989. 214/324-9575.

Honor Creditors Agency Inc.
PO Box 830398, Richardson TX 75083-0398. 972/235-1202.

UAI
PO Box 1931, Dallas TX 75221-1931. 214/965-8000.

CLEANING, MAINTENANCE, AND PEST CONTROL SERVICES

Dallas Pest Control Company
10210 Monroe Dr, Dallas TX 75229-5715. 972/263-9508.

Sears Termite & Pest Control
3015 Bryan St, Dallas TX 75204-6103. 214/826-9600.

CREDIT REPORTING SERVICES

Alliance Data Systems
PO Box 100, Dallas TX 75221-0100. 972/960-5100.

Equifax Credit Information Services
PO Box 833810, Richardson TX 75083-3810. 972/234-7200.

Experian Inc.
701 Experian Parkway, Allen TX 75013. 972/390-3000.

DETECTIVE, GUARD, AND ARMORED CAR SERVICES

Accu-Guard Inc.
8585 N Stemmons Freeway, Dallas TX 75247-3836. 214/637-6410.

Advance Security
1425 W Pioneer Dr, Ste 209, Irving TX 75061-7132. 972/254-1513.

Allied Security Inc.
1140 Empire Central Dr, Dallas TX 75247-4322. 214/631-6928.

American Commercial Security Services
2300 Valley View Lane, Irving TX 75062-1721. 972/570-3999.

American Guard Corporation
111 S Terry St, Ste 8, Malakoff TX 75148-9207. 903/489-3662.

American Protective Service
5944 Luther Lane, Ste 301, Dallas TX 75225-5910. 214/692-7844.

Armored Transport of Texas
PO Box 223646, Dallas TX 75222-3646. 214/631-5355.

Brinks Incorporated
2530 Century Lake Dr, Irving TX 75062-4964. 972/445-1800.

Burns International Security Services
8150 Brookriver Dr, Ste 1, Dallas TX 75247-4068. 214/638-1666.

Burns International Security Services
6707 Brentwood Stair Rd, Fort Worth TX 76112-3335. 817/492-8001.

Burns International Security Services
PO Box 749, Glen Rose TX 76043-0749. 254/897-5434.

City Center Security
201 Main St, Ste 1910, Fort Worth TX 76102-3105. 817/390-8787.

D&L Security Services
1420 W Mockingbird Lane, Dallas TX 75247-4931. 214/634-0146.

Guardsmark
PO Box 561125, Dallas TX 75356-1125. 214/638-4961.

Hawk Security Systems Inc.
PO Box 97, Hewitt TX 76643-0097. 254/666-7400.

International Total Service
PO Box 612368, Dallas TX 75261-2368. 214/574-3220.

Loomis Fargo Co.
1655 Vilbig Rd, Dallas TX 75208-1317. 214/742-4473.

Murray Guard Inc.
8500 N Stemmons Fwy, Dallas TX 75247-3832. 214/630-4525.

Murray Guard Inc.
1018 S Van Buren St, Amarillo TX 79101-3306. 806/376-1193.

NASG
PO Box 539, Dallas TX 75221-0539. 214/739-0777.

Pinkertons Inc.
4150 International Plz, Fort Worth TX 76109-4819. 817/731-7590.

Ruiz Protective Services
11029 Shady Trl, Ste 117, Dallas TX 75229-5621. 214/357-0820.

Silver Star Security Inc.
1616 Gateway Blvd, Richardson TX 75080-3529. 972/235-8910.

Smith Protective Services
2120 W Vickery Blvd, Fort Worth TX 76102-5830. 817/332-7981.

Supreme Security Inc.
788 S Floyd Rd, Richardson TX 75080-7403. 972/235-8844.

The Diamond Group
13101 Preston Rd, Ste 212, Dallas TX 75240-5220. 972/788-4413.

Triad Protective Services
1925 Beltline Rd, Ste 400, Carrollton TX 75006. 972/416-6169.

Wackenhut Corporation
3002 Gilmer Rd, Ste 5, Longview TX 75604-1412. 903/759-9341.

Wackenhut Corporation
6737 Brentwood Stair Rd, Fort Worth TX 76112-3348. 817/429-0672.

Wells Fargo Guard Services
3610 Avenue Q, Ste 226, Lubbock TX 79412-1248. 806/765-0006.

Wells Fargo Guard Services
8150 Brook River, Ste 104S,
Dallas TX 75247. 214/638-4906.

**SECRETARIAL AND COURT
REPORTING SERVICES**

Team Texas
1600 Airport Fwy, Ste 208,
Bedford TX 76022-6881.
817/354-7785.

**SECURITY SYSTEMS
SERVICES**

Access Protection Systems
6500 Greenville Ave, Dallas TX
75206-1014. 972/696-1800.

Brinks Home Security Inc.
8880 Esters Blvd, Irving TX
75063-2406. 972/871-3500.

Firstwatch Corporation
PO Box 36304, Dallas TX 75235-
1304. 214/630-6636.

Guardco
2510 W Mockingbird Ln, Dallas
TX 75235-5629. 214/352-5752.

Monitronics International
12801 N Stemmons Fwy, Dallas
TX 75234. 972/243-7443.

For more information on career opportunities in miscellaneous business services and non-scientific research:

<u>Associations</u>

AMERICAN SOCIETY OF APPRAISERS
P.O. Box 17265, Washington DC 20041. 703/478-
2228. Toll-free phone: 800/ASA-VALU. Fax:
703/742-8471. World Wide Web address:
http://www.appraisers.org. An international,
nonprofit, independent appraisal organization. ASA
teaches, tests, and awards designations.

**EQUIPMENT LEASING ASSOCIATION OF
AMERICA**
4301 North Fairfax Drive, Suite 550, Arlington VA
22203. 703/527-8655. World Wide Web address:
http://www.elaonline.com.

**NATIONAL ASSOCIATION OF PERSONNEL
SERVICES**
3133 Mt. Vernon Avenue, Alexandria VA 22305.
703/684-0180. Fax: 703/684-0071. World Wide Web
address: http://www.napsweb.org. Provides federal
legislative protection, education, certification, and
business products and services to its member
employment service agencies.

<u>Online Services</u>

**INTERNET BUSINESS OPPORTUNITIES
SHOWCASE**
http://www.clark.net./pub/ibos/busops.html. This
Website offers links to franchise, small business, and
related opportunities.

CHARITIES AND SOCIAL SERVICES

Charitable health organizations have come into the spotlight in recent years. The American Heart Association, the Arthritis Foundation, and the American Lung Association have all volunteered their names (for a fee) to promote the sale of brand name products. Many think that the charities are risking their reputations by choosing one product over another. Even with this controversy, there is still a growing need for professionals to work in charitable organizations. The industry faces a high turnover rate and opportunities are plentiful.

The need for qualified social workers continues to grow as the older population in need of such services increases. Other factors leading to increasing job opportunities include: rising crime and juvenile delinquency; a growing number of mentally ill, AIDS patients, and families in crisis; and the need for more social workers to administer discharge plans at medical facilities.

ABILENE REGIONAL MENTAL HEALTH & MENTAL RETARDATION CENTER
2616 South Clack, Suite 140, Abilene TX 79606. 915/690-5100. **Contact:** Personnel. **Description:** An outpatient counseling facility for people who are mentally challenged.

AMERICAN HEART ASSOCIATION (AHA)
7272 Greenville Avenue, Dallas TX 75231. 214/373-6300. **Contact:** Human Resources Department. **World Wide Web address:** http://www.amhrt.org. **Description:** One of the oldest and largest national nonprofit voluntary health associations dedicated to reducing disability and death from cardiovascular diseases and stroke. AHA-funded research has yielded such discoveries as CPR, bypass surgery, pacemakers, artificial heart valves, microsurgery, life-extending drugs, and new surgical techniques to repair heart defects. The American Heart Association's interactive public education programs emphasize quitting smoking, controlling high blood pressure, eating a low-fat, low-cholesterol diet, and being physically active. The AHA also teaches the warning signs of heart attack and stroke and what to do if they occur. The American Heart Association trains about 5 million Americans per year in emergency care procedures; these training systems are used by millions more worldwide. Founded in 1924. **Special programs:** Internships. **Corporate headquarters location:** This Location. **Other U.S. locations:** Nationwide.

BIG SKY RANCH
2234 Amy Lynn Avenue, Abilene TX 79603. 915/676-5671. **Contact:** Peter Brown, Administrator. **Description:** A group home for people who have mental retardation.

BOY SCOUTS OF AMERICA
1325 West Walnut Hill Lane, P.O. Box 152079, Irving TX 75015-2079. 972/580-2000. **Contact:** Professional Selection and Placement. **World Wide Web address:** http://www.bsa.scouting.org. **Description:** The national scouting organization for young male adults. The Boy Scouts of America has 340 local councils nationwide. **Common positions include:** Administrator; Customer Service Representative; Human Service Worker; Sales Representative. **Educational backgrounds include:** Bachelor of Arts; Business Administration; College Degree; Liberal Arts; Management/Planning; Master of Arts; MBA; Ph.D.; Social Science. **Benefits:** 401(k); Dental Insurance; Disability Coverage; Life Insurance; Medical Insurance; Pension Plan. **Special programs:** Internships. **Corporate headquarters location:** This Location. **Other U.S. locations:** Nationwide. **Listed on:** Privately held. **Number of employees nationwide:** 4,000.

E.O.A.C.
500 Franklin Avenue, Waco TX 76701. 254/753-0331. **Contact:** Employment. **Description:** This is the central office of E.O.A.C. Overall, the organization offers Head Start programs for three and

four year olds; charter school for children ages five years through third grade; Youth in Action, an alcohol and drug prevention program for teenagers; assistance with rent and utilities payments; weatherization of homes; and a variety of services for the homeless.

THE GLADNEY CENTER

2300 Hemphill, Fort Worth TX 76110. 817/926-3304. **Contact:** Human Resources. **World Wide Web address:** http://www.gladney.org. **Description:** A nonprofit adoption agency, providing services to young women experiencing unplanned pregnancies who seek to make an adoption plan for their infant; individuals seeking to build their families through adoptions; and adoptees. The Gladney Fund is a support organization that exists to provide continuous financial support and philanthropic funds management to The Gladney Center. Founded in 1887.

HARMONY FAMILY SERVICES

1111 Industrial Boulevard, Abilene TX 79602. 915/677-4663. **Contact:** Personnel. **Description:** A treatment facility that offers a residential center for runaway and homeless youths.

MEALS ON WHEELS

1416 West Eighth Avenue, Room 106, Amarillo TX 79101. 806/374-1521. **Contact:** Personnel. **Description:** Delivers meals to those who are 60 years of age or older.

PANHANDLE COMMUNITY SERVICES

P.O. Box 763, Clarendon TX 79226. 806/874-2573. **Contact:** Human Resources. **Description:** An agency that offers housing, energy, weatherization, transportation, and food banks for the homeless and low-income families.

UNITED WAY

901 Ross Avenue, Dallas TX 75202. 214/978-0000. **Contact:** Human Resources. **Description:** Helps to meet the health and human-care needs of millions of people. United Way includes approximately 1,900 organizations.

Note: Because addresses and telephone numbers of smaller companies can change rapidly, we recommend you call each company to verify the information below before inquiring about job opportunities. Mass mailings are not recommended.

Additional small employers:

MISC. SOCIAL SERVICES

American Heart Association
4808 Eastover Circle, Mesquite TX 75149-1048. 972/388-0495.

Career Design & Development
1881 Sylvan Ave, Ste 215, Dallas TX 75208-2031. 214/741-1097.

Community Access Inc.
1611 East Fifth Street, Tyler TX 75701-3432. 903/595-5644.

Community Action Home Health
PO Box 610, Levelland TX 79336-0610. 806/894-6104.

HBO & Company
601 East Corporate Drive, Lewisville TX 75057-6403. 972/219-4200.

United Way
210 E 9th St, Fort Worth TX 76102-6404. 817/878-0000.

For more information on career opportunities in charities and social services:

Associations

ASAE CAREER OPPORTUNITIES
1575 I Street NW, Suite 1190, Washington DC 20005-1168. 202/408-7900. Fax: 202/408-7907. World Wide Web address: http://www.entremkt.com/ceo. Publishes a lengthy newsletter of job openings at associations and nonprofit organizations nationwide and internationally. Each issue is organized by region. All jobs listed are in the $30,000 - $50,000 salary range. Subscription rates for non-members: $57 for 5 issues; $117 for 12 issues; $197 for 24 issues. Subscription

rates for members: $57 for 6 issues; $117 for 14 issues; $197 for 28 issues.

AMERICAN COUNCIL OF THE BLIND
1155 15th Street NW, Suite 720, Washington DC 20005. 202/467-5081. World Wide Web address: http://www.acb.org. Membership required. Offers an annual conference, a monthly magazine, and scholarships.

CATHOLIC CHARITIES USA
1731 King Street, Suite 200, Alexandria VA 22314. 703/549-1390. World Wide Web address:

http://www.catholiccharitiesusa.org. Membership required.

CLINICAL SOCIAL WORK FEDERATION
P.O. Box 3740, Arlington VA 22203. 703/522-3866. A lobbying organization. Offers newsletters and a conference every two years to member organizations.

FAMILY SERVICE ASSOCIATION OF AMERICA
11700 West Lake Park Drive, Park Place, Milwaukee WI 53224. 414/359-1040. World Wide Web address: http://www.fsanet.org. Membership required.

NATIONAL ASSOCIATION OF SOCIAL WORKERS
750 First Street NE, Suite 700, Washington DC 20002-4241. 202/408-8600. World Wide Web address: http://www.naswdc.org.

NATIONAL COUNCIL ON FAMILY RELATIONS
3989 Central Avenue NE, Suite 550, Minneapolis MN 55421. 612/781-9331. Fax: 612/781-9348. Membership required. Publishes two quarterly journals. Offers an annual conference and newsletters.

NATIONAL FEDERATION OF THE BLIND
1800 Johnson Street, Baltimore MD 21230. 410/659-9314. World Wide Web address: http://www.nfb.org. Membership of 50,000 in 600 local chapters. Publishes a monthly magazine.

NATIONAL MULTIPLE SCLEROSIS SOCIETY
733 Third Avenue, New York NY 10017. 212/986-3240. Toll-free phone: 800/344-4867. World Wide Web address: http://www.nmss.org. Publishes a quarterly magazine.

NATIONAL ORGANIZATION FOR HUMAN SERVICE EDUCATION
Brookdale Community College, 765 Newman Springs Road, Lyncroft NJ 07738. 732/842-1900x546.

Online Services

COOLWORKS
http://www.coolworks.com/. This Website includes information on volunteer openings. The site also provides links to 22,000 job openings in national parks, summer camps, ski areas, river areas, ranches, fishing areas, cruise ships, and resorts.

NONPROFIT JOBNET
http://www.nando.net/philant/philant.html. The *Philanthropy Journal*'s site lists jobs in nonprofit associations and philanthropic occupations.

CHEMICALS/RUBBER AND PLASTICS

 *Growth in the chemicals industry should be rather weak overall, with some sectors faring better than others. Since 1996, the industry has done poorly in terms of growth, trade, and earnings, according to the U.S. Department of Commerce.*

The two major industrial consumers of chemicals -- the housing and automotive industries -- both face overall sluggish growth for the next few years. However, a growing market for electronics and electronic components will feed the demand for products such as cleaners, resin, and other specialty chemicals. With production and prices at a low for large-volume industrial chemicals, both the inorganic and organic sectors are expected to see minimal growth in 1998.

The demand and production of plastics, on the other hand, continues to grow, especially in the automotive industry. Additionally, industrial use of rubber will expand as the demand for synthetic rubber by the automotive industry increases.

AMERICAN EXCELSIOR COMPANY
P.O. Box 5624, Arlington TX 76005. 817/640-2161. **Contact:** Randy Dark, Branch Manager. **World Wide Web address:** http://www.amexco.com. **Description:** A packaging company engaged in the production of environmentally sound, water-soluble packaging materials, foam protective shipping pads, fabricated polyurethane foam, shaped packaging, and other related packaging products. **Common positions include:** Blue-Collar Worker Supervisor; Cost Estimator; Customer Service Representative; Industrial Production Manager; Quality Control Supervisor. **Educational backgrounds include:** Business Administration; Marketing. **Benefits:** Dental Insurance; Life Insurance; Medical Insurance; Profit Sharing. **Operations at this facility include:** Administration; Manufacturing; Sales. **Number of employees at this location:** 30. **Number of employees nationwide:** 600.

BFX HOSPITALITY GROUP, INC.
226 Bailey Avenue, Suite 101, Fort Worth TX 76107. 817/332-4761. **Contact:** Personnel. **Description:** A manufacturer of a variety of plastic products.

BONAR PACKAGING, INC.
P.O. Box 818, Tyler TX 75710. 903/593-1793. **Contact:** Personnel Department. **Description:** Manufactures plastic films and sheets for packaging.

CAPROCK MANUFACTURING, INC.
2303 120th Street, Lubbock TX 79423. 806/745-6454. **Contact:** Ms. Yolanda Sanchez, Human Resources Department. **World Wide Web address:** http://www.caprock-mfg.com. **Description:** A plastic injection molding company that specializes in the manufacture of plastic parts for cellular phones including phone windows and battery cases. **NOTE:** Second and third shifts are offered. **Common positions include:** Advertising Clerk; Buyer; Controller; Customer Service Representative; Design Engineer; EKG Technician; General Manager; Human Resources Manager; Manufacturing Engineer; Production Manager; Purchasing Agent/Manager; Quality Control Supervisor; Secretary. **Educational backgrounds include:** Accounting; Art/Design; Business Administration; Chemistry; Communications; Computer Science; Engineering; Finance; Mathematics; Public Relations. **Benefits:** 401(k); Dental Insurance; Disability Coverage; Life Insurance; Medical Insurance; Savings Plan. **Corporate headquarters location:** This Location. **Listed on:** Privately held. **President:** Ryan Provenzano. **Annual sales/revenues:** $51 - $100 million. **Number of employees at this location:** 150. **Number of projected hires for 1998 - 1999 at this location:** 15.

CARROLL COMPANY
2900 West Kingsley Road, Garland TX 75041. 972/278-1304. **Toll-free phone:** 800/527-5722. **Fax:** 972/840-0678. **Recorded jobline:** 972/278-1304x600. **Contact:** Shirley Wren, Human Resources Manager. **World Wide Web address:** http://www.carrollco.com. **Description:** A manufacturer of institutional cleaning products. Founded in 1921. **NOTE:** Entry-level positions and second and third shifts are offered. **Common positions include:** Account Manager; Account Representative; Accountant; Administrative Assistant; Blue-Collar Worker Supervisor; Buyer; Chemist; Computer Programmer; Controller; Credit Manager; Customer Service Representative; Database Manager; Electrician; Graphic Artist; Human Resources Manager; Industrial Engineer; Marketing Manager; Production Manager; Purchasing Agent/Manager; Sales Executive; Sales Manager; Secretary; Video Production Coordinator. **Educational backgrounds include:** Accounting; Art/Design; Marketing. **Benefits:** 401(k); Dental Insurance; Disability Coverage; Employee Discounts; Life Insurance; Mass Transit Available; Medical Insurance; Tuition Assistance. **Corporate headquarters location:** This Location. **Other U.S. locations:** Carson CA. **Operations at this facility include:** Administration; Manufacturing; Regional Headquarters; Research and Development; Sales. **Listed on:** Privately held. **President/CEO:** Kyle Ogden. **Facilities manager:** Jim Coats. **Number of employees at this location:** 160. **Number of employees nationwide:** 180. **Number of projected hires for 1998 - 1999 at this location:** 50.

CHEMICAL LIME COMPANY
P.O. Box 985004, Fort Worth TX 76185. 817/732-8164. **Contact:** Earle Haley, Director of Human Resources. **Description:** A manufacturer and distributor of chemical lime products with facilities located in the West, Southwest, and Southeast. The company's principal products are high calcium limestone, dolomite limestone, dolomite glass flux, high calcium quicklime, dolomitic quicklime, calcium hydrated lime and dolomitic hydrated lime sold widely in the western U.S. in the construction field under the trade name Type S Hydrated Lime. **Common positions include:** Accountant/Auditor; Chemist; Civil Engineer; Computer Programmer; Electrical/Electronics Engineer; Financial Analyst; Geologist/Geophysicist; Industrial Engineer; Mechanical Engineer; Mining Engineer; Operations/Production Manager; Quality Control Supervisor; Systems Analyst; Transportation/Traffic Specialist. **Educational backgrounds include:** Accounting; Business Administration; Chemistry; Computer Science; Engineering; Geology. **Benefits:** Dental Insurance; Disability Coverage; Life Insurance; Medical Insurance; Profit Sharing; Savings Plan; Tuition Assistance. **Corporate headquarters location:** This Location.

CRYOVAC
1301 West Magnolia Avenue, Iowa Park TX 76367-1410. 940/592-2111. **Contact:** Human Resources Department. **Description:** This location manufactures plastic bags. **Parent company:** W.R. Grace & Company is one of the largest producers of specialty chemicals, as well as a provider of specialized health care. The major divisions of W.R. Grace include Grace Packaging, Grace Davison, Grace Construction Products, Grace Dearborn, Grace Container & Specialty Polymers, and Grace Health Care.

CYRO INDUSTRIES
101 East Park Boulevard, Suite 1039, Plano TX 75074. 972/424-6830. **Contact:** Human Resources. **World Wide Web address:** http://www.cyro.com. **Description:** This location is a sales office. Overall, Cyro Industries is a manufacturer of acrylite plastic sheets.

D&S PLASTICS INTERNATIONAL
1201 Avenue H East, Grand Prairie TX 75050-2702. 972/988-4200. **Contact:** Human Resources. **Description:** A manufacturer of plastic pellets. These pellets are sold to auto manufacturers and melted down to make various auto parts including bumpers.

FINA INC.
8350 North Central Expressway, Dallas TX 75206. 214/750-2400. **Contact:** Human Resources. **World Wide Web address:** http://www.fina.com. **Description:** Explores for crude oil and natural gas; markets natural gas; refines, supplies, transports, and markets petroleum products; manufactures and markets specialty chemicals, primarily petrochemicals and plastics, including polypropylene, polystyrene, styrene monomer, high-density polyethylene, and aromatics; licenses

certain chemical processes; and manufactures and markets paints and coatings. **Corporate headquarters location:** This Location.

FRITZ INDUSTRIES
P.O. Drawer 170040, Dallas TX 75217. 972/285-5471. **Contact:** Human Resources Department. **Description:** Fritz Industries manufactures a variety of chemicals for oil field and concrete production.

GAF MATERIALS CORPORATION
2600 Singleton Boulevard, Dallas TX 75212. 214/637-1060. **Contact:** Human Resources. **World Wide Web address:** http://www.gaf.com. **Description:** A multiproduct manufacturer with sales in both consumer and industrial markets. The company's product line includes building, roofing, and insulation materials for the construction trades; specialty chemicals and plastics; and reprographic products. **Common positions include:** Accountant/Auditor; Blue-Collar Worker Supervisor; Customer Service Representative; Electrical/Electronics Engineer; Industrial Engineer; Manufacturer's/Wholesaler's Sales Rep.; Operations/Production Manager; Production Worker; Purchasing Agent/Manager; Quality Control Supervisor. **Educational backgrounds include:** Accounting; Business Administration; Engineering; Manufacturing Management. **Benefits:** 401(k); Dental Insurance; Disability Coverage; Life Insurance; Medical Insurance; Pension Plan; Tuition Assistance. **Corporate headquarters location:** Wayne NJ. **Other U.S. locations:** Nationwide. **Operations at this facility include:** Manufacturing; Sales. **Listed on:** Privately held. **Number of employees at this location:** 235.

M.A. HANNA COLOR
9001 South Freeway, Fort Worth TX 76140. 817/293-1555. **Contact:** Ms. Mardell Everett, Personnel Manager. **Description:** M.A. Hanna Color is a manufacturer of inorganic pigment and colorants for plastics.

HUNTSMAN POLYMERS CORPORATION
5005 LBJ Freeway, Suite 450, Dallas TX 75244. 972/450-2340. **Contact:** Human Resources. **Description:** Manufactures plastic materials (including plastic films), thermoplastic resins, and other synthetic resins; polyethylene; and polypropylene. The company's products are used to make a wide variety of products ranging from dashboards to diapers and medical supplies. **Corporate headquarters location:** This Location. **Other U.S. locations:** DE; GA; UT; WI. **Number of employees at this location:** 1,000.

ICI EXPLOSIVES USA, INC.
15301 Dallas Parkway, Suite 1200, Dallas TX 75248. 972/450-1269. **Contact:** Human Resources. **World Wide Web address:** http://www.energeticsolutions.com. **Description:** A manufacturing company producing commercial explosives, nitrogen products, and chemicals. **Common positions include:** Accountant/Auditor; Biological Scientist; Chemical Engineer; Chemist; Computer Programmer; Manufacturer's/Wholesaler's Sales Rep. **Educational backgrounds include:** Accounting; Chemistry; Computer Science; Engineering. **Benefits:** Dental Insurance; Disability Coverage; Employee Discounts; Life Insurance; Medical Insurance; Pension Plan; Savings Plan; Tuition Assistance. **Corporate headquarters location:** This Location. **Parent company:** ICI, plc. **Operations at this facility include:** Administration; Sales. **Number of employees at this location:** 70. **Number of employees nationwide:** 1,200.

INDUSTRIAL MOLDING CORPORATION
616 East Slaton Road, Lubbock TX 79404. 806/474-1000. **Contact:** Amy Willingham, Personnel Manager. **World Wide Web address:** http://www.indmolding.com. **Description:** An injection molding company. **Corporate headquarters location:** This Location.

JAMAK FABRICATION, INC.
1401 North Bowie Drive, Weatherford TX 76086. 817/594-8771. **Contact:** Human Resources. **Description:** Manufacturers of synthetic silicone rubber products. **Corporate headquarters location:** Fort Worth TX. **Parent company:** JMK International. **Number of employees at this location:** 300.

JONES BLAIR COMPANY

P.O. Box 35286, Dallas TX 75235. 214/353-1661. **Contact:** Personnel. **Description:** A manufacturer of paints, resins, elastomers, and powder coatings. **Common positions include:** Chemical Engineer; Chemist; Industrial Engineer; Industrial Production Manager; Management Trainee; Operations/Production Manager. **Educational backgrounds include:** Chemistry; Engineering. **Benefits:** 401(k); Disability Coverage; Employee Discounts; Life Insurance; Medical Insurance; Tuition Assistance. **Corporate headquarters location:** This Location. **Other U.S. locations:** Chattanooga TN. **Operations at this facility include:** Administration; Manufacturing; Research and Development; Sales; Service. **Listed on:** Privately held. **Number of employees at this location:** 250. **Number of employees nationwide:** 450.

KELLY-SPRINGFIELD TIRE COMPANY

P.O. Box 4670, Tyler TX 75712-4670. 903/535-1500. **Contact:** Human Resources. **World Wide Web address:** http://www.kelly-springfield.com. **Description:** Manufactures tires and inner tubes. **Common positions include:** Accountant/Auditor; Blue-Collar Worker Supervisor; Buyer; Chemist; Computer Programmer; Electrical/Electronics Engineer; Industrial Engineer; Management Trainee; Mechanical Engineer; Purchasing Agent/Manager. **Educational backgrounds include:** Business Administration; Engineering. **Benefits:** 401(k); Dental Insurance; Life Insurance; Medical Insurance. **Corporate headquarters location:** Cumberland MD. **Other U.S. locations:** Freeport IL; Fayetteville NC. **Parent company:** Goodyear Tire & Rubber Company. **Listed on:** New York Stock Exchange.

LUBRICATION ENGINEERS INC.

P.O. Box 7128, Fort Worth TX 76111. 817/834-6321. **Physical address:** 3851 Airport Freeway, Fort Worth TX 76111. **Contact:** Karen May, Personnel Director. **Description:** Produces a variety of industrial lubricants. **Corporate headquarters location:** This Location.

MPI INC.

2341 North Main Street, Fort Worth TX 76106. 817/347-7200. **Contact:** Personnel Department. **Description:** A manufacturer and distributor of rubber carpet padding.

MOHAWK LABORATORIES

2730 Carl Road, Irving TX 75062. 972/438-0551. **Contact:** Human Resources Department. **Description:** Operates two laboratories that manufacture specialty cleaning and polishing chemicals.

NCH CORPORATION

P.O. Box 152170, Irving TX 75015-2170. 972/438-0211. **Physical address:** 2727 Chensearch Boulevard, Irving TX 75062. **Contact:** Human Resources. **Description:** A diverse chemical and construction products company. Chemical products include paints, varnishes, lacquers, and enamels for institutional, government, and industrial markets. Retail chemical products include deodorizers and stain removers. NCH Corporation also manufactures fasteners, welding supplies, electrical components, plumbing components, and safety products. Subsidiaries are located in Canada, Europe, Latin America, and the Far East. **Corporate headquarters location:** This Location. **Listed on:** New York Stock Exchange.

OCCIDENTAL CHEMICAL CORPORATION

P.O. Box 809050, Dallas TX 75380-9050. 972/404-3800. **Contact:** James F. Reder, Manager of Staff Planning and College Relations. **World Wide Web address:** http://www.oxychem.com. **Description:** Manufactures commodity and specialty chemicals, plastics, and petrochemicals. The company has approximately 35 manufacturing facilities nationwide. **Common positions include:** Accountant/Auditor; Chemical Engineer; Electrical/Electronics Engineer; Mechanical Engineer. **Educational backgrounds include:** Accounting; Engineering. **Benefits:** 401(k); Dental Insurance; Disability Coverage; Life Insurance; Medical Insurance; Pension Plan; Tuition Assistance. **Corporate headquarters location:** Los Angeles CA. **Other U.S. locations:** Nationwide. **Parent company:** Occidental Petroleum. **Operations at this facility include:** Divisional Headquarters. **Listed on:** New York Stock Exchange. **Annual sales/revenues:** More than $100 million. **Number of employees at this location:** 700. **Number of employees nationwide:** 8,000.

POLY-AMERICA INC.
2000 West Marshall Drive, Grand Prairie TX 75051. 972/647-4374. **Contact:** Human Resources Department. **World Wide Web address:** http://www.poly-america.com. **Description:** Produces plastics materials and synthetic resins.

RIBELIN SALES INC.
P.O. Box 461673, Garland TX 75046-1673. 972/272-1594. **Contact:** Human Resources. **World Wide Web address:** http://www.ribelin.com. **Description:** Ribelin Sales Inc. is a wholesale distributor of raw materials for the paint and coating industry.

THE SHERWIN-WILLIAMS COMPANY
P.O. Box 38469, Dallas TX 75238-0469. 214/553-2950. **Physical address:** 10440 East NW Highway, Dallas TX 75238. **Fax:** 214/553-3903. **Contact:** Division Recruiting Manager. **Description:** Engaged in the manufacturing, selling, and distribution of coatings and related products. Coatings are produced for original equipment manufacturers in various industries as well as for the automotive aftermarket, the industrial maintenance market, and the traffic paint market. The Sherwin-Williams labeled architectural and industrial coatings are sold through approximately 2,000 company-owned specialty paint and wall-covering stores, located in 48 states. The Sherwin-Williams Company also manufactures paint under the Dutch Boy, Martin-Senour, Kem-Tone, Lucas, Acme, and Rogers brand names, as well as private labels, and sells it to independent dealers, mass merchandisers, and home improvement centers. **Common positions include:** Management Trainee. **Corporate headquarters location:** Cleveland OH. **Other U.S. locations:** Nationwide. **Number of employees nationwide:** 17,000.

STYROCHEM INTERNATIONAL
3607 North Sylvania, Fort Worth TX 76111. 817/831-3541. **Contact:** Estella Hernandez, Human Resources Manager. **World Wide Web address:** http://www.styrochem.com. **Description:** StyroChem International manufactures raw plastic beads. **Common positions include:** Administrator; Blue-Collar Worker Supervisor; Buyer; Chemist; Claim Representative; Customer Service Representative; Draftsperson; Electrical/Electronics Engineer; General Manager; Human Resources Manager; Insurance Agent/Broker; Manufacturer's/Wholesaler's Sales Rep.; Marketing Specialist; Mechanical Engineer; Operations/Production Manager; Purchasing Agent/Manager; Quality Control Supervisor; Transportation/Traffic Specialist. **Educational backgrounds include:** Business Administration; Chemistry; Communications; Engineering; Marketing; Mathematics. **Benefits:** Dental Insurance; Disability Coverage; Life Insurance; Medical Insurance; Pension Plan; Savings Plan. **Operations at this facility include:** Administration; Manufacturing; Research and Development; Sales; Service.

SUNCOAST INDUSTRIES
PLASTICS MANUFACTURING COMPANY (PMC)
2700 South Westmoreland Avenue, Dallas TX 75233. 214/330-8671. **Contact:** Lee Hicks, Director of Personnel. **World Wide Web address:** http://www.azone.net/suncoast. **Description:** Manufactures a wide variety of resins, plastics, and glass-reinforced plastics for use in the electronics industry, as well as plastic tableware products used in the food service industry. A second Dallas location produces other plastic products used in the construction and food service industries. **Corporate headquarters location:** This Location.

TEXAS EASTMAN
P.O. Box 7444, Longview TX 75607. 903/237-5000. **Contact:** Human Resources Department. **Description:** A manufacturer of a wide variety of chemicals and plastics. **Parent company:** Eastman Chemicals.

TEXAS REFINERY CORPORATION
P.O. Box 711, Fort Worth TX 76101. 817/332-1161. **Contact:** Jan Peel, Personnel Director. **Description:** Manufactures specialty lubricant products and building maintenance products such as roof coatings. **Common positions include:** Chemist; Credit Manager; Manufacturer's/Wholesaler's Sales Rep. **Educational backgrounds include:** Chemistry. **Number of employees at this location:** 275.

VIRGINIA KMP CORPORATION
4100 Platinum Way, Dallas TX 75237. 214/330-7731. **Contact:** Vice President of Operations. **Description:** Manufactures and sells chemicals, filter driers, refrigeration accumulators, and air conditioners.

WELLMARK INTERNATIONAL
12200 Denton Drive, Farmers Branch TX 75234. 972/243-2321. **Contact:** Human Resources Specialist. **Description:** An international producer of a wide range of insecticide products, including strips, flea and tick collars for dogs and cats, and agricultural insecticides and dips. This company was formerly Sandoz Agro Inc. **Corporate headquarters location:** Bensonville IL. **Parent company:** Central Garden and Pet. **Operations at this facility include:** Divisional Headquarters.

Note: Because addresses and telephone numbers of smaller companies can change rapidly, we recommend you call each company to verify the information below before inquiring about job opportunities. Mass mailings are not recommended.

Additional small employers:

AGRICULTURAL CHEMICALS

Ennis Agri-Tech Inc.
PO Box 237, Ennis TX 75120-0237. 972/878-4400.

CARBON BLACK

Cabot Corp.
PO Box 5001, Pampa TX 79066-5001. 806/661-3100.

Darco Activated Carbon
PO Box 790, Marshall TX 75671-0790. 903/938-9211.

Sid Richardson Carbon & Gas
PO Box 3118, Borger TX 79008-3118. 806/274-7213.

CHEMICALS AND ALLIED PRODUCTS WHOLESALE

Ecolab Inc.
2305 Sherwin St, Garland TX 75041-1222. 972/278-6121.

Kem Manufacturing
1400 Northgate Dr, Irving TX 75062. 972/438-0265.

Tech Spray
PO Box 949, Amarillo TX 79105. 806/372-8523.

CLEANING, POLISHING, AND SANITATION PREPARATIONS

Arden Corporation
10901 Airport Blvd, Amarillo TX 79111-1202. 806/335-1147.

Magnolia Enterprises
PO Box 59089, Dallas TX 75229-1089. 972/247-7111.

Zep Manufacturing Company
PO Box 645, De Soto TX 75123-0645. 972/228-3388.

INDUSTRIAL GASES

Air Liquide America Corp.
13140 Floyd Rd, Dallas TX 75243-1508. 972/235-2388.

INDUSTRIAL INORGANIC CHEMICALS

Hoechst Corporation
PO Box 937, Pampa TX 79066-0937. 806/665-1801.

Huntsman Chemical Corporation
PO Box 8389, Longview TX 75607-8389. 903/234-1100.

INDUSTRIAL ORGANIC CHEMICALS

Hoechst Celanese Chemical
PO Box 819005, Dallas TX 75381-9005. 972/277-4000.

PAINTS, VARNISHES, AND RELATED PRODUCTS

Sherwin-Williams Company
2802 W Miller Rd, Garland TX 75041-1211. 972/271-2541.

Valspar
701 S Shiloh Rd, Garland TX 75042-7812. 972/276-5181.

PLASTIC MATERIALS WHOLESALE

Plastican Incorporated
2651 Santa Anna Ave, Dallas TX 75228-1673. 214/328-2721.

PLASTIC MATERIALS, SYNTHETICS, AND ELASTOMERS

Life-Like Products Inc.
1600 W US Highway 287 Byp, Waxahachie TX 75165-5068. 972/937-6512.

Rhone-Poulenc
201 Harrison St, Vernon TX 76384-3399. 940/552-9911.

Wilsonart International Inc.
600 General Bruce Dr, Temple TX 76504. 254/207-7000.

WNA Carthage Inc.
PO Box 668, Carthage TX 75633-0668. 903/693-7151.

PLASTIC PRODUCTS

AEP Industries Inc.
6250 N Interstate Highway, Waxahachie TX 75165-5602. 972/576-8193.

ALCOA Building Products
1601 Commerce Dr, Denison TX 75020-1905. 903/463-6095.

Atco
7101 Atco Dr, Fort Worth TX 76118-7029. 817/595-2894.

CANTEX Inc.
PO Box 340, Mineral Wells TX
76068-0340. 817/498-7070.

Carpenter Co.
PO Box 1007, Temple TX 76503-
1007. 254/778-8991.

Centron International Inc.
PO Box 490, Mineral Wells TX
76068-0490. 940/325-1341.

CKS Packaging Inc.
109 W Felix St, Fort Worth TX
76115-3531. 817/924-2205.

Constar Plastics Inc.
2210 Saint Germain Rd, Dallas
TX 75212-4811. 214/688-0714.

Creative Manufacturing Inc.
1016 W Harris Rd, Arlington TX
76001-6806. 817/465-1452.

Daltex Technologies Inc.
2300 N Hwy 121, Euless TX
76039. 817/540-2300.

Dolco Packaging Corp.
4700 S Westmoreland Rd, Dallas
TX 75237-1629. 214/337-4711.

Fibergrate Corporation
PO Box 208, Stephenville TX
76401-0208. 254/965-3148.

Flexible Foam Products Inc.
501 Industrial Blvd, Terrell TX
75160-5403. 972/563-1559.

Genpak Corporation
1101 W Harrison Rd, Longview
TX 75604-5610. 903/297-4445.

Hartzell Manufacturing Inc.
2200 Worthington Dr, Denton TX
76207. 940/387-3535.

Hefco Plastics Inc.
PO Box 638, Troup TX 75789-
0638. 903/842-3136.

Integral Corporation
PO Box 151369, Dallas TX
75315-1369. 972/263-9512.

ITW Meritex
PO Box 5508, Arlington TX
76005-5508. 817/640-5668.

Kysor/Needham
PO Box 14248, Fort Worth TX
76117-0248. 817/281-5121.

Miramar Designs Inc.
PO Box 15420, Fort Worth TX
76119-0420. 817/457-4981.

Molded Products Company
PO Box 37169, Fort Worth TX
76117-8169. 817/428-3636.

Paramount Packaging
800 Jordan Valley Rd, Longview
TX 75604-5221. 903/297-3242.

Pescor Plastics Inc.
3300 W Bolt St, Fort Worth TX
76110-5816. 817/926-5471.

Plexco
1601 W 287 Byp, Waxahachie
TX 75165. 972/923-6400.

Ring Can
2107 Franklin Dr, Fort Worth TX
76106-2206. 817/625-7214.

Roto-Plastics
PO Box 38, Gatesville TX 76528-
0038. 254/865-7221.

Sealed Air Corporation
4400 Diplomacy Rd, Fort Worth
TX 76155-2638. 817/540-2020.

Southern Plastics Inc.
PO Box 352, Kilgore TX 75663-
0352. 903/984-6229.

Supreme Plastics Inc.
PO Box 1072, White Oak TX
75693-1072. 903/759-3881.

Tallyho Plastics Inc.
PO Box 990, Jacksonville TX
75766-0990. 903/586-2263.

Texstar Plastics
925 Avenue H E, Arlington TX
76011-7721. 972/647-1366.

The Resource Group
3066 San Diego Dr, Dallas TX
75228-1726. 972/644-7074.

Thermo-Serv Inc.
PO Box 223886, Dallas TX
75222-3886. 214/631-0307.

Trinity Plastics Inc.
901 E Industrial Ave, Fort Worth
TX 76131-2715. 817/230-2020.

Tucker Housewares
721 111th St, Arlington TX
76011-7616. 817/640-5621.

Wilsonart International Inc.
2400 Wilson Place, Temple TX
76504. 254/207-6000.

WNA Cups Illustrated Inc.
PO Box 650037, Dallas TX
75265-0037. 972/224-8407.

RUBBER PRODUCTS

Fineline Packaging
1416 Upfield Dr, Carrollton TX
75006-6915. 972/242-2711.

Rex-Hide Inc.
PO Box 4726, Tyler TX 75712-
4726. 903/593-7387.

RGL
PO Box 1237, Corsicana TX
75151-1237. 903/872-3091.

Tenneco Packaging Inc.
4501 E Hwy 31, Corsicana TX
75110. 903/872-6540.

TIRES AND INNER TUBES

Oliver Rubber Company
6850 Forest Park Rd, Dallas TX
75235-4633. 214/350-7851.

**UNSUPPORTED PLASTIC
PRODUCTS**

Pak-Sher Co.
2500 N Longview St, Kilgore TX
75662-6840. 903/984-8596.

For more information on career opportunities in the chemicals/rubber and plastics industries:

Associations

AMERICAN ASSOCIATION FOR CLINICAL CHEMISTRY
2101 L Street NW, Suite 202, Washington DC 20037-
1526. 202/857-0717. Toll-free phone: 800/892-1400.
World Wide Web address: http://www.aacc.org.
International scientific/medical society of individuals

involved with clinical chemistry and other clinical lab
science-related disciplines.

AMERICAN CHEMICAL SOCIETY
Career Services, 1155 16th Street NW, Washington
DC 20036. 202/872-4600. World Wide Web address:
http://www.acs.org.

AMERICAN INSTITUTE OF CHEMICAL ENGINEERS
345 East 47th Street, New York NY 10017. 212/705-7338. Toll-free phone: 800/242-4363. World Wide Web address: http://www.aiche.org. Provides leadership in advancing the chemical engineering profession as it meets the needs of society.

CHEMICAL MANAGEMENT & RESOURCES ASSOCIATION
60 Bay Street, Suite 702, Staten Island NY 10301. 718/876-8800. Fax: 718/720-4666. Engaged in marketing, marketing research, business development, and planning for the chemical and allied process industries. Provides technical meetings, educational programs, and publications to members.

CHEMICAL MANUFACTURERS ASSOCIATION
1300 Wilson Boulevard, Arlington VA 22209. 703/741-5000. World Wide Web address: http://www.cmahq.com. A trade association that develops and implements programs and services and advocates public policy that benefits the industry and society.

THE ELECTROCHEMICAL SOCIETY
10 South Main Street, Pennington NJ 08534-2896. An international educational society dealing with electrochemical issues. Also publishes monthly journals.

SOAP AND DETERGENT ASSOCIATION
475 Park Avenue South, 27th Floor, New York NY 10016. 212/725-1262. World Wide Web address: http://www.sdahq.org. A trade association and research center.

SOCIETY OF PLASTICS ENGINEERS
14 Fairfield Drive, P.O. Box 403, Brookfield CT 06804-0403. 203/775-0471. World Wide Web address: http://www.4spe.org. Dedicated to helping members attain higher professional status through increased scientific, engineering, and technical knowledge.

THE SOCIETY OF THE PLASTICS INDUSTRY, INC.
1801 K Street NW, Suite 600K, Washington DC 20006. 202/974-5200. Promotes the development of the plastics industry and enhances public understanding of its contributions while meeting the needs of society.

Directories

CHEMICAL INDUSTRY DIRECTORY
State Mutual Book and Periodical Service, Order Department, 17th Floor, 521 Fifth Avenue, New York NY 10175. 516/537-1104.

CHEMICALS DIRECTORY
Cahners Publishing, 275 Washington Street, Newton MA 02158. 617/964-3030.

DIRECTORY OF CHEMICAL ENGINEERING CONSULTANTS
American Institute of Chemical Engineering, 345 East 47th Street, New York NY 10017. 212/705-7338.

DIRECTORY OF CHEMICAL PRODUCERS
SRI International, 333 Ravenswood Avenue, Menlo Park CA 94025. 650/326-6200. World Wide Web address: http://www.sri.com.

Magazines

CHEMICAL & ENGINEERING NEWS
American Chemical Society, 1155 16th Street NW, Washington DC 20036. 202/872-4600. World Wide Web address: http://www.pubs.acs.org/cen.

CHEMICAL MARKETING REPORTER
Schnell Publishing Company, 80 Brot Street, 23rd Floor, New York NY 10004. 212/791-4267.

CHEMICAL WEEK
888 Seventh Avenue, 26th Floor, New York NY 10106. 212/621-4900. World Wide Web address: http://www.chemweek.com.

COMMUNICATIONS: TELECOMMUNICATIONS AND BROADCASTING

The telecommunications industry was marked by radical changes in 1997, and more consolidation and intense competition among local and long-distance carriers were expected to follow in 1998, according to Business Week. *In reaction to price drops and increased competition across all segments of the industry, mergers and acquisitions have been an industry trend.*

The Telecommunications Act of 1996, coupled with promising new wireless technology, opened the door for major long-distance companies to break into the local phone market within their respective regions, which proved a very costly venture. However, a federal court decision to limit the FCC's regulation over long-distance carriers should give businesses more power over prices and the freedom to enter new territories.

Subscribers of wireless services were expected to increase substantially by the end of 1998, although declining prices of wireless minutes, driven by competition, will likely be detrimental to smaller wireless operators. Meanwhile, a strong demand for data and networking communications equipment will be beneficial to the industry.

Internet technologies continue to transform the telecommunications industry as companies begin to offer long-distance and fax services over the Internet. According to Action Information Services, these services will produce $1 billion in revenues by 2001, although companies must satisfy customers' demands for increasingly faster Internet access.

AT&T
4100 Bryan Street, Dallas TX 75204. 214/421-6400. **Recorded jobline:** 800/562-7288. **Contact:** Human Resources Department. **World Wide Web address:** http://www.att.com. **Description:** AT&T is a major long-distance telephone company which provides domestic and international voice and data communications and management services, telecommunications products, and leasing and financial services. The company manufactures data communications products, computer products, switching and transmission equipment, and components. **Corporate headquarters location:** Basking Ridge NJ. **Other U.S. locations:** Nationwide.

AT&T
5501 LBJ Freeway, Dallas TX 75240. 972/778-3600. **Contact:** Personnel. **World Wide Web address:** http://www.att.com. **Description:** AT&T is a major long-distance telephone company which provides domestic and international voice and data communications and management services, telecommunications products, and leasing and financial services. The company manufactures data communications products, computer products, switching and transmission equipment, and components. **Benefits:** Life Insurance; Pension Plan. **Corporate headquarters location:** Basking Ridge NJ. **Other U.S. locations:** Nationwide.

ABILENE RADIO AND TELEVISION INC.
4510 South 14th Street, Abilene TX 79605. 915/692-4242. **Fax:** 915/692-8265. **Contact:** Debbie Freeman, Personnel Director. **Description:** An NBC-affiliated television station. **Corporate headquarters location:** This Location. **Number of employees at this location:** 50.

ALCATEL NETWORK SYSTEMS
P.O. Box 833802, Mail Stop 401-152, Richardson TX 75083-3802. 972/996-5000. **Contact:** Human Resources Department. **World Wide Web address:** http://www.aud.alcatel.com. **Description:** Manufactures telecommunications equipment. **Corporate headquarters location:** This Location. **Other U.S. locations:** St. Louis MO; Raleigh NC.

ANDREW CORPORATION
2701 Mayhill Road, Denton TX 76208. 940/891-0965. **Contact:** Tim Bee, Human Resources Manager. **World Wide Web address:** http://www.andrew.com. **Description:** A manufacturer of telecommunications equipment including Earth station satellite, cellular, and microwave antennas, towers, shelters, cables, and associated equipment. **Common positions include:** Accountant/Auditor; Blue-Collar Worker Supervisor; Budget Analyst; Buyer; Civil Engineer; Construction and Building Inspector; Cost Estimator; Customer Service Representative; Designer; Draftsperson; Electrical/Electronics Engineer; Electrician; Financial Analyst; General Manager; Human Resources Manager; Industrial Engineer; Industrial Production Manager; Licensed Practical Nurse; Management Analyst/Consultant; Mechanical Engineer; Operations/Production Manager; Purchasing Agent/Manager; Quality Control Supervisor; Registered Nurse; Software Engineer; Structural Engineer; Technical Writer/Editor; Transportation/Traffic Specialist. **Educational backgrounds include:** Accounting; Business Administration; Communications; Computer Science; Engineering; Finance; Liberal Arts; Marketing. **Benefits:** 401(k); Dental Insurance; Disability Coverage; Employee Discounts; Life Insurance; Medical Insurance; Pension Plan; Profit Sharing; Savings Plan; Tuition Assistance. **Special programs:** Internships. **Corporate headquarters location:** Orland Park IL. **Other U.S. locations:** Torrance CA; Austin TX; Dallas TX; Garland TX; Richardson TX; Bothell WA. **Operations at this facility include:** Administration; Divisional Headquarters; Manufacturing; Regional Headquarters; Research and Development; Sales; Service. **Listed on:** New York Stock Exchange. **Number of employees at this location:** 600. **Number of employees nationwide:** 3,000.

A.H. BELO CORPORATION
P.O. Box 655237, Dallas TX 75265. 214/977-6600. **Contact:** Mr. Lee Smith, Employment Manager. **World Wide Web address:** http://www.dallasnews.com. **Description:** Owns and operates newspapers and network-affiliated television stations in seven U.S. metropolitan areas. The company traces its roots to The Galveston Daily News, which began publishing in 1842. **Subsidiaries include:** DFW Printing Company, Inc.; DFW Suburban Newspapers, Inc.

CONTINENTAL ELECTRONICS CORPORATION
P.O. Box 270879, Dallas TX 75227-0879. 214/381-7161. **Contact:** Employment. **World Wide Web address:** http://www.contelec.com. **Description:** A manufacturer and distributor of radio and television transmitters and machinery. **Common positions include:** Accountant/Auditor; Assistant Manager; Blue-Collar Worker Supervisor; Buyer; Computer Programmer; Credit Manager; Customer Service Representative; Department Manager; Draftsperson; Electrical/Electronics Engineer; Human Resources Manager; Manufacturer's/Wholesaler's Sales Rep.; Mechanical Engineer; Operations/Production Manager; Purchasing Agent/Manager; Quality Control Supervisor; Technical Writer/Editor. **Educational backgrounds include:** Accounting; Business Administration; Engineering; Marketing. **Benefits:** 401(k); Dental Insurance; Disability Coverage; Life Insurance; Medical Insurance; Tuition Assistance. **Corporate headquarters location:** Houston TX. **Parent company:** Tech-Sym Corporation. **Operations at this facility include:** Administration; Divisional Headquarters; Manufacturing; Research and Development; Sales. **Listed on:** New York Stock Exchange. **Number of employees at this location:** 250.

D.F.W. COMMUNICATIONS
2413 Gravel Drive, Fort Worth TX 76118. 817/589-7322. **Contact:** Human Resources. **Description:** A manufacturer of communications equipment and electronic products. **Other U.S. locations:** Nationwide.

DECIBEL PRODUCTS INC.
8635 Stemmons Freeway, Dallas TX 75247. 214/819-4265. **Fax:** 214/819-4262. **Contact:** Human Resources. **World Wide Web address:** http://www.decibelproducts.com. **Description:** A manufacturer and distributor of telecommunications products including cables, connectors, and

sway brace kits. **Common positions include:** Accountant/Auditor; Buyer; Electrical/Electronics Engineer; Industrial Engineer; Mechanical Engineer; Quality Control Supervisor; Technical Writer/Editor. **Educational backgrounds include:** Engineering. **Benefits:** 401(k); Dental Insurance; Disability Coverage; Life Insurance; Medical Insurance; Pension Plan; Profit Sharing; Savings Plan; Tuition Assistance. **Corporate headquarters location:** Beachwood OH. **Parent company:** Allen Telecom Systems. **Operations at this facility include:** Manufacturing. **Number of employees at this location:** 600.

ERICSSON INC.
PRIVATE RADIO SYSTEMS
4757 Irving Boulevard, Dallas TX 75247. 214/267-6907. **Contact:** Human Resources. **World Wide Web address:** http://www.ericsson.com. **Description:** Designs and manufactures advanced telecommunications equipment for wired and mobile communications in public and private networks. **Common positions include:** Electrical/Electronics Engineer; Software Engineer. **Educational backgrounds include:** Computer Science; Engineering. **Benefits:** 401(k); Daycare Assistance; Dental Insurance; Disability Coverage; Life Insurance; Medical Insurance; Pension Plan; Savings Plan; Tuition Assistance. **Corporate headquarters location:** Sweden. **Other U.S. locations:** New York NY; Lynchburg VA. **Operations at this facility include:** Research and Development. **Listed on:** New York Stock Exchange. **Number of employees nationwide:** 5,000.

FUJITSU AMERICA INC.
2801 Telecom Parkway, Richardson TX 75082. 972/690-6000. **Contact:** Sheila Reynolds, Human Resources. **World Wide Web address:** http://www.fnc.fujitsu.com. **Description:** This location is engaged in the repair of cellular telephones.

GTE SOUTHWEST
P.O. Box 152013, Irving TX 75015-2013. 972/717-7700. **Contact:** Human Resources. **World Wide Web address:** http://www.gte.com. **Description:** This location is the regional headquarters. Overall, GTE is a worldwide leader in developing, manufacturing, and marketing telecommunications, electrical, and electronic products, services, and systems, with operations in 43 states, Puerto Rico, and 18 foreign countries. The company is comprised of four principal groups: GTE Telephone Operating Group; GTE Electrical Products, operating through the GTE Lighting Products, GTE Precision Materials, and GTE Electrical Equipment divisions; GTE Communications Products Group, which produces a wide range of communications systems, equipment, and devices, including electronic digital central office switching equipment, digital private automatic exchanges, transmission equipment, telephone instruments, and electronic systems for defense and aerospace applications; and GTE Telenet Communications Group, which operates public data communications networks and markets specially designed data communications networks for business and government organizations throughout the world. The company is also engaged in advanced research and development work in such high-technology areas as fiberoptic communications, satellite communications, digital systems, microelectronics, precision materials, and packet switching. **Corporate headquarters location:** Stamford CT. **Listed on:** New York Stock Exchange.

GENERAL CABLE COMPANY
800 East Second Street, Bonham TX 75418. 903/583-2181. **Contact:** Human Resources. **World Wide Web address:** http://www.generalcable.com. **Description:** This location of General Cable Company produces commercial cable for telephone companies. Overall, the company's business units include the Electrical Group, the Telecommunications and Electronics Group, the Consumer Products Group, and the Manufacturing Group. The Electrical Group operates under the business units General Cable/Guardian, which manufactures and distributes a full line of copper building wire, tray cable, power cable, and other cable products; Carol Cable Electrical, which manufactures industrial, power, mining, and control cable, THHN building wire, entertainment cable, rubber portable cord, and cordsets insulated with plastic and thermosetting compounds; and Capital Wire and Cable, which manufactures insulated wire and cable using both aluminum and copper conductors. The Telecommunications and Electronics Group operates under the business units Outside Products, which markets wire and cable designed for use in the outside plant network; Premise Products, which manufactures wire products that support the central office and commercial premise markets; and Electronics, which manufactures computer and control cables, IBM cabling

products, ethernet, coaxial, twin axial, and fire alarm cables. The Consumer Products Group operates under the business units Carol Cable, which manufactures extension cords, portable lights, and home office power supplies; General/Capital Wire Retail, which sells building wire to the retail market; and the OEM Engineered Cordsets Division, which manufactures cord and cordsets for data processing equipment, tools, floor care products, and other appliances. The Manufacturing Group provides specialized support and expertise in the areas of purchasing, transportation, engineering, labor relations, manufacturing, and environmental and safety support. **Corporate headquarters location:** Highland Heights KY. **Operations at this facility include:** Manufacturing.

HERITAGE MEDIA CORPORATION
13355 Noel Road, Suite 1500, Dallas TX 75240. 972/702-7380. **Contact:** Human Resources. **Description:** A radio station and broadcasting company.

KAMC TELEVISION
1201 84th Street, Lubbock TX 79423. 806/745-2828. **Contact:** Human Resources. **World Wide Web address:** http://www.abc28.com. **Description:** A television broadcasting station affiliated with ABC.

KFDA-TV
NEWS CHANNEL 10
P.O. Box 10, Amarillo TX 79105. 806/383-1010. **Contact:** Human Resources. **World Wide Web address:** http://www.newschannel10.com. **Description:** A CBS-affiliated television broadcasting station.

KLBK-TV
7403 South University Avenue, Lubbock TX 79423. 806/745-2345. **Contact:** Human Resources. **Description:** A CBS-affiliated television broadcasting station.

KPLX/KLIF
3500 Maple Avenue, Suite 1600, Dallas TX 75219. 214/526-2400. **Contact:** Human Resources Department. **World Wide Web address:** http://www.kplx.com. **Description:** A radio station.

KRLD/TEXAS STATE NETWORKS
1080 Ballpark Way, Arlington TX 76011. 817/543-5400. **Contact:** Human Resources. **World Wide Web address:** http://www.krld.com. **Description:** A radio station.

KVII-TV
CHANNEL 7
One Broadcasting Center, Amarillo TX 79101. 806/373-1787. **Contact:** Human Resources. **E-mail address:** pronews7@kvii.com. **Description:** An ABC-affiliated television broadcasting station.

KVIL-AM/FM 103.7
9400 North Central Expressway, Suite 1600, Dallas TX 75231. 214/691-1037. **Fax:** 214/891-7975. **Contact:** Vice President/Treasurer. **World Wide Web address:** http://www.kvil.com. **Description:** An adult contemporary radio station broadcasting on AM and FM. **Common positions include:** Assistant Manager; Assistant Program Officer; Copywriter; Program Manager; Promotion Manager; Radio/TV Announcer/Broadcaster; Transportation/Traffic Specialist. **Parent company:** Infinity Broadcasting Corporation of Texas.

KXXV-TV
P.O. Box 2522, Waco TX 76702. 254/754-2525. **Contact:** Human Resources. **World Wide Web address:** http://www.kxxv.com. **Description:** A television station affiliated with ABC.

LUCENT TECHNOLOGIES
3000 Skyline Drive, Mesquite TX 75149. 972/284-2000. **Contact:** Human Resources Department. **World Wide Web address:** http://www.lucent.com. **Description:** This location manufactures electronic power components for the communications industry. Overall, Lucent Technologies manufactures communications products, including switching, transmission, fiberoptic cable,

wireless systems, and operations systems, to supply the needs of telephone companies and other communications services providers.

MCI TELECOMMUNICATIONS CORPORATION

2400 North Glenville Drive, Richardson TX 75082. 972/783-4900. **Contact:** Human Resources Department. **World Wide Web address:** http://www.mci.com. **Description:** Provides domestic interstate long-distance service throughout the continental U.S., plus Hawaii, Puerto Rico, the Virgin Islands, and all foreign countries. Overall, MCI is one of the nation's largest long-distance companies and international carriers, providing a full array of sophisticated domestic and international telecommunications services to millions of residential and business customers, state and federal government agencies, and other organizations. MCI has divisional offices in Atlanta GA, Rye Brook NY, and Arlington VA, and more than 65 overseas offices in 60 countries. **Corporate headquarters location:** Washington DC. **Other U.S. locations:** Nationwide. **Parent company:** MCI Communications Corporation.

MOBILECOMM

1320 Greenway Drive, Suite 150, Dallas TX 75234. 972/751-2500. **Contact:** Human Resources. **Description:** This location serves as the company's national call center. Overall, MobileComm provides paging and wireless communications services.

MOTOROLA, INC.

5555 North Beach Street, Fort Worth TX 76137. 817/245-6000. **Contact:** Lionel Sweeney, Jr., Human Resources Manager. **World Wide Web address:** http://www.mot.com. **Description:** This location manufactures pagers. Overall, Motorola manufactures communications equipment and electronic products including car radios, cellular phones, semiconductors, computer systems, cellular infrastructure equipment, pagers, cordless phones, and LAN systems. The company has production plants in the U.S. and 18 countries around the world. **Common positions include:** Computer Programmer; Electrical/Electronics Engineer; Industrial Engineer; Mechanical Engineer; Quality Control Supervisor; Software Engineer; Systems Analyst. **Educational backgrounds include:** Computer Science; Engineering; Physics. **Benefits:** 401(k); Dental Insurance; Disability Coverage; Employee Discounts; Life Insurance; Medical Insurance; Pension Plan; Profit Sharing; Savings Plan; Tuition Assistance. **Special programs:** Internships. **Corporate headquarters location:** Schaumburg IL. **Other U.S. locations:** Nationwide. **Operations at this facility include:** Administration; Manufacturing; Research and Development. **Listed on:** NASDAQ.

NEC AMERICA INC.

1525 West Walnut Hill Lane, Irving TX 75038. 972/580-9100. **Contact:** Human Resources Department. **World Wide Web address:** http://www.nec.com. **Description:** A telecommunications corporation. NEC America manufactures communications systems and equipment, computers, industrial electronic systems, electronic devices, and home electronic products.

ONCOR COMMUNICATIONS, INC.

3530 Forest Lane, Suite 195, Dallas TX 75234. 214/902-3601. **Contact:** Recruiting. **Description:** A provider of operator and information services. **Common positions include:** Customer Service Representative; Long Distance Operator; Sales Representative. **Educational backgrounds include:** Communications. **Benefits:** Dental Insurance; Life Insurance; Medical Insurance; Pension Plan; Profit Sharing. **Corporate headquarters location:** Bethesda MD. **Operations at this facility include:** Sales; Service. **Listed on:** Privately held. **Number of employees at this location:** 800.

PAGENET

4965 Preston Park Boulevard, Suite 800, Plano TX 75093. 972/985-4100. **Contact:** Human Resources. **World Wide Web address:** http://www.pagenet.com. **Description:** Provides paging services. **Corporate headquarters location:** This Location.

RF MONOLITHICS, INC.

4347 Sigma Road, Dallas TX 75244. 972/233-2903. **Contact:** Human Resources. **World Wide Web address:** http://www.rfm.com. **Description:** Designs, develops, manufactures, and sells a broad range of radio frequency components and modules for the low-power wireless, high-frequency timing, and telecommunications markets. The company's products are based on surface acoustic wave reduced power consumption, increased precision, and greater reliability and durability. The company markets its line of more than 500 resonators, filters, delay lines, and related modules to original equipment manufacturers worldwide. **Corporate headquarters location:** This Location. **Listed on:** NASDAQ. **Stock exchange symbol:** RFMI.

REL-TEC CORPORATION
P.O. Box 919, Bedford TX 76095. 817/267-3141. **Contact:** Employee Relations Manager. **World Wide Web address:** http://www.reltec.com. **Description:** Manufactures carrier equipment for telephone stations and related electronic products.

SIECOR CORPORATION
9275 Denton Highway, Keller TX 76248. 817/431-1521. **Contact:** Human Resources. **Description:** Manufactures fiberoptic telecommunications equipment.

SOUTHWESTERN BELL TELEPHONE COMPANY
3 Bell Plaza, 308 South Akard Street, Dallas TX 75202. 214/464-3171. **Contact:** Employment Office. **Description:** A telephone services holding company, Southwestern Bell Telephone and its subsidiaries provide residential and commercial telephone service to 13.5 million access lines in Arkansas, Kansas, Missouri, Oklahoma, and Texas, and cellular services to 2.4 million customers. Other subsidiaries are engaged in publishing, underwriting, and marketing classified directories, and selling telecommunications systems, services, and related products. Southwestern Bell Telephone Company has international interests in telephone services in Mexico, cable and telephone services in the United Kingdom, and directory services in Australia. Southwestern Bell Telephone Company jointly owns Bell Communications Research with six other regional Bell companies. **NOTE:** Jobseekers should call 800/613-JOBS and ask for extension JEL363 to speak with a recruiter. **Corporate headquarters location:** San Antonio TX. **Listed on:** New York Stock Exchange.

SPRINT CORPORATION
1520 East Rochelle Boulevard, Irving TX 75039. 972/405-8000. **Contact:** Human Resources. **Description:** A diversified telecommunications company, with a nationwide, all-digital, fiberoptic network. Sprint's divisions provide global long-distance voice, data, and video products and services; local telephone services in 19 states; and cellular operations that serve 42 metropolitan markets and more than 50 rural service areas. **NOTE:** Sprint's Staff Associate Program is a two- to three-year developmental program. Staff Associates are hired into one of three specific tracks: Financial, Technological, or General Management. Each candidate should have the opportunity to experience at least three of the following departments: Finance, Information Systems, Marketing, Network Operations, Customer Service, and International. Rotational assignments allow the individual to be an immediate contributor while gaining a broad understanding of industry issues and operations. The program incorporates formal training and individual development, including periodical assessment of leadership skills. Students should contact their placement offices regarding on-campus interviews. **Common positions include:** Budget Analyst; Credit Manager; Customer Service Representative; Financial Analyst; Human Resources Manager; Market Research Analyst; Public Relations Specialist; Services Sales Representative; Software Engineer; Telecommunications Manager. **Educational backgrounds include:** Accounting; Business Administration; Communications; Computer Science; Economics; Engineering; Finance; Marketing. **Benefits:** 401(k); Dental Insurance; Disability Coverage; Employee Discounts; Life Insurance; Medical Insurance; Pension Plan; Savings Plan; Tuition Assistance. **Corporate headquarters location:** Shawnee Mission KS. **Other U.S. locations:** Nationwide. **Operations at this facility include:** Administration; Regional Headquarters; Sales; Service. **Listed on:** NASDAQ. **Number of employees nationwide:** 55,000.

VERTEX COMMUNICATIONS CORPORATION
2600 Longview Street, Kilgore TX 75662. 903/984-0555. **Fax:** 903/984-1826. **Contact:** Ann Jerden, Manager, Personnel. **World Wide Web address:** http://www.vertexcomm.com. **Description:** Designs and manufactures satellite Earth station antennas which operate on domestic, international, and military radio frequencies. The company offers a complete line of standard antenna products. **NOTE:** Entry-level positions are offered. **Common positions include:** Buyer;

Civil Engineer; Computer Programmer; Design Engineer; Draftsperson; Electrical/Electronics Engineer; Mechanical Engineer; MIS Specialist; Operations/Production Manager; Software Engineer; Structural Engineer; Systems Analyst; Technical Writer/Editor; Transportation/Traffic Specialist. **Educational backgrounds include:** Accounting; Computer Science; Engineering; Finance; Marketing. **Benefits:** 401(k); Dental Insurance; Disability Coverage; Life Insurance; Medical Insurance; Pension Plan; Profit Sharing; Savings Plan; Tuition Assistance. **Corporate headquarters location:** This Location. **Other U.S. locations:** Torrance CA; State College PA. **Operations at this facility include:** Administration; Divisional Headquarters; Manufacturing; Research and Development; Sales; Service. **Listed on:** NASDAQ. **Annual sales/revenues:** $21 - $50 million. **Number of employees at this location:** 400. **Number of employees nationwide:** 575. **Number of employees worldwide:** 605.

WESTCOTT COMMUNICATIONS, INC.
1303 Marsh Lane, Carrollton TX 75006. 972/416-4100. **Contact:** Human Resources. **Description:** An educational, training, and information services company that serves clients with common interests in selected markets by providing value-added products and services using appropriate communication technologies. The company currently delivers programming to the following markets: the government and public services market through the Law Enforcement Television Network and Fire & Emergency Television Network satellite networks, and American Heat, Pulse, and the Government Services Television Network video subscription services; the automotive market through the Automotive Satellite Television Network satellite network; the health care market through the Health & Sciences Television Network and the Long Term Care Network satellite networks, and the American Hospital Association and Westcott Healthcare Teleconference Group video seminar operations; the corporate and professional market through the Professional Security Television Network, CPA Report and Accounting and Financial Television Network video subscription services, Excellence in Training Corporation single tape sales, and Industrial Training Systems Corporation and Tel-A-Train, Inc. single tape sales, videotape library services, and the Interactive Distance Training Network electronic classroom facilities; the primary and secondary education market through the TI-IN Network satellite network; and the financial services market through the Bankers Training and Consulting Company videotape library service.

Note: Because addresses and telephone numbers of smaller companies can change rapidly, we recommend you call each company to verify the information below before inquiring about job opportunities. Mass mailings are not recommended.

Additional small employers:

CABLE/PAY TELEVISION SERVICES

Cablevision
PO Box 7852, Waco TX 76714-7852. 254/776-2996.

Marcus Cable
PO Box 2666, Fort Worth TX 76113-2666. 817/737-4795.

Marcus Cable
2911 Turtle Creek Blvd, Dallas TX 75219-6223. 214/521-7898.

Optel Inc.
1111 W Mockingbird Ln, Dallas TX 75247-5028. 214/634-3800.

The People's Network
PO Box 111817, Carrollton TX 75011-1817. 972/860-0400.

Storer Cable Communications
1045 Venture Ct, Carrollton TX 75006-5411. 972/840-2288.

TCI of Arlington Inc.
PO Box 120, Arlington TX 76004. 817/265-7766.

TCI of Plano Inc.
PO Box 940109, Plano TX 75094-0109. 972/578-7573.

Vista Cablevision Corp.
3225 Maurine Street, Wichita Falls TX 76305. 940/855-5700.

COMMUNICATIONS EQUIPMENT

ADC Telecommunications Inc.
2240 Campbell Creek Blvd, Richardson TX 75082. 972/680-6906.

Alcatel
1227 West Marshall Ave, Longview TX 75604-5110. 903/236-5200.

Bosch Telecom Inc.
8360 LBJ Freeway, Dallas TX 75243-1213. 972/997-2568.

Decibel Products Inc.
PO Box 569610, Dallas TX 75356-9610. 214/634-8502.

Ericsson Inc.
740 E Campbell Rd, Richardson TX 75081-6708. 972/583-0000.

Gardiner Communications Corp.
3605 Security St, Garland TX 75042-7629. 214/348-4747.

Hikari Corporation
11512 Pagemill Rd, Dallas TX
75243-5507. 214/349-4788.

INET Inc.
1255 W 15th St, Ste 600, Plano
TX 75075-7262. 972/578-6100.

Intecom Inc.
PO Box 911790, Dallas TX
75391-1774. 972/855-8000.

Intecom Inc.
2621 Summit Ave, Plano TX
75074-7432. 972/447-8292.

**Intelect Network Technology
Co. Inc.**
1100 W Executive Dr,
Richardson TX 75081-2229.
972/437-1888.

JRC Canada Inc.
4000 Sandshell Dr, Fort Worth
TX 76137-2422. 817/847-2100.

Loss Prevention Electronics
1301 Waters Ridge Dr,
Lewisville TX 75057-6022.
972/280-9675.

Lucent Technologies Inc.
909 Las Colinas Blvd E, Irving
TX 75039-3908. 972/325-4700.

Nokia Inc.
2300 Valley View Ln, Irving TX
75062-1721. 972/257-9800.

Nokia Mobile Phones America
5650 Alliance Gateway Fwy, Fort
Worth TX 76178-3736. 817/491-
7800.

Teknekron Infoswitch Corp.
4425 Cambridge Rd, Fort Worth
TX 76155-2629. 817/267-3025.

**Tektronix Grass Valley
Products**
5628 SW Green Oaks Blvd,
Arlington TX 76017-1199.
817/483-7447.

**MISC. COMMUNICATIONS
SERVICES**

Audionet Inc.
2914 Taylor St, Dallas TX 75226-
1908. 214/748-6660.

**RADIO BROADCASTING
STATIONS**

Daybreak USA
2290 Springlake Rd, Dallas TX
75234-5874. 972/484-2020.

Heftel Broadcasting Corp.
100 Crescent Ct, Ste 1777, Dallas
TX 75201-7822. 214/855-8882.

KDGE/KZPS Radio
15851 Dallas Pkwy, Dallas TX
75248-3369. 972/770-7777.

KKDA-FM
PO Box 530860, Grand Prairie
TX 75053-0860. 972/263-9911.

KTXQ-FM
4131 Canal St, Ste 1200, Dallas
TX 75210-2035. 214/528-5500.

KYNG
12201 Merit Dr, Ste 930, Dallas
TX 75251-2200. 214/716-7800.

WBAP-KSCS Radio Inc.
2221 E Lamar Blvd, Ste 400,
Arlington TX 76006-7419.
817/695-1820.

**TELEGRAPH AND OTHER
MESSAGE
COMMUNICATIONS**

GTE Communications Corp.
5221 North O'Connor Blvd, Bldg
E, Irving TX 75062. 972/887-
4387.

Transceiver Network
PO Box 816348, Dallas TX
75381-6348. 972/620-8920.

USA Relay
4310 Iola Avenue, Lubbock TX
79407-3746. 806/788-8940.

**TELEPHONE
COMMUNICATIONS**

A&B Electronics Inc.
PO Box 6088, Abilene TX
79608-6088. 915/690-5700.

Able Communication Services
2100 Couch Dr, McKinney TX
75069-7315. 972/424-5680.

Citizens Communication
8800 N Central Expressway,
Dallas TX 75231-6433. 214/365-
3247.

Comm South Companies Inc.
6830 Walling Ln, Dallas TX
75231-7204. 972/690-9955.

Excel Telecommunications
PO Box 650582, Dallas TX
75265-0582. 214/863-8000.

GTE Business Phone Systems
8550 Esters Blvd, Irving TX
75063-2205. 972/258-2000.

GTE Customer Care Center
3622 North Garland Avenue,
Garland TX 75040-8523.
972/414-2301.

GTE North Inc.
600 Hidden Ridge, Irving TX
75038-3809. 972/718-5600.

GTE Southwest Inc.
309 West Oak Street, Denton TX
76201-9037. 940/383-2511.

GTE Southwest Inc.
2201 Ave I, Plano TX 75074.
972/578-1161.

GTE Southwest Inc.
2303 South Highway 1417,
Sherman TX 75092. 903/870-
5253.

GTE Southwest Inc.
1824 North 1st Street, Garland
TX 75040-4704. 972/487-5701.

GTE Southwest Inc.
PO Box 1997, Texarkana TX
75504-1997. 903/798-4201.

Highwaymaster Corporation
16479 Dallas Pkwy, Ste 710,
Dallas TX 75248-2621. 972/732-
2500.

Matrix Telecom Inc.
8721 Airport Fwy, Fort Worth TX
76180-7603. 817/581-9380.

**MCI Telecommunications
Corp.**
1122 Alma Rd, Richardson TX
75081-2259. 972/918-2044.

**MCI Telecommunications
Corp.**
901 International Pkwy,
Richardson TX 75081-2874.
972/498-1000.

**MCI Telecommunications
Corp.**
12790 Merit Dr, Dallas TX
75251-1226. 972/788-5111.

**MCI Telecommunications
Corp.**
13155 Noel Rd, Dallas TX
75240-5090. 972/774-3400.

MFS Intelenet Inc.
1950 N Stemmons Fwy, Dallas
TX 75207-3107. 214/939-8800.

Mobilecomm Inc.
8901 Autobahn Dr, Ste 100,
Dallas TX 75237-3939. 214/849-
1402.

Network Long Distance
PO Box 3529, Longview TX
75606-3529. 903/758-9350.

Nokia Telecommunications Inc.
7 Village Cir, Ste 100, Roanoke
TX 76262-5904. 817/491-5800.

Northern Telecom Inc.
2100 Lakeside Blvd, Richardson
TX 75082-4355. 972/234-5300.

NTS Communications Inc.
PO Box 10730, Lubbock TX
79408-3730. 806/762-4565.

Oncor Communications Inc.
1412 Main St, Ste 2600, Dallas
TX 75202-4018. 214/653-1247.

Operator Service Company
5302 Avenue Q, Ste 6, Lubbock
TX 79412-2729. 806/747-2474.

Pagemart Wireless Inc.
3333 Lee Pkwy, Ste 100, Dallas
TX 75219-5142. 214/765-4000.

Poka-Lambro Coop
PO Box 1340, Tahoka TX 79373-
1340. 806/924-7234.

**Primeco Personal
Communications**
5221 N O'Connor Blvd, Irving
TX 75061. 972/337-3000.

**Primeco Personal
Communications**
6 Campus Cir, Roanoke TX
76262-8220. 817/258-1000.

**Southwestern Bell Mobile
Systems**
17330 Preston Rd, S100A, Dallas
TX 75252-5619. 972/733-2000.

**Southwestern Bell Mobile
Systems**
17210 Campbell Rd, Dallas TX
75252-4202. 972/447-6213.

**Southwestern Bell Mobile
Systems**
13900 Midway Rd, Dallas TX
75244-4317. 214/733-2387.

**Southwestern Bell Telephone
Co.**
PO Box 480, Wichita Falls TX
76307-0480. 940/766-7011.

**Southwestern Bell Telephone
Co.**
1240 Park Place Blvd, Hurst TX
76053-5320. 817/338-6141.

**Southwestern Bell Telephone
Co.**
1405 Main St, Rm 501, Lubbock
TX 79401-3225. 806/321-6444.

**Southwestern Bell Telephone
Co.**
1255 Tavaros Ave, Dallas TX
75218-4018. 214/324-7883.

**Southwestern Bell Telephone
Co.**
1116 Houston St, Rm 900, Fort
Worth TX 76102-6416. 817/884-
8332.

**Southwestern Bell Telephone
Co.**
2200 N Greenville Ave,
Richardson TX 75082-4412.
972/454-6206.

**Southwestern Bell Telephone
Co.**
2010 Avenue R, Rm 218,
Lubbock TX 79411-1228.
806/321-7070.

Sprint Business
5420 Lyndon B. Johnson Fwy,
Dallas TX 75240-6222. 972/405-
5000.

Sprint Corporation
1603 Lyndon B. Johnson Fwy,
Dallas TX 75234-6040. 972/405-
6000.

United Telephone Co. of Texas
213 E Corsicana St, Athens TX
75751-2503. 903/675-9685.

Vartec Telecom Inc.
3200 W Pleasant Run Rd,
Lancaster TX 75146-1022.
972/230-7200.

**TELEVISION
BROADCASTING STATIONS**

Caprock Telecasting
5600 Avenue A, Lubbock TX
79404-4598. 806/744-1414.

KAMR TV Channel 4
PO Box 751, Amarillo TX 79105-
0751. 806/383-3321.

KCEN TV
PO Box 6103, Temple TX 76503-
6103. 254/773-1633.

KDAF-TV
8001 John Carpenter Freeway,
Dallas TX 75247. 214/634-8833.

KERA Channel 13
3000 Harry Hines Boulevard,
Dallas TX 75201-1012. 214/871-
1390.

KETK TV 56
4300 Richmond Road, Tyler TX
75703-1201. 903/581-5656.

KFXK Fox 51
701 North Access Road,
Longview TX 75602-4205.
903/758-1691.

KLTV
PO Box 957, Tyler TX 75710-
0957. 903/597-5588.

KTEN
PO Box 1450, Denison TX
75021-1450. 903/465-5836.

KTVT-TV
PO Box 2495, Fort Worth TX
76113-2495. 817/496-7111.

KTXS TV
PO Box 2997, Abilene TX
79604-2997. 915/677-2281.

KWTX TV
PO Box 2636, Waco TX 76702-
2636. 254/776-1330.

KWTX TV
4400-1 East Centex Expressway,
Killeen TX 76543-7313. 254/690-
7787.

KXII TV
PO Box 1175, Sherman TX
75091-1175. 903/892-8123.

KXTX-TV
3900 Harry Hines Boulevard,
Dallas TX 75219-3204. 214/521-
3900.

**Lin Television of Texas
Inc.**
3900 Barnett Street, Fort Worth
TX 76103-1400. 817/536-5555.

**Shooting Star Broadcasting/
KTAB**
PO Box 5309, Abilene TX
79608-5309. 915/695-2777.

For more information on career opportunities in the communications industries:

Associations

ACADEMY OF TELEVISION ARTS & SCIENCES
5220 Lankershim Boulevard, North Hollywood CA 91601. 818/754-2800. World Wide Web address: http://www.emmys.org.

AMERICAN DISC JOCKEY ASSOCIATION
World Wide Web address: http://www.adja.org. A membership organization for professional disc jockeys that publishes a newsletter of current events and new products.

AMERICAN WOMEN IN RADIO AND TELEVISION, INC.
1650 Tysons Boulevard, Suite 200, McLean VA 22102. 703/506-3290. World Wide Web address: http://www.awrt.org. A national, nonprofit professional organization for the advancement of women and men who work in electronic media and related fields. Services include *News and Views,* a fax newsletter transmitted biweekly to members; *Careerline,* a national listing of job openings available to members only; and the AWRT Foundation, which supports charitable and educational programs and annual awards.

THE COMPETITIVE TELECOMMUNICATIONS ASSOCIATION (COMPTEL)
http://www.comptel.org. A national association providing a wide variety of resources including telecommunications trade shows.

INTERACTIVE SERVICES ASSOCIATION
8403 Colesville Road, Suite 865, Silver Spring MD 20910. 301/495-4955. World Wide Web address: http://www.isa.net.

INTERNATIONAL TELEVISION ASSOCIATION
6311 North O'Connor Road, Suite 230, Irving TX 75309. 972/869-1112. World Wide Web address: http://www.itva.org. Membership required.

NATIONAL ASSOCIATION OF BROADCASTERS
1771 N Street NW, Washington DC 20036. 202/429-5300, ext. 5490. Fax: 202/429-5343. World Wide Web address: http://www.nab.org. Provides employment information.

NATIONAL CABLE TELEVISION ASSOCIATION
1724 Massachusetts Avenue NW, Washington DC 20036-1969. 202/775-3651. Fax: 202/775-3695. World Wide Web address: http://www.ncta.com. A trade association. Publications include *Cable Television Developments, Secure Signals, Kids and Cable, Linking Up, Only on Cable,* and *Producers' Sourcebook: A Guide to Program Buyers.*

PROMAX INTERNATIONAL
2029 Century Park East, Suite 555, Los Angeles CA 90067. 310/788-7600. Fax: 310/788-7616. A nonprofit organization for radio, film, television, video, and other broadcasting professionals. Ask for the jobline.

U.S. TELEPHONE ASSOCIATION
1401 H Street NW, Suite 600, Washington DC 20005-2136. 202/326-7300. World Wide Web address: http://www.usta.org. A trade association for local telephone companies.

Magazines

BROADCASTING AND CABLE
Broadcasting Publications Inc., 1705 DeSales Street NW, Washington DC 20036. 202/659-2340.

ELECTRONIC MEDIA
Crain Communications, 220 East 42nd Street, New York NY 10017. 212/210-0100.

Online Services

BROADCAST PROFESSIONALS FORUM
Go: BPForum. A CompuServe discussion group for professionals in radio and television.

CPB JOBLINE
http://www.cpb.org/jobline/index.html. The Corporation for Public Broadcasting, a nonprofit company, operates this site which provides a list of job openings in the public radio and television industries.

JOURNALISM FORUM
Go: Jforum. A CompuServe discussion group for journalists in print, radio, or television.

ON-LINE DISC JOCKEY ASSOCIATION
http://www.odja.com. Provides members with insurance, Internet advertising, a magazine, and networking resources. This site also posts job opportunities.

COMPUTER HARDWARE, SOFTWARE, AND SERVICES

As the computer industry's expansion continues to gain strength in a diverse and competitive marketplace, a plethora of new products and services will open up even more opportunities for employment into the next century.

The demand for software, particularly for education, entertainment, and communications, increased by about 12 percent in 1997, and International Data Corporation projected that global sales of packaged software would grow 12.8 percent in 1998. This fastest-growing segment of the industry continues to be dominated by Microsoft, whose office software products are chosen by over 85 percent of users worldwide. Furthermore, Internet-related software sales are expected to double each year through 2000, according to the U.S. Department of Labor.

Telephone and cable companies are investing in new technologies, including ASDL (asynchronous digital subscriber line), that promise to link users to the Internet at up to 200 times faster than traditional modems. According to Dataquest Inc., 80 percent of the nation's households will have these fast-access technologies available by the year 2001.

Services that aid business customers in areas such as technology strategy, employee training, and Internet access have grown considerably, including IBM Global Services, a division whose revenues account for 25 percent of IBM's overall sales, according to The New York Times. *Meanwhile, mainframe programmers and consultants are being actively hired to correct the "Year 2000 problem" due to anticipated system errors resulting from the year 2000. Personnel are needed who can read old programming codes, and according to Gartner Research, those with the required skills have a good chance at finding highly-paid jobs in this particular area. In effect, many qualified workers from other segments of the computer industry are leaving their current jobs to work as Year 2000 consultants.*

The U.S. Department of Commerce forecasted that the healthy demand for computer systems and networking equipment would boost product shipments by about 10 percent in 1998, especially as businesses upgrade to more powerful PCs. The continued drop in PC prices should also increase sales significantly.

AMERICAN SOFTWARE INC.
5605 North MacArthur Boulevard, Suite 850, Irving TX 75038. 972/580-8350. **Contact:** Human Resources. **Description:** This location is the regional sales department for the home office in Georgia. Overall, the company develops, markets, and supports integrated supply chain management and financial control systems. American Software Inc. also provides consulting and outsourcing services.

ANALYSTS INTERNATIONAL CORPORATION (AiC)
3030 LBJ Freeway, Suite 820, Dallas TX 75234. 972/243-2001. **Contact:** Human Resources Department. **World Wide Web address:** http://www.analysts.com. **Description:** AiC is an international computer consulting firm. The company assists clients in developing systems in a

variety of industries using different programming languages and software. This involves systems analysis, design, and development. **Corporate headquarters location:** Minneapolis MN.

BANC SOFTWARE SERVICES
981 East North Tent, Abilene TX 79601. 915/672-1363. **Contact:** Human Resources. **Description:** Designs, programs, and manages software packages specifically adapted for banks.

CALYX SOFTWARE
606 Northlake Drive, Dallas TX 75218. 214/320-3668. **Contact:** Human Resources. **World Wide Web address:** http://www.calyxsoftware.com. **Description:** Designs and markets Point for Windows and Point for DOS, designed to help process the paperwork created by the home buying procedure.

CANMAX RETAIL SYSTEMS, INC.
150 West Carpenter Freeway, Irving TX 75039. 972/541-1600. **Fax:** 972/541-1155. **Contact:** Don Thorn, Technical Recruiter. **E-mail address:** postmaster@canmax.com. **World Wide Web address:** http://www.canmax.com. **Description:** Develops software for convenience stores and gas stations. Founded in 1979. **NOTE:** The company offers entry-level positions. **Common positions include:** Applications Engineer; Computer Programmer; Software Engineer; Systems Analyst; Systems Manager; Technical Writer/Editor. **Educational backgrounds include:** Computer Science; Engineering. **Benefits:** 401(k); Dental Insurance; Disability Coverage; Employee Discounts; Life Insurance; Mass Transit Available; Medical Insurance; Profit Sharing; Tuition Assistance. **Corporate headquarters location:** This Location. **International locations:** Canada. **Parent company:** International Retail Systems. **Listed on:** NASDAQ. **Stock exchange symbol:** CNMX. **Annual sales/revenues:** $21 - $50 million. **Number of employees at this location:** 150.

CERNER CORPORATION
8235 Douglas, Suite 1000, Dallas TX 75225. 214/369-4210. **Contact:** Human Resources. **World Wide Web address:** http://www.cerner.com. **Description:** Cerner Corporation designs, installs, and supports software systems for the health care industry worldwide, including hospitals, HMOs, clinics, physicians' offices, and integrated health organizations. All Cerner Corporation applications are structured around a single architectural design, Health Network Architecture (HNA), which allows information to be shared among clinical disciplines and across multiple facilities. Cerner Corporation's information systems are focused in four areas: Clinical Management, Care Management, Repositories, and Knowledge. Clinical Management systems include PathNet, which automates the processes of the clinical laboratory; MedNet, which supports pulmonary medicine, respiratory care, and other internal medicine departments; RadNet, which focuses on automating radiology department operations; PharmNet, which automates the processes of the pharmacy; SurgiNet, which addresses the information management needs of the operating room team; and MSMEDS, which provides information management for the pharmacy. Care Management systems include ProNet, which automates the processes of patient management and registration, order communication, scheduling, and tracking. Repositories include the Open Clinical Foundation, an enterprisewide, relational database that contains information captured by various clinical systems to form the computer-based patient record; Open Management Foundation, a repository of process-related information to support management analysis and decision making; MRNet, which automates the chart management process for the medical records department; and Open Engine, an interface engine that collates interfaces, linking systems at a single point. Cerner Corporation's Knowledge system is Discern, a family of applications that provides support for improving the quality and effectiveness of care. All regional offices provide software implementation, sales, and support. **Corporate headquarters location:** Kansas City MO. **Other U.S. locations:** Irvine CA; Atlanta GA; Burlington MA; Southfield MI; Herndon VA; Bellevue WA. **Listed on:** NASDAQ. **Stock exchange symbol:** CERN. **Annual sales/revenues:** More than $100 million. **Number of employees worldwide:** 1,000.

COMPAQ COMPUTER CORPORATION
8404 Esters Boulevard, Irving TX 75063. 972/929-1700. **Contact:** Human Resources. **World Wide Web address:** http://www.compaq.com. **Description:** Manufactures Fast Ethernet networking hardware. The company was formerly known as Networth. **NOTE:** In January 1998, Compaq Computer Corporation and Digital Equipment Corporation announced plans to merge.

COMPUCOM INC.
7171 Forest Lane, Dallas TX 75230. 214/265-3600. **Contact:** Human Resources. **World Wide Web address:** http://www.compucom.com. **Description:** CompuCom is a leading PC services integration company providing product procurement, advanced configuration, network integration, and support services. CompuCom serves the needs of large businesses through more than 40 sales and service locations nationwide. **Common positions include:** Accountant/Auditor; Buyer; Computer Operator; Computer Programmer; Customer Service Representative; Software Engineer; Systems Analyst. **Educational backgrounds include:** Business Administration; Computer Science. **Corporate headquarters location:** This Location. **Operations at this facility include:** Administration; Divisional Headquarters; Regional Headquarters; Sales; Service. **Number of employees at this location:** 800. **Number of employees nationwide:** 1,600.

COMPUSERVE INC.
222 West Las Colinas Boulevard, Suite 1710, North Tower, Irving TX 75039. 972/869-6300. **Contact:** Human Resources. **Description:** This location of CompuServe is a sales office for the network services division. This division does not represent the CompuServe Information Service. There are approximately 25 other CompuServe branches across the U.S. The Network Services Division of CompuServe provides domestic and international public data network services. Services include fixed-X.25 and fixed-QLLC asynchronous dial access, frame relay, point-of-sale access, IBM enhanced protocol services, and hybrid public/private network solutions. **NOTE:** Send resumes to Human Resources, 5000 Arlington Center Boulevard, Columbus OH 43220. **Common positions include:** Account Manager; Manufacturer's/Wholesaler's Sales Rep. **Educational backgrounds include:** Business Administration; Communications; Computer Science; Marketing; MBA. **Benefits:** 401(k); Dental Insurance; Disability Coverage; Life Insurance; Medical Insurance; Profit Sharing; Tuition Assistance. **Corporate headquarters location:** Columbus OH. **Parent company:** H&R Block. **Listed on:** New York Stock Exchange.

COMPUTER ASSOCIATES INTERNATIONAL, INC.
909 Las Colinas Boulevard East, Irving TX 75039. 972/556-7100. **Contact:** Lavena Sipes, Human Resources Manager. **World Wide Web address:** http://www.cai.com. **Description:** This location develops and sells software, and offers support services. Overall, Computer Associates International develops, markets, and supports more than 500 integrated products including enterprise, systems and database management, business applications, application development, and consumer solutions. Computer Associates International, Inc. serves many of the world's businesses, governments, research organizations, and educational organizations. Founded in 1976. **NOTE:** Computer Associates International, Inc. looks for entry-level applicants or co-op students and grooms them internally to become productive members of the Computer Associates team. The majority of promotions are given internally, and the farm system approach has provided a career path for many employees. Employees are trained in all areas of the organization to make them part of the companywide team. The company recruits at universities nationwide. **Common positions include:** Administrative Manager; Clerical Supervisor; Computer Programmer; Customer Service Representative; Data Processor; Financial Services Sales Representative; Human Resources Manager; Manufacturer's/Wholesaler's Sales Rep.; Marketing Specialist; Quality Control Supervisor; Sales Representative; Services Sales Representative; Software Engineer; Support Personnel; Systems Analyst; Technical Writer/Editor. **Educational backgrounds include:** Accounting; Business Administration; Computer Science; Finance; Human Resources; Marketing. **Benefits:** 401(k); Dental Insurance; Disability Coverage; Employee Discounts; Life Insurance; Medical Insurance; Savings Plan; Smoke-free; Tuition Assistance. **Special programs:** Co-ops; Internships. **Corporate headquarters location:** Islandia NY. **Other U.S. locations:** Nationwide. **Operations at this facility include:** Administration; Divisional Headquarters; Research and Development; Sales; Service. **Listed on:** New York Stock Exchange. **Annual sales/revenues:** More than $100 million. **Number of employees at this location:** 350. **Number of employees worldwide:** 11,000.

COMPUTER IDENTICS ID MATRIX
6311 North O'Connor Road, Suite N50, Irving TX 75039. 972/869-7684. **Contact:** Human Resources. **Description:** This location is a sales office. Overall, Computer Identics ID Matrix is dedicated to providing data collection integrators with complete solutions, including scanning components, networking, software tools, and support services. Customers are primarily involved in

materials handling and factory automation environments, and include systems integrators, original equipment manufacturers, value-added resellers, and end users performing in-house systems integration. Products and related services fall into four major categories: omnidirectional scanning systems, intelligent fixed position line scanners, data collection terminals, and networking products. Computer Identics' foreign subsidiaries are located in Canada, Belgium, England, France, and Germany. **NOTE:** Send resumes to Human Resources, 5 Shawmut Road, Canton MA 02021. **Benefits:** 401(k). **Corporate headquarters location:** Canton MA. **Other U.S. locations:** Mission Viejo CA; San Jose CA; West Hartford CT; Roswell GA; Schaumburg IL; Southfield MI; Cincinnati OH. **Listed on:** NASDAQ.

COMPUTER SCIENCE, INC.
5525 LBJ Freeway, Dallas TX 75240. 972/386-0020. **Contact:** Human Resources. **Description:** Supplies integrated software products and support services to financial institutions worldwide.

CYBERTEK CORPORATION
7800 North Simmons Freeway, Suite 600, Dallas TX 75247. 214/637-1540. **Contact:** Human Resources. **World Wide Web address:** http://www.pmsc.com. **Description:** Develops and distributes software for life insurance companies. **Parent company:** Policy Management Systems Corporation.

CYRIX CORPORATION
2703 North Central Expressway, Richardson TX 75080. 972/968-8388. **Fax:** 972/699-9857. **Contact:** Human Resources. **World Wide Web address:** http://www.cyrix.com. **Description:** Cyrix Corporation supplies high-performance microprocessors to the personal computer industry. The company designs, manufactures, and markets x86 software-compatible processors for the desktop and portable computer markets. Product line includes the Cyrix 5x86, a high-performance, low-power processor aimed at the mobile computer market; the Cyrix 6x86, a sixth-generation architecture, high-performance processor designed to be competitive with Intel's Pentium; and the P200, P166, and P155 desktop PCs. **Corporate headquarters location:** This Location. **Listed on:** NASDAQ. **Stock exchange symbol:** CYRX. **Annual sales/revenues:** More than $100 million. **Number of employees nationwide:** 320.

DMR CONSULTING GROUP, INC.
13355 Noel Road, Suite 815, Dallas TX 75240. 972/503-3700. **Toll-free phone:** 800/259-0012. **Fax:** 972/371-0400. **Contact:** Randal Allison, Human Resources. **World Wide Web address:** http://www.dmr.com. **Description:** Provides computer consulting services including outsourcing solutions and systems integration. **Common positions include:** Account Manager; Account Representative; Applications Engineer; Computer Operator; Computer Programmer; Database Manager; IT Specialist; MIS Specialist; Operations Manager; Project Manager; Software Engineer; Systems Analyst; Systems Manager; Technical Writer/Editor; Telecommunications Manager. **Benefits:** 401(k); Dental Insurance; Disability Coverage; Financial Planning Assistance; Life Insurance; Pension Plan; Profit Sharing; Savings Plan; Tuition Assistance.

DALLAS DIGITAL CORPORATION
624 Krona, Suite 160, Plano TX 75074. 972/424-2800. **Contact:** Human Resources. **World Wide Web address:** http://www.daldig.com. **Description:** Provides businesses with networking computer systems hardware and software.

DATABASE CONSULTANTS INC.
4835 LBJ Freeway, Suite 900, Dallas TX 75244. 972/392-0955. **Contact:** Human Resources. **World Wide Web address:** http://www.dci-ltd.com. **Description:** Offers consulting services for businesses with Oracle databases.

DATAMATIC INC.
715 North Glenville Drive, Suite 450, Richardson TX 75081. 972/234-5000. **Contact:** Human Resources Department. **World Wide Web address:** http://www.datamatic.com. **Description:** Datamatic Inc. offers software integration solutions. Datamatic has an engineering team and an active sales force.

DECISIVE QUEST, INC.
735 North Plano Road, Richardson TX 75081. 972/480-9070. **Fax:** 972/480-0348. **Contact:** Human Resources. **World Wide Web address:** http://www.questmatch.com. **Description:** Provides online employment services through customer use of its company-developed software (QuestMatch). Founded in 1993.

DIGITAL EQUIPMENT CORPORATION
5310 Harvest Hill Road, Suite 200, Dallas TX 75230. 972/702-4000. **Contact:** Human Resources Department. **World Wide Web address:** http://www.digital.com. **Description:** This location is a sales and service office. Overall, Digital Equipment Corporation designs, manufactures, sells, and services computers, associated peripheral equipment, and related software and supplies. Applications and programs include scientific research, computation, communications, education, data analysis, industrial control, time sharing, commercial data processing, graphic arts, word processing, health care, instrumentation, engineering, and simulation. **NOTE:** Send resumes to the Resume Processing Center, 111 Powdermill Road, MSO/1-1C2, Maynard MA 01754. In January 1998, Digital Equipment Corporation and Compaq Computer Corporation announced plans to merge.

DURACOM COMPUTER SYSTEMS
2115 East Beltline Road, Carrollton TX 75006. 972/416-7600. **Contact:** Human Resources. **World Wide Web address:** http://www.duracom.com. **Description:** Manufactures and sells computers. Founded in 1989.

EDS (ELECTRONIC DATA SYSTEMS CORPORATION)
5400 Legacy Drive, Mail Slot H4-GB-35, Plano TX 75024. 972/605-2700. **Fax:** 800/562-6241. **Contact:** Human Resources. **E-mail address:** staffing@eds.com. **World Wide Web address:** http://www.eds.com. **Description:** Engaged in information management services including banking, insurance, retail, manufacturing, automotive, defense, telecommunications, transportation, distribution, utility, and government services. Electronic Data Systems Corporation offers consulting, systems design, systems integration, and systems management. Founded in 1962. **NOTE:** The company offers entry-level positions. **Common positions include:** Applications Engineer; Computer Programmer; Database Manager; Financial Analyst; Software Engineer; Systems Analyst; Systems Manager. **Educational backgrounds include:** Accounting; Business Administration; Communications; Computer Science; Engineering; Finance; Marketing. **Benefits:** Dental Insurance; Employee Discounts; Life Insurance; Medical Insurance. **Special programs:** Internships; Training. **Corporate headquarters location:** This Location. **Parent company:** General Motors Corporation. **Listed on:** New York Stock Exchange. **Annual sales/revenues:** More than $100 million. **Number of employees worldwide:** 95,000.

ENTERPRISING SERVICE SOLUTIONS
1100 Venture Court, Carrollton TX 75006. 972/386-2000. **Contact:** Human Resources Department. **World Wide Web address:** http://www.essc.com. **Description:** Enterprising Service Solutions provides networking and installation services, help desk support, and integration design.

EXECUTRAIN OF TEXAS
12201 Merit Drive, Suite 350, Dallas TX 75251. 972/387-1212. **Contact:** Human Resources. **World Wide Web address:** http://www.executrain.com/dallas. **Description:** Trains employees from client companies on software.

GE CAPITAL IT SOLUTIONS
12377 Merritt Drive, Suite 310, Dallas TX 75251. 972/387-6600. **Contact:** Human Resources. **World Wide Web address:** http://www.gecits.ge.com. **Description:** GE Capital IT Solutions, formerly AmeriData Technologies, Inc., is a nationwide reseller of computer products and services to commercial, governmental, and educational users. The company's products and services include value-added systems, systems integration, networking services, support, maintenance, facilities management, outsourcing, software and business consulting services, and rental services. GE Capital IT Solutions markets its computer products and business services through its offices in approximately 70 cities throughout the country. **Parent company:** GE Capital.

HEWLETT-PACKARD
3000 Waterview Parkway, Richardson TX 75080. 972/497-4000. **Contact:** Human Resources. **Description:** This location builds supercomputers. As a whole, Hewlett-Packard is engaged in the design and manufacture of measurement and computation products and systems used in business, industry, engineering, science, health care, and education. Principal products are integrated instrument and computer systems (including hardware and software), peripheral products, and medical electronic equipment and systems. **NOTE:** Jobseekers should send resumes to Employment Response Center, Event #2498, Hewlett-Packard Company, Mail Stop 20-APP, 3000 Hanover Street, Palo Alto CA 94304-1181. **Common positions include:** Accountant/Auditor; Electrical/Electronics Engineer; Financial Analyst; Software Engineer; Technical Writer/Editor. **Educational backgrounds include:** Computer Science; Engineering. **Benefits:** 401(k); Dental Insurance; Disability Coverage; Life Insurance; Medical Insurance; Tuition Assistance. **Special programs:** Internships. **Operations at this facility include:** Administration; Manufacturing; Research and Development; Sales; Service. **Listed on:** New York Stock Exchange. **Number of employees at this location:** 700. **Number of employees worldwide:** 93,000.

I-CONCEPTS
2607 Walnut Hill Lane, Suite 200, Dallas TX 75229. 214/956-7770. **Contact:** Human Resources. **Description:** A developer of software for the insurance industry.

IBM CORPORATION
1605 LBJ Freeway, Dallas TX 75234. 972/280-4000. **Toll-free phone:** 800/426-4968. **Recorded jobline:** 800/964-4473. **Contact:** IBM Staffing Services. **World Wide Web address:** http://www.ibm.com. **Description:** This location is a regional sales and marketing office. Overall, International Business Machines (IBM) is a developer, manufacturer, and marketer of advanced information processing products, including computers and microelectronic technology, software, networking systems and information technology-related services. IBM operates worldwide through its United States, Canada, Europe/Middle East/Africa, Latin America, and Asia Pacific business units providing comprehensive and complete product choices. **NOTE:** Jobseekers should send a resume to IBM Staffing Services, Department 1DP, Building 051, P.O. Box 12195, Research Triangle Park NC 27709-2195. **Corporate headquarters location:** Armonk NY. **Number of employees at this location:** 3,000. **Number of employees nationwide:** 220,000.

ICS COMPUTER SYSTEMS CORPORATION
2301 North Central Expressway, Suite 158, Plano TX 75075. 972/509-8000. **Contact:** Human Resources. **Description:** A computer reseller.

INTERPHASE CORPORATION
13800 Senlac, Dallas TX 75234. 214/654-5000. **Toll-free phone:** 800/777-3722. **Fax:** 214/654-5500. **Contact:** Jeff Simmons, Human Resources Manager. **E-mail address:** resumes@iphase.com. **World Wide Web address:** http://www.iphase.com. **Description:** Interphase Corporation is a developer, manufacturer, and marketer of networking and mass storage controllers, as well as stand alone networking devices for computer systems. Many of the networking products are sold to original equipment manufacturers and to value-added resellers, systems integrators, and large end users. **Common positions include:** Design Engineer; Electrical/Electronics Engineer; Software Engineer. **Educational backgrounds include:** Computer Science; Engineering. **Benefits:** 401(k); Dental Insurance; Disability Coverage; Life Insurance; Medical Insurance; Pension Plan; Tuition Assistance; Vision Insurance. **Corporate headquarters location:** This Location. **Operations at this facility include:** Administration; Manufacturing; Research and Development; Sales. **Listed on:** NASDAQ. **Annual sales/revenues:** Less than $5 million. **Number of employees at this location:** 200.

INTERVOICE, INC.
17811 Waterview Parkway, Dallas TX 75252. 972/454-8000. **Fax:** 972/907-1079. **Contact:** Human Resources. **World Wide Web address:** http://www.intervoice.com. **Description:** InterVoice, Inc. develops, sells, and services interactive voice response systems that allow individuals to access a computer database using a telephone keypad, computer keyboard, or human voice. Applications are currently functioning in industries including insurance, banking, higher

education, government, utilities, health care, retail distribution, transportation, and operator services. **Corporate headquarters location:** This Location.

ITAC SYSTEMS, INC.
3113 Benton Street, Garland TX 75042. 972/494-3073. **Fax:** 972/494-4159. **Contact:** Human Resources. **World Wide Web address:** http://www.mousetrak.com. **Description:** Manufactures the mouse-trak trackball, a computer peripheral product. Founded in 1993. **NOTE:** Entry-level positions are offered. **Common positions include:** Account Manager; Accountant/Auditor; Administrative Assistant; Controller; Credit Manager; Customer Service Representative; Database Manager; Design Engineer; Electrical/Electronics Engineer; Finance Director; Human Resources Manager; Internet Services Manager; Manufacturing Engineer; Marketing Specialist; Mechanical Engineer; Operations/Production Manager; Production Manager; Purchasing Agent/Manager; Sales Executive; Sales Manager; Systems Manager; Vice President of Operations; Webmaster. **Educational backgrounds include:** Accounting; Computer Science; Engineering; Marketing. **Benefits:** 401(k); Dental Insurance; Disability Coverage; Life Insurance; Medical Insurance; Tuition Assistance. **Corporate headquarters location:** This Location. **Operations at this facility include:** Administration; Manufacturing; Research and Development; Sales; Service. **Listed on:** Privately held. **Annual sales/revenues:** Less than $5 million. **Number of employees at this location:** 25.

JRA INFORMATION SERVICES, INC.
4100 McEwen, Suite 230, Dallas TX 75244. 972/702-8900. **Contact:** Human Resources. **World Wide Web address:** http://www.jrainfo.com. **Description:** Provides computer consulting and technical consulting services.

LINX DATA TERMINALS, INC.
625 Digital Drive, Suite 100, Plano TX 75075. 972/964-7090. **Contact:** Human Resources. **World Wide Web address:** http://www.linxdata.com. **Description:** A manufacturer of data collection terminals.

LUCKY COMPUTER COMPANY
1701 North Greenville Avenue, Suite 602, Richardson TX 75081. 972/705-2600. **Contact:** Human Resources. **Description:** A computer assembly company.

MENTOR GRAPHICS CORPORATION
5430 LBJ Freeway, Suite 1010, Dallas TX 75240. 972/450-2300. **Fax:** 972/991-7658. **Contact:** Human Resources. **World Wide Web address:** http://www.mentorg.com. **Description:** This location is a sales office. Overall, Mentor Graphics Corporation has researched advances in electronic design automation (EDA), the use of technically advanced computer software to automate the design, analysis, and documentation of electronic components and systems. The company is one of the world's leading suppliers of EDA software and professional services. Mentor Graphics products enable customers to become more competitive by increasing their productivity and product quality, while reducing their development costs and time to market. Founded in 1981. **Corporate headquarters location:** Wilsonville OR.

MERLIN SOFTWARE SERVICES
1420 Presidential Drive, Richardson TX 75081. 972/235-9551. **Contact:** Human Resources. **World Wide Web address:** http://www.merlinss.com. **Description:** A CD-ROM duplication firm.

MICRO COMPUTER SYSTEMS, INC.
2300 Valley View Lane, Suite 800, Irving TX 75062. 972/659-1514. **Fax:** 972/659-1624. **Contact:** Human Resources. **World Wide Web address:** http://www.mcsdallas.com. **Description:** A developer of software. Products include Local Area Network (LAN) communication systems and configuration utilities for EISA computers. Micro Computer Systems specializes in effecting network systems interoperability from LANs to the Internet to the World Wide Web.

MICROGRAFX, INC.
1303 East Arapahoe Road, Richardson TX 75081. 972/234-1769. **Fax:** 972/994-6036. **Contact:** Human Resources. **World Wide Web address:** http://www.micrografx.com. **Description:**

Micrografx, Inc. develops, markets, and supports a line of graphic application software products for IBM PCs and compatibles running under the Microsoft Windows operating environment. Its software is designed for both business and professional use and includes professional illustration, basic drawing and charting products, data-driven graphics, image editing, and reusable clip-art libraries. Micrografx, Inc. also offers systems software products designed to enhance the Windows and OS/2 operating environments. **Common positions include:** Account Representative; Applications Engineer; Computer Programmer; Sales Representative; Software Engineer; Systems Analyst. **Educational backgrounds include:** Business Administration; Computer Science; Engineering; Finance; Marketing. **Benefits:** 401(k); Dental Insurance; Disability Coverage; Employee Discounts; Life Insurance; Medical Insurance; Tuition Assistance. **Corporate headquarters location:** This Location. **International locations:** Australia; Italy; Japan; United Kingdom. **Listed on:** NASDAQ. **Annual sales/revenues:** $5 - $10 million. **Number of employees at this location:** 200. **Number of employees worldwide:** 300.

NCR CORPORATION
450 East John Carpenter Freeway, Irving TX 75062. 972/650-2710. **Contact:** Joy Maffeo, Human Resources Consultant. **E-mail address:** joy.maffeo@dallastx.ncr.com. **World Wide Web address:** http://www.ncr.com. **Description:** This is a sales and service location. Overall, NCR Corporation is a worldwide provider of computer products and services. The company provides computer solutions to three targeted industries: retail, financial, and communication. NCR Computer Systems Group develops, manufactures, and markets computer systems. NCR Financial Systems Group is an industry leader in three target areas: financial delivery systems, relationship banking data warehousing solutions, and payments systems/item processing. NCR Retail Systems Group is a world leader in end-to-end retail solutions serving the food, general merchandise, and hospitality industries. NCR Worldwide Services provides data warehousing services solutions; end-to-end networking services; and designs, implements, and supports complex open systems environments. NCR Systemedia Group develops, produces, and markets a complete line of information products to satisfy customers' information technology needs including transaction processing media, auto identification media, business form communication products, managing documents and media, and a full line of integrated equipment solutions. **Educational backgrounds include:** Business Administration; Computer Science. **Benefits:** 401(k); Dental Insurance; Disability Coverage; Life Insurance; Medical Insurance; Pension Plan; Savings Plan; Tuition Assistance. **Corporate headquarters location:** Dayton OH. **Other U.S. locations:** Nationwide. **Operations at this facility include:** Administration; Sales; Service. **Listed on:** New York Stock Exchange. **Annual sales/revenues:** More than $100 million. **Number of employees nationwide:** 19,000. **Number of employees worldwide:** 38,000.

NETWORK ASSOCIATES, INC.
4099 McEwen Road, Suite 500, Dallas TX 75244. 214/361-8086. **Contact:** Human Resources. **Description:** An international supplier of enterprisewide network security and management software. Products include VirusScan, an anti-virus software. The company has strategic relationships with numerous computer firms including Compaq, Hewlett-Packard, Novell, Microsoft, and AST. Network Associates was formerly McAfee. **Common positions include:** Software Engineer. **Other U.S. locations:** Tinton Falls NJ. **Annual sales/revenues:** $51 - $100 million. **Number of employees nationwide:** 350.

OPEN-CONNECT SYSTEMS INC.
2711 LBJ Freeway, Suite 800, Dallas TX 75234. 972/484-5200. **Contact:** Human Resources. **World Wide Web address:** http://www.oc.com. **Description:** A developer of Java software.

POLICY MANAGEMENT SYSTEMS CORPORATION (PMSC)
12001 North Central Expressway, Suite 500, Dallas TX 75243. 972/778-7000. **Contact:** Barbara McGalloway, Personnel. **World Wide Web address:** http://www.pmsc.com. **Description:** This location is a sales office. Overall, Policy Management Systems Corporation develops and licenses standardized insurance software systems and provides automation and administrative support and information services to the worldwide insurance industry. The company also provides professional support services, which include implementation and integration assistance; consulting and education services; and information and outsourcing services. **Common positions include:** Computer Programmer; Insurance Agent/Broker; Systems Analyst. **Educational backgrounds**

include: Computer Science. **Benefits:** 401(k); Dental Insurance; Disability Coverage; Employee Discounts; Life Insurance; Medical Insurance; Tuition Assistance. **Special programs:** Internships. **Corporate headquarters location:** Columbia SC. **Operations at this facility include:** Service. **Listed on:** New York Stock Exchange. **Number of employees nationwide:** 4,300.

RACAL-DATACOM

1100 Jupiter Road, Suite 190, Plano TX 75074. 972/509-4700. **Contact:** Personnel. **Description:** This location is a sales and technical service office. Racal-Datacom Inc. manufactures data communications equipment including WANs, LANs, and access products. The company also offers related services including project management, installation, consultation, network integration, maintenance, disaster recovery, and training. **NOTE:** Professional hiring is done primarily through the Florida office (1601 North Harrison Parkway, Sunrise FL 33323-2899). **Corporate headquarters location:** Sunrise FL.

RAYTHEON SYSTEMS, INC.

P.O. Box 660023, Dallas TX 75266. 972/272-0515. **Contact:** Human Resources. **E-mail address:** employment@esi.org. **World Wide Web address:** http://www.raytheon.com. **Description:** This location develops high-technology software. Overall, Raytheon Systems designs, manufactures, and installs state-of-the-art communications and integrated command-and-control systems for military and industrial customers worldwide. The company is a complete systems engineering company offering technological innovation in the commercial and defense electronics industry.

SEI

8585 North Stemmons Freeway, Suite 1100, Dallas TX 75247. 214/689-3200. **Contact:** Human Resources. **Description:** This location provides investment accounting software to over 400 banking institutions. Overall, SEI operates primarily in two business markets: trust and banking; and fund sponsor/investment advisory. The company invests for clients worldwide in both public and private markets, and also provides investment and business solutions to those in the investment business who in turn serve their own investor clients. SEI provides direct investment solutions for $50 billion of investable capital and delivers systems and business solutions to organizations investing nearly $1 trillion. SEI is one of the largest providers of trust systems in the world, claiming over 40 percent of the U.S. trust market. **NOTE:** Send resumes to Jim Ward, Recruiter, One Freedom Valley Drive, Oaks PA 19456. **Corporate headquarters location:** Wayne PA.

SEAGATE TECHNOLOGY

5000 Quorum Drive, Suite 485, Dallas TX 75240. 972/448-8050. **Contact:** Human Resources. **World Wide Web address:** http://www.seaweb.seagate.com. **Description:** This location is a sales and engineering office. Overall, Seagate Technology is a designer and manufacturer of data storage devices and related products including hard disk drives, tape drives, software, and systems for many different computer-related applications and operating systems. The company sells its products primarily through a sales force to OEMs (original equipment manufacturers) and through non-affiliated distributors. **NOTE:** Job seekers interested in applying should forward their resume to: Seagate Technology, P.O. Box 66360, Scotts Valley CA 95066. Attention: Brenda Rogers, Human Resources Manager. **Corporate headquarters location:** Scotts Valley CA. **Subsidiaries include:** Arcada Holdings, Inc., an information protection and storage management software company serving several operating systems; and Conners Storage Systems.

SEQUENT COMPUTER SYSTEMS, INC.

15303 Dallas Parkway, Suite 1350, Dallas TX 75248. 972/661-1900. **Contact:** Human Resources. **World Wide Web address:** http://www.sequent.com. **Description:** This location is a sales office. Overall, Sequent Computer Systems is a leading provider of enterprise architecture and open solutions for large corporations. The company's Enterprise Division provides architectural consulting, professional services, and industry-leading servers that enable customers to migrate successfully from host-based, proprietary computer environments to open, client/server architectures. Working closely with leading hardware and software partners, the Enterprise Division helps customers design and implement enterprisewide architectures and systems for online transaction processing, decision support, and workgroup computing. Sequent's Platform Division develops high-performance, Intel-based, symmetric multiprocessing servers that run on the UNIX and Microsoft Windows NT operating systems and support enterprisewide applications and information services. The Platform Division's products are sold by the Enterprise Division and through a variety of indirect channels, including OEM resellers, value-added resellers, and distributors. Founded in 1983.

7TH LEVEL, INC.
1110 East Collins Boulevard, Suite 122, Richardson TX 75081. 972/498-8100. **Fax:** 972/498-0111. **Contact:** Human Resources. **World Wide Web address:** http://www.7thlevel.com. **Description:** A developer and manufacturer of computer game software. **Corporate headquarters location:** This Location. **Listed on:** NASDAQ. **Stock exchange symbol:** SEVL.

SOFTWARE AG-REGIONAL OFFICES
5005 LBJ Freeway, Suite 700, Dallas TX 75244. 972/991-8900. **Contact:** Human Resources. **World Wide Web address:** http://www.sagafyi.com. **Description:** Distributes business applications for a German parent company. Software AG's Regional Offices supply businesses in the United States with customized applications for mainframe computers as well as offering technical support.

SOFTWARE SPECTRUM INC.
2140 Merritt Drive, Garland TX 75041. 972/840-6600. **Fax:** 972/864-5120. **Contact:** Human Resources. **World Wide Web address:** http://www.softwarespectrum.com. **Description:** A reseller of microcomputer software and services to businesses and government agencies. Software Spectrum also offers technical support and volume software license services. **Common positions include:** Accountant/Auditor; Advertising Clerk; Blue-Collar Worker Supervisor; Buyer; Collector; Computer Programmer; Credit Manager; Customer Service Representative; Electrical/Electronics Engineer; Human Resources Manager; Operations/Production Manager; Public Relations Specialist; Purchasing Agent/Manager; Quality Control Supervisor; Services Sales Representative; Systems Analyst; Technical Writer/Editor. **Educational backgrounds include:** Accounting; Art/Design; Business Administration; Communications; Computer Science; Economics; Engineering; Finance; Liberal Arts; Marketing. **Benefits:** 401(k); Dental Insurance; Disability Coverage; Employee Discounts; Life Insurance; Medical Insurance; Profit Sharing. **Corporate headquarters location:** This Location. **Other U.S. locations:** Nationwide. **International locations:** Worldwide. **Subsidiaries include:** Spectrum Integrated Services. **Operations at this facility include:** Administration; Sales; Service. **Listed on:** NASDAQ. **Number of employees at this location:** 500. **Number of employees nationwide:** 575.

SOURCE MEDIA, INC.
One Lincoln Center, 5400 LBJ Freeway, Suite 690, Dallas TX 75240. 972/701-5400. **Contact:** Judy Nunnenkamp, Human Resources Manager. **World Wide Web address:** http://www.srcm.com. **Description:** Operates the Interactive Channel, an online television browser and programming service. The Interactive Channel is broadcast over cable television networks, and provides on-demand information covering education, news, sports, entertainment, and shopping. **Corporate headquarters location:** This Location. **Listed on:** NASDAQ. **Stock exchange symbol:** SRCM.

STERLING SOFTWARE, INC.
300 Crescent Court, Suite 1200, Dallas TX 75201-7832. 214/981-1000. **Fax:** 214/981-1255. **Contact:** Personnel Department. **World Wide Web address:** http://www.sterling.com. **Description:** A worldwide developer and supplier of software products and services. The company's business segments include systems management, which provides software products for large computer companies; applications management, which provides customers with software products for developing new client/server applications; and federal systems, which provides technical services to the federal government including the U.S. Department of Defense and NASA. The company's products are sold through offices in 17 countries and distributed worldwide. **Common positions include:** Accountant/Auditor; Blue-Collar Worker Supervisor; Buyer; Chemical Engineer; Chemist; Designer; Draftsperson; Electrical/Electronics Engineer; Human Resources Manager; Mechanical Engineer; Public Relations Specialist; Purchasing Agent/Manager; Quality Control Supervisor; Registered Nurse. **Educational backgrounds include:** Accounting; Business Administration; Chemistry; Computer Science; Engineering; Finance; Marketing; Physics. **Benefits:** 401(k); Dental Insurance; Disability Coverage; Life

Insurance; Medical Insurance; Pension Plan; Profit Sharing; Tuition Assistance. **Corporate headquarters location:** This Location. **Operations at this facility include:** Administration; Manufacturing; Regional Headquarters; Sales. **Listed on:** New York Stock Exchange. **Stock exchange symbol:** SSW. **Number of employees nationwide:** 1,350.

STERLING SOFTWARE, INC.
15301 Dallas Parkway, Suite 400, Dallas TX 75248. 972/788-2580. **Contact:** Human Resources. **World Wide Web address:** http://www.sterling.com. **Description:** This location houses the Banking Systems Group. Overall, Sterling Software is a worldwide developer and supplier of software products and services. The company's business segments include systems management, which provides software products for large computer companies; applications management, which provides customers with software products for developing new client/server applications; and federal systems, which provides technical services to the federal government including the U.S. Department of Defense and NASA. The company's products are sold through offices in 17 countries and distributed worldwide. **Corporate headquarters location:** Dallas TX. **Listed on:** New York Stock Exchange. **Stock exchange symbol:** SSW. **Number of employees nationwide:** 1,350.

S2 SYSTEMS, INC.
15301 Dallas Parkway, Suite 600, Dallas TX 75248. 972/233-8356. **Contact:** Human Resources. **World Wide Web address:** http://www.s2systems.com. **Description:** S2 Systems, Inc. is a provider of software and professional services to the financial services, retail, and health care industries. **Corporate headquarters location:** Marlborough MA. **Parent company:** Stratus Computer, Inc. offers a broad range of computer platforms, application solutions, middleware, and professional services for critical online operations. Other Stratus subsidiaries include SoftCom Systems, Inc., a provider of data communications middleware and related professional services that bridge the gap between open distributed systems and legacy mainframe and mid-range systems used for online applications; and Isis Distributed Systems, Inc., a developer of advanced messaging middleware products that enable businesses to develop reliable, high-performance distributed computing applications involving networked desktop computers and shared systems.

TANDY WIRE AND CABLE COMPANY
3500 McCart Avenue, Fort Worth TX 76110. 817/921-2023. **Contact:** Marianne Wiestner, Human Resource Manager. **Description:** Engaged in the manufacture of wire and cable, including computer cable. **Common positions include:** Blue-Collar Worker Supervisor; Customer Service Representative; Draftsperson; Electrical/Electronics Engineer; Systems Analyst. **Educational backgrounds include:** Business Administration; Engineering. **Benefits:** Dental Insurance; Employee Discounts; Life Insurance; Medical Insurance; Profit Sharing; Savings Plan; Tuition Assistance. **Parent company:** Tandy Corporation. **Operations at this facility include:** Manufacturing. **Listed on:** New York Stock Exchange.

TECHNICAL DIRECTIONS
3030 LBJ Freeway, Suite 910, Lock Box 2, Dallas TX 75234. 972/243-1020. **Contact:** Human Resources Administrator. **Description:** A software consulting firm.

UNITED STATES DATA CORPORATION (USDATA)
2435 North Central Expressway, Richardson TX 75080-2722. 972/680-9700. **Fax:** 972/680-9324. **Contact:** Personnel Administrator. **World Wide Web address:** http://www.usdata.com. **Description:** Develops, markets, and supports application-enabler products that customers configure to implement a wide range of real-time monitoring, analysis, information management, and control solutions in worldwide industrial automation markets. USData also develops, markets, and supports integrated hardware, software, and systems solutions for automated identification and data collection applications that are sold to a broad base of customers throughout North America. The company acts as a full-service distributor and value-added remarketer for manufacturers of bar code equipment. **Common positions include:** Computer Programmer; Designer; Electrical/Electronics Engineer; Industrial Engineer; Manufacturer's/Wholesaler's Sales Rep.; Mathematician; Mechanical Engineer; Petroleum Engineer; Software Engineer; Systems Analyst; Technical Writer/Editor. **Educational backgrounds include:** Business Administration; Computer Science; Engineering; Marketing. **Benefits:** 401(k); Dental Insurance; Life Insurance; Medical

Insurance; Tuition Assistance. **Special programs:** Internships. **Corporate headquarters location:** This Location. **Other U.S. locations:** Atlanta GA; Chicago IL; Boston MA; Seattle WA. **Operations at this facility include:** Administration; Divisional Headquarters; Research and Development; Sales; Service. **Listed on:** Privately held. **Number of employees at this location:** 200. **Number of employees nationwide:** 300.

VIASOFT INC.
1231 Greenway Drive, Suite 380, Irving TX 75038. 972/550-1808. **Contact:** Human Resources. **World Wide Web address:** http://www.viasoft.com. **Description:** This location is a sales office. Overall, Viasoft develops a wide range of management application software.

Note: Because addresses and telephone numbers of smaller companies can change rapidly, we recommend you call each company to verify the information below before inquiring about job opportunities. Mass mailings are not recommended.

Additional small employers:

COMPUTER EQUIPMENT AND SOFTWARE WHOLESALE

Amdahl Corporation
13355 Noel Rd, Ste 900, Dallas TX 75240-6643. 972/239-8611.

AMR Distribution Systems
PO Box 155099, Fort Worth TX 76155-0099. 817/963-0989.

ASI Dallas
1355 N Glenville Dr, Richardson TX 75081-2414. 972/238-8899.

CompuCom Systems Inc.
10210 N Central Expressway, Dallas TX 75231-3425. 214/265-5500.

Globelle Inc.
1914 Hampshire St, Grand Prairie TX 75050-6312. 972/642-5695.

HBS Systems
PO Box 832030, Richardson TX 75083-2030. 972/234-4444.

Hughes Data Systems
13755 Diplomat Dr, Dallas TX 75234-8917. 972/488-1874.

JM Computers Inc.
1111 Digital Dr, Richardson TX 75081-1948. 972/231-2713.

Vektron International Inc.
PO Box 840874, Dallas TX 75284-0874. 972/606-0280.

COMPUTER FACILITIES MANAGEMENT SERVICES

CSSI
125 E. John Carpenter Freeway,

Irving TX 75062-2238. 972/869-3966.

Perot Systems Corporation
12377 Merit Dr, Ste 1100, Dallas TX 75251-3233. 972/383-5600.

COMPUTER MAINTENANCE AND REPAIR

Cyclix Engineering Corp.
2800 Story Rd W, Ste 200, Irving TX 75038-5248. 972/257-8855.

Dalworth Holdings Inc.
2895 113th St, Grand Prairie TX 75050-6481. 972/988-4888.

GE Computer Service
2200 Highway 121 N, Grapevine TX 76051-9504. 972/471-3325.

ICBS
2454 Merritt Dr, Garland TX 75041-6145. 972/271-7171.

COMPUTER MANUFACTURERS

IBM
1102 N Carrier Pkwy, Grand Prairie TX 75050-3364. 972/606-6200.

Mizar Inc.
2410 Luna Rd, Carrollton TX 75006-6529. 972/277-4600.

COMPUTER PERIPHERAL EQUIPMENT MANUFACTURERS

Cisco Systems Inc.
251 O'Connor Ridge Blvd, Irving TX 75038-6532. 972/887-2800.

Computer Cable Connection
3333 Earhart Dr, Ste 380, Carrollton TX 75006-5083. 972/490-5542.

Genicom Corporation
1100 Venture Ct, Carrollton TX 75006-5412. 972/386-2164.

COMPUTER PROCESSING AND DATA PREPARATION SERVICES

Advance Paradigm Inc.
14755 Preston Rd, Ste 200, Dallas TX 75240-7861. 972/851-0618.

Alliance Data Systems
17201 Waterview Parkway, Dallas TX 75252-8004. 972/643-4078.

Alltel Information Services
2300 Valley View Lane, Irving TX 75062-1721. 972/257-2001.

Amigos Bibliographic Council
12200 Park Central Dr, Dallas TX 75251-2100. 972/851-8000.

Bankline Texas Inc.
8400 John Carpenter Freeway, Dallas TX 75247. 214/879-9500.

BRC Holdings Inc.
1111 W Mockingbird Ln, Dallas TX 75247-5028. 214/905-2300.

Computer Data Systems Inc.
1638 Glenmore Dr, Lewisville TX 75067-2419. 972/317-8889.

CSC Logic
9330 LBJ Freeway, Dallas TX 75243-3436. 972/783-3509.

Data Services
100 W Weatherford St, Fort Worth TX 76102-2115. 817/884-1180.

Decision One
13800 Hutton Dr, Dallas TX 75234-9007. 972/484-4883.

EDS Bank Services
PO Box 10332, Lubbock TX 79408-3332. 806/762-6691.

EDS Bank Services
1163 N Jackson St, Jacksonville TX 75766-3805. 903/586-0871.

EDS Tech Products
1221 Coit Rd, Plano TX 75075-7761. 972/612-6500.

EDS/Business Services Group
4490 Alpha Rd, Dallas TX 75244-4505. 972/604-6000.

Financial Data Systems
1612 Shadywood Lane, Mount Pleasant TX 75455-5637. 903/572-4336.

Input of Texas Inc.
PO Box 535007, Grand Prairie TX 75053-5007. 972/988-3282.

Intellifile Inc.
3988 N Central Expy, Dallas TX 75204-3036. 214/818-3000.

International Benefit Services Co.
PO Box 309, Fort Worth TX 76101-0309. 817/737-1700.

Lomas Information Systems
PO Box 655644, Dallas TX 75265-5644. 214/665-6300.

Mailbox Data Services
1325 Capital Pkwy, Ste 123, Carrollton TX 75006-3645. 972/245-0030.

Mailing List Systems Corp.
PO Box 1909, Arlington TX 76004-1909. 817/640-7007.

McLane/PDI
3407 S 31st St, Ste 200, Temple TX 76502-1944. 254/771-7100.

MDS
730 E Park Blvd, Ste 104, Plano TX 75074-5451. 972/424-1212.

Microsoft Corporation
1321 Greenway Dr, Irving TX 75038-2504. 972/756-7000.

NCR Corporation
3330 W Royal Ln, Irving TX 75063-6013. 972/401-6000.

PRC
PO Box 5098, Fort Hood TX 76544-0098. 254/288-9801.

SMS
800 E Campbell Rd, Ste 295, Richardson TX 75081-1872. 972/783-6737.

Stat Cat Inc.
1605 N Stemmons Fwy, Ste C, Dallas TX 75207-3431. 214/720-0606.

Universal Cadworks Inc.
251 W Renner Pkwy, Richardson TX 75080-1347. 972/480-9644.

USLife Systems Corporation
6363 Forest Park Rd, Dallas TX 75235-5402. 214/637-1179.

COMPUTER RENTAL AND LEASING

Baylor Computer Services
3801 Main St, Fl 2, Dallas TX 75226-1227. 214/820-4242.

StorageTek
12770 Merit Dr, Ste 300, Dallas TX 75251-1212. 214/980-7799.

COMPUTER SOFTWARE, PROGRAMMING, AND SYSTEMS DESIGN

3Com Corporation
15301 Dallas Parkway, Dallas TX 75248-4629. 972/868-6500.

Acclaim Services Inc.
PO Box 595905, Dallas TX 75359-0905. 214/750-1818.

Accugraph Corporation
801 E Campbell Rd, Ste 500, Richardson TX 75081-6702. 972/907-1295.

ADP Dealer Services Ltd.
2735 N Stemmons Freeway, Dallas TX 75207-2211. 214/630-3041.

Akili Systems Group Inc.
3624 Oak Lawn Ave, Dallas TX 75219-4376. 214/526-3260.

Alliance Consulting
5944 Luther Lane, Ste 402, Dallas TX 75225-5916. 214/369-1379.

Allstar Systems Inc.
14202 Proton Rd, Dallas TX 75244-3605. 972/458-7766.

Alltel Information Services
4455 Lyndon B. Johnson Freeway, Dallas TX 75244-5903. 972/866-1135.

Andrew Electronic Center
2425 N Central Expressway, Richardson TX 75080-2756. 972/235-7300.

Answer Soft
2201 N Central Expressway, Richardson TX 75080-2799. 972/997-8300.

Antrim Corporation
101 E Park Blvd, Fl 12, Plano TX 75074-5483. 972/422-1022.

Argo Data Resource Corp.
12770 Coit Rd, Ste 600, Dallas TX 75251-1320. 972/866-3300.

ASC Solutions Inc.
3740 N Josey Lane, Ste 210, Carrollton TX 75007-2472. 972/492-0569.

AST
2400 Western Center Blvd, Fort Worth TX 76131-1322. 817/847-7800.

BEA Systems Inc.
PO Box 115, Dallas TX 75221-0115. 972/738-6100.

Candle Corporation
12790 Merit Dr, Ste 614, Dallas TX 75251-1229. 972/991-0111.

Care Systems Corporation
12377 Merit Dr, Ste 100, Dallas TX 75251-2224. 972/383-1100.

Clearsystems Inc.
4925 O'Connor Rd N 200, Irving TX 75039. 972/541-1771.

CompuPros Inc.
16479 Dallas Parkway, Ste 800, Dallas TX 75248-6800. 972/250-4504.

CompuSource Inc.
3214 West Park Row Dr, Arlington TX 76013-3168. 817/277-4057.

Computrac Inc.
222 Municipal Drive, Richardson TX 75080-3539. 972/234-4241.

CPS Systems Inc.
3400 Carlisle St, Ste 500, Dallas
TX 75204-1288. 214/855-5277.

Criterion
9425 N MacArthur Blvd, Irving
TX 75063-4706. 972/401-2100.

CTI Limited Inc.
5400 LBJ Freeway, Ste 910,
Dallas TX 75240-1009. 972/776-
3600.

Decision Consultants Inc.
5000 Quorum Dr, Ste 410, Dallas
TX 75240-7509. 972/386-8777.

Diamond Head Software Inc.
1217 Digital Dr, Ste 125,
Richardson TX 75081-1970.
972/479-9205.

Docucorp Inc.
5910 N Central Expressway,
Dallas TX 75206-5125. 214/891-
6500.

Efficient Networks Inc.
4201 Spring Valley Rd, Dallas
TX 75244-3631. 972/991-3884.

Ensemble Corporation
12655 N Central Expressway,
Dallas TX 75243-1700. 972/960-
2700.

Enstar
8304 Esters Blvd, Ste 840, Irving
TX 75063-2234. 972/929-5267.

Enterprise Systems
PO Box 869305, Plano TX
75086. 972/575-6696.

Erapmus
3031 Allen St, Dallas TX 75204-
1059. 214/720-7221.

Flashnet Communications
1812 N Forest Park Blvd, Fort
Worth TX 76102-5807. 817/332-
8883.

Geac
3150 Premier Dr, Ste 128, Irving
TX 75063-2672. 972/490-3482.

Glenayre Technologies
4975 Preston Park Boulevard,
Plano TX 75093-5164. 972/867-
3333.

Harbinger Enterprise Solutions
2425 North Central Expy,
Richardson TX 75080-2756.
972/479-1260.

HCC
PO Box 1230, Fort Worth TX
76101-1230. 817/531-8992.

Healthdyne
15301 Dallas Pkwy, Ste 950,
Dallas TX 75248-4675. 972/851-
7033.

I² Technologies Inc.
909 Las Colinas Blvd E, Irving
TX 75039-3908. 214/860-6000.

ICI Retail Systems
5429 LBJ Fwy, Dallas TX 75240-
2607. 972/716-8300.

ICW Network Services
3000 Technology Dr, Plano TX
75074-7436. 972/633-3000.

InfoExperts Inc.
100 N Central Expy, Richardson
TX 75080-5332. 972/671-1500.

Intactix International Inc.
2900 Gateway Dr, Ste 600, Irving
TX 75063-2667. 972/580-1733.

**Integrated Information
Solutions**
1330 River Bend Dr, Dallas TX
75247-4914. 214/631-5430.

Intelligent Control Corp.
12750 Merit Dr, Ste 800, Dallas
TX 75251-1209. 972/776-8500.

International Network Services
14160 Dallas Pkwy, Ste 600,
Dallas TX 75240-4367. 972/392-
3545.

Internet America
350 N Saint Paul St, Dallas TX
75201-4240. 214/861-2500.

IRM
1525 N I35 E, Carrollton TX
75006-3890. 972/242-2312.

Lacerte Software Corporation
13155 Noel Rd, Fl 22, Dallas TX
75240-5090. 972/490-8500.

Lakeloge
3800 Marina Dr, Fort Worth TX
76135-2835. 817/237-7231.

LANsystems
1201 Elm St, Ste 4241, Dallas TX
75270-2144. 214/571-6050.

Leardata Info-Services Inc.
5910 N Central Expy, Dallas TX
75206-5125. 214/360-9008.

**Level One Communications
Inc.**
2340 E Trinity Mills Rd,
Carrollton TX 75006-1942.
972/418-2956.

**Mantech Telecom & Info
Systems**
PO Box 810, Copperas Cove TX
76522-0810. 254/288-1901.

Microsoft Corporation
5080 Spectrum Dr, Ste 900E,
Dallas TX 75248-6411. 972/458-
8086.

Multimedia Learning Inc.
5215 N O'Connor Blvd, Irving
TX 75039-3713. 972/869-8282.

Newdata Strategies
16415 Addison Rd, Ste 500,
Dallas TX 75248-2418. 972/735-
0001.

Object Systems Group Inc.
1950 N Stemmons Fwy, Dallas
TX 75207-3107. 214/742-5840.

On-Ramp Technologies Inc.
1950 N Stemmons Fwy, Dallas
TX 75207-3107. 214/672-7267.

Oracle Corporation
222 Las Colinas Blvd W, Irving
TX 75039-5421. 972/401-5800.

Paradigm Entertainment Inc.
14900 Landmark Blvd, Dallas TX
75240-6783. 972/960-2301.

Peerless Systems Inc.
1212 E Arapaho Rd, Richardson
TX 75081-2441. 972/497-5500.

Pegasus Systems Inc.
3811 Turtle Creek Blvd, Dallas
TX 75219-4444. 214/528-5656.

PeopleSoft Inc.
5420 Lyndon B. Johnson Fwy,
Dallas TX 75240-6222. 972/866-
3000.

Platinum Technology Inc.
16415 Addison Rd, Ste 200,
Dallas TX 75248-2461. 972/735-
8020.

Prelude Systems Inc.
16901 Dallas Pkwy, Ste 100,
Dallas TX 75248-1901. 972/931-
9005.

Reverse Distribution Service
5339 Alpha Rd, Ste 200, Dallas
TX 75240-7306. 972/980-7825.

Reynolds and Reynolds Co.
1555 Valwood Pkwy, Ste 150,
Carrollton TX 75006-6828.
972/243-4343.

Sabre Decision Technologies
1 Kirkwood Dr, Southlake TX
76092-2100. 817/264-7841.

Sabre Decision Technologies
4255 Amon Carter Blvd, Fort
Worth TX 76155-2603. 817/967-
1468.

Security Technologies Inc.
15182 Marsh Ln, Dallas TX
75234-2621. 214/351-7100.

SEI
5228 Village Creek Dr, Plano TX
75093-5066. 972/407-9921.

Sensormatic Electronics Corp.
PO Box 816425, Dallas TX
75381-6425. 972/241-2000.

Sequel Systems Inc.
1220 E Campbell Rd, Richardson
TX 75081-1935. 972/997-9000.

Softsource
1303 W Walnut Hill Ln, Irving
TX 75038-3030. 972/550-8371.

Software Group Inc.
1120 Jupiter Rd, Ste 100, Plano
TX 75074-7069. 972/424-1579.

Stonebridge Technologies Inc.
14800 Landmark Blvd, Dallas TX
75240-7565. 972/404-9755.

Supertech Systems Inc.
4637 Ringgold Ln, Plano TX
75093-3947. 972/612-9466.

Sybase Inc.
5400 LBJ Fwy, Ste 1500, Dallas
TX 75240-1015. 972/687-6400.

Tandem Telecom
1255 W 15th St, Ste 8030, Plano
TX 75075-7299. 972/423-5383.

Tandy Electronics
Tandy Tech Sq, Fl 6, Fort Worth
TX 76102. 817/390-3588.

Technical Management Group
6100 Western Pl, Ste 105, Fort
Worth TX 76107-4602. 817/762-
8400.

Techsol
5420 LBJ, 2 Lincoln Ctr 1550,
Roanoke TX 76262. 972/726-
5000.

TSK
1505 Lyndon B. Johnson Fwy,
Dallas TX 75234-6069. 972/919-
1555.

Visible Systems
4012 Info Mart, Dallas TX
75207. 214/746-4372.

Visualsoft Inc.
8200 Brookriver Dr, Dallas TX
75247-4069. 214/630-1480.

Voice Control Systems Inc.
14140 Midway Rd, Ste 100,
Dallas TX 75244-3672. 972/726-
1200.

Willow Bend Communications
PO Box 797485, Dallas TX
75379-7485. 972/248-0451.

Xlconnect Solutions Inc.
4100 Spring Valley, Dallas TX
75244-3629. 972/404-0888.

Xpert Applications Inc.
222 Las Colinas Blvd W, Irving
TX 75039-5421. 972/831-9884.

**Yokogawa Industrial
Automation**
2155 Chenault Drive, Carrollton
TX 75006. 972/417-2400.

**MISC. COMPUTER
RELATED SERVICES**

Abacus Technical Service
1701 N Collins Blvd, Richardson
TX 75080-3564. 972/644-4105.

AGS Information Services
4925 N O'Connor Blvd, Irving
TX 75062. 972/650-1120.

Berger & Co.
2828 Routh Street, Ste 350,
Dallas TX 75201-1422. 214/922-
8010.

Cap Gemini America Inc.
13455 Noel Road, Ste 1600,
Dallas TX 75240-6634. 972/385-
3290.

Ciber Inc.
15770 Dallas Parkway, Ste 850,
Dallas TX 75248-6616. 972/391-
7696.

**Comforce Information
Technology**
5055 Keller Springs Road, Dallas
TX 75248-5997. 972/248-8555.

Computer Systems Authority
6380 LBJ Freeway, Ste 191,
Dallas TX 75240-6411. 972/960-
0180.

Comsys Technical Services
17304 Preston Rd, Ste 590,
Dallas TX 75252-5617. 972/931-
8200.

CSC Consulting Systems
3811 Turtle Creek Blvd, Dallas
TX 75219-4461. 214/523-8236.

IBM
1 W Kirkwood Blvd, Roanoke
TX 76262-9503. 817/962-4000.

IMI Systems Inc.
14180 Dallas Pkwy, Ste 450,
Dallas TX 75240-4370. 972/788-
2311.

JCS Consulting Services Inc.
4201 Spring Valley, Ste 1400,
Dallas TX 75244-3668. 972/458-
1609.

Just Technical Associates
600 N Pearl St, Ste 370, Dallas
TX 75201-2862. 214/880-8700.

National Techteam Inc.
10945 Estate Ln, Dallas TX
75238-2317. 214/503-3800.

NETC
1607 Lyndon B. Johnson Fwy,
Dallas TX 75234-6034. 972/481-
5761.

Objectspace Inc.
14850 Quorum Dr, Ste 500,
Dallas TX 75240-7566. 972/934-
2496.

RCG Information Technology
5430 Lyndon B. Johnson Fwy,
Dallas TX 75240-2601. 972/855-
2200.

Software Solutions
5080 Spectrum Dr, Ste 116W,
Dallas TX 75248-4621. 972/701-
2333.

Sykes Enterprises Inc.
4722 South Lindhurst Avenue,
Dallas TX 75229-6526. 972/869-
9062.

Vital Solutions Inc.
2301 Ohio Drive, Suite 236,
Plano TX 75093-3902. 972/612-
2684.

For more information on career opportunities in the computer industry:

Associations

AMERICAN INTERNET ASSOCIATION
World Wide Web address: http://www.amernet.org. A nonprofit association providing assistance in the use of the Internet. Membership required.

ASSOCIATION FOR COMPUTING MACHINERY
1515 Broadway, 17th Floor, New York NY 10036. 212/869-7440. World Wide Web address: http://www.acm.org. Membership required.

ASSOCIATION FOR MULTIMEDIA COMMUNICATIONS
P.O. Box 10645, Chicago IL 60610. 312/409-1032. E-mail address: amc@amcomm.org. World Wide Web address: http://www.amcomm.org. A multimedia and Internet association.

ASSOCIATION FOR WOMEN IN COMPUTING
41 Sutter Street, Suite 1006, San Francisco CA 94104. 415/905-4663. E-mail address: awc@acm.org. World Wide Web address: http://www.awc-hq.org/awc. A nonprofit organization promoting women in computing professions.

ASSOCIATION OF INTERNET PROFESSIONALS
1301 Fifth Avenue, Suite 3300, Seattle WA 98101. E-mail address: info@associp.org. World Wide Web address: http://www.associp.org. A nonprofit trade association providing a forum for Internet users and professionals.

BLACK DATA PROCESSING ASSOCIATES
1111 14th Street NW, Suite 700, Washington DC 20005-5603. Toll-free phone: 800/727-BDPA. E-mail address: nbdpa@bdpa.org. World Wide Web address: http://www.bdpa.org. An organization of information technology professionals serving the minority community.

THE CENTER FOR SOFTWARE DEVELOPMENT
111 West St. John, Suite 200, San Jose CA 95113. 408/494-8378. E-mail address: info@center.org. World Wide Web address: http://www.center.org. A nonprofit organization providing technical and business resources for software developers.

COMMERCIAL INTERNET EXCHANGE ASSOCIATION (CIX)
1041 Sterling Road, Suite 104A, Herndon VA 20170. 703/824-9249. E-mail address: helpdesk@cix.org. World Wide Web address: http://www.cix.org. A nonprofit trade association of data internetworking service providers.

HTML WRITERS GUILD
World Wide Web address: http://www.hwg.org. An international organization of Web page writers and Internet professionals.

THE IPG SOCIETY
World Wide Web address: http://www.ipgnet.com. A professional trade association representing programmers internationally.

INFORMATION TECHNOLOGY ASSOCIATION OF AMERICA
1616 North Fort Myer Drive, Suite 1300, Arlington VA 22209. 703/522-5055. World Wide Web address: http://www.itaa.org.

INTERNET DEVELOPERS ASSOCIATION
World Wide Web address: http://www.association. org. A trade association concerned with content development for the Internet.

MULTIMEDIA DEVELOPMENT GROUP
520 Third Street, Suite 225, San Francisco CA 94107. 415/512-3556. Fax: 415/512-3569. E-mail address: info@mdg.org. A nonprofit trade association dedicated to the business and market development of multimedia companies.

THE OPEN GROUP
11 Cambridge Center, Cambridge MA 02142-1405. 617/621-8700. World Wide Web address: http://www. opengroup.org. A consortium concerned with open systems technology in the information systems industry. Membership required.

SOCIETY FOR INFORMATION MANAGEMENT
401 North Michigan Avenue, Chicago IL 60611-4267. 312/644-6610. E-mail address: info@simnet.org. World Wide Web address: http://www.simnet.org. A forum for information technology professionals.

SOFTWARE FORUM
953 Industrial, Suite 117, Palo Alto CA 94303. 650/856-3706. World Wide Web address: http://www.softwareforum.org. An independent, nonprofit organization for software industry professionals.

SOFTWARE PUBLISHERS ASSOCIATION
1730 M Street NW, Suite 700, Washington DC 20036. 202/452-1600. World Wide Web address: http://www.spa.org.

SOFTWARE SUPPORT PROFESSIONALS ASSOCIATION
11858 Bernardo Plaza Court, Suite 101C, San Diego CA 92128. 619/674-4864. World Wide Web address: http://www.sspa-online.com. A forum for service and support professionals in the software industry.

USENIX ASSOCIATION
2560 Ninth Street, Berkeley CA 94710. 510/528-8649. World Wide Web address: http://www.usenix. org. An advanced computing systems professional association for engineers, systems administrators, scientists, and technicians.

WORLD WIDE WEB TRADE ASSOCIATION
World Wide Web address: http://www.web-

star.com/wwwta.html. An association promoting responsible use of the World Wide Web.

Magazines

COMPUTER-AIDED ENGINEERING
Penton Publishing, 1100 Superior Avenue, Cleveland OH 44114. 216/696-7000. World Wide Web address: http://www.penton.com/cae.

COMPUTERWORLD, INC.
International Data Group, 500 Old Connecticut Path, Framingham MA 01701. 508/879-0700.

DATA COMMUNICATIONS
McGraw-Hill, 1221 Avenue of the Americas, New York NY 10020. 212/512-2000.

DATAMATION
Cahners Publishing, 275 Washington Street, Newton MA 02158. 617/964-3030. World Wide Web address: http://www.datamation.com.

IDC REPORT
International Data Corporation, 5 Speen Street, Framingham MA 01701. 508/872-8200.

Online Services

COMPUTER CONSULTANTS
Go: Consult. A CompuServe discussion group for computer professionals interested in networking and business development.

COMPUTERWORLD
http://www.computerworld.com. A weekly online newspaper for information sciences professionals featuring the latest news and employment opportunities. *Computerworld* conducts a job search by skills, job level (entry-level or experienced), job title, company, and your choice of three cities and three states. One feature of this site is "CareerMail," a service which e-mails you when a job matches the skills you have submitted online. This site also has corporate profiles, an events calendar, *Computerworld's* publications, an index of graduate schools, and other informative and educational resources.

IT JOBS
http://www.internet-solutions.com/itjobs/us/usselect.htm. This Website provides links to companies that have job openings in the information technology industry.

JOBSERVE
http://www.jobserve.com. Provides information on job openings in the field of information technology for companies throughout Europe. The site also offers links to numerous company Web pages, resume posting services, and a directory of recruiters.

SELECTJOBS
http://www.selectjobs.com. Post a resume and search the job database by region, discipline, special requirements, and skills on *SelectJOBS*. Once your search criteria has been entered, this site will automatically e-mail you when a job opportunity matches your requests.

THE SOFTWARE JOBS HOMEPAGE
http://www.softwarejobs.com. This Website offers a searchable database of openings for jobseekers looking in the software industry. The site is run by Allen Davis & Associates.

EDUCATIONAL SERVICES

Job prospects remain favorable in educational services, due to a healthy demand for qualified teachers at all levels. The U.S. Department of Labor projects that over the next 10 years, an additional 2.2 million teaching jobs in elementary and secondary education will be created, and demand will also be strong for college and university faculty, education administrators, school counselors, and kindergarten teachers. Special education teachers are still in strong demand, with a 56 percent projected increase in openings through 2005.

As enrollment swells in elementary and secondary schools, and at higher learning institutions, the growth of operating costs will rise significantly as well, and the U.S. Department of Commerce projects a 1 percent annual cost increase through the year 2000. Among the cost pressures schools face is the implementation of computer technology in the classroom and curriculum changes.

According to Business Week, *colleges and universities, under fiscal constraints, are struggling to meet the challenge of sustaining a high level of teaching and curricula without increasing tuitions to the point that they are unaffordable for the majority of students.*

ABILENE CHRISTIAN UNIVERSITY
ACU Station, Box 29106, Abilene TX 79699-9106. 915/674-2000. **Contact:** Personnel. **World Wide Web address:** http://www.acu.edu. **Description:** A university with 117 undergraduate programs, 39 graduate fields of study, and one doctoral level program in theology. Approximately 4,500 students are enrolled in the university.

AMARILLO COLLEGE
P.O. Box 447, Amarillo TX 79178. 806/371-5000. **Contact:** Human Resources. **World Wide Web address:** http://www.actx.edu. **Description:** A two-year community college.

ART INSTITUTE OF DALLAS
2 Northpark, 8080 Park Lane, Dallas TX 75231. 214/692-8080. **Contact:** Personnel Office. **World Wide Web address:** http://www.aid.aii.edu. **Description:** The Art Institute of Dallas is a two-year accredited institute with associate programs in art, fashion, photography, interior design, and music and video production. **Common positions include:** Accountant/Auditor; Administrator; Commercial Artist; Customer Service Representative; Department Manager; Instructor/Trainer; Services Sales Representative. **Educational backgrounds include:** Accounting; Art/Design; Business Administration; Communications; Liberal Arts; Marketing. **Benefits:** Disability Coverage; Life Insurance; Medical Insurance; Pension Plan; Profit Sharing; Tuition Assistance. **Corporate headquarters location:** Pittsburgh PA.

BAYLOR COLLEGE OF DENTISTRY
P.O. Box 660677, Dallas TX 75266-0677. 214/828-8100. **Contact:** Sandy Howell, Personnel Director. **Description:** A dentistry school connected with Baylor University.

BROOKHAVEN COLLEGE
3939 Valley View Lane, Farmers Branch TX 75244. 972/860-4813. **Contact:** Human Resources Department. **World Wide Web address:** http://www.dcccd.edu. **Description:** Accredited by the Southern Association of Colleges and Schools, Brookhaven is a two-year community college offering a full range of transferable, freshman-level and sophomore-level college courses. Brookhaven College opened its doors in 1978 as part of the Dallas County Community College District. The college serves the northern portion of Dallas County, including North Dallas,

Carrollton, Farmers Branch, Addison, Lewisville, Flower Mound, and The Colony. Brookhaven College serves 2,400 international students representing more than 100 countries and 65 languages. **Corporate headquarters location:** This Location.

CISCO JUNIOR COLLEGE
841 North Judge Ely, Abilene TX 79601. 915/673-4567. **Contact:** Personnel. **World Wide Web address:** http://www.cisco.cc.tx.us. **Description:** A junior college. **NOTE:** Interested jobseekers should address inquiries to the personnel department located at Route 3, Box 3, Cisco TX 76437.

COLLIN COUNTY COMMUNITY COLLEGE
P.O. Box 8001, McKinney TX 75070-8001. 972/881-5660. **Physical address:** 2200 West University Drive, McKinney TX 75070-8001. **Fax:** 972/985-3778. **Recorded jobline:** 972/881-5627. **Contact:** Kim Russell, Director of Human Resources. **World Wide Web address:** http://www.ccccd.edu. **Description:** A community college offering courses in computer science, humanities, international studies, fine arts, mathematics/natural science, health sciences, education, and engineering. **Common positions include:** Clerical Supervisor; Computer Programmer; Customer Service Representative; Education Administrator; Human Resources Manager; Librarian; Library Technician; Purchasing Agent/Manager; Systems Analyst; Teacher/Professor. **Educational backgrounds include:** Business Administration; Computer Science. **Benefits:** Dental Insurance; Disability Coverage; Life Insurance; Medical Insurance; Pension Plan; Tuition Assistance. **Special programs:** Internships. **Corporate headquarters location:** This Location. **Operations at this facility include:** Administration.

DALLAS BAPTIST UNIVERSITY
3000 Mountain Creek Parkway, Dallas TX 75211-9299. 214/333-7100. **Contact:** Personnel. **World Wide Web address:** http://www.dbu.edu. **Description:** An accredited university offering 34 undergraduate majors and eight master's-level programs.

DALLAS CHRISTIAN COLLEGE
2700 Christian Parkway, Dallas TX 75234. 972/241-3371. **Contact:** Dr. Mike Young, Academic Dean. **Description:** Offers undergraduate programs in religious studies.

DALLAS COUNTY COMMUNITY COLLEGE DISTRICT
701 Elm Street, Dallas TX 75202. 214/860-2135. **Contact:** Human Resources. **World Wide Web address:** http://www.dcccd.edu. **Description:** A community college district. **NOTE:** Primary positions require higher education and administration experience. **Common positions include:** Accountant/Auditor; Administrator; Buyer; Education Administrator; Instructor/Trainer; Systems Manager. **Educational backgrounds include:** Accounting; Art/Design; Biology; Business Administration; Chemistry; Communications; Computer Science; Economics; Education; Engineering; Finance; Geology; Liberal Arts; Marketing; Mathematics; Physics. **Benefits:** Dental Insurance; Disability Coverage; Life Insurance; Medical Insurance; Pension Plan. **Corporate headquarters location:** This Location. **Operations at this facility include:** Administration; Research and Development.

DALLAS INDEPENDENT SCHOOL DISTRICT
3700 Ross Avenue, Dallas TX 75204. 214/989-8000. **Contact:** Personnel. **Description:** This location houses offices for the local school district.

DAY CARE ASSOCIATION/FORT WORTH AND TARRANT
P.O. Box 7935, Fort Worth TX 76111. 817/831-0374. **Contact:** Human Resources. **Description:** A nonprofit daycare association. The organization's primary function is assisting low-income families in finding affordable daycare.

DeVRY INSTITUTE OF TECHNOLOGY
4800 Regent Boulevard, Irving TX 75063. 972/929-6777x250. **Fax:** 972/929-6778. **Contact:** Mr. R. Glyn Williams, Human Resources Manager. **E-mail address:** gwilliams@dal.devry.edu. **World Wide Web address:** http://www.dal.devry.edu. **Description:** A fully-accredited college offering baccalaureate degrees in business and technology. **Common positions include:** Education Administrator; Electrical/Electronics Engineer; Teacher/Professor; Telecommunications Manager.

Educational backgrounds include: Computer Science; Engineering. **Benefits:** 401(k); Dental Insurance; Disability Coverage; Life Insurance; Mass Transit Available; Medical Insurance; Tuition Assistance. **Corporate headquarters location:** Oakbrook Terrace IL. **Operations at this facility include:** Administration. **Listed on:** New York Stock Exchange. **Stock exchange symbol:** DV. **Number of employees at this location:** 200. **Number of employees nationwide:** 3,000.

EASTFIELD COLLEGE
3737 Motley Drive, Mesquite TX 75150. 972/860-7100. **Contact:** Human Resources. **Description:** A community college.

EL CENTRO COLLEGE
Main & Lamar Street, Dallas TX 75202-3604. 214/860-2037. **Contact:** Human Resources. **World Wide Web address:** http://www.dcccd.edu. **Description:** Operates as part of the Dallas County Community College District.

FLIGHTSAFETY INTERNATIONAL, INC.
8900 Trinity Boulevard, Hurst TX 76053. 817/595-5450. **Fax:** 817/595-5479. **Contact:** Phyllis Lovelace, Manager of Human Resources. **World Wide Web address:** http://www.flightsafety.com. **Description:** Provides high-technology training to operators of aircraft and ships. **Common positions include:** Computer Programmer; Operations/Production Manager; Software Engineer; Systems Analyst; Technical Writer/Editor. **Educational backgrounds include:** Art/Design; Computer Science. **Benefits:** 401(k); Dental Insurance; Disability Coverage; Life Insurance; Medical Insurance; Pension Plan. **Corporate headquarters location:** Flushing NY. **Other U.S. locations:** Nationwide. **Listed on:** New York Stock Exchange. **Number of employees at this location:** 150. **Number of employees nationwide:** 2,000.

HARDIN-SIMMONS UNIVERSITY
HSU Box 16030, Abilene TX 79698. 915/670-1507. **Fax:** 915/670-5874. **Contact:** Earl T. Garrett, Director/Human Resources. **World Wide Web address:** http://www.hsutx.edu. **Description:** A Southern Baptist university with both graduate and undergraduate degrees. **Common positions include:** Accountant/Auditor; Administrative Manager; Blue-Collar Worker Supervisor; Budget Analyst; Clerical Supervisor; Computer Programmer; Counselor; Education Administrator; Fundraising Specialist; Human Resources Manager; Librarian; Library Technician; Licensed Practical Nurse; Public Relations Specialist; Registered Nurse; Reporter; Systems Analyst; Teacher/Professor. **Educational backgrounds include:** Accounting; Art/Design; Biology; Business Administration; Chemistry; Communications; Computer Science; Economics; Finance; Geology; Liberal Arts; Marketing; Mathematics; Physical Therapy; Physics; Religion. **Benefits:** 403(b); Cafeteria; Dental Insurance; Disability Coverage; Employee Discounts; Life Insurance; Medical Insurance; Pension Plan; Tuition Assistance. **Corporate headquarters location:** This Location. **Number of employees at this location:** 300.

INFOTECH
307 West Seventh Street, Suite 275, Fort Worth TX 76102. 817/332-3900. **Contact:** Human Resources. **Description:** A privately owned school that teaches computer, copier, and medical equipment software and repair.

McKINNEY INDEPENDENT SCHOOL DISTRICT
One Duvall Street, McKinney TX 75069. 972/569-6400. **Contact:** Human Resources Department. **Description:** This location houses the administrative offices of McKinney's school district.

McMURRY UNIVERSITY
McMurry Station, P.O. Box 308, Abilene TX 79697. 915/691-6200. **Contact:** Human Resources. **World Wide Web address:** http://www.mcm.edu. **Description:** A four-year university offering bachelor's degrees. Approximately 1,425 students attend McMurry University.

MIDWESTERN STATE UNIVERSITY
3410 Taft Boulevard, Personnel Office, Wichita Falls TX 76308. 940/397-4221. **Fax:** 940/397-4780. **Contact:** Steve Holland, Director of Personnel. **E-mail address:** steve.holland@nexus.mwsu.edu. **World Wide Web address:** http://www.mwsu.edu. **Description:**

Midwestern State University is a state university. **Common positions include:** Accountant/Auditor; Buyer; Computer Programmer; Counselor; Education Administrator; Electrician; Human Resources Manager; Librarian; Library Technician; Property and Real Estate Manager; Public Relations Specialist; Radiological Technologist; Registered Nurse; Systems Analyst; Teacher/Professor. **Educational backgrounds include:** Accounting; Art/Design; Biology; Business Administration; Chemistry; Communications; Computer Science; Economics; Engineering; Finance; Geology; Marketing; Mathematics; Ph.D.; Physics. **Benefits:** 401(k); Dental Insurance; Disability Coverage; Employee Discounts; Life Insurance; Medical Insurance; Pension Plan; Savings Plan; Tuition Assistance. **Corporate headquarters location:** This Location. **President:** Dr. Louis J. Rodriguez. **Facilities manager:** Al Hooten. **Number of employees at this location:** 900.

NORTH LAKE COLLEGE
5001 North MacArthur Boulevard, Irving TX 75038. 972/273-3000. **Contact:** Human Resources Department. **World Wide Web address:** http://www.dcccd.edu/nlc. **Description:** A two-year community college offering technical occupational courses as well as general studies. Approximately 6,200 students are enrolled.

RICHLAND COLLEGE
12800 Abrams Road, Dallas TX 75243-2199. 972/238-6240. **Contact:** Personnel Director. **World Wide Web address:** http://www.rlc.dcccd.edu. **Description:** Richland College is a junior college.

SKYLINE HIGH SCHOOL
7777 Forney Road, Dallas TX 75227. 214/388-5731. **Contact:** Human Resources Department. **Description:** A high school.

SOUTH PLAINS COLLEGE
1401 South College Avenue, Levelland TX 79336. 806/894-9611. **Fax:** 806/894-6880. **Contact:** LaNell Spears, Benefit Coordinator. **World Wide Web address:** http://www.spc.cc.tx.us. **Description:** A two-year, state funded college. South Plains College offers majors in education, arts & sciences, nursing, and continuing education. The college has an enrollment of approximately 5,400 students.

SOUTHERN METHODIST UNIVERSITY
P.O. Box 750232, Dallas TX 75275-0232. 214/768-1111. **Contact:** Employment Office. **Description:** Southern Methodist University is a university. **Common positions include:** Accountant/Auditor; Administrator; Attorney; Biological Scientist; Blue-Collar Worker Supervisor; Buyer; Chemist. **Benefits:** Dental Insurance; Disability Coverage; Employee Discounts; Life Insurance; Medical Insurance; Pension Plan; Tuition Assistance. **Special programs:** Internships. **Corporate headquarters location:** This Location. **Number of employees at this location:** 1,820.

SOUTHWESTERN ADVENTIST UNIVERSITY
300 North College Drive, Keene TX 76059. 817/477-2543. **Contact:** Personnel Department. **World Wide Web address:** http://www.swau.edu. **Description:** The university is affiliated with the Seventh Day Adventist Church and offers 40 undergraduate programs and two graduate level programs. There are over 1,100 students enrolled.

SOUTHWESTERN BAPTIST THEOLOGICAL SEMINARY
P.O. Box 22000, Fort Worth TX 76122. 817/923-1921. **Contact:** Office of Church/Minister Relations. **World Wide Web address:** http://www.swbts.edu. **Description:** Southwestern Baptist Theological Seminary is a seminary college offering a variety of religious training programs.

TARLETON STATE UNIVERSITY
Mail Stop T-510, Tarleton Station, Stephenville TX 76402. 254/968-9905. **Fax:** 254/968-9590. **Contact:** Ms. Mary Chenault, Human Resources Assistant. **World Wide Web address:** http://www.tarleton.edu. **Description:** Tarleton State University is a four-year state university. **Common positions include:** Accountant/Auditor; Buyer; Clerical Supervisor; Computer

Programmer; Counselor; Designer; Editor; Education Administrator; Electrician; Financial Analyst; General Manager; Human Resources Manager; Instructor/Trainer; Librarian; Library Technician; Management Analyst/Consultant; Psychologist; Public Relations Specialist; Registered Nurse; Research Assistant; Systems Analyst; Teacher/Professor; Technical Writer/Editor. **Educational backgrounds include:** Accounting; Biology; Business Administration; Chemistry; Communications; Computer Science; Hydrogeology; Liberal Arts; Marketing. **Benefits:** 403(b); Dental Insurance; Disability Coverage; Life Insurance; Medical Insurance; Pension Plan; Savings Plan. **Corporate headquarters location:** College Station TX. **Operations at this facility include:** Administration. **Number of employees at this location:** 675.

TARRANT COUNTY JUNIOR COLLEGE
1500 Houston Street, Fort Worth TX 76102. 817/515-5100. **Contact:** Human Resources. **World Wide Web address:** http://www.tcjc.cc.tx.us. **Description:** A two-year college. **Common positions include:** Accountant/Auditor; Clerical Supervisor; Teacher/Professor. **Benefits:** Dental Insurance; Life Insurance; Medical Insurance; Pension Plan; Tuition Assistance. **Corporate headquarters location:** This Location. **Operations at this facility include:** Administration.

TEXAS A&M UNIVERSITY
East Texas Station, Commerce TX 75429. 903/886-5668. **Fax:** 903/886-5670. **Recorded jobline:** 903/886-5665. **Contact:** Human Resources. **World Wide Web address:** http://www.tamu-commerce.edu. **Description:** A state university.

TEXAS CHRISTIAN UNIVERSITY
P.O. Box 298200, Fort Worth TX 76129. 817/921-7095. **Contact:** Sharon E. Barnes, Director of Employee Relations. **Description:** A university. **Common positions include:** Blue-Collar Worker Supervisor; Cashier; Construction Trade Worker; Dispatcher; Heating/AC/Refrigeration Technician; Library Technician; Payroll Clerk; Postal Clerk/Mail Carrier; Printing Press Operator; Secretary; Teacher/Professor; Typist/Word Processor. **Educational backgrounds include:** Accounting; Art/Design; Biology; Business Administration; Chemistry; Communications; Computer Science; Economics; Engineering; Finance; Geology; Liberal Arts; Marketing; Mathematics; Physics. **Benefits:** Dental Insurance; Disability Coverage; Employee Discounts; Life Insurance; Medical Insurance; Pension Plan; Tuition Assistance. **Corporate headquarters location:** This Location. **Number of employees at this location:** 1,300.

TEXAS TECH UNIVERSITY
P.O. Box 41093, Lubbock TX 79409. 806/742-2011. **Contact:** Jim Brown, Personnel Director. **World Wide Web address:** http://www.ttu.edu. **Description:** A four-year state university with a range of program offerings which provide the opportunity for a liberal education for all students and for professional training at the undergraduate and graduate levels. The university also has the following schools: Law, Applied Health, and Medicine. **Benefits:** Dental Insurance; Disability Coverage; Life Insurance; Medical Insurance; Pension Plan; Savings Plan. **Corporate headquarters location:** This Location.

TEXAS WESLEYAN UNIVERSITY
1201 Wesleyan Street, Fort Worth TX 76105. 817/531-4403. **Fax:** 817/531-4402. **Contact:** Human Resources. **Description:** A small, private university affiliated with the United Methodist Church. **Common positions include:** Accountant/Auditor; Administrative Manager; Administrator; Biological Scientist; Blue-Collar Worker Supervisor; Chemist; Clerical Supervisor; Computer Programmer; Construction Contractor; Counselor; Dietician/Nutritionist; Economist; Education Administrator; Financial Analyst; Food Scientist/Technologist; Librarian; Library Technician; Mathematician; Paralegal; Psychologist; Public Relations Specialist; Registered Nurse; Systems Analyst; Teacher/Professor. **Educational backgrounds include:** Accounting; Art/Design; Biology; Business Administration; Chemistry; Communications; Computer Science; Economics; Finance; Liberal Arts; Marketing; Mathematics; Physics. **Benefits:** Dental Insurance; Disability Coverage; Employee Discounts; Life Insurance; Medical Insurance; Pension Plan; Tuition Assistance. **Corporate headquarters location:** This Location. **Operations at this facility include:** Administration; Divisional Headquarters. **Number of employees at this location:** 285.

TEXAS WOMAN'S UNIVERSITY (TWU)
P.O. Box 425739, Denton TX 76204-3739. 940/898-3555. **Fax:** 940/898-3566. **Contact:** Annette Johnson, Assistant Manager of Employment. **World Wide Web address:** http://www.twu.edu. **Description:** A teaching and research institution, the university emphasizes liberal arts, specialized studies, and professional studies. The university awards bachelor's, master's, and doctoral degrees. There are over 8,000 students enrolled at the university, and 91 percent are women. Twenty-four percent of the students are minority or international students, and the majority of all students enrolled are from Texas. Founded in 1903. **Common positions include:** Accountant/Auditor; Computer Programmer; Counselor; Dispatcher; Electrician; Financial Analyst; Human Resources Manager; Librarian; Purchasing Agent/Manager; Receptionist; Registered Nurse; Secretary; Systems Analyst; Typist/Word Processor. **Educational backgrounds include:** Accounting; Business Administration; Computer Science; Finance; Marketing; Mathematics. **Benefits:** Dental Insurance; Disability Coverage; Life Insurance; Medical Insurance; Pension Plan. **Special programs:** Internships. **Corporate headquarters location:** This Location. **Other U.S. locations:** Dallas TX; Houston TX. **Number of employees at this location:** 1,000. **Number of employees nationwide:** 1,400.

UNIVERSITY OF NORTH TEXAS
P.O. Box 311010, Denton TX 76203. 940/565-2281. **Contact:** Personnel Department. **World Wide Web address:** http://www.unt.edu. **Description:** The university offers undergraduate, graduate, and doctoral programs. Approximately 25,000 students attend the university.

UNIVERSITY OF NORTH TEXAS HEALTH SCIENCE AT FORT WORTH
3500 Camp Bowie Boulevard, Suite 735, Fort Worth TX 76107-2699. 817/735-2690. **Contact:** Human Resources Services. **World Wide Web address:** http://www.hsc.unt.edu. **Description:** A health science education center. **Common positions include:** Accountant/Auditor; Biological Scientist; Biomedical Engineer; Buyer; Chemist; Claim Representative; Clinical Lab Technician; Computer Programmer; Graphic Artist; Library Technician; Licensed Practical Nurse; Receptionist; Registered Nurse; Science Technologist; Secretary; Systems Analyst; Typist/Word Processor. **Educational backgrounds include:** Accounting; Biology; Business Administration; Computer Science; Education; Mathematics. **Benefits:** Dental Insurance; Disability Coverage; Employee Discounts; Life Insurance; Medical Insurance; Pension Plan. **Corporate headquarters location:** This Location. **Operations at this facility include:** Administration; Education; Research and Development. **Number of employees at this location:** 1,000.

UNIVERSITY OF TEXAS AT ARLINGTON
1225 West Mitchell Street, P.O. Box 19176, Arlington TX 76019. 817/272-2011. **Fax:** 817/272-5798. **Contact:** Human Resources. **World Wide Web address:** http://www.uta.edu/human_resource/emply.html. **Description:** A campus of the state university. **Common positions include:** Accountant/Auditor; Administrative Manager; Administrative Worker/Clerk; Administrator; Aerospace Engineer; Architect; Attorney; Automotive Mechanic; Biomedical Engineer; Blue-Collar Worker Supervisor; Budget Analyst; Buyer; Chemical Engineer; Chemist; Civil Engineer; Clerical Supervisor; Computer Programmer; Construction and Building Inspector; Counselor; Customer Service Representative; Electrical/Electronics Engineer; Electrician; Environmental Engineer; Financial Analyst; Geologist/Geophysicist; Health Services Manager; Human Resources Manager; Industrial Engineer; Librarian; Library Technician; Licensed Practical Nurse; Management Trainee; Materials Engineer; Mathematician; Mechanical Engineer; Pharmacist; Physician; Property and Real Estate Manager; Public Relations Specialist; Registered Nurse; Science Technologist; Services Sales Representative; Social Worker; Software Engineer; Systems Analyst; Teacher/Professor; Technical Writer/Editor; Wholesale and Retail Buyer. **Educational backgrounds include:** Accounting; Business Administration; Communications; Computer Science; Engineering; Finance; Health Care; Liberal Arts. **Benefits:** Dental Insurance; Disability Coverage; Life Insurance; Medical Insurance; Pension Plan. **Special programs:** Internships. **Corporate headquarters location:** Austin TX. **Parent company:** University of Texas at Austin/System Office. **Number of employees at this location:** 4,000.

UNIVERSITY OF TEXAS AT DALLAS
2601 North Floyd Street, Richardson TX 75080-0688. 972/883-2221. **Contact:** Ms. Kim Lerwick, Human Resources Specialist. **World Wide Web address:** http://www.utdallas.edu. **Description:** A

state university offering programs at the undergraduate, graduate, and doctoral levels. Enrollment at the university is approximately 10,000.

UNIVERSITY OF TEXAS AT TYLER
3900 University Boulevard, Tyler TX 75799. 903/566-7234. **Fax:** 903/566-8368. **Contact:** Human Resources. **World Wide Web address:** http://www.uttyl.edu. **Description:** A university.

Note: Because addresses and telephone numbers of smaller companies can change rapidly, we recommend you call each company to verify the information below before inquiring about job opportunities. Mass mailings are not recommended.

Additional small employers:

CHILD DAYCARE SERVICES

Child Care Group
1221 River Bend Dr, Ste 250, Dallas TX 75247. 214/630-7911.

Clayton Childcare Inc.
1810 8th Ave, Fort Worth TX 76110-1352. 817/428-6619.

Dallas Christian School
1515 Republic Parkway, Mesquite TX 75150-6911. 972/681-3351.

Educare Community Living Co.
5047 Martin Luther King F, Fort Worth TX 76119-4169. 817/446-1591.

K&A Enterprises Inc.
9011 John Carpenter Fwy, Dallas TX 75247. 214/350-2422.

COLLEGES, UNIVERSITIES, AND PROFESSIONAL SCHOOLS

Amber University
1700 Eastgate Dr, Garland TX 75041-5511. 972/279-6511.

Austin College
900 N Grand Ave, Sherman TX 75090-4440. 903/813-2000.

Baylor University
PO Box 97043, Waco TX 76798-7043. 254/710-3731.

Dallas Theological Seminary
3909 Swiss Ave, Dallas TX 75204-6411. 214/824-3094.

East Texas Baptist University
1209 N Grove St, Marshall TX 75670-1423. 903/935-7963.

East Texas Police Academy
1100 Broadway Blvd, Kilgore TX 75662-3204. 903/984-8531.

Jarvis Christian College
PO Drawer G, Hawkins TX 75765-0650. 903/769-2174.

Le Tourneau University
PO Box 7001, Longview TX 75607-7001. 903/753-0231.

Lubbock Christian School
5601 19th St, Lubbock TX 79407-2031. 806/792-3221.

Parker College of Chiropractics
2550 Walnut Hill Ln, Dallas TX 75229-5631. 214/352-7332.

Paul Quinn College
3837 Simpson Stuart Road, Dallas TX 75241-4331. 214/376-1000.

Temple College
2600 S 1st St, Temple TX 76504-7435. 254/298-8282.

University of Dallas
1845 East Northgate Drive, Irving TX 75062-4736. 972/721-5000.

ELEMENTARY AND SECONDARY SCHOOLS

Abernathy Independent School District
505 7th St, Abernathy TX 79311-3318. 806/298-2563.

Abilene High School
2800 North 6th Street, Abilene TX 79603-7125. 915/677-1731.

Allen High School
601 E Main St, Allen TX 75002-3007. 972/727-0400.

AM Aikin Elementary School
3100 Pine Mill Rd, Paris TX 75460-4937. 903/737-7443.

Amarillo High School
4225 Danbury St, Amarillo TX 79109-5199. 806/354-4400.

Arlington Heights Senior High School
4501 W Rosedale St, Fort Worth TX 76107-5427. 817/377-7200.

Arlington High School
818 W Park Row Dr, Arlington TX 76013-3903. 817/460-2541.

Ascher Silberstein Elementary School
PO Box 351, Dallas TX 75221-0351. 214/381-8740.

Austin Elementary School
1500 Austin Dr, Ennis TX 75119-7508. 972/875-5571.

Bailey Junior High School
2411 Winewood St, Arlington TX 76013-3333. 817/460-3933.

Barnett Junior High School
2101 Harwood Rd, Arlington TX 76018-3101. 817/468-1952.

Belton High School
PO Box 300, Belton TX 76513-0300. 254/933-4600.

Belton Independent School District
PO Box 148, Belton TX 76513-0148. 254/933-4740.

Belton Junior High School
PO Box 360, Belton TX 76513-0360. 254/939-3535.

Berkner High School
1600 E Spring Valley Rd, Richardson TX 75081-5351. 972/301-4100.

Big Sandy Elementary School
PO Box 598, Big Sandy TX
75755-0598. 903/636-5287.

Billingham Intermediate School
1701 Gallagher Dr, Sherman TX
75090-1809. 903/892-6162.

Billy Ryan Senior High School
5101 E McKinney St, Denton TX
76208-4630. 940/566-7926.

Birdville Independent Schools
6125 E Belknap St, Fort Worth
TX 76117-4204. 817/831-5700.

Boles Junior High School
3900 SW Green Oaks Blvd,
Arlington TX 76017-4110.
817/483-5216.

**Booker T. Washington High
School**
2501 Flora St, Dallas TX 75201-
2417. 214/720-7300.

**Bowie Independent School
District**
PO Box 1168, Bowie TX 76230-
1168. 940/872-1151.

**Breckenridge Independent
School District**
PO Box 1738, Breckenridge TX
76424-1738. 254/559-2278.

Brewer High School
1000 S Cherry Ln, Fort Worth TX
76108-3215. 817/367-1200.

Brewer Middle School
1000 S Cherry Lane, Ste A, Fort
Worth TX 76108-3215. 817/367-
1267.

**Brownfield Independent School
District**
601 Tahoka Rd, Brownfield TX
79316-3631. 806/637-2591.

Brownsboro Jr. High School
PO Box 465, Brownsboro TX
75756-0465. 903/852-6931.

**Bruceville-Eddy Independent
School District**
PO Box 99, Eddy TX 76524-
0099. 254/859-5832.

Bryan Adams High School
2101 Millmar Dr, Dallas TX
75228-3357. 214/319-0140.

**Buffalo Independent School
District**
PO Box C, Buffalo TX 75831-
0168. 903/322-3765.

**Burkburnett Independent
School District**
416 Glendale St, Burkburnett TX
76354-2425. 940/569-1852.

Burleson High School
100 NW John Jones Dr, Burleson
TX 76028-5648. 817/447-5700.

Burleson Junior High School
316 SW Thomas St, Burleson TX
76028-4610. 817/447-5750.

**Carrollton-Farmers Branch
Independent School District**
PO Box 115186, Carrollton TX
75011-5186. 972/466-6100.

Carter Junior High School
701 Tharp St, Arlington TX
76010-2851. 817/460-3242.

**Carthage Independent School
District**
1 Bulldog Dr, Carthage TX
75633-2370. 903/693-3806.

**Cayuga Independent School
District**
PO Box 427, Cayuga TX 75832-
0427. 903/928-2102.

Cedar Hill High School
1 Longhorn Blvd, Cedar Hill TX
75104-2748. 972/291-4273.

Central Elementary School
PO Box 724, Belton TX 76513-
0724. 254/939-3512.

Chandler School
711 N Longview St, Kilgore TX
75662-5413. 903/984-2534.

Chapel Hill High School
13172 State Hwy 64 E, Tyler TX
75707-5340. 903/566-2311.

**Childress Independent School
District**
PO Box 179, Childress TX
79201-0179. 940/937-2501.

**Chisum Independent School
District**
3250 S Church St, Paris TX
75462-8909. 903/737-2830.

Clark High School
523 W Spring Creek Parkway,
Plano TX 75023-4602. 972/517-
5105.

Clear Creek Elementary School
4800 Washington St, Fort Hood
TX 76544-1741. 254/520-1500.

Colony High School
4301 Blair Oaks Dr, Lewisville
TX 75056-2718. 972/625-9000.

**Community Independent
School District**
PO Box 400, Nevada TX 75173-
0400. 972/853-2474.

Cooper High School
3639 Sayles Blvd, Abilene TX
79605-7050. 915/691-1000.

Copperas Cove High School
PO Box 580, Copperas Cove TX
76522-0580. 254/547-2534.

Coronado Senior High School
3307 Vicksburg Ave, Lubbock
TX 79410-2321. 806/766-0600.

Corprew Intermediate School
PO Box 1117, Mount Pleasant
TX 75456-1117. 903/575-2050.

Corsicana High School Inc.
3701 W Highway 22, Corsicana
TX 75110-2463. 903/874-8211.

Curtis Elementary School
501 W Russell St, Weatherford
TX 76086-5175. 817/598-2838.

Dallas Christian School
PO Box 28295, Dallas TX 75228-
0295. 972/270-5495.

**David G. Burnet Elementary
School**
3200 Kinkaid Dr, Dallas TX
75220-1623. 214/904-1220.

Decatur Elementary School
1300 Deer Park Rd, Decatur TX
76234-4403. 940/627-3332.

Denison High School
1901 S Mirick Ave, Denison TX
75020-6835. 903/465-2488.

**Denison Independent School
District**
PO Box 303, Denison TX 75021-
0303. 903/465-4244.

Dr. Ralph Poteet High School
3300 Poteet Dr, Mesquite TX
75150-4760. 972/270-8737.

Dumas Junior High School
5th Durratt St, Dumas TX 79029.
806/935-4155.

Dumas Senior High School
300 S Klein Ave, Dumas TX
79029-3744. 806/935-6461.

Duncan Elementary School
Muskogee Rd, Fort Hood TX
76544. 254/539-3596.

Duncanville High School
900 W Camp Wisdom Rd,
Duncanville TX 75116-3021.
972/298-6136.

East Texas Christian Academy
PO Box 8201, Tyler TX 75711-
8201. 903/561-8642.

Eastern Hills Middle School
300 Indian Trail, Killeen TX
76548-7206. 254/690-6016.

**Eastern Hills Senior High
School**
5701 Shelton St, Fort Worth TX
76112-3929. 817/496-7600.

**Eastland Independent School
District**
PO Box 31, Eastland TX 76448-
0031. 254/629-8221.

**Edgewood Independent School
District**
Hwy 80 E, Edgewood TX 75117.
903/896-4332.

**Edward Titche Elementary
School**
9560 Highfield Dr, Dallas TX
75227-8149. 214/381-8760.

EM Daggett Elementary School
958 Page Ave, Fort Worth TX
76110-2627. 817/922-6880.

**Ennis Independent School
District**
501 N Gaines St, Ennis TX
75119-3841. 972/875-3779.

Ennis Vocational School
800 W Denton St, Ennis TX
75119-2923. 972/875-3376.

Estacado High School
1504 E Itasca St, Lubbock TX
79403-3120. 806/766-1400.

Evers Park Elementary School
3300 Evers Parkway, Denton TX
76207-7208. 940/382-1576.

**Ewell D. Walker Special
Education School**
12532 Nuestra Dr, Dallas TX
75230-1718. 972/490-8701.

**Fort Worth Country Day
School**
4200 Country Day Lane, Fort

Worth TX 76109-4201. 817/732-
7718.

**Fort Worth Independent School
District**
100 North University Dr, Fort
Worth TX 76107-1360. 817/871-
2000.

Foster Middle School
410 S Green St, Longview TX
75601-7533. 903/753-1692.

Friona High School
909 E 11th St, Friona TX 79035-
1416. 806/247-2747.

**Garland Independent School
District**
PO Box 469026, Garland TX
75046-9026. 972/494-8201.

**George W. Carver Learning
Center**
3719 Greenleaf St, Dallas TX
75212-1522. 214/689-1540.

Granbury High School
2000 West Pearl Street, Granbury
TX 76048-1888. 817/579-2230.

Grapevine High School
3223 Mustang Dr, Grapevine TX
76051-5962. 817/488-9596.

Grapevine Middle School
730 E Worth St, Grapevine TX
76051-3653. 817/488-9588.

**Grapevine-Colleyville
Independent School**
3051 Ira E. Wood Ave,
Grapevine TX 76051-3817.
817/481-5575.

Greenhill School
4141 Spring Valley Road, Dallas
TX 75244-3615. 972/661-1211.

Greenville High School
3515 Lions Lair Rd, Greenville
TX 75402-7906. 903/457-2550.

Greenville Middle School
3611 Texas St, Greenville TX
75401-5046. 903/457-2620.

**Groesbeck Independent School
District**
PO Box 559, Groesbeck TX
76642-0559. 254/729-3808.

H. Grady Spruce High School
9733 Old Seagoville Road, Dallas
TX 75217-7744. 972/557-6200.

Halstead Elementary School
PO Box 580, Copperas Cove TX
76522-0580. 254/547-3440.

Haltom Senior High School
5501 Haltom Road, Fort Worth
TX 76137-2804. 817/581-5300.

Hankamer School of Business
PO Box 98001, Waco TX 76798.
254/755-1211.

Harmony High School
Rural Route 4, Box 653, Gilmer
TX 75644-9470. 903/725-5495.

**Harmony Independent School
District**
Rural Route 4, Box 652, Gilmer
TX 75644-9470. 903/725-5493.

**Hedley Samnorwood
Wellington**
609 15th St, Wellington TX
79095-3603. 806/447-2512.

Henderson High School
PO Box 728, Henderson TX
75653-0728. 903/657-1483.

**Henderson Independent School
District**
501 Richardson Drive, Henderson
TX 75654-3908. 903/657-1491.

**Hereford Independent School
District**
601 North 25 Mile Avenue,
Hereford TX 79045-3024.
806/364-0606.

Hereford Senior High School
200 Avenue F, Hereford TX
79045-4408. 806/363-7620.

Hico School District
PO Box 218, Hico TX 76457-
0218. 254/796-2181.

**Highland Park Elementary
School**
4220 Emerson Avenue, Dallas
TX 75205-1070. 214/526-4800.

**Highland Park Independent
School District**
PO Box 30430, Amarillo TX
79120-0430. 806/335-2821.

Highland Park Middle School
3555 Granada Avenue, Dallas TX
75205-2235. 214/523-2900.

Hillcrest High School
9924 Hillcrest Rd, Dallas TX
75230-5309. 214/987-8412.

Hooks Independent School District
PO Box 39, Hooks TX 75561-0039. 903/547-6077.

Hutcheson Junior High School
2101 Browning Dr, Arlington TX 76010-5949. 817/460-6572.

Iowa Park Consolidated Independent School District
PO Box 898, Iowa Park TX 76367-0898. 940/592-4193.

Irving Independent School District
PO Box 152637, Irving TX 75015-2637. 972/273-6000.

Italy Independent School District
300 S College St, Italy TX 76651. 972/483-7414.

Jacksonville High School
PO Box 631, Jacksonville TX 75766-0631. 903/586-3661.

James Bowie High School
2101 Highbank Dr, Arlington TX 76018-1980. 817/468-9370.

James Bowie Middle School
3001 E 12th Ave, Amarillo TX 79104-2521. 806/371-5580.

James Madison High School
3000 ML King Blvd, Dallas TX 75215. 214/565-6518.

Jasper High School
6800 Archgate Dr, Plano TX 75024-5214. 972/519-8887.

JL Long Middle School
6116 Reiger Ave, Dallas TX 75214-4534. 214/841-5270.

JN Ervin Elementary School
3722 Black Oak Dr, Dallas TX 75241-3307. 214/302-2310.

John B. Hood Middle School
7625 Hume Dr, Dallas TX 75227-8828. 214/381-8700.

John F. Kennedy Learning Center
1802 Moser Ave, Dallas TX 75206-7537. 214/824-8003.

John Tyler High School
1120 N Northwest Loop 323, Tyler TX 75702-3617. 903/531-6000.

Killeen High School
500 N 38th St, Killeen TX 76543-4161. 254/699-0392.

La Vega Independent School District
3100 Bellmead Dr, Waco TX 76705-3033. 254/799-4963.

La Vega Primary School
900 Ashleman St, Waco TX 76705-2957. 254/799-6229.

Lakeview Centennial High School
3505 Hayman Dr, Garland TX 75043-1920. 972/494-8592.

Lakewood Elementary School
3000 Hillbrook St, Dallas TX 75214-3412. 214/841-5250.

Lamar Middle School
4000 Timber Creek Rd, Flower Mound TX 75028-2102. 972/539-0886.

Lamar Senior High School
1400 W Lamar Blvd, Arlington TX 76012-1743. 817/460-4721.

Lancaster High School
822 W Pleasant Run Rd, Lancaster TX 75146-1446. 972/227-2418.

LD Bell High School
1601 Brown Trl, Hurst TX 76054-3703. 817/282-2551.

Leila Cowart Elementary School
1515 S Ravinia Dr, Dallas TX 75211-5742. 214/331-7870.

Leon Heights Elementary School
PO Box 709, Belton TX 76513-0709. 254/933-4720.

Lewisville High School
1098 West Main Street, Lewisville TX 75067-3518. 972/221-3535.

LG Pinkston High School
2200 Dennison St, Dallas TX 75212-2460. 214/689-1603.

Liberty Junior High School
10330 Lawler Rd, Dallas TX 75243-2634. 972/238-6760.

Little Elm High School
500 Lobo Ln, Little Elm TX 75068-5220. 972/292-1840.

Longview High School
PO Box 3268, Longview TX 75606-3268. 903/663-1301.

Lubbock Public Schools
1628 19th St, Lubbock TX 79401-4832. 806/766-1000.

Lubbock Senior High School
2004 19th St, Lubbock TX 79401-4606. 806/766-1444.

Lubbock-Cooper Independent School District
Rural Route 6, Box 400, Lubbock TX 79423-9530. 806/863-2282.

Lyles Middle School
4655 South Country Club Rd, Garland TX 75043-1846. 972/494-8648.

Mabank High School
PO Box 124, Mabank TX 75147-0124. 903/887-9333.

MacArthur High School
3700 North MacArthur Blvd, Irving TX 75062-3639. 972/255-2171.

Madison Middle School
PO Box 241, Abilene TX 79604-0241. 915/692-5661.

Malakoff School District
813 East Royall Boulevard, Malakoff TX 75148-9254. 903/489-1152.

Mann Middle School
2545 Mimosa Dr, Abilene TX 79603-2131. 915/672-8493.

Maple Lawn Elementary School
3120 Inwood Rd, Dallas TX 75235-7626. 214/904-1080.

Marcus High School
5707 Morriss Road, Flower Mound TX 75028-3730. 972/539-1591.

Mayfield Workman Junior High School
701 E Arbrook Blvd, Arlington TX 76014-3240. 817/465-4741.

McNair Elementary School
1530 W Hickory St, Denton TX 76201-3895. 940/383-4744.

Meadowbrook Middle School
2001 Ederville Rd S, Fort Worth TX 76103-1510. 817/531-6250.

Meadows Elementary School
27th St, Bldg 22, Fort Hood TX
76544. 254/532-2210.

Merkel High School
South 3rd & Ash Sts, Merkel TX
79536. 915/928-5511.

Mesquite High School
300 E Davis St, Mesquite TX
75149-4610. 972/285-8861.

**Mesquite Independent School
District**
405 E Davis St, Mesquite TX
75149-4701. 972/288-6411.

Mexia State School
PO Box 1132, Mexia TX 76667-
1132. 254/562-2821.

Midway High School
700 N Hewitt Dr, Hewitt TX
76643-2970. 254/666-5151.

Monterey Senior High School
3211 47th St, Lubbock TX
79413-4112. 806/766-0700.

**Morton Independent School
District**
500 Champion Dr, Morton TX
79346-3310. 806/266-5505.

Mount Pleasant High School
PO Box 1117, Mount Pleasant
TX 75456-1117. 903/572-1891.

**Mount Vernon Independent
School District**
PO Box 98, Mount Vernon TX
75457-0098. 903/537-2546.

Naaman Forest High School
4843 Naaman Forest Blvd,
Garland TX 75040-2732.
972/494-8670.

Nichols Junior High School
2201 Ascension Blvd, Arlington
TX 76006-5587. 817/460-7161.

Nimitz High School
100 W Oakdale Rd, Irving TX
75060-6833. 972/259-3621.

Nolan Middle School
505 E Jasper Dr, Killeen TX
76541-8940. 254/634-4646.

North Dallas High School
3120 N Haskell Ave, Dallas TX
75204-1510. 214/559-1900.

North Garland High School
2109 W Buckingham Rd, Garland
TX 75042-5031. 972/494-8451.

North Mesquite High School
18201 Lyndon B. Johnson Fwy,
Mesquite TX 75150-4124.
972/279-6721.

**Northwest Independent School
District**
RR 1, Box 39A, Justin TX
76247-9801. 940/648-2611.

OD Wyatt High School
2400 E Seminary Dr, Fort Worth
TX 76119-5502. 817/531-6300.

**Oliver W. Holmes Classical
Academy**
2001 E Kiest Blvd, Dallas TX
75216-3326. 214/302-2380.

Palestine High School
1600 S Loop 256, Palestine TX
75801-5847. 903/731-8005.

Palo Duro High School
1400 N Grant St, Amarillo TX
79107-3951. 806/381-7132.

**Paradise Independent School
District**
RR 2, Box 646, Paradise TX
76073-9622. 940/969-2501.

Paris High School
2400 Jefferson Rd, Paris TX
75460-7825. 903/737-7400.

Pascal High School
3001 Forest Park Blvd, Fort
Worth TX 76110-2828. 817/922-
6600.

**Pearl C. Anderson Middle
School**
3400 Garden Ln, Dallas TX
75215-4855. 214/565-6400.

**Pewitt Consolidated
Independent School District**
PO Box 1106, Omaha TX 75571-
1106. 903/884-2136.

Pine Tree Senior High School
PO Box 5878, Longview TX
75608-5878. 903/295-5031.

Plano East Senior High School
3000 Los Rios Blvd, Plano TX
75074-3513. 972/423-9664.

**Plano Independent School
District**
2700 W 15th St, Plano TX 75075-
7524. 972/519-8100.

Plano Senior High School
2200 Independence Pkwy, Plano
TX 75075-3143. 972/519-8500.

**Queen City Independent School
District**
PO Box 128, Queen City TX
75572-0128. 903/796-8256.

Quitman Independent School
1101 E Goode St, Quitman TX
75783-1651. 903/763-4593.

Red Oak High School
PO Box 9000, Red Oak TX
75154-9000. 972/617-3535.

**Reeces Creek Elementary
School**
400 W Stan Schlueter Loop,
Killeen TX 76542-3839. 254/634-
1200.

Richardson High School
1250 W Belt Line Rd, Richardson
TX 75080-5850. 972/301-4700.

**Richardson Independent School
District**
400 S Greenville Ave,
Richardson TX 75081-4181.
972/301-3333.

Richland High School
5201 Holiday Ln, Fort Worth TX
76180-6703. 817/581-5400.

**Rio Vista Independent School
District**
PO Box 369, Rio Vista TX
76093-0369. 817/373-2241.

RL Turner High School
1600 S Josey Ln, Carrollton TX
75006-7431. 972/323-5900.

Robert E. Lee High School
411 Ese Loop 323, Tyler TX
75701. 903/531-3900.

Rockwall High School
901 Yellow Jacket Ln, Rockwall
TX 75087-4839. 972/771-7339.

Roosevelt Independent School
RR 1, Box 402, Lubbock TX
79401-9643. 806/842-3282.

Rosemont Middle School
1501 W Seminary Dr, Fort Worth
TX 76115-1144. 817/922-6650.

Rutherford Elementary School
1607 Sierra Dr, Mesquite TX
75149-6135. 972/285-0151.

**S&S Consolidated Independent
School District**
PO Box 837, Sadler TX 76264-
0837. 903/564-6051.

Sabine Independent School District
RR 1, Box 189, Gladewater TX
75647-9723. 903/984-8564.

Salado High School
PO Box 98, Salado TX 76571-
0098. 254/947-5479.

Sam Houston High School
2000 Sam Houston Dr, Arlington
TX 76014-1660. 817/459-8200.

Seymour Independent School District
409 W Idaho St, Seymour TX
76380-1650. 940/888-3525.

Shallowater Independent School District
PO Box 220, Shallowater TX
79363-0220. 806/832-4531.

Shepton High School
5601 W Parker Rd, Plano TX
75093-7727. 972/519-8900.

Sherman High School
2201 E Lamar St, Sherman TX
75090-6501. 903/893-8101.

Sims Elementary School
PO Box 1117, Mount Pleasant
TX 75456-1117. 903/572-2218.

Solomon Schechter Academy
18011 Hillcrest Rd, Dallas TX
75252-5863. 972/248-3032.

South Garland High School
600 Colonel Dr, Garland TX
75043-2302. 972/494-8424.

South Grand Prairie High School
301 W Warrior Trl, Grand Prairie
TX 75052-5718. 972/264-4731.

South Oak Cliff High School
3601 S Marsalis Ave, Dallas TX
75216-5905. 214/371-4391.

South West High School
4100 Altamesa Blvd, Fort Worth
TX 76133-5420. 817/370-5800.

Stephenville Independent School District
2655 West Overhill Dr,
Stephenville TX 76401-1971.
254/968-7990.

Story Elementary School
PO Box 440, Palestine TX 75802-
0440. 903/731-8015.

Sulphur Springs Independent School District
631 Connally St, Sulphur Springs
TX 75482-2401. 903/885-2153.

Sweetwater High School
1205 Ragland St, Sweetwater TX
79556-2438. 915/235-4371.

Tascosa High School
3921 Westlawn St, Amarillo TX
79102-1795. 806/354-4500.

Temple High School
415 N 31st St, Temple TX 76504-
2426. 254/791-6300.

Texas High School
2112 Kennedy Ln, Texarkana TX
75503-2533. 903/794-3891.

The Hockaday School
11600 Welch Rd, Dallas TX
75229-2913. 214/363-6311.

Thomas Jefferson High School
4001 Walnut Hill Ln, Dallas TX
75229-6239. 214/904-1000.

Thompson Elementary School
5700 Bexar St, Dallas TX 75215-
5205. 214/565-6450.

Tibby Brine Middle School
3333 Sprague Dr, Dallas TX
75233-3123. 214/331-7944.

Travis Elementary School
1001 SE 7th St, Mineral Wells
TX 76067-6103. 940/325-7801.

Travis Elementary School
200 N Shawnee St, Ennis TX
75119-4157. 972/875-7325.

Travis Junior High School
1600 Finley Rd, Irving TX
75062-4349. 972/255-7161.

Trimble Tech Senior High School
1003 W Cannon St, Fort Worth
TX 76104-3030. 817/871-3400.

Trinity Christian Academy
17001 Addison Rd, Dallas TX
75248-1027. 972/931-8325.

Troup High School
PO Box 578, Troup TX 75789-
0578. 903/842-3065.

Troy Independent School District
PO Box 409, Troy TX 76579-
0409. 254/938-2595.

Turning Point Junior High School
4215 Little Rd, Arlington TX
76016-5602. 817/478-9139.

Turning Point Senior High School
5816 West Arkansas Ln,
Arlington TX 76016-1105.
817/492-3000.

Tye Elementary School
PO Box 430, Merkel TX 79536-
0430. 915/692-3809.

Tyler Independent School District
PO Box 2035, Tyler TX 75710-
2035. 903/531-3500.

Union Grove Independent School District
PO Box 1447, Gladewater TX
75647-1447. 903/845-5509.

Ursuline Academy of Dallas
4900 Walnut Hill Ln, Dallas TX
75229-6542. 214/363-6551.

Van Alstyne Independent School District
PO Box 518, Van Alstyne TX
75495-0518. 903/482-6617.

Venture Senior High School
2315 Stonegate St, Arlington TX
76010-3222. 817/801-2050.

Vines High School
1401 Highedge Dr, Plano TX
75075-7520. 972/596-4405.

Vivian Fowler Primary School
PO Box 1117, Mount Pleasant
TX 75456-1117. 903/572-2161.

Waco High School
2020 North 42nd Street, Waco
TX 76710-3012. 254/776-1150.

Waco Independent School District
PO Box 27, Waco TX 76703-
0027. 254/752-8341.

Walter Lois Curtis Middle School
1530 Rivercrest Blvd, Allen TX
75002-4547. 972/727-0340.

Waxahachie High School
1000 North Highway 77,
Waxahachie TX 75165-1754.
972/937-6800.

Waxahachie Independent School District
411 North Gibson Street, Waxahachie TX 75165-3007. 972/923-4631.

Weatherford High School
1007 South Main Street, Weatherford TX 76086-5357. 817/598-2858.

West Mesquite High School
2500 Memorial Boulevard, Mesquite TX 75149-3702. 972/288-5431.

Western Hills High School
3600 Boston Ave, Fort Worth TX 76116-6928. 817/560-5600.

Westwood Elementary School
PO Box 260, Palestine TX 75802-0260. 903/729-1771.

Westwood Junior High School
7630 Arapaho Rd, Dallas TX 75248-4343. 972/448-2800.

White Oak Independent School District
200 South White Oak Rd, White Oak TX 75693-1520. 903/759-4492.

White Settlement School District
PO Box 150187, Fort Worth TX 76108-0187. 817/367-1300.

Whiteface High School
PO Box 67, Whiteface TX 79379-0067. 806/287-1104.

Whitley Road Elementary School
7600 Whitley Rd, Fort Worth TX 76148-1211. 817/281-9542.

Whitney High School
PO Box 518, Whitney TX 76692-0518. 254/694-3457.

Wichita Falls School District
4611 Cypress Ave, Wichita Falls TX 76310-2540. 940/720-3000.

Wilmer Hutchins High School
5520 Langdon Rd, Dallas TX 75241-7148. 972/225-6143.

Wilmer Hutchins Independent School District
3820 E Illinois Ave, Dallas TX 75216-4140. 214/376-7311.

Wilson Junior High School
4402 31st St, Lubbock TX 79410-2404. 806/766-0799.

Winters Independent School
PO Box 125, Winters TX 79567-0125. 915/754-5574.

Woodrow Wilson High School
100 South Glasgow Drive, Dallas TX 75214-4518. 214/841-5100.

WT White High School
4505 Ridgeside Dr, Dallas TX 75244-7524. 972/308-8915.

WW Samuell High School
8928 Palisade Dr, Dallas TX 75217-2039. 214/309-7040.

Wylie High School
PO Box 490, Wylie TX 75098-0490. 972/442-2218.

Young Junior High School
3200 Woodside Dr, Arlington TX 76016-2359. 817/457-7300.

JUNIOR COLLEGES AND TECHNICAL INSTITUTES

Cedar Valley College
3030 North Dallas Avenue, Lancaster TX 75134-3705. 214/372-8250.

El Centro College
4343 Highway 67, Mesquite TX 75150-2018. 972/860-7709.

Frank Phillips College
PO Box 5118, Borger TX 79008-5118. 806/274-5311.

Grayson County Junior High School
6101 Grayson Dr, Denison TX 75020-8238. 903/465-6030.

Hill College
PO Box 619, Hillsboro TX 76645-0619. 254/582-2555.

Institute of Applied Science
PO Box 13078, Denton TX 76203-6078. 940/565-2694.

McLennan Community College
1400 College Dr, Waco TX 76708-1402. 254/299-8000.

Navarro College
1900 John Arden Drive, Waxahachie TX 75165-5220. 972/937-7612.

Navarro College
3200 West 7th Avenue, Corsicana TX 75110-4818. 903/874-6501.

North Central Texas College
1525 West California St, Gainesville TX 76240-4636. 940/668-7731.

North Central Texas College
601 East Hickory St, Ste B, Denton TX 76205-4305. 940/381-1142.

North East Texas Community College
PO Box 1307, Mount Pleasant TX 75456-9991. 903/572-1911.

Panola College
1109 West Panola Street, Carthage TX 75633-2341. 903/693-2000.

Paris Junior College
2400 Clarksville St, Paris TX 75460-6258. 903/785-7661.

TCJC
2100 TCJC Pkwy, Arlington TX 76018-3144. 817/467-1424.

Texarkana College
2500 N Robison Rd, Texarkana TX 75599-0002. 903/838-4541.

Texas State Technical College
PO Box 1269, Marshall TX 75671-1269. 903/935-1010.

Texas Tech University
1400 Wallace Blvd, Amarillo TX 79106-1708. 806/354-5403.

Trinity Valley Community College
500 S Prairieville St, Athens TX 75751-2734. 903/675-6200.

Texas State Technical College
3801 Campus Dr, Waco TX 76705-1607. 254/799-3611.

Tyler Junior College
PO Box 9020, Tyler TX 75711-9020. 903/510-2200.

Weatherford College
308 E Park Ave, Weatherford TX 76086-5618. 817/594-5471.

Western Texas College
6200 College Ave, Snyder TX 79549-6105. 915/573-8511.

Wilbarger County Junior College
4400 College Dr, Vernon TX 76384-4005. 940/552-6291.

MISC. SCHOOLS AND EDUCATIONAL SERVICES

Education Service Center
3001 North Freeway, Fort Worth TX 76106-6526. 817/625-5311.

Education Service Center
PO Box 23409, Waco TX 76702-3409. 254/666-0707.

Education Service Center
PO Box 831300, Richardson TX 75083-1300. 972/231-6301.

Education Service Center
PO Box 30600, Amarillo TX 79120-0600. 806/376-5521.

Microsoft University
5080 Spectrum Dr, Ste 115, Dallas TX 75248-4648. 972/458-7237.

Rio Brazos Education Co-op
PO Box 1970, Waco TX 76703-1970. 254/756-1974.

Sylvan Learning Center
5016 W Waco Dr, Waco TX 76710-7022. 254/772-7373.

Texas Transportation Institute
9441 Lyndon B. Johnson Fwy, Dallas TX 75243-4545. 972/994-0433.

VOCATIONAL SCHOOLS

American Airlines Flight Academy
PO Box 619617, Dallas TX 75261-9617. 817/967-5123.

Simuflite Training International
PO Box 619119, Dallas TX 75261-9119. 972/456-8000.

TSTI-Sweetwater
300 College Dr, Sweetwater TX 79556-4108. 915/235-7300.

For more information on career opportunities in educational services:

Associations

AMERICAN ASSOCIATION FOR HIGHER EDUCATION
One DuPont Circle, Suite 360, Washington DC 20036. 202/293-6440. World Wide Web address: http://www.aahe.org.

AMERICAN ASSOCIATION OF SCHOOL ADMINISTRATORS
1801 North Moore Street, Arlington VA 22209-1813. 703/528-0700. Fax: 703/841-1543. World Wide Web address: http://www.aasa.org. An organization of school system leaders. Membership includes a national conference on education; programs and seminars; *The School Administrator*, a monthly magazine; *Leadership News*, a bi-monthly newspaper; *The AASA Professor*, a quarterly publication; and a catalog of other publications and audiovisuals.

AMERICAN FEDERATION OF TEACHERS
555 New Jersey Avenue NW, Washington DC 20001. 202/879-4400. World Wide Web address: http://www.aft.org.

COLLEGE AND UNIVERSITY PERSONNEL ASSOCIATION
1233 20th Street NW, Suite 301, Washington DC 20036. 202/429-0311. World Wide Web address: http://www.cupa.org. Membership required.

NATIONAL ASSOCIATION OF BIOLOGY TEACHERS
11250 Roger Bacon Drive, Suite 19, Reston VA 20190-5202. 703/471-1134. Toll-free phone: 800/406-0775. Fax: 703/435-5582. E-mail address: nabter@aol.com. World Wide Web address: http://www.nabt.org. A professional organization for biology and life science educators.

NATIONAL ASSOCIATION OF COLLEGE ADMISSION COUNSELORS
1631 Prince Street, Alexandria VA 22314. 703/836-2222. World Wide Web address: http://www.nacac.com. An education association of secondary school counselors, college and university admission officers, and related individuals who work with students as they make the transition from high school to post-secondary education.

NATIONAL ASSOCIATION OF COLLEGE AND UNIVERSITY BUSINESS OFFICERS
2501 M Street NW, Suite 400, Washington DC 20037-1308. 202/861-2500. World Wide Web address: http://www.nacubo.org. An association for those involved in the financial administration and management of higher education. Membership required.

NATIONAL SCIENCE TEACHERS ASSOCIATION
1840 Wilson Boulevard, Arlington VA 22201-3000. 703/243-7100. World Wide Web address: http://www.nsta.org. A professional organization committed to the improvement of science education at all levels, preschool through college. Publishes five journals, a newspaper, and a number of special publications, and conducts national and regional conventions.

Books

HOW TO GET A JOB IN EDUCATION
Adams Media Corporation, 260 Center Street, Holbrook MA 02343. 781/767-8100. World Wide Web address: http://www.adamsmedia.com.

Directories

WASHINGTON EDUCATION ASSOCIATION DIRECTORY
Council for Advancement and Support of Education, 11 DuPont Circle, Suite 400, Washington DC 20036. 202/328-5900. World Wide Web address: http://www.case.org.

Online Services

ACADEMIC EMPLOYMENT NETWORK
http://www.academploy.com. This site offers

information for the educational professional. It allows you to search for positions using keywords or location. It also has information on other sites of interest, educational products, certification requirements by state, and relocation services.

CHRONICLE OF HIGHER EDUCATION
http://www.chronicle.merit.edu/.ads/.links.html. This Website provides job listings from the weekly published newspaper *The Chronicle of Higher Education*. Besides featuring articles from the paper, this site also offers employment opportunities. You can search for information by geographic location, type of position, and teaching fields.

EDUCATION & INSTRUCTION JOBS
http://csueb.sfsu.edu/jobs/educationjobs.html. Offers a long list of links to other sites around the country that provide job openings and information for jobseekers looking in education. This site is part of the California State University Employment Board.

EDUCATION FORUM
Go: Edforum. This CompuServe discussion group is open to educators of all levels.

JOBWEB SCHOOL DISTRICTS SEARCH
http://www.jobweb.org/search/schools/. Provides a search engine for school districts across the country. The site is run by the National Association of Colleges and Employers and it also provides information on colleges and career fairs.

THE TEACHER'S LOUNGE
Keyword: teacher's lounge. An America Online discussion group for teachers of kindergarten through the twelfth grade.

VISUAL NATION ARTS JOBS LINKS
http://fly.hiwaay.net/%7Edrewyor/art_job.html. Provides links to other sites that post academic and arts job openings and information.

ELECTRONIC/INDUSTRIAL ELECTRICAL EQUIPMENT

Intense international competition is prompting the U.S. electronics industry to become more globalized. Companies are being forced to seek less expensive materials and labor. Overall, employment in the industry has remained stable at about 551,000 since 1994. Foreign demand for U.S. electronic component exports is expected to reach $48 billion by the end of 1998, a 15.9 percent increase over 1997. Semiconductor manufacturing needs are expected to rise by 18 percent in North America in 1998 and to support this growth the industry continues to invest in new technology and equipment.

U.S. Industry and Trade Outlook 1998 projects the best opportunities for jobseekers to be in the production of analog and memory ICs, microcomponents, and discrete semiconductors. Industry observers worldwide predict that semiconductor markets will grow at an approximate rate of 15 percent annually through 2005. Sales of printed circuit boards should see an increase of 7 percent in 1998. The outlook for the switchgear sector is highly favorable. U.S. electric utilities are expected to spend more than $300 million to automate power substations by 2000; and shipments of switchgear are forecasted to grow at an average rate of 4 to 5 percent through 2000.

AMTECH CORPORATION
19111 Dallas Parkway, Suite 300, Dallas TX 75287. 972/733-6600. **Fax:** 972/733-6699. **Contact:** Michelle Ramacciotti, Human Resources Manager. **World Wide Web address:** http://www.amtech.com. **Description:** Manufactures electronic identification equipment. **Common positions include:** Computer Programmer; Editor; Electrical/Electronics Engineer; Software Engineer; Technical Writer/Editor. **Educational backgrounds include:** Business Administration; Engineering; Marketing. **Benefits:** 401(k); Dental Insurance; Life Insurance. **Corporate headquarters location:** This Location. **Operations at this facility include:** Regional Headquarters. **Listed on:** NASDAQ. **Number of employees at this location:** 300.

ARROW SCHWEBER
3220 Commander Drive, Carrollton TX 75006. 972/380-6464. **Contact:** Human Resources. **World Wide Web address:** http://www.arrow.com. **Description:** Arrow Schweber is a distributor of electronics components, systems, and related items through a network in North America, Europe, and Asia. The company operates 150 marketing facilities, 10 primary distribution centers, and over 4,000 remote computer terminals that supply components to about 125,000 original equipment manufacturers and commercial customers. Semiconductors account for more than half of Arrow Schweber's sales. The company has interests in Spoerle Electronic, one of the largest electronics distributors in Germany, and in 1993, acquired several distributing companies including CCI Electronique (France), Components Agent Ltd. (Asia), The ATD Group (Spain and Portugal), Microprocessor & Memory Distribution Limited (U.K.), and Zeus Components (U.S.). **Other U.S. locations:** Melville NY.

AVNET, INC.
11333 Pagemill Road, Dallas TX 75243. 214/343-5000. **Toll-free phone:** 800/459-1225. **Fax:** 214/343-5054. **Contact:** Human Resources. **World Wide Web address:** http://www.avnet.com. **Description:** This location is engaged in the distribution of company-manufactured electronics products. Overall, Avnet, Inc. is one of the nation's largest distributors of electronic components and computer products for industrial and military customers. The company also produces and

distributes electronic, electrical, and video communications products. **Common positions include:** Account Manager; Accountant/Auditor; Bookkeeper; Computer Programmer; Human Resources Manager; Inventory Control Specialist; Manufacturer's/Wholesaler's Sales Rep.; Marketing Specialist; Services Sales Representative; Stock Clerk; Warehouse/Distribution Worker. **Educational backgrounds include:** Accounting; Business Administration; Engineering; Finance; Liberal Arts; Marketing. **Benefits:** 401(k); Dental Insurance; Employee Discounts; Life Insurance; Medical Insurance; Pension Plan; Savings Plan; Tuition Assistance. **Corporate headquarters location:** Chandler AZ. **Operations at this facility include:** Divisional Headquarters. **Listed on:** American Stock Exchange; New York Stock Exchange.

AVO INTERNATIONAL
4271 Bronze Way, Dallas TX 75237. 214/333-3201. **Contact:** Manager of Human Resources. **World Wide Web address:** http://www.avointl.com. **Description:** Manufactures test equipment and measurement instruments for electric power applications. **Corporate headquarters location:** This Location. **Parent company:** TBG.

BANCTEC, INC.
2701 East Grauwyler Road, Irving TX 75061. 972/579-6000. **Fax:** 972/579-6877. **Recorded jobline:** 972/579-5888. **Contact:** Marylou Caro, Human Resources Manager. **World Wide Web address:** http://www.banctec.com. **Description:** Designs, manufactures, markets, and services information-processing systems which are used for data capture, document processing, and the management of information. Principal purchasers of these systems include major commercial banks, utilities, insurance firms, retail companies, and other businesses handling a high volume of machine-readable documents. **Common positions include:** Accountant/Auditor; Blue-Collar Worker Supervisor; Branch Manager; Budget Analyst; Buyer; Clerical Supervisor; Computer Programmer; Customer Service Representative; Draftsperson; Electrical/Electronics Engineer; Electrician; Financial Analyst; General Manager; Human Resources Manager; Management Analyst/Consultant; Mechanical Engineer; Purchasing Agent/Manager; Quality Control Supervisor; Software Engineer; Systems Analyst; Technical Writer/Editor. **Educational backgrounds include:** Accounting; Business Administration; Computer Science; Engineering; Marketing; Mathematics. **Benefits:** 401(k); Dental Insurance; Disability Coverage; Employee Discounts; Life Insurance; Medical Insurance; Spending Account; Tuition Assistance. **Corporate headquarters location:** Dallas TX. **Operations at this facility include:** Administration; Divisional Headquarters; Manufacturing; Research and Development; Sales; Service. **Listed on:** New York Stock Exchange.

BANCTEC, INC.
4435 Spring Valley Road, Dallas TX 75244. 972/450-7700. **Contact:** Human Resources Department. **World Wide Web address:** http://www.banctec.com. **Description:** Designs, manufactures, markets, and services information-processing systems which are used for data capture, document processing, and the management of information. **Common positions include:** Manufacturing Engineer. **Corporate headquarters location:** This Location.

COLLMER SEMICONDUCTOR, INC.
14368 Proton Road, Dallas TX 75244. 972/233-1589. **Contact:** Human Resources. **World Wide Web address:** http://www.fujielectric.com. **Description:** A manufacturer and distributor of semiconductors.

COOPER INDUSTRIES
1901 Farmers Avenue, Amarillo TX 79118. **Contact:** Human Resources. **World Wide Web address:** http://www.cooperlighting.com. **Description:** This location manufactures electrical conduit fittings. Overall, the company is engaged in three primary areas of manufacturing: tools and hardware, electrical and electronic products, and automotive products. **Other U.S. locations:** Nationwide.

DSC COMMUNICATIONS CORPORATION
1000 Coit Road, Mail Stop 210, Plano TX 75075-5813. 972/519-3000. **Contact:** Human Resources. **World Wide Web address:** http://www.dsccc.com. **Description:** Designs, manufactures, and markets electronic components for the telecommunications industry. Products

include digital switching, transmission, and private network system components. **Corporate headquarters location:** This Location. **Listed on:** NASDAQ.

DALLAS SEMICONDUCTOR
4401 South Beltwood Parkway, Dallas TX 75244-3292. 972/371-4000. **Contact:** Human Resources. **World Wide Web address:** http://www.dalsemi.com. **Description:** Manufactures semiconductors. **Common positions include:** Electrical/Electronics Engineer; Mechanical Engineer; Software Engineer. **Educational backgrounds include:** Computer Science; Engineering; Physics. **Benefits:** 401(k); Dental Insurance; Disability Coverage; Life Insurance; Medical Insurance; Profit Sharing; Tuition Assistance. **Corporate headquarters location:** This Location. **Operations at this facility include:** Administration; Manufacturing; Research and Development; Sales; Service. **Listed on:** New York Stock Exchange. **Number of employees at this location:** 1,250.

FAS TECHNOLOGIES
10480 Markison Road, Dallas TX 75238. 214/553-9991. **Fax:** 214/553-9919. **Contact:** Human Resources Manager. **E-mail address:** personnel@fas.com. **World Wide Web address:** http://www.fas.com. **Description:** Manufactures semiconductor processing equipment. Founded in 1988. **Common positions include:** Administrative Assistant; Buyer; Customer Service Representative; Draftsperson; Electrical/Electronics Engineer; Food Scientist/Technologist; Mechanical Engineer; Software Engineer; Technical Writer/Editor. **Educational backgrounds include:** Engineering. **Benefits:** Dental Insurance; Employee Discounts; Life Insurance; Medical Insurance; Tuition Assistance. **Corporate headquarters location:** This Location. **International locations:** Japan. **Subsidiaries include:** FAS-Asia, Ltd. **Listed on:** Privately held.

HONEYWELL MICROSWITCH
OPTOELECTRONICS DIVISION
830 East Arapaho Road, Richardson TX 75081. 972/470-4271. **Contact:** Jim Francis, Personnel Director. **World Wide Web address:** http://www.honeywell.com. **Description:** This location manufactures several different optoelectronics and fiberoptic systems and components, including light-emitting and sensing devices/systems; and optical switches and isolators applicable to data transmission and automation of the computer industry and the military worldwide. **Common positions include:** Accountant/Auditor; Buyer; Computer Programmer; Customer Service Representative; Draftsperson; Electrical/Electronics Engineer; Human Resources Manager; Industrial Engineer; Mechanical Engineer; Operations/Production Manager; Quality Control Supervisor. **Educational backgrounds include:** Accounting; Engineering; Physics. **Benefits:** Dental Insurance; Disability Coverage; Employee Discounts; Life Insurance; Medical Insurance; Pension Plan; Savings Plan; Tuition Assistance. **Corporate headquarters location:** Minneapolis MN. **Parent company:** Honeywell Inc. is an international company engaged in the research and development, manufacture, and sale of advanced technology products and services in satellite technology. **Operations at this facility include:** Administration; Divisional Headquarters; Manufacturing; Research and Development; Sales. **Listed on:** New York Stock Exchange.

HOWELL INSTRUMENTS, INC.
P.O. Box 985001, Fort Worth TX 76185-5001. 817/336-7411x 223. **Physical address:** 3479 West Vickery Boulevard, Fort Worth TX 76107. **Fax:** 817/336-7874. **Contact:** Corene Cloud, Personnel Manager. **E-mail address:** ccloud@howellinst.com. **World Wide Web address:** http://www.howellinst.com. **Description:** Manufactures turbine engine instrumentation and test equipment for military and commercial applications. **NOTE:** Entry-level positions are offered. **Common positions include:** Computer Programmer; Sales Engineer; Software Engineer. **Educational backgrounds include:** Computer Science; Engineering. **Benefits:** Dental Insurance; Disability Coverage; Life Insurance; Mass Transit Available; Medical Insurance; Pension Plan; Profit Sharing. **Corporate headquarters location:** This Location. **Listed on:** Privately held. **CEO:** John Howell. **Facilities manager:** H.G. White. **Annual sales/revenues:** $11 - $20 million. **Number of projected hires for 1998 - 1999 at this location:** 4.

LITTON ELECTRO-OPTICAL SYSTEMS
3414 Herrmann Drive, Garland TX 75041. 972/840-5600. **Contact:** Human Resources. **Description:** Manufactures a diverse line of military equipment and electro-optical systems,

including guided-missile launchers, optical sighting and fire control equipment, laser range finders, night-vision sights, and systems for weapons and high-intensity searchlights. **NOTE:** Entry-level positions and second and third shifts are offered. **Common positions include:** Accountant/Auditor; Administrator; Blue-Collar Worker Supervisor; Buyer; Computer Programmer; Department Manager; Draftsperson; Electrical/Electronics Engineer; Financial Analyst; Human Resources Manager; Industrial Engineer; Mechanical Engineer; Operations/Production Manager; Physicist; Purchasing Agent/Manager; Quality Control Supervisor; Systems Analyst. **Educational backgrounds include:** Accounting; Business Administration; Chemistry; Computer Science; Engineering; Marketing; Physics. **Benefits:** 401(k); Dental Insurance; Disability Coverage; Life Insurance; Medical Insurance; Pension Plan; Stock Option; Tuition Assistance. **Other U.S. locations:** Tempe AZ. **Parent company:** Litton Industries. **Operations at this facility include:** Administration; Manufacturing; Research and Development; Sales. **Listed on:** New York Stock Exchange. **Number of employees at this location:** 550.

OPTEK TECHNOLOGY INC.

1215 West Crosby Road, Carrollton TX 75006. 972/323-2200. **Contact:** Personnel Manager. **World Wide Web address:** http://www.optekinc.com. **Description:** Produces fiber optic, log-wavelength, light-emitting diodes; hybrid components; galium arsenide and galium aluminum arsenide circuits; and related products. **Common positions include:** Accountant/Auditor; Buyer; Ceramics Engineer; Chemical Engineer; Computer Programmer; Credit Manager; Customer Service Representative; Draftsperson; Electrical/Electronics Engineer; Financial Analyst; Human Resources Manager; Metallurgical Engineer; Purchasing Agent/Manager; Quality Control Supervisor; Technical Writer/Editor. **Educational backgrounds include:** Accounting; Chemistry; Computer Science; Engineering; Finance; Physics. **Benefits:** 401(k); Disability Coverage; Life Insurance; Medical Insurance; Tuition Assistance.

RAYTHEON E-SYSTEMS

P.O. Box 831359, Richardson TX 75083-1359. 972/470-2000. **Toll-free phone:** 800/933-5359. **Fax:** 972/301-5991. **Contact:** Lonnie Duke, Employment Manager. **E-mail address:** lonnie@koyote.com. **World Wide Web address:** http://www.rayjobs.com. **Description:** Engaged in the design, manufacture, and installation of state-of-the-art communications and integrated command-and-control systems for military and industrial customers worldwide. **NOTE:** The company offers entry-level positions. In January 1997, Raytheon purchased Hughes Aircraft from General Motors. **Common positions include:** Electrical/Electronics Engineer; Software Engineer; Technical Writer/Editor; Telecommunications Manager. **Benefits:** 401(k); Car Lease Plan; Car Purchase Plan; Dental Insurance; Disability Coverage; Employee Discounts; Life Insurance; Medical Insurance; Pension Plan; Savings Plan. **Special programs:** Internships. **Parent company:** Raytheon. **Operations at this facility include:** Administration; Divisional Headquarters; Manufacturing; Research and Development; Sales. **Listed on:** New York Stock Exchange. **Number of employees at this location:** 1,000. **Number of employees nationwide:** 72,000.

RAYTHEON SYSTEMS, INC.

P.O. Box 6056, Greenville TX 75403-6056. 903/455-3450. **Contact:** Human Resources. **Description:** Raytheon Systems, Inc. manufactures electronic equipment for the military and commercial electronics industries. Military products include reconnaissance and surveillance equipment; command, control, and communications equipment; navigation and control systems; and aircraft maintenance and navigation systems. Non-military products include mass media storage equipment, medical imaging devices, and data handling products. **Listed on:** New York Stock Exchange.

REXEL

P.O. Box 1085, Addison TX 75001. 972/387-3600. **Contact:** Human Resources. **World Wide Web address:** http://www.rexel.com. **Description:** A wholesaler of electrical products. **Common positions include:** Accountant/Auditor; Administrator; Credit Manager; Department Manager; Financial Analyst; Human Resources Manager; Management Trainee; Marketing Specialist; Operations/Production Manager. **Educational backgrounds include:** Accounting; Business Administration; Communications; Liberal Arts; Marketing. **Benefits:** Dental Insurance; Disability Coverage; Employee Discounts; Life Insurance; Medical Insurance; Pension Plan; Profit Sharing;

Savings Plan; Tuition Assistance. **Corporate headquarters location:** This Location. **Parent company:** BTR. **Operations at this facility include:** Administration.

ROBINSON NUGENT DALLAS, INC.

2640 Tarna Drive, Dallas TX 75229. 972/241-1738. **Contact:** Human Resources. **World Wide Web address:** http://www.robinsonnugent.com. **Description:** Manufactures electronic connectors. **Educational backgrounds include:** Chemistry; Engineering. **Benefits:** 401(k); Dental Insurance; Disability Coverage; Life Insurance; Medical Insurance; Pension Plan; Tuition Assistance. **Corporate headquarters location:** New Albany IN. **Operations at this facility include:** Manufacturing. **Listed on:** NASDAQ. **Number of employees at this location:** 180.

ROCHESTER GAUGES, INC.

P.O. Box 29242, Dallas TX 75229. 972/241-2161. **Contact:** Barbara Nitishin, Corporate Human Resources Generalist. **Description:** A manufacturer of gauges, thermometers, and measuring devices. **NOTE:** Entry-level positions are offered. **Common positions include:** Blue-Collar Worker Supervisor; Customer Service Representative; Manufacturer's/Wholesaler's Sales Rep.; Mechanical Engineer; MIS Specialist. **Educational backgrounds include:** Engineering. **Benefits:** 401(k); Dental Insurance; Disability Coverage; Life Insurance; Mass Transit Available; Medical Insurance; Pension Plan; Savings Plan; Tuition Assistance. **Corporate headquarters location:** This Location. **Operations at this facility include:** Manufacturing. **Listed on:** Privately held. **Annual sales/revenues:** $21 - $50 million. **Number of employees at this location:** 300. **Number of employees nationwide:** 500.

ROCKWELL INTERNATIONAL CORPORATION

P.O. Box 833807, Richardson TX 75083-3807. 972/705-1898. **Recorded jobline:** 972/705-1870. **Contact:** Human Resources. **World Wide Web address:** http://www.rockwell.com. **Description:** This location manufactures electronic equipment. Overall, Rockwell International provides products for the printing, military, automotive, and aerospace industries through its electronics, automotive, and graphics divisions. Products include military and commercial communication equipment, guidance systems, electronics, components for automobiles, and printing presses. A major client of Rockwell is the U.S. government. **Common positions include:** Electrical/Electronics Engineer; Mechanical Engineer; Software Engineer. **Educational backgrounds include:** Engineering. **Benefits:** Dental Insurance; Disability Coverage; Life Insurance; Medical Insurance; Pension Plan; Savings Plan; Tuition Assistance. **Corporate headquarters location:** Seal Beach CA. **Other U.S. locations:** Nationwide. **Operations at this facility include:** Administration; Divisional Headquarters; Manufacturing; Research and Development. **Listed on:** New York Stock Exchange. **Number of employees at this location:** 1,200.

SGS-THOMSON MICROELECTRONICS

1310 Electronics Drive, Carrollton TX 75006. 972/466-6000. **Contact:** Human Resources Department. **Description:** This location manufactures microchips. Overall, SGS-THOMSON Microelectronics designs, develops, manufactures, and markets a broad range of semiconductor integrated circuits and discrete devices used in a variety of microelectronic applications. These applications include telecommunications systems, computer systems, consumer products, automotive products, and industrial automation and control systems. **Corporate headquarters location:** Montgomeryville PA. **Listed on:** New York Stock Exchange. **Stock exchange symbol:** STM.

TECCOR ELECTRONICS INC.

1801 Hurd Drive, Irving TX 75038. 972/580-1515. **Contact:** Human Resources Department. **Description:** Manufactures electronic power controls and a wide variety of related equipment. A second plant at this location manufactures semiconductor power devices, solid state relays, and a variety of silicon chips and rectifiers. Markets for these products include manufacturers of lighting fixtures, appliances, heating and air conditioning equipment, and power hand tools. **Common positions include:** Accountant/Auditor; Administrator; Blue-Collar Worker Supervisor; Buyer; Ceramics Engineer; Chemical Engineer; Chemist; Computer Programmer; Customer Service Representative; Department Manager; Draftsperson; Electrical/Electronics Engineer; Industrial Engineer; Purchasing Agent/Manager; Quality Control Supervisor; Sales Executive; Systems

Analyst. **Educational backgrounds include:** Accounting; Business Administration; Chemistry; Engineering; Marketing. **Benefits:** Dental Insurance; Disability Coverage; Employee Discounts; Life Insurance; Medical Insurance; Pension Plan; Profit Sharing; Savings Plan; Tuition Assistance. **Corporate headquarters location:** This Location. **Listed on:** New York Stock Exchange.

TELEDYNE BROWN ENGINEERING
GEOTECH INSTRUMENTS
10755 Sanden Drive, Dallas TX 75238. 214/221-0000. **Contact:** Human Resources. **World Wide Web address:** http://www.tbe.com. **Description:** Manufactures earthquake monitoring equipment.

TEXAS INSTRUMENTS, INC.
P.O. Box 650311, Mail Station 3955, Dallas TX 75265. 972/995-2000. **Contact:** Human Resources. **World Wide Web address:** http://www.ti.com. **Description:** Engaged in the design, development, and manufacture of semiconductor memories, microprocessors, large-scale integrated circuits; electronic calculators; minicomputers; microcomputers; electronic data terminals; clad metal systems; opto-electronics, airborne, and ground-based radar systems; and electro-optics equipment. **Common positions include:** Computer Programmer; Electrical/Electronics Engineer; Industrial Engineer; Mechanical Engineer; Systems Analyst. **Educational backgrounds include:** Computer Science; Engineering. **Benefits:** Dental Insurance; Disability Coverage; Life Insurance; Medical Insurance; Pension Plan; Profit Sharing; Savings Plan; Tuition Assistance. **Corporate headquarters location:** This Location. **Operations at this facility include:** Divisional Headquarters; Research and Development. **Listed on:** New York Stock Exchange. **Number of employees at this location:** 25,000. **Number of employees nationwide:** 56,000.

THERMALLOY INC.
P.O. Box 810839, Dallas TX 75381-0839. 972/243-4321. **Contact:** Personnel. **World Wide Web address:** http://www.thermalloy.com. **Description:** Produces a variety of electronics components and systems, plastics, and machined products, including ceramic electrical products, electronic semiconductor equipment, semiconductor insulating covers, screw machine products, plastic injected molding products for electronics use, and printed circuit board guides. **Corporate headquarters location:** This Location.

ULTRAK INC.
1301 Waters Ridge Drive, Lewisville TX 75057. 972/353-6500. **Contact:** Human Resources. **World Wide Web address:** http://www.ultrak.com. **Description:** Manufactures security surveillance equipment.

ZIMMERMAN SIGN COMPANY
9846 Highway 31 East, Tyler TX 75705. 903/535-7400. **Contact:** Human Resources. **Description:** An electric sign manufacturer. **Common positions include:** Accountant/Auditor; Blue-Collar Worker Supervisor; Budget Analyst; Buyer; Cost Estimator; Customer Service Representative; Designer; Draftsperson; Human Resources Manager; Purchasing Agent/Manager; Quality Control Supervisor; Systems Analyst. **Educational backgrounds include:** Accounting; Art/Design; Business Administration; Computer Science; Engineering; Marketing. **Benefits:** Disability Coverage; Life Insurance; Medical Insurance. **Corporate headquarters location:** This Location. **Number of employees at this location:** 50. **Number of employees nationwide:** 400.

Note: Because addresses and telephone numbers of smaller companies can change rapidly, we recommend you call each company to verify the information below before inquiring about job opportunities. Mass mailings are not recommended.

Additional small employers:

ELECTRIC LIGHTING AND WIRING EQUIPMENT

Appleton Electric Co.
2150 W South Loop, Stephenville TX 76401-3922. 254/968-6071.

Corbett Lighting Inc.
2727 Northaven Rd, Dallas TX 75229-2324. 972/241-8800.

Crouse-Hinds Co.
RR 5, Box 6, Amarillo TX 79118-9805. 806/358-4585.

Genlyte Controls
2413 S Shiloh Rd, Garland TX
75041-1344. 972/840-1640.

Golden Eagle Systems Inc.
1201 W Crosby Rd, Carrollton
TX 75006-6905. 972/323-3400.

Philips Lighting Co.
3010 Clarksville St, Paris TX
75460-7913. 903/784-7453.

**ELECTRICAL ENGINE
EQUIPMENT**

Ennis Automotive Inc.
PO Box 400, Ennis TX 75120-
0400. 972/878-3896.

Federal Parts Corporation
9249 King James Dr, Dallas TX
75247-3603. 214/631-5942.

Unison Industries LP
2155 Eagle Pkwy, Fort Worth TX
76177-2311. 817/264-3100.

**ELECTRICAL EQUIPMENT
WHOLESALE**

Anixter Inc.
1601 Waters Ridge Dr,
Lewisville TX 75057-6013.
972/353-7000.

Brandon & Clark Inc.
PO Box 3159, Lubbock TX
79452-3159. 806/747-3861.

Grinnell Corporation
2425 Pearson Dr, Dallas TX
75214-3772. 972/721-9129.

ITEL
1620 W Crosby Rd, Ste 115,
Carrollton TX 75006-6664.
972/446-7337.

Simplex Time Recorder
8300 Esters Blvd, Ste 950, Irving
TX 75063-2233. 972/621-1900.

Texas Instruments Park Center
7800 Banner Dr, Dallas TX
75251-1602. 972/917-7622.

WW Grainger Inc.
3001 E Pioneer Pkwy, Arlington
TX 76010-5309. 817/640-1810.

**ELECTRICAL EQUIPMENT,
MACHINERY, AND
SUPPLIES**

Caddx Controls Inc.
1420 N Main St, Gladewater TX
75647-4518. 903/845-6941.

Hughes Training Inc.
PO Box 6171, Arlington TX
76005-6171. 817/619-2000.

Texas Instruments Inc.
PO Box 801, McKinney TX
75070-0801. 972/542-3301.

Tocom Inc.
1330 Capital Pkwy, Carrollton
TX 75006-3647. 972/323-4000.

**ELECTRICAL INDUSTRIAL
APPARATUS**

AMX Corporation
11995 Forestgate Dr, Dallas TX
75243-5412. 972/644-3048.

Crouzet Corporation
3237 Commander Dr, Carrollton
TX 75006-2506. 972/250-1647.

Mantek
PO Box 660196, Dallas TX
75266-0196. 972/438-0361.

Prescolite Controls
PO Box 173, Carrollton TX
75006. 972/242-6581.

Square D Company
1111 Regal Row, Dallas TX
75247-3611. 214/630-4521.

**ELECTRONIC
COMPONENTS AND
ACCESSORIES**

CompuRoute Incorporated
10365 Sanden Dr, Dallas TX
75238-2440. 214/340-0543.

Cuplex Inc.
1140 N Peak St, Dallas TX
75204-6709. 214/503-9988.

Cuplex Inc.
1500 Highway 66, Garland TX
75040-6727. 972/276-0333.

Flextronics Technologies
1299 Commerce Dr, Richardson
TX 75081-2406. 972/680-6520.

H-R Industries Inc.
1302 E Collins Blvd, Richardson
TX 75081-2403. 972/301-6600.

H-R Industries Inc.
2430 Albert Broadfoot St,
Bonham TX 75418-2020.
903/640-1200.

**McDonald Technologies
International**
2220 W Peter Smith St, Fort

Worth TX 76102-4316. 817/332-
3672.

MTI
2434 McIver Ln, Carrollton TX
75006-6511. 972/243-6767.

Sanmina Corporation
1250 American Pkwy,
Richardson TX 75081-2931.
972/669-1125.

STB Systems Inc.
PO Box 850957, Richardson TX
75085-0957. 972/234-8750.

Texas Instruments Inc.
PO Box 405, Lewisville TX
75067-0405. 972/462-5749.

**ELECTRONIC PARTS AND
EQUIPMENT WHOLESALE**

Airtech Wireless Inc.
1420 Zalwood Parkway, Ste 200,
Carrollton TX 75006. 972/247-
6611.

Allied Electronics Inc.
PO Box 1544, Fort Worth TX
76101-1544. 817/595-3500.

Bearcom Operating LP
11545 Pagemill Rd, Dallas TX
75243-5508. 972/680-9750.

Ericsson Inc.
1010 East Arapaho Rd,
Richardson TX 75081-2302.
972/669-9900.

Ericsson Inc.
701 N Glenville Dr, Bldg H,
Richardson TX 75081-2835.
972/907-7904.

GTE Supply
PO Box 169001, Irving TX
75038. 972/751-4528.

Jerrold General Instrument
1330 Capital Pkwy, Carrollton
TX 75006-3647. 972/248-7931.

Motorola Communications
1701 Valley View Lane, Dallas
TX 75234-9004. 972/888-6700.

Mouser Corporation
PO Box 714, Mansfield TX
76063-0714. 817/483-0165.

National Auto Cellular
1730 Briercroft Court, Carrollton
TX 75006-6400. 972/323-0600.

Samsung Telecom America
1130 E Arapaho Rd, Richardson
TX 75081-2328. 972/761-7000.

Source Inc.
14060 Proton Rd, Dallas TX
75244-3601. 972/450-2600.

Sterling Electronics Corp.
2200 William D. Tate Ave,
Grapevine TX 76051-3978.
817/949-1600.

Syncomm
4011 W Plano Pkwy, Ste 103,
Plano TX 75093. 972/867-5655.

TTI Inc.
2441 Northeast Pkwy, Fort Worth
TX 76106-1816. 817/740-9000.

Uniden America Corporation
4700 Amon Carter Blvd, Fort
Worth TX 76155. 817/858-3300.

Verifone Inc.
14881 Quorum Dr, Ste 800,
Dallas TX 75240. 972/701-0818.

**MISC. ELECTRONIC
COMPONENTS**

Comsat RSI
PO Box 458, Wortham TX
76693-0458. 254/765-3304.

**Precision Cable Manufacturing
Corp.**
PO Box 1448, Rockwall TX
75087-1448. 972/771-1233.

Tandy Magnetics
401 NE 38th St, Fort Worth TX
76106-3736. 817/390-8206.

**SEMICONDUCTORS AND
RELATED DEVICES**

Hitachi Semiconductor America
PO Box 167928, Irving TX
75016-7928. 972/518-1501.

MEMC Southwest Inc.
PO Box 9600, Sherman TX
75091. 903/891-5000.

National Semiconductor Corp.
1111 W Bardin Rd, Arlington TX
76017-5903. 817/468-6300.

Raytheon TI Systems Inc.
2501 S Highway 121, Lewisville
TX 75067-8122. 972/462-4111.

Texas Instruments
PO Box 10508, Lubbock TX
79408-3508. 806/741-2000.

Twinstar Semiconductor Inc.
PO Box 834104, Richardson TX
75083-4104. 972/994-3600.

**SWITCHGEAR AND
SWITCHBOARD
APPARATUS**

Aztec Manufacturing Company
PO Box 668, Crowley TX 76036-
0668. 817/297-4361.

TRANSFORMERS

Superior Magnetics Inc.
PO Box 308, Denison TX 75021-
0308. 903/415-2800.

For more information on career opportunities in the electronic/industrial electrical equipment industry:

Associations

AMERICAN CERAMIC SOCIETY
P.O. Box 6136, Westerville OH 43086-6136.
614/890-4700. World Wide Web address:
http://www.acers.org. Membership required.

ELECTROCHEMICAL SOCIETY
10 South Main Street, Pennington NJ 08534. 609/737-
1902. World Wide Web address:
http://www.electrochem.org. An international society
which holds bi-annual meetings internationally and
periodic meetings through local sections.

ELECTRONIC INDUSTRIES ASSOCIATION
2500 Wilson Boulevard, Arlington VA 22201.
703/907-7500. World Wide Web address:
http://www.eia.org.

ELECTRONICS TECHNICIANS ASSOCIATION
602 North Jackson Street, Greencastle IN 46135.
765/653-8262. World Wide Web address: http://www.
eta-sda.com. Offers published job-hunting advice
from the organization's officers and members. Also
offers educational material and certification programs.

FABLESS SEMICONDUCTOR ASSOCIATION
Galleria Tower I, 13355 Noel Road, Dallas TX
75240-6636. 972/239-5119. Fax: 972/774-4577.

World Wide Web address: http://www.fsa.org. A
semiconductor industry association.

**INSTITUTE OF ELECTRICAL AND
ELECTRONICS ENGINEERS (IEEE)**
345 East 47th Street, New York NY 10017. 212/705-
7900. Toll-free customer service line: 800/678-4333.
World Wide Web address: http://www.ieee.org.

**INTERNATIONAL SOCIETY OF CERTIFIED
ELECTRONICS TECHNICIANS**
2708 West Berry Street, Fort Worth TX 76109.
817/921-9101. World Wide Web address:
http://www.iscet.org.

**NATIONAL ELECTRONICS SERVICE
DEALERS ASSOCIATION**
2708 West Berry Street, Fort Worth TX 76109.
817/921-9101. World Wide Web address:
http://www.nesda.com. Provides newsletters and
directories to members.

**SEMICONDUCTOR EQUIPMENT AND
MATERIALS INTERNATIONAL**
805 East Middlefield Road, Mountain View CA
94043-4080. 650/964-5111. E-mail address:
semihq@semi.org. World Wide Web address:
http://www.semi.org. Membership required.

ENVIRONMENTAL AND WASTE MANAGEMENT SERVICES

The United States is the largest producer and consumer of environmental goods and services in the world. The industry continues to expand as a result of increasing public concern for the environment and the passing of both the Clean Air and Clean Water Acts. Global environmental revenues are expected to increase 33 percent by the year 2000. The Water Quality Association reports that Americans spent more than $1.3 billion on the filtration and purification of household water in 1995 and that number is expected to increase 70 percent by the year 2000.

Solid waste management remains the largest of the environmental business segments. Waste Management is a leader in the industry with the company's two main rivals, Browning-Ferris Industries and USA Waste, gaining ground. Job opportunities will continue to be found primarily in the areas of environmental protection, natural resources, and education.

ABATIX ENVIRONMENTAL CORPORATION
8311 Eastpoint Drive, Suite 400, Dallas TX 75227. 214/381-1146. **Contact:** Human Resources. **Description:** Supplies durable and nondurable goods to the following industry segments: asbestos and lead abatement, hazardous material remediation, and construction. Supplies include industrial safety products, construction tools, general safety products such as protective clothing and eyewear, and clean-up equipment. **Common positions include:** Sales Representative. **Corporate headquarters location:** This Location. **Other U.S. locations:** Phoenix AZ; Denver CO; Las Vegas NV; Corpus Christi TX; Seattle WA. **Listed on:** Boston Stock Exchange; NASDAQ. **Stock exchange symbol:** ABIX. **Number of employees nationwide:** 65.

DUNCAN DISPOSAL
1408 North Martin Luther King Boulevard, Lubbock TX 79403. 806/762-2650. **Contact:** Personnel. **Description:** Disposes of residential refuse.

GEO-MARINE INC.
550 East 15th Street, Plano TX 75074. 972/423-5480. **Contact:** Human Resources. **World Wide Web address:** http://www.geo-marine.com-gmi. **Description:** An environmental engineering and consulting firm.

Note: Because addresses and telephone numbers of smaller companies can change rapidly, we recommend you call each company to verify the information below before inquiring about job opportunities. Mass mailings are not recommended.

Additional small employers:

SANITARY SERVICES

Arlington Disposal Company
1212 Harrison Avenue, Arlington TX 76011-7332. 817/277-2641.

Laidlaw Waste Systems Inc.
PO Box 1139, Kilgore TX 75663-1139. 903/984-8621.

Safety-Kleen Corporation
1722 Cooper Creek Road, Denton TX 76208-1000. 940/383-2611.

Texas Waste Management
PO Box 719, Lewisville TX 75067-0719. 972/436-3512.

Waste Management of Dallas
12160 Garland Rd, Dallas TX 75218-1533. 214/328-8888.

Waste Management of Fort Worth Recycling
PO Box 911005, Fort Worth TX 76111-9105. 817/332-2251.

For more information on career opportunities in environmental and waste management services:

Associations

AIR & WASTE MANAGEMENT ASSOCIATION
One Gateway Center, 3rd Floor, Pittsburgh PA 15222. 412/232-3444. World Wide Web address: http://www.awma.org. A nonprofit, technical and educational organization providing a neutral forum where all points of view regarding environmental management issues can be addressed.

AMERICAN ACADEMY OF ENVIRONMENTAL ENGINEERS
130 Holiday Court, Suite 100, Annapolis MD 21401. 410/266-3311. World Wide Web address: http://www.enviro.engrs.org. Publishes the *Environmental Engineering Selection Guide*, a directory of engineering firms and educational institutions.

ENVIRONMENTAL INDUSTRY ASSOCIATION
4301 Connecticut Avenue NW, Suite 300, Washington DC 20008. 202/244-4700. World Wide Web address: http://www.envasns.org.

INSTITUTE OF CLEAN AIR COMPANIES
1660 L Street NW, Suite 1100, Washington DC 20036. 202/457-0911. World Wide Web address: http://www.icac.com.

Magazines

JOURNAL OF AIR AND WASTE MANAGEMENT ASSOCIATION
One Gateway Center, 3rd Floor, Pittsburgh PA 15222.

Toll-free phone: 800/275-5851. World Wide Web address: http://www.awma.org.

Online Services

ECOLOGIC
http://www.eng.rpi.edu/dept/union/pugwash/ecojobs.html. This Website provides links to a variety of environmental job resources. This site is run by the Rensselaer Student Pugwash.

ENVIRONMENTAL JOBS SEARCH PAGE/UBIQUITY
http://ourworld.compuserve.com/homepages/ubikk/env4.htm. This Website includes internships, tips, and links to other databases of environmental job openings.

INTERNATIONAL & ENVIRONMENTAL JOB BULLETINS
http://www.sas.upenn.edu/African_Studies/Publications/International_Environmental_16621.html. Provides a wealth of information on bulletins, magazines, and resources for jobseekers who are looking to get into the environmental field. Most of these resources are on a subscription basis and provide job openings and other information. This information was compiled by Dennis F. Desmond.

LINKS TO SOURCES OF INFORMATION ON ENVIRONMENTAL JOBS
http://www.host.cc.utexas.edu/ftp/student/scb/joblinks.html. Provides links to numerous sites that offer job openings and information in the environmental field. The site is run by the University of Texas at Austin.

FABRICATED/PRIMARY METALS AND PRODUCTS

 *The fabricated metals industry is on the rebound after a rough time in the early '90s. In 1996, domestic steel consumption reached 106 million tons, a 33 percent increase from the mid-'80s.* U.S. Industry and Trade Outlook 1998 *reported that employment in the steel industry remains stable. Steel makers have managed to cut costs and increase productivity while at the same time keeping employment levels steady. Forecasters predict that in 1998, shipments of steel mill products should increase by 2 percent as a result of demand from automobile manufacturers and the construction market. However, competition overseas could affect profits for U.S. companies.*

In 1998, aluminum supply will remain low with prices remaining solid. The transportation sector is expected to increase demand for metal castings, and commercial aircraft deliveries will still have a heavy reliance on plate products.

AIR SYSTEM COMPONENTS (ASC)
1200 Executive Drive East, Suite 90, Richardson TX 75081. 972/907-0791. **Fax:** 972/234-0354. **Contact:** Human Resources Department. **Description:** Engaged in sheet metal fabrication of heating and air conditioning components for the residential and commercial markets. **NOTE:** Entry-level positions are offered. **Common positions include:** Accountant/Auditor; Computer Programmer; Customer Service Representative; Design Engineer; Designer; Draftsperson; Human Resources Manager; Industrial Engineer; Mechanical Engineer; Operations/Production Manager; Systems Analyst; Typist/Word Processor; Video Production Coordinator. **Educational backgrounds include:** Business Administration; Engineering; Marketing. **Benefits:** 401(k); Dental Insurance; Disability Coverage; Employee Discounts; Life Insurance; Mass Transit Available; Medical Insurance; Profit Sharing; Savings Plan; Tuition Assistance. **Corporate headquarters location:** This Location. **Other U.S. locations:** AZ; OK. **Parent company:** Tomkins plc. **Operations at this facility include:** Administration; Divisional Headquarters; Research and Development; Sales; Service. **Listed on:** New York Stock Exchange. **Annual sales/revenues:** More than $100 million. **Number of employees at this location:** 100. **Number of employees nationwide:** 1,600.

ALUMAX BUILDING PRODUCTS, INC.
14651 Dallas Parkway, Suite 330, Dallas TX 75240. 972/701-4900. **Fax:** 972/701-4960. **Contact:** Linda Johnson, Human Resources Manager. **Description:** Alumax Building Products, Inc. is a diversified company that fabricates products of aluminum, steel, and vinyl for a variety of industries. The company sells its products to manufacturers of recreational vehicles and manufactured housing, retail building products suppliers, construction firms, and others. The facilities include 15 fabrication plants located throughout the United States. Founded in 1954. **Common positions include:** Accountant/Auditor; Agricultural Engineer; Branch Manager; Computer Programmer; Customer Service Representative; Human Resources Manager; Management Trainee; Mechanical Engineer; Operations/Production Manager; Purchasing Agent/Manager. **Educational backgrounds include:** Accounting; Business Administration; Engineering; Marketing. **Benefits:** 401(k); Dental Insurance; Disability Coverage; Life Insurance; Medical Insurance; Pension Plan; Savings Plan; Tuition Assistance; Vision Insurance. **Corporate headquarters location:** This Location. **Parent company:** Alumax, Inc. is one of America's largest aluminum companies. Alumax, Inc. employs approximately 14,000 people throughout North America, Europe, and the Far East. **Operations at this facility include:** Administration; Divisional

Headquarters; Manufacturing; Research and Development; Sales. **Listed on:** New York Stock Exchange. **Number of employees at this location:** 55. **Number of employees nationwide:** 750.

BROCKWAY STANDARD, INC.
13401 Denton Drive, Dallas TX 75234. 972/620-1530. **Toll-free phone:** 800/627-1530. **Fax:** 972/620-2318. **Contact:** Jeanie Gaines, Human Resources Manager/Safety Director. **E-mail address:** jeanie.gaines@bwaycorp.com. **Description:** Manufactures metal containers. **NOTE:** Second and third shifts are offered. **Common positions include:** Buyer; Controller; Electrician; Human Resources Manager; Industrial Engineer; Operations/Production Manager; Plant Manager; Purchasing Agent/Manager; Quality Control Supervisor; Sales Representative; Secretary. **Educational backgrounds include:** Business Administration; Engineering. **Benefits:** 401(k); Dental Insurance; Disability Coverage; Life Insurance; Medical Insurance; Profit Sharing. **Corporate headquarters location:** Atlanta GA. **Other U.S. locations:** Nationwide. **Operations at this facility include:** Administration; Manufacturing; Sales; Service. **Listed on:** NASDAQ; New York Stock Exchange. **Stock exchange symbol:** BWAY. **Facilities manager:** Charles Drake. **Number of employees at this location:** 80.

CHAPARRAL STEEL COMPANY
300 Ward Road, Midlothian TX 76065. 972/775-8241. **Contact:** Human Resources Department. **World Wide Web address:** http://www.chaparralsteel.com. **Description:** A steel works company.

G.H. HENSLEY INDUSTRIES, INC.
P.O. Box 29779, Dallas TX 75229. 972/241-2321. **Contact:** Tom McCormack, Personnel Director. **Description:** Operates a steel foundry producing steel castings and construction equipment parts. **Corporate headquarters location:** This Location.

KEYSTONE CONSOLIDATED INDUSTRIES, INC.
5430 LBJ Freeway, Dallas TX 75240. 972/458-0028. **Contact:** Human Resources Department. **Description:** Keystone Consolidated Industries operates a steel works and is also a blast furnace producer.

KOCH-GLITSCH INC.
4900 Singleton Boulevard, Dallas TX 75212. 214/631-3841. **Contact:** Chip Davis, Manager of Human Resources. **World Wide Web address:** http://www.kochind.com. **Description:** Fabricates metal plates and sheet metal and manufactures petroleum refinery processing equipment, pollution control equipment, and mesh products used in the automotive industry.

LEWIS & LAMBERT METAL
P.O. Box 14439, Fort Worth TX 76117. 817/834-7146. **Contact:** Linda Oberby, Personnel. **Description:** Provides sheet metal work and contracting services.

THE LOFLAND COMPANY
P.O. Box 35446, Dallas TX 75235. 214/631-5250. **Fax:** 214/637-1110. **Contact:** Gail Wachtendorf, Personnel Manager. **Description:** A steel fabricator and distributor of construction materials. **Corporate headquarters location:** This Location. **Other U.S. locations:** Little Rock AR; Keithvilla LA; Fort Worth TX; Waxahachie TX. **Operations at this facility include:** Administration; Manufacturing; Sales; Service. **Number of employees nationwide:** 260.

LONE STAR STEEL COMPANY
P.O. Box 803546, Dallas TX 75380. 972/386-3981. **Contact:** Personnel. **Description:** Manufactures steel tubular goods used for oil and gas drilling. **Corporate headquarters location:** This Location.

TEXAS STEEL COMPANY
P.O. Box 2976, Fort Worth TX 76113. 817/923-4611. **Contact:** Mr. W.O. Pender, Personnel Supervisor. **Description:** Manufactures carbon, stainless steel, alloy castings, and other metal products for use in construction. **Corporate headquarters location:** This Location.

THORNTON STEEL COMPANY INC.
2700 West Pafford, Fort Worth TX 76110. 817/926-3324. **Fax:** 817/926-0758. **Contact:** Hiring. **Description:** A structural steel fabricator. **Common positions include:** Computer Operator; Structural Engineer. **Educational backgrounds include:** Accounting; Business Administration; Engineering. **Corporate headquarters location:** This Location. **Operations at this facility include:** Manufacturing; Sales. **Number of employees at this location:** 15.

Note: Because addresses and telephone numbers of smaller companies can change rapidly, we recommend you call each company to verify the information below before inquiring about job opportunities. Mass mailings are not recommended.

Additional small employers:

ALUMINUM FOUNDRIES

Denison Industries
PO Box 1459, Denison TX 75021-1459. 903/786-4444.

Skotty Aluminum Products
2101 E Union Bower Rd, Irving TX 75061-8811. 972/438-4787.

United States Aluminum Corp.
200 Singleton Rd, Waxahachie TX 75165-5012. 972/937-9651.

COATING, ENGRAVING, AND ALLIED SERVICES

Ameron International
PO Box 878, Burkburnett TX 76354-0878. 940/569-1471.

DIECASTINGS

Cascade Die Casting
PO Box 460820, Garland TX 75046-0820. 972/278-3515.

Cercon
201 Cercon Dr, Hillsboro TX 76645-3064. 254/582-3413.

Texas Die Casting Inc.
PO Box 71, Gladewater TX 75647-0071. 903/845-2224.

FABRICATED METAL PRODUCTS

Charles W. Weaver Manufacturing Co.
3101 Justin Rd, Flower Mound TX 75028-2430. 972/539-1537.

FABRICATED STRUCTURAL METAL PRODUCTS

AA Manufacturing Inc.
3837 Dividend Dr, Garland TX 75042-7694. 972/494-2575.

Alpine Engineered Products
2820 N Great Southwest Park, Grand Prairie TX 75050-6472. 972/660-4422.

Baker Tank Co.
PO Box 40, Arp TX 75750-0040. 903/859-2111.

Challenge Door of Texas
PO Box 575, Sulphur Springs TX 75483-0575. 903/885-0660.

Danvid Company Inc.
1813 Kelly Blvd, Carrollton TX 75006-5511. 972/416-8140.

Double Eagle Structures
5400 S Interstate Hwy 35 E, Denton TX 76205. 940/497-7070.

Golden Manufacturing Inc.
322 Barnes Dr, Garland TX 75042. 972/272-6371.

H&S Manufacturing Co.
PO Box 1515, Rowlett TX 75030-1515. 972/475-4747.

Hirschfeld Steel Co. Inc.
PO Box 3695, Abilene TX 79604-3695. 915/676-1421.

Humanetics II
1700 Columbian Club Dr, Carrollton TX 75006-5517. 972/416-1304.

JHS Building Products Inc.
PO Box 934, Clarksville TX 75426-0934. 903/427-5666.

Karlee Company
PO Box 461207, Garland TX 75046-1207. 972/272-0628.

Lane Company
120 Fairview St, Arlington TX 76010-7221. 817/261-9116.

Logic Design Metals Inc.
3233 West Kingsley Road, Garland TX 75041-2205. 972/271-5525.

M&M Manufacturing Company
PO Box 9739, Fort Worth TX 76147-2739. 817/336-2311.

Magni-Fab Southwest Co.
PO Box 578, Howe TX 75459-0578. 903/532-5533.

Mesco Metal Buildings
PO Box 20, Grapevine TX 76099-0020. 817/488-8511.

Norris Cylinder Company
PO Box 7486, Longview TX 75607-7486. 903/757-7633.

North Texas Steel Company
PO Box 2497, Fort Worth TX 76113-2497. 817/927-5333.

Philips Inc.
PO Box 1240, Clarksville TX 75426-1240. 903/427-2256.

Rangaire
PO Box 177, Cleburne TX 76033-0177. 817/556-6500.

Robroy Industries Texas Inc.
PO Box 1828, Gilmer TX 75644-4828. 903/843-5591.

Rooftop Systems Inc.
2405 McIver Ln, Carrollton TX 75006-6512. 972/247-7447.

SBS
PO Box 15070, Fort Worth TX 76119-0070. 817/572-4029.

Simpson Strong-Tie Company
1720 Couch Dr, McKinney TX 75069-7326. 972/542-0326.

Special Products & Manufacturing
2455 Interstate 30, Rockwall TX 75087-9715. 972/771-8851.

Tranner Corp.
PO Box 2289, Wichita Falls TX 76307-2289. 940/723-7125.

Vistawall Architectural Products
PO Box 629, Terrell TX 75160. 972/551-6100.

W&W Steel Company
PO Box 2219, Lubbock TX 79408-2219. 806/765-5781.

FABRICATED WIRE PRODUCTS

Mapco
1671 South Broadway St, Carrollton TX 75006-7442. 972/466-0475.

Meadow Steel
7000 Will Rogers Blvd, Fort Worth TX 76140-6010. 817/293-9641.

IRON AND STEEL FOUNDRIES

Columbus Metals
PO Box 1043, Temple TX 76503-1043. 254/773-9055.

Consolidated Casting Corp.
1501 South Interstate 45, Hutchins TX 75141. 972/225-7305.

EBAA Iron Inc.
PO Box 877, Eastland TX 76448-0877. 254/629-1737.

Frazier & Frazier Industries
PO Box 279, Coolidge TX 76635-0279. 254/786-2293.

Oil City Iron Works Inc.
PO Box 1560, Corsicana TX 75151-1560. 903/872-6571.

Wichita Falls Casting
PO Box 1616, Wichita Falls TX 76307-7534. 940/855-8100.

METAL FORGINGS

Advantage Steel Service Inc.
PO Box 820040, Fort Worth TX 76182-0040. 817/589-0088.

Crosby Lebus Manufacturing
PO Box 271, Longview TX 75606-0271. 903/759-4424.

Trinity Forge Inc.
947 Trinity Drive, Mansfield TX 76063-2730. 817/473-1515.

METAL STAMPINGS

Johns International
PO Box 365, Winters TX 79567-0365. 915/754-4561.

NONFERROUS ROLLING AND DRAWING OF METALS

Aavid Thermal Products of Texas
250 Apache Trail, Terrell TX 75160-6591. 972/563-2843.

Airmax
PO Box 2704, Longview TX 75606-2704. 903/843-5666.

Alumax Mill Products
300 Alumax Drive, Texarkana TX 75501-0209. 903/832-8471.

Extruders
PO Box 1719, Wylie TX 75098-1719. 972/442-3535.

General Cable Industries Inc.
910 Tenth Street, Suite A, Plano TX 75074-6802. 972/423-6565.

International Extrusion Corp.
202 Singleton Road, Waxahachie TX 75165-5012. 972/937-7032.

Snow Coil
PO Box 2704, Longview TX 75606-2704. 903/984-0838.

Western Extrusions Corporation
PO Box 810219, Dallas TX 75381-0219. 972/245-7515.

Zexel Texas Division
1102 W North Carrier Pkwy, Grand Prairie TX 75050-1122. 972/641-7000.

SCREW MACHINE PRODUCTS

Automatic Products Corp.
PO Box 461088, Garland TX 75046-1088. 972/272-6422.

SMELTING AND REFINING OF NONFERROUS METALS

American Smelting & Refining Co.
PO Box 30200, Amarillo TX 79120-0200. 806/383-2201.

STEEL SHEET, STRIP, AND BARS

Niagara Southwest
1291 S Highway 67, Midlothian TX 76065-5488. 972/723-8500.

STEEL WIRE, NAILS, AND SPIKES

Sherman Wire
PO Box 729, Sherman TX 75091-0729. 903/893-0191.

STEEL WORKS, BLAST FURNACES, AND ROLLING MILLS

Ennis Steel Industries Inc.
PO Box 1360, Ennis TX 75120-1360. 972/878-0400.

Lone Star Steel Company
PO Box 1000, Lone Star TX 75668-1000. 903/656-6521.

Southwest Steel Casting
600 Foundry Dr, Longview TX 75604-5222. 903/759-3946.

WHOLESALE METALS SERVICE CENTERS AND OFFICES

Altair Company
PO Box 853900, Richardson TX 75085-3900. 972/231-5176.

Arrow Metals
1010 E Walnut St, Garland TX 75040-6614. 972/276-2676.

Davis Iron Works Inc.
PO Box 99, Hewitt TX 76643-0099. 254/666-1000.

Ryerson Steel
PO Box 655960, Dallas TX 75265-5960. 214/637-4710.

The Lofland Company
Hwy 35 E, Waxahachie TX 75165. 972/299-5106.

Triple A Wire
PO Box 215, Point TX 75472-0215. 903/598-2225.

For more information on career opportunities in the fabricated/primary metals and products industries:

Associations

ASM INTERNATIONAL: THE MATERIALS INFORMATION SOCIETY
9639 Kinsman Road, Materials Park OH 44073. 800/336-5152. World Wide Web address: http://www. asm-intl.org. Gathers, processes, and disseminates technical information to foster the understanding and application of engineered materials.

AMERICAN FOUNDRYMEN'S SOCIETY
505 State Street, Des Plaines IL 60016. 847/824-0181. World Wide Web address: http://www.afsinc.org.

AMERICAN WELDING SOCIETY
550 Northwest LeJeune Road, Miami FL 33126. 305/443-9353. World Wide Web address: http://www.aws.org.

Directories

DIRECTORY OF STEEL FOUNDRIES IN THE UNITED STATES, CANADA, AND MEXICO
Steel Founders' Society of America, 455 State Street, Des Plaines IL 60016. 847/299-9160. World Wide Web address: http://www.sfsa.org.

Magazines

AMERICAN METAL MARKET
825 Seventh Avenue, New York NY 10019. 212/887-8580.

IRON & STEEL ENGINEER
Association of Iron and Steel Engineers, 3 Gateway Center, Suite 1900, Pittsburgh PA 15222-1004. 412/281-6323. World Wide Web address: http://www.aise.org.

MODERN METALS
Trend Publishing, 625 North Michigan Avenue, Suite 1500, Chicago IL 60611. 312/654-2300.

FINANCIAL SERVICES

 *Riding on the waves of a steady economy, the future appears solid for the financial services sector. Merrill Lynch & Co. had a strong year in 1997, posting over $1 trillion in customer assets. Attempting to match Merrill Lynch's success, Morgan Stanley and Dean Witter merged and Discover & Co. purchased Saloman Inc. with the help of Travelers Group.*

Foreign investors are taking interest in American stocks. According to the Federal Reserve, at the end of the third quarter in 1997, foreigners had channeled $52 billion into U.S. equities. More and more investors are choosing U.S. stocks as the economy is strong, especially in contrast to the turmoil in Asia.

Despite all the good news, economists worry that the runaway U.S. stock market could be peaking, and fears of inflation are causing a downturn in the bond market, which could prompt the Federal Reserve to raise interest rates. The best opportunities through the end of the decade will be for investment managers, specifically those with experience in high-technology, natural resources, and emerging markets.

A.T.C. COMMUNICATIONS GROUP
5950 Berkshire Lane, Suite 1650, Dallas TX 75225. 214/361-9870. **Contact:** Jerry Sims, Controller. **World Wide Web address:** http://www.atct.com. **Description:** Conducts strategic funding and financial planning. **Corporate headquarters location:** This Location. **Listed on:** NASDAQ. **Number of employees nationwide:** 1,500.

AMERICREDIT CORPORATION
P.O. Box 9130, Fort Worth TX 76147. 817/332-7000. **Contact:** Human Resources. **Description:** Americredit Corporation specializes in car loans.

THE ASSOCIATES CORPORATION OF NORTH AMERICA
P.O. Box 660237, Dallas TX 75266-0237. 972/652-4000. **Contact:** Human Resources Department. **World Wide Web address:** http://www.theassociates.com. **Description:** A nondepository credit institution. **Common positions include:** Accountant/Auditor; Adjuster; Attorney; Budget Analyst; Buyer; Claim Representative; Clerical Supervisor; Computer Programmer; Credit Clerk and Authorizer; Credit Manager; Customer Service Representative; Department Manager; Employment Interviewer; Financial Analyst; Financial Services Sales Representative; Marketing Manager; Paralegal; Payroll Clerk; Purchasing Agent/Manager; Receptionist; Secretary; Securities Sales Representative; Systems Analyst; Technical Writer/Editor; Typist/Word Processor. **Educational backgrounds include:** Accounting; Business Administration; Communications; Computer Science; Economics; Finance; Marketing; Mathematics. **Benefits:** 401(k); Dental Insurance; Disability Coverage; Employee Discounts; Fitness Program; Life Insurance; Medical Insurance; Pension Plan; Profit Sharing; Savings Plan; Tuition Assistance. **Special programs:** Internships. **Corporate headquarters location:** This Location. **Parent company:** Ford Motor Company. **Number of employees at this location:** 3,500. **Number of employees nationwide:** 17,000.

ASSOCIATES RV FINANCE COMPANY
14901 Quorom Drive, Suite 750, Dallas TX 75240. 972/661-0595. **Contact:** Human Resources. **Description:** Provides financing for recreational vehicle loans.

ATLAS CREDIT COMPANY
118 East Cotton Street, Longview TX 75601. 903/758-1741. **Contact:** Human Resources. **Description:** Provides financing for customers in need of personal loans.

BANC ONE SECURITIES
1600 Redbud Boulevard, McKinney TX 75069. 972/647-1111. **Contact:** Human Resources. **World Wide Web address:** http://www.bankone.com. **Description:** Provides financial services in the areas of stocks, bonds, and mutual funds.

BARNETT MORTGAGE CORPORATION
1700 Alma Drive, Suite 365, Plano TX 75075. 817/267-2251. **Contact:** Human Resources. **Description:** Provides mortgage financing.

BEAR, STEARNS & COMPANY, INC.
300 Crescent Court, Suite 200, Dallas TX 75201. 214/979-7900. **Contact:** Human Resources. **World Wide Web address:** http://www.bearstearns.com. **Description:** A leading worldwide investment banking, securities trading, and brokerage firm. With over $5.7 billion in total capital, the company serves corporations, governments, institutions, and private investors worldwide. The firm's business includes corporate finance, mergers and acquisitions, public finance, institutional equities, fixed income sales and trading, private client services, foreign exchange, future sales and trading, derivatives, and asset management. **Corporate headquarters location:** New York NY. **Other U.S. locations:** Los Angeles CA; San Francisco CA; Atlanta GA; Chicago IL; Boston MA. **Parent company:** The Bear Stearns Companies Inc. also operates Bear, Stearns Securities Corporation, providing professional and correspondent clearing services, including securities lending; and Custodial Trust Company, providing master trust, custody, and government securities services. **Listed on:** New York Stock Exchange. **Annual sales/revenues:** More than $100 million. **Number of employees nationwide:** 7,800.

CENTEX CORPORATION
P.O. Box 199000, Dallas TX 75219. 214/981-5000. **Contact:** Human Resources. **World Wide Web address:** http://www.centex.com. **Description:** Provides home building, mortgage banking, contracting, and construction products and services. **Corporate headquarters location:** This Location. **Subsidiaries include:** Centex Homes is one of America's largest home builders; CTX Mortgage Company is among the top retail originators of single-family home mortgages; Centex Construction Company, Inc. is one of the largest general building contractors in the U.S., as well as one of the largest constructors of health care facilities; Centex Construction Products, Inc., which manufactures and distributes cement, ready-mix concrete, aggregates, and gypsum wallboard, is one of the largest U.S.-owned cement producers; Centex Development Company, LP conducts real estate development activities. **Listed on:** New York Stock Exchange.

COLONIAL FINANCE COMPANY
101 South Jennings Avenue, Suite 102, Fort Worth TX 76104. 817/877-1944. **Contact:** Human Resources. **Description:** Finances small businesses and offers personal loans.

COMMERCIAL CREDIT CORPORATION
P.O. Box 280, De Soto TX 75123. 972/228-5688. **Contact:** Human Resources. **Description:** Specializes in the financing of small personal loans.

CONTINENTAL CREDIT CORPORATION
706 10th Street, Wichita Falls TX 76301. 940/766-3122. **Contact:** Human Resources. **Description:** Specializes in the financing of small personal loans.

CONTINENTAL CREDIT CORPORATION
217 North Kentucky Street, McKinney TX 75069. 972/542-2916. **Contact:** Human Resources. **Description:** Provides financing for small personal loans.

DIAMOND SHAMROCK, INC.
P.O. Box 631, Amarillo TX 79105. 806/324-4601. **Contact:** Human Resources. **Description:** This location is the credit card center servicing over 500,000 accounts. Overall, Diamond Shamrock, Inc. is a regional petroleum company. The company operates 3,800 miles of pipeline, six terminals, and approximately 2,000 stores in eight southwestern states. Diamond Shamrock, Inc. also owns two refineries in Texas, and is engaged in crude oil refining, wholesale marketing, retail marketing,

and the storing, manufacturing, and marketing of gas liquids, petrochemicals, and ammonia fertilizer.

A.G. EDWARDS & SONS
2305 Cedars Spring Road, Suite 300, Dallas TX 75201. 214/954-1999. **Contact:** Human Resources. **Description:** A.G. Edwards & Sons is an investment firm.

EMPIRE FUNDING CORPORATION
800 West Airport Freeway, Suite 518, Irving TX 75062. 972/644-1071. **Contact:** Human Resources. **Description:** Provides financing for home improvement loans.

FIDELITY FINANCIAL
1220 North Town East Boulevard, Suite 120, Mesquite TX 75150. 972/686-0300. **Contact:** Human Resources. **Description:** Fidelity Financial provides financing for car loans.

FIDELITY INVESTMENTS
400 East Las Colinas Boulevard, Irving TX 75039. 972/584-7000. **Fax:** 972/584-7275. **Recorded jobline:** 972/584-6622. **Contact:** Human Resources Department. **World Wide Web address:** http://www.newjobs.com/fidelity. **Description:** One of the largest mutual fund/discount brokerage firms with over $500 billion in assets. **NOTE:** Entry-level positions are offered, as well as second and third shifts. **Common positions include:** Account Representative; Accountant; Administrative Assistant; Computer Operator; Computer Programmer; Customer Service Representative; Database Manager; Financial Analyst; Management Trainee; MIS Specialist; Operations Manager; Project Manager; Sales Representative; Secretary; Software Engineer; Systems Analyst; Systems Manager; Telecommunications Manager. **Educational backgrounds include:** Business Administration; Computer Science; Finance. **Benefits:** 401(k); Dental Insurance; Disability Coverage; Employee Discounts; Financial Planning Assistance; Flexible Schedule; Life Insurance; Medical Insurance; Pension Plan; Profit Sharing; Tuition Assistance. **Special programs:** Internships. **Internship information:** The company has an MIS internship program. Applications must be submitted by March 1st via e-mail or in writing. **Corporate headquarters location:** Boston MA. **Other U.S. locations:** New York NY; Cincinnati OH; Salt Lake City UT. **Operations at this facility include:** Regional Headquarters. **Listed on:** Privately held.

THE FINANCE COMPANY
2201 South WS Young Drive, Suite 105C, Killeen TX 76543. 254/526-8390. **Contact:** Human Resources. **Description:** Engaged primarily in buying and servicing installment contracts originated by used car dealers. Most of The Finance Company's income comes from interest charged on contracts and from the discounts at which it purchases contracts. The company also receives revenue from the commissions received on ancillary products, such as credit insurance, limited physical damage insurance, and product warranties offered by the company and underwritten by third-party vendors.

FIRST SOUTHWEST COMPANY
1700 Pacific Avenue, Suite 500, Dallas TX 75201. 214/953-4000. **Contact:** Personnel. **World Wide Web address:** http://www.firstsw.com. **Description:** A professional security brokerage.

FORD MOTOR CREDIT COMPANY
P.O. Box 833830, Richardson TX 75083. 972/669-0022. **Contact:** Human Resources. **World Wide Web address:** http://www.ford.com. **Description:** Ford Motor Credit Company is one of the largest providers of financial services in the United States, providing financing for automobiles. **Parent company:** Ford Motor Company is engaged in the design, development, manufacture, and sale of cars, trucks, tractors, and related components and accessories. The company has manufacturing, assembly, and sales affiliates in 29 countries outside the United States. Ford Motor Company's two core businesses are the Automotive Group and the Financial Services Group (Ford Motor Credit, The Associates, USL Capital, and First Nationwide). Ford is also engaged in a number of other businesses, including electronics, glass, electrical, and fuel-handling products; plastics; climate-control systems; automotive services and replacement parts; vehicle leasing and rental; and land development.

FORT WORTH MORTGAGE
5710 LBJ Freeway, Suite 190, Dallas TX 75240. 972/233-3722. **Contact:** Human Resources. **Description:** Fort Worth Mortgage provides financing for home mortgage loans.

GANIS CREDIT CORPORATION
222 West Las Colinas Boulevard, Suite 548, Irving TX 75039. 972/717-0194. **Contact:** Human Resources. **Description:** Provides financing for recreational vehicle and boat loans.

HAPPY LOANS & FINANCIAL SERVICE
817 North Travis Street, Sherman TX 75090. 903/892-1281. **Contact:** Human Resources. **Description:** Happy Loans specializes in personal loans.

JEFFERIES & COMPANY, INC.
13355 Noel Road, Suite 1400, Dallas TX 75240. 972/701-3000. **Contact:** Human Resources. **World Wide Web address:** http://www.jefco.com. **Description:** Jefferies & Company is engaged in equity, convertible debt and taxable fixed income securities brokerage and trading, and corporate finance. Jefferies is one of the leading national firms engaged in the distribution and trading of blocks of equity securities and conducts such activities primarily in the third market, which refers to transactions in listed equity securities effected away from national securities exchanges. **Parent company:** Jefferies Group, Inc. is a holding company which, through Jefferies & Company and its three other primary subsidiaries, Investment Technology Group, Inc., Jefferies International Limited, and Jefferies Pacific Limited, is engaged in securities brokerage and trading, corporate finance, and other financial services. Founded in 1962.

MFC FINANCE COMPANY
333 West Campbell Road, Suite 220, Richardson TX 75080. 972/918-0900. **Contact:** Human Resources. **Description:** MFC Finance Company provides financing for car loans and sometimes engages in financing personal loans for established customers.

MERRILL LYNCH
701 South Taylor Street, Suite 100, Amarillo TX 79101-2443. 806/376-4861. **Contact:** Hiring Manager. **World Wide Web address:** http://www.ml.com. **Description:** A diversified financial service organization. Merrill Lynch is a major broker in securities, option contracts, commodities and financial futures contracts, and insurance. The company also deals with corporate and municipal securities and investment banking. **NOTE:** Call for specific information on where to mail a resume.

PAINE WEBBER, INC.
2200 Ross Avenue, Suite 5000, Dallas TX 75201-2777. 214/978-6000. **Contact:** Branch Manager. **World Wide Web address:** http://www.painewebber.com. **Description:** A holding company that, together with operating subsidiaries, forms one of the world's largest investment services firms. Paine Webber assists corporations, governments, and individuals in meeting their long-term financial needs. The company also has operations in equity and fixed-income securities.

PRINCIPAL FINANCIAL SECURITIES INC.
P.O. Box 508, Dallas TX 75221-0508. 214/880-9000. **Contact:** Laura Mellor, Human Resources. **Description:** An investment banking company.

RAUSCHER PIERCE REFSNES, INC.
2711 North Haskell Avenue, Suite 2400, Dallas TX 75204. 214/989-1000. **Contact:** Human Resources. **Description:** A diversified brokerage and investment banking firm specializing in the origination and distribution of fixed income and equity securities for clients located primarily in the southwestern United States. The company is a leading municipal financing firm and has managed or co-managed billions of dollars in municipal bonds that generate funds for government entities, hospitals, school districts, and special authorities. Rauscher Pierce Refsnes is a member of the National Association of Securities Dealers, the SIPC, and the Securities Industry Association. Founded in 1933. **Common positions include:** Accountant/Auditor; Branch Manager; Brokerage Clerk; Financial Analyst; Human Resources Manager; Market Research Analyst; Public Relations Specialist; Securities Sales Representative; Services Sales Representative; Systems Analyst;

Typist/Word Processor. **Educational backgrounds include:** Accounting; Business Administration; Economics; Finance; Liberal Arts; Marketing. **Corporate headquarters location:** This Location. **Other U.S. locations:** AZ; CA; CO; NM; OK; TX. **Parent company:** Inter Regional Financial Group. **Listed on:** American Stock Exchange; NASDAQ; New York Stock Exchange. **Number of employees at this location:** 400. **Number of employees nationwide:** 3,200.

REPUBLIC FINANCIAL SERVICES, INC.
2727 Turtle Creek Boulevard, Dallas TX 75219. 214/559-1222. **Contact:** Larry Westerfield, Director of Employee Relations. **Description:** A diversified holding company whose principal assets are the Republic Insurance Group (offers a broad range of property and liability insurance), and the Allied Finance Company (principally engaged in making direct personal loans to individuals and purchasing discounted retail installment loans). **Common positions include:** Accountant/Auditor; Actuary; Administrator; Customer Service Representative; Human Resources Manager; Purchasing Agent/Manager; Systems Analyst; Underwriter/Assistant Underwriter. **Educational backgrounds include:** Accounting; Business Administration; Communications; Computer Science; Economics; Finance; Marketing; Mathematics. **Benefits:** Dental Insurance; Disability Coverage; Employee Discounts; Life Insurance; Medical Insurance; Pension Plan; Profit Sharing; Savings Plan; Tuition Assistance. **Special programs:** Internships. **Corporate headquarters location:** This Location. **Parent company:** Winterther Swiss.

SEACOAST EQUITIES INC.
2997 LBJ Freeway, Suite 115N, Dallas TX 75234. 972/620-9300. **Contact:** Human Resources. **Description:** Seacoast Equities Inc. provides financing for home improvement loans.

SOUTHWEST SECURITIES GROUP, INC.
1201 Elm Street, Suite 3500, Dallas TX 75270-2180. 214/651-1800. **Contact:** Human Resources. **Description:** A holding company with subsidiaries engaged in providing securities brokerage, investment banking, and investment advisory services. Founded in 1972. **Corporate headquarters location:** This Location. **Other U.S. locations:** Santa Fe NM; Tulsa OK; Albuquerque TX; Georgetown TX; Irving TX; Longview TX; Lufkin TX; Nacodoches TX; San Antonio TX. **Subsidiaries include:** Brokers Transaction Services, Inc.; SW Capital Corporation; The Trust Company of Texas; Westwood Management Corporation. **Number of employees worldwide:** 550.

TRADESTAR INVESTMENTS
8201 Preston Road, Suite 270, Dallas TX 75225. **Toll-free phone:** 800/622-5484. **Contact:** Human Resources. **Description:** A regional brokerage firm.

TRANSOUTH
3201 West Airport Freeway, Suite 103, Irving TX 75062. 972/255-4666. **Contact:** Human Resources. **Description:** A financial company that offers personal loans.

WORLD FINANCE
108 Gilmer Street, Sulphur Springs TX 75482. 903/885-0811. **Contact:** Human Resources. **Description:** World Finance provides financing for small personal loans. **Other area locations:** 1708 NW 28th Street, Fort Worth TX 76106.

Note: Because addresses and telephone numbers of smaller companies can change rapidly, we recommend you call each company to verify the information below before inquiring about job opportunities. Mass mailings are not recommended.

Additional small employers:

CREDIT AGENCIES AND INSTITUTIONS

Banc One Mortgage Corp.
1717 Main Street, Floor 14, Dallas TX 75201-4605. 214/290-2631.

Citicorp North America
2001 Ross Ave, Dallas TX 75201-8001. 214/953-3800.

Federal Home Loan Bank
PO Box 619026, Dallas TX 75261-9026. 972/714-8500.

Federal Information Systems
6201 Interstate Highway 3, Greenville TX 75402-7419. 903/408-4500.

First USA Financial Inc.
PO Box 650370, Dallas TX
75265-0370. 214/849-2000.

Montgomery Ward Credit Corp.
901 E Avenue K, Grand Prairie
TX 75050-2636. 972/647-0303.

NationsCredit Corporation
225 E John Carpenter Fwy, Irving
TX 75062-2731. 972/506-5000.

One Hour Acceptance
3301 Airport Fwy, Bedford TX
76021-6032. 817/459-1400.

Paymentech Inc.
PO Box 650370, Dallas TX
75265-0370. 214/849-3000.

Sallie Mae
777 N Twin Creek Dr, Killeen
TX 76543-4236. 254/554-4500.

Summit Acceptance Corporation
3939 Belt Line Rd, Ste 500,
Dallas TX 75244-2220. 972/247-0777.

The Associates
8201 Ridgepoint Dr, Irving TX
75063-3160. 972/831-3498.

WFS Financial Inc.
PO Box 168048, Irving TX
75016-8048. 972/409-3300.

INVESTMENT ADVISORS

American Express Financial Advisors
860 Airport Freeway, Ste 401,
Hurst TX 76054-3264. 817/428-9898.

Basic Capital Management
10670 N Central Expressway,
Dallas TX 75231-2111. 214/692-4700.

Fidelity Information Service Co.
6001 Campus Circle, Irving TX
75063. 972/830-7100.

Lone Star Securities Corp.
600 North Pearl St, Ste 1500,
Dallas TX 75201-2864. 214/754-8400.

Magna Management and Investment Co.
2727 Ruder St, Dallas TX 75212-4216. 214/638-8718.

MORTGAGE BANKERS

Amresco Inc.
700 N Pearl St, Ste 2400, Dallas
TX 75201-2840. 214/953-7700.

Banc One Mortgage Corp.
1825 Market Center Blvd, Dallas
TX 75207-3327. 214/744-8600.

Capstead Inc.
2711 N Haskell Ave, Dallas TX
75204-2911. 214/874-2323.

Carl Brown Mortgage
2974 LBJ Freeway, Dallas TX
75234-7602. 972/484-5600.

Countrywide Home Loans Inc.
5151 Beltline Rd, Dallas TX
75240. 972/980-4100.

CWF Home Loans
6400 Legacy Dr, Plano TX
75024-3628. 972/608-6000.

Dunwoody Mortgage
PO Box 809089, Dallas TX
75380-9089. 972/458-9200.

EMC Mortgage Corporation
PO Box 141358, Irving TX
75014-1358. 972/444-2800.

Fannie Mae
PO Box 650043, Dallas TX
75265-0043. 972/773-4663.

First Plus Financial Inc.
1600 Viceroy Dr, Dallas TX
75235-2306. 214/599-6300.

First Tennessee Bank Mortgage
8001 N Stemmons Freeway,
Dallas TX 75247-4101. 214/672-3000.

NationsBank Mortgage Corp.
1201 Main St, Fl 29, Dallas TX
75202-3903. 214/743-9800.

Sunbelt National Mortgage
2974 LBJ Fwy, Dallas TX 75234.
972/919-8077.

SECURITY BROKERS AND DEALERS

Antilles Investment Corp.
6808 Winterwood Lane, Dallas
TX 75248-5048. 972/701-8600.

Capital Institutional Services
750 N Saint Paul St, Dallas TX
75201-3233. 214/720-0055.

Dean Witter Reynolds Inc.
6310 LBJ Freeway, Dallas TX
75240-6401. 972/788-8500.

Dean Witter Reynolds Inc.
10000 N Central Expressway,
Dallas TX 75231-4177. 214/265-4452.

First Boston Mortgage Securities
2200 Ross Ave, Ste 3100, Dallas
TX 75201-2761. 214/740-5000.

HD Vest Financial Services
433 Las Colinas Blvd E, Irving
TX 75039-5581. 214/863-6000.

Hicks Muse Tate & Furst Inc.
200 Crescent Ct, Ste 1600, Dallas
TX 75201-1829. 214/740-7300.

Merrill Lynch Pierce Fenner Smith
2000 Premiere Pl, Dallas TX
75206. 214/750-4700.

Merrill Lynch Pierce Fenner Smith
201 Main St, Ste 850, Fort Worth
TX 76102-3112. 817/335-3751.

Merrill Lynch Pierce Fenner Smith
13355 Noel Rd, Fl 7, Dallas TX
75240-6602. 972/980-8600.

Merrill Lynch Pierce Fenner Smith
2121 San Jacinto St, Dallas TX
75201-2739. 214/969-0008.

Penson Financial Services
8080 North Central Expressway,
Dallas TX 75206-1838. 214/953-0016.

Prudential Securities Inc.
10440 North Central Expressway,
Dallas TX 75231-2221. 214/373-2700.

Royal Indemnity Company
PO Box 809016, Dallas TX
75380-9016. 972/490-1800.

Smith Barney Inc.
500 North Akard St, Ste 3900,
Dallas TX 75201-6604. 214/720-1200.

Smith Barney Inc.
5950 Berkshire Lane, Ste 600,
Dallas TX 75225-5834. 214/368-8555.

Smith Barney Inc.
12377 Merit Drive, Ste 800,
Dallas TX 75251-2224. 972/387-8989.

Smith Barney Inc.
200 Crescent Court, Suite 1200,
Dallas TX 75201-7837. 214/855-7900.

Sunpoint Securities Inc.
911 W Loop 281, Longview TX
75604-2900. 903/759-3530.

For more information on career opportunities in financial services:

Associations

FINANCIAL EXECUTIVES INSTITUTE
P.O. Box 1938, Morristown NJ 07962-1938. 973/898-4600. World Wide Web address: http://www.fei.org. Fee and membership required.

INSTITUTE OF FINANCIAL EDUCATION
55 West Monroe Street, Suite 2800, Chicago IL 60603-5014. 312/364-0100. World Wide Web address: http://www.theinstitute.com. Offers career development programs.

NATIONAL ASSOCIATION OF BUSINESS ECONOMISTS
1233 20th Street NW, Suite 505, Washington DC 20036. 202/463-6223. World Wide Web address: http://www.nabe.com. Offers a newsletter and Website that provide a list of job openings.

NATIONAL ASSOCIATION OF CREDIT MANAGEMENT
8815 Centre Park Drive, Suite 200, Columbia MD 21045-2158. 410/740-5560. World Wide Web address: http://www.nacm.org. Publishes a business credit magazine.

NATIONAL ASSOCIATION OF REITS
1129 20th Street NW, Suite 305, Washington DC 20036. 202/785-8717. World Wide Web address: http://www.nareit.com. Contact: Matt Lentz, Membership. Membership required.

PUBLIC SECURITIES ASSOCIATION
40 Broad Street, 12th Floor, New York NY 10004. 212/809-7000. Contact: Caroline Binn, extension 427.

SECURITIES INDUSTRY ASSOCIATION
120 Broadway, 35th Floor, New York NY 10271. 212/608-1500. World Wide Web address: http://www. sia.com. Contact: Phil Williams, Membership. Publishes a security industry yearbook. Membership required.

TREASURY MANAGEMENT ASSOCIATION
7315 Wisconsin Avenue, Suite 600-W, Bethesda MD 20814. 301/907-2862. World Wide Web address: http://www.tma-net.org/treasury.

Directories

DIRECTORY OF AMERICAN FINANCIAL INSTITUTIONS
Thomson Business Publications, 6195 Crooked Creek Road, Norcross GA 30092. 770/448-1011. Sales: 800/321-3373.

MOODY'S BANK AND FINANCE MANUAL
Moody's Investor Service, 99 Church Street, New York NY 10007. 212/553-0300. World Wide Web address: http://www.moodys.com.

Magazines

BARRON'S: NATIONAL BUSINESS AND FINANCIAL WEEKLY
Barron's, 200 Liberty Street, New York NY 10281. 212/416-2700.

FINANCIAL PLANNING
40 West 57th Street, 11th Floor, New York NY 10019. 212/765-5311.

FINANCIAL WORLD
1328 Broadway, 3rd Floor, New York NY 10001. 212/594-5030.

FUTURES: THE MAGAZINE OF COMMODITIES AND OPTIONS
250 South Wacker Drive, Suite 1150, Chicago IL 60606. 312/977-0999. World Wide Web address: http://www.futuresmag.com.

INSTITUTIONAL INVESTOR
488 Madison Avenue, 12th Floor, New York NY 10022. 212/303-3300.

Online Services

FINANCIAL/ACCOUNTING/INSURANCE JOBS PAGE
http://www.nationjob.com/financial. This Website provides a list of financial, accounting, and insurance job openings.

JOBS IN CORPORATE FINANCE
http://www.cob.ohio-state.edu/dept/fin/jobs/corpfin.htm. Provides information and resources for jobseekers looking to work in the field of corporate finance.

NATIONAL BANKING NETWORK: RECRUITING FOR BANKING AND FINANCE
http://www.banking-financejobs.com. Offers a searchable database of job openings in financial services and banking. The database is searchable by region, keyword, and job specialty.

FOOD AND BEVERAGES/AGRICULTURE

 *The food and beverages industry constitutes the nation's largest sector of manufacturing, and the demand for processed food and beverages should increase moderately as the market becomes more globalized. With the popularity of pre-cooked meals, supermarkets have increased spending on prepared foods; Technomic Inc., a food industry consulting firm, forecasted that these sales would rise by about 7 percent in 1998.*

According to Business Week, *about 15 percent of packaged food industry jobs were eliminated between 1996 and 1998. The trend in the packaged food business is toward cutbacks in the number of brands offered as well as less coupons for consumers. By reducing the number of brands, food companies are able to spend less money on marketing and focus on top-selling products. General Mills, for example, has eliminated all but its more profitable cereals.*

Overall, the U.S. Department of Labor projects a slow decline in food industry employment through the year 2005, particularly for those occupations hurt by rising operating costs, including food processors and butchers. Agricultural careers are also expected to decline through 2005. However, the dairy sector should see about 3 percent annual growth over the next five years, due mainly to strong demand for reduced fat milk, natural cheese, and frozen desserts.

ACCO FEEDS
P.O. Box 190666, Dallas TX 75219. 214/631-8280. **Contact:** Personnel. **Description:** Produces a variety of animal feeds.

AMERICAN PRODUCTS COMPANY, INC.
10741 Miller Road, Dallas TX 75238. 214/343-4816. **Contact:** Human Resources Department. **Description:** Produces a complete range of bakery products. **Common positions include:** Manufacturer's/Wholesaler's Sales Rep.; Operations/Production Manager. **Benefits:** Credit Union; Dental Insurance; Life Insurance; Medical Insurance; Pension Plan. **Corporate headquarters location:** St. Paul MN. **Other U.S. locations:** Kingswood TX; San Antonio TX. **Parent company:** Best Brands, Inc. **Operations at this facility include:** Administration; Divisional Headquarters; Manufacturing; Regional Headquarters; Research and Development; Sales; Service.

BEST MAID
P.O. Box 1809, Fort Worth TX 76101-1809. 817/335-5494. **Contact:** Human Resources Department. **Description:** Best Maid manufactures and distributes a variety of pickled fruits and vegetables.

BUNGE FOODS GROUP
P.O. Box 163289, Fort Worth TX 76161-3289. 817/625-2331. **Contact:** Human Resources Department. **Description:** A manufacturer of shortening and margarine. **Common positions include:** Accountant/Auditor; Blue-Collar Worker Supervisor; Customer Service Representative; Department Manager; Electrical/Electronics Engineer; Food Scientist/Technologist; Industrial Engineer; Manufacturer's/Wholesaler's Sales Rep.; Mechanical Engineer. **Educational backgrounds include:** Engineering. **Corporate headquarters location:** St. Louis MO. **Parent company:** Bunge Corporation. **Operations at this facility include:** Administration; Manufacturing; Sales.

CACTUS FEEDERS INC.
2209 West Seventh Street, Amarillo TX 79106-3050. 806/373-2333. **Contact:** Kevin Hazelwood, Director of Employment Development. **Description:** Feeds and prepares cattle to be delivered to meat packing plants and slaughterhouses.

CAMPBELL SOUP COMPANY
P.O. Box 9016, Paris TX 75461-9016. 903/737-2282. **Contact:** Human Resources. **World Wide Web address:** http://www.campbellsoup.com. **Description:** This location manufactures soup. Overall, the company manufactures commercial soups, juices, pickles, frozen foods, canned beans, canned pasta products, spaghetti sauces, and baked goods. The company's products are distributed worldwide. U.S. brand names include Campbell's, Vlasic, V8, Chunky, Home Cookin', Prego, Pepperidge Farm, Inc., LeMenu, and Swanson. European foods are sold under brand names such as Pleybin, Biscuits Delacre, Freshbake, Groko, Godiva, and Betis. Campbell Soup Company also owns Arnotts Biscuits of Australia. **Common positions include:** Accountant/Auditor; Biological Scientist; Chemist; Electrical/Electronics Engineer; Electrician; Food Scientist/Technologist; Human Resources Manager; Industrial Production Manager; Management Trainee; Mechanical Engineer; Purchasing Agent/Manager; Registered Nurse. **Educational backgrounds include:** Accounting; Biology; Chemistry; Engineering; Technology. **Benefits:** 401(k); Dental Insurance; Disability Coverage; Employee Discounts; Life Insurance; Medical Insurance; Pension Plan; Savings Plan; Tuition Assistance. **Corporate headquarters location:** Camden NJ. **Other U.S. locations:** Sacramento CA; Maxton NC; Napoleon OH. **Operations at this facility include:** Manufacturing. **Listed on:** New York Stock Exchange. **Number of employees at this location:** 1,600. **Number of employees nationwide:** 49,000.

CARGILL INC.
P.O. Box 79370, Saginaw TX 76179. 817/847-3400. **Contact:** Virginia Smith, Personnel. **World Wide Web address:** http://www.cargill.com. **Description:** This facility is a flour and grain mill processor and distributor. Overall, Cargill Inc., its subsidiaries, and its affiliates are involved in nearly 50 individual lines of business. Cargill is a major trader of grains and oilseeds, as well as a marketer of many other agricultural and non-agricultural commodities. As a transporter, it uses a complex network of rail and road systems, inland waterways, and ocean-going routes, combining its own fleet with transportation services purchased from outside sources to move bulk commodities from point of origin to point of consumption. As an agricultural supplier, Cargill is a leader in developing high-quality, competitively-priced farm products and in supplying them to growers. Agricultural products include a wide variety of feed, seed, fertilizers, and other goods and services required by producers worldwide. Cargill is also a leader in producing and marketing seed varieties and hybrids. Cargill Central Research, located at Cargill headquarters, is dedicated to developing new agricultural products to address the needs of customers around the world. Cargill also provides financial and technical services through Cargill's Financial Markets Division, which supports Cargill and its subsidiaries with financial products and services that address the full spectrum of market conditions. These include financial instrument trading, emerging markets instrument trading, value investing, and money management. Cargill's worldwide food processing businesses supply products ranging from basic ingredients used in food production to recognized name brands. Cargill also operates a number of industrial businesses, including the production of steel, industrial-grade starches, and ethane. **Corporate headquarters location:** Minneapolis MN. **Number of employees worldwide:** 70,000.

COCA-COLA BOTTLING COMPANY OF NORTH TEXAS
P.O. Box 2008, Dallas TX 75221. 214/357-1781. **Recorded jobline:** 214/902-2634. **Contact:** Brent Hansen, Senior Human Resources Administrator. **Description:** Coca-Cola Bottling Company of North Texas is a regional subsidiary of Coca-Cola Company, one of the world's largest marketers, distributors, and producers of bottle and can products of The Coca-Cola Company. The company also serves as a significant bottler of several other national and regional beverage brands such as Barq's and Dr. Pepper. **Common positions include:** Accountant/Auditor; Blue-Collar Worker Supervisor; Financial Analyst; Services Sales Representative. **Educational backgrounds include:** Accounting; Business Administration; Finance. **Benefits:** 401(k); Dental Insurance; Disability Coverage; Employee Discounts; Life Insurance; Medical Insurance; Pension Plan; Savings Plan; Tuition Assistance. **Special programs:** Internships. **Corporate headquarters location:** Atlanta GA. **Other U.S. locations:** Nationwide. **Parent company:** Coca-Cola

Enterprises Inc. is in the liquid nonalcoholic refreshment business, which extends the company's product line beyond traditional carbonated soft drink categories to beverages such as still and sparkling waters, juices, isotonics, and teas. The company operates in 38 states, the District of Columbia, the U.S. Virgin Islands, the Islands of Tortola and Grand Cayman, and the Netherlands. Coca-Cola Enterprises Inc. employs approximately 30,000 individuals who operate the 268 facilities, approximately 24,000 vehicles, and over 860,000 vending machines, beverage dispensers, and coolers used to market, distribute, and produce the company's products. **Operations at this facility include:** Administration; Divisional Headquarters; Regional Headquarters; Sales; Service. **Listed on:** New York Stock Exchange.

CONTINENTAL GRAIN COMPANY
P.O. Box 4277, Fort Worth TX 76164-0277. 817/624-4171. **Contact:** Mr. Kim Mathison, Superintendent. **Description:** An international food company involved principally in grain and grain-related businesses. Traders buy and sell grains and commodities in almost every market and are supported by the company's global network of storage and ocean freight facilities.

DALLAS CITY PACKING INC.
3049 Morrell Street, Dallas TX 75203. 214/948-3901. **Contact:** David Myers, Personnel. **Description:** A meat packing plant.

DARLING INTERNATIONAL INC.
251 O'Connor Ridge Boulevard, Suite 300, Irving TX 75038. 972/717-0300. **Contact:** Linda Crain, Director of Human Resources. **Description:** Manufacturers of animal by-products, including fats and proteins. **Common positions include:** Accountant/Auditor; Agricultural Engineer; Computer Programmer; Management Trainee; Systems Analyst. **Educational backgrounds include:** Accounting; Business Administration; Computer Science; Marketing. **Benefits:** 401(k); Dental Insurance; Disability Coverage; Medical Insurance; Pension Plan; Tuition Assistance. **Corporate headquarters location:** This Location. **Listed on:** Privately held. **Number of employees at this location:** 50. **Number of employees nationwide:** 1,450.

DECKER FOOD COMPANY
P.O. Box 472587, Garland TX 75047-2587. 972/278-6192. **Physical address:** 3200 West Kingsley, Garland TX 75041. **Contact:** Bill Mitchell, Human Resources. **Description:** Processes bacon, sausage, boiled ham, and smoked and cured pork.

DEEN MEAT
P.O. Box 4155, Fort Worth TX 76164. 817/335-2257. **Contact:** Personnel. **Description:** A local distributor of beef products.

DR. PEPPER/7-UP COMPANY
P.O. Box 869077, Plano TX 75086-9077. 972/673-7000. **Physical address:** 5301 Legacy Drive, Plano TX 75024. **Contact:** Personnel. **World Wide Web address:** http://www.drpepper.com. **Description:** Regional facility of the soft drink producer. Overall, Dr. Pepper/7-Up Company manufactures, markets, and distributes soft drink syrups, concentrates, and extracts to bottlers. A food service segment distributes products to restaurants and convenience stores. The premier beverages segment makes Welch's carbonated drinks. Dr. Pepper products are sold in 19 foreign countries. **Listed on:** New York Stock Exchange.

EARTHGRAINS COMPANY
3500 Manor Way, Dallas TX 75235. 214/357-1754. **Fax:** 214/350-1137. **Contact:** Jerry I. Riano, Director of Human Resources. **Description:** A bread manufacturing plant and product distribution center. **Common positions include:** Accountant/Auditor; Blue-Collar Worker Supervisor; Branch Manager; Buyer; Chemist; Clerical Supervisor; Credit Manager; Electrician; Human Resources Manager; Industrial Production Manager; Operations/Production Manager. **Benefits:** Dental Insurance; Employee Discounts; Life Insurance; Medical Insurance; Pension Plan. **Corporate headquarters location:** St. Louis MO. **Operations at this facility include:** Administration; Manufacturing; Sales. **Listed on:** New York Stock Exchange. **Number of employees at this location:** 420.

EXCEL CORPORATION
P.O. Box 910, Plainview TX 79072. 806/293-5181. **Fax:** 806/293-1897. **Contact:** Human Resources Manager. **Description:** A beef processing company. **Educational backgrounds include:** Accounting; Business Administration; Engineering; Nursing. **Benefits:** 401(k); Daycare Assistance; Dental Insurance; Disability Coverage; Life Insurance; Medical Insurance; Pension Plan; Savings Plan; Tuition Assistance. **Special programs:** Internships. **Corporate headquarters location:** Wichita KS. **Parent company:** Cargill Inc. **Number of employees at this location:** 1,750.

EXCEL CORPORATION
P.O. Box 579, Friona TX 79035-0579. 806/295-3201. **Contact:** Director of Human Resources. **Description:** A beef processing plant. **Special programs:** Internships. **Corporate headquarters location:** Wichita KS. **Parent company:** Cargill Inc.

FLEMING COMPANY
P.O. Box 469012, Garland TX 75046. 972/840-4400. **Contact:** Personnel. **Description:** A wholesale distributor of a wide variety of groceries, meats, dairy and delicatessen products, frozen foods, fresh produce, and a variety of general merchandise.

FLOWERS BAKING COMPANY
3521 East Avenue E, Arlington TX 76011-5236. 817/640-8752. **Contact:** Personnel. **Description:** Bakes and distributes a variety of bread products.

FRIONA INDUSTRIES
P.O. Box 15568, Amarillo TX 79105-5568. 806/374-1811. **Fax:** 806/374-1324. **Contact:** Dave Delaney, General Manager. **Description:** Friona Industries owns and operates cattle feed lots.

FRITO-LAY INC.
P.O. Box 225458, Dallas TX 75222-5458. 817/861-1784. **Contact:** Staffing Department. **World Wide Web address:** http://www.fritolay.com. **Description:** A worldwide manufacturer and wholesaler of snack products, including Fritos Corn Chips, Lays Potato Chips, Doritos Tortilla Chips, Ruffles Potato Chips, Chee-tos, and a wide range of other snack foods. In 1996, Frito-Lay acquired Eagle Snacks from Anheuser-Busch. **Common positions include:** Chemical Engineer; Computer Programmer; Electrical/Electronics Engineer; Financial Analyst; Mechanical Engineer; Purchasing Agent/Manager. **Educational backgrounds include:** Business Administration; Engineering; Finance. **Benefits:** 401(k); Dental Insurance; Disability Coverage; Employee Discounts; Life Insurance; Medical Insurance; Savings Plan; Tuition Assistance. **Special programs:** Internships. **Corporate headquarters location:** Plano TX. **Other U.S. locations:** Nationwide. **Parent company:** PepsiCo operates on a worldwide basis within two industry segments: beverages and snack foods. The beverage segment primarily markets its brands worldwide and manufactures concentrates for its brands for sale to franchised bottlers worldwide. The segment also operates bottling plants and distribution facilities of its own located in the U.S. and key international markets, and distributes ready-to-drink Lipton tea products under a joint-venture agreement. In addition, under separate distribution and joint-venture agreements, the segment distributes certain previously existing, as well as jointly developed Ocean Spray juice products. The international snack food business includes major operations in Mexico, the United Kingdom, and Canada. **Operations at this facility include:** Divisional Headquarters; Research and Development. **Listed on:** New York Stock Exchange. **Number of employees at this location:** 2,000. **Number of employees nationwide:** 29,000.

FRITO-LAY INC.
P.O. Box 569100, Dallas TX 75356-9100. 972/579-2111. **Physical address:** 701 North Wildwood, Irving TX 75061. **Contact:** Human Resources Department. **Description:** A worldwide manufacturer and wholesaler of snack products, including Fritos Corn Chips, Lays Potato Chips, Doritos Tortilla Chips, Ruffles Potato Chips, Chee-tos, and a wide range of other snack foods. In 1996, Frito-Lay acquired Eagle Snacks from Anheuser-Busch. **Special programs:** Internships. **Corporate headquarters location:** Plano TX. **Parent company:** PepsiCo operates on a worldwide basis within two industry segments: beverages and snack foods. The beverage segment primarily markets its brands worldwide and manufactures concentrates for its brands for sale to franchised

bottlers worldwide. The segment also operates bottling plants and distribution facilities of its own located in the U.S. and key international markets, and distributes ready-to-drink Lipton tea products under a joint-venture agreement. In addition, under separate distribution and joint-venture agreements, the segment distributes certain previously existing, as well as jointly developed Ocean Spray juice products. The international snack food business includes major operations in Mexico, the United Kingdom, and Canada. **Number of employees nationwide:** 29,000.

FRITO-LAY INC.

P.O. Box 660634, Dallas TX 75266-0634. 972/334-7000. **Physical address:** 7701 Legacy Drive, Plano TX 75024-4099. **Fax:** 972/334-2019. **Contact:** Staffing. **World Wide Web address:** http://www.fritolay.com. **Description:** Frito-Lay Inc. is a worldwide manufacturer and wholesaler of snack products, including Fritos Corn Chips, Lays Potato Chips, Doritos Tortilla Chips, Ruffles Potato Chips, Chee-tos, and a wide range of other snack foods. In 1996, Frito-Lay acquired Eagle Snacks from Anheuser-Busch. **Special programs:** Internships. **Corporate headquarters location:** This Location. **Parent company:** PepsiCo operates on a worldwide basis within two industry segments: beverages and snack foods. The beverage segment primarily markets its brands worldwide and manufactures concentrates for its brands for sale to franchised bottlers worldwide. The segment also operates bottling plants and distribution facilities of its own located in the U.S. and key international markets, and distributes ready-to-drink Lipton tea products under a joint-venture agreement. In addition, under separate distribution and joint-venture agreements, the segment distributes certain previously existing, as well as jointly developed Ocean Spray juice products. The international snack food business includes major operations in Mexico, the United Kingdom, and Canada.

FRITO-LAY INC.

3203 Avenue B, Lubbock TX 79404. 806/762-7700. **Contact:** Dave Keenan, Human Resources Director. **World Wide Web address:** http://www.fritolay.com. **Description:** A worldwide manufacturer and wholesaler of snack products, including Fritos Corn Chips, Lays Potato Chips, Doritos Tortilla Chips, and a wide range of other snack foods. In 1996, Frito-Lay acquired Eagle Snacks from Anheuser-Busch. **Corporate headquarters location:** Plano TX. **Parent company:** PepsiCo operates on a worldwide basis within two industry segments: beverages and snack foods. The beverage segment primarily markets its brands worldwide and manufactures concentrates for its brands for sale to franchised bottlers worldwide. The segment also operates bottling plants and distribution facilities of its own located in the U.S. and key international markets, and distributes ready-to-drink Lipton tea products under a joint-venture agreement. In addition, under separate distribution and joint-venture agreements, the segment distributes certain previously existing, as well as jointly developed Ocean Spray juice products. The international snack food business includes major operations in Mexico, the United Kingdom, and Canada.

GROCERY SUPPLY

1135 South Lamar Boulevard, Dallas TX 75215. 214/565-1311. **Contact:** Personnel. **Description:** A wholesaler of groceries.

H&M FOOD SYSTEMS

3709 East First Street, Fort Worth TX 76111-5804. 817/831-0981. **Contact:** Human Resources. **Description:** A meat packaging plant.

HOLLY SUGAR CORPORATION

P.O. Drawer 1778, Hereford TX 79045. 806/364-2590. **Contact:** Glen Boozer, Human Resources Manager. **World Wide Web address:** http://www.hollysugar.com. **Description:** This location grows, harvests, and processes sugar beets, which are then used to produce granulated sugar. Sugar is packaged at this location year round. Overall, Holly Sugar produces sugar and sugar products such as beet pulp and molasses. **Parent company:** Imperial Holly Corporation (Sugar Land TX). **Number of employees at this location:** 350.

HORMEL FOODS CORPORATION

700 Highlander Boulevard, Suite 540, Arlington TX 76015. 817/465-4772. **Contact:** Office Manager. **World Wide Web address:** http://www.hormel.com. **Description:** One of the leading processors and marketers of branded, value-added meat and food products. Principal products of

the company are branded, processed meat and food entrees which are sold fresh, frozen, cured, smoked, cooked, and canned. Included are sausages, hams, franks, bacon, canned luncheon meats, shelf-stable microwaveable entrees, stews, chili, hash, meat spreads, and frozen processed products. The majority of the company's products are sold under the Hormel brandmark. Other trademarks of the company include Farm Fresh, Little Sizzlers, Quick Meal, Kid's Kitchen, Chi Chi's, House of Tsang, Mary Kitchen, Dinty Moore, Light & Lean, Chicken by George, Black Label, and SPAM. **Corporate headquarters location:** Austin MN. **Other U.S. locations:** CA; GA; IA; KS; NE; OK; WI. **International locations:** Australia; England; Japan; Korea; Panama; Philippines. **Subsidiaries include:** Dan's Prize, Inc.; Dubuque Foods; Farm Fresh Catfish Company; Jennie-O Foods. **Listed on:** New York Stock Exchange. **Number of employees nationwide:** 10,000.

IBP INC.
P.O. Box 30500, Amarillo TX 79187. 806/335-1531. **Contact:** Human Resources Department. **World Wide Web address:** http://www.ibpinc.com. **Description:** A slaughterhouse and meat packing plant.

INTERNATIONAL HOME FOODS INC.
P.O. Box 1867, Fort Worth TX 76101. 817/336-5581. **Contact:** Personnel. **Description:** Produces ranch-style beans.

KINGS LIQUOR INC.
6659 Camp Bowie Boulevard, Fort Worth TX 76116. 817/732-0661. **Contact:** Harry Labovitz, Personnel Director. **Description:** A liquor distiller, distributor, and retailer.

KRAFT FOODS, INC.
2340 Forest Lane, Garland TX 75042. 972/272-7511. **Contact:** Mark Niggemeyer, Human Resources Supervisor. **Description:** This location produces a variety of food products including barbecue sauce, mayonnaise, tartar sauce, Miracle Whip, Catalina dressing, and salad products. Overall, Kraft Foods, Inc. is one of the world's leading producers of packaged grocery products. The company's products are supplied to more than 100 countries worldwide.

LEON'S TEXAS CUISINE
P.O. Box 1850, McKinney TX 75070-1850. 972/529-5050. **Fax:** 972/529-2244. **Contact:** Cindy Stephens, Human Resources Director. **Description:** A food production company.

LIPTON FOODS
1729 Irving Boulevard, Dallas TX 75207. 214/741-5481. **Contact:** Personnel Supervisor. **Description:** A producer of margarine and non-dairy spreads.

MILLER BREWING COMPANY
7001 South Freeway, Fort Worth TX 76134. 817/551-3200. **Contact:** Personnel Department. **World Wide Web address:** http://www.reddog.com. **Description:** Miller Brewing Company produces and distributes beer and other malt beverages. Principal beer brands include Miller Lite, Lite Ice, Miller Genuine Draft, Miller Genuine Draft Light, Miller High Life, Miller Reserve, Lowenbrau, Milwaukee's Best, Meister Brau, as well as Red Dog and Icehouse brewed at the Plank Road Brewery. Miller also produces Sharp's, a non-alcoholic brew. **Corporate headquarters location:** Milwaukee WI. **Subsidiaries include:** Jacob Leinenkugel Brewing Company (Chippewa Falls WI) brews Leinenkugel's Original Premium, Leinenkugel's Light, Leinie's Ice, Leinenkugel's Limited, Leinenkugel's Red Lager, and four seasonal beers: Leinenkugel's Genuine Bock, Leinenkugel's Honey Weiss, Leinenkugel's Autumn Gold, and Leinenkugel's Winter Lager. Miller owns and operates one of the largest beer importers in the United States, Molson Breweries U.S.A., Inc. (Reston VA), which imports Molson beers from Canada, as well as Australia's Foster's Lager and many other brands. **Parent company:** Philip Morris Companies Inc. (New York). **Number of employees nationwide:** 155,000.

MINUTE MAID COMPANY
8400 Imperial, Waco TX 76712. **Contact:** Human Resources. **Description:** This location manufactures Powerade, Nestea, Fruitopia, and other Minute Maid brand juice products. **NOTE:** This firm does not accept unsolicited resumes. Please only respond to advertised openings.

MONFORT INC.
P.O. Box 524, Dumas TX 79029. 806/966-5103. **Contact:** Edye Cunningham, Personnel Manager. **Description:** This location is a meat processing and packing facility. Overall, Monfort's business activities are divided into two groups: food products and consumer products. The food products division slaughters livestock and poultry; and processes, purchases, and sells meats, animal products, and animal by-products including eggs, butter, cheese, vegetable oils, margarine, and shortenings. The food products division also operates seven livestock slaughtering plants, 37 meat processing and distribution facilities, 11 poultry and dairy facilities, and three other facilities in the United States producing bacon, hot dogs, and other processed meats. The consumer products division manufactures and sells a variety of personal care products, household goods, and handcraft goods; and operates 14 United States facilities producing soap, ammonia, toiletries, and other products.

MORNINGSTAR GROUP, INC.
5956 Sherry Lane, Suite 1500, Dallas TX 75225. 214/360-4700. **Contact:** Human Resources. **Description:** A food preparations company.

MRS. BAIRD'S BAKERIES
P.O. Box 417, Dallas TX 75221. 214/526-7201. **Contact:** Sharon King, Personnel Director. **Description:** Bakes bread and other goods. The company has 11 facilities located throughout Texas. **Corporate headquarters location:** This Location.

NORTH CENTRAL DISTRIBUTORS INC.
2445 Santa Ana, Dallas TX 75228. 214/328-2821. **Contact:** Personnel. **Description:** A distributor of tobacco products.

OSCAR MAYER FOODS CORPORATION
4700 Highway 75 South, Sherman TX 75090. 903/893-5151. **Fax:** 903/813-5632. **Contact:** Monique Hoppess, Associate Human Resources Manager. **Description:** This location processes meat and poultry products. **NOTE:** The company offers entry-level positions. **Common positions include:** Accountant/Auditor; Computer Programmer; Electrical/Electronics Engineer; Electrician; Environmental Engineer; Food Scientist/Technologist; Health Services Manager; Human Resources Manager; Industrial Engineer; Mechanical Engineer; Quality Control Supervisor. **Educational backgrounds include:** Accounting; Business Administration; Engineering; Finance; Food Science. **Benefits:** 401(k); Dental Insurance; Disability Coverage; Life Insurance; Medical Insurance; Pension Plan; Profit Sharing; Tuition Assistance. **Special programs:** Internships; Training. **Corporate headquarters location:** Northfield IL. **Other U.S. locations:** Davenport IA; Madison WI. **Subsidiaries include:** Claussen; Louis Rich. **Parent company:** Kraft Foods, Inc. **Operations at this facility include:** Manufacturing. **Listed on:** New York Stock Exchange. **Number of employees at this location:** 750.

OWENS COUNTRY SAUSAGE INC.
P.O. Box 830249, Richardson TX 75083. 972/235-7181. **Contact:** Human Resources. **World Wide Web address:** http://www.owensinc.com. **Description:** Produces sausage and other pork products. **Corporate headquarters location:** This Location.

PEPSI-COLA COMPANY
4532 Highway 67, Mesquite TX 75150. 214/324-8500. **Contact:** Human Resources. **World Wide Web address:** http://www.pepsi.com. **Description:** This location is a bottler and distributor of Pepsi-Cola beverages. **Parent company:** PepsiCo operates on a worldwide basis within two industry segments: beverages and snack foods. The beverage segment primarily markets its brands worldwide, and manufactures concentrates for its brands for sale to franchised bottlers worldwide. The beverage segment also operates bottling plants and distribution facilities in the U.S. and in key international markets, and distributes ready-to-drink Lipton tea products under a joint venture agreement. In addition, under separate distribution and joint-venture agreements, the beverage segment distributes certain previously existing, as well as jointly developed, Ocean Spray juice products. The international snack food business includes major operations in Mexico, the United Kingdom, and Canada.

PILGRIM'S PRIDE CORPORATION

P.O. Box 1268, Mt. Pleasant TX 75456-1268. 903/575-1000. **Contact:** Human Resources. **Description:** Pilgrim's Pride Corporation is a producer of chicken products and eggs for the restaurant, institutional, food service, grocery, and wholesale markets. The company's operations include breeding, hatching, growing, processing, packaging, and preparing poultry. Pilgrim's Pride Corporation also produces animal feeds and ingredients. The company is one of the largest producers of chicken products in the United States and Mexico. The company's primary domestic distribution is handled through restaurants and retailers in central, southwestern, and western United States, and through the food service industry throughout the country. **Corporate headquarters location:** Pittsburg TX. **Other U.S. locations:** AR; AZ; OK. **Listed on:** New York Stock Exchange.

PILGRIM'S PRIDE CORPORATION

P.O. Box 93, Pittsburg TX 75686-0093. 903/855-1000. **Contact:** Human Resources. **Description:** Pilgrim's Pride Corporation is a producer of chicken products and eggs for the restaurant, institutional, food service, grocery, and wholesale markets. The company's operations include breeding, hatching, growing, processing, packaging, and preparing poultry. Pilgrim's Pride Corporation also produces animal feeds and ingredients. The company is one of the largest producers of chicken products in the United States and Mexico. The company's primary domestic distribution is handled through restaurants and retailers in central, southwestern, and western United States, and through the food service industry throughout the country. **Common positions include:** Accountant/Auditor; Blue-Collar Worker Supervisor; Computer Programmer; Credit Manager; Customer Service Representative; Food Scientist/Technologist; Human Resources Manager; Management Trainee; Manufacturer's/Wholesaler's Sales Rep. **Benefits:** 401(k); Daycare Assistance; Disability Coverage; ESOP; Life Insurance; Medical Insurance; Tuition Assistance. **Corporate headquarters location:** This Location. **Other U.S. locations:** AR; AZ; OK. **Listed on:** New York Stock Exchange.

PLAINS COTTON COOPERATIVE ASSOCIATION

P.O. Box 2827, Lubbock TX 79408. 806/763-8011. **Physical address:** 3301 East 50th Street, Lubbock TX 79404. **Contact:** Mr. Lee Phenix, Personnel Manager. **World Wide Web address:** http://www.pcca.com. **Description:** A marketing firm that buys and sells cotton. Plains Cotton Cooperative Association acts as the middle step between buyers and sellers by marketing raw cotton worldwide. The company sells to cotton merchants and textile mills.

PLANTATION FOODS INC.

P.O. Box 20788, Waco TX 76702. 254/799-6211. **Contact:** Human Resources. **World Wide Web address:** http://www.plantation-foods.com. **Description:** A turkey processing plant.

THE QUAKER OATS COMPANY

13745 Jupiter Road, Dallas TX 75238. 214/340-0370. **Contact:** Personnel Director. **World Wide Web address:** http://www.quakeroats.com. **Description:** A grocery products company. The Quaker Oats Company is best known for Old Fashioned Quaker Oats. Other products include Van Camps' canned pork and beans, and specialty products such as Beanee Weenee canned beans and wieners. The Quaker Oats Company is also the primary producer of Gatorade, one of the leading sports beverages in the United States. **Corporate headquarters location:** Chicago IL. **Listed on:** New York Stock Exchange.

QUIK-TO-FIX PRODUCTS INC.

209 Range Road, Garland TX 75040. 972/272-5521. **Contact:** Human Resources. **Description:** A food processing plant.

REDDY ICE

4320 Duncanville Road, Dallas TX 75236. 972/296-4271. **Contact:** Personnel. **Description:** Manufactures ice.

REPUBLIC BEVERAGE

4332 Empire Road, Fort Worth TX 76155. 817/868-4444. **Contact:** Personnel Representative. **Description:** A wine and alcohol distributor.

RODRIGUEZ FESTIVE FOODS
P.O. Box 4369, Fort Worth TX 76106. 817/624-2123. **Contact:** Pam Harris, Personnel Director. **Description:** Produces a line of frozen Mexican foods.

SCHEPPS DAIRY INC.
P.O. Box 279000, Dallas TX 75227. 214/824-8163. **Contact:** Personnel. **Description:** A producer and distributor of dairy products.

SEED RESOURCE, INC.
P.O. Box 326, Tulia TX 79088. 806/995-3882. **Contact:** Gary Regner, Human Resources Manager. **Description:** Distributes forage seed (including Sorghum Sudans, which it produces), alfalfa, turf grass seed, and wheat seed. The company also produces wheat. **Parent company:** ABT (AgriBioTech, Inc.) is a specialized distributor of forage (hay crops) and turf grass seed. The forage and turf grass seed industry supplies seed to the forage and turf cash crop sectors. The company distributes the following non-seed products: Bloatenz Plus, a liquid bloat preventative administered to the drinking water of cattle, permitting them to graze on alfalfa safely; PDS-1000, marketed in conjunction with Bloatenz Plus, is a microprocessor controlled precision dispensing system designed to dispense solutions into the drinking water of livestock at a preset dosage rate. Other subsidiaries of ABT include: Scott Seed Company; Hobart Seed Company; Halsey Seed Company; and Sphar & Company. Combined, these companies cover the following distribution territories: IN; KY; NM; NY; OK; OR; PA; TX; WA. The product specialties of these companies includes forage, turf grass, corn, vegetables, wheat, alfalfa, sorghum sudans, birdseed, and clover.

SEED RESOURCE, INC.
P.O. Box 439, Cactus TX 79013. 806/966-5165. **Contact:** Human Resources. **Description:** Distributes forage seed (including Sorghum Sudans, which it produces), alfalfa, turf grass seed, and wheat seed. The company also produces wheat. **Parent company:** ABT (AgriBioTech, Inc.) is a specialized distributor of forage (hay crops) and turf grass seed. The forage and turf grass seed industry supplies seed to the forage and turf cash crop sectors. The company distributes the following non-seed products: Bloatenz Plus, a liquid bloat preventative administered to the drinking water of cattle, permitting them to graze on alfalfa safely; PDS-1000, marketed in conjunction with Bloatenz Plus, is a microprocessor controlled precision dispensing system designed to dispense solutions into the drinking water of livestock at a preset dosage rate. Other subsidiaries of ABT include: Scott Seed Company; Hobart Seed Company; Halsey Seed Company; and Sphar & Company. Combined, these companies cover the following distribution territories: IN; KY; NM; NY; OK; OR; PA; TX; WA. The product specialties of these companies includes forage, turf grass, corn, vegetables, wheat, alfalfa, sorghum sudans, birdseed, and clover.

SIMEUS FOODS INTERNATIONAL
812 South Fifth Avenue, Mansfield TX 76063. 817/473-1562. **Contact:** Human Resources. **Description:** A food processing plant.

SOUTHWEST COCA-COLA BOTTLING COMPANY
6101 Avenue A, Lubbock TX 79404. 806/745-3261. **Contact:** Human Resources. **World Wide Web address:** http://www.coca-cola.com. **Description:** A bottling company packaging Coca-Cola, Barq's, and Dr. Pepper. **Parent company:** Coca-Cola Enterprises, Inc. is in the liquid non-alcoholic refreshment business, which includes traditional carbonated soft drinks, still and sparkling waters, juices, isotonics, and teas. The company operates in 38 states, the District of Columbia, the U.S. Virgin Islands, the Islands of Tortola and Grand Cayman, and the Netherlands. Including recent acquisitions, Coca-Cola Enterprises franchise territories encompass a population of over 154 million people, representing 54 percent of the population of the United States. Coca-Cola Enterprises operates 268 facilities, approximately 24,000 vehicles, and over 860,000 vending machines, beverage dispensers, and coolers used to market, distribute, and produce the company's products.

STANDARD FRUIT & VEGETABLE
P.O. Box 225027, Dallas TX 75222-5027. 214/428-3600. **Contact:** Ms. Francis McBride, Office Manager. **Description:** A distributor of produce.

SUPREME BEEF PROCESSORS
5219 Second Avenue, Dallas TX 75210. 214/428-1761. **Contact:** Gayla Hensley, Personnel Director. **Description:** A beef processing plant.

TYSON FOODS INC.
P.O. Box 648, Carthage TX 75633. 903/693-7101. **Contact:** Tim Hooper, Personnel Manager. **Description:** This location is a poultry processing plant. Overall, Tyson Foods Inc. is one of the world's largest fully integrated producers, processors, and marketers of poultry-based food products. The company also produces other entrees and convenience food items. Tyson products include Tyson Holly Farms Fresh Chicken, Weaver, Louis Kemp Crab, Lobster Delights, Healthy Portion, Beef Stir Fry, Crab Delights Stir Fry, Chicken Fried Rice Kits, Pork Chops with Cinnamon Apples, Salmon Grill Kits, Fish 'n Chips Kits, and Rotisserie Chicken. **Common positions include:** Accountant/Auditor; Agricultural Engineer; Agricultural Scientist; Architect; Biological Scientist; Blue-Collar Worker Supervisor; Branch Manager; Budget Analyst; Clerical Supervisor; Computer Programmer; Construction and Building Inspector; Construction Contractor; Cost Estimator; Counselor; Customer Service Representative; Draftsperson; Electrical/Electronics Engineer; Electrician; Emergency Medical Technician; Financial Analyst; Food Scientist/Technologist; General Manager; Human Resources Manager; Industrial Engineer; Industrial Production Manager; Insurance Agent/Broker; Licensed Practical Nurse; Management Trainee; Mechanical Engineer; Purchasing Agent/Manager; Quality Control Supervisor; Registered Nurse; Software Engineer; Systems Analyst; Veterinarian. **Educational backgrounds include:** Accounting; Business Administration; Engineering. **Benefits:** 401(k); Dental Insurance; Disability Coverage; Employee Discounts; Life Insurance; Medical Insurance; Pension Plan; Profit Sharing; Savings Plan. **Special programs:** Internships. **Corporate headquarters location:** Springdale AR. **Operations at this facility include:** Administration; Divisional Headquarters; Manufacturing; Regional Headquarters; Research and Development. **Listed on:** American Stock Exchange; NASDAQ; New York Stock Exchange. **Number of employees at this location:** 900.

VANDERVOORT DAIRY
900 South Main Street, Fort Worth TX 76104. 817/332-7551. **Contact:** Personnel. **Description:** A large producer of ice cream and other dairy products.

Note: Because addresses and telephone numbers of smaller companies can change rapidly, we recommend you call each company to verify the information below before inquiring about job opportunities. Mass mailings are not recommended.

Additional small employers:

ALCOHOL WHOLESALE

Budweiser Beer
7001 Will Rodgers Blvd, Fort Worth TX 76140. 817/568-4000.

Coors Distributing Company
PO Box 162869, Fort Worth TX 76161-2869. 817/838-1600.

Coors Distributing Company
3508 Avenue F, Arlington TX 76011-5225. 817/649-5626.

Miller Distributing of Dallas
PO Box 566187, Dallas TX 75356-6187. 214/630-0777.

Miller Distributing of Fort Worth
PO Box 3062, Fort Worth TX 76113-3062. 817/877-5960.

Oley Distributing Company Inc.
PO Box 4389, Fort Worth TX 76164-0389. 817/625-8251.

Republic Beverage
2535 Manana Drive, Dallas TX 75220-1241. 214/357-8300.

Stroh Brewery Company
PO Box 2709, Longview TX 75606-2709. 903/753-0371.

BAKERY PRODUCTS

Earthgrains Baking Companies
1950 Texas Ave, Lubbock TX 79405-1117. 806/747-3244.

Earthgrains Baking Companies
PO Box 110457, Carrollton TX 75011-0457. 972/416-4395.

Flowers Baking Co.
PO Box 360, Tyler TX 75710-0360. 903/595-2421.

Lance Inc.
PO Box 1061, Greenville TX 75403-1061. 903/455-3362.

Lil Dutch Maid Cookies
5425 N 1st St, Abilene TX 79603-6424. 915/691-5425.

Mrs. Baird's Bakeries Inc.
PO Box 1496, Lubbock TX 79408-1496. 806/763-9304.

Mrs. Baird's Bakeries Inc.
PO Box 937, Fort Worth TX 76101-0937. 817/293-6230.

Mrs. Baird's Bakeries Inc.
PO Box 5086, Abilene TX 79608-5086. 915/692-3141.

Orowheat
10701 Harry Hines Boulevard,
Dallas TX 75220-1311. 972/263-1537.

BEVERAGES

Abtex Beverage Corporation
650 Colonial Dr, Abilene TX
79603-3104. 915/673-7171.

Coca-Cola Bottling Co.
PO Box 15050, Amarillo TX
79105-5050. 806/376-5421.

Dr. Pepper Bottling Co.
PO Box 655024, Dallas TX
75265-5024. 972/579-1024.

Dr. Pepper Bottling Co.
2817 Braswell Dr, Fort Worth TX
76111-1814. 817/926-8151.

**North Texas Coca-Cola
Company**
3400 Fossil Creek Blvd, Fort
Worth TX 76137-2402. 817/232-8600.

**Southwest Coca-Cola Bottling
Co.**
PO Box 1441, Abilene TX
79604-1441. 915/672-3232.

Southwest Fountain Supply
PO Box 655024, Dallas TX
75265-5024. 972/721-8197.

Tyler Coca-Cola Bottling Co.
3200 W Gentry Pkwy, Tyler TX
75702-1311. 903/597-9325.

CHIPS AND SNACKS

Frito-Lay Inc.
555 S Town East Blvd, Mesquite
TX 75149-2815. 972/288-9375.

Frito-Lay Inc.
948 Avenue H E, Arlington TX
76011-7722. 817/649-3266.

Leo's Foods Inc.
3200 Northern Cross Blvd, Fort
Worth TX 76137-3601. 817/834-3200.

Tom's Foods Inc.
3001 E Highway 31, Corsicana
TX 75110-9048. 903/874-6553.

COFFEE

Folgers Coffee Company
PO Box 3125, Sherman TX
75091-3125. 903/893-5166.

CROP SERVICES

Azteca Milling Co. Inc.
PO Box 620, Plainview TX
79073-0620. 806/293-0110.

Birdsong Peanuts
PO Box 698, Gorman TX 76454-0698. 254/734-2266.

DAIRY FARMS

Borden Dairy
PO Box 1739, Dallas TX 75221-1739. 214/565-0332.

Oak Farms Dairies
PO Box 655178, Dallas TX
75265-5178. 214/941-0302.

RJ Smelley Company Inc.
4750 Cattlebaron Drive, Fort
Worth TX 76108-9351. 817/448-8520.

DAIRY PRODUCTS

Bell Dairy Products Inc.
PO Box 2588, Lubbock TX
79408-2588. 806/765-8833.

Dannon Yogurt
1300 W Peter Smith St, Fort
Worth TX 76104-2116. 817/332-1264.

Morningstar Foods Inc.
PO Box 488, Sulphur Springs TX
75483-0488. 903/885-0881.

Southwest Ice Cream
1220 North Tennessee St,
McKinney TX 75069-2116.
972/542-9391.

**FLORICULTURE AND
NURSERY PRODUCTS**

Gandy's Nursery Inc.
PO Box 337, Ben Wheeler TX
75754-0337. 903/833-5869.

Mill Creek Farm Nursery
RR 9, Box 9184, Winnsboro TX
75494-9809. 903/857-2222.

Powell Farms
RR 3, Box 1058, Troup TX
75789-9160. 903/842-3123.

FOOD CROPS

Campbells Fresh Inc.
PO Box 639, Hillsboro TX
76645-0639. 254/582-3458.

FOOD PREPARATIONS

CPC Baking Business
10701 Harry Hines Blvd, Dallas
TX 75220-1311. 214/956-2030.

Kraft Foods Inc.
8150 Springwood Dr, Irving TX
75063-5810. 972/432-3464.

Nabisco Holdings Corp.
PO Box 3988, Lubbock TX
79452-3988. 806/745-5675.

Portion Pac Inc.
11461 Hillguard Rd, Dallas TX
75243-5501. 214/349-6125.

Prime Deli Corporation
1301A Ridgeview, Ste 200,
Lewisville TX 75057-6016.
972/219-7110.

FOOD WHOLESALE

Affiliated Foods Inc.
PO Box 30300, Amarillo TX
79120-0300. 806/372-3851.

Affiliated Foods Inc.
4109 Vine St, Abilene TX 79602-6922. 915/692-1440.

AMPI
PO Box 5288, Arlington TX
76005-5288. 817/461-2674.

Bassham Wholesale Foods
PO Box 6296, Fort Worth TX
76115-0296. 817/429-6910.

Ben E. Keith Company
PO Box 2628, Fort Worth TX
76113-2628. 817/332-9171.

CD Hartnett Company
4151 Blue Mound Rd, Fort Worth
TX 76106-1926. 817/625-8921.

Dutch Regale Bakery
5531 East University Boulevard,
Dallas TX 75206-4113. 214/369-0079.

Dynamic Foods
1001 E 33rd St, Lubbock TX
79404-1816. 806/747-2777.

Fresh Advantage
PO Box 535789, Grand Prairie
TX 75053-5789. 972/988-8553.

Grocery Supply Company
PO Box 638, Sulphur Springs TX
75483-0638. 903/885-7621.

John Soules Foods Inc.
PO Box 4579, Tyler TX 75712-
4579. 903/592-9800.

Loggins Meat Co. Inc.
PO Box 164, Tyler TX 75710-
0164. 903/595-1011.

Lone Star Donut Co.
PO Box 225979, Dallas TX
75222-5979. 214/946-2185.

Luke Soules/Southwest LP
1920 Westridge Dr, Irving TX
75038-2901. 972/518-1442.

Martin-Brower Company
1350 Avenue S, Ste 110, Grand
Prairie TX 75050-1256. 972/647-
2666.

McLane Company Inc.
PO Box 6115, Temple TX 76503-
6115. 254/771-7500.

McLane High Plains Inc.
PO Box 5550, Lubbock TX
79408-5550. 806/766-2900.

MDS
901 Railhead Dr, Fort Worth TX
76177-3904. 817/224-9050.

Multifoods
5225 Investment Dr, Dallas TX
75236-1422. 972/709-3001.

PFG
PO Box 6104, Temple TX 76501.
254/778-4519.

PFS
14841 Dallas Pkwy, Dallas TX
75240-7552. 972/338-7280.

PFS
3901 Scientific Drive, Arlington
TX 76014-4515. 817/557-0100.

Pritchard Brokerage Co.
PO Box 12010, Lubbock TX
79452-2010. 806/745-7404.

Tree of Life
5101 Highland Place Dr, Dallas
TX 75236-1449. 972/298-2957.

Tree of Life SW
105 Bluebonnet Dr, Cleburne TX
76031-9140. 817/641-6678.

GRAIN MILL PRODUCTS

Cerestar USA Inc.
PO Box 169, Dimmitt TX 79027-
0169. 806/647-4141.

Morrison Milling Company
PO Box 719, Denton TX 76202-
0719. 940/387-6111.

HOGS

**Premium Standard Farms
Texas**
HC 3, Box 322, Dalhart TX
79022-9408. 806/377-6289.

Texas Farms Co.
9 SW 2nd Ave, Perryton TX
79070-2509. 806/435-5935.

**MEAT AND POULTRY
PROCESSING**

Beltex Corporation
3801 N Grove St, Fort Worth TX
76106-3720. 817/624-1136.

H&M Food Systems Company
6350 Browning Ct, Fort Worth
TX 76180-6013. 817/656-5507.

Kennedy Sausage Co.
PO Box 598, Weatherford TX
76086-0598. 817/594-3316.

Pilgrim's Pride Corporation
PO Box 150129, Dallas TX
75315-0129. 214/421-9091.

Quality Sausage Company Ltd.
1925 Lone Star Dr, Dallas TX
75212-6302. 214/634-3400.

Rosani Foods
4114 Mint Way, Dallas TX
75237-1606. 214/331-1010.

Supreme Beef Packers Inc.
1000 E Main St, Ladonia TX
75449. 903/367-7255.

Wright Brand Foods Inc.
PO Box 1779, Vernon TX 76385-
1779. 940/553-1811.

**PREPARED FEEDS AND
INGREDIENTS FOR
ANIMALS**

Gore Hilltop
PO Box 1000, Comanche TX
76442. 915/356-3045.

Vigortone Ag Products Inc.
1050 Vigortone Blvd,
Weatherford TX 76086-1554.
817/594-9628.

**PRESERVED FRUITS AND
VEGETABLES**

Calidad Foods
PO Box 535008, Grand Prairie
TX 75053-5008. 972/933-4100.

Food Source Inc.
181 Industrial Blvd, McKinney
TX 75069-7220. 972/548-9001.

Jon-Lin Corporation
PO Box 428, Marlin TX 76661-
0428. 254/883-2591.

Mrs. Crockett's Kitchens Inc.
8821G Forum Way, Fort Worth
TX 76140-5009. 817/293-8164.

Ocean Spray Cranberries Inc.
419 Industrial Dr E, Sulphur
Springs TX 75482-4883.
903/885-8676.

State Fair Foods Inc.
PO Box 561223, Dallas TX
75356-1223. 214/630-1500.

**SUGAR AND
CONFECTIONERY
PRODUCTS**

Kennedy Gourmet
1313 Energy Dr, Kilgore TX
75662-5539. 903/986-3227.

M&M Mars
PO Box 7955, Waco TX 76714-
7955. 254/776-2100.

**For more information on career opportunities in the food, beverage, and agriculture
industries:**

Associations

**AMERICAN ASSOCIATION OF CEREAL
CHEMISTS (AACC)**
3340 Pilot Knob Road, St. Paul MN 55121. 612/454-
7250. World Wide Web address: http://www.scisoc.
org/aacc. Dedicated to the dissemination of technical

information and continuing education in cereal
science.

**AMERICAN CROPS PROTECTION
ASSOCIATION**
1156 15th Street NW, Suite 400, Washington DC

20005. 202/296-1585. World Wide Web address: http://www.acpa.org.

AMERICAN FROZEN FOOD INSTITUTE
2000 Corporate Ridge, Suite 1000, McLean VA 22102. 703/821-0770. World Wide Web address: http://www.affi.com. A national trade association representing the interests of the frozen food industry.

AMERICAN SOCIETY OF AGRICULTURAL ENGINEERS
2950 Niles Road, St. Joseph MI 49085-9659. 616/429-0300. Contact: Julie Swim. World Wide Web address: http://www.asae.org.

AMERICAN SOCIETY OF BREWING CHEMISTS
3340 Pilot Knob Road, St. Paul MN 55121. 612/454-7250. World Wide Web address: http://www.scisoc.org/asbc. Works to improve and bring uniformity to the brewing industry on a technical level. Founded in 1934.

CIES - THE FOOD BUSINESS FORUM
5549 Lee Highway, Arlington VA 22209. 703/534-8880. World Wide Web address: http://www.ciesnet.com. A global food business network. Membership is on a company basis. Members learn how to manage their businesses more effectively and gain access to information and contacts.

DAIRY AND FOOD INDUSTRIES SUPPLY ASSOCIATION (DFISA)
1451 Dolly Madison Boulevard, McLean VA 22101. 703/761-2600. Contact: Dorothy Brady. World Wide Web address: http://www.iafis.org. A trade association whose members are suppliers to the food, dairy, liquid processing, and related industries.

DAIRY MANAGEMENT, INC.
10255 West Higgins Road, Suite 900, Rosemont IL 60018. 847/803-2000. World Wide Web address: http://www.dairyinfo.com. A federation of state and regional dairy promotion organizations that develop and execute effective programs to increase consumer demand for U.S.-produced milk and dairy products.

MASTER BREWERS ASSOCIATION OF THE AMERICAS (MBAA)
2421 North Mayfair Road, Suite 310, Wauwatosa WI 53226. 414/774-8558. World Wide Web address: http://www.mbaa.com. Promotes, advances, improves, and protects the professional interests of brew and malt house production and technical personnel. Disseminates technical and practical information.

NATIONAL BEER WHOLESALERS' ASSOCIATION
1100 South Washington Street, Alexandria VA 22314-4494. 703/683-4300. Fax: 703/683-8965. Contact: Karen Craig.

NATIONAL FOOD PROCESSORS ASSOCIATION
1401 New York Avenue NW, Suite 400, Washington DC 20005. 202/639-5900. World Wide Web address: http://www.nfpa-food.org.

NATIONAL SOFT DRINK ASSOCIATION
1101 16th Street NW, Washington DC 20036. 202/463-6732. World Wide Web address: http://www.nsda.org.

Directories

THOMAS FOOD INDUSTRY REGISTER
Thomas Publishing Company, Five Penn Plaza, New York NY 10001. 212/695-0500. World Wide Web address: http://www.thomaspublishing.com.

Magazines

BEVERAGE WORLD
Keller International Publishing Corporation, 150 Great Neck Road, Great Neck NY 11021. 516/829-9210. E-mail address: kellpub@worldnet.att.net.

FROZEN FOOD AGE
Progressive Grocer Associates, 23 Old Kings Highway South, Darien CT 06820. 203/325-3500.

GOVERNMENT

Choosing a job in politics or government has never been for the faint of heart. But even with all the controversy that continues to surround the White House, the government remains the nation's largest employer. Be advised, however, that the number of federal jobs is on the decline. The Defense Department is expected to reduce the size of its workforce through attrition over the next decade. The outlook for state and local government workers is somewhat better. While opportunities vary from state to state, the Bureau of Labor Statistics forecasts a 16 percent increase in state and local positions through 2005.

The U.S. Postal Service delivered the best profits in 1997, recorded at over $1 billion for the third straight year. This phenomenal success is a result of cost cuts, the elimination of 23,000 administrative jobs, improved delivery times, and the 1997 United Parcel Service strike. In order to remain competitive, the U.S. Postal Service is looking for ways to increase first-class mail business which has been sharply reduced by the convenience and efficiency of electronic mail, faxes, and teleconferencing.

There will be a growing need for correctional officers and prison guards as many leave due to low salaries and unattractive rural locations. Positions in fire departments and police departments will be hardest to come by as the number of candidates will exceed new openings.

The Armed Forces are reducing personnel as a result of relative international peace. As of 1997, the number of active duty personnel remained constant with decreased recruiting levels and tougher advancement standards. However, there are still opportunities for persons wishing to enter the military in the late '90s. These candidates will finish their first enlistments in 2000 when personnel reductions will be complete. It is estimated that there will then be a need for 190,000 enlisted personnel and 15,000 officers to replace retirees and those who have completed their enlistments.

ABILENE, CITY OF
P.O. Box 60, Abilene TX 79604. 915/676-6347. **Contact:** Judy Potter, Human Resources Specialist. **World Wide Web address:** http://www.abilenetx.com. **Description:** Administrative offices for the city of Abilene.

DALLAS, CITY OF
2014 Main Street, Room 104, Dallas TX 75201. **Recorded jobline:** 214/670-5908. **Contact:** Human Resources. **Description:** Provides civil services for the city of Dallas.

DALLAS POLICE DEPARTMENT
2014 Main Street, Room 201, Dallas TX 75201. 214/670-4407. **Toll-free phone:** 800/527-2948. **Fax:** 214/670-5093. **Contact:** Doug Chaney, Recruiting Sergeant. **World Wide Web address:** http://www.ci.dallas.tx.us/dpd. **Description:** Provides law enforcement services. **NOTE:** The department requires 45 semester hours from an accredited college or university with a "C" or better average. Entry-level positions and second and third shifts are offered. **Common positions include:** Police/Law Enforcement Officer. **Benefits:** 401(k); Dental Insurance; Disability Coverage; Life Insurance; Medical Insurance; Pension Plan; Savings Plan; Tuition Assistance; Vision Insurance.

DALLAS PUBLIC WORKS AND TRANSPORTATION DEPARTMENT
320 East Jefferson Boulevard, Room 208, Dallas TX 75203. 214/948-4200. **Contact:** Mr. Kerry Rhines, Human Resources Representative. **Description:** This location houses the administrative offices for the city public works and transportation department. **Common positions include:** Budget Analyst; Property and Real Estate Manager; Surveyor. **Educational backgrounds include:** Business Administration; Engineering; Finance. **Benefits:** 401(k); Disability Coverage; Life Insurance; Medical Insurance; Pension Plan; Tuition Assistance. **Operations at this facility include:** Administration; Divisional Headquarters. **Number of employees at this location:** 775.

CITY OF DALLAS SHERIFF'S DEPARTMENT
133 North Industrial Boulevard, Dallas TX 75207. 214/749-8641. **Contact:** Human Resources Department. **Description:** Works to enforce justice, promote public order, and ensure safety for the citizens of Dallas.

DEPARTMENT OF TRANSPORTATION
P.O. Box 150, Abilene TX 79602. 915/676-6800. **Recorded jobline:** 800/893-6848. **Contact:** Employment. **World Wide Web address:** http://www.dot.state.tx.us/txdot.htm. **Description:** Designs, builds, and maintains roads and highways throughout the state of Texas.

PLANO, CITY OF
1520 Avenue K, Plano TX 75074. 972/461-7000. **Contact:** Human Resources Department. **World Wide Web address:** http://www.ci.plano.tx.us. **Description:** Administrative offices for the city of Plano.

ROBERTSON UNIT
12071 FM 3522, Abilene TX 79601. 915/548-9035. **Contact:** Joyce Lee, Human Resources Manager. **Description:** A maximum security prison.

U.S. ENVIRONMENTAL PROTECTION AGENCY
1445 Ross Avenue, Dallas TX 75202-2733. 214/665-6444. **Contact:** Personnel Services. **World Wide Web address:** http://www.epa.gov. **Description:** As part of Region 6, this location of the EPA serves Arkansas, Louisiana, New Mexico, Oklahoma, and Texas. The EPA was created in 1970 through an executive reorganization plan designed to consolidate the environmental activities of the federal government into a single agency. The agency is committed to ensuring that federal environmental laws are implemented and enforced effectively; U.S. policy, both foreign and domestic, fosters the integration of economic development and environmental protection so that economic growth can be sustained over the long term; and public and private decisions affecting energy, transportation, agriculture, industry, international trade, and natural resources fully integrate considerations of environmental quality. **Benefits:** Daycare Assistance; Fitness Program; Flextime Plan; Incentive Plan; Leave Time; Retirement Plan. **Special programs:** Internships. **Corporate headquarters location:** Washington DC. **Other U.S. locations:** San Francisco CA; Denver CO; Atlanta GA; Chicago IL; Kansas City KS; Boston MA; New York NY; Philadelphia PA; Seattle WA. **Number of employees nationwide:** 19,000.

U.S. POSTAL SERVICE
401 DFW Turnpike, Dallas TX 75260. 214/760-4400. **Contact:** Human Resources. **Description:** The federal mail delivery service.

WACO, CITY OF
P.O. Box 2570, Waco TX 76702-2570. 254/750-5600. **Contact:** Personnel. **Description:** Administrative offices for the city of Waco.

Note: Because addresses and telephone numbers of smaller companies can change rapidly, we recommend you call each company to verify the information below before inquiring about job opportunities. Mass mailings are not recommended.

Additional small employers:

ADMINISTRATION OF ECONOMIC PROGRAMS

Bureau of Census
6303 Harry Hines Blvd, Dallas TX 75235-5269. 214/640-4400.

ADMINISTRATION OF PUBLIC HEALTH PROGRAMS

Amarillo State Center
PO Box 3070, Amarillo TX 79116-3070. 806/358-1681.

City of Fort Worth Health Dept.
1800 University Dr, Rm 232, Fort Worth TX 76107-3405. 817/870-7239.

Health Care Financing Administration
1200 Main Tower, Bldg 2000, Dallas TX 75202-4325. 214/767-6423.

Martin Luther King Center
2922 Martin Luther King Jr, Dallas TX 75215-2321. 214/670-8367.

Public Health Region 4 & 5
PO Box 2501, Tyler TX 75710-2501. 903/595-3585.

ADMINISTRATION OF SOCIAL AND MANPOWER PROGRAMS

Human Services Department
1540 New York Avenue, Arlington TX 76010-4722. 817/461-8273.

Social Security Administration
1200 Main Tower, Dallas TX 75202-4325. 214/767-0853.

Texas Department of Human Services
2010 La Salle Avenue, Waco TX 76706-3443. 254/750-4839.

Texas Department of Human Services
PO Box 6635, Abilene TX 79608-6635. 915/695-5750.

Texas Department of Human Services
3128 South Riverside Dr, Fort Worth TX 76119-3009. 817/921-5511.

COURTS

Bowie County Judge
100 N State Line Ave, Texarkana TX 75501-5666. 903/798-3040.

Dallas County District Court
509 Main St, Dallas TX 75202-5701. 214/653-7131.

Gregg County Courthouse
101 E Methvin St, Ste 204, Longview TX 75601-7234. 903/758-6181.

EXECUTIVE, LEGISLATIVE, AND GENERAL GOVERNMENT

Addison, Town of
PO Box 144, Addison TX 75001-0144. 972/450-7000.

Amarillo Transit System
PO Box 1971, Amarillo TX 79186-0001. 806/378-3011.

Anderson, County of
PO Box 1158, Palestine TX 75802-1158. 903/723-7426.

Bell, County of
PO Box 768, Belton TX 76513-0768. 254/939-3521.

Borger, City of
PO Box 5250, Borger TX 79008-5250. 806/273-0900.

Breckenridge, City of
209 N Breckenridge Ave, Breckenridge TX 76424-3503. 254/559-8287.

Carrollton, City of
PO Box 110535, Carrollton TX 75011-0535. 972/466-3000.

Cass, County of
PO Box 152, Linden TX 75563-0152. 903/756-5067.

Cedar Hill, City of
PO Box 96, Cedar Hill TX 75106-0096. 972/291-5100.

Cleburne City Hall
PO Box 657, Cleburne TX 76033-0657. 817/645-0901.

Collin, County of
210 South McDonald St, McKinney TX 75069-5655. 972/548-4100.

Coppell City Hall
PO Box 478, Coppell TX 75019-0478. 972/462-0022.

Corsicana, City of
200 North 12th Street, Corsicana TX 75110-4616. 903/654-4800.

County Court House
PO Box 10536, Lubbock TX 79408-3536. 806/775-1086.

Dawson, County of
PO Box 1268, Lamesa TX 79331-1268. 806/872-7474.

De Soto, City of
PO Box 550, De Soto TX 75123-0550. 972/230-9643.

Duncanville, City of
PO Box 380280, Duncanville TX 75138-0280. 972/780-5000.

Falls County Judge's Office
PO Box 458, Marlin TX 76661-0458. 254/883-3182.

Flower Mound, Town of
2121 Cross Timbers Road, Flower Mound TX 75028. 972/539-6006.

Gaines, County of
PO Box 847, Seminole TX 79360-0847. 915/758-5411.

Gainesville, City of
200 South Rusk Street, Gainesville TX 76240-4851. 940/668-4500.

Gregg, County of
101 E Methvin St, Ste 300, Longview TX 75601-7236. 903/236-8420.

Harrison, County of
County Courthouse, Marshall TX 75670. 903/935-4818.

Hunt, County of
PO Box 1097, Greenville TX 75403-1097. 903/408-4120.

Irving, City of
PO Box 152288, Irving TX 75015-2288. 972/721-2600.

Johnson, County of
2 North Main Street, Cleburne TX 76031-5573. 817/556-6300.

Lamesa, City of
601 S 1st St, Lamesa TX 79331-6247. 806/872-2124.

Lancaster, City of
PO Box 940, Lancaster TX 75146-0940. 972/227-2111.

Longview, City of
PO Box 1952, Longview TX 75606-1952. 903/237-1000.

Navarro, County of
300 W 3rd Ave, Corsicana TX 75110-4672. 903/654-3025.

North Richland Hills, City of
PO Box 820609, Fort Worth TX 76182-0609. 817/581-5500.

Pampa, City of
PO Box 2499, Pampa TX 79066-2499. 806/669-5750.

Paris, City of
PO Box 9037, Paris TX 75461-9037. 903/785-7511.

Richardson, City of
PO Box 830309, Richardson TX 75083-0309. 972/238-4100.

Robinson Justice Center
900 E 15th St, Plano TX 75074-5808. 972/516-2199.

Rusk, County of
115 N Main St, Henderson TX 75652-3147. 903/657-0307.

Stephenville, City of
298 W Washington St, Stephenville TX 76401-4257. 254/965-7887.

Sulphur Springs, City of
125 Davis St S, Sulphur Springs TX 75482-2717. 903/885-7541.

Taylor, County of
300 Oak St, Abilene TX 79602-1521. 915/677-1711.

Texarkana, City of
PO Box 1967, Texarkana TX 75504-1967. 903/794-3434.

Titus, County of
100 W 1st St, Ste 200, Mount Pleasant TX 75455-4443. 903/572-8723.

Upshur, County of
PO Box 730, Gilmer TX 75644-0730. 903/843-4001.

Van Zandt, County of
121 East Dallas Street, Canton TX 75103-1465. 903/567-2551.

Vernon, City of
PO Box 1423, Vernon TX 76385-1423. 940/552-2581.

Weatherford, City of
PO Box 255, Weatherford TX 76086-0255. 817/598-4221.

White Settlement, City of
214 Meadow Park Dr, Fort Worth TX 76108-2424. 817/246-4971.

Yoakum, County of
PO Box 516, Plains TX 79355-0516. 806/456-2422.

FINANCE, TAXATION, AND MONETARY POLICY BODIES

Assessor & Collector of Taxes
PO Box 819010, Dallas TX 75381-9010. 972/247-3131.

General Accounting Office
1999 Bryan Street, Ste 2200, Dallas TX 75201-6812. 214/855-2600.

Tax Assessor-Collector
100 W Weatherford St, Fort Worth TX 76102-2115. 817/884-1860.

Tax Office
PO Box 299002, Lewisville TX 75029-9002. 972/219-3400.

HOUSING AND URBAN DEVELOPMENT PROGRAMS

Dallas Housing Authority
PO Box 569660, Dallas TX 75356-9660. 214/951-8300.

HUD
PO Box 2905, Fort Worth TX 76113-2905. 817/978-9000.

LAND, MINERAL, AND WILDLIFE CONSERVATION PROGRAMS

Department of Parks & Recreation
PO Box 152288, Irving TX 75015-2288. 972/721-2501.

NRCS State Office
101 South Main Street, Temple TX 76501-7602. 254/742-9700.

PUBLIC ENVIRONMENTAL QUALITY PROGRAMS

Midlothian Water District
235 N 8th St, Midlothian TX 76065-2943. 972/775-3481.

Trinity River Authority Texas
PO Box 531196, Grand Prairie TX 75053-1196. 972/262-5186.

Trinity River Authority Texas
6500 Singleton Blvd, Dallas TX 75212-3038. 972/263-2251.

PUBLIC ORDER AND SAFETY

Abilene Police Dept.
PO Box 174, Abilene TX 79604-0174. 915/676-6600.

Amarillo City Fire Dept.
400 S Van Buren St, Amarillo TX 79101-1354. 806/378-3061.

Arlington Police Department
PO Box 1065, Arlington TX 76004-1065. 817/265-3311.

Bowie County Correctional Facility
105 W Front St, Texarkana TX 75501-5610. 903/798-3515.

Central Fire Station
1019 Austin St, Garland TX 75040-5608. 972/205-2275.

City of Dallas Fire Dept.
2014 Main St, Ste 401, Dallas TX 75201-4426. 214/670-4319.

County Jail of Canyon
501 16th St, Canyon TX 79015-3842. 806/655-6302.

County Jail of McKinney
200 S McDonald St, McKinney TX 75069-5686. 972/548-4700.

County Jail of Waco
3201 E Highway 6, Waco TX 76705-3734. 254/757-5120.

Denton County Sheriff's Dept.
127 Woodrow Lane, Denton TX 76205. 940/898-5600.

Drug Enforcement Administration
1880 Regal Row, Dallas TX 75235-2302. 214/640-0801.

Ellis County Sheriff's Dept.
300 S Jackson St, Waxahachie
TX 75165-3750. 972/923-4900.

**Federal Correctional Institute
of Seagoville**
PO Box 1000, Seagoville TX
75159-1000. 972/287-2911.

**Federal Correctional Institute
of Texarkana**
PO Box 9500, Texarkana TX
75505-9500. 903/838-4587.

Fire Department
217 N 5th St, Fl 4, Garland TX
75040-6313. 972/205-2250.

Fire Department
201 S 28th St, Killeen TX 76541-
6220. 254/634-3131.

FMC
3150 Horton Rd, Fort Worth TX
76119-5905. 817/535-2111.

Fort Worth Police Department
2500 N Houston St, Fort Worth
TX 76106-7147. 817/871-6454.

Gainesville State School
4701 E Farm Road 678,
Gainesville TX 76240. 940/665-
0701.

Grapevine Police Department
307 W Dallas Rd, Grapevine TX
76051-5505. 817/481-0326.

**Highway Department District
Office**
2709 W Front St, Tyler TX
75702-7712. 903/593-0111.

**Highway Department District
Office**
PO Box 1010, Waco TX 76703-
1010. 254/867-2700.

**Highway Department District
Office**
PO Box 3067, Dallas TX 75221-
3067. 214/320-6100.

Hilltop Unit
1500 State School Rd, Gatesville
TX 76598-0001. 254/865-8901.

Hutchins State Jail Facility
1500 E Langdon Rd, Dallas TX
75241-7136. 972/225-1304.

Immigration & Naturalization
7701 N Stemmons Fwy, Dallas
TX 75247-4232. 214/767-7013.

Johnson County Sheriff's Office
1800 Ridgemar Dr, Cleburne TX
76031-1353. 817/556-6060.

Jordan Unit
1992 Hilton Rd, Pampa TX
79065-9655. 806/665-7070.

Killeen Police Department
402 N 2nd St, Killeen TX 76541-
5207. 254/526-8311.

Killeen Police Department
4205 Hickory Rd, Temple TX
76502-2910. 817/760-4011.

Lewisville City Police
184 N Valley Pkwy, Lewisville
TX 75067-3429. 972/219-3600.

Limestone County Detention
910 N Tyus St, Groesbeck TX
76642-2011. 254/729-8615.

Longview City Police Dept.
302 W Cotton St, Longview TX
75601-6222. 903/237-1199.

Lubbock County Youth Center
2025 N Akron Ave, Lubbock TX
79415-1118. 806/775-1800.

McLennan County Jail
3201 E Highway 6, Waco TX
76705-3734. 254/757-2555.

Mount View Unit
RR 4, Box 4400, Gatesville TX
76528. 254/865-6663.

North Richland Hills Fire
PO Box 820609, Fort Worth TX
76182-0609. 817/281-1000.

Plano Police Department
909 14th St, Plano TX 75074-
5803. 972/424-5678.

Police Department
217 N 5th St, Garland TX 75040-
6313. 972/205-2010.

Police Department
2000 Forest Ridge Dr, Bedford
TX 76021-5713. 817/952-2100.

Police Dept.
PO Box 152288, Irving TX
75015-2288. 972/721-2650.

Police Dept.
PO Box 2570, Waco TX 76702-
2570. 254/750-7500.

Police Station
PO Box 831078, Richardson TX
75083-1078. 972/238-3800.

Powledge Unit
RR 2, Box 2250, Palestine TX
75882-0001. 903/723-2403.

Protective Services Intake Unit
2727 Avenue E East, Ste 802,
Arlington TX 76011-5240.
817/640-9600.

Sheriff's Office
PO Box 749, Belton TX 76513-
0749. 254/933-5400.

Smith County Court House
Smith County Courthouse, Tyler
TX 75702. 903/535-0500.

Smith County Sheriff's Dept.
PO Box 90, Tyler TX 75710-
0090. 903/535-0911.

Smith Unit
HCR 07, Box 187-A, Lamesa TX
79331. 806/872-6741.

South Central Regional Office
4211 Cedar Springs Rd, Dallas
TX 75219-2698. 214/767-9700.

Tarra County Juvenile Services
2701 Kimbo Rd, Fort Worth TX
76111-3007. 817/838-4600.

**Texas Department of Public
Safety**
PO Box 420, Lubbock TX 79408-
0420. 806/747-4491.

**Texas Department of Public
Safety**
PO Box 130040, Tyler TX
75713-0040. 903/566-9740.

Texas Dept. of Criminal Justice
RR 2, Box 500, Teague TX
75860-8671. 254/739-5555.

Texas Highway Patrol
1617 E Crest Dr, Waco TX
76705-1555. 254/867-4628.

Tl Roach Unit
RR 2, Box 500, Childress TX
79201-9553. 940/937-6364.

Tulia Unit
HC 3, Box 5C, Tulia TX 79088-
9512. 806/995-4109.

United States Customs Service
PO Box 619050, Dallas TX
75261-9050. 972/574-2170.

**Victory Fields Youth
Commission**
8407 FM 433, Vernon TX 76384.
940/552-9347.

Young County Rural Fire Department
200 Oak St, Graham TX 76450-2007. 940/846-3251.

REGULATION OF MISC. COMMERCIAL SECTORS

Office of the Comptroller
500 N Akard St, Dallas TX 75201-3320. 214/720-0656.

Office of Thrift Supervision
PO Box 619027, Dallas TX 75261-9027. 972/281-2000.

Public Works Department
PO Box 8005, Dallas TX 75205-0005. 214/987-5402.

REGULATORY ADMINISTRATION OF TRANSPORTATION

Department of Transportation
PO Box 1210, Atlanta TX 75551-1210. 903/796-2851.

Department of Transportation
PO Box 6868, Fort Worth TX 76115-0868. 817/370-6500.

Federal Aviation Administration
2601 Meacham Blvd, Fort Worth TX 76137-4204. 817/222-5200.

SITA
125 East John Carpenter Fwy, Irving TX 75062-2238. 972/444-0100.

Texas Department of Transportation
PO Box 1010, Waco TX 76703-1010. 254/867-2854.

Texas Department of Transportation
PO Box 900, Childress TX 79201-0900. 940/937-2571.

Texas Department of Transportation
PO Box 771, Lubbock TX 79408-0771. 806/745-4411.

REGULATORY ADMINISTRATION OF UTILITIES

US Nuclear Regulatory Agency
611 Ryan Plaza Dr, Arlington TX 76011-4005. 817/860-8232.

UNITED STATES POSTAL SERVICE

Bent Tree Station
PO Box 9998, Dallas TX 75372-9998. 972/380-8895.

Burleson Post Office
232 SW Johnson Ave, Burleson TX 76028-9998. 817/295-8158.

Carrolton Post Office
2030 E Jackson Rd, Carrollton TX 75006-9998. 972/418-7858.

Dallas Post Office
6640 Abrams Rd, Dallas TX 75231-7210. 214/553-8894.

Garland Main Post Office
1000 W Walnut St, Garland TX 75040-9998. 972/272-5541.

Greenville Main Post Office
PO Box 9998, Greenville TX 75401. 903/455-5363.

Hurst Post Office
825 Precinct Line Rd, Hurst TX 76053-9998. 817/284-3464.

Lewisville Post Office
194 Civic Cir, Lewisville TX 75067-3424. 972/221-2755.

Longview Main Post Office
2336 S Mobberly Ave, Longview TX 75602-3864. 903/753-7644.

Marshall Post Office
202 E Travis St, Marshall TX 75670-4167. 903/938-4086.

Melear Post Office
3903 Melear Dr, Arlington TX 76015-4151. 817/465-3868.

Mesquite Main Post Office
120 E Grubb Dr, Mesquite TX 75149-9998. 972/288-4476.

Northaven Post Office
2736 Royal Ln, Dallas TX 75229-4716. 972/243-6121.

Prestonwood Post Office
PO Box 9998, Dallas TX 75372-9998. 972/380-8441.

Richardson Main Post Office
433 Belle Grove Dr, Richardson TX 75080-9998. 972/235-8353.

Saginaw Branch
101 S Belmont St, Fort Worth TX 76179-9998. 817/232-0808.

Spring Valley Station
13770 Noel Rd, Dallas TX 75240-4324. 972/233-3780.

Temple Post Office
PO Box 9998, Temple TX 76501. 254/773-0792.

Tyler Processing & Distribution Center
2100 Martin Luther, Tyler TX 75712. 903/595-8645.

United States Postal Service
PO Box 152091, Irving TX 75015-9998. 972/986-6557.

University Station
5606 Yale Blvd, Dallas TX 75206-5018. 214/739-3331.

US Post Office
2301 Ross St, Amarillo TX 79120-9998. 806/379-2142.

US Post Office
341 Pine St, Abilene TX 79601-5943. 915/673-6485.

Waco Main Post Office
470 W State Highway 6, Waco TX 76712-3973. 254/757-6516.

Watson Community Station
1975 Ballpark Way, Arlington TX 76006-6609. 817/649-5532.

Wedgwood Station
3701 Altamesa Blvd, Fort Worth TX 76133-9998. 817/294-0785.

For more information about career opportunities in the government:

Online Services

FEDERAL JOB OPPORTUNITIES BOARD
fjob.opm.gov. A Telnet bulletin board that allows jobseekers to search for government jobs by department, agency, or state. The site includes information about the application process as well as opportunities overseas.

FEDERAL JOBS CENTRAL
http://www.fedjobs.com. This resourceful site has only one drawback: Its services require a fee. Federal

Jobs Central offers a subscription to a 64-page biweekly publication containing over 3,500 job listings; online listings that are accessible by occupation, salary, and location; and a service that pairs you with the job you are seeking.

FEDERAL JOBS DIGEST
http://www.jobsfed.com. An excellent site for jobseekers hoping to work for the government, this site offers over 3,500 opportunities in fields such as engineering, medical, administration, management, secretarial, computer services, and law enforcement. The site also includes employment links to government agencies. For a fee, you can let *FJD*'s matching service perform the job hunt for you.

FEDWORLD
http://www.fedworld.gov. Provides a wealth of information on all aspects of the government. Besides an employment link to federal job opportunities, this site also offers access to all government agencies and many government documents.

JOBS IN GOVERNMENT
http://www.jobsingovernment.com. E-mail address: info@jobsingovernment.com. A helpful search engine for individuals seeking employment in government or the public sector. The site offers profile-based searches for thousands of open positions, the ability to post and e-mail resumes, and information about current topics and resources in government.

LIBRARY JOB LEADS/GOVERNMENT JOB LISTINGS
http://www.emporia.edu/s/www/slim/resource/jobs/govjob.htm. This Website provides many links to sites that post government job openings and information for jobseekers.

HEALTH CARE: SERVICES, EQUIPMENT, AND PRODUCTS

The rising cost of health care in the United States is influencing the move from the traditional fee-for-service plans to more cost-conscious managed care plans. Cost control is also creating a more demanding nation of health care customers who want the most for their money. In 1996, the average cost of health care per person was $3,760. Overall, spending increases have stabilized from rising at an average annual rate of 13.6 percent between 1975 and 1980 to approximately 6 percent between 1996 and 1997. If managed care continues to revolutionize the industry, the nation can expect a 6 to 7 percent average annual rate of growth through 2000. Cost-cutting improvements in the field are beginning to take shape with the advent of new technology such as the use of telemedicine. This process allows electronic images of X-rays and test results to be transmitted anywhere in the world for further consultation and diagnosis.

Consolidation is still a dominant factor in the industry. Small, independent hospitals are being purchased by large corporations to form multi-hospital enterprises. Recently, Columbia/HCA (an industry powerhouse) has been targeted in one of the largest federal investigations of health care fraud ever. Industry analysts expect the company will be sold, renamed, and split into four new smaller companies in an attempt to restructure and boost stock prices.

Health care services are still a major source of job creation in the economy. That distinction is not expected to change as the population over the age of 85 continues to grow faster than the nation's total population. With a growing elderly population, the number of home health care agencies has doubled since 1992.

Industry trends point to a stronger demand for primary care physicians, rather than specialists. Non-traditional forms of medicine such as acupuncture and home-infusion therapy are gaining acceptance by consumers, as well as insurers, which should create more job opportunities. Overall, occupations in health care will account for one-fifth of the nation's job growth from 1998 through 2005.

ALL SAINTS EPISCOPAL HOSPITAL
1400 Eighth Avenue, Fort Worth TX 76104. 817/926-2544. **Contact:** Human Resources. **Description:** A hospital with over 500 beds.

ARCADIA HEALTH CARE
1660 South Stemmons, Suite 360, Lewisville TX 75067. 972/436-5229. **Fax:** 972/221-1076. **Contact:** Wendy Tellor, RN Supervisor. **Description:** A home health care agency. **Common positions include:** Bookkeeper; Claim Representative; Computer Operator; Data Entry Clerk; Nurse; Occupational Therapist; Physical Therapist; Receptionist; Secretary; Social Worker.

BAPTIST/ST. ANTHONY HEALTH SYSTEM
P.O. Box 950, Amarillo TX 79176. 806/376-4411. **Contact:** Human Resource Manager. **Description:** An acute health care facility that houses 255 beds. **Common positions include:**

Clerical Supervisor; Food Service Manager; Laboratory Technician; Nurse; Physical Therapist; Registered Nurse; Retail Manager; Secretary. **Number of employees at this location:** 1,000.

BAYLOR MEDICAL CENTER
2300 Marie Curie Boulevard, Garland TX 75042. 972/487-5000. **Contact:** Human Resources Department. **Description:** An acute care medical center licensed for over 200 beds.

BAYLOR RICHARDSON MEDICAL CENTER
401 West Campbell Road, Richardson TX 75080. 972/498-4737. **Fax:** 972/498-4978. **Recorded jobline:** 972/498-4875. **Contact:** Employment Coordinator. **Description:** A nonprofit medical, surgical, and psychiatric hospital. **Common positions include:** Accountant/Auditor; Buyer; Claim Representative; Clerical Supervisor; Collector; Counselor; Dietician/Nutritionist; EEG Technologist; EKG Technician; Human Resources Manager; Licensed Practical Nurse; Medical Records Technician; Nuclear Medicine Technologist; Occupational Therapist; Pharmacist; Physical Therapist; Public Relations Specialist; Purchasing Agent/Manager; Radiological Technologist; Recreational Therapist; Registered Nurse; Respiratory Therapist; Social Worker; Speech-Language Pathologist; Surgical Technician; Systems Analyst. **Educational backgrounds include:** Health Care; M.D./Medicine. **Benefits:** 401(k); 403(b); Dental Insurance; Disability Coverage; Employee Discounts; Life Insurance; Medical Insurance; Tuition Assistance. **Corporate headquarters location:** This Location. **Operations at this facility include:** Administration. **Number of employees at this location:** 680.

BAYLOR SENIOR HEALTH CENTER
820 West Arapaho Road, Suite 200, Richardson TX 75080. 972/498-4500. **Contact:** Human Resources. **Description:** An outpatient facility that offers comprehensive services to senior citizens. Founded in 1995.

BAYLOR UNIVERSITY MEDICAL CENTER
3500 Gaston Avenue, Dallas TX 75246. 214/820-2525. **Contact:** Personnel. **Description:** A regional medical facility. **NOTE:** This location also houses the Baylor Rehabilitation Center. The center can be reached at 214/826-7030. **Common positions include:** Accountant/Auditor; Biomedical Engineer; Blue-Collar Worker Supervisor; Buyer; Computer Programmer; Customer Service Representative; Dietician/Nutritionist; General Manager; Human Resources Manager; Marketing Specialist; Purchasing Agent/Manager; Technical Writer/Editor. **Educational backgrounds include:** Accounting; Biology; Business Administration; Chemistry; Communications; Computer Science; Engineering; Finance; Liberal Arts; Marketing. **Benefits:** Daycare Assistance; Dental Insurance; Disability Coverage; Employee Discounts; Life Insurance; Medical Insurance; Pension Plan; Retirement Plan; Tuition Assistance. **Corporate headquarters location:** This Location. **Operations at this facility include:** Administration; Research and Development.

CENTRAL TEXAS VETERANS HEALTHCARE SYSTEM
4800 Memorial Drive, Waco TX 76711. 254/752-6581. **Contact:** Personnel. **World Wide Web address:** http://www.va.gov. **Description:** A medical center. From 54 hospitals in 1930, the VA health care system has grown to include 171 medical centers; more than 364 outpatient, community, and outreach clinics; 130 nursing home care units; and 37 domiciliaries. The VA operates at least one medical center in each of the 48 contiguous states, Puerto Rico, and the District of Columbia. With approximately 76,000 medical center beds, the VA treats nearly one million patients in VA hospitals; 75,000 in nursing home care units; and 25,000 in domiciliaries. The VA's outpatient clinics register approximately 24 million visits per year. **NOTE:** Central Texas Veterans Healthcare System hires current or former federal employees, veterans, and disabled veterans. Central Texas Veterans Healthcare System is currently under hiring constraints. Applications from the general public are not accepted. **Parent company:** U.S. Department of Veterans Affairs.

CHILDREN'S MEDICAL CENTER OF DALLAS
1935 Motor Street, Dallas TX 75235. 214/539-2161. **Fax:** 214/539-6099. **Contact:** Human Resource Services. **Description:** A private, children's medical center. **Common positions include:** Claim Representative; Clinical Lab Technician; Computer Programmer; Customer Service

Representative; EEG Technologist; EKG Technician; Emergency Medical Technician; Human Resources Manager; Medical Records Technician; Nuclear Medicine Technologist; Occupational Therapist; Pharmacist; Physical Therapist; Psychologist; Public Relations Specialist; Radiological Technologist; Registered Nurse; Respiratory Therapist; Social Worker; Speech-Language Pathologist; Surgical Technician; Systems Analyst. **Educational backgrounds include:** Business Administration; Communications; Computer Science; Health Care. **Corporate headquarters location:** This Location. **Operations at this facility include:** Administration. **Listed on:** Privately held. **Number of employees at this location:** 2,100.

COLUMBIA LONGVIEW REGIONAL MEDICAL CENTER
P.O. Box 14000, Longview TX 75607. 903/232-3725. **Fax:** 903/232-3888. **Recorded jobline:** 903/232-3726. **Contact:** Veronica Franks, Employment Coordinator. **Description:** A 115-bed, acute care, medical center providing cardiovascular, pediatric, dialysis, intensive care, intermediate care, outpatient, and laboratory services. **NOTE:** Entry-level positions and second and third shifts are offered. **Common positions include:** Administrative Assistant; Certified Nurses Aide; Clinical Lab Technician; Dietician/Nutritionist; EKG Technician; Emergency Medical Technician; Licensed Practical Nurse; Medical Records Technician; Nuclear Medicine Technologist; Occupational Therapist; Pharmacist; Physical Therapist; Registered Nurse; Respiratory Therapist; Secretary; Social Worker; Speech-Language Pathologist; Surgical Technician. **Benefits:** 401(k); Dental Insurance; Disability Coverage; Life Insurance; Medical Insurance; Pension Plan; Profit Sharing. **Corporate headquarters location:** Nashville TN. **Other U.S. locations:** Nationwide. **Listed on:** American Stock Exchange. **CEO:** Velinda Stevens. **Number of employees at this location:** 600. **Number of projected hires for 1998 - 1999 at this location:** 150.

COLUMBIA MEDICAL ARTS HOSPITAL
6161 Harry Hines Boulevard, Dallas TX 75235. 214/688-1111. **Fax:** 214/689-8599. **Contact:** Ms. Shana Kadane, Human Resources Director. **Description:** A medical hospital. **Common positions include:** Accountant/Auditor; Adjuster; Collector; Computer Programmer; Dietician/Nutritionist; EEG Technologist; EKG Technician; Environmental Engineer; Financial Analyst; Human Resources Manager; Investigator; Licensed Practical Nurse; Medical Records Technician; Occupational Therapist; Pharmacist; Physical Therapist; Physician; Registered Nurse; Respiratory Therapist. **Educational backgrounds include:** Health Care; M.D./Medicine. **Benefits:** 401(k); Dental Insurance; Disability Coverage; Life Insurance; Medical Insurance; Pension Plan; Profit Sharing; Savings Plan; Tuition Assistance. **Special programs:** Internships. **Corporate headquarters location:** Nashville TN. **Other U.S. locations:** Nationwide. **Operations at this facility include:** Administration. **Listed on:** New York Stock Exchange. **Number of employees at this location:** 200.

COLUMBIA MEDICAL CENTER
One Medical Plaza, Pampa TX 79065. 806/665-3721. **Contact:** Personnel. **Description:** An acute care hospital licensed for 107 beds.

COLUMBIA MEDICAL CENTER OF PLANO
3901 West 15th Street, Plano TX 75075. 972/596-6800. **Contact:** Human Resources. **World Wide Web address:** http://www.columbia.net. **Description:** A 300-bed medical center providing acute and residential care.

COLUMBIA MEDICAL CITY DALLAS HOSPITAL
7777 Forest Lane, Dallas TX 75230. 972/661-7000. **Contact:** Human Resources Department. **Description:** A hospital.

COLUMBIA PLAZA MEDICAL CENTER
900 Eighth Avenue, Fort Worth TX 76104. 817/336-2100. **Contact:** Human Resources. **Description:** A hospital. **Common positions include:** Dietician/Nutritionist; Nuclear Medicine Technologist; Pharmacist; Physical Therapist; Registered Nurse; Respiratory Therapist. **Educational backgrounds include:** Health Care; Nursing. **Benefits:** 401(k); Dental Insurance; Disability Coverage; Employee Discounts; Life Insurance; Medical Insurance; Pension Plan; Profit Sharing; Savings Plan; Tuition Assistance. **Number of employees at this location:** 700.

COLUMBIA/HCA

13455 Noel Road, Suite 2000, Dallas TX 75240. 972/701-2200. **Contact:** Human Resources. **World Wide Web address:** http://www.columbia.net. **Description:** This location is a regional administrative office. Overall, Columbia/HCA was formed in 1992 to combine the outpatient surgical centers of Medical Care International, Inc. and the home infusion therapy business of Critical Care America, Inc. Today, Columbia/HCA owns several hundred surgical centers and hospitals. **Number of employees at this location:** 5,000.

COOK CHILDREN'S MEDICAL CENTER
COOK CHILDREN'S HEALTH CARE NETWORK

801 Seventh Avenue, Fort Worth TX 76104-2733. 817/885-4419. **Fax:** 817/885-3947. **Recorded jobline:** 817/885-4414. **Contact:** Kay Kirby, Employment Specialist. **World Wide Web address:** http://www.cookchildrens.org. **Description:** A pediatric health care center. Founded in 1985. **NOTE:** Entry-level positions and second and third shifts are offered. **Common positions include:** Accountant; Applications Engineer; Buyer; Certified Nurses Aide; Chief Financial Officer; Computer Operator; Computer Programmer; Counselor; Customer Service Representative; Database Manager; Dietician/Nutritionist; EEG Technologist; EKG Technician; Emergency Medical Technician; Financial Analyst; Fund Manager; Human Resources Manager; Librarian; Licensed Practical Nurse; Marketing Specialist; Medical Records Technician; MIS Specialist; Nuclear Medicine Technologist; Occupational Therapist; Pharmacist; Physical Therapist; Physician; Psychologist; Public Relations Specialist; Radiological Technologist; Registered Nurse; Respiratory Therapist; Secretary; Social Worker; Speech-Language Pathologist; Surgical Technician; Systems Analyst; Systems Manager; Typist/Word Processor; Webmaster. **Educational backgrounds include:** Accounting; Computer Science; Health Care; Marketing; Nutrition; Public Relations. **Benefits:** 403(b); Dental Insurance; Disability Coverage; Employee Discounts; Flexible Schedule; Life Insurance; Mass Transit Available; Medical Insurance; Tuition Assistance. **Listed on:** Privately held. **Facilities manager:** Harry Delks. **Annual sales/revenues:** More than $100 million. **Number of employees at this location:** 2,000. **Number of projected hires for 1998 - 1999 at this location:** 500.

DALLAS-FORT WORTH MEDICAL CENTER

2709 Hospital Boulevard, Grand Prairie TX 75051. 972/641-5000. **Contact:** Human Resources Department. **Description:** An acute care hospital with 160 beds.

DE SOTO ANIMAL HOSPITAL

201 North Lyndalyn, De Soto TX 75115. 972/223-4840. **Contact:** Human Resources. **Description:** De Soto Animal Hospital provides general medical and surgical services to domestic animals. Other services include radiology, dentistry, behavior counseling, allergy testing, and boarding.

DOCTORS HOSPITAL

9440 Poppy Drive, Dallas TX 75218. 214/324-6297. **Fax:** 214/324-6547. **Recorded jobline:** 214/324-6700. **Contact:** Marlene Rothman, Assistant Director of Human Resources. **World Wide Web address:** http://www.tenethealth.com. **Description:** A hospital. **Common positions include:** Dietician/Nutritionist; EEG Technologist; EKG Technician; Electrician; Human Resources Manager; Medical Records Technician; Nuclear Medicine Technologist; Pharmacist; Physical Therapist; Purchasing Agent/Manager; Radiological Technologist; Recreational Therapist; Registered Nurse; Respiratory Therapist; Social Worker; Surgical Technician. **Educational backgrounds include:** Health Care; Nursing. **Benefits:** 401(k); Dental Insurance; Disability Coverage; Employee Discounts; Life Insurance; Medical Insurance; Tuition Assistance. **Special programs:** Internships. **Other U.S. locations:** CA; FL; LA; MO; TN. **Parent company:** Tenet Healthcare Corporation. **Operations at this facility include:** Administration. **Listed on:** New York Stock Exchange. **Number of employees at this location:** 900.

HARRINGTON CANCER CENTER

1500 Wallace Avenue, Amarillo TX 79106. 806/359-4673. **Contact:** Human Resources Department. **World Wide Web address:** http://www.harringtoncc.org. **Description:** Harrington Cancer Center is a medical facility that specializes in providing cancer treatments and researching cures for the disease.

HARRIS METHODIST FORT WORTH
1301 Pennsylvania Avenue, Fort Worth TX 76104. 817/882-2000. **Contact:** Human Resources. **Description:** Harris Methodist Fort Worth is a hospital that also has a Community Cancer Center which provides coordinated, multidisciplinary cancer treatment. **Parent company:** Harris Methodist Health System.

HEALTHSOUTH
2124 Research Row, Dallas TX 75235. 214/358-8363. **Contact:** Judy Webster, Director of Human Resources. **Description:** A comprehensive, medical rehabilitation hospital specializing in orthopedic surgery. HealthSouth also operates an outpatient facility. **Common positions include:** Accountant/Auditor; Biomedical Engineer; Clinical Lab Technician; Counselor; Dietician/Nutritionist; Electrician; Human Resources Manager; Licensed Practical Nurse; Mechanical Engineer; Medical Records Technician; Occupational Therapist; Physical Therapist; Purchasing Agent/Manager; Registered Nurse; Respiratory Therapist; Speech-Language Pathologist; Systems Analyst. **Educational backgrounds include:** Nursing; Physical Therapy. **Benefits:** 401(k); Dental Insurance; Disability Coverage; Life Insurance; Medical Insurance; Profit Sharing; Tuition Assistance. **Corporate headquarters location:** Birmingham AL. **Other U.S. locations:** Nationwide. **Listed on:** New York Stock Exchange. **Number of employees at this location:** 345. **Number of employees nationwide:** 15,065.

HENDERSON MEMORIAL HOSPITAL
300 Wilson Street, Henderson TX 75652. 903/657-7541. **Toll-free phone:** 800/329-7541. **Fax:** 903/657-0125. **Contact:** Daniel Hart, Director of Human Resources. **Description:** A private, nonprofit, acute care hospital. **NOTE:** The hospital offers entry-level positions, as well as second and third shifts. **Common positions include:** Account Representative; Accountant; Adjuster; Administrative Assistant; Biomedical Engineer; Certified Nurses Aide; Claim Representative; Clerical Supervisor; Clinical Lab Technician; Computer Operator; Counselor; Customer Service Representative; Dietician/Nutritionist; Education Administrator; EEG Technologist; EKG Technician; Emergency Medical Technician; Environmental Engineer; Financial Analyst; Food Scientist/Technologist; Licensed Practical Nurse; Licensed Vocational Nurse; Medical Records Technician; Operations Manager; Pharmacist; Physical Therapist; Physician; Purchasing Agent/Manager; Quality Control Supervisor; Radiological Technologist; Recreational Therapist; Registered Nurse; Respiratory Therapist; Restaurant/Food Service Manager; Secretary; Social Worker; Surgical Technician; Systems Analyst; Systems Manager; Typist/Word Processor. **Educational backgrounds include:** Accounting; Biology; Business Administration; Chemistry; Health Care; Nursing. **Benefits:** 403(b); Dental Insurance; Disability Coverage; Employee Discounts; Flexible Schedule; Life Insurance; Medical Insurance; Pension Plan; Tuition Assistance. **Special programs:** Internships; Apprenticeships. **Office hours:** Monday - Friday, 7:30 a.m. - 5:00 p.m. **Corporate headquarters location:** This Location. **Operations at this facility include:** Administration; Service. **Listed on:** Privately held. **Annual sales/revenues:** $21 - $50 million. **CEO:** George Roberts. **Number of employees at this location:** 385. **Number of projected hires for 1998 - 1999 at this location:** 40.

HENDRICK HEALTH SYSTEM
1242 North 19th Street, Abilene TX 79601-2316. 915/670-2000. **Contact:** Human Resources Department. **World Wide Web address:** http://www.hendrickhealth.org. **Description:** Operates a general hospital. **Common positions include:** Accountant/Auditor; Database Manager; Marketing Specialist; Medical Assistant; Medical Records Technician; Medical Secretary; MIS Specialist; Nurse; Pharmacist; Pharmacy Technician; Physical Therapist; Surgical Technician.

HORIZON SPECIALTY HOSPITAL
7850 Brookhollow Road, Dallas TX 75235. 214/637-0000. **Contact:** Human Resources Department. **Description:** A long-term, acute care hospital. **Parent company:** Horizon/CMS Healthcare Corporation acquires and operates long-term care facilities throughout the United States; provides health care services, such as nursing care, rehabilitation, and other therapies; provides institutional pharmacy services; provides specialty care to Alzheimer's patients; and offers subacute care.

HORIZON/CMS HEALTHCARE CORPORATION
CENTRAL HOSPITAL DIVISION
3700 West 15th Street, Woodburn Corners, Building B, Suite 200, Plano TX 75075. 972/596-1155. **Contact:** Human Resources. **Description:** This location is the Central Hospital Division for Horizon/CMS Healthcare's hospital group. Overall, Horizon/CMS Healthcare acquires and operates long-term care facilities throughout the United States; provides health care services, such as nursing care, rehabilitation, and other therapies; provides institutional pharmacy services; provides specialty care to Alzheimer's patients; and offers subacute care. The company operates over 280 clinics in 25 states.

HORIZON/CMS HEALTHCARE CORPORATION
MIDWEST DIVISION AND SPECIALTY HOSPITAL DIVISION
9535 Forest Lane, Suite 211, Dallas TX 75243. 972/783-2393. **Contact:** Human Resources. **Description:** This location houses Midwest and Specialty Hospital divisions of Horizon/CMS Healthcare Corporation. Overall, Horizon/CMS Healthcare acquires and operates long-term care facilities throughout the United States; provides health care services, such as nursing care, rehabilitation, and other therapies; provides institutional pharmacy services; provides specialty care to Alzheimer's patients; and offers subacute care. The company operates over 280 clinics in 25 states.

HUGULEY MEMORIAL MEDICAL CENTER
11801 South Freeway, P.O. Box 6337, South Fort Worth TX 76115-0337. 817/551-2703. **Fax:** 817/551-2455. **Contact:** Jane Yingst, Employment Specialist. **Description:** An acute care facility with 220 beds. Huguley Memorial Medical Center also owns Willow Creek, a mental health facility in Arlington TX. **Common positions include:** Accountant/Auditor; Buyer; Clerical Supervisor; Clinical Lab Technician; Counselor; Customer Service Representative; Dietician/Nutritionist; Emergency Medical Technician; Licensed Practical Nurse; Medical Records Technician; Nuclear Medicine Technologist; Occupational Therapist; Pharmacist; Physical Therapist; Recreational Therapist; Registered Nurse; Respiratory Therapist; Social Worker; Speech-Language Pathologist; Surgical Technician. **Educational backgrounds include:** Nursing. **Benefits:** 403(b); Credit Union; Dental Insurance; Disability Coverage; Employee Discounts; Life Insurance; Medical Insurance; Savings Plan; TSAs; Tuition Assistance. **Special programs:** Internships. **Corporate headquarters location:** Orlando FL. **Operations at this facility include:** Administration; Service. **Number of employees at this location:** 1,100. **Number of employees nationwide:** 1,400.

IRVING HOSPITAL
IRVING HEALTH CARE SYSTEM
1901 North MacArthur Boulevard, Irving TX 75061. 972/579-8100. **Contact:** Human Resources Department. **Description:** An acute care hospital licensed for 288 beds.

JOHNSON & JOHNSON MEDICAL, INC.
P.O. Box 90130, Arlington TX 76004-3130. 817/467-0211. **Contact:** Human Resources Department. **Description:** This location of Johnson & Johnson Medical manufactures and markets an extensive line of disposable packs and gowns, surgical products, decontamination and disposal systems, latex gloves, and surgical antiseptics. **Common positions include:** Accountant/Auditor; Biological Scientist; Buyer; Chemical Engineer; Chemist; Clinical Lab Technician; Computer Programmer; Human Resources Manager; Industrial Production Manager; Operations/Production Manager; Purchasing Agent/Manager; Quality Control Supervisor; Software Engineer; Systems Analyst. **Educational backgrounds include:** Accounting; Biology; Business Administration; Chemistry; Computer Science; Engineering; Finance; Marketing. **Benefits:** 401(k); Dental Insurance; Disability Coverage; Employee Discounts; Life Insurance; Medical Insurance; Pension Plan; Tuition Assistance. **Special programs:** Internships. **Corporate headquarters location:** This Location. **Other U.S. locations:** Irvine CA; Southington CT; Tampa FL; El Paso TX; Jacksonville TX; Sherman TX. **Parent company:** Johnson & Johnson, Inc. (New Brunswick NJ). **Operations at this facility include:** Administration; Manufacturing; Research and Development; Sales. **Number of employees at this location:** 400. **Number of employees nationwide:** 2,500.

JORDAN HEALTH SERVICES
P.O. Box 1387, Mount Vernon TX 75457. 903/537-3012. **Contact:** John McAuley, Human Resources Manager. **Description:** A diversified home health care agency. **Common positions include:** Licensed Practical Nurse; Occupational Therapist; Physical Therapist; Registered Nurse; Respiratory Therapist; Social Worker; Speech-Language Pathologist. **Educational backgrounds include:** Health Care. **Benefits:** 401(k); Disability Coverage; Life Insurance; Medical Insurance. **Corporate headquarters location:** This Location. **Operations at this facility include:** Administration. **Listed on:** Privately held. **Annual sales/revenues:** $21 - $50 million. **Number of employees at this location:** 500.

KIMBERLY-CLARK TECNOL INC.
7201 Industrial Park Boulevard, Fort Worth TX 76180. 817/577-3404. **Fax:** 817/577-7777. **Recorded jobline:** 817/577-6429. **Contact:** Human Resources. **World Wide Web address:** http://www.kimberlyclark.com. **Description:** A supplier of disposable hospital products including surgical masks and ice packs.

MEDICAL CENTER HOSPITAL/TYLER
P.O. Drawer 6400, Tyler TX 75711. 903/597-0351. **Contact:** Human Resources. **Description:** A hospital.

MEDICAL CENTER OF PLANO
3901 West 15th Street, Plano TX 75075. 972/519-1174. **Fax:** 972/519-1423. **Recorded jobline:** 972/596-5300. **Contact:** Human Resources Department. **World Wide Web address:** http://www.columbia.net. **Description:** A medical center. **Common positions include:** EEG Technologist; EKG Technician; Emergency Medical Technician; Medical Records Technician; Nuclear Medicine Technologist; Occupational Therapist; Physical Therapist; Radiological Technologist; Registered Nurse; Respiratory Therapist. **Benefits:** 401(k); Dental Insurance; Life Insurance; Medical Insurance; Tuition Assistance. **Parent company:** Columbia/HCA. **Listed on:** New York Stock Exchange. **Number of employees at this location:** 1,200.

MESQUITE COMMUNITY HOSPITAL
3500 Interstate 30, Mesquite TX 75150. 972/698-3300. **Fax:** 972/698-2580. **Recorded jobline:** 972/698-2463. **Contact:** Debbie Ottwell, Executive Assistant. **Description:** A hospital with 172 beds.

METHODIST HOSPITAL
3615 19th Street, Lubbock TX 79410. 806/792-1011. **Contact:** Personnel. **World Wide Web address:** http://www.methodisthospital.com. **Description:** A hospital with approximately 760 beds.

METHODIST MEDICAL CENTER
1441 North Beckley Avenue, Dallas TX 75203. 214/947-8181. **Contact:** Human Resources Department. **Description:** An acute care medical center licensed for 478 beds.

NORTHWEST TEXAS HEALTHCARE SYSTEM
P.O. Box 1110, Amarillo TX 79175-0001. 806/354-1000. **Contact:** Human Resources. **World Wide Web address:** http://www.nwths.com. **Description:** An acute care, 357-bed health facility. **Number of employees at this location:** 1,700.

OMEGA OPTICAL COMPANY, INC.
13515 North Stemmons Freeway, Dallas TX 75234. 972/241-4141. **Contact:** Personnel Manager. **Description:** A manufacturer of prescription optical lenses and ophthalmic goods. **Common positions include:** Accountant/Auditor; Blue-Collar Worker Supervisor; Clerical Supervisor; Computer Programmer; Credit Manager; Customer Service Representative; Electrician; General Manager; Human Resources Manager; Operations/Production Manager; Quality Control Supervisor; Systems Analyst. **Educational backgrounds include:** Accounting; Business Administration. **Benefits:** 401(k); Dental Insurance; Disability Coverage; Employee Discounts; Life Insurance; Medical Insurance. **Corporate headquarters location:** This Location. **Parent**

company: Benson Eyecare. **Operations at this facility include:** Administration; Manufacturing. **Number of employees at this location:** 600.

183 ANIMAL HOSPITAL
1010 West Airport Freeway, Irving TX 75062. 972/579-0115. **Contact:** Human Resources. **Description:** 183 Animal Hospital provides general medical and surgical services along with diagnostic testing, radiography, and dentistry for small animals.

ORTHOFIX INC.
250 East Arapaho Road, Richardson TX 75081. 972/918-8300. **Fax:** 972/918-8311. **Recorded jobline:** 972/918-8327. **Contact:** Human Resources. **Description:** Orthofix Inc. develops, manufactures, markets, and distributes medical devices to promote bone healing. Products are primarily used by orthopedic surgeons. **Common positions include:** Chemical Engineer; Customer Service Representative; Electrical/Electronics Engineer; Mechanical Engineer; Services Sales Representative. **Benefits:** 401(k); Dental Insurance; Disability Coverage; Life Insurance; Medical Insurance; Profit Sharing; Savings Plan; Tuition Assistance. **Parent company:** Orthofix N.V. (Henly, England). **Operations at this facility include:** Administration; Divisional Headquarters; Manufacturing; Research and Development; Sales; Service. **Listed on:** NASDAQ. **Annual sales/revenues:** $21 - $50 million. **Number of employees at this location:** 240. **Number of employees worldwide:** 350.

PALO PINTO GENERAL HOSPITAL
400 SW 25th Avenue, Mineral Wells TX 76067. 940/328-6390. **Fax:** 940/328-6389. **Contact:** Barbara Stagner, Director of Human Resources. **Description:** An acute care hospital. **Common positions include:** Dietician/Nutritionist; Emergency Medical Technician; Licensed Practical Nurse; Medical Records Technician; Nuclear Medicine Technologist; Occupational Therapist; Pharmacist; Physical Therapist; Public Relations Specialist; Purchasing Agent/Manager; Radiological Technologist; Registered Nurse; Respiratory Therapist; Social Worker. **Educational backgrounds include:** Biology; Chemistry; Health Care. **Benefits:** Dental Insurance; Disability Coverage; Employee Discounts; Life Insurance; Medical Insurance; Pension Plan; Savings Plan; Tuition Assistance. **Corporate headquarters location:** This Location. **Operations at this facility include:** Administration; Service. **Annual sales/revenues:** $11 - $20 million. **Number of employees at this location:** 415.

PARKLAND MEMORIAL HOSPITAL
5201 Harry Hines Boulevard, Dallas TX 75235. 214/590-8064. **Contact:** Employment Services. **Description:** Part of the Dallas County hospital district, Parkland Memorial Hospital is a Level I trauma center, and a 900-bed teaching hospital affiliated with the University of Texas Health Science Center at Dallas. **Common positions include:** Accountant/Auditor; Administrator; Biological Scientist; Biomedical Engineer; Blue-Collar Worker Supervisor; Buyer; Chemist; Civil Engineer; Claim Representative; Computer Programmer; Credit Manager; Customer Service Representative; Department Manager; Dietician/Nutritionist; Electrician; Financial Analyst; Human Resources Manager; Management Trainee; Public Relations Specialist; Purchasing Agent/Manager; Quality Control Supervisor; Systems Analyst. **Educational backgrounds include:** Accounting; Biology; Business Administration; Chemistry; Computer Science; Engineering. **Benefits:** Disability Coverage; Employee Discounts; Life Insurance; Medical Insurance; Pension Plan; Savings Plan; Tuition Assistance. **Corporate headquarters location:** This Location.

PRESBYTERIAN HOSPITAL OF DALLAS
PRESBYTERIAN HEALTHCARE SYSTEM
8440 Walnut Hill Lane, Suite 300, Lockbox 28, Dallas TX 75231. 214/345-4251. **Toll-free phone:** 800/749-6877. **Fax:** 214/345-4003. **Recorded jobline:** 214/345-7863. **Contact:** Camilla Norder, Employment Manager. **E-mail address:** norderc@wpmail.phscare.org. **World Wide Web address:** http://www.phscare.com. **Description:** A 700-bed, nonprofit hospital and teaching facility. **NOTE:** Second and third shifts are offered. **Common positions include:** Account Representative; Accountant; Administrative Assistant; Certified Nurses Aide; Claim Representative; Clerical Supervisor; Clinical Lab Technician; Collector; Computer Operator; Computer Programmer; Customer Service Representative; Database Manager; Daycare Worker;

Dietician/Nutritionist; EEG Technologist; EKG Technician; Financial Aid Officer; Health Services Manager; Health Services Worker; Human Resources Manager; Investigator; Medical Records Technician; MIS Specialist; Nuclear Medicine Technologist; Occupational Therapist; Pharmacist; Physical Therapist; Physician; Physicist; Preschool Worker; Registered Nurse; Respiratory Therapist; Secretary; Social Worker; Speech-Language Pathologist; Surgical Technician; Systems Analyst; Telecommunications Manager. **Educational backgrounds include:** Health Care; M.D./Medicine; Nursing. **Benefits:** 403(b); Dental Insurance; Disability Coverage; Life Insurance; Long-Term Care; Medical Insurance; On-Site Daycare; Retirement Plan; Scholarship Program; Tuition Assistance. **Corporate headquarters location:** This Location. **Other U.S. locations:** Greenville TX; Kaufman TX; Plano TX; Winnsboro TX. **Operations at this facility include:** Administration; Regional Headquarters. **Number of employees at this location:** 3,000. **Number of employees nationwide:** 12,000.

PROVIDENCE HEALTH CENTER
P.O. Box 2589, Waco TX 76702. 254/751-4000. **Contact:** Human Resources. **Description:** A hospital.

QUEST MEDICAL, INC.
One Allentown Parkway, Allen TX 75002-4211. 972/390-9800. **Contact:** Human Resources. **Description:** Develops, manufactures, and markets cardiovascular surgery products (valves, instrumentation, filters, traps, and surgical retracting tapes); intravenous fluid delivery tubing; and neuromodulators. **Corporate headquarters location:** This Location. **Subsidiaries include:** Quest Advanced Neuromodulation Systems. **Listed on:** NASDAQ. **Stock exchange symbol:** QMED. **Number of employees at this location:** 250.

RHD MEMORIAL MEDICAL CENTER
7 Medical Parkway, Dallas TX 75234. 972/247-1000. **Contact:** Personnel Department. **Description:** A hospital with 190 acute care beds.

ROYAL OPTICAL U.S. VISION
1334 Inwood Road, Dallas TX 75247. 214/630-5791. **Contact:** Personnel Department. **Description:** Manufactures frames, grinds lenses, and distributes a line of eyewear.

ST. JOSEPH'S HOSPITAL & HEALTH CENTER
P.O. Box 9070, Paris TX 75461-9070. 903/737-3253. **Fax:** 903/737-3887. **Contact:** Human Resources Department. **Description:** A licensed 216-bed, acute care hospital. St. Joseph's Hospital and Health Center provides comprehensive heart programs, inpatient and outpatient dialysis, rehabilitation services, oncology, radiation therapy, and nuclear medicine. **Common positions include:** Accountant/Auditor; Administrative Manager; Blue-Collar Worker Supervisor; Budget Analyst; Buyer; Claim Representative; Clerical Supervisor; Clinical Lab Technician; Computer Programmer; Construction Contractor; Counselor; Credit Manager; Customer Service Representative; Dietician/Nutritionist; EEG Technologist; EKG Technician; Electrician; Emergency Medical Technician; Environmental Engineer; Financial Analyst; Food Scientist/Technologist; Health Services Manager; Human Service Worker; Library Technician; Licensed Practical Nurse; Medical Records Technician; Nuclear Medicine Technologist; Occupational Therapist; Pharmacist; Physical Therapist; Physician; Psychologist; Public Relations Specialist; Purchasing Agent/Manager; Quality Control Supervisor; Radiological Technologist; Recreational Therapist; Registered Nurse; Respiratory Therapist; Restaurant/Food Service Manager; Social Worker; Speech-Language Pathologist; Surgical Technician; Systems Analyst; Teacher/Professor. **Educational backgrounds include:** Accounting; Biology; Business Administration; Chemistry; Computer Science; Finance; Health Care; M.D./Medicine; Marketing. **Benefits:** 403(b); Dental Insurance; Disability Coverage; EAP; Employee Discounts; Life Insurance; Medical Insurance; Pension Plan; Tuition Assistance. **Corporate headquarters location:** San Antonio TX. **Parent company:** IWHS. **Operations at this facility include:** Administration; Service. **Listed on:** Privately held. **Number of employees at this location:** 800.

ST. PAUL MEDICAL CENTER
5909 Harry Hines Boulevard, Dallas TX 75235. 214/879-1000. **Contact:** Human Resources Department. **Description:** A 600-bed medical center.

JOHN PETER SMITH HEALTH NETWORK
1500 South Main Street, Fort Worth TX 76104. 817/921-3431. **Contact:** Human Resources. **Description:** An acute care hospital with over 160 beds.

SOUTHERN MANOR
4320 West 19th Street, Lubbock TX 79407. 806/795-7147. **Contact:** Personnel Department. **Description:** A nursing home. **Number of employees at this location:** 100.

SOUTHWESTERN MEDICAL CENTER AT DALLAS
UNIVERSITY OF TEXAS
5323 Harry Hines Boulevard, Dallas TX 75235-9023. 214/648-3111. **Fax:** 214/648-9874. **Contact:** Annette Brannan, Human Resources. **World Wide Web address:** http://www.swmed.edu. **Description:** A medical center providing patient care, medical education, and research. **NOTE:** Entry-level positions are offered. **Common positions include:** Accountant; Administrative Assistant; Administrative Manager; Attorney; Auditor; Biochemist; Biological Scientist; Budget Analyst; Buyer; Claim Representative; Clinical Lab Technician; Computer Operator; Computer Programmer; Database Manager; Emergency Medical Technician; Financial Analyst; Librarian; Licensed Practical Nurse; Licensed Vocational Nurse; Medical Records Technician; Network Engineer; Nurse Practitioner; Physical Therapist; Registered Nurse; Secretary; Social Worker; Systems Analyst; Systems Manager; Veterinarian. **Educational backgrounds include:** Accounting; Biology; Business Administration; Chemistry; Computer Science; Finance; Health Care; Medical Technology; Physics. **Benefits:** 403(b); Dental Insurance; Disability Coverage; Life Insurance; Mass Transit Available; Medical Insurance; Pension Plan; Savings Plan. **Special programs:** Internships. **Corporate headquarters location:** This Location. **Operations at this facility include:** Administration; Research and Development. **Number of employees at this location:** 5,000.

STAFF BUILDERS HOME HEALTH
7929 Brook River Drive, Suite 550, Dallas TX 75247. 214/630-9241. **Contact:** Human Resources. **World Wide Web address:** http://www.staffbuilders.com. **Description:** A home health care agency. **Common positions include:** Home Health Aide; Licensed Practical Nurse; Registered Nurse. **Corporate headquarters location:** Lake Success NY. **Other U.S. locations:** Nationwide.

STERN EMPIRE
1918 East Front Street, Tyler TX 75702. 903/597-3198. **Contact:** Human Resources. **Description:** A dental laboratory that makes dental prosthetics. **Benefits:** 401(k); Incentive Plan; Stock Option. **Other U.S. locations:** Arlington TX; Houston TX. **Parent company:** National Dentex Corporation (Wayland MA) is one of the largest operators of dental laboratories in the United States. National Dentex Corporation serves an active customer base of approximately 6,200 dentists through its 20 full-service and three branch laboratories located in 18 states. These dental laboratories provide a full range of custom-made dental prosthetic appliances, divided into three main groups: restorative products (crowns and bridges); reconstructive products (partial and full dentures); and cosmetic products (porcelain veneers and ceramic crowns). Each lab is operated as a stand-alone facility under the direction of a local manager. All sales and marketing is done through each lab's own direct sales force. **Listed on:** NASDAQ. **Number of employees nationwide:** 840.

STERN REED ASSOCIATES
4203 Beltway, Suite 5, Dallas TX 75244. 817/640-8341. **Contact:** Human Resources. **Description:** A dental laboratory that makes dental prosthetics. **Benefits:** 401(k); Incentive Plan; Stock Option. **Other U.S. locations:** Houston TX; Tyler TX. **Parent company:** National Dentex Corporation (Wayland MA) is one of the largest operators of dental laboratories in the United States. National Dentex Corporation serves an active customer base of approximately 6,200 dentists through its 20 full-service and three branch laboratories located in 18 states. These dental laboratories provide a full range of custom-made dental prosthetic appliances, divided into three main groups: restorative products (crowns and bridges); reconstructive products (partial and full dentures); and cosmetic products (porcelain veneers and ceramic crowns). Each lab is operated as a stand-alone facility under the direction of a local manager. All sales and marketing is done through each lab's own direct sales force. **Listed on:** NASDAQ. **Number of employees nationwide:** 840.

TENET HEALTHCARE CORPORATION

P.O. Box 809088, Dallas TX 75380-9088. 972/789-2324. **Fax:** 972/980-2685. **Contact:** Mike Duda, Manager of Recruitment. **World Wide Web address:** http://www.tenethealth.com. **Description:** A multibillion-dollar, multi-hospital corporation with facilities nationwide. **Common positions include:** Accountant/Auditor; Administrative Manager; Computer Programmer; Human Resources Manager; Public Relations Specialist; Systems Analyst. **Benefits:** 401(k); Credit Union; Dental Insurance; Disability Coverage; Employee Discounts; Life Insurance; Medical Insurance; Tuition Assistance. **Corporate headquarters location:** Santa Monica CA. **Other U.S. locations:** AL; AR; CA; FL; GA; IN; LA; MO; NC; NE; SC; TN. **Operations at this facility include:** Administration; Regional Headquarters. **Listed on:** New York Stock Exchange; Pacific Stock Exchange. **Number of employees at this location:** 300. **Number of employees nationwide:** 68,000.

TEXAS MEDICAL

8440 Walnut Hill Lane, Dallas TX 75231. 214/823-4151. **Contact:** Personnel. **Description:** A private clinic.

TEXOMA MEDICAL CENTER (TMC)
TEXOMA HEALTHCARE SYSTEMS, INC.

1000 Memorial Drive, Denison TX 75021. 903/416-4050. **Fax:** 903/415-4087. **Recorded jobline:** 800/566-1211. **Contact:** Mike Botello, Employment Coordinator. **Description:** Texoma Medical Center (TMC) is an acute care hospital with 300 beds. TMC offers general medical and surgical services, an intensive care unit, and pediatric care. Also at this location is the headquarters for the parent company, Texoma Healthcare Systems, and an office building for physicians. Founded in 1965. **NOTE:** Summer jobs for students and second and third shifts are offered. **Common positions include:** Accountant; Administrative Assistant; Buyer; Certified Nurses Aide; Clerical Supervisor; Clinical Lab Technician; Computer Operator; Controller; Customer Service Representative; Database Manager; Dietician/Nutritionist; EEG Technologist; EKG Technician; Electrician; Human Resources Manager; Licensed Practical Nurse; Marketing Specialist; Medical Records Technician; Nuclear Medicine Technologist; Occupational Therapist; Pharmacist; Physical Therapist; Radiological Technologist; Registered Nurse; Respiratory Therapist; Secretary; Speech-Language Pathologist; Surgical Technician; Systems Analyst; Systems Manager. **Educational backgrounds include:** Computer Science; Health Care. **Benefits:** 403(b); Dental Insurance; Disability Coverage; Job Sharing; Life Insurance; Medical Insurance; Pension Plan; Profit Sharing; Tuition Assistance. **Special programs:** Co-op. **Corporate headquarters location:** This Location. **Other U.S. locations:** Durant OK; Bonham TX; Sherman TX; Trenton TX; Whitewright TX. **Subsidiaries include:** Times Medical Equipment. **Operations at this facility include:** Administration; Support Services. **CEO/President:** Arthur L. Hohenberger. **Number of employees nationwide:** 1,200.

TRI-CITY HOSPITAL

7525 Scyene Road, Dallas TX 75227. 214/381-7171. **Contact:** Human Resources Department. **Description:** A 131-bed, acute care hospital.

UNITED REGIONAL HEALTHCARE SYSTEMS

1600 Eighth Street, Wichita Falls TX 76301. 940/723-1960. **Toll-free phone:** 800/221-9750. **Fax:** 940/761-8223. **Recorded jobline:** 940/723-1960x19. **Contact:** Patra Linderkamp, Recruitment Coordinator. **Description:** This location is a licensed, 300-bed, acute care facility. United Regional Healthcare Systems is the result of the merger between Wichita General Hospital (formerly this location) and Bethania Regional Health Care Center.

UNIVERSITY MEDICAL CENTER

602 Indiana Avenue, Lubbock TX 79415. 806/743-3111. **Recorded jobline:** 806/743-3352. **Contact:** Human Resources Manager. **Description:** A hospital. **Common positions include:** Accountant/Auditor; Buyer; Clerical Supervisor; Clinical Lab Technician; Computer Programmer; Dietician/Nutritionist; EEG Technologist; EKG Technician; Health Services Manager; Licensed Practical Nurse; Medical Records Technician; Nuclear Medicine Technologist; Occupational Therapist; Pharmacist; Physical Therapist; Registered Nurse; Respiratory Therapist; Restaurant/Food Service Manager; Social Worker; Speech-Language Pathologist; Surgical

Technician; Systems Analyst. **Educational backgrounds include:** Accounting; Business Administration; Health Care. **Benefits:** 401(k); Dental Insurance; Employee Discounts; Life Insurance; Medical Insurance; Profit Sharing. **Special programs:** Internships. **Operations at this facility include:** Administration; Service. **Number of employees at this location:** 1,850.

UNIVERSITY OF TEXAS HEALTH CENTER AT TYLER
P.O. Box 2003, Tyler TX 75710. 903/877-7740. **Recorded jobline:** 903/877-7071. **Contact:** Human Resources. **World Wide Web address:** http://www.pegasus.uthct.edu/hr/hrhome.html. **Description:** A nonprofit hospital. **Common positions include:** Accountant/Auditor; Biological Scientist; Budget Analyst; Buyer; Chemist; Clerical Supervisor; Clinical Lab Technician; Computer Programmer; Dietician/Nutritionist; EEG Technologist; EKG Technician; Electrician; Hotel Manager; Human Resources Manager; Librarian; Library Technician; Licensed Practical Nurse; Meteorologist; Nuclear Medicine Technologist; Occupational Therapist; Pharmacist; Physical Therapist; Physician; Radiological Technologist; Registered Nurse; Respiratory Therapist; Social Worker; Surgical Technician; Systems Analyst. **Educational backgrounds include:** Health Care. **Benefits:** Dental Insurance; Disability Coverage; Employee Discounts; Life Insurance; Medical Insurance; Tuition Assistance. **Corporate headquarters location:** This Location. **Operations at this facility include:** Administration; Research and Development; Service. **Number of employees at this location:** 1,300.

VA MEDICAL CENTER
6010 Amarillo Boulevard West, Amarillo TX 79106. 806/355-9703. **Contact:** Human Resources. **World Wide Web address:** http://www.va.gov. **Description:** A medical center operated by the U.S. Department of Veterans Affairs. From 54 hospitals in 1930, the VA health care system has grown to include 171 medical centers; more than 364 outpatient, community, and outreach clinics; 130 nursing home care units; and 37 domiciliaries. The VA operates at least one medical center in each of the 48 contiguous states, Puerto Rico, and the District of Columbia. With approximately 76,000 medical center beds, the VA treats nearly 1 million patients in VA hospitals; 75,000 in nursing home care units; and 25,000 in domiciliaries. The VA's outpatient clinics register approximately 24 million visits per year.

VA NORTH TEXAS HEALTHCARE SYSTEM
4500 South Lancaster Road, Dallas TX 75216. 214/376-5451. **Contact:** Personnel. **World Wide Web address:** http://www.va.gov. **Description:** This location houses administrative offices. From 54 hospitals in 1930, the VA health care system has grown to include 171 medical centers; more than 364 outpatient, community, and outreach clinics; 130 nursing home care units; and 37 domiciliaries. The VA operates at least one medical center in each of the 48 contiguous states, Puerto Rico, and the District of Columbia. With approximately 76,000 medical center beds, the VA treats nearly one million patients in VA hospitals; 75,000 in nursing home care units; and 25,000 in domiciliaries. The VA's outpatient clinics register approximately 24 million visits per year. **Common positions include:** Accountant/Auditor; Attorney; Clerical Supervisor; Clinical Lab Technician; Computer Programmer; Counselor; Dental Assistant/Dental Hygienist; Dental Lab Technician; Dentist; Designer; Dietician/Nutritionist; Education Administrator; EEG Technologist; EKG Technician; Electrical/Electronics Engineer; Electrician; Emergency Medical Technician; Environmental Engineer; Financial Analyst; Human Resources Manager; Human Service Worker; Industrial Engineer; Librarian; Library Technician; Licensed Practical Nurse; Management Analyst/Consultant; Management Trainee; Materials Engineer; Mechanical Engineer; Medical Records Technician; Nuclear Engineer; Nuclear Medicine Technologist; Occupational Therapist; Operations/Production Manager; Pharmacist; Physical Therapist; Physician; Physicist; Psychologist; Public Relations Specialist; Purchasing Agent/Manager; Radiological Technologist; Recreational Therapist; Registered Nurse; Respiratory Therapist; Social Worker; Sociologist; Software Engineer; Speech-Language Pathologist; Surgical Technician; Systems Analyst. **Benefits:** 401(k); Dental Insurance; Disability Coverage; Employee Discounts; Life Insurance; Medical Insurance; Pension Plan; Savings Plan; Tuition Assistance. **Special programs:** Internships. **Operations at this facility include:** Administration.

VENCOR HOSPITAL OF DALLAS
1600 Abrams Road, Dallas TX 75214. 214/818-2400. **Contact:** Business Office. **Description:** An acute care hospital licensed for 609 beds.

VISITING NURSE ASSOCIATION
1440 West Mockingbird Lane, Suite 500, Dallas TX 75247. 214/689-0000. **Contact:** Human Resources. **Description:** A home health care agency that provides intermittent in-home visits. **Common positions include:** Dietician/Nutritionist; Licensed Practical Nurse; Occupational Therapist; Physical Therapist; Registered Nurse.

WADLEY REGIONAL MEDICAL CENTER
1000 Pine Street, Texarkana TX 75501. 903/798-7160. **Fax:** 903/798-7177. **Contact:** Jan Loveall, Employment Coordinator. **E-mail address:** loveall@wadleyrmc.com. **World Wide Web address:** http://www.wadley.com. **Description:** A nonprofit, acute care hospital with 448 beds. The services offered at Wadley include a skilled nursing facility, a Cancer Treatment & Diagnostic Imaging Center, a day surgery center, and a Community Oriented Medical Plan Clinic. Founded in 1959. **NOTE:** Summer jobs for students and second and third shifts are offered. **Company slogan:** To improve the health and healthcare of those we serve. **Common positions include:** Accountant; Certified Nurses Aide; Chief Financial Officer; Customer Service Representative; Daycare Worker; Dietician/Nutritionist; EEG Technologist; EKG Technician; Electrical/Electronics Engineer; Electrician; Emergency Medical Technician; Nuclear Medicine Technologist; Pharmacist; Registered Nurse; Respiratory Therapist; Social Worker; Speech-Language Pathologist; Surgical Technician. **Educational backgrounds include:** Health Care. **Benefits:** 401(k); 403(b); Dental Insurance; Disability Coverage; Employee Discounts; Life Insurance; Medical Insurance; On-Site Daycare; Pension Plan; Tuition Assistance. **CEO:** Hugh Hallgren. **Number of employees at this location:** 1,200.

WICHITA FALLS STATE HOSPITAL
P.O. Box 300, Wichita Falls TX 76038. 940/689-5260. **Fax:** 940/689-5735. **Recorded jobline:** 940/689-5378. **Contact:** Human Resources. **Description:** A hospital specializing in providing services to the mentally retarded. **Common positions include:** Human Service Worker; Physician; Registered Nurse. **Educational backgrounds include:** Health Care. **Benefits:** Dental Insurance; Disability Coverage; Life Insurance; Medical Insurance; Pension Plan. **Special programs:** Internships. **Corporate headquarters location:** Austin TX. **Parent company:** Texas Department of Mental Health/Mental Retardation. **Operations at this facility include:** Administration. **Number of employees at this location:** 1,200.

ZALE LIPSHY UNIVERSITY HOSPITAL
SOUTHWESTERN MEDICAL CENTER
5151 Harry Hines Boulevard, Dallas TX 75235-7786. 214/590-3150. **Fax:** 214/590-3193. **Recorded jobline:** 214/590-3484. **Contact:** Dara Biegert, Director of Human Resources. **E-mail address:** response@zluh.org. **Description:** Zale Lipshy University Hospital at Southwestern Medical Center was built to serve University of Texas Southwestern Medical Center at Dallas as its private, nonprofit, adult referral hospital for specialized tertiary care. The facilities consist of 152 hospital beds (20 intensive care unit beds, 89 medical/surgical beds, 22 rehabilitation beds, and 21 psychiatric beds) and 12 operating room suites for specialized surgical care in the areas of neurological surgery, orthopedics, urology, gynecology, otorhinolaryngology (ear, nose, and throat), ophthalmology, cardiothoracic surgery, oral and maxillofacial surgery, vascular surgery, and plastic and reconstructive surgery. Founded in 1989. **NOTE:** Second and third shifts are offered. **Common positions include:** Accountant/Auditor; Biomedical Engineer; Buyer; Certified Nurses Aide; Chemist; Chief Financial Officer; Clinical Lab Technician; Computer Programmer; Dietician/Nutritionist; Electrician; Financial Analyst; Health Services Manager; Medical Records Technician; Nuclear Medicine Technologist; Occupational Therapist; Pharmacist; Physical Therapist; Radiological Technologist; Registered Nurse; Respiratory Therapist; Restaurant/Food Service Manager; Secretary; Social Worker; Surgical Technician; Systems Analyst. **Educational backgrounds include:** Accounting; Business Administration; Computer Science; Health Care. **Benefits:** 403(b); Dental Insurance; Disability Coverage; Employee Discounts; Incentive Plan; Life Insurance; Medical Insurance; Pension Plan; Tuition Assistance. **Corporate headquarters location:** This Location. **Operations at this facility include:** Administration; Service. **Annual sales/revenues:** More than $100 million. **Number of employees at this location:** 600.

Note: Because addresses and telephone numbers of smaller companies can change rapidly, we recommend you call each company to verify the information below before inquiring about job opportunities. Mass mailings are not recommended.

Additional small employers:

DENTISTS' OFFICES AND CLINICS

Managed Dental Care Centers
4445 Alpha Rd, Ste 100, Dallas
TX 75244-4507. 972/458-2449.

HOME HEALTH CARE SERVICES

Caprock Primary Home Care
PO Box 53803, Lubbock TX
79453-3803. 806/793-3615.

Cedar Lake Nursing Services
PO Box 2034, Malakoff TX
75148-2034. 903/489-2043.

Cherokee Home Health Care
615A E Rusk St, Jacksonville TX
75766-5017. 903/586-3173.

Columbia Home Care
1800 Teague Dr, Sherman TX
75090-2640. 903/870-2000.

Companion Care Home Health
3502 Slide Rd, Lubbock TX
79414-2500. 806/792-0192.

Concepts of Care
PO Box 5767, Abilene TX
79608-5767. 915/698-1613.

Delta Home Health Care Inc.
207 S McDonald St, McKinney
TX 75069-5658. 972/542-8600.

Family Service Inc.
1424 Hemphill St, Fort Worth TX
76104-4703. 817/927-8884.

Girling Health Care Inc.
6301 Gaston Ave, Ste 800, Dallas
TX 75214-6207. 214/824-3621.

Harris Methodist Northwest
108 Denver Trl, Azle TX 76020-
3614. 817/444-8676.

Healthcor Holdings Inc.
8150 N Central Expy, Dallas TX
75206-1815. 972/233-7744.

Heaven Sent Home Health
RR 1, Box 302P, Hughes Springs
TX 75656-9775. 903/639-2878.

HHCA Texas Health Services
7502 Greenville Ave, Dallas TX
75231-3832. 817/338-4855.

Hi Plains Hospital & Nursing Home
PO Drawer H, Hale Center TX
79041-1260. 806/839-2471.

Home Care Service Inc.
10 Richardson Heights Ctr,
Richardson TX 75080-6316.
972/690-5875.

Home Health of Tarrant County
923 Pennsylvania Ave, Fort
Worth TX 76104-2254. 817/338-
9595.

Home Health Services of Dallas
2929 Carlisle St, Ste 375A,
Dallas TX 75204-1084. 214/720-
4473.

Interim Healthcare Inc.
8330 Meadow Rd, Ste 114,
Dallas TX 75231-3750. 214/360-
9090.

Interim Healthcare Lubbock
166 S Willis St, Abilene TX
79605-1734. 915/677-2047.

Jackson Healthcare Systems
PO Box 3945, Temple TX 76505-
3945. 254/778-4210.

LHS Common Community Care
8150 Brookriver Dr, Dallas TX
75247-4068. 214/951-7381.

Magnolia Home Health Care
110 S Collegiate Dr, Paris TX
75460-6319. 903/784-4014.

Olsten Kimberly Quality Care
4004 Call Field Rd, Wichita Falls
TX 76308-2634. 940/691-2106.

Omnicare Home Health
PO Box 689, De Soto TX 75123-
0689. 972/228-4584.

PDN Inc.
101 E Park Blvd, Ste 115, Plano
TX 75074-5445. 972/578-0924.

PFI Corporation
1320 South University Dr, Fort
Worth TX 76107-5764. 817/338-
0042.

Professional Home Health
PO Box 1236, Granbury TX
76048-8236. 817/573-0171.

PT Home Service
8200 Brookriver Dr, Grand
Prairie TX 75050. 972/263-9619.

Quality Home Health Care Inc.
2626 Hilltop Dr, Ste 2, Sherman
TX 75090-2248. 903/892-9281.

Signature Home Care
2006 N Highway 360, Grand
Prairie TX 75050-1423. 972/714-
7800.

Signature Home Care
810 Office Park Cir, Lewisville
TX 75057-3181. 972/420-8711.

Texoma Community Health Services
3821 Wilbarger St, Vernon TX
76384-3262. 940/552-9365.

TLC Inc.
520 E Central Pkwy, Plano TX
75074-5527. 972/422-1375.

TNF Homehealth Service Inc.
PO Box 521, Atlanta TX 75551-
0521. 903/796-9922.

Trinity Mother Frances Home Care
423 S Beckham Ave, Tyler TX
75702-8309. 903/592-8001.

Visiting Nurse Association
PO Box 91, Texarkana TX
75504-0091. 903/794-3102.

Visiting Nurse Association of Texas
2414 W University Dr,
McKinney TX 75070-2810.
972/562-0140.

Wichita Home Health
1100 Alma St, Wichita Falls TX
76301-5702. 940/322-7113.

MEDICAL EQUIPMENT

B. Braun/McGaw Inc.
1601 Wallace Dr, Ste 150,
Carrollton TX 75006-6652.
972/245-2243.

Baxter Convertors
PO Box 2046, Jacksonville TX
75766-2046. 903/586-6502.

Benedict Optical Inc.
651 E Corporate Dr, Lewisville
TX 75057-6403. 972/221-4141.

Black Sheep Inc.
3220 W Gentry Parkway, Tyler
TX 75702-1311. 903/592-3853.

Bledsoe Brace Systems
2601 Pinewood St, Grand Prairie
TX 75051-3516. 972/647-0884.

DAC Vision Incorporated
PO Box 402147, Garland TX
75046. 972/494-4555.

Guard Line Inc.
PO Box 1030, Atlanta TX 75551-
1030. 903/796-4111.

Johnson & Johnson Medical
PO Box 9100, Sherman TX
75091-9100. 903/868-9000.

Spenco Medical Corporation
PO Box 2501, Waco TX 76702-
2501. 254/772-6000.

Struckmeyer Corp.
13737 N Stemmons Fwy, Dallas
TX 75234-5761. 972/247-0407.

**NURSING AND PERSONAL
CARE FACILITIES**

A-1 Nursing Care & Placement
PO Box 397988, Dallas TX
75339-7988. 214/467-7048.

American Habilitation Services
117 W Walker St, Breckenridge
TX 76424-3538. 254/559-3336.

**Atria Briarcliff Village Health
Care**
3403 S Vine Ave, Tyler TX
75701-8539. 903/581-5714.

Autumn Years Lodge
424 S Adams St, Fort Worth TX
76104-1003. 817/335-5781.

Bell Haven Nursing Center
1002 Medical Dr, Killeen TX
76543-3525. 254/634-0374.

Bellmire Healthcare Facility
1101 Rock St, Bowie TX 76230-
3115. 940/872-2283.

Bivins Memorial Nursing Home
PO Box 1727, Amarillo TX
79105-1727. 806/355-7453.

Brentwood II
8059 Scyene Circle, Dallas TX
75227-5534. 214/388-0519.

Brentwood Place
8069 Scyene Circle, Dallas TX
75227-5534. 214/388-0609.

**Buckner Ryburn Nursing
Center**
4810 Samuell Blvd, Dallas TX
75228-6831. 214/388-0426.

Capital Senior Living Inc.
14160 Dallas Parkway, Ste 300,
Dallas TX 75240-4383. 972/770-
5600.

Carriage House Manor Inc.
PO Box 914, Sulphur Springs TX
75483-0914. 903/885-3589.

CC Young Memorial Home
4829 W Lawther Dr, Dallas TX
75214-1823. 214/827-8080.

Cherry Street Annex
2185 E Cherry St, Paris TX
75460-4747. 903/784-7108.

Christian Care Center
1000 Wiggins Parkway, Mesquite
TX 75150-1409. 972/686-3100.

Clarksville Nursing Center
300 E Baker St, Clarksville TX
75426-5034. 903/427-2236.

Clifton Lutheran Sunset Home
PO Box 71, Clifton TX 76634-
0071. 254/675-8637.

Collins Care Center
3100 S Rigsbee Dr, Plano TX
75074-7008. 972/423-6217.

Colonial Manor
2035 N Grandbury, Cleburne TX
76031. 817/645-9134.

Colonial Manor
400 S Beach St, Fort Worth TX
76105-1102. 817/535-2135.

Colonial Manor
930 S Baxter Ave, Tyler TX
75701-2209. 903/597-2068.

Colonial Park Nursing Home
PO Box 1869, Marshall TX
75671-1869. 903/935-7886.

Coronado Nursing Center
1751 N 15th St, Abilene TX
79603-4430. 915/673-3531.

Corsicana Nursing Home
1500 N 45th St, Corsicana TX
75110-1703. 903/872-4606.

Creekview Retirement Center
123 Lions Club Park Rd,
Lancaster TX 75146-3108.
972/227-1205.

**Dallas Nursing &
Rehabilitation Center**
11301 Dennis Rd, Dallas TX
75229-2305. 972/247-4866.

Denton Development Center
909 N Loop 288, Denton TX
76201-3607. 940/387-8525.

Denton Good Samaritan Village
2500 Hinkle Dr, Denton TX
76201-0739. 940/383-2651.

**Denton Rehabilitation &
Nursing Center**
2229 N Carroll Blvd, Denton TX
76201-1833. 940/387-8508.

Edmond Oaks Center
1680 S Edmonds Lane,
Lewisville TX 75067-5803.
972/436-4538.

Elmwood Nursing Center
221 Virginia Ave, Marlin TX
76661-2160. 254/883-5548.

Farwell Medical Clinic
PO Box 890, Farwell TX 79325-
0890. 806/481-9027.

Four Seasons Nursing Center
7625 Glenview Dr, Fort Worth
TX 76180-8331. 817/284-1427.

Four States Care Center
8 E Midway Dr, Texarkana TX
75501-5884. 903/838-9526.

Gardendale Nursing Home
PO Box 911, Jacksonville TX
75766-0911. 903/586-3626.

Gardens Care Center
901 Penn St, Fort Worth TX
76102-3415. 817/335-3030.

Glen Rose Nursing Home
PO Box 2099, Glen Rose TX
76043-2099. 254/897-2215.

Glenview Nursing Home
PO Box 4878, Tyler TX 75712-
4878. 903/593-6441.

Golden Acres
2525 Centerville Rd, Dallas TX
75228-2634. 214/327-4503.

Grace Presbyterian Village
550 E Ann Arbor Ave, Dallas TX
75216-6718. 214/376-1701.

Graham Oak Center Inc.
1325 1st St, Graham TX 76450-
3603. 940/549-8787.

Granbury Care Center
301 S Park St, Granbury TX
76048-1800. 817/573-3726.

Greenbelt Nursing & Rehab
4301 Hospital Dr, Vernon TX
76384-3135. 940/552-2568.

Greenville Nursing Home
4910 Wellington St, Greenville
TX 75402-6007. 903/454-3772.

Hansford Manor
707 Roland St, Spearman TX
79081-3441. 806/659-2535.

Health Center at Broadway
5301 Bryant Irvin Rd, Fort Worth
TX 76132-4030. 817/346-9407.

**Health Enterprises of
Wisconsin**
401 N Elm St, Denton TX 76201-
4137. 940/387-4388.

Heartland Health Care
2001 Forest Ridge Dr, Bedford
TX 76021-5712. 817/571-6804.

Heritage Estates
201 Sycamore School Rd, Fort
Worth TX 76134-5009. 817/293-
7610.

Heritage Gardens
2135 Denton Dr, Carrollton TX
75006-3103. 972/242-0666.

Heritage Manor
601 Midwestern Pkwy E, Wichita
Falls TX 76302-2401. 940/723-
0885.

Heritage Manor Longview
112 Ruthlynn Dr, Longview TX
75605-5634. 903/753-8611.

Heritage Manor Plano
1621 Coit Rd, Plano TX 75075-
6141. 972/596-7930.

Heritage Nursing Home
PO Box 728, Quitman TX 75783-
0728. 903/763-2284.

Heritage Oaks Nursing Center
1112 Gibbins Rd, Arlington TX
76011-5618. 817/274-2584.

Heritage Place
825 W Kearney St, Mesquite TX
75149-3206. 972/288-7668.

Heritage Place Grand Prairie
820 Small St, Grand Prairie TX
75050-5856. 972/262-1351.

Heritage Village
1111 Rockingham Ln,
Richardson TX 75080-4309.
972/231-8833.

Heritage Western Hills
8001 Western Hills Blvd, Fort
Worth TX 76108-3524. 817/246-
4953.

Hilltop Haven Nursing Center
PO Box 39, Gunter TX 75058-
0039. 903/433-2415.

Holiday Lodge Nursing Home
1301 Eden Dr, Longview TX
75605-4102. 903/753-7651.

Homestead of Denison
1101 Reba McEntire Ln, Denison
TX 75020-9059. 903/463-4663.

Homestead of McKinney
1801 Pearson Avenue, McKinney
TX 75069-3464. 972/562-8880.

IHS at Benbrook-Trinity Hil
1000 McKinley St, Fort Worth
TX 76126-3474. 817/249-0020.

IHS at Woodridge
1500 Autumn Dr, Grapevine TX
76051-3103. 817/481-3622.

**Integrated Health Services of
America**
5601 Plum Creek Dr, Amarillo
TX 79124-1801. 806/351-1000.

**James L. West Presbyterian
Care Center**
PO Box 1348, Fort Worth TX
76101-1348. 817/877-1199.

Juliette Fowler Homes
PO Box 140129, Dallas TX
75214-0129. 214/827-0813.

Louisana Healthcare Partners
207 East Parkerville Road, De
Soto TX 75115-6251. 972/230-
1000.

**Lubbock Regional Mental
Health Center**
3801 Avenue J, Lubbock TX
79412-2017. 806/766-0277.

Lynn Lodge
111 Ruthlynn Dr, Longview TX
75605-5635. 903/757-2557.

Mansfield Nursing Center
1402 E Broad St, Mansfield TX
76063-1806. 817/477-2176.

Mariner Health Fort Worth
4825 Wellesley Ave, Fort Worth
TX 76107-6148. 817/732-6608.

New Boston Nursing Center
210 Rice St, New Boston TX
75570-2929. 903/628-5551.

Oak Brook Health Care Center
PO Box 520, Whitehouse TX
75791-0520. 903/839-5050.

Palo Pinto Nursing Center
PO Box 23, Mineral Wells TX
76068-0023. 940/325-7813.

Park Central
6110 W 34th Ave, Amarillo TX
79109-4004. 806/337-5292.

Park Haven Healthcare Center
2108 15th St, Bridgeport TX
76426-2055. 940/683-5023.

Park Place Nursing Center
PO Box 132100, Tyler TX
75713-2100. 903/592-6745.

Park Place Nursing Home
PO Box 2430, Palestine TX
75802-2430. 903/729-3246.

Park Plaza Care Center
929 Hemphill St, Fort Worth TX
76104-3111. 817/336-9191.

**Post Oak Health &
Rehabilitation**
1518 S Sam Rayburn Fwy,
Sherman TX 75090-8736.
903/893-5553.

Prairie House Living Center
1301 Mesa Dr, Plainview TX
79072-3905. 806/293-4855.

Presbyterian Village North
8600 Skyline Dr, Dallas TX
75243-4198. 214/345-9000.

Quality Convalescent Center
1000 6th Ave, Fort Worth TX
76104-2808. 817/336-2586.

Randol Mill Manor
2645 W Randol Mill Rd,
Arlington TX 76012-4228.
817/277-6789.

Red River Haven Nursing Home
PO Box 790, Bogata TX 75417-0790. 903/632-5293.

Regis/St. Elizabeth Centers
PO Box 1909, Waco TX 76703-1909. 254/756-5441.

Renfro Nursing Home Inc.
1413 W Main St, Waxahachie TX 75165-2298. 972/937-2298.

Ridgecrest Retirement Center
1900 W Highway 6, Waco TX 76712-9729. 254/776-9681.

Robinson Nursing & Development Center
305 S Andrews Dr, Waco TX 76706-5705. 254/662-4010.

Rose Haven Retreat
PO Box 240, Atlanta TX 75551-0240. 903/796-4127.

Rowlett Nursing Center
9300 Hwy 66, Rowlett TX 75088. 972/475-4700.

Senior Care at Lake Pointe
PO Box 1907, Rowlett TX 75030-1907. 972/412-4000.

Shady Oaks Nursing Center
1000 E Highway 82, Sherman TX 75090-1704. 903/893-9636.

Silver Haven Health Care
600 Maple Ave, Burleson TX 76028-5810. 817/295-8118.

Southland Villa
2222 S 5th St, Temple TX 76504-7446. 254/773-1641.

Sweetwater Healthcare
1600 Josephine St, Sweetwater TX 79556-3599. 915/236-6653.

The Clairmont
3201 N 4th St, Longview TX 75605-5145. 903/236-4291.

The Clairmont
900 S Baxter Ave, Tyler TX 75701-2209. 903/597-8192.

The Convalescent Center
4005 Gaston Ave, Dallas TX 75246-1514. 214/826-3891.

Truman W. Smith Children's Center
PO Box 1468, Gladewater TX 75647-1468. 903/845-2181.

Twilight Home
3001 W 4th Ave, Corsicana TX 75110-3913. 903/872-2521.

Tyler Skilled Nursing Rehabilitation
810 S Porter Ave, Tyler TX 75701-2300. 903/593-2463.

Ware Memorial Care Center
1300 S Harrison St, Amarillo TX 79101-4204. 806/376-1177.

Wedgewood Nursing Home
6621 Dan Danciger Rd, Fort Worth TX 76133-4905. 817/292-6330.

West Resthaven Inc.
300 W Haven St, West TX 76691-1011. 254/826-5354.

West Side Care Center
950 S Las Vegas Trl, Fort Worth TX 76108-2920. 817/246-4995.

Western Hill Nursing Home
RR 5, Box 26, Comanche TX 76442-9702. 915/356-2571.

Westgate Nursing Home
PO Box 1999, Hereford TX 79045-1999. 806/364-0661.

Whitewright Nursing Home
PO Box 725, Whitewright TX 75491-0725. 903/364-2774.

Willaben Care Center
2231 E Highway 80, Mesquite TX 75150-5510. 972/279-3601.

Wind Crest Nursing Center
607 W Avenue B, Copperas Cove TX 76522-1553. 254/547-1033.

Woodland Springs Nursing Home
PO Box 154216, Waco TX 76715-4216. 254/752-9774.

RESIDENTIAL CARE

Buckner Baptist Children's Hospital
5202 S Buckner Blvd, Dallas TX 75227-2006. 214/319-3444.

Dallas County Mental Health
1380 River Bend Dr, Dallas TX 75247-4914. 214/743-1200.

Dallas County Mental Health
1425 W Pioneer Dr, Ste 135, Irving TX 75061-7124. 972/254-9353.

Emerald Point Home
PO Box 196, Cleburne TX 76033-0196. 817/558-1121.

Ennis Care Center
1200 S Hall St, Ennis TX 75119-6318. 972/875-9051.

Professional Care Center
1950 N Record St, Dallas TX 75202-1840. 214/630-1491.

Sears Heritage Place
3202 S Willis St, Abilene TX 79605-6650. 915/691-5519.

Skyview Living Center
1519 Scripture St, Denton TX 76201-3915. 940/383-3576.

The Forum at Park Lane
7831 Park Ln, Dallas TX 75225-2000. 214/369-9902.

Wichita Falls Rehabilitation Hospital
PO Box 3449, Wichita Falls TX 76301-0449. 940/720-5700.

For more information on career opportunities in the health care industry:

<u>Associations</u>

ACCREDITING COMMISSION ON EDUCATION FOR HEALTH SERVICES ADMINISTRATION
1911 North Fort Myer Drive, Suite 503, Arlington VA 22209. 703/524-0511.

AMBULATORY INFORMATION MANAGEMENT ASSOCIATION BAY VALLEY MEDICAL GROUP
27212 Calaroga Avenue, Hayward CA 94545. 510/293-5688. World Wide Web address: http://www.aim4.org. E-mail address: info@aim4.org.

AMERICAN ACADEMY OF ALLERGY, ASTHMA, AND IMMUNOLOGY
611 East Wells Street, Milwaukee WI 53202.

414/272-6071. World Wide Web address: http://www.aaaai.org.

AMERICAN ACADEMY OF FAMILY PHYSICIANS
8880 Ward Parkway, Kansas City MO 64114. 816/333-9700. World Wide Web address: http://www.aafp.org. Promotes continuing education for family physicians.

AMERICAN ACADEMY OF PEDIATRIC DENTISTRY
211 East Chicago Avenue, Suite 700, Chicago IL 60611-2626. 312/337-2169. World Wide Web address: http://www.aapd.org.

AMERICAN ACADEMY OF PERIODONTOLOGY
737 North Michigan Avenue, Suite 800, Chicago IL 60611-2690. 312/573-3218. World Wide Web address: http://www.perio.org.

AMERICAN ACADEMY OF PHYSICIAN ASSISTANTS
950 North Washington Street, Alexandria VA 22314-1552. 703/836-2272. World Wide Web address: http://www.aapa.org. Promotes the use of physician assistants.

AMERICAN ASSOCIATION FOR CLINICAL CHEMISTRY
2101 L Street NW, Suite 202, Washington DC 20037-1526. 202/857-0717. World Wide Web address: http://www.aacc.org. A nonprofit association for clinical, chemical, medical, and technical doctors.

AMERICAN ASSOCIATION FOR ORAL AND MAXILLOFACIAL SURGEONS
9700 West Bryn Mawr Avenue, Rosemont IL 60018-5701. 847/678-6200. World Wide Web address: http://www.aaoms.org.

AMERICAN ASSOCIATION FOR RESPIRATORY CARE
11030 Ables Lane, Dallas TX 75229-4593. 972/243-2272. World Wide Web address: http://www.aarc.org. Promotes the art and science of respiratory care, while focusing on the needs of the patients.

AMERICAN ASSOCIATION OF COLLEGES OF OSTEOPATHIC MEDICINE
5550 Friendship Boulevard, Suite 310, Chevy Chase MD 20815. 301/968-4190. World Wide Web address: http://www.aacom.org. Provides application processing services for colleges of osteopathic medicine.

AMERICAN ASSOCIATION OF COLLEGES OF PODIATRIC MEDICINE
1350 Piccard Drive, Suite 322, Rockville MD 20850. 301/990-7400. World Wide Web address: http://www.aacpm.org. Provides applications processing services for colleges of podiatric medicine.

AMERICAN ASSOCIATION OF DENTAL SCHOOLS
1625 Massachusetts Avenue NW, Suite 600, Washington DC 20036-2212. 202/667-9433. Fax: 202/667-0642. E-mail address: aads@aads.jhu.edu. World Wide Web address: http://www.aads.jhu.edu. Represents all 54 of the dental schools in the U.S. as well as individual members. This organization works to expand postdoctoral training and increase the number of women and minorities in the dental field.

AMERICAN ASSOCIATION OF HEALTHCARE CONSULTANTS
11208 Waples Mill Road, Suite 109, Fairfax VA 22030. 703/691-2242. World Wide Web address: http://www.aahc.net.

AMERICAN ASSOCIATION OF HOMES AND SERVICES FOR THE AGING
901 E Street NW, Suite 500, Washington DC 20001. 202/783-2242. World Wide Web address: http://www.aahsa.org.

AMERICAN ASSOCIATION OF MEDICAL ASSISTANTS
20 North Wacker Drive, Suite 1575, Chicago IL 60606. 312/899-1500. World Wide Web address: http://www.aama-ntl.org.

AMERICAN ASSOCIATION OF NURSE ANESTHETISTS
222 South Prospect Avenue, Park Ridge IL 60068-4001. 847/692-7050. World Wide Web address: http://www.aana.com

AMERICAN CHIROPRACTIC ASSOCIATION
1701 Clarendon Boulevard, Arlington VA 22209. 703/276-8800. World Wide Web address: http://www.amerchiro.org/aca. A national, nonprofit professional membership organization offering educational services (through films, booklets, texts, and kits), regional seminars and workshops, and major health and education activities that provide information on public health, safety, physical fitness, and disease prevention.

AMERICAN COLLEGE OF HEALTHCARE ADMINISTRATORS
325 South Patrick Street, Alexandria VA 22314. 703/549-5822. World Wide Web address: http://www.achca.org. A professional membership society for individual long-term care professionals. Sponsors educational programs, supports research, and produces a number of publications, including the *Journal of Long-Term Care Administration* and *The Long-Term Care Administrator.*

AMERICAN COLLEGE OF HEALTHCARE EXECUTIVES
One North Franklin Street, Suite 1700, Chicago IL 60606-3491. 312/424-2800. World Wide Web address: http://www.ache.org. Offers credentialing and educational programs. Publishes *Hospital & Health Services Administration* (a journal), and *Healthcare Executive* (a magazine).

AMERICAN COLLEGE OF MEDICAL PRACTICE EXECUTIVES
104 Inverness Terrace East, Englewood CO 80112-

5306. 303/397-7869. World Wide Web address: http://www.mgma.com.

AMERICAN COLLEGE OF OBSTETRICIANS AND GYNECOLOGISTS
409 12th Street SW, P.O. Box 96920, Washington DC 20090-6920. World Wide Web address: http://www.acog.org.

AMERICAN COLLEGE OF PHYSICIAN EXECUTIVES
4890 West Kennedy Boulevard, Suite 200, Tampa FL 33609-2575. 813/287-2000. Fax: 813/287-8993. World Wide Web address: http://www.acpe.org.

AMERICAN DENTAL ASSOCIATION
211 East Chicago Avenue, Chicago IL 60611. 312/440-2500. World Wide Web address: http://www.ada.com.

AMERICAN DENTAL HYGIENISTS ASSOCIATION
444 North Michigan Avenue, Suite 3400, Chicago IL 60611. 312/440-8900. World Wide Web address: http://www.adha.org.

AMERICAN DIETETIC ASSOCIATION
216 West Jackson Boulevard, Suite 800, Chicago IL 60606-6995. 312/899-0040. Toll-free phone: 800/877-1600. Promotes optimal nutrition to improve public health and well-being.

AMERICAN HEALTH INFORMATION MANAGEMENT ASSOCIATION
919 North Michigan Avenue, Suite 1400, Chicago IL 60611. 312/787-2672. World Wide Web address: http://www.ahima.org.

AMERICAN HOSPITAL ASSOCIATION
One North Franklin Street, 27th Floor, Chicago IL 60606. 312/422-3000. World Wide Web address: http://www.aha.org.

AMERICAN MEDICAL ASSOCIATION
515 North State Street, Chicago IL 60610. 312/464-5000. World Wide Web address: http://www.ama.org. An organization for medical doctors.

AMERICAN MEDICAL INFORMATICS ASSOCIATION
4915 St. Elmo Avenue, Suite 401, Bethesda MD 20814. 301/657-1291. World Wide Web address: http://www.amia2.amia.org.

AMERICAN MEDICAL TECHNOLOGISTS
710 Higgins Road, Park Ridge IL 60068. 847/823-5169.

AMERICAN MEDICAL WOMEN'S ASSOCIATION
Fax: 703/838-0500. E-mail address: director@amwa-doc.org. World Wide Web address: http://www. amwa-doc.org/index.html. Supports the advancement of women in medicine.

AMERICAN NURSES ASSOCIATION
600 Maryland Avenue SW, Suite 100W, Washington DC 20024-2571. 202/554-4444.

AMERICAN OCCUPATIONAL THERAPY ASSOCIATION
4720 Montgomery Lane, P.O. Box 31220, Bethesda MD 20824-1220. 301/652-2682. Toll-free phone: 800/377-8555. Fax: 301/652-7711. World Wide Web address: http://www.aota.org.

AMERICAN OPTOMETRIC ASSOCIATION
243 North Lindbergh Boulevard, St. Louis MO 63141. 314/991-4100. Offers publications, discounts, and insurance programs for members.

AMERICAN ORGANIZATION OF NURSE EXECUTIVES
One North Franklin Street, 34th Floor, Chicago IL 60606. 312/422-2800. World Wide Web address: http://www.aone.org.

AMERICAN ORTHOPAEDIC ASSOCIATION
6300 North River Road, Suite 300, Rosemont IL 60018. 847/318-7330. World Wide Web address: http://www.aoassn.org.

AMERICAN PHYSICAL THERAPY ASSOC.
111 North Fairfax Street, Alexandria VA 22314. 703/684-2782. World Wide Web address: http://www.apta.org. Small fee required for information.

AMERICAN PODIATRIC MEDICAL ASSOCIATION
9312 Old Georgetown Road, Bethesda MD 20814-1698. 301/571-9200. World Wide Web address: http://www.apma.org.

AMERICAN PSYCHIATRIC ASSOCIATION
World Wide Web address: http://www.psych.org. Professional association for mental health professionals.

AMERICAN PUBLIC HEALTH ASSOCIATION
1015 15th Street NW, Suite 300, Washington DC 20005. 202/789-5600. World Wide Web address: http://www.apha.org.

AMERICAN SOCIETY OF ANESTHESIOLOGISTS
520 North NW Highway, Park Ridge IL 60068. 847/825-5586. World Wide Web address: http://www.asahq.org.

AMERICAN SPEECH-LANGUAGE-HEARING ASSOCIATION
10801 Rockville Pike, Rockville MD 20852. Toll-free phone: 800/498-2071. World Wide Web address: http://www.asha.org. Professional, scientific, and credentialing association for audiologists, speech-language pathologists, and speech, language, and hearing, scientists.

AMERICAN SUBACUTE CARE ASSOCIATION
1720 Kennedy Causeway, Suite 109, North Bay

Village FL 33141. 305/864-0396. World Wide Web address: http://members.aol.com.

AMERICAN VETERINARY MEDICAL ASSOCIATION
1931 North Meacham Road, Suite 100, Schaumburg IL 60173-4360. 847/925-8070. World Wide Web address: http://www.avma.org. Provides a forum for the discussion of important issues in the veterinary profession.

ASSOCIATION OF AMERICAN MEDICAL COLLEGES
2450 N Street NW, Washington DC 20037-1126. 202/828-0400. World Wide Web address: http://www.aamc.org.

ASSOCIATION OF MENTAL HEALTH ADMINISTRATORS
60 Revere Drive, Suite 500, Northbrook IL 60062. 847/480-9626.

ASSOCIATION OF UNIVERSITY PROGRAMS IN HEALTH ADMINISTRATION
1110 Vermont Avenue, Suite 220, Washington DC 20005. 202/822-8550.

BAYER QUALITY NETWORK
11511 West 73rd Place, Burr Ridge IL 60525. Toll-free phone: 888/BAYERNET. World Wide Web address: http://www.bayerquality.org. A cooperative educational forum for health care professionals.

HEALTH INFORMATION AND MANAGEMENT SYSTEMS SOCIETY
230 East Ohio Street, Suite 500, Chicago IL 60611-3201. 312/664-4467. World Wide Web address: http://www.himss.org.

HEALTHCARE FINANCIAL MANAGEMENT ASSOCIATION
2 Westbrook Corporate Center, Suite 700, Westchester IL 60154. 708/531-9600. World Wide Web address: http://www.hfma.org.

NATIONAL ASSOCIATION FOR CHIROPRACTIC MEDICINE
15427 Baybrook Drive, Houston TX 77062. 281/280-8262. World Wide Web address: http://www.chiromed.org.

NATIONAL COALITION OF HISPANIC HEALTH AND HUMAN SERVICES ORGANIZATIONS
1501 16th Street NW, Washington DC 20036. 202/387-5000. World Wide Web address: http://www.cossmho.org. Strives to improve the health and well-being of Hispanic communities throughout the United States.

NATIONAL HOSPICE ORGANIZATION
1901 North Moore Street, Suite 901, Arlington VA 22209. 703/243-5900. World Wide Web address: http://www.nho.org. Educates and advocates for the principles of hospice care to meet the needs of the terminally ill.

NATIONAL MEDICAL ASSOCIATION
1012 10th Street NW, Washington DC 20001. 202/347-1895.

<u>Magazines</u>

AMERICAN MEDICAL NEWS
American Medical Association, 515 North State Street, Chicago IL 60605. 312/464-5000.

HEALTH CARE EXECUTIVE
American College of Health Care Executives, One North Franklin, Suite 1700, Chicago IL 60606-3491. 312/424-2800.

MODERN HEALTHCARE
Crain Communications, 740 North Rush Street, Chicago IL 60611. 312/649-5374. World Wide Web address: http://www.modernhealthcare.com.

NURSEFAX
Springhouse Corporation, 1111 Bethlehem Pike, P.O. Box 908, Springhouse PA 19477. 215/646-8700. World Wide Web address: http://www.springnet.com. This is a jobline service designed to be used in conjunction with *Nursing* magazine. Please call to obtain a copy of a magazine or the *Nursing* directory.

<u>Online Services</u>

AMIA/MEDSIG
Go: MedSIG. A CompuServe forum for health care professionals to discuss and exchange information about topics in medicine.

ACADEMIC PHYSICIAN AND SCIENTIST
Gopher://aps.acad-phy-sci.com/. A great resource for jobseekers interested in administrative or clinical positions at teaching hospitals.

HEALTH CARE JOBS ONLINE JOB BULLETIN BOARD
http://www.hcjobsonline.com/bbs.html. This Website is for jobseekers who are looking for job opportunities in the health care industry. This site is maintained by Images, Ink.

MEDSEARCH AMERICA
http://www.medsearch.com. Site geared for medical professionals and a definite "must see" for those seeking positions in this area, *Medsearch America* offers national and international job searches, career forums, a resume builder, resume posting, recruiters' sites, listings of professional associations, and employer profiles. Precise and extensive searches can be done by job category, association or company name, keyword, or location.

MEDZILLA
E-mail address: info@medzilla.com. World Wide Web address: http://www.medzilla.com. Lists job openings for professionals in the fields of biotechnology, health care, medicine, and science related industries.

NURSING NETWORK FORUM
Go: Custom 261. A CompuServe bulletin board for

nurses that provides periodic "live" discussions with special guests.

SALUDOS WEB CAREER GUIDE: HEALTH CARE
http://www.saludos.com/cguide/hcguide.html.

Provides information for jobseekers looking in the health care field. The site includes links to several health care associations and other sites that are sources of job openings in health care. This site is run by Saludos Hispanos.

HOTELS AND RESTAURANTS

Employment in the hotel and restaurant industry has increased from 1.66 million workers in 1993 to 1.85 million workers in 1998. Hotels are doing considerable business with a shortage of new lodging facilities (many are under construction) and the booming economy. As a result room rates have risen more than 12 percent over the past two years and are expected to rise another 5.3 percent in 1998. This will be offset by new construction which will increase the number of rooms faster than the demand. This is especially true in cities such as Las Vegas, where the construction of 7,200 additional rooms in 1997 and a new 3,000-room hotel and casino owned by Mirage Resorts Inc. slated to open in 1998 will outpace demand. U.S. Industry and Trade Outlook 1998 *reports that numerous U.S. cities are banking on the success of business meetings and conventions and are making significant investments in new and expanded convention facilities.*

Jobs are plentiful for candidates with degrees in hotel or restaurant management. Meanwhile, a shortage of young adult workers between 16 and 24 years of age to fill many of the industry's entry-level positions is causing hotels to rely more heavily on computer-based property management and check-in systems that require fewer employees.

According to the National Restaurant Association, 44 percent of every dollar Americans spend on food goes toward dining out. Nine million people are employed in food services and that number is expected to climb to 11 million in the year 2005. Across the industry, fast-food chains are experiencing tremendous growth and are moving into less traditional sites such as airports and college campuses.

BLACK-EYED PEA RESTAURANT U.S.A., INC.
2212 Arlington Downs Road, Suite 204, Arlington TX 76011. 817/633-6992. **Contact:** Human Resources. **Description:** A full-service restaurant chain specializing in homestyle cooking. Black-Eyed Pea operates over 130 locations nationwide. **Common positions include:** Restaurant/Food Service Manager. **Benefits:** Dental Insurance; Disability Coverage; Life Insurance; Medical Insurance; Profit Sharing; Savings Plan; Stock Option; Tuition Assistance. **Corporate headquarters location:** This Location. **Other U.S. locations:** AR; DC; GA; IN; KS; MD; NC; NM; OK; SC; TN; VA. **Parent company:** Unigate plc. **Operations at this facility include:** Administration; Research and Development.

BONANZA RESTAURANTS
12404 Park Central Drive, Dallas TX 75251-1899. 972/404-5850. **Fax:** 972/404-5705. **Contact:** Personnel. **Description:** Operates a chain of restaurants. **Corporate headquarters location:** This Location.

BRINKER INTERNATIONAL INC.
6820 LBJ Freeway, Dallas TX 75240. 972/980-9917. **Fax:** 972/770-9386. **Contact:** Corporate Recruiting. **World Wide Web address:** http://www.brinker.com. **Description:** Operates a chain of full-service, casual dining restaurants including the Chili's Grill & Bar restaurant chain, which has 400 units in operation. Brinker also operates 150 other restaurants under the following names: Cozymel's, On the Border, Romano's Macaroni Grill, and Spageddie's Italian Foods. **Common positions include:** Accountant/Auditor; Architect; Attorney; Buyer; Computer Programmer;

Construction Contractor; Designer; General Manager; Management Trainee; Property and Real Estate Manager; Systems Analyst. **Educational backgrounds include:** Accounting; Computer Science; Finance; Hotel Administration. **Benefits:** 401(k); Daycare Assistance; Dental Insurance; Disability Coverage; Employee Discounts; Life Insurance; Mass Transit Available; Medical Insurance; Profit Sharing; Stock Option; Tuition Assistance. **Corporate headquarters location:** This Location. **Other U.S. locations:** Nationwide. **Operations at this facility include:** Administration; Divisional Headquarters; Regional Headquarters. **Listed on:** New York Stock Exchange. **Annual sales/revenues:** More than $100 million. **Number of employees at this location:** 750. **Number of employees nationwide:** 65,000.

CULINAIRE INTERNATIONAL, INC.
2121 San Jacinto Street, Suite 3100, Dallas TX 75201. 214/754-1880. **Contact:** Human Resources. **Description:** Provides food and beverage services for the Dallas Convention Center as well as the Embassy Suites Hotels.

DAVE & BUSTER'S, INC.
2751 Electronic Lane, Dallas TX 75220. 214/357-9588. **Contact:** Margo Manning, Recruiter. **Description:** Operates a chain of restaurants located in Dallas (two locations), Houston, Chicago (two locations), Atlanta, Philadelphia, and Hollywood FL. **Corporate headquarters location:** This Location. **Listed on:** NASDAQ. **Stock exchange symbol:** DANB.

EL CHICO RESTAURANTS
12200 Stemmons Freeway, Suite 100, Dallas TX 75234. 972/241-5500. **Contact:** Corporate Recruiter. **Description:** Operates a chain of full-service restaurants. **Common positions include:** Management Trainee; Restaurant/Food Service Manager. **Educational backgrounds include:** Business Administration; Chemistry; Marketing; Restaurant Management. **Corporate headquarters location:** This Location. **Operations at this facility include:** Administration; Manufacturing; Research and Development.

EMBASSY SUITES HOTEL
4250 Ridgemont Drive, Abilene TX 79605. 915/698-1234. **Contact:** Human Resources. **World Wide Web address:** http://www.embassy-suites.com. **Description:** A 176-room hotel.

FOODMAKER INC./JACK-IN-THE-BOX
7700 Bent Branch Drive, Suite 130, Irving TX 75063. 972/263-4403. **Contact:** Human Resources. **World Wide Web address:** http://www.foodmaker.com. **Description:** Foodmaker Inc. operates Jack-in-the-Box restaurants primarily in the western and southwestern United States. International operations include restaurants in Hong Kong and Mexico. **Other U.S. locations:** Houston TX.

FOUR SEASONS RESORT AND CLUB
4150 North MacArthur Boulevard, Irving TX 75038. 972/717-0700. **Contact:** Human Resources. **Description:** A 315-room resort and club that offers two championship golf courses, 12 tennis courts, a spa, and a conference center. The resort also offers a racquet sports center, indoor and outdoor pools and tracks, and personal training facilities. The conference center contains 26 meeting and function rooms.

FURR'S/BISHOP'S CAFETERIAS
P.O. Box 6747, Lubbock TX 79493. 806/792-7151. **Contact:** Human Resources. **Description:** Operates a national chain of cafeteria-style restaurants.

HARVEY HOTEL/DFW AIRPORT
4545 West John Carpenter Freeway, Irving TX 75063. 972/929-4500. **Fax:** 972/929-5793. **Contact:** Human Resources. **Description:** A hotel with over 500 rooms, including 64 multi-use suites. Harvey Hotel's business center offers typing, copying, fax, car rental information, travel agency information, and word processing. The hotel also offers Benton's Grill and Scoops Diner. **NOTE:** Entry-level positions and second and third shifts are offered. **Common positions include:** Accountant/Auditor; Administrative Assistant; Auditor; General Manager; Human Resources Manager; Management Trainee; Marketing Manager; Sales Manager; Systems Manager. **Educational backgrounds include:** Accounting; Business Administration; Communications;

Marketing; Public Relations. **Benefits:** 401(k); Dental Insurance; Disability Coverage; Employee Discounts; Flexible Schedule; Life Insurance; Medical Insurance; Savings Plan. **Special programs:** Internships; Training. **Corporate headquarters location:** Addison TX. **Parent company:** Bristol Hotel Company. **Listed on:** New York Stock Exchange. **Number of employees at this location:** 350.

HYATT REGENCY DALLAS AT REUNION
300 Reunion Boulevard, Dallas TX 75207. 214/651-1234. **Contact:** Mark Spinelli, Human Resources Manager. **World Wide Web address:** http://www.hyatt.com. **Description:** A hotel that offers dining and entertainment facilities including a pool, a fully-equipped fitness center, tennis and basketball courts, three restaurants, and a rooftop revolving lounge. **Parent company:** Hyatt Corporation.

MARRIOTT SOUTH CENTRAL REGIONAL OFFICE
5151 Beltline Road, Suite 500, Dallas TX 75240. 972/385-1600. **Contact:** Regional Director. **World Wide Web address:** http://www.marriott.com. **Description:** This location houses regional offices for the chain of hotels. Overall, the company is a nationwide, diversified food service, retail merchandising, and hospitality company, doing business in more than 25 United States airports, as well as operating restaurants under various names throughout the United States. **Common positions include:** Human Resources Manager. **Educational backgrounds include:** Culinary Arts/Cooking; Hospitality/Restaurant. **Benefits:** Dental Insurance; Disability Coverage; Employee Discounts; Life Insurance; Medical Insurance; Pension Plan; Profit Sharing; Savings Plan; Tuition Assistance. **Special programs:** Internships. **Corporate headquarters location:** Washington DC. **Parent company:** Marriott Corporation. **Operations at this facility include:** Regional Headquarters. **Listed on:** New York Stock Exchange.

McDONALD'S RESTAURANTS
SULLINS & ASSOCIATES
122 South 12th Street, Suite 105, Corsicana TX 75110. 903/872-5611. **Fax:** 903/872-5613. **Contact:** Human Resources. **Description:** A leader in the fast-food industry, McDonald's offers quick-service meals, specializing in hamburgers. **Common positions include:** Branch Manager; General Manager; Management Trainee; Restaurant/Food Service Manager. **Educational backgrounds include:** Business Administration; Communications. **Benefits:** Dental Insurance; Employee Discounts; Life Insurance; Medical Insurance. **Special programs:** Internships. **Other U.S. locations:** Ennis TX; Palestine TX; Terrell TX. **Parent company:** McDonald's Corporation. **Operations at this facility include:** Administration. **Number of employees at this location:** 250.

METROMEDIA RESTAURANT GROUP
S&A RESTAURANT CORPORATION
12404 Park Central Drive, Dallas TX 75251. 972/404-5902. **Fax:** 972/404-5467. **Contact:** Julie Bottoms, Corporate Recruiter. **Description:** One of the largest full-service restaurant chains in the nation. The company operates 1,200 restaurants in 45 states and two countries. **NOTE:** Entry-level positions and second and third shifts are offered. **Common positions include:** Accountant; Administrative Assistant; Attorney; Auditor; Budget Analyst; Buyer; Chief Financial Officer; Claim Representative; Computer Programmer; Controller; Customer Service Representative; Database Manager; Financial Analyst; Food Scientist/Technologist; Human Resources Manager; MIS Specialist; Paralegal; Purchasing Agent/Manager; Quality Control Supervisor; Secretary; Systems Analyst; Typist/Word Processor; Video Production Coordinator. **Educational backgrounds include:** Accounting; Business Administration; Finance; Liberal Arts. **Benefits:** 401(k); Dental Insurance; Disability Coverage; Employee Discounts; Fitness Program; Flexible Schedule; Life Insurance; Medical Insurance; Profit Sharing; Savings Plan; Tuition Assistance. **Corporate headquarters location:** This Location. **Listed on:** Privately held. **Annual sales/revenues:** $51 - $100 million. **Number of employees at this location:** 450.

MOTEL 6
14651 Dallas Parkway, Suite 500, Dallas TX 75240. 972/386-6161. **Contact:** Cheryl Beuttas, Director of Corporate Human Resources. **World Wide Web address:** http://www.motel6.com. **Description:** This location houses the corporate offices only. Overall, Motel 6 operates a chain of motels with over 50 locations throughout Texas. **Common positions include:** Administrative

Assistant; Auditor; Customer Service Representative; General Manager; Human Resources Generalist; Instructor/Trainer; IT Specialist; Management Trainee; Marketing Specialist. **Educational backgrounds include:** Accounting; Business Administration; Computer Science; Liberal Arts. **Benefits:** 401(k); Disability Coverage; Life Insurance; Medical Insurance; Pension Plan; Tuition Assistance. **Corporate headquarters location:** This Location. **Parent company:** Accor (Paris, France). **Operations at this facility include:** Administration. **Number of employees at this location:** 275. **Number of employees nationwide:** 17,000.

MOTEL 6
4951 West Stamford Street, Abilene TX 79603. 915/672-8462. **Contact:** Manager. **World Wide Web address:** http://www.motel6.com. **Description:** One location of the motel chain, with over 50 locations throughout Texas. **Corporate headquarters location:** Dallas TX.

OMNI HOTELS
420 Decker Drive, Suite 200, Irving TX 75062-3952. 972/730-6664. **Fax:** 972/871-5669. **Contact:** Alison Brody, Corporate Recruiting Manager. **World Wide Web address:** http://www.omnihotels.com. **Description:** Operates an international chain of hotels, motels, and resorts. **NOTE:** Entry-level positions are offered. **Common positions include:** Accountant/Auditor; Computer Programmer; Credit Manager; Electrician; Financial Analyst; General Manager; Hotel Manager; Human Resources Manager; Management Trainee; MIS Specialist; Public Relations Specialist; Purchasing Agent/Manager; Quality Control Supervisor; Restaurant/Food Service Manager; Systems Analyst; Technical Writer/Editor; Typist/Word Processor. **Educational backgrounds include:** Accounting; Finance; Hospitality/Restaurant; Liberal Arts; Marketing; Mathematics. **Benefits:** 401(k); Dental Insurance; Disability Coverage; Employee Discounts; Job Sharing; Life Insurance; Medical Insurance; Pension Plan; Profit Sharing; Savings Plan; Tuition Assistance. **Special programs:** Internships; Training. **Corporate headquarters location:** This Location. **Other U.S. locations:** Nationwide. **Subsidiaries include:** Shoreline Operating Company. **Parent company:** TRT Holdings, Inc. **Operations at this facility include:** Administration; Divisional Headquarters. **Listed on:** Privately held. **Annual sales/revenues:** More than $100 million. **Number of employees at this location:** 30. **Number of employees nationwide:** 7,000. **Number of employees worldwide:** 8,000.

OMNI RICHARDSON HOTEL
701 East Campbell Road, Richardson TX 75081. 972/231-9600. **Contact:** Human Resources. **Description:** A hotel. **Corporate headquarters location:** Hampton NH. **Parent company:** Omni Hotels operates an international chain of hotels, motels, and resorts.

PANCHO'S MEXICAN BUFFET, INC.
P.O. Box 7407, Fort Worth TX 76111. 817/831-0081. **Physical address:** 3500 Noble Street, Fort Worth TX. **Contact:** Human Resources. **Description:** A Mexican restaurant with a buffet-style format. Pancho's Mexican Buffet operates over 70 restaurants in Texas, Arizona, Louisiana, New Mexico, and Oklahoma. Founded in 1966. **Corporate headquarters location:** This Location. **Listed on:** NASDAQ. **Stock exchange symbol:** PAMX.

PIZZA INN INC.
5050 Quorum Drive, Suite 500, Dallas TX 75240. 972/701-9955. **Contact:** Sandra Feinglas, Assistant to Chief Operating Officer. **Description:** Operates and franchises a chain of pizza restaurants. Pizza Inn operates more than 740 restaurants in 33 states, Mexico, Puerto Rico, Japan, the Philippines, and South Africa. **Common positions include:** Accountant/Auditor; Advertising Clerk; Architect; Computer Programmer; Draftsperson; General Manager; Human Resources Manager; Management Trainee; Marketing Specialist; Operations/Production Manager. **Benefits:** Dental Insurance; Disability Coverage; Life Insurance; Medical Insurance. **Operations at this facility include:** Administration; Sales. **Listed on:** American Stock Exchange.

SHOWBIZ PIZZA TIME, INC.
dba CHUCK E. CHEESE
4441 West Airport Freeway, Irving TX 75015. 972/258-8507. **Contact:** Human Resources. **Description:** Operates over 200 family restaurant/entertainment centers nationwide. **Common positions include:** Account Representative; Attorney; Claim Representative; Computer

Programmer; Construction Contractor; General Manager; Human Resources Manager; Operations/Production Manager; Paralegal; Property and Real Estate Manager; Purchasing Agent/Manager; Restaurant/Food Service Manager; Systems Analyst. **Educational backgrounds include:** Accounting; Business Administration; Computer Science; Finance; Marketing. **Benefits:** 401(k); Daycare Assistance; Dental Insurance; Disability Coverage; Employee Discounts; Life Insurance; Medical Insurance. **Corporate headquarters location:** This Location. **Operations at this facility include:** Divisional Headquarters. **Listed on:** NASDAQ.

SPAGHETTI WAREHOUSE, INC.
402 West Interstate 30, Garland TX 75043. 972/226-6000. **Fax:** 972/203-9589. **Contact:** Human Resources. **World Wide Web address:** http://www.meatballs.com. **Description:** An international chain of 36 company-owned and seven franchised Italian restaurants in 17 states and Canada. **Corporate headquarters location:** This Location. **Number of employees nationwide:** 3,300.

TGI FRIDAY'S INC.
P.O. Box 809062, Dallas TX 75380. 972/450-5400. **Contact:** Employee Relations. **World Wide Web address:** http://www.tgifridays.com. **Description:** This location houses corporate offices only. Overall, TGI Friday's operates a nationwide chain of restaurants. **Corporate headquarters location:** This Location.

U.S. FOOD SERVICE
1550 Norwood Drive, Suite 225, Hurst TX 76054. 817/285-8999. **Contact:** Personnel. **Description:** An institutional food production and distribution company.

U.S. FOOD SERVICE
P.O. Box 2804, Lubbock TX 79408. 806/747-5204. **Contact:** Personnel. **Description:** An institutional food production and distribution company.

WYATT'S CAFETERIAS INC.
16970 Dallas Parkway, Suite 701, Dallas TX 75248. 972/248-4145. **Fax:** 972/248-8116. **Contact:** Human Resources Director. **Description:** An employee-owned cafeteria chain with over 60 locations in five states. **Common positions include:** Accountant; Claim Representative; Food Scientist/Technologist; General Manager; Management Trainee; Restaurant/Food Service Manager. **Educational backgrounds include:** Business Administration. **Benefits:** Dental Insurance; Employee Discounts; ESOP; Life Insurance; Medical Insurance; Pension Plan. **Corporate headquarters location:** This Location. **Operations at this facility include:** Administration; Divisional Headquarters; Regional Headquarters; Research and Development. **Listed on:** Privately held. **Number of employees at this location:** 60. **Number of employees nationwide:** 3,500.

WYNDHAM ANATOLE HOTEL
2201 Stemmons Freeway, Dallas TX 75207. 214/748-1200. **Contact:** Personnel. **Description:** A luxury convention hotel with over 1,600 rooms. **Common positions include:** Accountant/Auditor; Chef/Cook/Kitchen Worker; Department Manager; Hotel Manager; Operations/Production Manager; Restaurant/Food Service Manager; Services Sales Representative. **Educational backgrounds include:** Business Administration; Liberal Arts; Marketing. **Benefits:** 401(k); Dental Insurance; Employee Discounts; Life Insurance; Medical Insurance; Tuition Assistance. **Corporate headquarters location:** New York NY. **Number of employees at this location:** 1,500.

Note: Because addresses and telephone numbers of smaller companies can change rapidly, we recommend you call each company to verify the information below before inquiring about job opportunities. Mass mailings are not recommended.

Additional small employers:

DRINKING PLACES

Cabaret Royale
10723 Composite Dr, Dallas TX
75220-1207. 214/350-0303.

Million Dollar Saloon
6848 Greenville Ave, Dallas TX
75231-6404. 214/363-4506.

On the Border Cafe
1801 N Lamar St, Dallas TX
75202-1748. 214/855-0296.

EATING PLACES

50th Street Caboose Restaurant & Bar
5027 50th St, Lubbock TX 79414-3420. 806/796-2240.

Apple South Inc.
5710 LBJ Freeway, Ste 350, Dallas TX 75240-6399. 972/991-0509.

Applebee's
614 N Valley Mills Dr, Waco TX 76710-6047. 254/751-9084.

Applebee's
543 E Round Grove Rd, Lewisville TX 75067-8310. 972/315-6002.

Applebee's
1820 W University Dr, McKinney TX 75069-3221. 972/562-8016.

Applebee's
1009 N Central Expressway, Plano TX 75075-8806. 972/881-1100.

Applebee's
1610 E Belt Line Rd, Richardson TX 75081-4620. 972/238-0875.

Applebee's
6645 NE Loop 820, Fort Worth TX 76180-6040. 817/788-9797.

Applebee's
707 S Interstate 35 E, Denton TX 76205-8101. 940/591-9353.

Applebee's
7004 Wesley St, Greenville TX 75402-7133. 903/455-9862.

Applebee's
5110 Summerhill Road, Texarkana TX 75503-1824. 903/792-9476.

Applebee's
2700 E Central Texas Expressway, Killeen TX 76543-5331. 254/526-9711.

Applebee's
3790 Belt Line Rd, Dallas TX 75244-2201. 972/243-8025.

Art Bar Cafe
14902 Preston Rd, Ste 700, Dallas TX 75240-9108. 972/458-0458.

Benale Holdings Corporation
12404 Park Central Dr, Dallas TX 75251-1810. 972/404-5000.

Bennigan's
2290 S Stemmons Freeway, Lewisville TX 75067-8759. 972/420-8541.

Bennigan's
5751 Bridge St, Fort Worth TX 76112-2402. 817/457-1966.

Bennigan's
4000 S Cooper St, Arlington TX 76015-4125. 817/467-3363.

Brinker International Inc.
1505 N Central Expy, Ste 9, Plano TX 75075-7022. 972/881-2257.

Brinker International Inc.
4400 Belt Line Rd, Dallas TX 75244-2413. 972/788-4400.

Brinker International Inc.
2011 E Copeland Rd, Arlington TX 76011-5135. 817/261-3598.

Burger King
6100 Southwest Blvd, Fort Worth TX 76109-3930. 817/731-1845.

Burger King
4215 Beltwood Parkway, Dallas TX 75244-3227. 972/458-8300.

Cheddar's Inc.
2400 N Central Expressway, Plano TX 75074-5411. 972/422-4240.

Cheddar's Inc.
39640 LBJ Freeway, Dallas TX 75237-3901. 972/780-1200.

Cheddar's Inc.
12355 Greenville Ave, Dallas TX 75243-3511. 972/235-5595.

Cheddar's Inc.
8126 Flags Dr, Arlington TX 76011. 817/640-6073.

Cheddar's Inc.
1937 Airport Freeway, Bedford TX 76021-5732. 817/540-0778.

Chili's Grill & Bar
3421 W Airport Freeway, Irving TX 75062-5924. 972/255-2727.

Chili's Grill & Bar
1129 S Stemmons Freeway, Lewisville TX 75067-5359. 972/221-8521.

Chili's Grill & Bar
7567 Greenville Ave, Dallas TX 75231-3801. 214/361-4371.

Chili's Grill & Bar
1540 S University Dr, Fort Worth TX 76107-6500. 817/429-2002.

Chili's Grill & Bar
5288 S Hulen St, Fort Worth TX 76132-1912. 817/572-1195.

Chili's Grill & Bar
2624 N Josey Lane, Carrollton TX 75007-5516. 972/466-1350.

Chili's Grill & Bar
3710 Call Field Rd, Wichita Falls TX 76308-2724. 940/692-4995.

Chili's Grill & Bar
531 W Shaw St, Tyler TX 75701-2932. 903/581-7813.

Chili's Grill & Bar
9239 Skillman St, Dallas TX 75243-7328. 214/553-0444.

Chili's Grill & Bar
924 E Copeland Rd, Arlington TX 76011-4944. 817/261-3891.

Chili's Grill and Bar
191 Walnut Hill Village, Dallas TX 75220-4941. 214/352-9327.

Copeland Restaurant
5353 Belt Line Rd, Dallas TX 75240-7605. 972/661-1883.

Cozymel's
5021 W Park Blvd, Plano TX 75093-2514. 972/964-2809.

Cozymel's
1300 E Copeland Rd, Arlington TX 76011-4952. 817/469-9595.

Cracker Barrel
4008 N Interstate 35, Denton TX 76207. 940/382-5277.

Cracker Barrel
4691 Gemini Court, Arlington TX 76016. 817/624-8050.

Dave & Buster's
10727 Composite Dr, Dallas TX 75220-1207. 214/353-0649.

Dave & Buster's
8021 Walnut Hill Lane, Dallas TX 75231-4349. 214/361-5553.

Don Pablo's Restaurant
1933 Airport Freeway, Bedford TX 76021-5732. 817/685-8868.

East Side Mario's
4757 W Park Blvd, Plano TX
75093-2329. 972/612-1011.

Fifty Yard Line
PO Box 54212, Lubbock TX
79453-4212. 806/745-3991.

Firehall Marketplace Deli
203 Commerce St, Fort Worth
TX 76102-7206. 817/877-4191.

Golden Corral Corporation
420 SW W Loop 323, Tyler TX
75701. 903/534-0281.

Good Eats
1101 N Central Expy, Plano TX
75075-7116. 972/516-3287.

Good Eats
2225 S Stemmons Fwy,
Lewisville TX 75067-8760.
972/315-5998.

Hard Rock Cafe
2601 McKinney Ave, Dallas TX
75204-2519. 214/855-0007.

Harrigan's Restaurant
3801 50th St, Lubbock TX
79413-3807. 806/792-4648.

Houston's Restaurant
8141 Walnut Hill Ln, Dallas TX
75231-4360. 214/691-8991.

Houston's Restaurant
5318 Belt Line Rd, Dallas TX
75240-7606. 972/960-1752.

Humperdink's
1601 N Central Expy, Richardson
TX 75080-3504. 972/690-4867.

Humperdink's
700 Six Flags Dr, Arlington TX
76011-6327. 817/640-8553.

**International House of
Pancakes**
6300 Ridglea Pl, Ste 320, Fort
Worth TX 76116-5705. 817/377-
5226.

Iron Skillet
PO Box 32245, Amarillo TX
79120-2245. 806/372-3682.

Joe's Crab Shack
5802 W Loop South 289,
Lubbock TX 79414. 806/797-
8600.

Josie's Restaurant Inc.
318 N University Ave, Lubbock
TX 79415-2318. 806/744-6262.

Kentucky Fried Chicken
PO Box 5949, Texarkana TX
75505-5949. 903/793-4100.

Luby's Cafeterias Inc.
1350 N Hampton Rd, Dallas TX
75208-1306. 214/946-0862.

McDonald's
2505 Lakeview Dr, Ste 100,
Amarillo TX 79109-1525.
806/358-4845.

McDonald's
4439 Lemmon Ave, Dallas TX
75219-2143. 214/520-2596.

McDonald's
PO Box 1623, Mount Pleasant
TX 75456-1623. 903/572-5380.

McDonald's
2102 Business Hwy 190, Killeen
TX 76541. 254/699-1659.

McDonald's
PO Box 699, Marshall TX 75671-
0699. 903/938-7745.

Medieval Times
PO Box 567706, Dallas TX
75356-7706. 214/761-1801.

Mexican Inn Cafe
4200 S Cooper St, Arlington TX
76015-4139. 817/467-0505.

Mi Piaci Restaurant
14854 Montfort Dr, Dallas TX
75240-7518. 972/934-8424.

Mr. Gatti's of Amarillo
4412 S Western St, Amarillo TX
79109-6007. 806/355-5601.

Multi Restaurants Group
8008 Aviation Pl, Fl 2, Dallas TX
75235-2824. 214/353-3959.

Multi Restaurants Group
4108 Amon Carter Blvd, Fort
Worth TX 76155-2649. 817/858-
0146.

Old San Francisco Steak House
10965 Composite Dr, Dallas TX
75220-1211. 214/357-0484.

Olive Garden Restaurant
4001 W Airport Fwy, Irving TX
75062-5935. 972/258-5191.

Olive Garden Restaurant
5921 W Waco Dr, Waco TX
76710-6356. 254/751-1667.

Olive Garden Restaurant
4121 I-40 W, Amarillo TX
79109-1530. 806/355-9973.

Olive Garden Restaurant
5702 Slide Rd, Lubbock TX
79414-4106. 806/791-3575.

Olive Garden Restaurant
4700 SW Loop 820, Fort Worth
TX 76109-4419. 817/377-8091.

Olive Garden Restaurant
925 Alta Mere Dr, Fort Worth TX
76114-4001. 817/732-0618.

Olive Garden Restaurant
3210 S Clack St, Abilene TX
79606-2200. 915/691-0388.

Olive Garden Restaurant
3816 N Town East Blvd,
Mesquite TX 75150-3751.
972/270-1582.

Olive Garden Restaurant
3916 Kemp Blvd, Wichita Falls
TX 76308-2141. 940/692-4714.

Olive Garden Restaurant
9079 Vantage Point Dr, Dallas
TX 75243-3581. 972/234-3292.

Olive Garden Restaurant
4604 S Cooper St, Arlington TX
76017-5826. 817/472-9733.

Olive Garden Restaurant
8020 Bedford Euless Rd, Bedford
TX 76022. 817/581-9511.

Outback Steakhouse
3510 W Airport Fwy, Irving TX
75062-5922. 972/399-1477.

Outback Steakhouse
3903 Towne Crossing Blvd,
Mesquite TX 75150-6121.
972/686-0555.

Palomino
500 Crescent Ct, Ste 165, Dallas
TX 75201-1896. 214/999-1222.

Papacita's Mexican Restaurant
305 W Loop 281, Longview TX
75605-4426. 903/663-1700.

Pappadeaux Seafood Kitchen
3420 Oak Lawn Ave, Dallas TX
75219-4214. 214/520-8988.

Pappadeaux Seafood Kitchen
725 S Central Expy, Dallas TX
75201-6001. 972/235-1181.

Pappasito's Cantina
723 S Central Expy, Richardson
TX 75080-7410. 972/480-8595.

Perfect Pizza Ltd.
2661 Buffalo Gap Rd, Abilene
TX 79605-6105. 915/692-6326.

Pizza Hut
227 W University Dr, Denton TX
76201-1837. 940/383-1670.

Pizza Hut
14841 Dallas Pkwy, Dallas TX
75240-7552. 972/338-7700.

Red Lobster
5034 50th St, Lubbock TX
79414-3421. 806/792-4805.

Red Lobster
7800 Bedford Euless Rd, Hurst
TX 76053. 817/281-7540.

Red Lobster
8312 Waterfront Ct, Fort Worth
TX 76179-2502. 817/244-7766.

Red Lobster
3906 Towne Crossing Blvd,
Mesquite TX 75150-6122.
972/613-1444.

Romano's Macaroni Grill
5858 W Northwest Hwy, Dallas
TX 75225-3201. 214/265-0770.

Romano's Macaroni Grill
4535 Belt Line Rd, Dallas TX
75244-2416. 972/386-3831.

Romano's Macaroni Grill
1670 Interstate 20 W, Arlington
TX 76017-5840. 817/784-1197.

Ryan's Family Steak Houses
301 S Valley Mills Dr, Waco TX
76710-7302. 254/751-7595.

Santa Fe Restaurant & Bar
401 Avenue N, Lubbock TX
79401. 806/763-6114.

Snuffer & Addison
14910 Midway Rd, Dallas TX
75244-2607. 972/991-8811.

Snuffers Restaurants Inc.
3526 Greenville Ave, Dallas TX
75206-5630. 214/826-6850.

Souper Salads Franchises
13154 Coit Road, Suite 210,
Dallas TX 75240-5787. 972/238-5653.

Spaghetti Warehouse
600 E Exchange Ave, Fort Worth
TX 76106-8246. 817/625-4171.

Spaghetti Warehouse
1815 N Market St, Dallas TX
75202-1809. 214/651-8475.

Stagecoach Inn
PO Box 97, Salado TX 76571-0097. 254/947-5111.

Star Canyon Inc.
3102 Oak Lawn Ave, Ste 144,
Dallas TX 75219-4257. 214/520-7827.

Steak & Ale
4650 Little Rd, Arlington TX
76017-1038. 817/483-5108.

Steak Kountry Restaurant
153 S Central Expy, McKinney
TX 75070-3743. 972/542-3192.

Taco Cabana
5601 Slide Rd, Lubbock TX
79414-4104. 806/795-4516.

TGI Friday's
8605 Airport Freeway, Fort
Worth TX 76180-7254. 817/498-2527.

TGI Friday's
1041 State Hwy 114, Grapevine
TX 76051. 817/421-8443.

TGI Friday's
10811 Composite Dr, Dallas TX
75220-1209. 214/350-0349.

TGI Friday's
5100 Beltline Rd, Dallas TX
75240. 972/386-5824.

The Big Texan Steak Ranch
PO Box 37000, Amarillo TX
79120. 806/372-6000.

The Fare
5030 Greenville Ave, Dallas TX
75206-4006. 214/369-4070.

Tippins Restaurants Inc.
3321 S Cooper St, Arlington TX
76015-2345. 817/467-7437.

**Two Rows Restaurant &
Brewery**
5500 Greenville Ave, Dallas TX
75206-2941. 214/696-2739.

Uncle Julio's Corporation
5301 Camp Bowie Blvd, Fort
Worth TX 76107. 817/377-2777.

Uncle Julio's Restaurant
4125 Lemmon Ave, Dallas TX
75219-3739. 214/520-6620.

Uncle Julio's Restaurant
7557 Greenville Ave, Dallas TX
75231-3801. 214/987-9900.

Weiss Enterprises Inc.
PO Box 150406, Dallas TX
75315-0406. 214/565-1511.

HOTELS AND MOTELS

Arlington Hilton
2401 E Lamar Blvd, Arlington
TX 76006-7503. 817/640-3322.

Arlington Marriott
1500 Convention Center Dr,
Arlington TX 76011-5116.
817/261-8200.

Circle R Ranch Inc.
PO Box 270420, Lewisville TX
75027-0420. 972/539-9121.

Clarion Hotel
1981 N Central Expressway,
Richardson TX 75080-3509.
972/644-4000.

Crown Sterling
4650 W Airport Freeway, Irving
TX 75062-5825. 972/790-0093.

Dallas Medallion Hotel
4099 Valley View Lane, Dallas
TX 75244-5002. 972/385-9000.

Dallas Parkway Hilton Hotel
4801 Lyndon B Johnson
Freeway, Dallas TX 75244-6002.
972/661-3600.

Days Inn
4213 South Freeway, Fort Worth
TX 76115-1501. 817/923-1987.

DePalma Hotel Corp.
5701 S Broadway Ave, Tyler TX
75703-4350. 903/561-5800.

Dominion Equity Corporation
1106 N Highway 360, Grand
Prairie TX 75050-2559. 972/641-6641.

DoubleTree Hotel
8250 N Central Expressway,
Dallas TX 75206-1803. 214/691-8700.

Econolodge Dalhart
123 Liberal St, Dalhart TX
79022-2732. 806/249-6464.

Embassy Suites
3880 W Northwest Hwy, Dallas
TX 75220-5139. 214/357-4500.

Embassy Suites Market Center
2727 N Stemmons Freeway,
Dallas TX 75207. 214/630-5332.

Fairmont Hotel
1717 N Akard St, Dallas TX
75201-2301. 214/720-2020.

Harvey Hotel Addison
14315 Midway Rd, Dallas TX
75244-3507. 972/980-8877.

Harvey Hotel Downtown
400 Olive St, Dallas TX 75201-
4048. 214/922-0314.

Holiday Inn
2000 Beach St, Fort Worth TX
76103-2319. 817/534-4801.

Holiday Inn
801 Avenue Q, Lubbock TX
79401-2617. 806/763-1200.

Holiday Inn De Soto
1515 N Beckley Ave, De Soto
TX 75115-2600. 972/224-9100.

Holiday Inn DFW Airport North
4441 W State Highway 114,
Irving TX 75063. 972/929-8181.

Holiday Inn DFW South
4440 West Airport Freeway,
Irving TX 75062-5821. 972/399-
1010.

Holiday Inn DFW West
3005 Airport Fwy, Bedford TX
76021-6011. 817/267-3181.

Holiday Inn Select Dallas
10650 N Central Expy, Dallas TX
75231-2102. 214/373-6000.

Holiday Inn-Paris
3560 NE Loop 286, Paris TX
75460-5051. 903/785-5545.

Hotel Crescent Court
400 Crescent Ct, Dallas TX
75201-1838. 214/871-3200.

Ironside Motor Inn
404 S Forthood St, Killeen TX
76541. 254/526-4632.

ITT Sheraton Corporation
2101 N Stemmons Fwy, Dallas
TX 75207-3004. 214/747-3000.

ITT Sheraton Corporation
2150 Market Center Blvd, Dallas
TX 75207-3321. 214/653-1166.

La Guinta Inn
825 N Watson Rd, Arlington TX
76011-5152. 817/640-4142.

La Meridien Dallas
650 N Pearl St, Dallas TX 75201-
2818. 214/979-9000.

Marriott Corp.
PO Box 612427, Grapevine TX
76051. 972/453-0600.

Marriott DFW Airport Hotel
PO Box 612427, Irving TX
75063. 972/929-8800.

Marriott Hotel Quorum
14901 Dallas Pkwy, Dallas TX
75240-7551. 972/661-2800.

Marriott Solana
5 Village Cir, Roanoke TX
76262-5901. 817/430-3848.

Melrose Hotel
3015 Oak Lawn Ave, Dallas TX
75219-4134. 214/521-5151.

Metro Hotels Inc.
8080 N Central Expy, Dallas TX
75206-1838. 214/891-8881.

Omni Dallas Hotel Parkwest
1590 LBJ Fwy, Dallas TX 75234.
972/869-4300.

Omni Mandalay Hotel
221 Las Colinas Blvd E, Irving
TX 75039-5504. 972/556-0800.

Park Suite Hotel
13131 N Central Expy, Dallas TX
75243-1115. 972/234-3300.

Pratt Hotel Management Corp.
13455 Noel Road, Suite 22,
Dallas TX 75240. 972/386-9777.

Radisson Hotel Dallas
1893 W Mockingbird Ln, Dallas
TX 75235-5012. 214/634-8850.

Radisson Hotel Denton
2211 I35 East N, Denton TX
76205. 940/565-8499.

Ramada Airport Hotel
14180 Dallas Pkwy, Ste 700,
Dallas TX 75240. 972/490-9600.

Ramada Plaza Hotel
1011 S Akard St, Dallas TX
75215-1002. 214/421-1083.

Ramada Plaza Hotel
1701 Commerce St, Fort Worth
TX 76102-6511. 817/335-7000.

Sheraton Grand Hotel
PO Box 619765, Dallas TX
75261-9765. 972/929-8400.

Sheraton Park Central Hotel
12720 Merit Dr, Dallas TX
75251-1206. 972/385-3000.

Sheraton Texarkana Inc.
5301 N State Line Ave,
Texarkana TX 75503-5301.
903/792-3222.

Stoneleigh Hotel
2927 Maple Ave, Dallas TX
75201-1444. 214/871-7111.

Stouffer Renaissance Dallas
2222 N Stemmons Fwy, Dallas
TX 75207-2802. 214/631-2222.

Sunburst Hospitality Corp.
17950 Preston Rd, Ste 780,
Dallas TX 75252-5635. 972/733-
3361.

Terraces at GTE Place
2200 W Airfield Dr, Dallas TX
75261-4008. 972/615-5362.

Westin Galleria Hotel Dallas
13340 Dallas Pkwy, Dallas TX
75240-6603. 972/934-9494.

Worthington Hotel
200 Main St, Fort Worth TX
76102-3011. 817/870-1000.

For more information on career opportunities in hotels and restaurants:

Associations

AMERICAN HOTEL AND MOTEL ASSOCIATION
1201 New York Avenue NW, Suite 600, Washington

DC 20005-3931. 202/289-3100. World Wide Web
address: http://www.ahma.com. Provides lobbying
services and educational programs, maintains and
disseminates industry data, and produces a variety of
publications.

THE EDUCATIONAL FOUNDATION OF THE NATIONAL RESTAURANT ASSOCIATION
250 South Wacker Drive, Suite 1400, Chicago IL 60606. 312/715-1010. World Wide Web address: http://www.restaurant.com. Offers educational products, including textbooks, manuals, instruction guides, manager and employee training programs, videos, and certification programs.

NATIONAL RESTAURANT ASSOCIATION
1200 17th Street NW, Washington DC 20036. 202/331-5900. World Wide Web address: http://www.restaurant.org. Provides a number of services, including government lobbying, communications, research, and information, and operates the Educational Foundation

Directories

DIRECTORY OF CHAIN RESTAURANT OPERATORS
Business Guides, Inc., Lebhar-Friedman, Inc., 3922 Coconut Palm Drive, Suite 300, Tampa FL 33619-8321. 813/664-6700.

DIRECTORY OF HIGH-VOLUME INDEPENDENT RESTAURANTS
Lebhar-Friedman, Inc., 3922 Coconut Palm Drive, Tampa FL 33619-8321. 813/664-6800.

Magazines

CORNELL HOTEL AND RESTAURANT ADMINISTRATION QUARTERLY
Cornell University School of Hotel Administration,

Statler Hall, Ithaca NY 14853-6902. 607/255-9393. World Wide Web address: http://www.cornell.edu.

INNKEEPING WORLD
P.O. Box 84108, Seattle WA 98124. 206/362-7125.

NATION'S RESTAURANT NEWS
Lebhar-Friedman, Inc., 3922 Coconut Palm Drive, Tampa FL 33619. 813/664-6700. World Wide Web address: http://www.lf.com.

Online Services

COOLWORKS
http://www.coolworks.com. This Website provides links to 22,000 job openings at resorts, summer camps, ski areas, river areas, ranches, fishing areas, and cruise ships. This site also includes information on volunteer openings.

HOSPITALITY NET VIRTUAL JOB EXCHANGE
http://www.hospitalitynet.nl/job. This site allows jobseekers to search for job opportunities worldwide in the hospitality industry including accounting, food and beverage, marketing and sales, and conference and banqueting positions. Jobseekers can also post resume information and a description of the job they want.

JOBNET: HOSPITALITY INDUSTRY
http://www.westga.edu/~coop/hospitality.html. This Website provides links to job openings and information for hotels.

INSURANCE

 Shaped by a changing marketplace of consolidation and competitive pressures, the insurance industry will face a tough year. *According to* Business Week, *after record earnings in 1997, analysts are expecting that pretax operating income for insurance companies will drop to $26.3 billion in 1998, down from $35.5 billion in 1997. This is due in part to lower projected margins and higher projected claims.*

Property/casualty insurance is likely to see poor sales growth, and industry analysts blame this on companies' diminishing financial reserves from prior years that tend to boost earnings. More consolidations are also expected in this sector. Homeowner insurers are also doing poorly, while automobile insurers are faring better, but Business Week *projects that increases in car premiums should slow in 1998.*

In contrast, the life insurance sector is stable, driven by increased consumer demand due to increasing consumer savings and an aging population.

BLUE CROSS BLUE SHIELD OF TEXAS
P.O. Box 655730, Dallas TX 75265-5730. 972/766-6440. **Physical address:** 901 South Central Expressway, Richardson TX 75080. **Fax:** 972/766-6102. **Recorded jobline:** 972/766-5364. **Contact:** Paulette Smith, Director of Employment. **World Wide Web address:** http://www.bcbstx.com. **Description:** A health and life insurance company. **Common positions include:** Accountant/Auditor; Actuary; Administrative Manager; Attorney; Blue-Collar Worker Supervisor; Budget Analyst; Buyer; Claim Representative; Claims Investigator; Clerical Supervisor; Computer Programmer; Credit Manager; Customer Service Representative; Dentist; Draftsperson; Electrician; Financial Analyst; Health Services Manager; Human Resources Manager; Human Service Worker; Industrial Engineer; Instructor/Trainer; Insurance Agent/Broker; Investigator; Licensed Practical Nurse; Mathematician; Medical Records Technician; Paralegal; Pharmacist; Physician; Psychologist; Public Relations Specialist; Purchasing Agent/Manager; Registered Nurse; Restaurant/Food Service Manager; Social Worker; Sociologist; Software Engineer; Statistician; Systems Analyst; Technical Writer/Editor; Underwriter/Assistant Underwriter. **Educational backgrounds include:** Accounting; Computer Science; Liberal Arts; Mathematics. **Benefits:** 401(k); Daycare Assistance; Dental Insurance; Disability Coverage; EAP; Employee Discounts; Life Insurance; Medical Insurance; Pension Plan; Savings Plan; Tuition Assistance. **Corporate headquarters location:** This Location. **Number of employees at this location:** 5,000.

CNA INSURANCE COMPANIES
P.O. Box 819006, Dallas TX 75381-9006. 214/220-1300. **Fax:** 214/220-5519. **Contact:** Human Resources. **World Wide Web address:** http://www.cna.com. **Description:** A property and casualty insurance writer offering commercial and personal policies.

CENTRA BENEFIT SERVICES
1255 West 15th Street, Plano TX 75075. 972/516-2604. **Contact:** Human Resources. **Description:** A third-party insurance administrator providing a complete range of health benefits and managed care services.

CHUBB INSURANCE
1445 Ross Avenue, Suite 4200, Dallas TX 75202. 214/754-0777. **Contact:** Gary Killbreath, Personnel Manager. **World Wide Web address:** http://www.chubb.com. **Description:** Offers a multiple-line of property and casualty insurance services, serving the public through independent agents and brokers. Founded in 1882. **Number of employees nationwide:** 60,000.

COMMERCIAL UNION INSURANCE COMPANIES
9229 LBJ Freeway, Suite 200, Dallas TX 75243. 972/783-6100. **Contact:** Richard G. Tremblay, Director of Personnel. **World Wide Web address:** http://www.cuusa.com. **Description:** A carrier of property, casualty, and life insurance, licensed in all 50 states, and has offices throughout the country. Commercial Union Insurance Companies is comprised of the U.S. property-casualty and life insurance subsidiaries of Commercial Union Corporation which is a wholly-owned subsidiary of Commercial Union plc of London, England. The principal operating companies are: Commercial Union Insurance Company; American Employers' Insurance Company; The Employers' Fire Insurance Company; The Northern Assurance Company of America; American Central Insurance Company; CU Homeland Insurance Company; Commercial Union Midwest Insurance Company; Commercial Union Life Insurance Company of America; CU Life Insurance Company of New York. **Corporate headquarters location:** Boston MA.

CRUM & FORSTER INSURANCE
6404 International Parkway, Suite 1000, Plano TX 75093. 972/380-3000. **Contact:** Human Resources. **Description:** An insurance company.

FAMILY SERVICE LIFE INSURANCE COMPANY
P.O. Box 8070, McKinney TX 75070. 972/540-6509. **Contact:** Human Resources Department. **Description:** An insurance company.

FIRST HEALTH
222 West Las Colinas Boulevard, Suite 1350, Irving TX 75039-5426. 972/830-7300. **Contact:** Human Resources. **Description:** A health care cost containment company that operates a national PPO network. **Common positions include:** Claim Representative; Clerical Supervisor; Computer Programmer; Customer Service Representative; Licensed Practical Nurse; Registered Nurse; Services Sales Representative; Systems Analyst. **Educational backgrounds include:** Business Administration; Communications; Computer Science; Health Care. **Benefits:** 401(k); Dental Insurance; Disability Coverage; Employee Discounts; Life Insurance; Medical Insurance; Stock Option; Tuition Assistance. **Corporate headquarters location:** Downers Grove IL. **Other U.S. locations:** Nationwide. **Operations at this facility include:** Sales; Service. **Listed on:** NASDAQ. **Annual sales/revenues:** More than $100 million. **Number of employees at this location:** 35. **Number of employees nationwide:** 1,700.

GENERAL REINSURANCE CORPORATION
8144 Walnut Hill Lane, Suite 1250, Dallas TX 75231-3309. 214/691-3000. **Contact:** Human Resources. **Description:** Provides property and casualty reinsurance to primary insurers on a direct basis. The company formerly operated as National Reinsurance Corporation. **Parent company:** General Re Corporation.

GILES INSURANCE AGENCY
2002 North Galloway Avenue, Suite A, Mesquite TX 75149. 972/288-9810. **Contact:** Human Resources. **Description:** An insurance agency.

J&H MARSH & McLENNAN
2200 Ross Avenue, Suite 3300, Dallas TX 75201-7988. 214/979-9900. **Contact:** Personnel. **World Wide Web address:** http://www.marshmc.com. **Description:** Provides advice and services worldwide through an insurance brokerage and risk management firm, reinsurance intermediary facilities, and a consulting and financial services group. Specific services include insurance and risk management services, reinsurance, financial services, consulting, merchandising, and investment management. Marsh & McLennan Companies has subsidiaries and affiliates in 57 countries, and correspondents in 20 others. **Listed on:** New York Stock Exchange.

LAWYERS TITLE INSURANCE CORPORATION
600 North Pearl Street, Suite 700, LB 182, Dallas TX 75201. 214/720-7600. **Contact:** Human Resources. **World Wide Web address:** http://www.ltic.com. **Description:** Provides title insurance and other real estate-related services on commercial and residential transactions in the United States, Canada, the Bahamas, Puerto Rico, and the U.S. Virgin Islands. Lawyers Title Insurance Corporation also provides search and examination services and closing services for a broad-based

customer group that includes lenders, developers, real estate brokers, attorneys, and home buyers. This location covers Kansas, New Mexico, Oklahoma, and Texas. **Corporate headquarters location:** Richmond VA. **Other U.S. locations:** Pasadena CA; Tampa FL; Chicago IL; Boston MA; Troy MI; White Plains NY; Westerville OH; Memphis TN. **Subsidiaries include:** Datatrace Information Services Company, Inc. (Richmond VA) markets automated public record information for public and private use. Genesis Data Systems, Inc. (Englewood CO) develops and markets computer software tailored specifically to the title industry. Lawyers Title Exchange Company operates out of 10 of Lawyers Title Insurance Corporation's regional offices and functions as an intermediary for individual and corporate investors interested in pursuing tax-free property exchanges. **Parent company:** Lawyers Title Corporation. **Listed on:** NASDAQ.

METROPOLITAN LIFE INSURANCE COMPANY
3010 LBJ Freeway, Suite 1550, Dallas TX 75234. 972/241-8841. **Contact:** Branch Manager. **World Wide Web address:** http://www.metlife.com. **Description:** Offers a wide range of individual and group insurance including life, annuity, disability, and mutual funds. **Common positions include:** Insurance Agent/Broker; Services Sales Representative. **Educational backgrounds include:** Business Administration; Finance; Liberal Arts; Marketing. **Benefits:** Dental Insurance; Disability Coverage; Life Insurance; Medical Insurance; Pension Plan; Profit Sharing; Savings Plan; Tuition Assistance. **Corporate headquarters location:** New York NY. **Number of employees at this location:** 15. **Number of employees nationwide:** 13,500.

MILLERS GROUP
P.O. Box 2269, Fort Worth TX 76113. 817/332-7761. **Contact:** Human Resources. **Description:** A fire, marine, and casualty insurance company.

NATIONAL FOUNDATION LIFE INSURANCE COMPANY
777 Main Street, Suite 900, Fort Worth TX 76102. 817/878-3300. **Contact:** Human Resources. **Description:** A life insurance company. **Common positions include:** Accountant/Auditor; Actuary; Attorney; Claim Representative; Clerical Supervisor; Computer Programmer; Human Resources Manager; Paralegal; Purchasing Agent/Manager; Systems Analyst; Underwriter/Assistant Underwriter. **Educational backgrounds include:** Accounting; Business Administration; Computer Science. **Benefits:** 401(k); Dental Insurance; Disability Coverage; Life Insurance; Medical Insurance. **Corporate headquarters location:** This Location. **Operations at this facility include:** Administration; Regional Headquarters. **Number of employees at this location:** 225.

REPUBLIC FINANCIAL SERVICES, INC.
2727 Turtle Creek Boulevard, Dallas TX 75219. 214/559-1222. **Contact:** Larry Westerfield, Director of Employee Relations. **Description:** A diversified holding company whose principal assets are the Republic Insurance Group (offers a broad range of property and liability insurance), and the Allied Finance Company (principally engaged in making direct personal loans to individuals and purchasing discounted retail installment loans). **Common positions include:** Accountant/Auditor; Actuary; Administrator; Customer Service Representative; Human Resources Manager; Purchasing Agent/Manager; Systems Analyst; Underwriter/Assistant Underwriter. **Educational backgrounds include:** Accounting; Business Administration; Communications; Computer Science; Economics; Finance; Marketing; Mathematics. **Benefits:** Dental Insurance; Disability Coverage; Employee Discounts; Life Insurance; Medical Insurance; Pension Plan; Profit Sharing; Savings Plan; Tuition Assistance. **Special programs:** Internships. **Corporate headquarters location:** This Location. **Parent company:** Winterther Swiss.

SCOR REINSURANCE
222 West Las Colinas Boulevard, Suite 650-E, Irving TX 75039. 972/401-1066. **Fax:** 972/869-2311. **Contact:** Human Resources. **Description:** A property and casualty insurance and reinsurance company. **Corporate headquarters location:** New York NY. **Other U.S. locations:** San Francisco CA; Hartford CT; Chicago IL. **Parent company:** SCOR U.S. Corporation.

SOUTHWESTERN LIFE INSURANCE
P.O. Box 2699, Dallas TX 75221. 214/954-7703. **Contact:** Human Resources Department. **Description:** An insurance company.

STATE FARM MUTUAL INSURANCE COMPANY
P.O. Box 799100, Dallas TX 75379-9100. 972/732-5000. **Contact:** Human Resources. **Description:** An insurance company. **Operations at this facility include:** Regional Headquarters.

TRAVELERS INSURANCE COMPANIES
P.O. Box 660456, Dallas TX 75266-0456. 972/866-4748. **Contact:** Susan Oliver, Human Resources Coordinator. **Description:** An insurance and financial services organization marketing virtually all forms of insurance, bond, and pension products on an individual and group basis. Operations include real estate development, business finance, and technology enterprises.

UNITED AMERICAN INSURANCE COMPANY
P.O. Box 8080, McKinney TX 75070-8080. 972/529-5085. **Contact:** Human Resources Department. **Description:** An insurance company.

UNITED INSURANCE COMPANIES INC.
4001 McEwen, Suite 200, Dallas TX 75244. 972/960-8497. **Fax:** 972/392-6737. **Contact:** Human Resources. **Description:** Engaged in health and life insurance. **NOTE:** Entry-level positions are offered. **Common positions include:** Accountant/Auditor; Actuary; Claim Representative; Clerical Supervisor; Computer Programmer; Customer Service Representative; MIS Specialist; Systems Analyst; Typist/Word Processor; Underwriter/Assistant Underwriter. **Educational backgrounds include:** Accounting; Computer Science; Health Care. **Benefits:** 401(k); Daycare Assistance; Dental Insurance; Disability Coverage; Employee Discounts; Life Insurance; Medical Insurance; Profit Sharing; Tuition Assistance. **Special programs:** Training. **Corporate headquarters location:** This Location. **Other U.S. locations:** Glendale AZ; Lakewood CO; St. Petersburg FL; Norcross GA; Oklahoma City OK; Sioux Falls SD. **Operations at this facility include:** Administration; Service. **Listed on:** NASDAQ. **Number of employees at this location:** 400. **Number of employees nationwide:** 780.

WAUSAU INSURANCE COMPANIES
P.O. Box 152800, Irving TX 75015-2800. 972/650-1955. **Contact:** Human Resources. **Description:** Offers a full line of commercial insurance services, including casualty, property, and group insurance products through 100 service offices located throughout the United States. **NOTE:** Entry-level positions are offered. **Common positions include:** Accountant/Auditor; Adjuster; Attorney; Customer Service Representative; Data Analyst; Human Resources Manager; Insurance Agent/Broker; Safety Engineer; Underwriter/Assistant Underwriter. **Educational backgrounds include:** Business Administration; Economics; Engineering; Finance; Liberal Arts. **Benefits:** 401(k); Dental Insurance; Disability Coverage; Life Insurance; Medical Insurance; Pension Plan; Telecommuting; Tuition Assistance. **Corporate headquarters location:** Wausau WI. **Other U.S. locations:** Nationwide. **Operations at this facility include:** Administration; Divisional Headquarters; Sales. **Annual sales/revenues:** More than $100 million. **Number of employees at this location:** 150. **Number of employees nationwide:** 5,500.

Note: Because addresses and telephone numbers of smaller companies can change rapidly, we recommend you call each company to verify the information below before inquiring about job opportunities. Mass mailings are not recommended.

Additional small employers:

INSURANCE AGENTS, BROKERS, AND SERVICES

Aetna Services Inc.
700 Highlander Blvd, Arlington TX 76015-4330. 817/784-5500.

Alexander & Alexander
2711 N Haskell Ave, Dallas TX 75204-2911. 214/989-0000.

Allstate Insurance Company
8711 Freeport Parkway, Irving TX 75063-2578. 972/915-5171.

Allstate Life Insurance Co.
2601 Victory Dr, Marshall TX 75672-4507. 903/935-1484.

Cigna Group Insurance
12225 Greenville Ave, Dallas TX 75243-9362. 972/907-6500.

Cigna Healthcare
PO Box 542588, Dallas TX 75354-2588. 972/401-5200.

Cigna Property Casualty Co.
PO Box 152041, Irving TX 75015-2041. 972/751-3500.

Crawford & Company
1210 River Bend Dr, Dallas TX 75247-4969. 214/631-7560.

CUNA Mutual Insurance Group
4455 LBJ Freeway, Ste 1008, Dallas TX 75244. 972/661-8485.

First National Life & Health Insurance
PO Box 7007, Fort Worth TX 76111-0007. 817/838-0806.

GPA
300 Municipal Dr, Richardson TX 75080-3541. 972/238-7900.

Hartford Insurance Group
PO Box 927, Dallas TX 75221. 972/980-1900.

Insurance Advisors Inc.
3909 Hulen St, Ste 400, Fort Worth TX 76107-7298. 817/732-0657.

James Sedgwick Inc.
3811 Turtle Creek Blvd, Dallas TX 75219-4461. 214/651-4000.

Jarrett Insurance Brokers
5910 N Central Expy, Dallas TX 75206-5125. 214/696-4700.

John Hancock Mutual Life Insurance
1661 Gateway Blvd, Richardson TX 75080-3530. 972/699-6500.

Kemper Insurance Co.
PO Box 479500, Garland TX 75047-9500. 972/270-6601.

Liberty Mutual Insurance
PO Box 152067, Irving TX 75015-2067. 972/550-7899.

Lindsey Morden Claim Services
7929 Brookriver Dr, Dallas TX 75247-4900. 214/630-3730.

Motors Insurance Corporation
PO Box 221048, Dallas TX 75266. 972/659-6000.

Nobel Holdings Inc.
8001 Lyndon B. Johnson Fwy, Dallas TX 75251-1337. 972/644-0434.

PFL Life Insurance Company
PO Box 930005, Bedford TX 76021. 817/285-3300.

Prudential Health Care Plan
4100 Alpha Rd, Ste 400, Dallas TX 75244-4327. 972/263-3861.

Rigg Group Inc.
309 W 7th St, Ste 200, Fort Worth TX 76102-6902. 817/335-4444.

Signal Aviation Underwriter
PO Box 797408, Dallas TX 75379-7408. 972/447-2000.

The Resource Group
1345 River Bend Dr, Dallas TX 75247-4915. 214/634-7014.

Transport Insurance Company
4100 Harry Hines Blvd, Dallas TX 75219-3207. 214/520-4520.

US Risk Insurance Group Inc.
5910 N Central Expy, Dallas TX 75206-5125. 214/265-7090.

Zurich American Insurance Group
9330 LBJ Freeway, Ste 1200, Dallas TX 75243-3446. 972/231-7001.

INSURANCE COMPANIES

Aetna Services Inc.
2350 Lakeside Blvd, Richardson TX 75082-4361. 972/470-7878.

Allstate Insurance Company
222 Las Colinas Blvd W, Irving TX 75039-5421. 972/869-6200.

American Amicable Life Insurance
PO Box 2549, Waco TX 76702-2549. 254/753-7311.

American Eagle Insurance Co.
12801 N Central Expressway, Dallas TX 75243-1716. 972/448-1400.

American Hallmark Insurance
14651 Dallas Parkway, Ste 900, Dallas TX 75240-8807. 972/934-2400.

American Income Life Insurance
PO Box 2608, Waco TX 76702-2608. 254/751-8600.

Ameriplan Corporation
14180 Dallas Parkway, Ste 504, Dallas TX 75240-4371. 972/702-9856.

Anthem Benefit Services Inc.
PO Box 660238, Dallas TX 75266-0238. 972/732-2130.

Anthem Life Insurance Co.
PO Box 660238, Dallas TX 75266-0238. 972/732-2000.

Associates Financial Life Insurance Co.
250 E Carpenter Freeway, Irving TX 75062-2710. 972/541-3800.

Blue Cross Blue Shield
3101 Woodlawn Blvd, Denison TX 75020-7441. 903/465-1239.

Continental Insurance Co.
PO Box 960, Dallas TX 75221. 214/220-1421.

Cornerstone National Market
2000 E Lamar Blvd, Ste 330, Arlington TX 76006-7347. 817/860-2620.

Crum & Forster Insurance
18383 Preston Rd, Ste 500, Dallas TX 75252-5490. 214/430-3000.

Employers General Insurance Group
PO Box 219010, Dallas TX 75221-9010. 214/665-6100.

Farmers Mutual Protective Association
PO Box 6106, Temple TX 76503-6106. 254/773-2181.

Federal Deposit Insurance Corp.
PO Box 214155, Dallas TX 75221. 214/754-0098.

Fireman's Fund Insurance Co.
PO Box 2519, Dallas TX 75221-2519. 214/220-4000.

Gainsco Inc.
PO Box 2933, Fort Worth TX 76113-2933. 817/336-2500.

Geico Insurance
PO Box 650253, Dallas TX 75265-0253. 972/701-8700.

Great Southern Life Insurance Co.
PO Box 219040, Dallas TX 75221-9040. 214/954-8100.

Houston General Insurance
PO Box 2932, Fort Worth TX 76113-2932. 817/377-6000.

Insurance Investors Life Insurance
1300 W Mockingbird Ln, Dallas TX 75247-4921. 214/638-9206.

InsurData
2121 Precinct Line Rd, Hurst TX 76054-3136. 817/428-4200.

JCPenney Life Insurance Co.
2700 W Plano Pkwy, Plano TX 75075-8205. 972/881-6000.

Kaiser Permanente
12720 Hillcrest Rd, Dallas TX 75230-2035. 972/458-5000.

Kemper Insurance Co.
PO Box 479503, Garland TX 75047-9503. 214/342-4600.

Leader National Insurance
PO Box 19706, Dallas TX 75301. 214/526-3876.

Lone Star Life Insurance Co.
PO Box 879008, Dallas TX 75287. 972/447-6400.

LSW
PO Box 569080, Dallas TX 75356-9080. 214/638-7100.

MetLife
433 Las Colinas Blvd E, Irving TX 75039-5581. 972/556-2094.

National Health Insurance
PO Box 619999, Dallas TX 75261-6199. 817/640-1900.

National Union Fire Insurance Co.
1999 Bryan St, Ste 1700, Dallas TX 75201-6848. 214/220-6000.

New York Life Insurance Co.
12201 Merit Dr, Ste 1000, Dallas TX 75251-2265. 972/387-2929.

North Texas Healthcare Network
PO Box 167768, Irving TX 75016-7768. 972/751-0047.

Nylcare Passport PPO
4500 Fuller Dr, Irving TX 75038-6529. 972/650-5500.

Old American County Mutual Fire Insurance
PO Box 802325, Dallas TX 75380-2325. 972/661-0400.

Pioneer Life Insurance Co.
5005 Royal Ln, Dallas TX 75229-4310. 972/915-2000.

Prudential Insurance of America Inc.
1521 N Cooper St, Ste 300, Arlington TX 76011-5537. 817/277-0006.

Rodney D. Young Insurance Agency
PO Box 224467, Dallas TX 75222-4467. 214/333-4002.

Safeco Insurance Company
PO Box 869012, Plano TX 75086-9012. 972/516-8600.

Security National Insurance Co.
PO Box 655028, Dallas TX 75265-5028. 214/360-8000.

Signature Group
4520 S Buckner Blvd, Ste B, Dallas TX 75227. 214/381-3355.

St. Paul Companies
2301 E Lamar Blvd, Ste 400, Arlington TX 76006-7427. 817/695-1400.

State National Insurance Co.
PO Box 24622, Fort Worth TX 76124-1622. 817/265-2000.

Texas Life Insurance Company
PO Box 830, Waco TX 76703-0830. 254/752-6521.

TIG Insurance Company
5205 North O'Connor Boulevard, Irving TX 75039. 972/831-5000.

Union Standard Insurance Co.
PO Box 152180, Irving TX 75015-2180. 972/719-2400.

United Benefit Life Insurance Co.
3909 Hulen St, Ste 300, Fort Worth TX 76107-7255. 817/732-0399.

Voyager Indemnity Insurance Co.
PO Box 901045, Fort Worth TX 76101-2045. 817/390-1700.

Zurich American Home Insurance
PO Box 742288, Dallas TX 75374-2288. 972/997-1800.

For more information on career opportunities in insurance:

Associations

ALLIANCE OF AMERICAN INSURERS
1501 Woodfield Road, Suite 400 West, Schaumburg IL 60173-4980. 847/330-8500. World Wide Web address: http://www.allianceai.org.

HEALTH INSURANCE ASSOCIATION OF AMERICA
555 13th Street NW, Suite 600E, Washington DC 20004. 202/824-1600. World Wide Web address: http://www.hiaa.org.

INSURANCE INFORMATION INSTITUTE
110 William Street, 24th Floor, New York NY 10038. 212/669-9200. World Wide Web address: http://www.iii.org. Provides information on property/casualty insurance issues.

NATIONAL ASSOCIATION OF PROFESSIONAL INSURANCE AGENTS
400 North Washington Street, Alexandria VA 22314. 703/836-9340. World Wide Web address: http://www.pianet.com.

SOCIETY OF ACTUARIES
475 North Martingale Road, Suite 800, Schaumburg IL 60173-2226. 847/706-3500. World Wide Web address: http://www.soa.org.

Directories

AMERICAN ASSOCIATION OF HEALTH PLANS
Managed Health Care Directory, 1129 20th Street NW, Suite 600, Washington DC 20036. 202/778-3200. World Wide Web address: http://www.aahp.org.

INSURANCE ALMANAC
Underwriter Printing and Publishing Company, 50 East Palisade Avenue, Englewood NJ 07631. 201/569-8808. Hardcover annual, 639 pages, $115.00. Available at libraries.

INSURANCE PHONE BOOK AND DIRECTORY
Reed Reference Publishing, 121 Chanlon Road, New Providence NJ 07974. Toll-free phone: 800/521-8110.

$89.95, new editions available every other year. Also available at libraries.

Magazines

BEST'S REVIEW
A.M. Best Company, A.M. Best Road, Oldwick NJ 08858-9988. 908/439-2200. World Wide Web address: http://www.ambest.com. Monthly.

INSURANCE JOURNAL
Wells Publishing, 9191 Towne Centre Drive, Suite 550, San Diego, CA 92122-1231 619/455-7717. World Wide Web address: http://www. insurancejrnl.com. A biweekly magazine covering the insurance industry. Subscription: $78.00 per year, $3.00 for a single issue.

Online Services

FINANCIAL/ACCOUNTING/INSURANCE JOBS PAGE
http://www.nationjob.com/financial. This Website provides a list of financial, accounting, and insurance job openings.

THE INSURANCE CAREER CENTER
http://connectyou.com/talent. Offers job openings, career resources, and a resume database for jobseekers looking to get into the insurance field.

INSURANCE NATIONAL SEARCH
http://www.insurancerecruiters.com/insjobs/jobs.htm. Provides a searchable database of job openings in the insurance industry. The site is run by Insurance National Search, Inc.

LEGAL SERVICES

Prospective lawyers will continue to face intense competition through the year 2005, due to the overabundance of law school graduates. Consequently, fewer lawyers are working for major law firms, opting instead for smaller firms, corporations, and associations, according to the U.S. Department of Commerce. Legal firms have reduced their support staffs, while large corporations are establishing in-house legal departments to avoid paying for expensive, big-name law offices.

Paralegals comprise the fastest-growing profession in legal services, and the U.S. Department of Labor projects that opportunities will continue to expand rapidly through 2005. Paralegals are taking on more responsibilities in areas such as real estate and trademark law. Private law firms will hire the most paralegals, but a vast array of other organizations also employ them, including insurance companies, real estate agencies, and banks.

ACKELS, ACKELS & ACKELS
624 North Good-Latimer Expressway, Suite 200, Dallas TX 75204. 214/826-1111. **Contact:** Wanda Nabors, Office Manager. **Description:** Specializes in civil, criminal, and commercial litigation, and also practices personal injury, juvenile, and entertainment law.

JOHN ATWOOD LAW OFFICE
3500 Oak Lawn, Suite 400, Dallas TX 75219. 214/523-9520. **Contact:** Personnel Department. **Description:** Specializes in corporate, real estate, administrative, and taxation law.

BAILEY AND WILLIAMS
7502 Greenville Avenue, Suite 500, Dallas TX 75231. 214/890-4006. **Contact:** Personnel. **Description:** A law firm specializing in litigation. **Common positions include:** Attorney; Paralegal. **Benefits:** Dental Insurance; Life Insurance; Medical Insurance; Pension Plan. **Corporate headquarters location:** This Location. **Operations at this facility include:** Service.

BAKER & BOTTS LLP
2001 Ross Avenue, Suite 600, Dallas TX 75201-2980. 214/953-6500. **Contact:** Personnel. **World Wide Web address:** http://www.bakerbotts.com. **Description:** Baker & Botts ranks among the largest law firms in the United States. **Common positions include:** Attorney; Librarian; Secretary; Typist/Word Processor. **Educational backgrounds include:** Business Administration; Liberal Arts. **Benefits:** Dental Insurance; Disability Coverage; Life Insurance; Medical Insurance; Pension Plan; Profit Sharing; Travel Allowance; Tuition Assistance. **Corporate headquarters location:** Houston TX.

BARON & BUDD
3102 Oak Lawn Avenue, Suite 1100, Dallas TX 75219. 214/521-3605. **Contact:** Personnel. **Description:** A law firm.

BICKEL & BREWER
1717 Main Street, Suite 4800, Dallas TX 75201. 214/653-4000. **Contact:** Human Resources. **Description:** A law firm specializing in corporate litigation including bankruptcy.

CANTEY HANGER
801 Cherry Street, Suite 2100, Fort Worth TX 76102. 817/877-2800. **Contact:** Personnel. **World Wide Web address:** http://www.canteyhanger.com. **Description:** A law firm specializing in corporate law.

CRENSHAW DUPREE & MILAM
P.O. Box 1499, Lubbock TX 79408. 806/762-5281. **Contact:** Human Resources. **Description:** A law firm.

DILTS AND LAW
9500 Forest Lane, Suite 435, Dallas TX 75243. 214/343-8752. **Contact:** Connie Womack, Personnel Manager. **Description:** A general civil and trial law firm handling corporate, probate, estate planning, and taxation law.

EUGENE, ZEMP, DUBOSE, P.C.
3303 Lee Parkway, Suite 210, Dallas TX 75219. 214/520-2983. **Contact:** Personnel. **Description:** A law firm specializing in antitrust and bankruptcy litigation.

JOHN EZELL
2815 Gaston Avenue, Dallas TX 75226. 214/827-3080. **Contact:** Personnel. **Description:** A litigation practice specializing in personal injury, negligence, and products liability.

FRED MISKO JR., P.C.
3811 Turtle Creek Boulevard, Suite 1900, Dallas TX 75219. 214/443-8000. **Contact:** Personnel. **World Wide Web address:** http://www.misko.com. **Description:** A trial practice specializing in personal injury law.

NOVAKOV DAVIDSON & FLYNN
750 North St. Paul Street, Suite 2000, Dallas TX 75201-3286. 214/922-9221. **Contact:** Human Resources. **World Wide Web address:** http://www.novakov.com. **Description:** A law firm.

THOMPSON & KNIGHT
1700 Pacific Avenue, Suite 3300, Dallas TX 75201. 214/969-1700. **Contact:** Human Resources Department. **World Wide Web address:** http://www.t&klaw.com. **Description:** A law firm.

WINSTEAD SECHREST & MINICK P.C.
5400 Renaissance Tower, 1201 Elm Street, Dallas TX 75270. 214/745-5211. **Contact:** Patty Stewart, Human Resources Manager. **Description:** A law firm.

OFFICES OF NORMAN A. ZABLE, PC
5340 Alpha Road, Dallas TX 75240. 972/386-6900. **Contact:** Human Resources Department. **Description:** A civil law practice specializing in business and bankruptcy law.

Note: Because addresses and telephone numbers of smaller companies can change rapidly, we recommend you call each company to verify the information below before inquiring about job opportunities. Mass mailings are not recommended.

Additional small employers:

LEGAL SERVICES

Arter & Hadden
1717 Main St, Ste 4100, Dallas TX 75201-7302. 214/761-2100.

Baker & McKenzie
2001 Ross Ave, Dallas TX 75201-8001. 214/978-3000.

Barrett Burke & Wilson
6750 Hillcrest Plaza Drive, Dallas TX 75230-1400. 972/386-5040.

Burford & Ryburn
500 N Akard St, Ste 3100, Dallas TX 75201-3327. 214/740-3100.

Burt Barr & Associates
304 S Record St, Dallas TX 75202-4712. 214/742-8001.

Calhoun & Stacy
901 Main St, Ste 5700, Dallas TX 75202-3713. 214/748-5000.

Carrington Coleman Sloman & Blumenthal
200 Crescent Court, Ste 1500, Dallas TX 75201-7839. 214/855-3000.

Cooper Aldous & Scully
900 Jackson St, Ste 100, Dallas TX 75202-4426. 214/712-9500.

Cowles & Thompson
901 Main St, Ste 4000, Dallas TX 75202-3746. 214/672-2000.

Decker Jones McMackin
301 Commerce St, Ste 2400, Fort Worth TX 76102-4124. 817/336-2400.

Dehay and Elliston
901 Main St, Ste 3500, Dallas TX 75202-3736. 214/210-2400.

Fanning Harper Martinson
8117 Preston Rd, Fl 3, Dallas TX 75225-6332. 214/369-1300.

Figari & Davenport
901 Main St, Ste 4800, Dallas TX 75202-3758. 214/939-2000.

Fowler Wiles & Keith
2711 N Haskell Ave, Dallas TX 75204-2911. 214/841-3000.

Fulbright & Jaworski
2200 Ross Ave, Ste 2800, Dallas TX 75201-2750. 214/855-8000.

Gardere & Wynne
1601 Elm St, Ste 3000, Dallas TX 75201-4757. 214/999-3000.

Geary Porter Donovan
16475 Dallas Pkwy, Ste 550, Dallas TX 75248-2639. 972/931-9901.

Gibson Dunn & Crutcher
1717 Main St, Ste 5400, Dallas TX 75201-7367. 214/698-3100.

Glast Phillips & Murray PC
13355 Noel Rd, Ste 2200, Dallas TX 75240-6612. 972/419-8300.

Godwin & Carlton PC
901 Main St, Ste 2500, Dallas TX 75202-3727. 214/939-4465.

Gwinn & Roby
1201 Elm St, Ste 4100, Dallas TX 75270-2109. 214/742-5191.

Haynes and Boone LLP
201 Main St, Ste 2200, Fort Worth TX 76102-3126. 817/347-6600.

Heard Goggan Blair & Williams
2323 Bryan St, Ste 1720, Dallas TX 75201-2644. 214/880-0089.

Hill & Gilstrap PC
1400 W Abram St, Arlington TX 76013-1705. 817/261-2222.

Hinkle Cox Eaton Coffield
PO Box 9238, Amarillo TX 79105-9238. 806/372-5569.

Hopkins & Sutter
1717 Main St, Ste 3700, Dallas TX 75201-4605. 214/653-2100.

Hughes & Luce LLP
1717 Main St, Ste 2800, Dallas TX 75201-7342. 214/939-5500.

Jackson & Walker LLP
901 Main St, Ste 6000, Dallas TX 75202-3748. 214/953-6000.

Jones Day Reavis & Pogue
PO Box 660623, Dallas TX 75266-0623. 214/969-4594.

Kane Russell Coleman Logan
3700 Thanksgiving Tower, Dallas TX 75201. 214/777-4200.

Kelly Hart & Hallman PC
201 Main St, Ste 2500, Fort Worth TX 76102-3129. 817/332-2500.

Legal Services of North Texas
1515 Main St, Dallas TX 75201-4841. 214/748-1234.

Liddell Sapp Zivley
2200 Ross Ave, Ste 900, Dallas TX 75201-6700. 214/220-4800.

Locke Purnell Rain Harrell
2200 Ross Ave, Ste 2200, Dallas TX 75201-2748. 214/740-8000.

Malouf Lynch Jackson Kessler
8117 Preston Rd, Ste 700W, Dallas TX 75225-6332. 214/750-0722.

McCauley McDonald Love Devin
1201 Elm St, Ste 3800, Dallas TX 75270-2130. 214/744-3300.

McDonald Sanders
1300 Continental Plz, Fort Worth TX 76102. 817/336-8651.

McKool Smith PC
300 Crescent Ct, Ste 1500, Dallas TX 75201-7856. 214/978-4000.

McMackin Decker Jones
301 Commerce St, Ste 2400, Fort Worth TX 76102. 817/336-0361.

McWhorter Cobb & Johnson
PO Box 2547, Lubbock TX 79408-2547. 806/762-0214.

Michener Larimore Swindle
3500 City Center, Tower 2, Fort Worth TX 76102. 817/335-4417.

Munsch Hardt Kopf
1445 Ross Ave, Ste 4000, Dallas TX 75202-2743. 214/855-7500.

Naman Howell Smith & Lee
PO Box 1470, Waco TX 76703-1470. 254/755-4100.

National Corporate Network
600 N Pearl St, Ste 2100, Dallas TX 75201-2825. 214/777-6400.

Page & Addison PC
15770 Dallas Pkwy, Fl 5, Dallas TX 75248-3329. 214/528-7010.

Payne & Blanchard
PO Box 393, Dallas TX 75221-0393. 214/953-1313.

Peirson & Patterson
4400 Alpha Rd, Dallas TX 75244-4505. 972/490-9027.

Potter Minton Roberts Davis
PO Box 359, Tyler TX 75710-0359. 903/597-8311.

Ramey & Flock
PO Box 629, Tyler TX 75710-0629. 903/597-3301.

Robertson-Railsback Inc.
705 Ross Ave, Dallas TX 75202-2007. 214/748-9211.

Silber & Pearlman PC
2711 N Haskell Ave, Dallas TX 75204-2911. 214/874-7000.

Sprouts Mozola Smith Rowley
PO Box 15008, Amarillo TX 79105-5008. 806/345-5005.

Thompson Coe Cousins & Iron
200 Crescent Ct, Fl 11, Dallas TX 75201-1875. 214/871-8200.

Touchstone Bernys Johnston
4700 Renaissance Tower, Dallas TX 75270. 214/741-1166.

True Rohde Sewell
8080 N Central Expy, Ste 9, Dallas TX 75206-1806. 214/368-1500.

Underwood Wilson Berry
PO Box 9158, Amarillo TX 79105-9158. 806/376-5613.

Vial Hamilton Koch & Knox
1717 Main St, Ste 4400, Dallas TX 75201-7357. 214/712-4400.

Vinson & Elkins LP
2001 Ross Ave, Ste 3700, Dallas TX 75201-2965. 214/220-7700.

Weil Gotshal & Manges
100 Crescent Ct, Ste 1300, Dallas
TX 75201-6900. 214/746-7700.

Windle Turley & Associates
6440 N Central Expressway,
Dallas TX 75206-4101. 214/691-
4025.

Worsham Forsythe Wooldridge
1601 Bryan St, Fl 30, Dallas TX
75201-3402. 214/979-3000.

For more information on career opportunities in legal services:

Associations

AMERICAN BAR ASSOCIATION
750 North Lake Shore Drive, Chicago IL 60611.
312/988-5000. World Wide Web address:
http://www.abanet.org.

FEDERAL BAR ASSOCIATION
1815 H Street NW, Suite 408, Washington DC 20006-
3697. 202/638-0252. World Wide Web address:
http://www.fedbar.org.

**NATIONAL ASSOCIATION OF LEGAL
ASSISTANTS**
1516 South Boston Avenue, Suite 200, Tulsa OK
74119-4013. 918/587-6828. World Wide Web
address: http://www.nala.org. An educational
association that administers the National Voluntary
Association Exam. Memberships are available.

**NATIONAL FEDERATION OF PARALEGAL
ASSOCIATIONS**
P.O. Box 33108, Kansas City MO 64114-0108.
816/941-4000. World Wide Web address:
http://www.paralegals.org. Offers magazines,
seminars, and Internet job listings.

NATIONAL PARALEGAL ASSOCIATION
P.O. Box 406, Solebury PA 18963. 215/297-8333.

Directories

MARTINDALE-HUBBELL LAW DIRECTORY
121 Chanlon Road, New Providence NJ 07974. Toll-
free phone: 800/526-4902. World Wide Web address:
http://www.martindale.com. A directory consisting of
the names of legal employers. In all, the database has
listings for over 900,000 lawyers and law firms. In
addition to information regarding firms and practices,
the database includes biographies of many individual
lawyers. Thus, you can do searches by firm name, law
school attended, and field of law. While it lists some
foreign law firms, the database consists primarily of
firms in the United States.

Online Services

COURT REPORTERS FORUM
Go: CrForum. A CompuServe networking forum that
includes information from the *Journal of Court
Reporting*.

LEGAL EXCHANGE
Jump to: Legal Exchange. A debate forum for lawyers
and other legal professionals, offered through Prodigy.

LEGAL INFORMATION NETWORK
Keyword: LIN. An America Online networking
resource for paralegals, family law specialists, social
security specialists, and law students.

MANUFACTURING: MISCELLANEOUS CONSUMER

Greater globalization is the trend in consumer manufacturing as worldwide and regional trade agreements reduce barriers and provide more uniform trade standards. Demand for household goods is cyclical and depends on the state of the economy and the disposable income of consumers. Now, the distribution of these goods is more dependent on large discount retailers. Household appliance shipments are expected to grow by 2 percent in 1998.

The best opportunities for jobseekers will be in the manufacture of home entertainment products. Baby boomers are reaching their peak earning potential and spending money on big-screen televisions and upgraded sound equipment for home stereos. There is also a renewed interest overseas in "Made in the U.S.A." products such as Harley-Davidson motorcycles, golfing equipment, fishing boats, and mountain bikes.

In general, manufacturing jobs in the United States will continue to disappear as the economy continues shifting toward service industries. Factory automation -- including wireless communications, distributed intelligence, and centralized computer control -- is one major cause for the loss of manufacturing jobs. Growing competition has forced some companies to streamline production by replacing workers with computers in the areas of inventory tracking, shipping, and ordering. Individuals who have a working knowledge of these software applications will have an edge over less technically experienced jobseekers.

AMC (ATLAS MATCH CORPORATION)
1801 South Airport Circle, Euless TX 76040. 817/267-1500. **Contact:** Personnel. **Description:** Manufactures a wide variety of matchbooks with advertisements.

ACTION COMPANY
P.O. Box 8008, McKinney TX 75070. 972/542-8700. **Contact:** Human Resources. **Description:** Manufactures leather riding saddles.

AMERICAN PERMANENT WARE COMPANY
P.O. Box 150069, Dallas TX 75389. 214/421-7366. **Contact:** Personnel. **Description:** Manufactures stainless steel hardware and kitchen utensils.

AMERICAN RECREATION PRODUCTS INC.
2125 West Broad Street, Mineola TX 75773. 903/569-3882. **Contact:** Human Resources. **World Wide Web address:** http://www.slumberjack.com. **Description:** A manufacturer of sleeping bags and dog beds.

ARROW INDUSTRIES
2625 Belt Line Road, Carrollton TX 75006. 972/416-6500x238. **Contact:** Kyle Marlin, Vice President of Human Resources. **Description:** A private label manufacturer, processor, and packager of polyethylene bags, household aluminum foil, paper plates, charcoal, lighter fluid, beans, rice, popcorn, and spices. **Common positions include:** Accountant/Auditor; Blue-Collar Worker Supervisor; Computer Programmer; Department Manager; Human Resources Manager;

Manufacturer's/Wholesaler's Sales Rep.; Mechanical Engineer; Operations/Production Manager; Purchasing Agent/Manager; Quality Control Supervisor; Transportation/Traffic Specialist. **Educational backgrounds include:** Accounting; Business Administration; Computer Science; Engineering; Marketing. **Benefits:** Dental Insurance; Life Insurance; Medical Insurance; Profit Sharing. **Corporate headquarters location:** This Location. **Operations at this facility include:** Administration; Manufacturing; Sales.

CARLTON MANUFACTURING
P.O. Box 539, Mt. Vernon TX 75457. 903/537-4591. **Contact:** Human Resources. **Description:** Manufactures wooden household furniture.

CURTIS MATHES HOLDING CORPORATION
10911 Petal Street, Dallas TX 75238. 214/503-8880. **Fax:** 214/503-8515. **Contact:** Human Resources. **World Wide Web address:** http://www.curtismathes.com. **Description:** Markets both consumer and commercial electronics products. Founded in 1901. **NOTE:** Entry-level positions are offered. **Common positions include:** Administrative Assistant; Public Relations Specialist; Secretary; Technical Writer/Editor. **Educational backgrounds include:** Accounting; Computer Science. **Benefits:** 401(k); Dental Insurance; Employee Discounts; Life Insurance; Medical Insurance; Pension Plan. **Corporate headquarters location:** This Location. **Subsidiaries include:** Curtis Mathes Corporation, which designs and markets home entertainment products including televisions, VCRs, audio systems, and other complementary products. The company's products are marketed by independent dealers throughout the United States. **Listed on:** NASDAQ. **Stock exchange symbol:** CRTM. **Number of employees at this location:** 50.

DALLAS WOODCRAFT
2829 Sea Harbour Road, Dallas TX 75212. 214/631-2782. **Contact:** Personnel. **Description:** Manufactures wooden picture frames.

DART CONTAINER CORPORATION
850 Solon Road, Waxahachie TX 75165. 972/937-7270. **Contact:** Human Resources. **Description:** A manufacturer and wholesaler of Styrofoam products such as cups, plates, and beverage coolers.

FOSSIL INC.
2280 North Greenville Avenue, Richardson TX 75082-4412. 214/348-7400. **Contact:** Human Resources. **World Wide Web address:** http://www.fossil.com. **Description:** Manufactures several products including watches, leather products, T-shirts, and sunglasses.

HICKORY-WHITE FURNITURE
P.O. Box 421068, Dallas TX 75342-1068. 214/742-8234. **Contact:** Human Resources. **Description:** A manufacturer of wooden and upholstered furniture for the home.

JOSTENS, INC.
P.O. Box AC, Denton TX 76202. 940/891-0434. **Contact:** Human Resources. **Description:** Jostens, Inc. is a manufacturer of jewelry. The company's jewelry is sold to consumers through independent contract salespeople.

JUMPKING INC.
901 West Miller Road, Garland TX 75041. 972/271-5867. **Contact:** Human Resources. **Description:** Jumpking Inc. is a manufacturer of trampolines.

KIMBERLY-CLARK CORPORATION
P.O. Box 619100, Dallas TX 75261. 972/281-1200. **Contact:** Human Resources. **World Wide Web address:** http://www.kimberly-clark.com. **Description:** Kimberly-Clark Corporation manufactures and markets products for personal, business, and industrial uses throughout the world. The name brands of Kimberly-Clark Corporation include Kleenex facial and bathroom tissue, Huggies diapers and baby wipes, Pull-Ups training pants, Kotex and New Freedom feminine care products, Depend and Poise incontinence care products, Hi-Dri household towels, Kimguard sterile wrap, Kimwipes industrial wipers, and Classic business and correspondence papers. Most of the company's products are made from natural and synthetic fibers using advanced technologies in

absorbency, fibers, and nonwovens. Kimberly-Clark Corporation has extensive operations overseas in Europe and Asia. **Corporate headquarters location:** Neenah WI.

KIRSCH
P.O. Box 154186, Waco TX 76704. 254/799-5523. **Contact:** Human Resources Department. **Description:** Kirsch specializes in the manufacture of window dressings, including wooden and mini- blinds.

LASTING PRODUCTS
2115 West Valley View Lane, Farmers Branch TX 75234. 972/247-9696. **Contact:** Personnel Director. **Description:** Manufactures decorative home products made of wood, metal, ceramic, and glass.

MARY KAY, INC.
16251 North Dallas Parkway, Dallas TX 75248-2696. 972/687-6300. **Contact:** Human Resources Department. **World Wide Web address:** http://www.marykay.com. **Description:** A manufacturer and distributor of cosmetics and other health and beauty aids. Production and development is conducted at a facility in Texas, while distribution is carried out by approximately 300,000 direct sales consultants. Products are sold in 16 countries.

MATTEL SALES CORPORATION
2310 Ridge Road, Suite C, Rockwall TX 75087. 972/771-2400. **Contact:** Human Resources. **Description:** A manufacturer and distributor of toys, electronic products, games, books, hobby products, and family entertainment products.

NASH MANUFACTURING COMPANY, INC.
315 West Ripy Street, Fort Worth TX 76110. 817/926-5225. **Contact:** Human Resources Department. **Description:** A manufacturer of sports and athletic equipment, including skateboards and water skis.

NATIONAL BANNER COMPANY
11938 Harry Hines Boulevard, Dallas TX 75234. 972/241-2131. **Contact:** Human Resources Department. **World Wide Web address:** http://www.nationalbannerco.com. **Description:** National Banner Company is a manufacturer and wholesaler of flags, banners, and pennants.

NU-KOTE INTERNATIONAL
17950 Preston Road, Suite 690, Dallas TX 75252-5634. 972/250-2785. **Contact:** Human Resources. **Description:** A holding company with a subsidiary which manufactures and markets supplies for office and home printing devices including inked fabric and coated film ribbons for impact printers, and toner supplies for laser printers, fax machines, and copiers. **Number of employees nationwide:** 1,250.

NUTONE INC.
850 North Lake Drive, Suite 500, Coppell TX 75019. 972/462-7627. **Contact:** Human Resources. **Description:** An electric housewares manufacturer.

PRO LINE CORPORATION
2121 Panoramic Circle, Dallas TX 75212. 214/631-4247. **Contact:** Human Resources. **Description:** Manufactures hair care products.

RUBBERMAID, INC.
7121 Shelby Avenue, Greenville TX 75402-5898. 903/455-0011. **Contact:** Human Resources Department. **Description:** This location specializes in the manufacture of a variety of household products such as plastic food storage containers. Overall, Rubbermaid manufactures and sells rubber and plastic products for the consumer and commercial markets. The company's product line includes over 2,500 items for home organization, kitchen and bath, household repairs/do-it-yourself, and agricultural, industrial, and institutional use. **Corporate headquarters location:** Wooster OH.

SAMSILL CORPORATION
4301 Mansfield Highway, Fort Worth TX 76119. 817/535-0203. **Contact:** Human Resources. **Description:** Samsill Corporation is a manufacturer of office products such as plastic binders and sheet protectors.

SIMMONS COMPANY
P.O. Box 814869, Dallas TX 75381-4869. 972/241-9100. **Fax:** 972/241-9508. **Contact:** Tony Zuniga, Human Resources Manager. **World Wide Web address:** http://www.simmonsco.com. **Description:** A mattress and boxspring manufacturer. Simmons has 15 other plants in the U.S. **Common positions include:** Blue-Collar Worker Supervisor; Production Worker. **Benefits:** 401(k); Dental Insurance; Disability Coverage; Employee Discounts; Life Insurance; Medical Insurance; Profit Sharing; Savings Plan; Tuition Assistance. **Corporate headquarters location:** Atlanta GA. **Operations at this facility include:** Manufacturing. **Number of employees at this location:** 100.

SPORTS SUPPLY GROUP, INC.
P.O. Box 7726, Dallas TX 75209. 972/484-9484. **Contact:** Human Resources Department. **World Wide Web address:** http://www.sportsgroup.com. **Description:** Manufactures and sells a wide variety of sports equipment.

STANLEY MECHANICS TOOLS
12827 Valley Branch Lane, Dallas TX 75234. 972/247-1367. **Contact:** Human Resources Department. **Description:** Stanley Mechanics Tools specializes in the manufacture of hand tools such as socket wrenches.

SWEETHEART CUP COMPANY, INC.
4444 West Ledbetter Drive, Dallas TX 75236. 214/339-3131. **Contact:** Human Resources. **Description:** Engaged in the manufacture and distribution of a variety of food serviceware including plates, cups, bowls, drinking straws, and ice cream cones, as well as containers for use in packaging food and dairy products. **Common positions include:** Blue-Collar Worker Supervisor; Department Manager; Electrician; Millwright; Printing Press Operator. **Educational backgrounds include:** Business Administration; Engineering; Liberal Arts. **Corporate headquarters location:** Chicago IL. **Other U.S. locations:** Nationwide. **Operations at this facility include:** Manufacturing; Sales. **Number of employees at this location:** 850. **Number of employees nationwide:** 8,000.

TEMPO LIGHTING
P.O. Box 421403, Dallas TX 75342-1403. 214/742-2685. **Contact:** Human Resources Department. **Description:** Tempo Lighting is a manufacturer of household floor and table lamps.

TEMTEX INDUSTRIES INC.
5400 LBJ Freeway, Suite 1375, Dallas TX 75240. 972/726-7175. **Contact:** Human Resources Department. **World Wide Web address:** http://www.hearth.com/temco. **Description:** Specializes in the manufacture of ceramic logs for fireplaces. **Corporate headquarters location:** This Location.

TEXAS RECREATION CORPORATION
908 North Beverly Drive, Wichita Falls TX 76305. 940/322-4463. **Contact:** Human Resources Department. **Description:** Texas Recreation Corporation is a manufacturer of soft foam products including pool flotation devices.

THIRD COAST TECHNOLOGIES
1571 North Glenville Street, Richardson TX 75081. 972/238-9123. **Contact:** Human Resources. **Description:** A manufacturer of toner cartridges.

UNIVEX INTERNATIONAL
7325 Imperial Drive, Waco TX 76712. 972/660-7400. **Contact:** Human Resources. **Description:** Manufactures audiotape and videotape albums and loose-leaf binders. **Common positions include:**

Advertising Clerk; Blue-Collar Worker Supervisor; Clerical Supervisor; Cost Estimator; Customer Service Representative; Environmental Engineer; General Manager; Industrial Production Manager; Management Trainee; Manufacturer's/Wholesaler's Sales Rep.; Operations/Production Manager; Purchasing Agent/Manager; Quality Control Supervisor. **Benefits:** 401(k). **Corporate headquarters location:** Denver CO. **Operations at this facility include:** Administration; Divisional Headquarters; Manufacturing; Research and Development; Sales; Service. **Number of employees at this location:** 80. **Number of employees nationwide:** 200.

Note: Because addresses and telephone numbers of smaller companies can change rapidly, we recommend you call each company to verify the information below before inquiring about job opportunities. Mass mailings are not recommended.

Additional small employers:

COSMETICS AND RELATED PRODUCTS

Aloe Vera of America Inc.
PO Box 801428, Dallas TX 75380-1428. 214/343-5700.

CBI Laboratories Inc.
PO Box 841058, Dallas TX 75284-1058. 972/241-7546.

HOUSEHOLD APPLIANCES

Lasko Metal Products Inc.
1700 Meacham Blvd, Fort Worth TX 76106-2109. 817/625-6381.

HOUSEHOLD AUDIO AND VIDEO EQUIPMENT

Anacomp Inc.
1715 4th St, Graham TX 76450-2927. 940/549-4500.

Atlas Soundolier
PO Box 1359, Ennis TX 75120-1359. 972/875-8413.

M&S Systems Inc.
PO Box 541777, Dallas TX 75354-1777. 214/358-3196.

Primo Microphones Inc.
PO Box 1570, McKinney TX 75070-1570. 972/548-9807.

HOUSEHOLD FURNITURE

Duro Metal Manufacturing
PO Box 17520, Dallas TX 75217-0520. 214/391-3181.

Leathertech
3700 Eagle Place Dr, Dallas TX 75236-1450. 972/296-9599.

Mattress Giant Corporation
1200 Trend Dr, Carrollton TX 75006-5408. 972/418-6644.

Mayo Brothers
PO Box 5338, Texarkana TX 75505-5338. 903/838-0518.

Smith Furniture Manufacturing Co.
PO Box 7973, Waco TX 76714-7973. 254/772-2760.

Towne Square Furniture Inc.
PO Box 419, Hillsboro TX 76645-0419. 254/582-7444.

MISC. FURNITURE AND FIXTURES

CH Industries Inc.
PO Box 29923, Dallas TX 75229-0923. 972/242-2164.

POWER-DRIVEN HAND TOOLS

National Hand Tools
2801 Production Blvd, Wichita Falls TX 76302-5920. 940/767-0555.

TOYS AND SPORTING GOODS

Adams Golf Inc.
2901 Summit Avenue, Ste 100, Plano TX 75074-7497. 972/422-7060.

Hebb Industries Inc.
PO Box 1698, Whitehouse TX 75791-1698. 903/534-3832.

Pacer Treadmill
5101 Pulaski St, Dallas TX 75247-5931. 214/630-7092.

For more information on career opportunities in consumer manufacturing:

Associations

ASSOCIATION FOR MANUFACTURING EXCELLENCE
380 West Palatine Road, Wheeling IL 60090. 847/520-3282.

ASSOCIATION FOR MANUFACTURING TECHNOLOGY
7901 Westpark Drive, McLean VA 22102. 703/893-2900. World Wide Web address: http://www.mfgtech.org. Offers research services.

ASSOCIATION OF HOME APPLIANCE MANUFACTURERS
20 North Wacker Drive, Suite 1231, Chicago IL

60606. 312/984-5800. World Wide Web address: http://www.aham.org.

NATIONAL ASSOCIATION OF MANUFACTURERS
1331 Pennsylvania Avenue NW, Suite 600, Washington DC 20004. 202/637-3000. World Wide Web address: http://www.nam.org. A lobbying association for manufacturers.

NATIONAL HOUSEWARES MANUFACTURERS ASSOCIATION
6400 Schafer Court, Suite 650, Rosemont IL 60018. 847/292-4200. World Wide Web address: http://www.housewares.org. Offers shipping discounts and other services.

SOCIETY OF MANUFACTURING ENGINEERS
P.O. Box 930, One SME Drive, Dearborn MI 48121.
313/271-1500. World Wide Web address:
http://www.sme.org. Offers educational events and
educational materials on manufacturing.

Directories

AMERICAN MANUFACTURER'S DIRECTORY
5711 South 86th Circle, P.O. Box 37347, Omaha NE
68127. Toll-free phone: 800/555-5211. Made by the
same company that created *American Big Business
Directory*, *American Manufacturer's Directory* lists
over 531,000 manufacturing companies of all sizes
and industries. The directory contains product and
sales information, company size, and a contact name
for each company.

**APPLIANCE MANUFACTURER ANNUAL
DIRECTORY**
Appliance Manufacturer, 5900 Harper Road, Suite
105, Solon OH 44139. 216/349-3060. $25.00.

**HOUSEHOLD AND PERSONAL PRODUCTS
INDUSTRY BUYERS GUIDE**
Rodman Publishing Group, 17 South Franklin
Turnpike, Ramsey NJ 07446. 201/825-2552. World
Wide Web address: http://www.happi.com. $12.00.

Magazines

APPLIANCE
1110 Jorie Boulevard, Oak Brook IL 60522-9019.
630/990-3484. World Wide Web address:
http://www.appliance.com. Monthly. $70.00 for a
one-year subscription.

COSMETICS INSIDERS REPORT
Advanstar Communications, 131 West First Street,
Duluth MN 55802. Toll-free phone: 800/346-0085.
World Wide Web address: http://www.advanstar.com.
$189.00 for a one-year subscription; 24 issues
annually. Features timely articles on cosmetics
marketing and research.

Online Services

CAREER PARK - MANUFACTURING JOBS
http://www.careerpark.com/jobs/manulist.html. This
Website provides a list of current job openings in the
manufacturing industry. The site is run by Parker
Advertising Service, Inc.

**MO'S GATEWAY TO MANUFACTURING-
RELATED JOBS LISTINGS**
http://www.chesapk.com/mfgjobs.html. Provides links
to sites that post job openings in manufacturing.

MANUFACTURING: MISCELLANEOUS INDUSTRIAL

Industrial manufacturing is rising at a surprising rate in an attempt to keep up with foreign demand which has been strengthened by improving growth abroad. Industrial production in January 1997 rose 4.7 percent from the previous year, while the output of business equipment rose 0.8 percent. According to Business Week, *industrial machinery has seen the greatest increase in amount of exports,* specifically to South America and Mexico.

However, rising productivity and a strong economy are not indicative of an increase in jobs. Manufacturers are choosing to put money into technology rather than an increased workforce. On the whole, employment in industrial manufacturing is on the decline, as the national economy continues to shift its focus from producing goods to providing services. Companies that specialize in equipment for thriving industries, such as health care and construction, will show the most gains in the future.

ABCO INDUSTRIES INC.
P.O. Box 268, Abilene TX 79604. 915/677-2011. **Contact:** Charlotte Murch, Personnel. **World Wide Web address:** http://www.abcoboilers.com. **Description:** Manufactures industrial boilers.

AIR SYSTEM COMPONENTS (ASC)
800 Airport Road, Terrell TX 75160. 972/563-2605. **Contact:** Human Resources. **Description:** Manufactures air system registers, grills, and diffusers. **Corporate headquarters location:** Richardson TX. **Parent company:** Tomkins Industries. **Listed on:** New York Stock Exchange. **Number of employees nationwide:** 1,600.

BOOTH CRYSTAL TIPS
2007 Royal Lane, Dallas TX 75229. 972/488-1030. **Contact:** Administrative Assistant. **Description:** An industrial manufacturing company specializing in the production of air conditioning and heating systems, as well as soft drink fountain equipment.

THE BRINKMANN CORPORATION
4215 McEwen Road, Dallas TX 75244. 972/387-4939. **Contact:** Milly S. Hall, Executive Vice President. **World Wide Web address:** http://www.thebrinkmanncorp.com. **Description:** A diversified manufacturer producing items such as meat smokers, spotlights, and metal detectors. **Common positions include:** Accountant/Auditor; Advertising Clerk; Blue-Collar Worker Supervisor; Computer Programmer; Credit Manager; Customer Service Representative; Financial Analyst; Human Resources Manager; Manufacturer's/Wholesaler's Sales Rep.; Mechanical Engineer; Operations/Production Manager; Purchasing Agent/Manager; Systems Analyst; Transportation/Traffic Specialist. **Educational backgrounds include:** Accounting; Business Administration; Engineering; Finance; Marketing. **Benefits:** Employee Discounts; Life Insurance; Medical Insurance. **Corporate headquarters location:** This Location. **Operations at this facility include:** Manufacturing; Regional Headquarters; Sales.

CENTERCORE SYSTEMS
8700 West Royal Lane, Irving TX 75063. 972/915-6822. **Contact:** Human Resources. **World Wide Web address:** http://www.centercore.com. **Description:** A manufacturer of wooden office furniture.

CONVEYORS, INC.
P.O. Box 50817, Fort Worth TX 76105. 817/477-3155. **Contact:** Human Resources Department. **Description:** Specializes in the manufacture and retail of conveyors and conveyor-related equipment.

DANA CORPORATION/LANCASTER HYDRAULICS PLANT
FLUID DRIVES DIVISION
600 West Beltline Road, Lancaster TX 75146-3019. 972/218-3100. **Contact:** Personnel. **Description:** This location manufactures hydraulic cylinders (rod cylinders and telescopic cylinders) for dump trucks; dump trailers; and construction, mining, and material equipment. Overall, Dana Corporation is a global leader in engineering, manufacturing, and marketing products and systems for the worldwide vehicular, industrial, and mobile off-highway original equipment markets and is a major supplier to the related aftermarkets. Dana is also a leading provider of lease financing services in selected markets. The company's products include drivetrain components, such as axles, driveshafts, clutches, and transmissions; engine parts, such as gaskets, piston rings, seals, pistons, and filters; chassis products, such as vehicular frames and cradles and heavy-duty side rails; fluid power components, such as pumps, motors, and control valves; and industrial products, such as electrical and mechanical brakes and clutches, drives, and motion control devices. Dana's vehicular components and parts are used on automobiles, pickup trucks, vans, minivans, sport utility vehicles, medium and heavy trucks, and off-highway vehicles. The company's industrial products include mobile off-highway and stationary equipment applications. Dana Corporation has approximately 700 facilities in 27 countries. Founded in 1905. **Common positions include:** Accountant/Auditor; Blue-Collar Worker Supervisor; Buyer; Customer Service Representative; Department Manager; Design Engineer; Draftsperson; Industrial Engineer; Manufacturer's/Wholesaler's Sales Rep.; Mechanical Engineer; Operations/Production Manager; Quality Control Supervisor. **Educational backgrounds include:** Accounting; Business Administration; Computer Science; Engineering. **Benefits:** Dental Insurance; Disability Coverage; Life Insurance; Medical Insurance; Pension Plan; Retirement Plan; Savings Plan; Stock Option; Tuition Assistance. **Corporate headquarters location:** Toledo OH. **Operations at this facility include:** Administration; Manufacturing. **Listed on:** New York Stock Exchange. **Number of employees worldwide:** 55,000.

DRY MANUFACTURING
P.O. Box 427, Winters TX 79567-0427. 915/754-4571. **Contact:** Human Resources. **Description:** A manufacturer of grilles and registers for duct and air systems. **Corporate headquarters location:** Dallas TX. **Parent company:** Eljer Industries Inc., through its subsidiaries, is a leading manufacturer of building products for residential construction, commercial construction, and repair and remodeling markets. Eljer Industries Inc. manufactures and markets plumbing, heating, ventilating, and air conditioning (HVAC) products in North America. The company markets its products through wholesale distribution channels and, in North America, directly to building products retailers. In North America, Eljer Industries Inc. is one of only a few full line suppliers of bath and kitchen fixtures and faucets. In Europe, the company is a leading manufacturer of prefabricated chimneys and venting systems.

EAGLE-PICHER INDUSTRIES, INC.
1802 East 50th Street, Lubbock TX 79404. 806/747-4663. **Contact:** Human Resources Department. **World Wide Web address:** http://www.epcorp.com. **Description:** Manufactures and distributes Caterpillar-brand industrial machinery and equipment. **Corporate headquarters location:** Cincinnati OH. **Other U.S. locations:** Nationwide. **Number of employees at this location:** 460.

FERGUSON MANUFACTURING AND EQUIPMENT
4900 Harry Hines Boulevard, Dallas TX 75235. 214/631-3000. **Contact:** Personnel. **Description:** Manufactures and distributes construction machines and equipment.

FISHER CONTROLS INTERNATIONAL
310 East University, McKinney TX 75069. 972/542-5512. **Contact:** Human Resources. **Description:** Manufactures gas pressure regulators.

FLOWSERVE CORPORATION
222 West Las Colinas Boulevard, Suite 1500, Irving TX 75039. 972/443-6500. **Contact:** Human Resources. **World Wide Web address:** http://www.flowserve.com. **Description:** Manufactures valves for the chemical and petroleum industries. **Corporate headquarters location:** This Location.

FORNEY CORPORATION
3405 Wiley Post Road, Carrollton TX 75006. 972/458-6100. **Contact:** Personnel. **Description:** Manufactures industrial boiler burners, and burner and process control equipment and systems. **Common positions include:** Accountant/Auditor; Designer; Draftsperson; Electrical/Electronics Engineer; Mechanical Engineer. **Educational backgrounds include:** Accounting; Engineering; Finance. **Benefits:** 401(k); Dental Insurance; Disability Coverage; Life Insurance; Medical Insurance; Tuition Assistance. **Parent company:** Kidde International, Inc. **Operations at this facility include:** Divisional Headquarters. **Number of employees at this location:** 320.

GNB TECHNOLOGIES INC.
P.O. Box 819023, Dallas TX 75381-9023. 972/243-1011. **Contact:** Calvin Wright, Regional Human Resources Manager. **Description:** This location manufactures batteries for automobiles, trucks, farm equipment, and industrial uses. Overall, GNB Technologies has three divisions: Automotive Battery, Industrial Battery, and Resource Recycling, with primary operations in North America. **Common positions include:** Environmental Engineer; Human Resources Manager; Industrial Engineer; Quality Control Supervisor. **Educational backgrounds include:** Business Administration; Chemistry; Engineering. **Benefits:** 401(k); Dental Insurance; Disability Coverage; Life Insurance; Medical Insurance; Pension Plan; Profit Sharing; Tuition Assistance. **Operations at this facility include:** Manufacturing. **Number of employees at this location:** 350.

HOBART CORPORATION
8120 Jetstar Drive, Suite 100, Irving TX 75063. 972/915-3822. **Contact:** Human Resources. **Description:** Manufactures food equipment for restaurants and supermarkets. Products include slicers, mixers, scales, fryers, food cutters, and toasters. **Common positions include:** Accountant/Auditor; Electronics Technician; Manufacturer's/Wholesaler's Sales Rep. **Educational backgrounds include:** Accounting; Marketing. **Corporate headquarters location:** Troy OH. **Parent company:** Premark International. **Operations at this facility include:** Sales; Service.

HUCK INTERNATIONAL
P.O. Box 8117, Waco TX 76714. 254/776-2000. **Contact:** Human Resources. **World Wide Web address:** http://www.huck.com. **Description:** Manufactures industrial fasteners.

INGERSOLL-RAND COMPANY
P.O. Box 462288, Garland TX 75046. 972/495-8181. **Contact:** Human Resources. **World Wide Web address:** http://www.ingersoll-rand.com. **Description:** Manufactures compressors, pumps, and other non-electrical industrial equipment and machinery. Ingersoll-Rand Company's products include air compression systems, antifriction systems, construction equipment, air tools, bearings, locks, tools, and pumps. The company operates 93 production facilities throughout the world.

JOHN DEERE COMPANY
P.O. Box 540598, Dallas TX 75354-0598. 972/385-1701. **Contact:** Human Resources. **World Wide Web address:** http://www.deere.com. **Description:** This office is the agricultural equipment sales office for the region. Overall, John Deere manufactures, distributes, and finances the sale of heavy equipment and machinery for use in the agricultural equipment and industrial equipment industries. The agricultural equipment sector manufactures tractors, soil, seeding, and harvesting equipment. The industrial equipment segment manufactures a variety of earth moving equipment, tractors, loaders, and excavators; while the consumer products division manufactures a variety of tractors and products for the homeowner. Financial services, including personal and commercial lines of insurance, retail, and managed health care services, are also offered.

JOHNSON CONTROLS, INC.
3021 West Bend Drive, Irving TX 75063. 972/869-4494. **Contact:** Human Resources. **World Wide Web address:** http://www.johnsoncontrols.com. **Description:** Manufactures and markets

automobile, marine, and commercial storage batteries for sale to private labels (Interstate, Sears Die Hard, Autozone, Wal-Mart, and others). **Common positions include:** Accountant/Auditor; Blue-Collar Worker Supervisor; Buyer; Customer Service Representative. **Educational backgrounds include:** Accounting; Business Administration; Computer Science; Engineering; Finance. **Benefits:** Dental Insurance; Disability Coverage; Employee Discounts; Life Insurance; Medical Insurance; Pension Plan; Savings Plan; Stock Option; Tuition Assistance. **Corporate headquarters location:** Milwaukee WI. **Operations at this facility include:** Manufacturing; Sales; Service. **Listed on:** New York Stock Exchange. **Number of employees at this location:** 300.

KEVCO
P.O. Box 947015, Fort Worth TX 76147-9015. 817/332-2758. **Contact:** Human Resources. **Description:** A group of nationwide manufacturing and distribution companies supplying a wide array of products used in the production of manufactured housing, modular housing, and RVs.

MADIX INC.
P.O. Box 729, Terrell TX 75160-0729. 972/524-5744. **Contact:** Human Resources. **World Wide Web address:** http://www.madix.com. **Description:** A manufacturer of store fixtures such as grocery store shelving.

MARTIN SPROCKET & GEAR INC.
P.O. Box 91588, Arlington TX 76015. 817/467-5181. **Contact:** Guy Young, Personnel Manager. **Description:** Manufactures chain sprockets and gears. **Corporate headquarters location:** This Location. **Other U.S. locations:** Nationwide. **Listed on:** Privately held. **Number of employees nationwide:** 1,200.

MARTIN SPROCKET & GEAR INC.
P.O. Box 1038, Fort Worth TX 76110. 817/924-4255. **Contact:** Jeffrey V. Hatley, Personnel Manager. **Description:** Manufactures, installs, and services conveyor equipment. **Common positions include:** Accountant/Auditor; Administrative Manager; Blue-Collar Worker Supervisor; Branch Manager; Buyer; Computer Programmer; Designer; Draftsperson; Electrician; Financial Analyst; General Manager; Human Resources Manager; Management Trainee; Manufacturer's/Wholesaler's Sales Rep.; Medical Records Technician; Operations/Production Manager; Purchasing Agent/Manager; Transportation/Traffic Specialist. **Educational backgrounds include:** Business Administration. **Benefits:** 401(k); Dental Insurance; Disability Coverage; Employee Discounts; Life Insurance; Medical Insurance; Pension Plan; Profit Sharing; Tuition Assistance. **Corporate headquarters location:** Arlington TX. **Other U.S. locations:** Nationwide. **Operations at this facility include:** Administration; Manufacturing; Sales; Service. **Listed on:** Privately held. **Number of employees at this location:** 400. **Number of employees nationwide:** 1,200.

MILLIPORE SPAN TYLON
2201 Avenue K, Plano TX 75074. 972/423-5320. **Contact:** Human Resources. **World Wide Web address:** http://www.millipore.com. **Description:** Manufactures pressure gauges used by pharmaceutical, agricultural, and oil and gas companies.

NCH CORPORATION
P.O. Box 152170, Irving TX 75015-2170. 972/438-0211. **Physical address:** 2727 Chensearch Boulevard, Irving TX 75062. **Contact:** Human Resources Department. **Description:** NCH Corporation is a diverse chemical and construction products company. Chemical products include paints, varnishes, lacquers, and enamels for institutional, government, and industrial markets. Retail chemical products include deodorizers and stain removers. NCH Corporation also manufactures fasteners, welding supplies, electrical components, plumbing components, and safety products. Subsidiaries are located in Canada, Europe, Latin America, and the Far East. **Corporate headquarters location:** This Location. **Listed on:** New York Stock Exchange.

PVI INDUSTRIES INC.
P.O. Box 7124, Fort Worth TX 76111. 817/335-9531. **Contact:** Personnel. **Description:** A manufacturer of commercial water heaters and boilers.

PARKER-HANNIFIN CORPORATION
STRATOFLEX AEROSPACE/MILITARY CONNECTORS DIVISION
P.O. Box 10398, Fort Worth TX 76114. 817/738-6543. **Fax:** 817/738-0598. **Contact:** Human Resources. **World Wide Web address:** http://www.parker.com. **Description:** A manufacturer of hose fittings and hose assemblies for the aerospace, military, and marine markets. Overall, the company makes motion control products, including fluid power systems, electromechanical controls, and related components. Products are sold through direct sales employees and more than 4,900 distributors. The Motion and Control Group makes hydraulic pumps, power units, control valves, accumulators, cylinders, actuators, and automation devices to remove contaminants from air, fuel, oil, water, and other fluids. The Fluid Connectors Group makes connectors, tube and hose fittings, hoses, and couplers which transmit fluid. The Seal Group makes sealing devices, gaskets, and packing materials which insure leak-proof connections. The Automotive and Refrigeration Groups make components for use in industrial and automotive air conditioning and refrigeration systems. **Common positions include:** Account Representative; Accountant; Blue-Collar Worker Supervisor; Buyer; Computer Programmer; Customer Service Representative; Draftsperson; Electrician; Human Resources Manager; Industrial Engineer; Manufacturing Engineer; Marketing Specialist; Mechanical Engineer; MIS Specialist; Operations/Production Manager; Quality Control Supervisor; Secretary; Systems Analyst. **Educational backgrounds include:** Business Administration; Engineering. **Benefits:** Dental Insurance; Disability Coverage; Life Insurance; Medical Insurance; Pension Plan; Profit Sharing; Savings Plan; Tuition Assistance. **Corporate headquarters location:** Cleveland OH. **Listed on:** New York Stock Exchange. **Number of employees at this location:** 425. **Number of projected hires for 1998 - 1999 at this location:** 50.

PERRY EQUIPMENT CORPORATION
P.O. Box 640, Mineral Wells TX 76068-0640. 940/325-2575. **Contact:** Doug Harcourt, Vice President/Human Resources. **Description:** Perry Equipment Corporation produces filtration separation cartridges, flow-measurement systems, and systems for the oil, gas, and chemical processing industries. **Common positions include:** Accountant/Auditor; Blue-Collar Worker Supervisor; Buyer; Chemical Engineer; Computer Programmer; Customer Service Representative; Designer; Draftsperson; Electrical/Electronics Engineer; General Manager; Industrial Engineer; Industrial Production Manager; Manufacturer's/Wholesaler's Sales Rep.; Mechanical Engineer; Operations/Production Manager; Purchasing Agent/Manager; Quality Control Supervisor; Systems Analyst; Transportation/Traffic Specialist. **Educational backgrounds include:** Accounting; Business Administration; Computer Science; Engineering; Marketing. **Benefits:** Disability Coverage; Life Insurance; Medical Insurance; Pension Plan; Profit Sharing; Tuition Assistance. **Corporate headquarters location:** This Location. **Other U.S. locations:** Amarillo TX; Houston TX. **Operations at this facility include:** Administration; Divisional Headquarters; Manufacturing; Regional Headquarters; Research and Development; Sales; Service. **Listed on:** Privately held. **Number of employees at this location:** 500.

SIEMENS ELECTROCOM L.P.
2910 Avenue F East, Arlington TX 76011-5276. 817/640-5690. **Contact:** Human Resources. **World Wide Web address:** http://www.siemenselectrocom.com. **Description:** Designs, manufactures, integrates, and services high-speed automated document processing, materials handling systems, mobile data and voice communication systems, and products under long-term contracts. Primary customers are the U.S. Postal Service and other government agencies.

STEELCASE INC.
3131 McKinney Avenue, Suite 300, Dallas TX 75204-2442. 214/871-3044. **Contact:** Human Resources. **World Wide Web address:** http://www.steelcase.com. **Description:** Steelcase Inc. is a manufacturer of metal and wood office furniture.

STEVENS INTERNATIONAL
5500 Airport Freeway, Fort Worth TX 76117-5985. 817/831-3911. **Contact:** Personnel Department. **Description:** Manufactures machinery for the printing industry.

THE TRANE COMPANY
P.O. Box 814609, Dallas TX 75381. 972/406-6000. **Fax:** 972/488-7415. **Contact:** Michele Bomer, Human Resources Representative. **Description:** Engaged in the development, manufacture, and

sale of air conditioning equipment designed for use in central air conditioning systems for commercial, institutional, industrial, and residential buildings. The Trane Company's products are designed to cool water, and to cool, heat, humidify, dehumidify, move, and filter air. Other products include similar systems for buses and rapid transit vehicles, refrigeration equipment for trucks, and pollution control equipment. **NOTE:** Entry-level positions are offered. **Common positions include:** Administrative Assistant; Credit Manager; Market Research Analyst; Mechanical Engineer; Project Manager; Systems Analyst; Typist/Word Processor. **Educational backgrounds include:** Accounting; Business Administration; Communications; Engineering. **Benefits:** 401(k); Dental Insurance; Disability Coverage; Life Insurance; Medical Insurance. **Special programs:** Apprenticeships; Training. **Corporate headquarters location:** La Crosse WI. **Parent company:** American Standard. **Number of employees at this location:** 200.

TRINITY INDUSTRIES, INC.
P.O. Box 568887, Dallas TX 75356-8887. 214/631-4420. **Contact:** Human Resources Department. **World Wide Web address:** http://www.trin.net. **Description:** Manufactures an assortment of railroad and construction equipment and replacement parts. Trinity Industries also offers related services for the transportation, construction, aerospace, commercial, and industrial markets. Products include railcars, gas processing systems, petroleum transportation systems, guard rails, bridge girders and beams, airport boarding bridges, barges, tug boats, military marine vessels, and precision welding products. Trinity Industries also makes concrete and aggregates in Texas and produces metal components for the petrochemical, industrial, processing, and power markets. **Common positions include:** Accountant/Auditor; Data Entry Clerk. **Educational backgrounds include:** Accounting; Business Administration; Computer Science; Engineering. **Benefits:** Daycare Assistance; Disability Coverage; Employee Discounts; Life Insurance; Medical Insurance; Pension Plan; Profit Sharing; Savings Plan; Tuition Assistance. **Corporate headquarters location:** This Location. **Operations at this facility include:** Administration; Sales; Service. **Listed on:** New York Stock Exchange.

TYLER PIPE INDUSTRIES, INC.
P.O. Box 2027, Tyler TX 75710. 903/882-5511. **Contact:** Human Resources. **Description:** Manufactures fabricated pipe and pipe fittings.

UNITED STATES BRASS CORPORATION
P.O. Box 3033, Abilene TX 79604-3033. 915/673-5046. **Contact:** Human Resources. **Description:** This company manufactures various kinds of brass faucets. **Corporate headquarters location:** Dallas TX.

VECTA
1800 South Great SW Parkway, Grand Prairie TX 75051. 972/660-0888. **Contact:** Human Resources. **Description:** Vecta is a manufacturer of custom office furniture.

VIRGINIA KMP CORPORATION
4100 Platinum Way, Dallas TX 75237. 214/330-7731. **Contact:** Vice President of Operations. **Description:** Manufactures and sells chemicals, filter driers, refrigeration accumulators, and air conditioners.

WATSON FOOD SERVICE
5950 Cedar Springs, Suite 125, Dallas TX 75235. 214/350-3561. **Contact:** Personnel. **Description:** A food service equipment manufacturing company that also designs restaurants.

XEROX CORPORATION
1301 Ridgeview Drive, Lewisville TX 75057. 972/830-4000. **Contact:** Human Resources. **World Wide Web address:** http://www.xerox.com. **Description:** This location is a sales and service office. Overall, Xerox is a global company in the document processing market. The company's document processing activities encompass the designing, developing, manufacturing, marketing, and servicing of a complete range of document processing products and systems that make office work more productive. Xerox copiers, duplicators, electronic scanners, facsimile machines, networks, multifunction publishing machines and related products, and software and supplies are marketed in more than 130 countries.

Note: Because addresses and telephone numbers of smaller companies can change rapidly, we recommend you call each company to verify the information below before inquiring about job opportunities. Mass mailings are not recommended.

Additional small employers:

AMMUNITION

Pantex
PO Box 30020, Amarillo TX 79120-0020. 806/477-3000.

COMMERCIAL FURNITURE AND FIXTURES

American Desk Inc.
PO Box 6129, Temple TX 76503-6129. 254/773-1776.

Anderson Hickey Company
PO Box 80, Henderson TX 75653-0080. 903/657-9531.

Artco-Bell Corporation
PO Box 608, Temple TX 76503-0608. 254/778-1811.

Contract Network
10390 Brockwood Rd, Dallas TX 75238-1611. 214/340-6400.

Faubion Associates Incorporated
PO Box 150159, Dallas TX 75315-0159. 214/565-1000.

Fixture Concepts
726 E Highway 121, Lewisville TX 75057-4159. 972/420-0955.

Full Vue Display Systems
3300 Enterprise Drive, Rowlett TX 75088-4085. 972/475-2954.

Furniture Contractors Inc.
2000 East Richmond Avenue, Fort Worth TX 76104. 817/531-3682.

Inca Manufacturing Corporation
PO Box 897, Lewisville TX 75067-0897. 972/436-5581.

Rodgers-Wade Manufacturing
PO Box 158, Paris TX 75461-0158. 903/785-1619.

Royal Seating Corp.
PO Box 753, Cameron TX 76520-0753. 254/697-6421.

Smith System Manufacturing
PO Box 860415, Plano TX 75086-0415. 972/424-6591.

Stempel Manufacturing Company
PO Box 9278, Amarillo TX 79105-9278. 806/342-3536.

Superior Chair Craft
1 Industrial Park Rd, Belton TX 76513-1922. 254/939-3517.

Tandy Cabinets
701 N Hampton St, Fort Worth TX 76102-1657. 817/336-1777.

United Interior Resources
8200 Lovett Ave, Dallas TX 75227-4230. 214/381-0101.

Universal Display & Fixtures Co.
613 Easy St, Garland TX 75042-6812. 972/276-8335.

Weber Aircraft Inc.
2000 Weber Dr, Gainesville TX 76240-9699. 940/668-8541.

COMMERCIAL LAUNDRY, DRY-CLEANING, AND PRESSING MACHINES

Washex Machinery Co.
5000 Central Freeway N, Wichita Falls TX 76306-1502. 940/855-3990.

CONSTRUCTION MACHINERY AND EQUIPMENT

Brown & Root Inc.
3120 S Precinct Line Rd, Hurst TX 76053-7615. 817/280-0502.

Condor
PO Box 21447, Waco TX 76702-1447. 254/666-4545.

Trencor Inc.
1400 E Highway 26, Grapevine TX 76051-3713. 817/424-1968.

CONVEYORS AND CONVEYING EQUIPMENT

BAE Automated Systems Inc.
PO Box 819002, Dallas TX 75381-9002. 972/245-9411.

KWS Manufacturing Company
PO Box 809, Joshua TX 76058-0809. 817/295-2247.

Metro Automation Inc.
1475 Avenue S, Ste 300, Grand Prairie TX 75050-1207. 972/606-2184.

ENGINE PARTS

Holley Replacement Parts
4001 Surestart Dr, Cooper TX 75432. 903/395-2412.

Precise Hard Chrome
PO Box 1067, Temple TX 76503-1067. 254/778-4701.

FABRICATED PIPE AND PIPE FITTINGS

Anvil Products
PO Box 2789, Longview TX 75606-2789. 903/759-4417.

Tube Forming Inc.
1533 Crescent Drive, Carrollton TX 75006-3628. 972/446-3550.

FANS, BLOWERS, AND AIR PURIFICATION EQUIPMENT

Burgess-Manning Inc.
8505 Jacksboro Hwy, Wichita Falls TX 76302-9703. 940/723-4355.

Glassfloss Industries
PO Box 150469, Dallas TX 75315-0469. 214/741-7056.

Precisionaire Inc.
100 Hwy 148 S, Terrell TX 75160. 972/563-1545.

FARM MACHINERY AND EQUIPMENT

Agco Corporation
PO Box 1120, Lockney TX 79241-1120. 806/652-3367.

Big Tex Trailer World Incorporated
Rural Route 6, Box 1369, Mount Pleasant TX 75455-9596. 903/575-0300.

Cantrell International
PO Box 11216, Fort Worth TX 76110-0216. 817/923-7382.

Priefert Manufacturing Co. Inc.
PO Box 1540, Mount Pleasant
TX 75456-1540. 903/572-1741.

INDUSTRIAL AND COMMERCIAL MACHINERY AND EQUIPMENT

Packless Industries
PO Box 20668, Waco TX 76702-0668. 254/666-7700.

SPM
7601 Wyatt Dr, Fort Worth TX
76108-2530. 817/246-2461.

INDUSTRIAL PROCESS FURNACES AND OVENS

Steelman Industries Inc.
PO Box 1461, Kilgore TX 75663-1461. 903/984-3061.

INDUSTRIAL WELDING AND SOLDERING EQUIPMENT

Victor Equipment Company
PO Box 1007, Denton TX 76202-1007. 940/566-2000.

MEASURING AND CONTROLLING EQUIPMENT

Delphi Energy & Engine Management
PO Box 97504, Wichita Falls TX
76307-7504. 940/855-7097.

Ludlum Measurement
PO Box 810, Sweetwater TX
79556-0810. 915/235-4947.

Mactronix Inc.
2050 N Plano Rd, Ste 300,
Richardson TX 75082-4430.
972/690-0028.

MEASURING AND DISPENSING PUMPS

Schlumberger Limited
1300 Bicentennial St, Bonham
TX 75418-2265. 903/583-3134.

METAL HARDWARE

Kwikset Corporation
2600 North Highway 75A,
Denison TX 75020-9042.
903/463-1313.

Progressive Inc.
1030 Commercial Blvd N,
Arlington TX 76001-7119.
817/467-0031.

METALWORKING MACHINERY

Custom Metal Services Inc.
PO Box 8129, Wichita Falls TX
76307-8129. 940/766-4545.

Delta Brands Inc.
2204 Century Center Blvd, Irving
TX 75062-4900. 972/438-7150.

MISC. INDUSTRIAL MACHINE TOOLS

Hughes Christensen Company
1600 S Great Southwest Pk,
Grand Prairie TX 75051-2516.
972/988-2602.

Valenite
RR 2, Box 150, Gainesville TX
76240-9765. 940/665-5501.

MISC. PIPE FITTINGS AND/OR VALVES

Dynamco Inc.
410 Industrial Boulevard,
McKinney TX 75069-7323.
972/548-9961.

Fisher Controls
PO Box 1658, Sherman TX
75091-1658. 903/868-3200.

Fujikoki America Inc.
4040 Bronze Way, Dallas TX
75237-1027. 214/333-4266.

Nordstrom Valves Inc.
PO Box 501, Sulphur Springs TX
75483-0501. 903/885-3151.

Plumb Shop
300 E Pecan St, Lancaster TX
75146-3811. 972/227-5511.

PLUMBING FIXTURE FITTINGS AND TRIM

Dearborn Brass
PO Box 1020, Tyler TX 75710-1020. 903/877-3468.

Weather-Matic
PO Box 180205, Dallas TX
75218-0205. 972/278-6131.

PUMPS AND PUMPING EQUIPMENT

Commercial Pump Service
10717 Harry Hines Blvd, Dallas
TX 75220-1311. 214/357-1320.

Production Oil Tools
PO Box 166469, Irving TX
75016-6469. 972/751-1788.

SERVICE INDUSTRY MACHINERY

Dallas H&K Inc.
PO Box 180729, Dallas TX
75218-0729. 214/821-2740.

TEXTILE MACHINERY

Poser Binder & Index
2621 S Cooper St, Arlington TX
76015-2414. 817/261-6431.

For more information on career opportunities in industrial manufacturing:

Associations

ASSOCIATION FOR MANUFACTURING EXCELLENCE
380 West Palatine Road, Wheeling IL 60090.
847/520-3282. World Wide Web address:
http://www.ame.org.

ASSOCIATION FOR MANUFACTURING TECHNOLOGY
7901 Westpark Drive, McLean VA 22102. 703/893-2900. A trade association. World Wide Web address:
http://www.mfgtech.org.

INSTITUTE OF INDUSTRIAL ENGINEERS
25 Technology Park, Norcross GA 30092-2988.
770/449-0460. World Wide Web address:
http://www.iienet.org. A nonprofit organization with
27,000 members. Conducts seminars and offers
reduced rates on its books and publications.

NATIONAL ASSOCIATION OF MANUFACTURERS
1331 Pennsylvania Avenue NW, Suite 1500,
Washington DC 20004. 202/637-3000. World Wide
Web address: http://www.nam.org. A lobbying
association.

NATIONAL TOOLING AND MACHINING ASSOCIATION
9300 Livingston Road, Fort Washington MD 20744. 301/248-1250. World Wide Web address: http://www.ntma.org. Reports on wages and operating expenses, produces monthly newsletters, and offers legal advice.

PRECISION MACHINED PRODUCTS ASSOCIATION
6700 West Snowville Road, Brecksville OH 44141. 440/526-0300. World Wide Web address: http://www.pmpa.org. Provides resource information.

SOCIETY OF MANUFACTURING ENGINEERS
P.O. Box 930, One SME Drive, Dearborn MI 48121. 313/271-1500. World Wide Web address: http://www.sme.org. Offers educational events and educational materials on manufacturing.

Directories

AMERICAN MANUFACTURER'S DIRECTORY
5711 South 86th Circle, P.O. Box 37347, Omaha NE 68127. 800/555-5211. Made by the same company that created *American Big Business Directory*,

American Manufacturer's Directory lists over 531,000 manufacturing companies of all sizes and industries. The directory contains product and sales information, company size, and a key contact name for each company.

Online Services

CAREER PARK - MANUFACTURING JOBS
http://www.careerpark.com/jobs/manulist.html. This Website provides a list of current job openings in the manufacturing industry. The site is run by Parker Advertising Service, Inc.

MO'S GATEWAY TO MANUFACTURING-RELATED JOBS LISTINGS
http://www.chesapk.com/mfgjobs.html. Provides links to sites that post job openings in manufacturing.

Special Programs

BUREAU OF APPRENTICESHIP AND TRAINING
U.S. Department of Labor, 200 Constitution Avenue NW, Room N4649, Washington DC 20210. 202/219-5921.

MINING/GAS/PETROLEUM/ENERGY RELATED

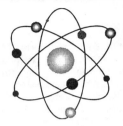

Crude oil prices have fallen 28 percent since October 1997 due to ailing economies in the Far East, mild winters in the U.S. and Europe, and a growing supply. The average price for crude oil was $4 lower in 1997 than 1996 and industry experts expect that to drop another $1 in 1998. The trend is likely to continue with Asia in turmoil and a surplus of everything from heating oil to gasoline. This is good news for consumers who have benefited from lower prices. Business Week *reports that nationwide, the average price of regular unleaded gasoline has dropped to $1.12 per gallon, down more than 8 percent from 1997.*

What does all this mean for the industry as a whole? Analysts expect profits to rise by a mere 5 percent in 1998 (half the rate of 1997). Oil companies are likely to see profits drop by 2 percent. Other sectors will remain steady, specifically service companies and drillers. These companies will continue spending on exploration and production projects, and projections indicate that a majority of gas exploration companies intend to increase domestic spending in 1998.

In other mining sectors, the average price of gold has remained stable in recent years with a slight dip toward the end of 1996 and early 1997. Lime production has been reaching higher levels since 1993 and this growth is predicted through 1998. The coal mining industry has undergone some changes in order to regain profits. Total coal production is expected to rise 1 percent yearly through 2002. Factors that may negatively affect this sector include higher transportation costs, labor disruptions, and government restrictions.

ARCH PETROLEUM INC.
777 Taylor Street, Suite II-A, Fort Worth TX 76102. 817/332-9209. **Toll-free phone:** 800/772-8558. **Contact:** Human Resources. **Description:** Arch Petroleum Inc. is a petroleum and natural gas acquisition and exploration company. **Common positions include:** Accountant/Auditor; Geologist/Geophysicist. **Educational backgrounds include:** Accounting; Geology. **Benefits:** Dental Insurance; Disability Coverage; Life Insurance; Medical Insurance. **Corporate headquarters location:** This Location. **Operations at this facility include:** Administration.

ARCO (ATLANTIC RICHFIELD COMPANY)
2300 West Plano Parkway, Plano TX 75075. **Contact:** Human Resources Department. **Description:** ARCO (Atlantic Richfield Company) is an oil and gas extraction company involved in all phases of the petroleum energy business. The company also manufactures and markets petrochemicals; has interests in coal, copper, molybdenum, and other minerals; and produces a wide range of metal products and solar energy devices. **NOTE:** This firm does not accept unsolicited resumes. Please only respond to advertised openings.

ATMOS ENERGY CORPORATION
P.O. Box 650205, Dallas TX 75265. 972/934-9227. **Recorded jobline:** 972/450-9966. **Contact:** Gary S. Manley, Manager of Compensation & Employment. **Description:** A natural gas distributor. **Common positions include:** Accountant/Auditor; Computer Programmer; Mechanical Engineer; Petroleum Engineer. **Educational backgrounds include:** Accounting; Computer Science; Engineering. **Benefits:** Dental Insurance; Disability Coverage; Life Insurance; Medical Insurance; Pension Plan; Profit Sharing. **Corporate headquarters location:** This Location. **Other U.S.**

locations: CO; KY; LA. **Subsidiaries include:** Energas; Greeley Gas; Trans Louisiana Gas; Western Kentucky Gas. **Operations at this facility include:** Administration. **Listed on:** New York Stock Exchange. **Number of employees at this location:** 200. **Number of employees nationwide:** 1,700.

BRIGGS-WEAVER-VINSON COMPANIES, INC.

3010 LBJ Freeway, Suite 800, Dallas TX 75234. 972/919-5770. **Toll-free phone:** 800/914-8443. **Fax:** 972/919-5781. **Contact:** Don R. Gathright, Vice President, Human Resources. **Description:** A distributor of industrial, marine, oil field tubing and instrumentation to related industries throughout the Southwest. **Common positions include:** Manufacturer's/Wholesaler's Sales Rep. **Educational backgrounds include:** Business Administration; Marketing. **Benefits:** Dental Insurance; Disability Coverage; Employee Discounts; Life Insurance; Medical Insurance; Pension Plan; Profit Sharing; Tuition Assistance. **Corporate headquarters location:** This Location. **Parent company:** Sammons Corporation. **Operations at this facility include:** Administration. **Listed on:** Privately held. **Annual sales/revenues:** More than $100 million. **Number of employees at this location:** 300. **Number of employees nationwide:** 700.

CALTEX PETROLEUM CORPORATION

125 East Carpenter Freeway, Irving TX 75062-2794. 972/830-1000. **Contact:** Professional Recruiter. **Description:** Refines and markets petroleum products. **Common positions include:** Accountant/Auditor; Chemical Engineer; Data Processor; Financial Analyst; Mechanical Engineer.

W.R. CHILDRESS OIL COMPANY

P.O. Box 7496, Fort Worth TX 76111. 817/834-1901. **Contact:** Linda Bookman, Secretary. **Description:** A distributor of petroleum and related products.

CODA ENERGY INC.

5735 Pineland Drive, Suite 300, Dallas TX 75231. 214/692-1800. **Contact:** Personnel. **Description:** A local distributor of petroleum and natural gas.

COMPUTALOG
WIRELINE PRODUCTS, INC.

500 Winscott Road, Fort Worth TX 76126. 817/249-1391. **Fax:** 817/249-7284. **Contact:** Human Resources Manager. **World Wide Web address:** http://www.computalog.com. **Description:** Manufactures, sells, and services oil well equipment for the oil field service industry. **Common positions include:** Accountant; Electrical/Electronics Engineer; Mechanical Engineer; Sales Engineer; Software Engineer. **Educational backgrounds include:** Accounting; Engineering; Geology. **Benefits:** 401(k); Dental Insurance; Disability Coverage; Life Insurance; Medical Insurance; Tuition Assistance. **Office hours:** Monday - Friday, 8:00 a.m. - 5:00 p.m. **Number of employees at this location:** 200. **Number of employees nationwide:** 430.

DIAMOND SHAMROCK, INC.

HCR 1, Box 36, Sunray TX 79086-9705. 806/935-2141. **Contact:** Tonja Bilbrey, Human Resources Director. **Description:** This location is an oil refinery. Overall, Diamond Shamrock is a regional petroleum refining, transporting, and marketing company. The company operates 3,800 miles of pipeline, six terminals, and approximately 2,000 stores in eight southwestern states. Diamond Shamrock is engaged in crude oil refining; wholesale marketing; retail marketing; and the storing, manufacturing, and marketing of gas liquids, petrochemicals, and ammonia fertilizer. The company also operates a credit card program with over 500,000 active accounts. **Corporate headquarters location:** San Antonio TX. **Number of employees at this location:** 400.

DRESSER INDUSTRIES

2001 Ross Avenue, Dallas TX 75201. 214/740-6000. **Contact:** Human Resources. **World Wide Web address:** http://www.dresser.com. **Description:** Supplies engineered products and technical services to energy and natural resources industries throughout the world. Operations are divided into several industry segments: petroleum operations; energy processing and conversion equipment; and industrial specialty products. More than 80 manufacturing plants are located in the United States, Canada, and various foreign countries. **Common positions include:** Accountant/Auditor; Buyer; Chemist; Computer Programmer; Draftsperson; Human Resources

Manager; Industrial Engineer; Mechanical Engineer; Metallurgical Engineer; Purchasing Agent/Manager; Quality Control Supervisor. **Educational backgrounds include:** Business Administration; Chemistry; Computer Science; Engineering. **Benefits:** Credit Union; Dental Insurance; Disability Coverage; Life Insurance; Medical Insurance; Pension Plan; Stock Option; Tuition Assistance. **Corporate headquarters location:** This Location. **Operations at this facility include:** Manufacturing. **Listed on:** New York Stock Exchange.

ENSCO (ENERGY SERVICES COMPANY)
2700 Fountain Place, 1445 Ross Avenue, Dallas TX 75202. 214/922-1500. **Contact:** Human Resources. **World Wide Web address:** http://www.enscous.com. **Description:** ENSCO is an oil and drilling company.

ENSERCH CORPORATION
300 South Saint Paul, Dallas TX 75201. 214/651-8700. **Contact:** Scott Brock, Personnel Director. **Description:** Engaged in all phases of exploration, extraction, production, and processing of oil and natural gas. **Corporate headquarters location:** This Location. **Subsidiaries include:** Pool Company owns and operates specialized drilling equipment at approximately 385 rigs worldwide; Ebasco Services provides engineering and consulting services; Lone Star Gas Company provides natural gas service to 1.2 million customers in Texas and southern Oklahoma.

EXXON CORPORATION
5959 Las Colinas Boulevard, Irving TX 75039-2298. 972/444-1000. **Fax:** 972/444-1348. **Contact:** Human Resources. **World Wide Web address:** http://www.exxon.com. **Description:** An integrated petroleum, natural gas, and chemical company with large coal and mineral holdings. Exxon Corporation is engaged in the production, marketing, refining, and distribution of chemicals, oil, coal, and other energy products. **Corporate headquarters location:** This Location. **Listed on:** New York Stock Exchange.

FINA INC.
8350 North Central Expressway, Dallas TX 75206. 214/750-2400. **Contact:** Human Resources. **World Wide Web address:** http://www.fina.com. **Description:** Explores for crude oil and natural gas; markets natural gas; refines, supplies, transports, and markets petroleum products; manufactures and markets specialty chemicals, primarily petrochemicals and plastics, including polypropylene, polystyrene, styrene monomer, high-density polyethylene, and aromatics; licenses certain chemical processes; and manufactures and markets paints and coatings. **Corporate headquarters location:** This Location.

GAS EQUIPMENT COMPANY
11616 Harry Hines Boulevard, Dallas TX 75229. 972/241-2333. **Contact:** Human Resources Department. **Description:** A wholesale distributor of LP (liquefied petroleum) gas products. **Common positions include:** Administrative Manager; Manufacturer's/Wholesaler's Sales Rep. **Educational backgrounds include:** Marketing. **Benefits:** 401(k); Dental Insurance; Disability Coverage; Employee Discounts; Life Insurance; Mass Transit Available; Medical Insurance; Pension Plan; Savings Plan; Tuition Assistance. **Corporate headquarters location:** This Location. **Operations at this facility include:** Regional Headquarters; Sales; Service. **Listed on:** Privately held. **Annual sales/revenues:** $21 - $50 million. **Number of employees at this location:** 30. **Number of employees nationwide:** 75.

GEER TANK TRUCKS INC.
P.O. Drawer J, Jacksboro TX 76458. 940/567-2677. **Contact:** Human Resources. **Description:** Geer Tank Trucks Inc. is a crude oil purchaser. The company also hauls various substances including oil and saltwater.

HALLIBURTON ENERGY SERVICES, INC.
P.O. Box 1936, Fort Worth TX 76101. 817/293-1300. **Contact:** Human Resources Manager. **World Wide Web address:** http://www.halliburton.com. **Description:** Provides evaluation services in connection with the drilling and completion of gas and oil wells and manufactures and sells the equipment and supplies required to perform well evaluation services. **Common positions include:** Accountant/Auditor; Architect; Blue-Collar Worker Supervisor; Budget Analyst; Buyer;

Chemist; Computer Programmer; Customer Service Representative; Draftsperson; Electrical/Electronics Engineer; Electrician; Environmental Engineer; General Manager; Geologist/Geophysicist; Human Resources Manager; Industrial Engineer; Industrial Production Manager; Materials Engineer; Mechanical Engineer; Operations/Production Manager; Petroleum Engineer; Production Manager; Property and Real Estate Manager; Purchasing Agent/Manager; Quality Control Supervisor; Registered Nurse; Systems Analyst. **Educational backgrounds include:** Business Administration; Engineering. **Benefits:** 401(k); Dental Insurance; Disability Coverage; Employee Discounts; Life Insurance; Medical Insurance; Pension Plan; Profit Sharing; Savings Plan; Tuition Assistance. **Special programs:** Internships. **Other U.S. locations:** Nationwide. **Subsidiaries include:** Brown & Root. **Parent company:** Halliburton Company. **Operations at this facility include:** Administration; Manufacturing; Sales; Service. **Listed on:** New York Stock Exchange. **Number of employees at this location:** 450.

HARBISON-FISCHER MANUFACTURING INC.
P.O. Box 2477, Fort Worth TX 76113-2477. 817/297-2211. **Fax:** 817/297-2178. **Contact:** Leon Gregory, Personnel Director. **Description:** Manufactures subsurface oil well pumping equipment. **Common positions include:** Accountant/Auditor; Blue-Collar Worker Supervisor; Buyer; Claim Representative; Clerical Supervisor; Computer Programmer; Designer; Draftsperson; Electrician; General Manager; Human Resources Manager; Management Trainee; Metallurgical Engineer; Petroleum Engineer; Systems Analyst. **Educational backgrounds include:** Accounting; Business Administration; Engineering. **Benefits:** Bonus Award/Plan; Dental Insurance; Disability Coverage; Life Insurance; Medical Insurance; Pension Plan; Savings Plan; Tuition Assistance. **Corporate headquarters location:** This Location. **Other U.S. locations:** Eugene OR; Odessa TX; Whitehouse TX. **Subsidiaries include:** Challenger Tank (Whitehouse TX); National Steelcrafters (Eugene OR). **Operations at this facility include:** Administration; Divisional Headquarters; Manufacturing; Regional Headquarters; Research and Development; Sales; Service. **Number of employees at this location:** 270. **Number of employees nationwide:** 500.

HOLLY CORPORATION
100 Crescent Court, Suite 1600, Dallas TX 75201-6927. 214/871-3555. **Contact:** Human Resources. **Description:** Holly Corporation is engaged in the refining and marketing of petroleum products through its subsidiaries, Navaho Refining Company (Artesia NM) and Montana Refining Company (Great Falls MT). The company also operates a jet fuel terminal in Idaho for the U.S. government. **Listed on:** American Stock Exchange. **Number of employees at this location:** 440.

HUNT OIL COMPANY
1445 Ross Avenue, Dallas TX 75202. 214/978-8022. **Fax:** 214/978-8911. **Contact:** Diane E. Brown, Personnel. **Description:** A petroleum and natural gas refinery and distributor. **Common positions include:** Accountant/Auditor; Clerical Supervisor; Computer Programmer; Draftsperson; Environmental Engineer; Financial Analyst; General Manager; Geologist/Geophysicist; Human Resources Manager; Paralegal; Petroleum Engineer; Purchasing Agent/Manager. **Educational backgrounds include:** Accounting; Business Administration; Computer Science; Engineering; Finance; Geology. **Benefits:** 401(k); Dental Insurance; Disability Coverage; Life Insurance; Medical Insurance; Pension Plan; Tuition Assistance. **Special programs:** Internships. **Corporate headquarters location:** This Location. **Operations at this facility include:** Administration. **Listed on:** Privately held. **Number of employees at this location:** 600.

IRI INTERNATIONAL COMPANY
P.O. Box 1101, Pampa TX 79065. 806/665-3701. **Fax:** 806/665-3216. **Contact:** Les Howard, Vice President of Human Resources. **Description:** Designs and manufactures a complete line of oil and gas drilling and workover rigs, together with related equipment and accessories. Through its specialty steel division, the company produces a wide array of alloy steel forging and bar stock for use in industries ranging from aerospace to nuclear energy. Founded in 1925. **Common positions include:** Account Manager; Accountant; Civil Engineer; Computer Programmer; Controller; Design Engineer; Draftsperson; Electrician; Human Resources Manager; Industrial Engineer; Metallurgical Engineer; Purchasing Agent/Manager; Quality Control Supervisor; Sales Manager. **Educational backgrounds include:** Accounting; Engineering. **Benefits:** 401(k); Dental Insurance; Disability Coverage; Life Insurance; Medical Insurance; Profit Sharing; Tuition Assistance. **Corporate headquarters location:** This Location. **Other U.S. locations:** Alice TX; Beaumont

TX; Houston TX; Odessa TX. **International locations:** Moscow, Russia; United Kingdom. **Operations at this facility include:** Administration; Manufacturing; Research and Development; Sales; Service. **Listed on:** New York Stock Exchange. **Annual sales/revenues:** More than $100 million. **Number of employees at this location:** 400. **Number of employees nationwide:** 600. **Number of projected hires for 1998 - 1999 at this location:** 10.

KANEB PIPE LINE PARTNERS

2435 North Central Expressway, Suite 700, Richardson TX 75080. 972/699-4000. **Contact:** Human Resources. **Description:** Kaneb Pipe Line Partners is a holding company specializing in industrial services and whose subsidiaries deal with refined petroleum products. **Corporate headquarters location:** This Location. **Listed on:** New York Stock Exchange.

LA GLORIA OIL AND GAS COMPANY

P.O. Box 840, Tyler TX 75710. 903/535-2200. **Contact:** Human Resources. **Description:** A wholesaler of petroleum products.

MAGUIRE OIL COMPANY

1201 Elm Street, Suite 4000, Dallas TX 75250. 214/741-5137. **Contact:** Vicki Snider, Personnel Manager. **Description:** A petroleum and natural gas producing and exploring company. **Common positions include:** Accountant/Auditor; Administrator; Geologist/Geophysicist; Petroleum Engineer. **Benefits:** Dental Insurance; Disability Coverage; Life Insurance; Medical Insurance; Profit Sharing; Tuition Assistance. **Corporate headquarters location:** This Location.

MAXUS ENERGY CORPORATION

717 North Harwood Street, Dallas TX 75201. 214/953-2000. **Contact:** Director of Human Resources. **Description:** A crude oil and natural gas exploration and production company. Most oil production operations are located in Indonesia. Gas production is conducted primarily in Texas, Oklahoma, and the Gulf of Mexico. **Common positions include:** Accountant/Auditor; Computer Programmer; Geologist/Geophysicist; Petroleum Engineer; Systems Analyst. **Educational backgrounds include:** Accounting; Business Administration; Computer Science; Engineering; Geology. **Benefits:** 401(k); Dental Insurance; Disability Coverage; Life Insurance; Medical Insurance; Pension Plan; Tuition Assistance. **Corporate headquarters location:** This Location. **Listed on:** New York Stock Exchange. **Number of employees at this location:** 300.

MERIDIAN OIL INC.

801 Cherry Street, Suite 700, Fort Worth TX 76102. 817/347-2542. **Fax:** 817/347-2263. **Contact:** Linda Harris, Senior Human Resources Representative. **Description:** A petroleum and natural gas exploration and production company. **Common positions include:** Accountant/Auditor; Administrative Manager; Architect; Assistant Manager; Blue-Collar Worker Supervisor; Chemical Engineer; Civil Engineer; Claim Representative; Clerical Supervisor; Computer Operator; Computer Programmer; Construction and Building Inspector; Construction Contractor; Credit Manager; Dispatcher; Draftsperson; Emergency Medical Technician; Employment Interviewer; Financial Analyst; General Manager; Geographer; Geologist/Geophysicist; Human Service Worker; Industrial Engineer; Interviewing Clerk; Mechanical Engineer; Metallurgical Engineer; Mining Engineer; New Accounts Clerk; Payroll Clerk; Petroleum Engineer; Postal Clerk/Mail Carrier; Public Relations Specialist; Purchasing Agent/Manager; Receptionist; Secretary; Software Engineer; Systems Analyst; Typist/Word Processor; Underwriter/Assistant Underwriter; Welder. **Educational backgrounds include:** Accounting; Biology; Business Administration; Communications; Computer Science; Economics; Engineering; Finance; Geology; Marketing; Mathematics; Physics. **Benefits:** Daycare Assistance; Dental Insurance; Disability Coverage; Life Insurance; Medical Insurance; Pension Plan; Savings Plan; Tuition Assistance. **Corporate headquarters location:** Houston TX. **Other U.S. locations:** Denver CO; Farmington NM; Midland TX. **Number of employees at this location:** 450. **Number of employees nationwide:** 2,000.

MOBIL OIL CORPORATION

P.O. Box 819047, Dallas TX 75381. 972/851-8111. **Physical address:** 13777 Midway Road, Dallas TX. **Contact:** Human Resources Department. **World Wide Web address:** http://www.mobil.com. **Description:** This location is a research facility. Overall, Mobil Oil

Corporation is an integrated oil company engaged in petroleum and chemical products marketing, refining, manufacturing, exploration, production, transportation, and research and development in more than 100 countries. Exploration is conducted in 34 countries. The company has interests in 21 refineries in 12 countries, owns 28 oil tankers, and has interests in over 36,000 miles of pipeline worldwide. Mobil markets its products through more than 19,000 company owned retail outlets in over 90 countries. Other products include fabricated plastics, films, food bags, houseware, garbage bags, and building materials. **Common positions include:** Chemical Engineer; Civil Engineer; Geologist/Geophysicist; Metallurgical Engineer; Petroleum Engineer; Science Technologist. **Educational backgrounds include:** Engineering; Geology; Physics. **Corporate headquarters location:** Fairfax VA. **Operations at this facility include:** Research and Development. **Number of employees at this location:** 850. **Number of employees worldwide:** 58,500.

MOBIL OIL CORPORATION
1201 Elm Street, Dallas TX 75270. 214/658-2111. **Contact:** Human Resources. **World Wide Web address:** http://www.mobil.com. **Description:** This location houses administrative offices. Overall, Mobil Oil Corporation is an integrated oil company engaged in petroleum and chemical products marketing, refining, manufacturing, exploration, production, transportation, and research and development in more than 100 countries. Exploration is conducted in 34 countries. The company has interests in 21 refineries in 12 countries, owns 28 oil tankers, and has interests in over 36,000 miles of pipeline worldwide. Mobil markets its products through more than 19,000 company owned retail outlets in over 90 countries. Other products include fabricated plastics, films, food bags, houseware, garbage bags, and building materials. The company also has subsidiaries involved in real estate development and mining operations. **Corporate headquarters location:** Fairfax VA. **Number of employees worldwide:** 58,500.

NORTON DRILLING COMPANY
5211 Brownfield Highway, Suite 230, Lubbock TX 79407. 806/785-8400. **Contact:** Human Resources. **Description:** Owns and operates 13 oil and gas drilling rigs and provides contract drilling services to the oil and gas industry.

ORYX ENERGY COMPANY
P.O. Box 2880, Dallas TX 75221-2880. 972/715-4000. **Contact:** Laura Dronzek, Employment. **Description:** Explores for, acquires, develops, produces, and sells oil and natural gas worldwide. **Common positions include:** Accountant/Auditor; Attorney; Chemist; Computer Programmer; Draftsperson; Electrical/Electronics Engineer; Financial Analyst; Geologist/Geophysicist; Petroleum Engineer; Systems Analyst. **Educational backgrounds include:** Accounting; Computer Science; Engineering; Finance; Geology. **Benefits:** Dental Insurance; Disability Coverage; Life Insurance; Medical Insurance; Pension Plan; Savings Plan; Tuition Assistance. **Corporate headquarters location:** This Location. **International locations:** Algeria; Australia; Ecuador; Indonesia. **Listed on:** New York Stock Exchange.

PATTERSON DRILLING COMPANY, INC.
P.O. Drawer 1416, Snyder TX 79550. 915/573-1104. **Contact:** Human Resources. **Description:** Engaged in onshore drilling for oil and gas, and, to a lesser extent, in the exploration, development, and production of oil and gas. The company's operations are conducted primarily in the Permian Basin in west Texas and southeastern New Mexico, and in south and southeast Texas, primarily in the Austin Chalk Trend. The company has been engaged in the contract drilling business since its inception in 1978 and in the oil and gas exploration, development, and production business since 1982.

PENNZOIL PRODUCTS
900 North Great SW Parkway, Suite 116, Arlington TX 76011. 817/640-1452. **Contact:** Human Resources. **World Wide Web address:** http://www.pennzoil.com. **Description:** A distributor of Pennzoil products.

PHILLIPS COAL COMPANY
2929 North Central Expressway, Richardson TX 75080. 972/669-1200. **Contact:** Human Resources. **Description:** This location houses administrative offices. Overall, Phillips Coal Company is engaged in surface mining.

PIONEER NATURAL RESOURCES
P.O. Box 2009, Amarillo TX 79101. 806/378-1000. **Contact:** Human Resources. **Description:** Pioneer Natural Resources is a petroleum oil and natural gas company specializing in exploration and production. **Listed on:** New York Stock Exchange.

PRIDE COMPANIES, L.P.
P.O. Box 3237, Abilene TX 79604. 915/674-8000. **Contact:** John Pearson, Human Resources. **Description:** A limited partnership that owns and operates a modern simplex petroleum refinery facility; a crude oil gathering system that gathers, transports, resells, and redelivers crude oil; and certain product pipelines.

PRIMROSE OIL COMPANY
P.O. Box 29665, Dallas TX 75229. 972/241-1100. **Contact:** Ryan Miller, Credit Manager. **Description:** An oil refinery and distributor of petroleum products.

QUAKER STATE CORPORATION
225 East John Carpenter Freeway, Irving TX 75062-2732. 972/868-0400. **Contact:** Human Resources Department. **Description:** Produces and markets Quaker State brand lubricants, and sells related petroleum and automotive aftermarket products to distributors and national and regional retailers. The company also packages, sells, and distributes private label lubricants, antifreeze, and greases, and collects and transports used motor oil, brake fluid, antifreeze, and used oil filters. Q-Lube is a fast service automobile oil change and lubrication business operated through company-owned and franchised centers. **Common positions include:** Accountant/Auditor; Attorney; Blue-Collar Worker Supervisor; Branch Manager; Chemist; Computer Programmer; Credit Manager; Customer Service Representative; Economist; Financial Analyst; General Manager; Human Resources Manager; Public Relations Specialist; Purchasing Agent/Manager; Quality Control Supervisor; Systems Analyst. **Educational backgrounds include:** Accounting; Business Administration; Chemistry; Computer Science; Finance; Marketing. **Benefits:** 401(k); Dental Insurance; Disability Coverage; Life Insurance; Medical Insurance; Pension Plan; Profit Sharing; Savings Plan; Tuition Assistance. **Corporate headquarters location:** This Location. **Other U.S. locations:** Nationwide. **Operations at this facility include:** Administration. **Listed on:** New York Stock Exchange. **Number of employees at this location:** 275. **Number of employees nationwide:** 5,400.

REPUBLIC SUPPLY COMPANY
5646 Milton Street, Suite 800, Dallas TX 75206. 214/987-9868. **Contact:** Personnel. **Description:** A distributor of oil field supplies and industrial machine equipment. **Common positions include:** Accountant/Auditor; Clerical Supervisor; Computer Programmer; Cost Estimator; Credit Manager; Manufacturer's/Wholesaler's Sales Rep.; Operations/Production Manager; Purchasing Agent/Manager; Services Sales Representative. **Educational backgrounds include:** Accounting; Business Administration; Computer Science. **Benefits:** Life Insurance; Medical Insurance. **Corporate headquarters location:** This Location. **Operations at this facility include:** Administration; Regional Headquarters. **Listed on:** Privately held. **Number of employees at this location:** 30. **Number of employees nationwide:** 170.

SANTA FE INTERNATIONAL CORPORATION
2 Lincoln Centre, 5420 LBJ Freeway, Dallas TX 75240. 972/701-7300. **Contact:** Human Resources. **World Wide Web address:** http://www.sfdrill.com. **Description:** An oil well drilling company.

SOUTHWESTERN PETROLEUM CORPORATION
534 North Main Street, Fort Worth TX 76106. 817/332-2336. **Fax:** 817/877-4047. **Contact:** Human Resources. **World Wide Web address:** http://www.swepcousa.com. **Description:** Manufactures protective coatings and specialty lubricants for the energy industry. **Common positions include:** Chemist; Management Trainee; Manufacturer's/Wholesaler's Sales Rep.; Petroleum Engineer. **Educational backgrounds include:** Business Administration; Marketing. **Benefits:** 401(k); Life Insurance; Medical Insurance. **Corporate headquarters location:** This Location. **Listed on:** Privately held. **Number of employees at this location:** 100.

SUNSHINE MINING AND REFINING COMPANY
5956 Sherry Lane, Suite 1621, Dallas TX 75225. 214/265-1377. **Fax:** 214/265-0324. **Contact:** Human Resources. **World Wide Web address:** http://www.sunshinemining.com. **Description:** A leading supplier of silver to the world market. In addition to refining its own silver concentrates, the company refines silver-bearing concentrates, emulsions, and ashes for various customers. The company's Sunshine Mine is located in Coeur d'Alene ID. **Corporate headquarters location:** Boise ID.

TOREADOR ROYALTY CORPORATION
8117 Preston Road, Suite 530, Dallas TX 75225. 214/369-0080. **Contact:** John McLaughlin, Chairman. **Description:** Holds mineral rights to drilling and refinery oil fields.

TRITON ENERGY CORPORATION
6688 North Central Expressway, Suite 1400, Dallas TX 75206. 214/691-5200. **Contact:** Human Resources. **World Wide Web address:** http://www.tritonenergy.com. **Description:** An international oil and gas exploration company. **Common positions include:** Accountant/Auditor; Administrative Assistant; Chemical Engineer; Computer Programmer; Financial Analyst; Geologist/Geophysicist. **Educational backgrounds include:** Engineering. **Benefits:** 401(k); Dental Insurance; Disability Coverage; Life Insurance; Medical Insurance; Pension Plan; Savings Plan; Tuition Assistance. **Special programs:** Internships. **Corporate headquarters location:** This Location. **International locations:** Argentina; China; Colombia; Ecuador; Guatemala; Indonesia; Italy; Malaysia; Thailand. **Operations at this facility include:** Administration. **Listed on:** New York Stock Exchange.

UNION PACIFIC RESOURCES
P.O. Box 7, Fort Worth TX 76101. 817/877-6000. **Physical address:** 801 Cherry Street, Fort Worth TX 76102. **Contact:** Human Resources. **Description:** Engaged in oil, gas, and mineral exploration and production.

VAREL MANUFACTURING COMPANY
P.O. Box 540157, Dallas TX 75354. 214/351-6487. **Contact:** Personnel Director. **Description:** Manufactures mining and oil well drilling bits and equipment and tungsten carbide products. **Corporate headquarters location:** This Location.

Note: Because addresses and telephone numbers of smaller companies can change rapidly, we recommend you call each company to verify the information below before inquiring about job opportunities. Mass mailings are not recommended.

Additional small employers:

COAL MINING

Maxim/Southwestern
PO Box 224227, Dallas TX 75222-4227. 214/631-2700.

Monticello Mine
PO Box 1636, Mount Pleasant TX 75456-1636. 903/524-3461.

Northwestern Resources Co.
PO Box 915, Jewett TX 75846-0915. 903/626-5485.

COAL MINING SERVICES

Sabine Mining Company
PO Box 659, Hallsville TX 75650-0659. 903/660-4200.

DRILLING OIL AND GAS WELLS

Hudson Leonard Drilling Co.
PO Box 1876, Pampa TX 79066-1876. 806/665-1816.

Key Energy Group Inc.
4549 Loop 322, Abilene TX 79602-8041. 915/695-9694.

Martex-Gibson Drilling Company
PO Box 2069, Marshall TX 75671-2069. 903/938-9949.

Ringo Drilling Co.
PO Box 2894, Abilene TX 79604-2894. 915/695-5600.

MINING MACHINERY AND EQUIPMENT

Reedrill Texoma
PO Box 998, Sherman TX 75091-0998. 903/786-2981.

OIL AND GAS FIELD MACHINERY AND EQUIPMENT

Antelope Oil Tool Manufacturing Co.
912 Hood Rd, Mineral Wells TX 76067-9202. 940/325-8989.

Dresser Oil Tool
PO Box 2427, Longview TX 75606-2427. 903/757-6650.

NATCO
PO Box 1072, Electra TX 76360-1072. 940/495-4333.

Tyler Petrofac Inc.
PO Box 131859, Tyler TX 75713-1859. 903/581-8755.

OIL AND GAS FIELD SERVICES

BJ Western
7609 White Settlement Rd, Fort Worth TX 76108-1902. 817/731-5100.

Bonner Hoffman Oil Well Service
PO Box 658, Seminole TX 79360-0658. 915/758-5858.

Brooks Well Servicing
PO Box 1240, Kilgore TX 75663-1240. 903/984-8528.

Burlington Resources
801 Cherry St, Ste 200, Fort Worth TX 76102-6842. 817/261-2227.

Five Star Consolidated
PO Box 1506, Denver City TX 79323-1506. 806/592-3113.

Halliburton Energy Services
300 Kirby, Garland TX 75042. 972/276-8561.

Halliburton Energy Services
2601 E Belt Line Rd, Carrollton TX 75006-5401. 972/418-3020.

Lone Star Pipeline Company
301 S Harwood St, Dallas TX 75201-5601. 214/741-3711.

Longview Inspection
PO Box 8204, Longview TX 75607-8204. 903/753-2375.

Pool Company
404 Ambassador Row, Longview TX 75604-5942. 903/753-7915.

Pride International Inc.
PO Drawer 870, Snyder TX 79550-0870. 915/573-0195.

Sundown Operating Inc.
PO Box 938, Sundown TX 79372-0938. 806/229-6102.

Well-Co
PO Box 631, Brownfield TX 79316-0631. 806/894-5820.

Well-Co
PO Box 1326, Levelland TX 79336-1326. 806/894-4974.

Yale E. Key Inc.
PO Box 861, Lamesa TX 79331-0861. 806/872-8331.

PETROLEUM AND COAL PRODUCTS

Candle Corporation
303 Falvey Ave, Texarkana TX 75501-6620. 903/832-8615.

PETROLEUM AND NATURAL GAS

Amoco Production Company
PO Box 9460, Longview TX 75608-9460. 903/297-4005.

Bass Enterprises Products
201 Main St, Ste 300, Fort Worth TX 76102-3107. 817/390-8400.

Crescendo Resources
112 W 8th Ave, Amarillo TX 79101-2300. 806/371-4625.

Cross Timbers Oil Company
810 Houston St, Ste 2000, Fort Worth TX 76102. 817/870-2800.

Gulf-Petro Trading Company
PO Box 8163, Dallas TX 75205-0163. 214/987-2211.

Hill Development Corporation
3400 Thanksgiving Tower, Dallas TX 75202. 214/922-1000.

Mercury Production Company
1619 Pennsylvania Ave, Fort Worth TX 76104-2030. 817/332-9133.

Midguard Energy Company
112 W 8th Ave, Amarillo TX 79101-2300. 806/371-4400.

North American Gas Corp.
5400 Lyndon B. Johnson Fwy, Dallas TX 75240-1000. 972/701-9106.

Petro-Hunt Corporation
1601 Elm St, Ste 3900, Dallas TX 75201-7201. 214/880-8400.

Phillips Petroleum Company
PO Box 126, Gruver TX 79040-0126. 806/339-3353.

Pioneer Natural Resources
5205 N O'Connor, Ste 1400, Irving TX 75039. 972/444-9001.

Rosewood Corporation
100 Crescent Ct, Suite 1700, Dallas TX 75201-7822. 214/871-8400.

Shell Western E&P Inc.
PO Drawer MM, Denver City TX 79323-1700. 806/592-2193.

Texaco Exploration and Production
PO Box 860, Levelland TX 79336-0860. 806/894-3118.

PETROLEUM AND PETROLEUM PRODUCTS WHOLESALE

Amerada Hess Corporation
PO Box 840, Seminole TX 79360-0840. 915/758-6700.

Nexus Fuels Inc.
6311 N O'Connor Blvd, Irving TX 75039. 972/501-0115.

For more information on career opportunities in the mining, gas, petroleum, and energy industries:

Associations

AMERICAN ASSOCIATION OF PETROLEUM GEOLOGISTS
P.O. Box 979, Tulsa OK 74101. 918/584-2555. World Wide Web address: http://www.geobyte.com. International headquarters for the association of petroleum geologists.

AMERICAN GEOLOGICAL INSTITUTE
4220 King Street, Alexandria VA 22302-1502. 703/379-2480. World Wide Web address: http://www.agiweb.org. Publishes monthly *Geotimes*. Offers job listings. Scholarships available.

AMERICAN NUCLEAR SOCIETY
555 North Kensington Avenue, La Grange Park IL 60526. 708/352-6611. World Wide Web address: http://www.ans.org. Offers educational services.

AMERICAN PETROLEUM INSTITUTE
1220 L Street NW, Suite 900, Washington DC 20005.
202/682-8000. World Wide Web address:
http://www.api.org. A trade association.

GEOLOGICAL SOCIETY OF AMERICA
3300 Penrose Place, P.O. Box 9140, Boulder CO
80301. 303/447-2020. World Wide Web address:
http://www.geosociety.org. Offers sales items and
publications, and conducts society meetings.
Membership is over 17,000.

NUCLEAR ENERGY INSTITUTE
1776 I Street NW, Suite 400, Washington DC 2006-
3708. 202/739-8000. World Wide Web address:
http://www.nei.org. Provides a wide variety of
information on nuclear energy issues and offers
complimentary educational packets for students and
teachers.

**SOCIETY FOR MINING, METALLURGY, AND
EXPLORATION, INC.**
P.O. Box 625002, Littleton CO 80162-5002. 303/973-
9550. World Wide Web address:
http://www.smenet.org.

**SOCIETY OF EXPLORATION
GEOPHYSICISTS**
P.O. Box 702740, Tulsa OK 74170-2740. 918/493-
3516. World Wide Web address: http://www.seg.org.
A membership association offering publications.

SOCIETY OF PETROLEUM ENGINEERS
222 Palisades Creek Drive, Richardson TX 75080.
972/952-9393. World Wide Web address:
http://www.spe.org.

Directories

**BROWN'S DIRECTORY OF NORTH
AMERICAN AND INTERNATIONAL GAS
COMPANIES**
Advanstar Communications, 7500 Old Oak
Boulevard, Cleveland OH 44130. Toll-free phone:

800/225-4569. World Wide Web address:
http://www.advanstar.com.

OIL AND GAS DIRECTORY
Geophysical Directory, Inc., P.O. Box 130508,
Houston TX 77219. 713/529-8789.

Magazines

AMERICAN GAS
American Gas Association, 1515 Wilson Boulevard,
Arlington VA 22209. 703/841-8686.

GAS INDUSTRIES
Gas Industries News, Inc., 6300 North River Road,
Suite 505, Rosemont IL 60018. 847/696-2394.

NATIONAL PETROLEUM NEWS
Adams Business Media, 2101 South Arlington
Heights Road, Suite 150, Arlington Heights IL 60005-
4142. 847/427-9512. World Wide Web address:
http://www.NPN-Net.com.

OIL AND GAS JOURNAL
PennWell Publishing Company, 1421 South Sheridan
Road, P.O. Box 74112, Tulsa OK 74101. 918/835-
3161. World Wide Web address:
http://www.ogjonline.com.

Online Services

**NATIONAL CENTRE FOR PETROLEUM
GEOLOGY AND GEOPHYSICS**
http://www.ncpgg.adelaide.edu.au/jobfind.htm. This
Website provides links to sites that post job openings
in mining, petroleum, energy, and related fields.

**PETROLEUM & GEOSYSTEMS
ENGINEERING**
http://www.pe.utexas.edu/dept/reading/pejb.html.
Offers a vast list of links to sites that are posting
current job openings in petroleum and geosystems
engineering and related fields. Links to many relevant
associations are also offered. The site is run by the
University of Texas at Austin.

PAPER AND WOOD PRODUCTS

 *Despite an increased demand for U.S. market pulp, employment growth in this sector should be relatively sluggish. According to the U.S. Department of Commerce, while the pulp sector is expected to enjoy higher sales through the year 2002, overseas shipment growth should be slower, at 1.8 percent annually.*

Newsprint and writing paper costs have plummeted, but with declining operating costs, paper producers should increase prices in 1998.

A 1998 rebound was forecasted for the paper and paperboard mills sector as global demand increases, and shipments should continue steady annual growth for the next several years. At the same time, shipments of corrugated boxes should be even stronger.

Automation is causing a decline in employment opportunities for precision woodworkers and woodworking machine operators, according to the U.S. Department of Labor. However, woodworkers who specialize in furniture, cabinets, moldings, and fixtures should find more opportunities. A significant upswing in the demand for household furniture should result in improved employment prospects.

ADVANCE EXCELSIOR COMPANY
2704 Dawson Street, Dallas TX 75226. 214/428-2535. **Contact:** Human Resources. **Description:** Manufactures paper and paperboard products.

BATES CONTAINER INC.
P.O. Box 822028, North Richland Hills TX 76182-2028. 817/498-3200. **Contact:** Sally Hackfeld, Personnel Manager. **Description:** A manufacturer and distributor of corrugated containers.

CHAMPION INTERNATIONAL CORPORATION/DAIRY PAK
1901 Windsor Place, Fort Worth TX 76110. 817/926-6661. **Contact:** Personnel Department. **Description:** This location manufactures polyethylene coated milk cartons. Overall, Champion International Corporation manufactures paper, lumber, plywood, and forest products for the printing, construction, and home improvement markets. The company has the capacity to produce 6.2 million tons of paper, board, and market pulp per year. Champion International Corporation owns or controls over five million acres of timberland in the United States. The company's business units include: Printing and Writing Papers; Publication Papers; Newsprint and Kraft; Forest Products; Marketing, which includes nationwide newspapers; Champion Export; and Pulp Sales. The company's paper operations include the production of business papers, coated papers, bleached paperboard, and packaging materials. **Subsidiaries include:** Weldwood of Canada; Champion Papel e Celulose (Brazil). **Listed on:** New York Stock Exchange.

FURMAN LUMBER COMPANY
9708 Skillman, Suite 102, Dallas TX 75243. 214/341-9000. **Contact:** Personnel Director. **World Wide Web address:** http://www.furmanlumber.com. **Description:** A lumber and plywood distributor.

INTERNATIONAL PAPER COMPANY
P.O. Box 870, Texarkana TX 75504-0870. 903/796-7101. **Contact:** Human Resources. **World Wide Web address:** http://www.ipaper.com. **Description:** This location manufactures folding cartons. Overall, International Paper is a manufacturer of pulp and paper, packaging, and wood products as well as a range of specialty products. The company is organized into five business segments: Printing Papers, in which principal products include uncoated papers, coated papers,

bristles, and pulp; Packaging, which includes industrial packaging, consumer packaging, and kraft and specialty papers; Distribution, which includes sales of printing papers, graphic arts equipment and supplies, packaging materials, industrial supplies, and office products; Specialty Products, which includes imaging products, specialty panels, nonwovens, chemicals, and minerals; and Forest Products, including logs and wood products. **Corporate headquarters location:** Purchase NY. **Number of employees worldwide:** 72,500.

JEFFERSON SMURFIT CORPORATION
6701 South Freeway, Fort Worth TX 76134. 817/568-3400. **Contact:** Holly Burch, Personnel. **Description:** This location manufactures corrugated fibreboard boxes. Overall, Jefferson Smurfit Corporation is a national producer of paperboard packaging. The company operates mills that produce a wide variety of forest-based products, including containerboard, boxboard, shipping containers, and recycled cylinder board, as well as facilities that collect and recycle wastepaper. Jefferson Smurfit Corporation also operates converting facilities that produce containers, folding cartons, paper tubes, labels, and flexible packaging, as well as newsprint mills that manufacture cladfood, an exterior panel used by the housing industry. **Other U.S. locations:** Nationwide. **International locations:** Dublin, Ireland. **Subsidiaries include:** CCA Enterprises Inc.; CCA Du Baja California; Container Corporation of American; Corfab, Inc.; Groveton Paper Board, Inc.; JSC Enterprises Inc.; JSC International Sales, Inc.; Jefferson Smurfit Finance Corporation; Packaging Unlimited, Inc.; Smurfit Newsprint Corporation.

MEAD PAPER
5215 North O'Connor Boulevard, Suite 200, Irving TX 75039. 972/868-9060. **Contact:** Human Resources. **World Wide Web address:** http://www.mead.com. **Description:** This location is a sales office. Overall, Mead Paper manufactures, sells, and markets pulp, paper, paperboard, shipping containers, packaging, lumber, school supplies, office supplies, stationery products, and electronic publishing and information retrieval systems.

REDI PACKAGING
P.O. Box 210629, Dallas TX 75211. 214/330-9286. **Contact:** Linda Pennington, Personnel Director. **Description:** A manufacturer of corrugated paper products.

SLAUGHTER INDUSTRIES INC.
P.O. Box 551699, Dallas TX 75355-1699. 214/342-4900. **Contact:** Personnel Department. **Description:** A lumber and plywood distributor. **Corporate headquarters location:** Memphis TN. **Parent company:** International Paper Company (Purchase NY). **Operations at this facility include:** Sales. **Listed on:** New York Stock Exchange. **Number of employees at this location:** 65.

TRIANGLE PACIFIC CORPORATION
16803 Dallas Parkway, Dallas TX 75248. 972/931-3000. **Contact:** Human Resources. **World Wide Web address:** http://www.trianglepacific.com. **Description:** Manufactures hardwood dimension and flooring.

WILLAMETTE INDUSTRIES, INC.
BUSINESS FORMS DIVISION
8800 Sterling Street, Irving TX 75063. 972/929-8581. **Contact:** Human Resources. **Description:** This location makes computer paper. Overall, Willamette Industries is a diversified, integrated forest products company with 90 plants and mills manufacturing containerboard, bag paper, fine paper, bleached hardwood market pulp, specialty printing papers, corrugated containers, business forms, cut sheet paper, paper bags, inks, lumber, plywood, particleboard, medium-density fiberboard, laminated beams, and value-added wood products. The company owns or controls over 1.2 million acres of forests. **Common positions include:** Accountant/Auditor; Branch Manager; Department Manager; General Manager; Manufacturer's/Wholesaler's Sales Rep. **Educational backgrounds include:** Accounting; Business Administration. **Benefits:** Dental Insurance; Disability Coverage; Life Insurance; Medical Insurance; Pension Plan; Savings Plan; Stock Option; Tuition Assistance. **Corporate headquarters location:** Portland OR. **Other U.S. locations:** Nationwide.

Note: Because addresses and telephone numbers of smaller companies can change rapidly, we recommend you call each company to verify the information below before inquiring about job opportunities. Mass mailings are not recommended.

Additional small employers:

CONVERTED PAPER AND PAPERBOARD PRODUCTS

Ennis Business Forms
PO Drawer D, Wolfe City TX 75496-0190. 903/496-2244.

HFS Holding Corporation
8900 Ambassador Row, Dallas TX 75247-4510. 214/634-8900.

Paragon Trade Brands Inc.
4920 Franklin Ave, Waco TX 76710-6918. 254/776-7570.

DIE-CUT PAPER AND PAPER PRODUCTS

Data Documents Inc.
601 S Interstate Highway, Hutchins TX 75141-9567. 972/225-2361.

Smead Manufacturing Company
PO Box 447, McGregor TX 76657-0447. 254/840-2861.

INDUSTRIAL PAPER AND RELATED PRODUCTS WHOLESALE

Pollock Paper Distributors
PO Box 660005, Dallas TX 75266-0005. 972/263-2126.

LUMBER AND WOOD WHOLESALE

Brandom Kitchens Manufacturing Co.
211 Campus Dr, Keene TX 76059-2340. 817/477-2414.

International Paper Company
PO Box 809024, Dallas TX 75380-9024. 972/934-6000.

International Paper Company
PO Box 460, Henderson TX 75653-0460. 903/657-4575.

Primesource Building Products
1800 John Connally Dr, Carrollton TX 75006-5403. 972/417-1976.

Texas Plywood & Lumber Co.
PO Box 531110, Grand Prairie TX 75053-1110. 972/262-1331.

Universal Forest Products
Hwy 81, Grandview TX 76050. 817/866-3306.

MILLWORK, PLYWOOD, AND STRUCTURAL MEMBERS

Annona Manufacturing Co.
PO Box 287, Annona TX 75550-0287. 903/697-3591.

Atrium Door & Window Co.
PO Box 226957, Dallas TX 75222-6957. 214/634-9663.

Clifton Moulding Corp.
PO Box 77, Clifton TX 76634-0077. 254/675-8641.

Daven Products Company
1000 W Crosby Rd, Ste 120, Carrollton TX 75006-6936. 972/245-5457.

Premdor Corporation
PO Box 1887, Greenville TX 75403-1887. 903/454-9500.

PAPER BAGS

Arrow Industries Flexible Packaging Division
3401 Garden Brook Dr, Dallas TX 75234-2435. 972/620-2902.

Printpack Inc.
PO Box 534030, Grand Prairie TX 75053. 972/641-4421.

Super Sack Manufacturing Co.
PO Box 245, Savoy TX 75479-0245. 903/965-7713.

PAPER MILLS

Corrugated Services Inc.
PO Box 847, Forney TX 75126-0847. 972/552-2267.

Gulf States Paper
PO Box 1129, Waco TX 76703-1129. 254/299-6500.

Rock-Tenn Co.
6702 Highway 66, Greenville TX 75402-5815. 903/455-0147.

Rock-Tenn Co.
PO Box 1291, Dallas TX 75221-1291. 214/941-3400.

Tufco Technologies Inc.
4750 Simonton Rd, Dallas TX 75244-5315. 972/387-0500.

Union Camp Corporation
3100 Jim Christal Rd, Denton TX 76207-2600. 940/566-3254.

PAPERBOARD CONTAINERS AND BOXES

Acco USA Inc.
1346 N Main St, Duncanville TX 75116-2312. 972/298-4225.

Box USA Group Inc.
PO Box 17009, Dallas TX 75217-0009. 972/285-8865.

Bulk-Pack Inc.
1501 Commerce Dr, Denison TX 75020-1903. 903/463-1612.

Central Texas Corrugated Inc.
PO Box 21539, Waco TX 76702-1539. 254/776-6902.

Gaylord Container Corporation
PO Box 38008, Dallas TX 75238-0008. 214/342-7200.

International Paper Company
1655 S I35 E, Carrollton TX 75006-7415. 972/446-9890.

Liberty Carton Co.-Texas Inc.
PO Box 14989, Fort Worth TX 76117-0989. 817/577-6100.

Lux Packaging
9200 Old McGregor Rd, Waco TX 76712. 254/776-8890.

Nekoosa Packaging Corp.
5800 N Interstate Highway, Waxahachie TX 75165-5717. 972/937-8804.

O'Grady Containers
2400 Shamrock Ave, Fort Worth TX 76107-1429. 817/338-4000.

Precision Printing and Packaging
PO Box 1155, Paris TX 75461-1155. 903/785-6411.

Simkins Industries
2801 E Abram St, Arlington TX 76010-1402. 817/633-7311.

Stone Container Corp.
PO Box 534028, Grand Prairie
TX 75053. 972/647-1333.

Stone Container Corp.
PO Box 1356, Tyler TX 75710-
1356. 903/877-3421.

Temple-Inland Inc.
2605 East Belt Line Rd,
Carrollton TX 75006-5444.
972/416-2691.

**Tenneco Packaging
Incorporated**
PO Box 5787, Arlington TX
76005-5787. 817/640-1888.

Waxahachie Folding
6200 N Interstate Highway,
Waxahachie TX 75165-5602.
972/617-0111.

Willamette Industries
PO Box 539501, Grand Prairie
TX 75053-9501. 972/641-3891.

WOOD MILLS

Dean Lumber Co. Inc.
PO Box 610, Gilmer TX 75644-
0610. 903/843-2457.

International Paper Company
PO Box 578, New Boston TX
75570-0578. 903/628-2506.

Snider Industries Inc.
PO Box 668, Marshall TX 75671-
0668. 903/938-9221.

WOOD PALLETS AND SKIDS

Arrington Lumber & Pallet Co.
PO Box 1898, Jacksonville TX
75766-1898. 903/586-4070.

M&H Crates Inc.
RR 7, Box 96, Jacksonville TX
75766-9117. 903/683-5351.

National Pallet Company
PO Box 560041, Dallas TX
75356-0041. 214/688-4108.

For more information on career opportunities in the paper and wood products industries:

Associations

FOREST PRODUCTS SOCIETY
2801 Marshall Court, Madison WI 53705-2295.
608/231-1361. An international, nonprofit,
educational association that provides an information
network for all segments of the forest products
industry, as well as an employment referral service.

NATIONAL PAPER TRADE ASSOCIATION
111 Great Neck Road, Great Neck NY 11021.
516/829-3070. World Wide Web address: http://www.
papertrade.com. Offers management services to paper
wholesalers, as well as books, seminars, and research
services.

PAPERBOARD PACKAGING COUNCIL
201 North Union Street, Suite 220, Alexandria VA
22314. 703/836-3300. Offers statistical and lobbying
services.

**TECHNICAL ASSOCIATION OF THE PULP
AND PAPER INDUSTRY**
P.O. Box 105113, Atlanta GA 30348. 770/446-1400.
World Wide Web address: http://www.tappi.org. A
nonprofit organization offering conferences and
continuing education.

Directories

**DIRECTORY OF THE FOREST PRODUCTS
INDUSTRY**
Miller Freeman Publications, Inc., 600 Harrison
Street, San Francisco CA 94107. 415/905-2200.
World Wide Web address: http://www.mfi.com.

**LOCKWOOD-POST'S DIRECTORY OF THE
PAPER AND ALLIED TRADES**
Miller Freeman Publications, Inc., 600 Harrison
Street, San Francisco CA 94107. 415/905-2200.
World Wide Web address: http://www.mfi.com.

POST'S PULP AND PAPER DIRECTORY
Miller Freeman Publications, Inc., 600 Harrison
Street, San Francisco CA 94107. 415/905-2200.
World Wide Web address: http://www.pulp-
paper.com.

Magazines

PAPERBOARD PACKAGING
Advantstar Communications, 131 West First Street,
Duluth MN 55802. 218/723-9200. World Wide Web
address: http://www.advantstar.com.

PULP AND PAPER WEEK
Miller Freeman Publications, Inc., 600 Harrison
Street, San Francisco CA 94107. 415/905-2200.
World Wide Web address: http://www.mfi.com.

WOOD TECHNOLOGIES
Miller Freeman Publications, Inc., 600 Harrison
Street, San Francisco CA 94107. 415/905-2200.
World Wide Web address:
http://www.woodtechmag.com.

Online Services

**COLE'S PAPER INDUSTRY RECRUITERS,
INC.: HOTTEST JOBS THIS WEEK**
http://www.staffing.net/MI4301/hotjobs.htm. This
Website offers detailed information on the most recent
job openings in the paper industry.

PRINTING AND PUBLISHING

 *Digital technology took the book publishing industry by storm in 1997. New printing production and editorial systems, Web publishing software, and digital color proofs are just a few of the high-tech offerings. At this point, technology is outpacing the industry and analysts think it will be well into 1998 before these new technologies are fully integrated into book publishing.*

A recent survey by Arthur Andersen reveals that 1998 could be another big year for mergers in the industry. Results showed that 79 percent of book publishing executives are considering a merger or acquisition transaction. There are already several well-known companies on the market including Bender, Mosby, Simon & Schuster, and Waverly. According to Publishers Weekly, *many other companies are restructuring and cutting loose smaller divisions that do not fit into their core businesses. The Arthur Andersen survey also indicates that publishers are motivated to agree to these deals in order to broaden product lines and increase market share in the industry. It seems more efficient for publishers to expand through mergers/acquisitions versus international expansion.*

Children's titles are the fastest growing segment of book publishing, with U.S. sales rising 30 percent from 1990 - 1997. According to the Association of American Publishers, the best book sales in 1997 were in education and professional book publishing. Another area that will be looking to expand is travel publishing. The World Tourism Organization predicts that by 2020 travel will be one of the leading industries in the United States. Look for publishers to expand their selections of travel books in an attempt to capture very specific audiences.

Newspaper publishers are on the rebound thanks in large part to lower paper prices, a healthy economy, and online services. MSNBC reports that more than half of the nation's Internet users now regularly obtain news from the World Wide Web and that nearly one-quarter of these individuals use it on a daily basis. Job seekers with Internet experience should look to Web publishing as a career possibility.

Consolidation of magazine wholesalers caused distribution problems in the mid-'90s. As a result, publishers will actively pursue foreign markets such as Asia and Latin America for their wares. Photographic and digital imaging professionals will see little employment growth in 1998.

AMARILLO GLOBE TIMES
P.O. Box 2091, Amarillo TX 79166. 806/376-4488. **Contact:** Human Resources. **World Wide Web address:** http://www.amarillonet.com. **Description:** Publishes morning and afternoon daily papers. The Sunday paper has a circulation of approximately 74,000.

AMERICAN BANK NOTE COMPANY
5307 East Mockingbird Lane, Suite 705, Dallas TX 75206. 214/823-2700. **Fax:** 214/821-9026. **Contact:** Human Resources. **Description:** This location is a national sales office. Overall, the

company is a printer of counterfeit-resistant documents and one of the largest security printers in the world. American Bank Note creates secure documents of value for governments and corporations worldwide. Products include currencies; passports; stock and bond certificates; and bank, corporate, government, and traveler's cheques; food coupons; gift vouchers and certificates; driver's licenses; product authentication labels; and vital documents. **Corporate headquarters location:** New York NY. **Other U.S. locations:** Burbank CA; Long Beach CA; San Francisco CA; Washington DC; Atlanta GA; Bedford Park IL; Needham MA; St. Louis MO; Horsham PA; Huntington Valley PA; Philadelphia PA; Pittsburgh PA. **Parent company:** American Bank Note Corporation also operates two other subsidiaries: American Bank Note Holographics, Inc., one of the world's largest producers of the laser-generated, three-dimensional images that appear on credit cards and products requiring proof of authenticity; and American Bank Note Company Brazil, one of Brazil's largest private security printers and a provider of personalized checks, financial transaction cards, and pre-paid telephone cards. **Listed on:** New York Stock Exchange.

AMERICAN WAY
AMERICAN AIRLINES MAGAZINE PUBLICATIONS
P.O. Box 619640, Mail Drop 5598, DFW Airport Texas, Fort Worth TX 75261-9640. 817/967-1804. **Contact:** Personnel. **World Wide Web address:** http://www.americanair.com/away. **Description:** An in-flight magazine produced by American Airlines.

BANKERS DIGEST
7515 Greenville Avenue, Suite 901, Dallas TX 75231. 214/373-4544. **Contact:** Editor. **Description:** A trade magazine that provides Texas banking news. *Bankers Digest* has a circulation of 4,800. Founded in 1942.

A.H. BELO CORPORATION
P.O. Box 655237, Dallas TX 75265. 214/977-6600. **Contact:** Mr. Lee Smith, Employment Manager. **World Wide Web address:** http://www.dallasnews.com. **Description:** Owns and operates newspapers and network-affiliated television stations in seven U.S. metropolitan areas. The company traces its roots to *The Galveston Daily News*, which began publishing in 1842. **Subsidiaries include:** DFW Printing Company, Inc.; DFW Suburban Newspapers, Inc.

DAILY SUN
P.O. Box 622, Corsicana TX 75151. 903/872-3931. **Contact:** Human Resources. **Description:** Publishes a daily newspaper with a circulation of 7,100 during the week and 8,100 on Sunday.

DALLAS BUSINESS JOURNAL
10670 North Central Expressway, Suite 710, Dallas TX 75231. 214/696-5959. **Contact:** Personnel. **World Wide Web address:** http://www.amcity.com. **Description:** A weekly business periodical with a circulation of 18,000.

THE DALLAS MORNING NEWS
P.O. Box 655237, Dallas TX 75265. 214/977-8222. **Contact:** Mr. Lee Smith, Human Resources. **World Wide Web address:** http://www.dallasnews.com. **Description:** A newspaper with a circulation of 550,000 during the week and 800,000 on Sunday.

R.R. DONNELLEY & SONS COMPANY
1722 Two Tandy Center, Fort Worth TX 76102. 817/335-6000. **Contact:** Gary Kohl, Vice President. **World Wide Web address:** http://www.rrdonnelley.com. **Description:** This facility is a regional sales office. Also known as The Lakeside Press, R.R. Donnelley & Sons is one of the world leaders in managing, reproducing, and distributing print and digital information for publishing, merchandising, and information technology customers. The company is one of the largest commercial printers in the world, producing catalogs, inserts, magazines, books, directories, computer documentation, and financial printing. R.R. Donnelley has more than 180 sales offices and production facilities. Principal services offered by the company are conventional and digital prepress operations, computerized printing and binding, and sophisticated pool shipping and distribution services for printed products; information repackaging into multiple formats (print, magnetic, and optical media); database management, list rental, list enhancement, and direct mail production services; turnkey computer documentation services (outsourcing, translation, printing,

binding, diskette replication, kitting, licensing, republishing, and fulfillment); reprographics and facilities management; creative design and communication services; and digital and conventional map creation and related services. Founded in 1864. **Corporate headquarters location:** Chicago IL. **Other U.S. locations:** Nationwide. **International locations:** Worldwide. **Listed on:** New York Stock Exchange. **Stock exchange symbol:** DNY. **Annual sales/revenues:** More than $100 million. **Number of employees nationwide:** 30,000. **Number of employees worldwide:** 35,000.

ENNIS BUSINESS FORMS
107 North Sherman Street, Ennis TX 75119. 972/875-6581. **Contact:** Human Resources. **Description:** Engaged in commercial printing.

FORT WORTH STAR-TELEGRAM
P.O. Box 1870, Fort Worth TX 76102. 817/390-7459. **Fax:** 817/336-3739. **Contact:** Maricar Frazer, Employment Coordinator. **World Wide Web address:** http://www.startext.net. **Description:** Publishes a daily newspaper. **NOTE:** Entry-level positions are offered. **Common positions include:** Account Representative; Advertising Clerk; Blue-Collar Worker Supervisor; Budget Analyst; Buyer; Credit Manager; Customer Service Representative; Database Manager; Editor; Editorial Assistant; Graphic Artist; Human Resources Manager; Internet Services Manager; Production Manager; Reporter; Sales Executive; Sales Manager; Sales Representative; Secretary; Typist/Word Processor. **Educational backgrounds include:** Art/Design; Business Administration; Communications; Liberal Arts; Marketing. **Benefits:** 401(k); Dental Insurance; Disability Coverage; Employee Discounts; Life Insurance; Medical Insurance; Pension Plan; Tuition Assistance. **Special programs:** Internships. **Corporate headquarters location:** Orlando FL. **Parent company:** Walt Disney Company. **Operations at this facility include:** Administration; Manufacturing; Sales. **Listed on:** New York Stock Exchange. **Number of employees at this location:** 1,200.

GTE DIRECTORIES
P.O. Box 619810, DFW Airport TX 75261-9810. 972/453-7000. **Contact:** Human Resources. **World Wide Web address:** http://www.gte.net. **Description:** This location prints GTE telephone directories. Overall, GTE provides a wide variety of communications services ranging from local telephone services for the home and office to highly complex voice and data services for industry. GTE is one of the largest publicly-held telecommunications companies in the world, one of the largest U.S.-based local telephone companies, and one of the largest cellular-service providers in the United States. In the U.S., GTE Telephone Operations serves 17.4 million access-lines in 28 states.

GREAT WESTERN DIRECTORIES
2400 Lakeview Drive, Suite 109, Amarillo TX 79101. 806/353-5155. **Contact:** Human Resources. **Description:** A publisher of telephone directories. Overall, the company is a commercial printer. **Corporate headquarters location:** This Location.

GREAT WESTERN PRESS
13465 Jupiter Road, Dallas TX 75238. 214/341-3010. **Contact:** Human Resources. **Description:** A printing company.

IMAGE BANK
2777 Stemmons Freeway, Suite 600, Dallas TX 75207. 214/863-4900. **Contact:** Human Resources. **World Wide Web address:** http://www.theimagebank.com. **Description:** Image Bank stocks and sells photographs obtained from many different photographers. **Corporate headquarters location:** This Location. **Other U.S. locations:** Worldwide.

LEGAL DIRECTORIES PUBLISHING
P.O. Box 189000, Dallas TX 75218. 214/321-3238. **Contact:** Human Resources Department. **World Wide Web address:** http://www.legaldirectories.com. **Description:** A publishing company.

LEHIGH PRESS/CARROLLTON
1228 Crowley Road, Carrollton TX 75006. 972/446-1900. **Contact:** Human Resources. **Description:** A commercial lithograph printer.

LUBBOCK AVALANCHE-JOURNAL

P.O. Box 491, Lubbock TX 79408. 806/762-8844. **Contact:** Linda Mills, Personnel. **World Wide Web address:** http://www.lubbockonline.com. **Description:** A daily newspaper. The *Lubbock Avalanche-Journal* has a circulation of 67,000 daily and 74,000 on Sundays.

McGRAW-HILL
EDUCATIONAL/PROFESSIONAL PUBLISHING GROUP

220 East Danieldale Road, De Soto TX 75115. 972/224-1111. **Contact:** Human Resources Department. **World Wide Web address:** http://www.mcgraw-hill.com. **Description:** A book publishing company. McGraw-Hill is a provider of information and services through books, magazines, newsletters, software, CD-ROMs, online data, fax, and TV broadcasting services. The company operates four network-affiliated TV stations and also publishes *Business Week* magazine and books for college, medical, international, legal, and professional markets. McGraw-Hill also offers financial services including *Standard & Poor's*, commodity items, and international and logistics management products and services.

MILLER FREEMAN INC.
IMPRESSIONS MAGAZINE

13760 Noel Road, Suite 500, Dallas TX 75240. 972/239-3060. **Contact:** Personnel Department. **World Wide Web address:** http://www.mfi.com. **Description:** Miller Freeman publishes a monthly trade magazine for the imprinted sportswear and textile screen printing industry. *Impressions* magazine was founded in 1977 and has a circulation of 30,000.

MOTHERAL PRINTING COMPANY

P.O. Box 629, Fort Worth TX 76101. 817/335-1481. **Contact:** Personnel Department. **Description:** A commercial lithography and printing company. **Common positions include:** Bindery Worker; Blue-Collar Worker Supervisor; Customer Service Representative; Department Manager; Printing Press Operator. **Educational backgrounds include:** Business Administration; Communications; Computer Science; Engineering. **Benefits:** Disability Coverage; Employee Discounts; Life Insurance; Medical Insurance; Pension Plan; Profit Sharing; Tuition Assistance. **Special programs:** Internships. **Corporate headquarters location:** This Location. **Operations at this facility include:** Administration; Manufacturing; Sales.

PADGETT PRINTING CORPORATION

1313 North Industrial Boulevard, Dallas TX 75207. 214/742-4261. **Contact:** Personnel. **Description:** A printing company. **Common positions include:** Accountant/Auditor; Bindery Worker; Customer Service Representative; Prepress Worker. **Benefits:** 401(k); Disability Coverage; Life Insurance; Medical Insurance; Profit Sharing; Savings Plan. **Corporate headquarters location:** This Location. **Operations at this facility include:** Administration; Manufacturing; Sales. **Listed on:** Privately held. **Number of employees at this location:** 110.

POLITICAL RESEARCH, INC.

16850 Dallas Parkway, Dallas TX 75248. 972/931-8827. **Contact:** Personnel Director. **Description:** A publisher of reference services on current state, federal, and international governments. Primary customers include educational institutions, libraries, government offices, and businesses. **Common positions include:** Accountant/Auditor; Customer Service Representative; Marketing Specialist; Purchasing Agent/Manager; Reporter; Researcher; Services Sales Representative; Technical Writer/Editor. **Educational backgrounds include:** Accounting; Economics; Liberal Arts; Marketing; Political Science. **Corporate headquarters location:** This Location. **Operations at this facility include:** Administration; Research and Development; Sales; Service. **Number of employees at this location:** 35.

PRINTING CENTER MEDIA

4600 Blue Mound Road, Fort Worth TX 76106. 817/626-1476. **Contact:** Carmen Hoggard, Human Resources. **Description:** A printer engaged in commercial lithography.

QUEBECOR DALLAS

4800 Spring Valley Road, Dallas TX 75244. 972/233-3400. **Contact:** Human Resources. **Description:** A commercial printing company. Quebecor Dallas handles large print runs for commercial magazines, including *Time* magazine and *Sports Illustrated* for the regional market. The company also prints retail inserts and catalogs.

RICHARDS, BROCK, MILLER, MITCHELL & ASSOCIATES
7007 Twin Hills, Suite 200, Dallas TX 75231-5184. 214/987-4800. **Contact:** Steven P. Miller, Designer. **E-mail address:** rbmm@usnetworks.com. **Description:** A graphic design company.

SCHUTZMAN COMPANY
P.O. Box 1529, Dallas TX 75221-1529. 214/443-1600. **Contact:** Human Resources. **Description:** A commercial printing and lithography firm. **Common positions include:** Credit Manager; Customer Service Representative; Department Manager; Manufacturer's/Wholesaler's Sales Rep.; Operations/Production Manager. **Benefits:** Employee Discounts; Medical Insurance; Savings Plan. **Corporate headquarters location:** Houston TX. **Operations at this facility include:** Manufacturing; Sales; Service.

SHOPPER'S GUIDE
1302 Avenue T, Grand Prairie TX 75050. 972/641-7690. **Contact:** Personnel. **Description:** A weekly shopper's newspaper with a circulation of approximately 430,000.

THE SHOPPING NEWS
4808 South Buckner Boulevard, Dallas TX 75227. 214/388-3431. **Contact:** Personnel Department. **Description:** A weekly consumer publication. *The Shopping News* was founded in 1955 and has a circulation of 101,000. **Common positions include:** Advertising Clerk. **Educational backgrounds include:** Art/Design. **Benefits:** Dental Insurance; Life Insurance; Medical Insurance. **Corporate headquarters location:** This Location. **Parent company:** J.C. Harty Publications. **Listed on:** Privately held. **Number of employees at this location:** 30.

TAYLOR PUBLISHING COMPANY
1550 West Mockingbird Lane, Dallas TX 75235. 214/819-8458. **Fax:** 214/819-8141. **Contact:** Stacey Waller, Employment Supervisor. **World Wide Web address:** http://www.taylorpub.com. **Description:** A publisher of yearbooks and some specialty books. **Common positions include:** Accountant/Auditor; Adjuster; Collector; Computer Programmer; Editor; Investigator; Purchasing Agent/Manager; Systems Analyst. **Educational backgrounds include:** Business Administration; Computer Science; Liberal Arts. **Benefits:** 401(k); Dental Insurance; Employee Discounts; Life Insurance; Medical Insurance; Pension Plan; Tuition Assistance. **Parent company:** Insilco. **Operations at this facility include:** Administration; Manufacturing; Research and Development; Service. **Number of employees at this location:** 1,300.

TRAVELHOST
10701 North Stemmons Freeway, Dallas TX 75220-2419. 972/556-0541. **Fax:** 972/402-0721. **Contact:** Mr. Chung-Ping Chang, Controller. **World Wide Web address:** http://www.travelhost.com. **Description:** A travel, business, and entertainment magazine published weekly. Founded in 1967.

UMR COMMUNICATIONS
P.O. Box 660275, Dallas TX 75266-0275. 214/630-6495. **Contact:** Personnel Department. **World Wide Web address:** http://www.umr.org. **Description:** Publishes religious articles, including the *United Methodist Reporter* and the *National Christian Reporter*. Founded in 1847.

WACO TRIBUNE-HERALD/A COX NEWSPAPER
P.O. Box 2588, Waco TX 76702-2588. 254/757-5757. **Contact:** Human Resources. **World Wide Web address:** http://www.waco.com. **Description:** A daily newspaper.

THE WALL STREET JOURNAL
DOW JONES & COMPANY, INC.
1233 Regal Row, Dallas TX 75247. 214/631-7250. **Contact:** Personnel Department. **Description:** A regional office of the well-known financial and business newspaper. *The Wall Street Journal's* southwest edition has a circulation of approximately 170,000.

WILLIAMSON PRINTING CORPORATION
6700 Denton Drive, Dallas TX 75235. 214/904-2670. **Toll-free phone:** 800/843-5423. **Fax:** 214/352-5698. **Recorded jobline:** 214/904-2603. **Contact:** Melissa Oujesky, Human Resources Administrator. **E-mail address:** jobs@twpc.com. **World Wide Web address:** http://www.twpc.com. **Description:** A commercial printing company. **NOTE:** Summer jobs for students, entry-level positions, and second and third shifts are offered. **Common positions include:** Cost Estimator; Customer Service Representative; Graphic Artist; Sales Representative. **Educational backgrounds include:** Art/Design. **Benefits:** 401(k); Dental Insurance; Life Insurance; Medical Insurance; Tuition Assistance. **Corporate headquarters location:** This Location. **Subsidiaries include:** Classic Colbr Corporation; Image Express; The Fulfillment Center. **Operations at this facility include:** Administration; Manufacturing; Sales. **Listed on:** Privately held. **CEO:** Jerry Williamson. **Number of employees nationwide:** 400.

Note: Because addresses and telephone numbers of smaller companies can change rapidly, we recommend you call each company to verify the information below before inquiring about job opportunities. Mass mailings are not recommended.

Additional small employers:

BLANK BOOKS AND BOOKBINDING

Big D Bindery Inc.
737 Regal Row, Dallas TX 75247-5211. 214/634-8060.

BOOKS, PERIODICALS, AND NEWSPAPERS WHOLESALE

JA Majors Company
PO Box 819074, Dallas TX 75381-9074. 972/247-2929.

BOOKS: PUBLISHING AND/OR PRINTING

Dryden Press
301 Commerce St, Ste 3700, Fort Worth TX 76102-4137. 817/334-7786.

Great Impression Printing & Graphics
444 West Mockingbird Lane, Dallas TX 75247-6614. 214/631-2665.

Houghton Mifflin Company
13400 Midway Rd, Dallas TX 75244-5122. 972/980-1100.

Knowles Publishing Inc.
PO Box 911004, Fort Worth TX 76111-9104. 817/838-0202.

Pritchett & Associates
13155 Noel Road, Ste 1600, Dallas TX 75240-5029. 972/789-7999.

Taylor Reunion Services
PO Box 597, Dallas TX 75221-0597. 214/637-2800.

BUSINESS FORMS

Reynolds and Reynolds Company
1010 East Avenue J, Grand Prairie TX 75050-2619. 972/647-1722.

Safeguard Business Systems
8585 North Stemmons Fwy, Dallas TX 75247-3836. 214/905-4732.

Wallace Computer Services
PO Box 600, Marlin TX 76661-0600. 254/883-9281.

COMMERCIAL ART AND GRAPHIC DESIGN

CDS
2623 Manana Dr, Dallas TX 75220-1301. 214/357-7041.

Wace-The Imaging Network
1221 River Bend Dr, Dallas TX 75247-4958. 214/630-9171.

COMMERCIAL PHOTOGRAPHY

Laser Tech Color Inc.
2010 Westridge Drive, Irving TX 75038-2900. 972/242-5700.

COMMERCIAL PRINTING

AJ Bart Inc.
4130 Lindberg Drive, Dallas TX 75244-2309. 972/960-8300.

Color Dynamics
200 East Bethany Drive, Allen TX 75002-3804. 972/390-6500.

Global Group Inc.
4901 North Beach Street, Fort Worth TX 76137-3404. 817/831-2631.

Grand Slam Acquisition Corporation
1845 Woodall Rodgers Fwy, Dallas TX 75201. 214/981-8100.

Graphic Arts
4601 Pylon St, Fort Worth TX 76106-1918. 817/625-1116.

Harland
4055 Corporate Dr, Ste 100, Grapevine TX 76051-2000. 817/329-7113.

Heritage Press Inc.
8939 Premier Row, Dallas TX 75247-5418. 214/637-2700.

Jarvis Press Inc.
9112 Viscount Row, Dallas TX 75247-5414. 214/637-2340.

Newman & Melton Printing
2800 Taylor St, Dallas TX 75226-1906. 214/749-2222.

Performance Printing Corp.
1174 Quaker St, Dallas TX 75207-5604. 214/819-1050.

Screencraft Advertising Inc.
PO Box 7612, Fort Worth TX 76111-0612. 817/834-5555.

Tarrant Dallas Printing Inc.
PO Box 1850, Euless TX 76039-
1850. 817/571-9966.

Uarco of Paris
PO Box 9079, Paris TX 75461-
9079. 903/785-5501.

MISC. PUBLISHING

**Harcourt Brace College
Publishing**
301 Commerce St, Ste 3700, Fort
Worth TX 76102-4137. 817/334-
7500.

Harmon Publishing Company
15400 Knoll Trail Dr, Dallas TX
75248-3467. 972/701-0244.

Henington Publishing Co.
PO Box N, Wolfe City TX
75496-0618. 903/496-2226.

JCP Media Corporation
6501 Legacy Dr, Plano TX
75024-3612. 972/431-1000.

New Lifestyles
3625 N Hall St, Ste 890, Dallas
TX 75219-5119. 214/526-6090.

**Southwestern Bell Yellow
Pages**
6707 Brentwood Stair Rd, Fort
Worth TX 76112-3335. 817/496-
7084.

**NEWSPAPERS: PUBLISHING
AND/OR PRINTING**

Abilene Reporter News
PO Box 30, Abilene TX 79604-
0030. 915/673-4271.

Arlington Morning News
1112 East Copeland Road,
Arlington TX 76011-4910.
817/461-6397.

Denton Record-Chronicle
PO Box 369, Denton TX 76202-
0369. 940/387-3811.

Greenville Herald Banner
PO Box 6000, Greenville TX
75403-6000. 903/455-4220.

**Herald Palestine Press
Company**
PO Box 379, Palestine TX 75802-
0379. 903/729-0281.

Hopkins County Echo
PO Box 598, Sulphur Springs TX
75483-0598. 903/885-8663.

Killeen Daily Herald
PO Box 1300, Killeen TX 76540-
1300. 254/634-2125.

Lewisville Daily Leader
PO Box 308, Lewisville TX
75067-0308. 972/436-3566.

Longview News Journal
PO Box 1792, Longview TX
75606-1792. 903/757-3311.

Plano Star Courier
PO Box 86248, Plano TX 75086.
972/424-6565.

Sherman Democrat
PO Box 1128, Sherman TX
75091-1128. 903/893-8181.

Star Telegram Northeast
3201 Airport Fwy, Ste 108,
Bedford TX 76021-6000.
817/685-3930.

Temple Daily Telegram
PO Box 6114, Temple TX 76503-
6114. 254/778-4444.

Texarkana Gazette
PO Box 621, Texarkana TX
75504-0621. 903/794-3311.

The Dallas Greensheet
7929 Brookriver Dr, Dallas TX
75247-4900. 214/905-8200.

The Mid-Cities News
PO Box 5546, Arlington TX
76005-5546. 817/695-0500.

Times Publishing Co.
PO Box 120, Wichita Falls TX
76307-0120. 940/723-7287.

**PERIODICALS:
PUBLISHING AND/OR
PRINTING**

Auto Trader
2985 S Highway 360, Grand
Prairie TX 75052-7615. 972/988-
0044.

**Squadron/
Signal Publication**
1115 Crowley Dr, Carrollton TX
75006-1312. 972/242-1485.

Statabase
15850 Dallas Pkwy, Dallas TX
75248-3308. 972/991-6657.

**Stevens Publishing
Corporation**
5151 Beltline Rd, Ste 1010,
Dallas TX 75240. 972/687-6700.

**PHOTOGRAPHIC
EQUIPMENT AND SUPPLIES**

**Photronics-Toppan Texas
Incorporated**
PO Box 655012, Dallas TX
75265-5012. 972/889-6273.

**PRINTING TRADE
SERVICES**

Bowne of Dallas Inc.
1931 Market Center Boulevard,
Dallas TX 75207-3307. 214/651-
1001.

**Process Engraving
Company**
PO Box 535338, Grand Prairie
TX 75053-5338. 972/601-6000.

Taxex Inc.
PO Box 2660, Waco TX 76702-
2660. 254/799-4911.

For more information on career opportunities in printing and publishing:

Associations

AMERICAN BOOKSELLERS ASSOCIATION
828 South Broadway, Tarrytown NY 10591. 914/591-
2665. World Wide Web address: http://www.
bookweb.org. Publishes *American Bookseller*,
Bookselling This Week, and *Bookstore Source Guide*.

AMERICAN INSTITUTE OF GRAPHIC ARTS
164 Fifth Avenue, New York NY 10010. 212/807-
1990. World Wide Web address: http://www.aiga.org.

A 36-chapter, nationwide organization sponsoring
programs and events for graphic designers and related
professionals.

**AMERICAN SOCIETY OF NEWSPAPER
EDITORS**
11690-B Sunrise Valley Drive, Reston VA 20191.
703/453-1122. World Wide Web address:
http://www.asne.org.

ASSOCIATION OF GRAPHIC ARTS
330 Seventh Avenue, 9th Floor, New York NY
10001-5010. 212/279-2100. World Wide Web
address: http://www.agcomm.org. Offers educational
classes and seminars.

BINDING INDUSTRIES OF AMERICA
70 East Lake Street, Suite 300, Chicago IL 60601.
312/372-7606. Offers credit collection, government
affairs, and educational services.

THE DOW JONES NEWSPAPER FUND
P.O. Box 300, Princeton NJ 08543-0300. 609/520-
4000. World Wide Web address:
http://www.dowjones.com.

GRAPHIC ARTISTS GUILD
90 John Street, Suite 403, New York NY 10038.
212/791-3400. World Wide Web address:
http://www.gag.org. A union for artists.

**INTERNATIONAL GRAPHIC ARTS
EDUCATION ASSOCIATION**
200 Deer Run Road, Sewickley PA 15143. 412/741-
6860. World Wide Web address: http://www.gatf.org.

MAGAZINE PUBLISHERS ASSOCIATION
919 Third Avenue, 22nd Floor, New York NY 10022.
212/752-0055. World Wide Web address: http://www.
magazine.org. A membership association.

**NATIONAL ASSOCIATION OF PRINTERS
AND LITHOGRAPHERS**
780 Pallisade Avenue, Teaneck NJ 07666. 201/342-
0700. World Wide Web address: http://www.napl.org.
Membership required. Offers consulting services and
a publication.

NATIONAL NEWSPAPER ASSOCIATION
1525 Wilson Boulevard, Arlington VA 22209.
703/907-7900. World Wide Web address:
http://www.oweb.com/nna.

NATIONAL PRESS CLUB
529 14th Street NW, 13th Floor, Washington DC
20045. 202/662-7500. World Wide Web address:
http://www.npc.press.org. Offers professional
seminars, career services, and conference facilities, as
well as members-only restaurants and a health club.

NEWSPAPER ASSOCIATION OF AMERICA
1921 Gallows Road, Suite 600, Vienna VA 22182.
703/902-1600. World Wide Web address:
http://www.naa.org. The technology department
publishes marketing research.

PRINTING INDUSTRIES OF AMERICA
100 Dangerfield Road, Alexandria VA 22314.
703/519-8100. World Wide Web address:
http://www.printing.org. Members are offered
publications and insurance.

**TECHNICAL ASSOCIATION OF THE
GRAPHIC ARTS**
68 Lomb Memorial Drive, Rochester NY 14623.
716/475-7470. World Wide Web address:

http://www.taga.org. Conducts an annual conference
and offers newsletters.

WRITERS GUILD OF AMERICA WEST
7000 West Third Street, Los Angeles CA 90048.
310/550-1000. World Wide Web address: http://www.
wga.org. A membership association which registers
scripts.

<u>Directories</u>

**EDITOR & PUBLISHER INTERNATIONAL
YEARBOOK**
Editor & Publisher Company Inc., 11 West 19th
Street, New York NY 10011. 212/675-4380. World
Wide Web address: http://www.mediainfo.com.
$100.00. Offers newspapers to editors in both the
United States and foreign countries.

GRAPHIC ARTS BLUE BOOK
A.F. Lewis & Company, 245 Fifth Avenue, Suite
2201, New York NY 10016. 212/679-0770. $80.00.
Manufacturers and dealers.

**JOURNALISM CAREER AND SCHOLARSHIP
GUIDE**
The Dow Jones Newspaper Fund, P.O. Box 300,
Princeton NJ 08543-0300. 609/520-4000.

<u>Magazines</u>

AIGA JOURNAL
American Institute of Graphic Arts, 164 Fifth Avenue,
New York NY 10010. 212/807-1990. World Wide
Web address: http://www.aiga.org. $21.50. A 56-page
magazine, published three times per year, that deals
with contemporary issues.

EDITOR & PUBLISHER
Editor & Publisher Company Inc., 11 West 19th
Street, New York NY 10011. 212/675-4380. World
Wide Web address: http://www.mediainfo.com.

GRAPHIS
141 Lexington Avenue, New York NY 10016.
212/532-9387. $89.00. A magazine that covers
portfolios, articles, designers, advertising, and photos.

PRINT
104 Fifth Avenue, 19th Floor, New York NY 10011.
212/463-0600. A graphic design magazine. $55.00 for
subscription.

PUBLISHERS WEEKLY
245 West 17th Street, New York NY 10011. 212/645-
9700. World Wide Web address: http://www.
bookwire.com. Weekly publication for book
publishers and sellers.

<u>Special Book and Magazine Programs</u>

**THE NEW YORK UNIVERSITY SUMMER
PUBLISHING PROGRAM**
11 West 42nd Street, Room 400, New York NY
10003. 212/790-3232.

THE RADCLIFFE PUBLISHING COURSE
6 Ash Street, Cambridge MA 02138. 617/495-8678.

RICE UNIVERSITY PUBLISHING PROGRAM
6100 Main Street, MS 550, Houston TX 70005-1892.
713/527-4803. World Wide Web address:
http://www.rice.edu/scs.

**THE STANFORD PROFESSIONAL
PUBLISHING COURSE**
Box PW, Stanford Alumni Association, Stanford CA
97305-4005. 650/725-6259. Fax: 650/725-9712. E-
mail address: publishing.courses@stanford.edu.

**UNIVERSITY OF DENVER PUBLISHING
INSTITUTE**
2075 South University Boulevard, #D-114, Denver
CO 80210. 303/871-2570.

<u>**Online Services**</u>

BOOKS AND WRITING
Jump to: Books and Writing BB. A bulletin board
service, available through Prodigy, that allows writers
to discuss issues in publishing and gain advice on
writing style.

JOURNALISM FORUM
Go: Jforum. A CompuServe discussion group for
journalists in print, radio, or television.

PHOTO PROFESSIONALS
Go: Photopro. A CompuServe forum for imaging
professionals.

PROPUBLISHING FORUM
Go: Propub. CompuServe charges a fee for this forum
which caters to publishing and graphic design
professionals.

REAL ESTATE

 *It's smooth sailing in the real estate sector. Employment has risen from 7.96 million in 1993 to 9.14 million in 1997. With the healthy condition of the economy, sales of single-family homes are projected to reach 4.11 million by the end of 1998. Low interest rates and strong consumer confidence are causing a surge in home buying. Office vacancy rates are down and rental rates of commercial real estate will remain stable.*

The trend that is sweeping the industry is ownership of real estate investments trusts (REITs). REITs are companies that own, manage, and develop a number of diversified properties. These companies must follow strict guidelines and in the end remain exempt from corporate taxation. The REIT industry has seen profits soar from $8 billion in 1990 to $120 billion at the end of 1997.

The best opportunities for investment and sales are in office space. Industry analysts say that suburbs and downtowns, specifically in the Boston, Chicago, New York, San Francisco, and Seattle areas, will be the hot-spots for new construction. Forecasters predict the development of 190 million square feet of office space in 1998, a 10 percent gain over the previous year.

Business Week reports that the retail sector may be the hardest hit in 1998. Overbuilding and changes in shopping habits have produced a glutted market of malls and shopping centers. Another negative is a potential overabundance in apartment space most noticeably in the Sunbelt.

ADLETA & POSTON, REALTORS
5956 Sherry Lane, Suite 100, Dallas TX 75225. 214/696-0900. **Fax:** 214/369-6996. **Contact:** Linda Adleta, Partner. **World Wide Web address:** http://www.adletaposton.com. **Description:** A residential real estate brokerage specializing in the executive market. **Common positions include:** Real Estate Agent; Receptionist; Secretary. **Benefits:** Medical Insurance; Profit Sharing. **Special programs:** Internships. **Corporate headquarters location:** This Location. **Operations at this facility include:** Administration; Sales. **Number of employees at this location:** 10.

CENTURY 21
3637 Highway 80, Mesquite TX 75150. 972/270-7521. **Contact:** Human Resources. **Description:** A local branch of the national realty company specializing in residential and commercial properties. **Other U.S. locations:** Nationwide.

CENTURY 21
150 Westpark Way, Suite 120, Euless TX 76040-3704. 817/354-7653. **Contact:** Human Resources. **Description:** A local branch of the national realty company specializing in residential and commercial properties. **Other U.S. locations:** Nationwide.

COLDWELL BANKER
3636 North MacArthur, Suite 100, Irving TX 75062. 972/659-1525. **Contact:** Human Resources. **World Wide Web address:** http://www.coldwellbanker.com. **Description:** One of the largest residential real estate companies in the United States and Canada in terms of total home sales transactions. Coldwell Banker is also a leader in meeting corporate America's specialized relocation needs on a worldwide basis. **NOTE:** This office hires agents only. Please send resumes to: Personnel, 15443 Knoll Trail, Suite 200, Dallas TX 75248. **Corporate headquarters location:** Mission Viejo CA.

COLDWELL BANKER
PAULA STRINGER REALTORS
15443 Knoll Trail, Suite 200, Dallas TX 75248. 972/385-0700. **Contact:** Personnel. **World Wide Web address:** http://www.coldwellbanker.com. **Description:** This location operates as the regional headquarters for 12 local branch sales offices in the Dallas-Fort Worth Metroplex. Overall, Coldwell Banker is one of the largest residential real estate companies in the United States and Canada in terms of total home sales transactions. Coldwell Banker also is a leader in meeting corporate America's specialized relocation needs on a worldwide basis. **Common positions include:** Accountant/Auditor; Advertising Clerk. **Educational backgrounds include:** Business Administration. **Benefits:** Dental Insurance; Disability Coverage; Life Insurance; Medical Insurance; Profit Sharing; Savings Plan. **Corporate headquarters location:** Mission Viejo CA. **Operations at this facility include:** Administration; Regional Headquarters; Service. **Listed on:** American Stock Exchange; New York Stock Exchange.

GRUBB & ELLIS
5420 LBJ Freeway, Suite 1600, Dallas TX 75240. 972/450-3300. **Contact:** Personnel. **World Wide Web address:** http://www.grubb-ellis.com. **Description:** A real estate agency operating numerous local offices.

KELLER WILLIAMS REALTORS
1206 Northwest Highway, Garland TX 75041. 972/240-4416. **Contact:** Tom Hall, Real Estate Agent. **Description:** A real estate company specializing in both residential and commercial properties.

LINCOLN PROPERTY COMPANY
500 North Akard Street, Suite 3300, Dallas TX 75201. 214/740-3300. **Contact:** Human Resources. **World Wide Web address:** http://www.lincolnpc.com. **Description:** A property management company with commercial, residential, and industrial properties.

McFARLAN REAL ESTATE
3838 Oak Lawn Avenue, Suite 400, Dallas TX 75219. 214/559-4599. **Contact:** Human Resources. **Description:** A commercial real estate agency. **Corporate headquarters location:** This Location.

PACIFIC UNITED DEVELOPMENT CORPORATION
2445 Midway Road, Suite 106, Carrollton TX 75006. 972/447-0401. **Contact:** Human Resources. **Description:** A land development company.

WILLIAM RIGG RELOCATION
17950 Preston Road, Suite 175, Dallas TX 75252. 972/931-5565. **Contact:** Hiring Manager. **Description:** A real estate agency specializing in residential properties.

TOWN EAST REALTORS
2220 Town East Boulevard, Mesquite TX 75150. 972/270-8733. **Contact:** Fern Hardin, Broker. **E-mail address:** towneastrealtors@attworldnet.com. **Description:** A real estate agency.

TRAMMELL CROW COMPANY
3400 Trammell Crow Center, 2001 Ross Avenue, Dallas TX 75201-2997. 214/863-3000. **Contact:** Employment. **Description:** A national real estate development company. **Common positions include:** Accountant/Auditor; Financial Analyst; Marketing Specialist; Property and Real Estate Manager; Real Estate Agent. **Educational backgrounds include:** Accounting; Business Administration; Finance; Marketing; Real Estate. **Benefits:** Dental Insurance; Disability Coverage; Employee Discounts; Life Insurance; Medical Insurance; Savings Plan. **Special programs:** Internships. **Operations at this facility include:** Administration.

WYNNE/JACKSON, INC.
600 North Pearl Street, Suite 650, Lock Box 149, Dallas TX 75201. 214/880-8600. **Contact:** Frank Murphy, Vice President. **Description:** A commercial real estate development and property management company. **Corporate headquarters location:** This Location.

Note: Because addresses and telephone numbers of smaller companies can change rapidly, we recommend you call each company to verify the information below before inquiring about job opportunities. Mass mailings are not recommended.

Additional small employers:

CEMETERY SUBDIVIDERS AND DEVELOPERS

Laurel Land Memorial Park
PO Box 829000, Dallas TX 75382-9000. 214/371-1336.

Restland Memorial Park
PO Box 82900, Dallas TX 75382. 972/238-7111.

LAND SUBDIVIDERS AND DEVELOPERS

Lazarus Property Corporation
5949 Sherry Ln, Ste 1255, Dallas TX 75225-8008. 214/691-8881.

REAL ESTATE AGENTS AND MANAGERS

Associates Relocation Management Co.
PO Box 650042, Dallas TX 75265-0042. 972/652-6700.

Axiom Real Estate Management
1600 South Second Avenue, Dallas TX 75210-1020. 972/450-3332.

Capital Consultants Management
7557 Rambler Road, Ste 850, Dallas TX 75231-2310. 214/696-8883.

Cencor Realty
3102 Maple Avenue, Ste 500, Dallas TX 75201-1262. 214/954-0300.

Fairfield Properties
PO Box 5407, Arlington TX 76005-5407. 817/640-9450.

L&B Group
8750 North Central Expressway,

Dallas TX 75231-6436. 214/989-0800.

REAL ESTATE OPERATORS

Carillon Inc.
1717 Norfolk Ave, Ste B, Lubbock TX 79416-6099. 806/791-6000.

MAC Company
PO Box 841, Corsicana TX 75151. 903/872-4611.

McDougal Property
7008 Salem Ave, Ste 200, Lubbock TX 79424-2234. 806/797-3162.

Sabine Valley Properties Incorporated
11255 Highway 80 W, Aledo TX 76008-3692. 817/560-8801.

For more information on career opportunities in real estate:

<u>Associations</u>

INSTITUTE OF REAL ESTATE MANAGEMENT
430 North Michigan Avenue, P.O. Box 109025, Chicago IL 60610-9025. 312/661-1930. World Wide Web address: http://www.irem.org. Dedicated to educating and identifying real estate managers who are committed to meeting the needs of real estate owners and investors.

INTERNATIONAL ASSOCIATION OF CORPORATE REAL ESTATE EXECUTIVES
440 Columbia Drive, Suite 100, West Palm Beach FL 33409. 561/683-8111. World Wide Web address: http://www.nacore.com. An international association of real estate brokers.

INTERNATIONAL REAL ESTATE INSTITUTE
8383 East Evans Road, Scottsdale AZ 85260. 602/998-8267. Fax: 602/998-8022. Offers seminars on issues relating to the real estate industry.

NATIONAL ASSOCIATION OF REALTORS
430 North Michigan Avenue, Chicago IL 60611. 312/329-8200. World Wide Web address: http://www.realtor.com. A membership organization

compiling statistics, advising the government, and publishing several magazines including *Real Estate Today* and *Today's Realtor*.

<u>Magazines</u>

JOURNAL OF PROPERTY MANAGEMENT
Institute of Real Estate Management, 430 North Michigan Avenue, P.O. Box 109025, Chicago IL 60610-9025. 312/661-1930. World Wide Web address: http://www.irem.org.

NATIONAL REAL ESTATE INVESTOR
6151 Powers Ferry Road NW, Suite 200, Atlanta GA 30339. 770/955-2500. World Wide Web address: http://www.intertec.com.

<u>Online Services</u>

JOBS IN REAL ESTATE
http://www.cob.ohio-state.edu/dept/fin/jobs/realest.htm.

REAL JOBS
http://www.real-jobs.com. This Website is designed to help real estate professionals who are looking for job.

RETAIL

 *Online buying is the new option in retailing. Internet shoppers will spend an estimated $4.8 billion in 1998, double the sales of 1997. Computers and high-tech wares seem to be the most popular items and the sale of these items is expected to increase by 85 percent in 1998. Despite this, the growth of sales in the retail industry* overall will slow to about 2 percent annually through 2002. With a glutted market of malls and shopping centers, increasing competition for expendable income, retail purchases are losing profits to entertainment and travel spending. Low unemployment rates and a hike in the minimum wage is good news for discounters like Wal-Mart, Kmart, and Target, as low-end consumers have more money in their pockets. Discount retailers posted a 10 percent sales gain in 1997. On the opposite end of the spectrum, luxury goods are expected to boast sales gains as long as the stock market is flourishing. Supermarkets are reaping the benefits of lower food prices but facing increased competition.*

In order to see profits continue to rise, retailers will need to consistently offer lower, fair prices. Stores that also provide consumers with added incentives and reward benefits will draw more customers. Jobs for retail salespersons and cashiers will continue to increase significantly through 2005.

BABBAGE'S, INC.
2250 William D. Tate Avenue, Grapevine TX 76051. 817/424-2000. **Fax:** 817/424-2002. **Contact:** Human Resources. **Description:** Operates a chain of computer hardware and software stores. **Corporate headquarters location:** This Location.

W.O. BANKSTON LINCOLN MERCURY SAAB
4747 LBJ Freeway, Dallas TX 75244. 972/233-1441. **Contact:** Human Resources. **Description:** A car dealer.

BECK IMPORTS OF TEXAS
3737 Airport Freeway, Bedford TX 76021. 817/571-3737. **Contact:** Personnel Department. **World Wide Web address:** http://www.becktex.com. **Description:** A new and used car dealership.

BESTWAY RENTAL, INC.
7800 Stemmons Freeway, Suite 320, Dallas TX 75247. 214/630-6655. **Contact:** Payroll. **Description:** A rent-to-own furniture and appliances service.

BLOCKBUSTER ENTERTAINMENT GROUP
1201 Elm Street, Suite 2100, Dallas TX 75270. 214/854-3259. **Fax:** 214/854-3241. **Contact:** Tom Grissom, Manager of Recruiting. **E-mail address:** career@blockbuster.com. **World Wide Web address:** http://www.blockbuster.com. **Description:** Operates a chain of video rental and music retail stores. There are approximately 6,000 Blockbuster locations worldwide. **NOTE:** The company offers entry-level positions. **Common positions include:** Accountant/Auditor; Buyer; Computer Operator; Financial Analyst; Market Research Analyst; MIS Specialist; Systems Analyst. **Educational backgrounds include:** Accounting; Business Administration; Computer Science; Finance. **Benefits:** 401(k); Dental Insurance; Disability Coverage; Employee Discounts; Financial Planning Assistance; Life Insurance; Medical Insurance; Tuition Assistance. **Office hours:** Monday - Friday, 8:30 a.m. - 5:30 p.m. **Corporate headquarters location:** This Location. **Other U.S. locations:** Nationwide. **International locations:** Australia; Canada; U.K. **Parent company:** Viacom. **Listed on:** New York Stock Exchange. **CEO:** John Antioco. **Annual**

sales/revenues: More than $100 million. **Number of employees at this location:** 1,600. **Number of employees nationwide:** 58,000.

THE BOMBAY COMPANY, INC.
550 Bailey Avenue, Suite 300, Fort Worth TX 76107-2111. 817/870-1847. **Fax:** 817/347-7553. **Recorded jobline:** 817/339-3799. **Contact:** Human Resources. **World Wide Web address:** http://www.bombayco.com. **Description:** A specialty retailer of ready-to-assemble home furnishings, prints, and accessories through over 400 Bombay Company and Alex & Ivy Stores throughout the United States and Canada. **Common positions include:** Accountant/Auditor; Buyer; Customer Service Representative; Designer; Financial Analyst; Management Trainee; Retail Sales Worker; Secretary; Systems Analyst; Wholesale and Retail Buyer. **Educational backgrounds include:** Accounting; Art/Design; Business Administration; Finance; Liberal Arts; Marketing. **Benefits:** 401(k); Dental Insurance; Disability Coverage; Employee Discounts; Life Insurance; Medical Insurance; Profit Sharing; Stock Option; Tuition Assistance. **Special programs:** Internships. **Corporate headquarters location:** This Location. **Operations at this facility include:** Administration; Sales. **Listed on:** New York Stock Exchange. **Number of employees nationwide:** 8,000.

BRIDGESTONE/FIRESTONE, INC.
RETAIL DIVISION
9901 East Valley Ranch Parkway, Suite 3020, Irving TX 75063. 972/869-2303. **Contact:** Steve Kratohvil, Human Resources Manager. **World Wide Web address:** http://www.bridgestone-firestone.com. **Description:** A zone office of the tire and automotive services company. **Common positions include:** Automotive Mechanic; Retail Sales Worker. **Corporate headquarters location:** Rolling Meadows IL. **Operations at this facility include:** Administration; Service.

CHIEF AUTO PARTS, INC.
829 Greenview Drive, Grand Prairie TX 75050. 972/602-0027. **Contact:** Human Resources. **Description:** A retailer of automotive parts. **Corporate headquarters location:** Dallas TX. **Operations at this facility include:** Regional Headquarters.

COMPUSA INC.
14951 North Dallas Parkway, Dallas TX 75240. 972/982-4000. **Contact:** Human Resources. **Description:** This location houses corporate offices only. Overall, CompUSA Inc. operates over 77 high-volume computer superstores in 40 metropolitan areas throughout the U.S. Each computer superstore offers more than 5,000 computer products, including hardware, software, accessories, and related products, at discount prices to retail, business, governmental, and institutional customers. The computer superstores also offers full-service technical departments and classroom facilities. **Common positions include:** Accountant/Auditor; Adjuster; Administrative Manager; Advertising Clerk; Attorney; Buyer; Clerical Supervisor; Collector; Computer Programmer; Credit Manager; Customer Service Representative; General Manager; Human Resources Manager; Investigator; Operations/Production Manager; Property and Real Estate Manager; Public Relations Specialist; Purchasing Agent/Manager; Services Sales Representative; Systems Analyst; Technical Writer/Editor; Wholesale and Retail Buyer. **Educational backgrounds include:** Accounting; Advertising; Business Administration; Computer Science; Finance. **Benefits:** 401(k); Dental Insurance; Disability Coverage; Employee Discounts; Life Insurance; Medical Insurance. **Corporate headquarters location:** This Location. **Other U.S. locations:** Nationwide. **Operations at this facility include:** Administration. **Listed on:** New York Stock Exchange. **Number of employees at this location:** 620. **Number of employees nationwide:** 8,000.

DORAN CHEVROLET AND GEO INC.
P.O. Box 801089, Dallas TX 75380. 972/233-3500. **Contact:** Victor Mullino, Office Manager. **Description:** A new and used car dealership.

DUNLAP COMPANY
200 Greenleaf, Fort Worth TX 76107. 817/336-4985. **Contact:** Human Resources. **Description:** Operates a chain of department stores under various names, with 50 locations throughout the United States. **Other U.S. locations:** Nationwide. **Operations at this facility include:** Administration.

EVANS PONTIAC GMC
12100 East NW Highway, Dallas TX 75218. 214/328-8411. **Contact:** Dick Manuel, Vice President. **World Wide Web address:** http://www.evanspontiacgmc.com. **Description:** A new and used car dealer.

F.F.P./NU-WAY OIL COMPANY, INC.
2801 Glenda Avenue, Fort Worth TX 76117. 817/838-4700. **Contact:** Controller. **Description:** Operates a chain of convenience stores that also offer drive-up gasoline pumps.

FIRST CASH, INC.
690 East Lamar Boulevard, Suite 400, Arlington TX 76011. 817/460-3947. **Contact:** Human Resources. **Description:** Acquires, establishes, and operates pawn stores that lend money on collateral of pledged personal property and retail previously owned merchandise acquired in forfeited transactions. **Corporate headquarters location:** This Location. **Other U.S. locations:** Washington DC; MD; OK; TX. **Listed on:** NASDAQ. **Stock exchange symbol:** PAWN.

FORT WORTH LUMBER YARD
P.O. Box 969, Fort Worth TX 76101. 817/293-5211. **Contact:** Personnel. **Description:** A retail lumber yard.

FOXWORTH-GALBRAITH
P.O. Box 799002, Dallas TX 75379-9002. 972/437-6100. **Contact:** Human Resources. **World Wide Web address:** http://www.foxgal.com. **Description:** A building materials retailer. **Listed on:** Privately held.

FRIENDLY CHEVROLET COMPANY, INC.
5601 Lemmon Avenue, Dallas TX 75209. 214/526-8811. **Contact:** Hiring Manager. **World Wide Web address:** http://www.friendlychevy.com. **Description:** A dealership of both new and used automobiles.

HIT OR MISS, INC.
Plano Market Square, 1717 East Spring Creek Parkway #144, Plano TX 75074. 972/422-7738. **Contact:** Store Manager. **Description:** A women's fashion store. Hit or Miss operates over 330 stores in 35 states. **Common positions include:** Assistant Manager; Buyer; District Manager; Management Trainee; Sales Executive; Store Manager. **Educational backgrounds include:** Business Administration; Fashion; Liberal Arts; Marketing; Merchandising; Retail Management. **Benefits:** 401(k); Dental Insurance; Disability Coverage; Employee Discounts; Life Insurance; Medical Insurance; Pension Plan; Referral Bonus Plan; Tuition Assistance. **Special programs:** Internships. **Corporate headquarters location:** Stoughton MA. **Other U.S. locations:** Nationwide. **Operations at this facility include:** Sales. **Number of employees nationwide:** 3,500.

HYPERMART U.S.A.
3159 Garland Road, Garland TX 75041. 972/278-8077. **Contact:** Personnel. **Description:** A retailer of general merchandise.

INTERTAN INC.
201 Main Street, Suite 1805, Fort Worth TX 76102. 817/348-9715. **Contact:** Human Resources. **World Wide Web address:** http://www.intertan.com. **Description:** A consumer electronics retailer that operates company retail stores and dealer outlets in Canada, the United Kingdom, and Australia. InterTan carries a broad range of brand name and private label consumer electronics products, including audio and video, computers and computer software, games and toys, communications products, and electronic accessories. **Parent company:** Tandy Corporation. **Listed on:** New York Stock Exchange.

JCPENNEY COMPANY, INC.
P.O. Box 10001, Dallas TX 75301. 972/431-1000. **Contact:** Human Resources. **World Wide Web address:** http://www.jcpenney.com. **Description:** This location houses corporate offices only. Overall, JCPenney Company is a national, $11 billion retail merchandise sales and service corporation with department stores nationwide. JCPenney sells apparel, home furnishings, and

leisure lines in catalogs and 1,900 stores. Other operations include JCPenney Life Insurance Company, which sells life, health, and credit insurance; and JCPenney National Bank. **Corporate headquarters location:** This Location. **Listed on:** New York Stock Exchange.

JCPENNEY COMPANY, INC.
6002 Clyde Road, P.O. Box 150, Lubbock TX 79414. 806/792-6841. **Contact:** Human Resources. **World Wide Web address:** http://www.jcpenney.com. **Description:** A retail department store that sells apparel, home furnishings, and leisure lines. **Corporate headquarters location:** Dallas TX. **Other U.S. locations:** Nationwide.

KROGER'S
3612 North Beltline, Irving TX 75062. 972/252-7413. **Contact:** Human Resources. **Description:** A supermarket. **Parent company:** The Kroger Company (Cincinnati OH) is a major supermarket and convenience store operator and food processor. The company operates over 1,250 supermarkets in 24 states and over 900 convenience stores in 16 states. The Kroger Company also has 37 food processing plants which supply over 4,000 private label products to its supermarkets.

LORD & TAYLOR
450 North Park Center, Dallas TX 75225. 214/691-6600. **Contact:** Human Resources. **Description:** A full-line department store carrying clothing, accessories, home furnishings, and a wide range of other items. **Corporate headquarters location:** New York NY.

LORD & TAYLOR
15350 Dallas Parkway, Dallas TX 75248. 972/387-0588. **Contact:** Human Resources. **Description:** A full-line department store carrying clothing, accessories, home furnishings, and a wide range of other items. **Corporate headquarters location:** New York NY.

BRUCE LOWRIE CHEVROLET
711 SW Loop 820, Fort Worth TX 76134. 817/293-5811. **Contact:** Personnel. **World Wide Web address:** http://www.carpoint.msn.com. **Description:** A new and used car dealership.

MASSEY CADILLAC
11501 East Northwest Highway, Dallas TX 75218. 214/348-2211. **Contact:** Personnel Department. **Description:** A new and used auto dealership. Massey Cadillac also offers maintenance and repair services.

MICHAEL'S STORES, INC.
P.O. Box 619566, Dallas TX 75261. 972/409-1300. **Physical address:** 8000 Bent Branch Drive, Irving TX 75063. **Contact:** Human Resources. **World Wide Web address:** http://www.michaels.com. **Description:** A nationwide specialty retailer of art, crafts, and decorative items and supplies, offering over 30,000 items, from picture framing materials to seasonal and holiday merchandise. Michael's Stores operates approximately 180 stores in 26 states. **Corporate headquarters location:** This Location.

MINYARD FOOD STORES, INC.
P.O. Box 518, Coppell TX 75019. 972/393-8700. **Fax:** 972/304-3828. **Contact:** Lester Burrell, Personnel Department. **Description:** A retail grocery chain of over 80 stores. Minyard Food Stores, Inc. also operates a large distribution center located in the Dallas-Fort Worth Metroplex. **Common positions include:** Computer Programmer; Management Trainee; Pharmacist; Systems Analyst. **Educational backgrounds include:** Computer Science; Pharmacology. **Benefits:** 401(k); Dental Insurance; Disability Coverage; Life Insurance; Medical Insurance. **Corporate headquarters location:** This Location. **Listed on:** Privately held. **Number of employees at this location:** 350. **Number of employees nationwide:** 6,100.

MONTGOMERY WARD & COMPANY, INC.
2700 East Pioneer Parkway, Arlington TX 76010. 817/633-1100. **Contact:** Personnel. **Description:** Operates specialty stores, distribution centers, and product service centers nationwide. The company focuses on apparel, fine jewelry, appliances and electronics, home products, and automotive services. **Common positions include:** Branch Manager; Department

Manager; Human Resources Manager; Management Trainee; Operations/Production Manager; Services Sales Representative. **Educational backgrounds include:** Business Administration; Finance; Marketing; Merchandising. **Benefits:** Dental Insurance; Disability Coverage; Employee Discounts; Life Insurance; Medical Insurance; Pension Plan; Profit Sharing; Savings Plan. **Corporate headquarters location:** Chicago IL. **Operations at this facility include:** Divisional Headquarters.

E.B. MOTT COMPANY
P.O. Box 769500, Dallas TX 75376. 214/339-5113. **Contact:** Personnel Department. **Description:** Owns and operates a chain of variety stores.

THE NEIMAN MARCUS GROUP, INC.
1618 Main Street, Dallas TX 75201. 214/573-5688. **Contact:** Crystal Curren, Manager of Executive Recruitment. **World Wide Web address:** http://www.neimanmarcus.com. **Description:** The Neiman Marcus Group, Inc. operates two specialty retailing businesses: Neiman Marcus and Bergdorf Goodman. Combined, these two chains offer high-quality men's and women's apparel, fashion accessories, precious jewelry, fine china, and moderately-priced crystal and silver. Neiman Marcus has 29 stores nationwide. NM Direct, another subsidiary, is a direct marketing company, which advertises primarily through the use of such specialty catalogs as Neiman Marcus and Horchow. **Corporate headquarters location:** This Location.

NICHOLS FORD
2401 East Route 20, Fort Worth TX 76119. 817/535-3673. **Contact:** Personnel Administrator. **Description:** A car dealership.

NICHOLS MACHINERY
1311 South Ervay Street, Dallas TX 75215. 214/421-3581. **Contact:** Personnel. **Description:** Engaged in the retail sale of street sweepers, street pavers, and Bobcats.

OLD AMERICA STORES, INC.
P.O. Box 370, Howe TX 75459. 903/532-5547. **Physical address:** 811 North Collins Freeway, Howe TX. **Contact:** Human Resources. **World Wide Web address:** http://www.oldamerica.com. **Description:** A specialty retailer of framing, floral, craft, and decorative accent products. The company's stores also offer a broad selection of decorative accent products, craft supplies, and seasonal merchandise for do-it-yourself home decorators and craft hobbyists. **Corporate headquarters location:** This Location.

PARK PLACE MOTOR CARS
4023 Oak Lawn Avenue, Dallas TX 75219. 214/526-8701. **Toll-free phone:** 800/336-7073. **Fax:** 214/443-8270. **Contact:** Michelle Joseph, Human Resources. **World Wide Web address:** http://www.parkplacetexas.com. **Description:** A new and pre-owned car dealership for Mercedes Benz, Porsche/Audi, Lexus, and BodyWerks Body Shop. **NOTE:** Entry-level positions are offered. **Common positions include:** Administrative Assistant; Assistant Manager; Chief Financial Officer; Clerical Supervisor; Computer Operator; Computer Programmer; Controller; Finance Director; General Manager; Human Resources Manager; Management Analyst/Consultant; Management Trainee; Quality Control Supervisor; Sales Executive; Sales Manager; Sales Representative; Secretary; Typist/Word Processor. **Educational backgrounds include:** Accounting; Business Administration; Finance. **Benefits:** 401(k); Dental Insurance; Disability Coverage; Employee Discounts; Life Insurance; Medical Insurance; Savings Plan. **Corporate headquarters location:** This Location. **Other U.S. locations:** Houston TX; Plano TX. **Number of employees at this location:** 230. **Number of employees nationwide:** 430.

PEARLE VISION, INC.
2534 Royal Lane, Dallas TX 75229. 972/277-5000. **Fax:** 972/277-5982. **Contact:** Human Resources. **Description:** A manufacturer and retailer of prescription eyewear. **Common positions include:** Accountant/Auditor; Advertising Clerk; Attorney; Computer Programmer; Customer Service Representative; Department Manager; Financial Analyst; Human Resources Manager; Management Trainee; Manufacturer's/Wholesaler's Sales Rep.; Marketing Specialist; Purchasing Agent/Manager; Systems Analyst. **Educational backgrounds include:** Accounting; Business

Administration; Computer Science; Finance; Marketing; Merchandising. **Benefits:** Dental Insurance; Disability Coverage; Employee Discounts; Life Insurance; Medical Insurance; Profit Sharing; Savings Plan; Tuition Assistance. **Corporate headquarters location:** This Location. **Parent company:** Grand Met USA is a health care firm engaged in three business segments: Research, Development, and the Optical Group. **Operations at this facility include:** Administration; Manufacturing. **Listed on:** London Stock Exchange.

PIER 1 IMPORTS

P.O. Box 961020, Fort Worth TX 76161-0020. 817/878-8000. **Contact:** Tawny McCarty, Staffing Manager. **World Wide Web address:** http://www.pier1.com. **Description:** This location houses corporate offices only. Overall, Pier 1 Imports is engaged in the specialty retailing of handcrafted decorative home furnishings and accessories imported from approximately 44 countries around the world. Pier 1 Imports currently operates over 600 stores located in most major markets in the U.S. and Canada. **Common positions include:** Accountant/Auditor; Assistant Manager; Computer Programmer; Distribution Manager; Management Trainee; Real Estate Agent; Retail Merchandiser; Transportation/Traffic Specialist. **Educational backgrounds include:** Accounting; Business Administration; Communications; Finance; Liberal Arts; Merchandising. **Benefits:** Accident/Emergency Insurance; Dental Insurance; Disability Coverage; Employee Discounts; Life Insurance; Medical Insurance; Retirement Plan; Stock Option; Tuition Assistance; Vision Plan. **Corporate headquarters location:** This Location. **Listed on:** New York Stock Exchange. **Number of employees at this location:** 520. **Number of employees nationwide:** 8,500.

PIONEER OIL COMPANY

P.O. Box 1838, Fort Worth TX 76101. 817/531-3776. **Fax:** 817/531-2271. **Contact:** Hiring Manager. **Description:** Owns and operates a chain of self-service gas stations. **Common positions include:** Accountant/Auditor; Clerical Supervisor; General Manager; Management Trainee; Property and Real Estate Manager. **Educational backgrounds include:** Business Administration. **Benefits:** Dental Insurance; Life Insurance; Medical Insurance; Pension Plan. **Corporate headquarters location:** This Location. **Other U.S. locations:** AR; KS; MS; TN. **Operations at this facility include:** Administration; Divisional Headquarters. **Listed on:** Privately held. **Number of employees at this location:** 10.

SAKS FIFTH AVENUE

13250 Dallas Parkway, Dallas TX 75240. 972/458-7000. **Contact:** Human Resources Manager. **Description:** A specialized department store, operating as part of a 52-store chain. Stores vary in size, but all emphasize soft-goods products, particularly apparel for men, women, and children. **Corporate headquarters location:** New York NY.

SOUTHLAND CORPORATION

P.O. Box 711, Dallas TX 75221. 214/828-7011. **Fax:** 214/841-6688. **Contact:** Beth Marquardt, Staff Personnel Manager. **World Wide Web address:** http://www.7-11.com. **Description:** Owns and operates 7-Eleven convenience stores. **Common positions include:** Accountant/Auditor; Management Trainee. **Benefits:** Daycare Assistance; Dental Insurance; Disability Coverage; Life Insurance; Medical Insurance; Profit Sharing. **Corporate headquarters location:** This Location. **Listed on:** NASDAQ. **Number of employees at this location:** 870. **Number of employees nationwide:** 35,000.

STEAKLY CHEVROLET-GEO-SUBARU INC.

6411 East NW Highway, Dallas TX 75231. 214/363-8341. **Contact:** Personnel. **Description:** A new and used car dealership.

STRIPLING & COX

6370 Camp Bowie Boulevard, Fort Worth TX 76116. 817/738-7361. **Contact:** Human Resources. **Description:** Owns and operates a large chain of department stores.

TANDY CORPORATION/RADIO SHACK

100 Throckmorton Street, Suite 500, Fort Worth TX 76102. 817/390-3011. **Contact:** Jeff Bland, Senior Director. **World Wide Web address:** http://www.tandy.com. **Description:** Retails a wide variety of consumer electronic parts and equipment through more than 7,000 stores nationwide.

Common positions include: Accountant/Auditor; Advertising Clerk; Computer Programmer; Customer Service Representative; Services Sales Representative; Systems Analyst. **Educational backgrounds include:** Accounting; Computer Science. **Benefits:** Dental Insurance; Employee Discounts; Life Insurance; Medical Insurance; Pension Plan; Tuition Assistance. **Corporate headquarters location:** This Location. **Operations at this facility include:** Administration; Advertising; Customer Service. **Listed on:** New York Stock Exchange.

TANDYCRAFTS, INC.
1400 Everman Parkway, Fort Worth TX 76140-5006. 817/551-9600. **Contact:** Human Resources. **Description:** Engaged in the production and retail sale of leather and leather kits. **Benefits:** 401(k); Employee Discounts; Medical Insurance. **Corporate headquarters location:** This Location. **Subsidiaries include:** Joshua's Christian Stores; Sav-On Office Supplies; Tandy Leather. **Listed on:** New York Stock Exchange.

TOM THUMB FOOD & PHARMACY
14303 Inwood Road, Dallas TX 75244. 972/661-9700. **Contact:** Lisa Hill, Training & Development. **World Wide Web address:** http://www.tomthumb.com. **Description:** A supermarket. **Common positions include:** Customer Service Representative; Management Trainee; Pharmacist; Restaurant/Food Service Manager; Retail Sales Worker. **Educational backgrounds include:** Accounting; Business Administration; Communications; Economics; Finance; Liberal Arts; Marketing. **Benefits:** Dental Insurance; Disability Coverage; Life Insurance; Medical Insurance; Stock Option; Tuition Assistance. **Special programs:** Internships. **Corporate headquarters location:** Houston TX. **Parent company:** Randalls. **Operations at this facility include:** Sales; Service. **Listed on:** Privately held. **Number of employees nationwide:** 20,000.

TOYOTA OF DALLAS INC.
2610 Forest Lane, Dallas TX 75234. 972/241-6655. **Contact:** Paula Beaver, Controller. **Description:** Specializes in the retail sale of new and used Toyota cars. **Common positions include:** Accountant/Auditor; Credit Manager; Customer Service Representative; Department Manager; General Manager; Management Trainee; Operations/Production Manager; Retail Sales Worker; Technician. **Benefits:** Employee Discounts; Medical Insurance; Profit Sharing. **Corporate headquarters location:** This Location. **Operations at this facility include:** Administration; Sales; Service.

TROY AIKMAN AUTO MALL
P.O. Box 121819, Fort Worth TX 76121-1819. 817/560-0500. **Fax:** 817/560-2365. **Contact:** Personnel Office. **Description:** A new and used car dealership specializing in Chevrolet and Chrysler-Plymouth-Jeep lines. Founded in 1996. **NOTE:** Entry-level positions are offered. **Common positions include:** Administrative Assistant; Automotive Mechanic; Controller; Finance Director; General Manager; Human Resources Manager; Receptionist; Sales Executive; Sales Manager. **Educational backgrounds include:** Accounting; Business Administration; Finance. **Benefits:** 401(k); Dental Insurance; Disability Coverage; Employee Discounts; Life Insurance; Medical Insurance. **Special programs:** Apprenticeships; Training. **Office hours:** Monday - Friday, 8:30 a.m. - 9:00 p.m. and Saturday, 8:30 a.m. - 7:00 p.m. **Corporate headquarters location:** This Location. **General manager:** Jim Hardick. **Facilities manager:** Jim Kappler. **Number of employees at this location:** 200. **Number of projected hires for 1998 - 1999 at this location:** 100.

TUESDAY MORNING CORPORATION
14621 Inwood Road, Dallas TX 75244. 972/387-3562. **Contact:** Human Resources. **World Wide Web address:** http://www.tuesdaymorning.com. **Description:** Operates a chain of over 235 discount retail stores under the name Tuesday Morning Inc. The stores sell close-out gift and houseware merchandise at prices ranging from 50 percent to 80 percent below retail prices. The stores only open to the public four times a year for four- to eight-week sales events. **Corporate headquarters location:** This Location.

ZALE CORPORATION
901 West Walnut Hill Lane, Mail Station 5A-1, Irving TX 75038. 972/580-4000. **Fax:** 972/580-5266. **Contact:** Manager of Corporate Staffing. **Description:** A specialty retail firm engaged in

selling fine jewelry and related products. **NOTE:** Entry-level positions are offered. **Common positions include:** Accountant/Auditor; Administrative Assistant; Architect; Attorney; Buyer; Computer Programmer; Customer Service Representative; Financial Analyst; Human Resources Manager; MIS Specialist; Property and Real Estate Manager; Systems Analyst; Typist/Word Processor. **Educational backgrounds include:** Accounting; Communications; Computer Science; Finance; Marketing. **Benefits:** 401(k); Daycare Assistance; Dental Insurance; Disability Coverage; Employee Discounts; Life Insurance; Medical Insurance; Profit Sharing; Savings Plan; Tuition Assistance. **Special programs:** Internships. **Corporate headquarters location:** This Location. **Other U.S. locations:** Nationwide. **Subsidiaries include:** Corrigan's; Gordon's; Linz. **Operations at this facility include:** Divisional Headquarters. **Listed on:** NASDAQ. **Stock exchange symbol:** ZALE. **Annual sales/revenues:** More than $100 million. **Number of employees at this location:** 1,000. **Number of employees nationwide:** 10,000.

Note: Because addresses and telephone numbers of smaller companies can change rapidly, we recommend you call each company to verify the information below before inquiring about job opportunities. Mass mailings are not recommended.

Additional small employers:

AUTO DEALERS

Allen Samuels Chevrolet Geo
PO Box 7978, Waco TX 76714-7978. 254/772-8850.

Arrow Ford Inc.
PO Box 5166, Abilene TX 79608-5166. 915/692-9500.

Autonation USA Corporation
11990 N Central Expressway, Dallas TX 75243-3714. 972/761-4100.

Bankston Nissan of Irving
1500 East Airport Freeway, Irving TX 75062-4821. 972/438-4300.

Big Billy Barrett Inc.
16200 LBJ Freeway, Mesquite TX 75150-1526. 214/327-9361.

Buz Post Isuzu
PO Box 1568, Arlington TX 76004-1568. 817/467-1234.

Charlie King Hillard Ford
5000 Bryant Irvin Road, Fort Worth TX 76132-3802. 817/370-5000.

Classic Chevrolet Inc.
PO Box 1717, Grapevine TX 76099-1717. 817/421-1200.

Crest Cadillac Inc.
2701 N Central Expressway, Plano TX 75075-2597. 972/578-7511.

Discount Motors
PO Box 490, Arlington TX 76004-0490. 817/461-2222.

Don Davis Toyota
1661 Wet 'n Wild Way, Arlington TX 76011. 817/469-7711.

Don Snell Buick Inc.
11400 N Central Expressway, Dallas TX 75243-6602. 214/363-7251.

Five Star Ford
PO Box 1278, Hurst TX 76053-1278. 817/498-8838.

Frank Kent Cadillac Inc.
PO Box 121219, Fort Worth TX 76121-1219. 817/763-5000.

Frank Parra Autoplex
1000 E Airport Freeway, Irving TX 75062-4813. 972/721-4300.

Frank Parra Used Cars
1015 W Airport Freeway, Irving TX 75062-6219. 972/594-8890.

Freeman Oldsmobile-Mazda-Hyundai
1800 E Airport Freeway, Irving TX 75062-4827. 972/438-2121.

Freeman Pontiac-Mazda
701 NE Loop 820, Hurst TX 76053-4604. 817/589-7956.

Frontier Automotive Inc.
PO Box 64540, Lubbock TX 79464-4540. 806/798-4500.

George Grubbs Enterprises
PO Box 845, Bedford TX 76095-0845. 817/268-6333.

Grand Prairie Ford Inc.
1102 W Pioneer Pkwy, #303, Grand Prairie TX 75051-4704. 972/641-1334.

Grubbs Oldsmobile
2900 Alta Mere Dr, Fort Worth TX 76116-4115. 817/560-9000.

Herb Easley Motors Inc.
1125 Central Fwy, Wichita Falls TX 76304-1801. 940/723-6631.

Hudiburg Chevrolet
7769 Grapevine Hwy, Fort Worth TX 76180-7101. 817/498-2400.

Huffines Chevrolet-Subaru-Geo
PO Box 338, Lewisville TX 75067-0338. 972/221-8686.

Huffines Hyundai
PO Box 869270, Plano TX 75086. 972/867-5000.

James Wood Auto Park Inc.
PO Box 50779, Denton TX 76206-0779. 940/591-9663.

James Wood Motors Inc.
PO Box 479, Decatur TX 76234-0479. 940/627-2177.

Jerry's Chevrolet-Buick Inc.
PO Box 839, Weatherford TX 76086-0839. 817/594-8784.

Jim Allee Oldsmobile Jeep/Eagle
12277 Shiloh Rd, Dallas TX 75228-1510. 214/321-5030.

King Chevrolet Company
PO Box 870, Tyler TX 75710-0870. 903/595-4531.

Larry Hilcher Hyundai
PO Box 170659, Arlington TX
76003-0639. 817/467-3673.

Lawrence Hall Mazda
1300 S Clack St, Abilene TX
79605-4606. 915/695-8811.

Leadership Ford Inc.
10510 N Central Expy, Dallas TX
75231-2202. 214/361-8100.

Lee Jarmon Ford Inc.
PO Box 110098, Carrollton TX
75011-0098. 972/242-6415.

Lute Riley Honda
PO Box 2557, Richardson TX
75080. 972/238-1700.

Mac Churchill Auto Group
3435 W Loop 820 S, Fort Worth
TX 76116-6646. 817/244-1111.

McKinney Garry Toyota
8901 Highway 80 W, Fort Worth
TX 76116-6032. 817/560-1500.

Middlekauff Kia
4400 W Plano Pkwy, Plano TX
75093-5608. 972/985-3600.

North Central Ford
PO Box 830908, Richardson TX
75083-0908. 972/231-3491.

Park Cities Ford
3333 Inwood Rd, Dallas TX
75235-7629. 214/358-8800.

**Park Cities Jeep Eagle
Volkswagon**
4801 Lemmon Ave, Dallas TX
75219-1417. 214/443-6900.

**Patterson Auto Center Used
Cars**
PO Box 5168, Wichita Falls TX
76307-5168. 940/766-0293.

Payton-Wright Ford Sales
440 W Highway 114, Grapevine
TX 76051-4015. 817/481-3531.

Performance Chevrolet
103 Hwy 59 S, Atlanta TX
75551. 903/796-2848.

**Pioneer Lincoln-Mercury-
Nissan**
PO Box 65210, Lubbock TX
79464-5210. 806/794-2511.

Plains Chevrolet Inc.
PO Box 322679120, Amarillo TX
79103. 806/374-4611.

Plano Lincoln-Mercury Inc.
3333 W Plano Pkwy, Plano TX
75075-8010. 972/964-5000.

Pollard Friendly Ford
PO Box 1978, Lubbock TX
79408-1978. 806/797-3441.

Ray Huffines Chevrolet Inc.
PO Box 869269, Plano TX
75086. 972/867-4000.

Red Bird Ford Inc.
PO Box 210709, Dallas TX
75211-0709. 972/296-1411.

Reliable Chevrolet Inc.
PO Box 831240, Richardson TX
75083-1240. 972/952-1500.

**Rodger Meier Cadillac
Company**
PO Box 810009, Dallas TX
75381-0009. 972/386-9000.

**Scoggin-Dickey Chevrolet-
Buick**
PO Box 64910, Lubbock TX
79464-4910. 806/798-4000.

Sewell Lexus
6421 Lemmon Avenue, Dallas
TX 75209-5721. 214/352-8100.

Sewell Motor Company
7310 Lemmon Avenue, Dallas
TX 75209-3014. 214/350-2000.

Shamrock Chevrolet
3907 Avenue Q, Lubbock TX
79412-1638. 806/747-3211.

Texas Motors Ford
2020 South Cherry Ln, Fort
Worth TX 76108-3602. 817/246-
4921.

Town East Ford Sales Inc.
18411 LBJ Fwy, Mesquite TX
75150-4128. 972/270-6441.

Toyota of Irving Inc.
1999 West Airport Freeway,
Irving TX 75062-6004. 972/258-
1200.

Toyota of Richardson
400 Monte Blaine Lane,
Richardson TX 75080-4674.
972/783-0065.

Trophy Nissan
5031 North Galloway Ave,
Mesquite TX 75150-1557.
972/613-2200.

Van Chevrolet Co. Inc.
PO Box 113149, Carrollton TX
75011-3149. 972/242-5181.

Vandergriff Chevrolet-Geo
PO Box 180189, Arlington TX
76096-0189. 817/784-2661.

Village Ford of Lewisville
1144 N Stemmons Fwy,
Lewisville TX 75067-2503.
972/221-2900.

Vista Ridge Buick
2700 N Interstate 35, Carrollton
TX 75007-4402. 972/242-4000.

Westway Ford
801 W Airport Freeway, Irving
TX 75062-6314. 972/659-0333.

WO Bankston Nissan Inc.
13130 Preston Rd, Dallas TX
75240-5204. 972/450-2400.

Young Chevrolet Inc.
9301 ERL Thornton Freeway,
Dallas TX 75228-6112. 214/328-
9111.

**CATALOG AND MAIL-
ORDER HOUSES**

ASD Catalogs Inc.
10812 Alder Circle, Dallas TX
75238-1347. 214/348-3600.

ASD Catalogs Inc.
3737 Grader St, Ste 110, Garland
TX 75041-6180. 972/348-7200.

**Merck-Medco Rx Services
Texas**
8111 Royal Ridge Pkwy, Irving
TX 75063-2834. 972/915-2737.

RX America Fort Worth
5450 N Riverside Dr, Fort Worth
TX 76137-2436. 817/850-5000.

Viking Office Products Inc.
PO Box 819064, Dallas TX
75381-9064. 972/929-4547.

**COMPUTER AND
SOFTWARE STORES**

CompUSA
18325 Waterview Parkway,
Dallas TX 75252-8026. 972/528-
7000.

Computer City Inc.
300 W 3rd St, Ste 2000, Fort
Worth TX 76102-2905. 817/415-
3000.

CONSUMER ELECTRONICS STORES

Best Buy
2460 S Stemmons Freeway, Lewisville TX 75067-8755. 972/315-6024.

Best Buy
4255 LBJ Freeway, Dallas TX 75244-5802. 972/239-9980.

Best Buy
3915 West Airport Freeway, Irving TX 75062-5900. 972/258-0001.

Best Buy
6241 Slide Rd, Lubbock TX 79414-4611. 806/795-8090.

Best Buy
9600 N Central Expressway, Dallas TX 75231-5004. 214/696-2089.

Best Buy
2333 N Central Expressway, Plano TX 75075-2534. 972/578-8000.

Best Buy
6750 West Freeway, Fort Worth TX 76116-2160. 817/731-9983.

Best Buy
7600 Northeast Loop 820, Fort Worth TX 76180-8343. 817/788-2213.

Best Buy
1330 N Town East Blvd, Mesquite TX 75150-4159. 972/270-9793.

Best Buy
1730 Pleasant Place, Arlington TX 76015-4500. 817/467-3155.

Best Buy
5515A Arapaho Road, Dallas TX 75248-3421. 972/392-4288.

Incredible Universe
12710 Executive Drive, Dallas TX 75238-3295. 214/342-5800.

CONSUMER SUPPLY STORES

Chief Auto Parts Inc.
301 Neal Street, Seagoville TX 75159-2836. 972/287-7474.

Super Shops Inc.
510 Fountain Parkway, Grand Prairie TX 75050-1405. 972/641-5811.

DEPARTMENT STORES

Bealls Distribution Center
506 Bealls Boulevard, Jacksonville TX 75766-5122. 903/589-5644.

Dillard's
3901 Irving Mall, Irving TX 75062-5166. 972/258-4968.

Dillard's
2401 S Stemmons Freeway, Lewisville TX 75067-8794. 972/315-3333.

Dillard's
7701 West Interstate 40, Amarillo TX 79160-0999. 806/358-7771.

Dillard's
6002 Slide Rd, Lubbock TX 79414-4310. 806/792-6871.

Dillard's
100 Northpark Center, Dallas TX 75225-2222. 214/373-7000.

Dillard's
1700 Green Oaks Road, Fort Worth TX 76116-1701. 817/731-4711.

Dillard's
4850 Overton Ridge Blvd, Fort Worth TX 76132-1932. 817/294-1449.

Dillard's
581 South Plano Road, Richardson TX 75081-4510. 972/783-5511.

Dillard's
4800 Texoma Parkway, Ste 400, Sherman TX 75090-2085. 903/868-1065.

Dillard's
4310 Buffalo Gap Road, Abilene TX 79606-2724. 915/695-2200.

Dillard's
2201 S I 35 E, Denton TX 76205. 940/566-6210.

Dillard's
5000 Town East Mall, Mesquite TX 75150-4122. 972/681-9231.

Dillard's
3001 S 31st St, Temple TX 76502-1926. 254/778-1854.

Dillard's
33 Central Mall I-30, Texarkana TX 75503-2422. 903/838-6591.

Dillard's
3500 McCann Rd, Longview TX 75605-4406. 903/758-4436.

Dillard's
3111 Midwestern Parkway, Wichita Falls TX 76308-2823. 940/692-9310.

Dillard's
4601 S Broadway Ave, Tyler TX 75703-1330. 903/561-1221.

Dillard's
1101 Melbourne Rd, Hurst TX 76053-6205. 817/284-6511.

Dillard's
3560 W Camp Wisdom Rd, Dallas TX 75237-2506. 972/298-4229.

Dillard's
13343 Preston Rd, Dallas TX 75240-5207. 972/386-1511.

Dillard's
2917 E Division St, Ste 2931, Arlington TX 76011. 817/649-7788.

Dillard's
6001 W Waco Dr, Waco TX 76710-6306. 254/776-3560.

Dillard's
3821 S Cooper St, Arlington TX 76015-4122. 817/465-0718.

Dillard's
15151 Prestonwood Blvd, Dallas TX 75248-4701. 972/458-1400.

Foley's Department Store
2401 S Stemmons Freeway, Lewisville TX 75067-8794. 972/385-6533.

Foley's Department Store
8300 Douglas Ave, Dallas TX 75225-5603. 214/385-6533.

Foley's Department Store
8335 Westchester Dr, Dallas TX 75225-5703. 214/987-6990.

Foley's Department Store
801 N Central Expressway, Plano TX 75075-8809. 972/422-8910.

Foley's Department Store
4650 S Hulen St, Fort Worth TX 76132-1402. 817/294-6996.

Foley's Department Store
7650 Grapevine Hwy, Fort Worth
TX 76180-8306. 817/284-6910.

Foley's Department Store
4000 Town East Mall, Mesquite
TX 75150-4121. 972/681-6919.

Foley's Department Store
4700 S Broadway Ave, Tyler TX
75703-1308. 903/534-6990.

Foley's Department Store
2901 E Division St, Arlington TX
76011-6710. 817/640-5910.

Foley's Department Store
3841 S Cooper St, Arlington TX
76015-4122. 817/472-4639.

JCPenney
3701 Irving Mall, Irving TX
75062-5157. 972/252-7541.

JCPenney
6001 W Waco Dr, Waco TX
76710-6306. 254/776-1250.

JCPenney
7701 W Interstate 40, Amarillo
TX 79160-0999. 806/355-7241.

JCPenney
1105 Melbourne Rd, Hurst TX
76053-6211. 817/284-4761.

JCPenney
821 N Central Expy, Plano TX
75075-8809. 972/578-8666.

JCPenney
1900 Green Oaks Rd, Fort Worth
TX 76116-1703. 817/731-6371.

JCPenney
4310 Buffalo Gap Rd, Abilene
TX 79606-2724. 915/695-2292.

JCPenney
2400 Richmond Rd, Ste 61,
Texarkana TX 75503-2461.
903/832-1561.

JCPenney
3550 McCann Rd, Longview TX
75605-4488. 903/758-4441.

JCPenney
3111 Midwestern Pkwy, Wichita
Falls TX 76308-2823. 940/692-
9630.

JCPenney
2100 SW Young Dr, Killeen TX
76543. 254/699-1919.

JCPenney
4401 S Broadway Ave, Tyler TX
75703-1304. 903/561-3333.

JCPenney
7202 SW Moreland Rd, Dallas
TX 75237. 972/296-1461.

JCPenney
2801 E Division St, Arlington TX
76011-6732. 817/649-1600.

Kmart
5701 Broadway Blvd, Garland
TX 75043-5819. 972/240-1626.

Kmart
PO Box 461119, Garland TX
75046-1119. 972/276-9411.

Kmart
3500 W Airport Fwy, Irving TX
75062-5997. 972/986-4000.

Kmart
4324 W Waco Dr, Waco TX
76710-7043. 254/772-8440.

Kmart
3503 NE 24th Ave, Amarillo TX
79107-6919. 806/381-0286.

Kmart
712 S Walton Walker Blvd,
Dallas TX 75211-4295. 214/330-
9103.

Kmart
6701 University Ave, Lubbock
TX 79413-6303. 806/745-5166.

Kmart
1405 W Pipeline Rd, Hurst TX
76053-4628. 817/284-1491.

Kmart
9334 E RL Thornton Fwy, Dallas
TX 75228-6100. 214/328-4367.

Kmart
6000 Skillman St, Dallas TX
75231-7721. 214/361-9547.

Kmart
800 W 15th St, Plano TX 75075-
8825. 972/423-0600.

Kmart
1701 S Cherry Ln, Fort Worth TX
76108-3601. 817/246-4941.

Kmart
3540 Altamesa Boulevard, Fort
Worth TX 76133-5602. 817/294-
0000.

Kmart
2222 US Hwy 75 N, Sherman TX
75090. 903/892-3591.

Kmart
4220 N 1st St, Abilene TX
79603-6720. 915/673-5191.

Kmart
229 FM 1382, Cedar Hill TX
75104. 972/291-0187.

Kmart
845 N Beckley Ave, De Soto TX
75115-4806. 972/223-1070.

Kmart
2300 W University Dr, Denton
TX 76201-1650. 940/383-2602.

Kmart
3809 S General Bruce Dr, Temple
TX 76502-1017. 254/773-0156.

Kmart
199 Planters Rd, Mesquite TX
75182-9601. 972/226-0295.

Kmart
2747 Duniven Cir, Amarillo TX
79109-1620. 806/352-5253.

Kmart
4520 W 7th St, Texarkana TX
75501-6354. 903/832-1588.

Kmart
3050 N Josey Ln, Carrollton TX
75007-5310. 972/492-0661.

Kmart
1100 McCann Rd, Longview TX
75601-4541. 903/758-8266.

Kmart
877 NE Alsbury Blvd, Burleson
TX 76028-2659. 817/447-8010.

Kmart
3712 Call Field Rd, Wichita Falls
TX 76308-2724. 940/691-0522.

Kmart
1101 S Fort Hood St, Killeen TX
76541-7451. 254/526-9541.

Kmart
2540 E Pioneer Pkwy, Arlington
TX 76010-8786. 817/860-2177.

Macy's
13375 Noel Rd, Dallas TX
75240-5061. 972/851-5185.

Marshall Field's
13550 Dallas Pkwy, Dallas TX
75240-6609. 972/851-1515.

Mervyn's
6002 Slide Rd, Lubbock TX
79414-4310. 806/793-1800.

Mervyn's
4800 Texoma Pkwy, Sherman TX
75090-2072. 903/868-1990.

Mervyn's
2625 Old Denton Rd, Carrollton
TX 75007-5125. 972/446-8833.

Mervyn's
103 W Loop 281, Longview TX
75605-4653. 903/663-4890.

Mervyn's
3663 W Camp Wisdom Rd,
Dallas TX 75237-2507. 972/780-
8800.

Mervyn's
3881 S Cooper St, Arlington TX
76015-4122. 817/468-8888.

Mervyn's
5556 Arapaho Rd, Dallas TX
75248-3422. 972/233-8840.

Montgomery Ward
282 W Irving Blvd, Irving TX
75060-2919. 972/790-0653.

Montgomery Ward
2428 S Stemmons Fwy,
Lewisville TX 75067-8779.
972/219-1411.

Montgomery Ward
2201 S Western Plz, Unit 29,
Amarillo TX 79109. 806/354-
3400.

Montgomery Ward
5015 Boston Ave, Lubbock TX
79413-4413. 806/795-8221.

Montgomery Ward
6000 Northeast Mall, Hurst TX
76053. 817/284-4700.

Montgomery Ward
800 Wynnewood Vlg, Dallas TX
75224. 214/944-4021.

Montgomery Ward
603 S Plano Rd, Richardson TX
75081-4512. 972/680-7421.

Montgomery Ward
100 N Town Mall, Dallas TX
75234-7757. 972/620-8500.

Montgomery Ward
2600 W 7th St, Fort Worth TX
76107-2217. 817/336-1170.

Montgomery Ward
401 Carroll St, Fort Worth TX
76107-2245. 817/338-3215.

Montgomery Ward
4900 S Hulen St, Fort Worth TX
76132-1408. 817/294-9930.

Montgomery Ward
4601 S 1st St, Abilene TX 79605-
1463. 915/692-1260.

Montgomery Ward
500 E Pike Rd, Mesquite TX
75149. 214/320-6944.

Montgomery Ward
3170 S 31st St, Temple TX
76502-1803. 254/778-4871.

Montgomery Ward
10 Oaklawn Vlg, Texarkana TX
75501-4158. 903/838-6571.

Montgomery Ward
PO Box 8175, Waco TX 76714-
8175. 254/776-1050.

Montgomery Ward
1814 Roseland Blvd, Tyler TX
75701-4244. 903/531-7000.

Montgomery Ward
Westmoreland Rd, Dallas TX
75237. 972/296-6372.

Neiman Marcus
5285 Belt Line Rd, Dallas TX
75240-7505. 972/233-1100.

Sears Roebuck & Co.
2501 Irving Mall, Irving TX
75062-5161. 972/570-8400.

Sears Roebuck & Co.
6001 West Waco Drive, Waco
TX 76710-6306. 254/776-5224.

Sears Roebuck & Co.
2400 S Stemmons Fwy,
Lewisville TX 75067-8777.
972/315-4200.

Sears Roebuck & Co.
7701 West I 40, Ste 400,
Amarillo TX 79160. 806/354-
7700.

Sears Roebuck & Co.
6002 Slide Rd, Lubbock TX
79414-4310. 806/796-4333.

Sears Roebuck & Co.
851 N Central Expy, Plano TX
75075-8816. 972/422-8484.

Sears Roebuck & Co.
201 S Plano Rd, Richardson TX
75081-4504. 972/470-5500.

Sears Roebuck & Co.
PO Box 660200, Dallas TX
75266-0200. 214/265-3435.

Sears Roebuck & Co.
110 Seminary Dr, Fort Worth TX
76115. 817/927-3400.

Sears Roebuck & Co.
1800 Green Oaks Rd, Fort Worth
TX 76116-1702. 817/735-6895.

Sears Roebuck & Co.
5000 N Frisco Rd, Sherman TX
75090-2150. 903/870-2261.

Sears Roebuck & Co.
4310 Buffalo Gap Rd, Abilene
TX 79606-2724. 915/691-7700.

Sears Roebuck & Co.
2201 N Interstate 35 E, Denton
TX 76205-5735. 940/566-8901.

Sears Roebuck & Co.
3000 Town East Mall, Mesquite
TX 75150-4120. 972/686-3601.

Sears Roebuck & Co.
3060 Clarksville St, Paris TX
75460-7914. 903/737-2100.

Sears Roebuck & Co.
1 Central Mall, Texarkana TX
75503-2420. 903/832-2511.

Sears Roebuck & Co.
1101 Melbourne Rd, Hurst TX
76053-6205. 817/595-5200.

Sears Roebuck & Co.
3510 McCann Rd, Longview TX
75605-4420. 903/757-1680.

Sears Roebuck & Co.
3111 Midwestern Pkwy, Wichita
Falls TX 76308-2823. 940/689-
7000.

Sears Roebuck & Co.
4701 S Broadway Ave, Tyler TX
75703-1382. 903/534-2334.

Sears Roebuck & Co.
3450 W Camp Wisdom Rd,
Dallas TX 75237-2504. 972/780-
4500.

Sears Roebuck & Co.
13131 Preston Rd, Dallas TX
75240-5290. 972/458-3500.

Sears Roebuck & Co.
2921 E Division St, Arlington TX
76011-6710. 817/649-4300.

Target
3212 N Jupiter Rd, Garland TX
75044-6553. 972/530-1177.

Target
601 W State Highway 6, Waco
TX 76710-5575. 254/776-8790.

Target
2325 S Stemmons Fwy,
Lewisville TX 75067-2311.
972/315-0134.

Target
1720 W University Dr,
McKinney TX 75069-3217.
972/542-0391.

Target
7302 University Ave, Lubbock
TX 79423-1423. 806/745-7579.

Target
1101 Ira E. Wood Ave,
Grapevine TX 76051-4020.
817/488-1800.

Target
1400 Precinct Line Rd, Hurst TX
76053-3828. 817/282-2533.

Target
212 Medallion Shopping Ctr,
Dallas TX 75214-1579. 214/361-
2026.

Target
120 W Parker Rd, Plano TX
75075-2331. 972/424-9575.

Target
2600 S Cherry Ln, Fort Worth TX
76116-3920. 817/244-9350.

Target
3710 Ridgemont Dr, Abilene TX
79606-2726. 915/695-4470.

Target
1629 N Town East Blvd,
Mesquite TX 75150-4105.
972/681-9071.

Target
2315 Richmond Rd, Ste 9,
Texarkana TX 75503-2447.
903/838-6555.

Target
2620 N Josey Ln, Carrollton TX
75007-5516. 972/245-7526.

Target
4317 Kemp Blvd, Wichita Falls
TX 76308-3717. 940/691-3310.

Target
2500 E Central Texas Expy,
Killeen TX 76543-5311. 254/526-
8010.

Target
5001 S Broadway Ave, Tyler TX
75703-3767. 903/561-0044.

Target
8201 I-40 W, Amarillo TX
79121-1104. 806/358-4030.

Target
4343 Gannon Ln, Dallas TX
75237-2901. 972/709-0031.

Target
13131 Montfort Dr, Dallas TX
75240-5112. 972/239-8161.

Target
1400 W Arbrook Blvd, Arlington
TX 76015-4103. 817/465-5502.

Target
3333 W Airport Fwy, Irving TX
75062-5921. 972/252-9888.

Target
1122 W Centerville Rd, Garland
TX 75041-5903. 972/279-6711.

Target
2417 N Haskell Ave, Dallas TX
75204-3707. 214/826-0331.

Venture Stores Inc.
3200 W Irving Blvd, Irving TX
75061-1622. 972/986-1892.

Venture Stores Inc.
600 Accent Dr, Plano TX 75075-
8962. 972/422-4382.

Wal-Mart
2615 W Pioneer Pkwy, Grand
Prairie TX 75051-3536. 972/660-
4200.

Wal-Mart
1000 Loop 340, Bellmead TX
76705. 254/867-0280.

Wal-Mart
300 N Valley Mills Dr, Waco TX
76710-7039. 254/751-0464.

Wal-Mart
1404 W Wilson St, Borger TX
79007-4420. 806/247-7257.

Wal-Mart
SW Dumas Ave & 14th St,
Dumas TX 79029. 806/935-9075.

Wal-Mart
2225 N Hobart St, Pampa TX
79065-3417. 806/665-0727.

Wal-Mart
1001 N Interstate 27, Plainview
TX 79072-3904. 806/293-4278.

Wal-Mart
FM 5000 Hwy 423, Lewisville
TX 75067. 972/625-6000.

Wal-Mart
1670 W University Dr,
McKinney TX 75069-3444.
972/542-2619.

Wal-Mart
2211 Avenue F NW, Childress
TX 79201-2221. 940/937-6166.

Wal-Mart
RR 1, Brownfield TX 79316-
9708. 806/637-8778.

Wal-Mart
400 Clubview Dr, Levelland TX
79336-6306. 806/894-2993.

Wal-Mart
PO Box 1807, Seminole TX
79360-1807. 915/758-9225.

Wal-Mart
4215 S Loop 289, Lubbock TX
79423-1100. 806/793-8828.

Wal-Mart
3620 US Highway 180 W,
Mineral Wells TX 76067-8236.
940/325-7808.

Wal-Mart
200 N Kimball Ave, Southlake
TX 76092-6676. 817/421-4770.

Wal-Mart
1401 S Cherry Ln, Fort Worth TX
76108-3622. 817/246-6666.

Wal-Mart
6300 Oakmont Blvd, Fort Worth
TX 76132-2813. 817/249-5931.

Wal-Mart
6360 Lake Worth Blvd, Fort
Worth TX 76135-3604. 817/237-
0400.

Wal-Mart
4515 College Ave, Snyder TX
79549-6012. 915/573-1967.

Wal-Mart
465 N Judge Ely Blvd, Abilene
TX 79601-5553. 915/677-5584.

Wal-Mart
1901 Preston Rd, Plano TX
75093-5102. 972/931-9846.

Wal-Mart
603 E Highway 243, Canton TX
75103-2420. 903/567-6598.

Wal-Mart
3500 W 7th Ave, Corsicana TX
75110-4869. 903/872-6691.

Wal-Mart
6401 NE Loop 820, Fort Worth
TX 76180-6041. 817/577-2100.

Wal-Mart
4350 Southwest Dr, Abilene TX
79606-8200. 915/695-3092.

Wal-Mart
1000 Park Ave, Bowie TX 76230.
940/872-1166.

Wal-Mart
I-45 Texas Hwy, Ennis TX
75119. 972/875-9671.

Wal-Mart
800 S Cockrell Hill Rd,
Duncanville TX 75137-2622.
972/709-1400.

Wal-Mart
804 E Highway 82, Gainesville
TX 76240-2719. 940/668-6898.

Wal-Mart
150 N Beckley St, Lancaster TX
75146-1844. 972/228-2185.

Wal-Mart
200 US Hwy 80 E, Mesquite TX
75149. 972/289-5478.

Wal-Mart
3732 West Walker St,
Breckenridge TX 76424-3917.
254/559-6570.

Wal-Mart
1547 4th St, Graham TX 76450-
2920. 940/549-7714.

Wal-Mart
State Hwy 205 US 80, Terrell TX
75160. 972/563-7638.

Wal-Mart
1201 N Highway 77, Waxahachie
TX 75165-5115. 972/937-8768.

Wal-Mart
12300 Lake June Rd, Mesquite
TX 75180-1636. 972/286-8600.

Wal-Mart
PO Box 871, Stamford TX
79553-0871. 915/773-2775.

Wal-Mart
1025 W Trinity Mills Rd,
Carrollton TX 75006-1324.
972/245-0111.

Wal-Mart
201 US Highway 59 Loop,
Atlanta TX 75551-2011. 903/796-
7916.

Wal-Mart
401 N McCoy Blvd, New Boston
TX 75570-2307. 903/628-5557.

Wal-Mart
6750 Mandy Ln, Loop 820, Fort
Worth TX 76112-8619. 817/496-
8700.

Wal-Mart
1905 Gilmer Rd, Longview TX
75604-2510. 903/297-1121.

Wal-Mart
423 W Loop 436, Carthage TX
75633. 903/693-8881.

Wal-Mart
2309 Hwy 79 S, Henderson TX
75654. 903/657-9528.

Wal-Mart
PO Box 618, Mansfield TX
76063-0618. 817/473-1189.

Wal-Mart
1811 US Highway 259 N, Kilgore
TX 75662-5529. 903/983-1494.

Wal-Mart
3705 Kell Blvd, Wichita Falls TX
76308-1604. 940/692-0771.

Wal-Mart
106 S Red River Expy,
Burkburnett TX 76354-3725.
940/569-2248.

Wal-Mart
3401 S 31st St, Temple TX
76502-1902. 254/778-9234.

Wal-Mart
2180 N Main St, Belton TX
76513-1919. 254/939-0962.

Wal-Mart
2401 S Highway 36, Gatesville
TX 76528-2517. 254/865-8991.

Wal-Mart
801 W Main St, Lewisville TX
75067-3556. 972/436-9597.

Wal-Mart
303 N Northwest Loop 323, Tyler
TX 75702-8729. 903/597-2888.

Wal-Mart
PO Box 132039, Tyler TX
75713-2039. 903/534-1333.

Wal-Mart
13739 N Central Expy, Dallas TX
75243-1003. 972/437-9146.

Wal-Mart
2309 N 3rd Ave, Canyon TX
79015-3104. 806/655-1175.

Wal-Mart
13307 Midway Rd, Dallas TX
75244-5121. 972/980-2195.

Wal-Mart
6001 N Central Expy, Plano TX
75023-4702. 972/422-3000.

Wal-Mart
3600 Harwood Rd, Bedford TX
76021-4012. 817/571-3841.

Wal-Mart
4100 W Airport Fwy, Irving TX
75062-5913. 972/252-5990.

Wal-Mart
1320 Corsicana Hwy, Hillsboro
TX 76645-2614. 254/582-2523.

Wal-Mart
1007 E Milam St, Mexia TX
76667-2599. 254/562-3831.

Wal-Mart
1616 W Henderson St, Cleburne
TX 76031-3423. 817/641-1575.

Wal-Mart
735 E Highway 377, Granbury
TX 76048-2578. 817/573-8824.

Wal-Mart
3700 I-40 E, Amarillo TX 79103-
6127. 806/342-3030.

Wal-Mart
4610 Coulter Rd, Amarillo TX
79119-6403. 806/354-9300.

Wal-Mart
1836 S Main St, Weatherford TX
76086-5561. 817/599-4188.

Wal-Mart
401 E Highway 82, Sherman TX
75092-2561. 903/813-4825.

Wal-Mart
1515 S Loop 288, Denton TX
76205-4729. 940/484-1717.

Wal-Mart
1200 W Main St, Mabank TX
75147-8020. 903/887-2033.

Wal-Mart
2765 W Washington St,
Stephenville TX 76401-3742.
254/968-6002.

Wal-Mart
7401 Interstate Highway 3,
Greenville TX 75402-7121.
903/455-1954.

Wal-Mart
2021 Highway 121 N, Bonham
TX 75418-2340. 903/583-9591.

Wal-Mart
2311 S Jefferson Ave, Mount
Pleasant TX 75455-6011.
903/572-7979.

Wal-Mart
3855 Lamar Ave, Paris TX
75462-5210. 903/785-7168.

Wal-Mart
4000 New Boston Rd, Texarkana
TX 75501-2819. 903/838-4007.

Wal-Mart
515 E Loop 281, Longview TX
75605-5001. 903/757-2514.

Wal-Mart
1701 E End Blvd N, Marshall TX
75670-0713. 903/938-0072.

Wal-Mart
1405 E Tyler St, Athens TX
75751-4613. 903/677-1090.

Wal-Mart
1311 S Jackson St, Jacksonville
TX 75766-3021. 903/589-3434.

Wal-Mart
135 N NE Loop 564, Mineola TX
75773. 903/569-0180.

Wal-Mart
2223 S Loop 256, Palestine TX
75801-4701. 903/729-4441.

Wal-Mart
1521 Interstate 35 N, Waco TX
76705-2466. 254/867-8084.

Wal-Mart
405 N Highway 75, Denison TX
75020-1526. 903/465-3020.

Wal-Mart
4801 S Cooper St, Arlington TX
76017-5940. 817/465-1000.

Wal-Mart
951 SW Wilshire Blvd, Burleson
TX 76028-5749. 817/447-2307.

DRUG STORES

Eckerd Drugs
5715 Interstate 20 W, Arlington
TX 76017-1142. 817/483-4995.

**GROCERY AND
CONVENIENCE STORES**

Albertson's
5710 Broadway Blvd, Garland
TX 75043-5818. 972/240-7339.

Albertson's
4126 S Carrier Parkway, Grand
Prairie TX 75052-3214. 972/642-
2692.

Albertson's
833 NE Alsbury Blvd, Burleson
TX 76028-2659. 817/447-9106.

Albertson's
4801 Colleyville Blvd,
Colleyville TX 76034-3936.
817/428-8011.

Albertson's
1900 N Valley Mills Dr, Waco
TX 76710-2559. 254/776-7064.

Albertson's
1087 W Main St, Lewisville TX
75067-3517. 972/420-1969.

Albertson's
1565 W Main St, Lewisville TX
75067-2603. 972/436-5533.

Albertson's
4215 W 45th Ave, Amarillo TX
79109-5401. 806/355-7456.

Albertson's
3249 50th St, Lubbock TX
79413-4105. 806/795-6457.

Albertson's
5402 4th St, Lubbock TX 79416-
4349. 806/792-8251.

Albertson's
2100 W Northwest Hwy,
Grapevine TX 76051-7808.
817/488-8037.

Albertson's
1495 Precinct Line Rd, Hurst TX
76053-3866. 817/284-5066.

Albertson's
6464 E Mockingbird Lane, Dallas
TX 75214-2406. 214/827-4870.

Albertson's
4349 W Northwest Hwy, Dallas
TX 75220-3808. 214/357-8374.

Albertson's
10020 Marsh Lane, Dallas TX
75229-6006. 214/350-6663.

Albertson's
2201 W Southlake Blvd,
Southlake TX 76092-6700.
817/421-0880.

Albertson's
13100 Josey Ln, Dallas TX
75234-6351. 972/241-0531.

Albertson's
1341 W Campbell Rd,
Richardson TX 75080-2815.
972/437-2896.

Albertson's
111 N Plano Rd, Richardson TX
75081-3827. 972/234-3337.

Albertson's
2165 Buckingham Rd,
Richardson TX 75081-5477.
972/680-1711.

Albertson's
850 E Loop 820, Fort Worth TX
76112-1796. 817/451-0306.

Albertson's
5109 E Lancaster Ave, Fort
Worth TX 76112-6350. 817/457-
2460.

Albertson's
3525 Sycamore School Rd, Fort
Worth TX 76133-7805. 817/346-
6497.

Albertson's
6308 Lake Worth Blvd, Fort
Worth TX 76135-3602. 817/237-
8124.

Albertson's
4400 Western Center Blvd, Fort
Worth TX 76137-2044. 817/232-
2180.

Albertson's
7580 Oak Grove Rd, Fort Worth
TX 76140-6000. 817/568-3900.

Albertson's
6249 Rufe Snow Dr, Fort Worth
TX 76148-3316. 817/581-7233.

Albertson's
100 E Taylor St, Sherman TX
75092-2830. 903/868-9686.

Albertson's
6524 Slide Rd, Lubbock TX
79424-1310. 806/794-4674.

Albertson's
901 N Polk St, De Soto TX
75115-4013. 972/224-3544.

Albertson's
2321 W University Dr, Denton
TX 76201-1649. 940/383-2391.

Albertson's
4701 S 14th St, Abilene TX
79605-4732. 915/698-3202.

Albertson's
4450 Buffalo Gap Rd, Abilene
TX 79606-2703. 915/695-5300.

Albertson's
2106 N Galloway Ave, Mesquite
TX 75150-5730. 972/289-1647.

Albertson's
2661 Midway Rd, Carrollton TX
75006-2359. 972/248-9911.

Albertson's
2315 Richmond Rd, Texarkana
TX 75503-2447. 903/832-2561.

Albertson's
2150 N Josey Ln, Ste 400,
Carrollton TX 75006-2998.
972/446-8226.

Albertson's
3040 N Josey Lane, Carrollton
TX 75007-5310. 972/492-6107.

Albertson's
4650 SW Loop 820, Fort Worth
TX 76109-4417. 817/738-5293.

Albertson's
1809 Gilmer Rd, Longview TX
75604-2616. 903/297-1391.

Albertson's
3603 McCann Rd, Longview TX
75605-5309. 903/663-2082.

Albertson's
2720 Southwest Parkway,
Wichita Falls TX 76308-3704.
940/691-0420.

Albertson's
3100 Custer Rd, Plano TX 75075-
2060. 972/985-1456.

Albertson's
3614 Call Field Rd, Wichita Falls
TX 76308-2723. 940/696-2531.

Albertson's
2001 W Adams Ave, Temple TX
76504-3915. 254/778-4311.

Albertson's
902 Central W Texas
Expressway, Killeen TX 76541.
254/634-6169.

Albertson's
2121 S Buckner Blvd, Dallas TX
75227-8602. 214/388-0626.

Albertson's
1900 E Southeast Loop 323,
Tyler TX 75701-8337. 903/597-
7223.

Albertson's
4101 W Wheatland Rd, Dallas
TX 75237-3312. 972/780-8991.

Albertson's
11170 N Central Expswy, Dallas
TX 75243. 214/363-9424.

Albertson's
9779 Forest Ln, Dallas TX
75243-5701. 972/234-0903.

Albertson's
301 S West St, Arlington TX
76010-1023. 817/478-4291.

Albertson's
1010 N Collins St, Arlington TX
76011-6134. 817/277-6152.

Albertson's
2121 N Collins St, Arlington TX
76011-2878. 817/548-1414.

Albertson's
2200 Bell St, Amarillo TX
79106-4602. 806/359-9425.

Albertson's
110 W Sandy Lake Rd, Coppell
TX 75019-2577. 972/462-9190.

Albertson's
200 W Crawford St, Denison TX
75020-4604. 903/463-6076.

Albertson's
131 W Spring Creek Parkway,
Plano TX 75023-4609. 972/517-
8104.

Albertson's
535 W Airport Freeway, Irving
TX 75062-6307. 972/257-3884.

Albertson's
6921 Independence Parkway,
Plano TX 75023-1406. 972/618-
1268.

Albertson's
1050 W Arkansas Lane,
Arlington TX 76013-6308.
817/277-8126.

Albertson's
1300 Airport Freeway, Bedford
TX 76022-6700. 817/354-0622.

Albertson's
2506 NE 8th St, Grand Prairie TX
75050-9641. 972/264-4771.

Albertson's
7007 Arapaho Rd, Dallas TX
75248-4158. 972/387-8996.

Albertson's
822 E Centerville Rd, Garland
TX 75041-3619. 972/271-3607.

Brookshire's
3500 Hwy 66, Rowlett TX 75088.
972/475-0466.

Brookshire's
109 N Greenville Ave, Allen TX
75002-2235. 972/727-9106.

Brookshire's
510 W Southwest Loop 323,
Tyler TX 75701-9405. 903/595-
2118.

Brookshire's
PO Box 1411, Tyler TX 75710-
1411. 903/534-3000.

Brookshire's
PO Box 880, Lindale TX 75771-
0880. 903/882-3167.

Diamond Food Markets Inc.
616 W McLeroy Blvd, Saginaw
TX 76179-1404. 817/847-0155.

Farm Country Mart
PO Box 777, Plainview TX
79073-0777. 806/293-8579.

Fiesta Mart Inc.
5334 Ross Ave, Dallas TX
75206-7453. 214/827-1653.

HEB Food Store
3801 N 19th St, Waco TX 76708-
1675. 254/752-0359.

HEB Food Store
1301 Wooded Acres Dr, Waco
TX 76710-4437. 254/776-7040.

HEB Food Store.
435 Live Oak St, Marlin TX
76661-2367. 254/883-5501.

HEB Food Store
600 W Henderson St, Cleburne
TX 76031-4830. 817/641-6203.

HEB Food Store
2300 E Waco Dr, Waco TX
76705-3206. 254/799-0253.

HEB Food Store
105 Hewitt Dr, Waco TX 76712-
6419. 254/751-7190.

HEB Food Store
201 S 15th St, Corsicana TX
75110-5138. 903/874-4778.

HEB Food Store
1345 Barrow St, Abilene TX
79605-5171. 915/690-5000.

HEB Food Store
2150 W Washington St,
Stephenville TX 76401-3928.
254/965-7063.

HEB Food Store
Loop 363 & 31st St, Temple TX
76501. 254/778-4820.

HEB Food Store
525 N Main St, Belton TX
76513-3071. 254/939-0856.

Homeland Stores
4111 Plains Blvd, Amarillo TX
79106-6449. 806/354-0235.

Kroger's
303 Corn Valley Rd, Grand
Prairie TX 75052-6457. 972/264-
2384.

Kroger's
1617 W Henderson St, Cleburne
TX 76031-3422. 817/641-0771.

Kroger's
1060 N Main St, Euless TX
76039-3300. 817/571-1008.

Kroger's
1420 E Highway 377, Granbury
TX 76048-2646. 817/573-8887.

Kroger's
515 S MacArthur Blvd, Irving TX
75060-2730. 972/259-8023.

Kroger's
2201 W Grauwyler Rd, Irving TX
75061-4349. 972/790-5745.

Kroger's
17194 Preston Rd, Dallas TX
75248-1221. 972/931-5794.

Kroger's
1610 S Westmoreland Rd, Dallas
TX 75211-5767. 214/330-0366.

Kroger's
1515 S Buckner Blvd, Dallas TX
75217-1706. 214/398-6631.

Kroger's
752 Wynnewood Village Shop,
Dallas TX 75224-1831. 214/941-
8311.

Kroger's
1740 Highway 157 N, Mansfield
TX 76063-3921. 817/473-0264.

Kroger's
102 College Park Dr,
Weatherford TX 76086-6212.
817/599-9405.

Kroger's
2524 W Ledbetter Dr, Dallas TX
75233-4018. 214/333-3542.

Kroger's
1750 E Belt Line Rd, Richardson
TX 75081-4621. 972/690-0120.

Kroger's
9114 Highway 80 W, Fort Worth
TX 76116-6023. 817/244-2576.

Kroger's
3304 Denton Hwy, Fort Worth
TX 76117-3203. 817/838-6974.

Kroger's
3510 Altamesa Blvd, Fort Worth
TX 76133-5602. 817/294-5911.

Kroger's
6246 Rufe Snow Dr, Fort Worth
TX 76148-3315. 817/281-9433.

Kroger's
405 Interstate 30, Rockwall TX
75087-5406. 972/771-8021.

Kroger's
1820 Loy Lake Rd, Sherman TX
75090-0203. 903/893-6788.

Kroger's
2400 Preston Rd, Plano TX
75093-2321. 972/867-8808.

Kroger's
235 E FM 1382, Cedar Hill TX
75104-2147. 972/291-7333.

Kroger's
1001 E I 35, De Soto TX 75115.
972/228-2143.

Kroger's
500 W University Dr, Denton TX
76201-1844. 940/566-6791.

Kroger's
2231 S Loop 288, Denton TX
76205-4973. 940/387-0531.

Kroger's
200 W Camp Wisdom Rd,
Duncanville TX 75116-3329.
972/298-9962.

Kroger's
525 Galloway St, Mesquite TX
75149. 972/288-5477.

Kroger's
3600 Gus Thomasson Rd,
Mesquite TX 75150-6200.
972/270-3589.

Kroger's
500 Hwy 77, Waxahachie TX
75165. 972/937-7843.

Kroger's
11925 Elam Rd, Mesquite TX
75180-2820. 972/557-1272.

Kroger's
1310 Clarksville St, Paris TX
75460-6033. 903/785-5591.

Kroger's
3044 Old Denton Rd, Carrollton
TX 75007-5016. 972/242-2787.

Kroger's
2515 E Rosemeade Pkwy,
Carrollton TX 75007-2036.
972/306-6601.

Kroger's
3616 Forest Ln, Dallas TX
75234-7922. 214/358-5366.

Kroger's
701 W Marshall Ave, Longview
TX 75601-6218. 903/758-1726.

Kroger's
300 E End Blvd, Marshall TX
75670. 903/938-7711.

Kroger's
10677 E Northwest Hwy, Dallas
TX 75238-4812. 214/553-0607.

Kroger's
3035 N Buckner Blvd, Dallas TX
75228-5262. 214/324-3466.

Kroger's
325 E Spring St, Palestine TX
75801-2941. 903/729-5108.

Kroger's
2475 Ascension Blvd, Arlington
TX 76006-4205. 817/467-2825.

Kroger's
7100 Independence Pkwy, Plano
TX 75025-5703. 972/491-2594.

Kroger's
1200 E Parker Rd, Plano TX
75074-5350. 972/423-8030.

Kroger's
715 W Lamar Blvd, Arlington TX
76012-2010. 817/261-8224.

Kroger's
301 S Bowen Rd, Arlington TX
76013-1255. 817/277-5289.

Kroger's
2580 East Arkansas Lane,
Arlington TX 76014-1706.
817/861-2255.

Kroger's
5701 W Pleasant Ridge Rd,
Arlington TX 76016-4424.
817/483-0666.

Kroger's
5330 S Cooper St, Arlington TX
76017-5938. 817/472-9491.

Kroger's
140 N Garland Ave, Garland TX
75040-6107. 972/494-3456.

Kroger's
1040 Centerville LBJ, Garland
TX 75041. 972/270-5419.

Kroger's
532 West Interstate 30, Garland
TX 75043-5700. 972/226-2681.

Lowes Market Place
2705 50th St, Lubbock TX
79413-4321. 806/792-6057.

Lowes Market Place
5201 82nd St, Lubbock TX
79424-2831. 806/794-9728.

Max Food & Drug
4008 S Polk St, Dallas TX 75224-
4925. 214/371-1357.

Minyard Food Store
4906 North Jupiter Road, Garland
TX 75044-5464. 972/530-0198.

Minyard Food Store
1706 W Irving Blvd, Irving TX
75061-7137. 972/254-4220.

Minyard Food Store
2240 Justin Rd, Lewisville TX
75067-7165. 972/317-5662.

Minyard Food Store
2128 Fort Worth Ave, Dallas TX
75211-1811. 214/941-0400.

Minyard Food Store
2118 Abrams Rd, Dallas TX
75214-3918. 214/823-4961.

Minyard Food Store
714 Preston Royal Shopping
Plaza, Dallas TX 75230-3837.
214/691-4529.

Minyard Food Store
1212 N Beach St, Fort Worth TX
76111-6027. 817/429-9332.

Minyard Food Store
2610 Pioneer St, Fort Worth TX
76119-4631. 817/265-4863.

Minyard Food Store
112 W Beltline, Cedar Hill TX
75104. 972/291-0191.

Minyard Food Store
125 Hall Rd, Seagoville TX
75159-2915. 972/287-5488.

Minyard Food Store
610 Ferris Ave, Waxahachie TX
75165-3030. 972/937-8330.

Sack-N-Save
1200 Richland Dr, Waco TX
76710-8008. 254/776-0422.

Sack-N-Save
1280 W Main St, Lewisville TX
75067-3420. 972/221-5585.

Sack-N-Save
3037 South Fwy, Fort Worth TX
76104-7234. 817/654-2306.

Sack-N-Save
3563 Alton Rd, Fort Worth TX
76109-2834. 817/429-2571.

Sack-N-Save
1220 N Town East Blvd,
Mesquite TX 75150-7605.
972/279-5552.

Sack-N-Save
106 Walnut Creek Shopping Ctr,
Garland TX 75040. 972/276-
7189.

Super 1 Foods
2301 W Loop 281, Longview TX
75604-2563. 903/297-6952.

Super 1 Foods
1801 W Parker Rd, Plano TX
75023-7502. 972/612-2564.

Super Save Food Warehouse
1314 S Main St, Weatherford TX
76086-5529. 817/599-0607.

Tom Thumb Food & Drug
451 W I 30 Beltline, Garland TX
75043. 972/240-1724.

Tom Thumb Food & Drug
3625 N Belt Line Rd, Irving TX
75062-7806. 972/257-3420.

Tom Thumb Food & Drug
2200 14th St, Plano TX 75074-
6454. 972/423-4105.

Tom Thumb Food & Drug
314 S Hampton Rd, Dallas TX
75208-5617. 214/943-7763.

Tom Thumb Food & Drug
7117 Inwood Rd, Dallas TX
75209-4803. 214/352-1781.

Tom Thumb Food & Drug
600 Grapevine Hwy, Hurst TX
76054-2758. 817/498-8480.

Tom Thumb Food & Drug
6333 E Mockingbird Ln, Dallas
TX 75214-2692. 214/824-1265.

Tom Thumb Food & Drug
3322 N Buckner Blvd, Dallas TX
75228-5604. 214/328-2830.

Tom Thumb Food & Drug
522 Preston Royal Shopping,
Dallas TX 75230-3835. 214/363-
7685.

Tom Thumb Food & Drug
6770 Abrams Rd, Dallas TX
75231-7115. 214/340-1119.

Tom Thumb Food & Drug
14280 Marsh Ln, Dallas TX
75234-3865. 972/241-4485.

Tom Thumb Food & Drug
39 Arapaho Village Ctr,
Richardson TX 75080-5001.
972/235-3917.

Tom Thumb Food & Drug
6377 Camp Bowie Blvd, Fort
Worth TX 76116-5423. 817/654-
0256.

Tom Thumb Food & Drug
4720 Bryant Irvin Rd, Fort Worth
TX 76132-3604. 817/572-5763.

Tom Thumb Food & Drug
4836 W Park Blvd, Plano TX
75093-2330. 972/964-8190.

Tom Thumb Food & Drug
633 W Wheatland Rd,
Duncanville TX 75116-4517.
972/780-0792.

Tom Thumb Food & Drug
206 N Grand Ave, Gainesville
TX 76240-4320. 940/665-3801.

Tom Thumb Food & Drug
2810 E Trinity Mills Rd,
Carrollton TX 75006-2545.
972/416-1605.

Tom Thumb Food & Drug
8698 Skillman St, Dallas TX
75243-8265. 214/340-1266.

Tom Thumb Food & Drug
820 South McArthur, Ste 130,
Coppell TX 75019. 972/393-
0411.

Tom Thumb Food & Drug
3945 Legacy Dr, Plano TX
75023-8320. 972/491-2200.

Tom Thumb Food & Drug
302 S Park Blvd, Grapevine TX
76051-7835. 817/481-5669.

Tom Thumb Food & Drug
745 Cross Timbers Rd, Flower
Mound TX 75028-1365. 972/539-
6828.

Tom Thumb Food & Drug
2611 W Park Row Dr, Arlington
TX 76013-2257. 817/792-2047.

Tom Thumb Food & Drug
4010 N MacArthur Blvd, Irving
TX 75038-6413. 972/717-9727.

Tom Thumb Food & Drug
7104 Campbell Rd, Dallas TX
75248-1503. 972/931-7023.

Tom Thumb Food & Drug
925 Northwest Hwy, Garland TX
75041-5827. 972/271-0582.

Tom Thumb Food & Drug
9 Highland Park Vlg, Dallas TX
75205-2710. 214/521-5025.

United Supermarkets
3501 Olton Rd, Plainview TX
79072-6605. 806/293-4402.

United Supermarkets
1401 Tahoka Rd, Brownfield TX
79316-4828. 806/637-2706.

United Supermarkets
1701 50th St, Lubbock TX
79412-2701. 806/744-7475.

United Supermarkets
106 N University Ave, Lubbock
TX 79415-2845. 806/762-5656.

United Supermarkets
2703 82nd St, Lubbock TX
79423-1429. 806/745-1273.

Whole Foods Market Southwest
2201 Preston Rd, Ste C, Plano TX
75093-2306. 972/612-6729.

Winn-Dixie
1100 N Carrier Pkwy, Grand
Prairie TX 75050-3364. 972/262-
2084.

Winn-Dixie
320 E Main St, Crowley TX
76036-2611. 817/297-3854.

Winn-Dixie
305 W Euless Blvd, Euless TX
76040-4578. 817/283-8561.

Winn-Dixie
4501 N I 35, Waco TX 76705.
254/799-5725.

Winn-Dixie
7524 Bosque Blvd, Waco TX
76712-3779. 254/772-3576.

Winn-Dixie
143 E Harwood Rd, Hurst TX
76054-3005. 817/281-1683.

Winn-Dixie
10325 Lake June Rd, Dallas TX
75217-5312. 972/289-6189.

Winn-Dixie
1101 N Walnut Creek Dr,
Mansfield TX 76063-2501.
817/473-2797.

Winn-Dixie
194 Garrett Morris Pkwy, Mineral
Wells TX 76067-9038. 940/328-
1083.

Winn-Dixie
PO Box 1540, Fort Worth TX
76101-1540. 817/921-1286.

Winn-Dixie
3320 Mansfield Hwy, Fort Worth
TX 76119-6026. 817/536-9002.

Winn-Dixie
6601 Watauga Rd, Fort Worth
TX 76148-3330. 817/485-3660.

Winn-Dixie
501 E Broadway St, Sweetwater
TX 79556-4623. 915/235-8426.

Winn-Dixie
1450 W Pleasant Run Rd,
Lancaster TX 75115-2726.
972/227-8584.

Winn-Dixie
7201 Grapevine Hwy, Fort Worth
TX 76180-8605. 817/281-4007.

Winn-Dixie
719 I 35 E, Denton TX 76205.
940/382-3655.

Winn-Dixie
3164 5th St, Wichita Falls TX
76301-1800. 940/723-2313.

Winn-Dixie
800 N Kilgore St, Kilgore TX
75662-5836. 903/984-6393.

Winn-Dixie
714 S Fort Hood St, Killeen TX
76541-7431. 254/526-3434.

Winn-Dixie
219 S Palestine St, Athens TX
75751-2507. 903/675-5311.

Winn-Dixie
1824 S Jackson St, Jacksonville
TX 75766-5800. 903/586-6135.

Winn-Dixie
3770 Beltline Rd, Dallas TX
75244-2201. 972/247-3814.

Winn-Dixie
1050 S Moore St, Dallas TX
75216-1356. 214/339-7294.

Winn-Dixie
1300 E Pioneer Pkwy, Arlington
TX 76010-6411. 817/548-1150.

Winn-Dixie
1701 W Randol Mill Rd,
Arlington TX 76012-3037.
817/460-8551.

Winn-Dixie
2210 South Fielder Road,
Arlington TX 76013-6258.
817/277-3505.

Winn-Dixie
1423 N Beltline Rd, Irving TX
75061-1517. 972/986-4034.

Winn-Dixie
4900 W Arkansas Ln, Arlington
TX 76016-1911. 817/451-3192.

Winn-Dixie
808 SW Green Oaks Blvd,
Arlington TX 76017-6233.
817/465-7977.

Winn-Dixie
5781 SW Green Oaks Blvd,
Arlington TX 76017-1202.
817/478-3531.

Winn-Dixie
5450 Peachtree Pkwy, Burleson
TX 76028. 817/295-6551.

**HOBBY, TOY, AND GAME
SHOPS**

MJ Designs
335 S Cedar Ridge Dr,
Duncanville TX 75116-4526.
972/780-8913.

MJD Mouldings
500 Airline Dr, Coppell TX
75019-4609. 972/304-2200.

MISC. FOOD STORES

Ozarka Spring Water
4250 Cambridge Rd, Fort Worth
TX 76155-2626. 817/354-2900.

Whole Foods Market Southwest
60 Dal Rich Village, Richardson
TX 75080-5714. 972/699-8075.

Whole Foods Market Southwest
2218 Greenville Ave, Dallas TX
75206-7122. 214/824-1744.

**MISC. GENERAL
MERCHANDISE STORES**

Sam's Club
2625 W Hwy 303, Grand Prairie
TX 75051. 972/660-7061.

Sam's Club
3520 W Airport Fwy, Irving TX
75062-5922. 972/790-5393.

Sam's Club
2201 Ross Osage Dr, Amarillo
TX 79102. 806/374-6651.

Sam's Club
4303 W Loop 289, Lubbock TX
79407-3729. 806/793-7184.

Sam's Club
5555 S Buckner Blvd, Dallas TX
75228-6101. 214/320-2824.

Sam's Club
8282 Park Ln, Dallas TX 75231-
6023. 214/373-3058.

Sam's Club
301 Coit Rd, Plano TX 75075-
5711. 972/612-8041.

Sam's Club
1451 S Cherry Ln, Fort Worth TX
76108-3622. 817/245-5502.

Sam's Club
7500 Baker Blvd, Fort Worth TX
76118-5902. 817/589-1357.

Sam's Club
2440 SE Loop 820, Fort Worth
TX 76140-1008. 817/293-9225.

Sam's Club
3333 N Highway 75, Sherman
TX 75090-2525. 903/813-0444.

Sam's Club
5301 S 1st St, Abilene TX 79605-
1336. 915/691-5480.

Sam's Club
1414 Marlandwood Rd, Temple
TX 76502-3309. 254/774-8402.

Sam's Club
3610 Saint Michael Dr,

Texarkana TX 75503-2341.
903/838-4338.

Sam's Club
3310 N 4th St, Longview TX
75605-5146. 903/663-5588.

Sam's Club
3801 Kell Blvd, Wichita Falls TX
76308-1605. 940/691-0463.

Sam's Club
2025 S Loop SW, Tyler TX
75701. 903/597-2296.

Sam's Club
2900 W Wheatland Rd, Dallas
TX 75237-3535. 972/283-1704.

Sam's Club
2301 E Waco Dr, Bellmead TX
76705-3207. 254/799-2408.

Sam's Club
12000 McCree Rd, Dallas TX
75238-3275. 214/342-9810.

Sam's Club
4150 Beltline Rd, Addison TX
75244. 972/934-9243.

Sam's Club
4915 S Cooper St, Arlington TX
76017-5930. 817/557-2011.

Service Merchandise Company
2021 N Town East Blvd,
Mesquite TX 75150-4050.
972/681-7024.

**RECORD AND
PRERECORDED TAPE
STORES**

Anderson Merchandisers Inc.
2301 Chovanetz Court, Irving TX
75038-4305. 972/550-0323.

Blockbuster Music
3000 Redbud Blvd, McKinney
TX 75069. 972/683-8800.

For more information on career opportunities in retail:

<u>Associations</u>

**INTERNATIONAL ASSOCIATION OF CHAIN
STORES**
5549 Lee Highway, Arlington VA 22207. 703/534-
8880. Fax: 703/534-9080.

**INTERNATIONAL COUNCIL OF SHOPPING
CENTERS**
665 Fifth Avenue, New York NY 10022-5370.
212/421-8181. World Wide Web address: http://www.
icsc.org. Offers conventions, research, education, a
variety of publications, and awards programs.

**NATIONAL AUTOMOTIVE DEALERS
ASSOCIATION**
8400 Westpark Drive, McLean VA 22102. 703/821-
7000. World Wide Web address: http://www.nadanet.
com.

**NATIONAL INDEPENDENT AUTOMOTIVE
DEALERS ASSOCIATION**
2521 Brown Boulevard, Suite 100, Arlington TX
76006. 817/640-3838. World Wide Web address:
http://www.niada.com.

NATIONAL RETAIL FEDERATION
325 7th Street NW, Suite 1000, Washington DC
20004. 202/783-7971. World Wide Web address:
http://www.nrf.com. Provides information services,
industry outlooks, and a variety of educational
opportunities and publications.

Directories

AUTOMOTIVE NEWS MARKET DATA BOOK
Automotive News, Crain Communication, 1400
Woodbridge Avenue, Detroit MI 48207-3187.
313/446-6000.

Online Services

THE INTERNET FASHION EXCHANGE
http://www.fashionexch.com. An excellent site for
those industry professionals interested in apparel and
retail. The extensive search engine allows you to
search by job title, location, salary, product line,
industry, and whether you want a permanent,
temporary, or freelance position. The Internet Fashion
Exchange also offers career services such as
recruiting, and outplacement firms that place fashion
and retail professionals.

RETAIL JOBNET
http://www.retailjobnet.com. Sponsored by Retail
Search Consultants, Inc. and Barnes & Associates
Retail Search, this site is geared toward recruiting
professionals for the retail industry. The resume
database has a fee of $15 for three months or $25 for
six months.

STONE, CLAY, GLASS, AND CONCRETE PRODUCTS

Largely dependent on the success of the construction market, the stone, clay, glass, and concrete industry should experience steady demand in 1998, as new construction projects begin nationwide. Manufacturers of float glass (a raw material used in producing windows, windshields, and door panes) are projected to see flat sales in 1998 until increases in vehicle demand and non-residential construction pick up later in the year. Six of the largest float glass plants are located in the United States. Among these are Guardian Industries, PPG Industries, and Ford Motor Company's glass division.

The primary market for clay and brick is in the construction of single-family housing; the demand should grow at an average of less than 1 percent annually through 2002. By the end of the decade, ceramic tile imports are likely to increase due to Mexico's duty-free access to the U.S. market and a projected 10 percent cut in tariffs.

AMERICAN FLAT GLASS DISTRIBUTORS, INC. (AFGD)
1201 Highway 67 East, Alvarado TX 76009. 817/477-1144. **Fax:** 817/783-7123. **Contact:** Carl Frey, Branch Manager. **World Wide Web address:** http://www.afg.com/afgd. **Description:** Specializes in architectural insulated glass units and custom tempering. AFGD manufactures a complete line of insulated glass units for commercial and residential applications. The product line includes clear, tint, and reflective glass; wire glass; and equipment for the handling, storage, and transportation of glass. There are 19 AFGD locations throughout the United States in metropolitan areas. **Common positions include:** Blue-Collar Worker Supervisor; Branch Manager; Clerical Supervisor; Credit Manager; Customer Service Representative; Industrial Engineer; Industrial Production Manager; Management Trainee; Manufacturer's/Wholesaler's Sales Rep.; Mechanical Engineer; Metallurgical Engineer; Operations/Production Manager; Production Manager. **Educational backgrounds include:** Business Administration; Engineering; Finance; Marketing; Sales. **Benefits:** 401(k); Disability Coverage; Life Insurance; Medical Insurance; Profit Sharing; Savings Plan; Tuition Assistance. **Corporate headquarters location:** Atlanta GA. **Parent company:** AFG Industries, Inc. **Operations at this facility include:** Manufacturing; Sales. **Listed on:** Privately held. **Number of employees at this location:** 75. **Number of employees nationwide:** 1,000.

AMERICAN FLAT GLASS DISTRIBUTORS, INC. (AFGD)
2148 Royal Lane, Dallas TX 75229. 972/241-0943. **Contact:** Rick Ogle, Branch Manager. **World Wide Web address:** http://www.afg.com/afgd. **Description:** Specializes in architectural insulated glass units and custom tempering. AFGD manufactures a complete line of insulated glass units for commercial and residential applications. The product line includes clear, tint, and reflective glass; wire glass; and equipment for the handling, storage, and transportation of glass. There are 19 AFGD locations throughout the United States in metropolitan areas. **Common positions include:** Blue-Collar Worker Supervisor; Branch Manager; Clerical Supervisor; Credit Manager; Customer Service Representative; Industrial Engineer; Industrial Production Manager; Management Trainee; Manufacturer's/Wholesaler's Sales Rep.; Mechanical Engineer; Metallurgical Engineer; Operations/Production Manager; Production Manager. **Educational backgrounds include:** Business Administration; Engineering; Finance; Marketing; Sales. **Benefits:** 401(k); Disability Coverage; Life Insurance; Medical Insurance; Profit Sharing; Savings Plan; Tuition Assistance. **Corporate headquarters location:** Atlanta GA. **Parent company:** AFG Industries, Inc. **Operations at this facility include:** Manufacturing; Sales. **Listed on:** Privately held. **Number of employees at this location:** 75. **Number of employees nationwide:** 1,000.

DAL TILE NATIONAL
P.O. Box 170130, Dallas TX 75217. 214/398-1411. **Fax:** 214/309-4192. **Contact:** Steve Smith, Director of Human Resources. **World Wide Web address:** http://www.daltile.com. **Description:** Manufactures wall and floor tile. **Common positions include:** Accountant/Auditor; Credit Manager; Systems Analyst. **Educational backgrounds include:** Accounting; Business Administration; Computer Science; Finance; Marketing. **Benefits:** 401(k); Employee Discounts; Life Insurance; Medical Insurance; Profit Sharing. **Corporate headquarters location:** This Location. **Operations at this facility include:** Administration; Manufacturing; Research and Development. **Listed on:** Privately held. **Number of employees at this location:** 1,100. **Number of employees nationwide:** 3,300.

ELK CORPORATION OF TEXAS
202 Cedar Drive, Ennis TX 75119. 972/875-9611. **Fax:** 972/872-2392. **Contact:** Human Resources. **World Wide Web address:** http://www.elcor.com. **Description:** Manufactures residential roofing products and fiberglass mats. **Common positions include:** Accountant/Auditor; Blue-Collar Worker Supervisor; Chemical Engineer; Clerical Supervisor; Designer; Electrical/Electronics Engineer; Human Resources Manager; Manufacturer's/Wholesaler's Sales Rep.; Mechanical Engineer. **Educational backgrounds include:** Accounting; Engineering; Marketing. **Benefits:** 401(k); Disability Coverage; Life Insurance; Medical Insurance; Profit Sharing; Savings Plan; Tuition Assistance. **Corporate headquarters location:** Dallas TX. **Other U.S. locations:** Tuscaloosa AL; Shafter CA. **Parent company:** Elcor Corporation. **Operations at this facility include:** Administration; Manufacturing; Sales. **Listed on:** New York Stock Exchange.

GIFFORD-HILL-AMERICAN, INC.
P.O. Box 569470, Dallas TX 75356-9470. 972/262-1571. **Contact:** Personnel Manager. **Description:** Produces concrete pressure pipe and pipe fittings.

GUARDIAN INDUSTRIES CORPORATION
3801 South Highway 287, Corsicana TX 75110. 903/872-4871. **Fax:** 903/872-4263. **Contact:** Employee Relations Manager. **Description:** Guardian Industries Corporation manufactures tempered, reflexive coatings and insulated glass. **Common positions include:** Accountant/Auditor; Blue-Collar Worker Supervisor; Ceramics Engineer; Chemical Engineer; Computer Programmer; Credit Manager; Electrical/Electronics Engineer; Electrician; Human Resources Manager; Industrial Production Manager; Management Trainee; Mechanical Engineer; Operations/Production Manager; Purchasing Agent/Manager; Systems Analyst. **Educational backgrounds include:** Accounting; Business Administration; Chemistry; Engineering. **Benefits:** 401(k); Dental Insurance; Disability Coverage; Employee Discounts; Life Insurance; Medical Insurance; Pension Plan; Profit Sharing; Savings Plan; Tuition Assistance. **Corporate headquarters location:** Auburn Hills MI. **Other U.S. locations:** Nationwide. **Operations at this facility include:** Administration; Manufacturing; Sales. **Number of employees at this location:** 330. **Number of employees nationwide:** 10,000.

HGP GLASS
14160 Dallas Parkway, Suite 850, Dallas TX 75240. 972/663-3800. **Fax:** 972/663-3838. **Contact:** Mollie Hines, Human Resources Manager. **Description:** A manufacturer of glass. **Common positions include:** Accountant/Auditor; Credit Manager. **Educational backgrounds include:** Accounting; Finance. **Benefits:** 401(k); Dental Insurance; Disability Coverage; Life Insurance; Medical Insurance; Tuition Assistance. **Corporate headquarters location:** This Location. **Parent company:** Old Castle. **Operations at this facility include:** Administration; Divisional Headquarters; Sales. **Number of employees at this location:** 10. **Number of employees nationwide:** 1,550.

LONE STAR INDUSTRIES, INC.
1801 Lone Star Drive, Dallas TX 75212. 972/386-0400. **Contact:** Human Resources Department. **Description:** Lone Star Industries manufactures and distributes cement products. **Other area locations:** Sweetwater TX.

MUR-TEX FIBERGLASS
P.O. Box 31240, Amarillo TX 79120. 806/373-7418. **Contact:** Human Resources. **Description:** A manufacturer of fiberglass tanks for industrial usage. **Corporate headquarters location:** This Location.

OWENS-CORNING FIBERGLAS CORPORATION
P.O. Box 8000, Amarillo TX 79114-8000. 806/622-1582. **Physical address:** 1701 Hollywood Road, Amarillo TX. **Contact:** Human Resources. **World Wide Web address:** http://www.owenscorning.com. **Description:** Manufactures and sells thermal and acoustical insulation products for appliances, roof insulation, and industrial asphalt. Other products of the company include windows, wet process chopped strands and specialty mats, and polyester resins. **Subsidiaries include:** Barbcorp, Inc.; Dansk-Svensk Glasfiber AS; Eric Co.; European Owens-Corning Fiberglas SA; IPM Inc.; Kitsons Insulations Products Ltd.; Owens-Corning AS; Owens-Corning Building Products; Owens-Corning FSC, Inc.; Owens-Corning Finance.

STRUCTURAL OF TEXAS INC.
P.O. Box 210579, Dallas TX 75211. 214/638-8933. **Contact:** Personnel Department. **Description:** A manufacturer and distributor of concrete products.

TXI, INC.
1341 West Mockingbird Lane, Dallas TX 75247-6913. 972/647-6700. **Contact:** Human Resources. **World Wide Web address:** http://www.txi.com. **Description:** A producer of cement, aggregates, steel, and concrete for the construction industry. Cement is produced at two facilities in Texas. Aggregate products, which include sand, gravel, limestone, and lightweight aggregates, are sold primarily in Texas and Louisiana. Concrete is made at 19 plants in Texas and 10 plants in Louisiana. **Common positions include:** Accountant/Auditor; Civil Engineer; Environmental Engineer; Financial Analyst; Human Resources Manager; Mining Engineer; Systems Analyst. **Educational backgrounds include:** Accounting; Business Administration; Engineering; Finance; Marketing. **Benefits:** 401(k); Dental Insurance; Disability Coverage; Life Insurance; Medical Insurance; Tuition Assistance. **Special programs:** Internships. **Corporate headquarters location:** This Location. **Other U.S. locations:** LA. **Subsidiaries include:** Chaparral Steel Company is a manufacturer of reinforced steel and related components. **Operations at this facility include:** Regional Headquarters; Sales. **Listed on:** New York Stock Exchange. **Number of employees at this location:** 380. **Number of employees nationwide:** 1,800.

VETROTEX CERTAINTEED CORPORATION
4515 Allendale Road, Wichita Falls TX 76310. 940/691-0020. **Contact:** Human Resources. **Description:** Manufactures fiberglass products.

Note: Because addresses and telephone numbers of smaller companies can change rapidly, we recommend you call each company to verify the information below before inquiring about job opportunities. Mass mailings are not recommended.

Additional small employers:

ASPHALT

Atlas Roofing
PO Box 700, Daingerfield TX 75638-0700. 903/645-3988.

CEMENT

Lone Star Industries, Inc.
PO Box 1639, Sweetwater TX 79556-1639. 915/288-4221.

North Texas Cement Co.
PO Box 520, Midlothian TX 76065-0520. 972/723-2301.

DIMENSION STONE

Chemical Lime Co.
PO Box 473, Clifton TX 76634-0473. 254/675-8668.

EARTH AND MINERALS

ICI Americas Inc.
4300 Jackson Street, Greenville TX 75402-5721. 903/457-8500.

Poco Graphite Inc.
1601 South State Street, Decatur TX 76234-2742. 940/627-2121.

GLASS AND GLASS PRODUCTS

Ball-Foster Glass Container Company
2400 Interstate 35 East, Waxahachie TX 75165. 972/937-3430.

D&S Insulated Glass Company
PO Box 59209, Dallas TX 75229-1209. 972/484-8892.

Johns Manville International Group
200 W Industrial Blvd, Cleburne TX 76031-1362. 817/645-9101.

TILE

Acme Brick Company
220 Daniels St, Denton TX 76205-7601. 940/387-5804.

Acme Brick Company
PO Box 425, Fort Worth TX 76101-0425. 817/332-4101.

American Marazzi Tile Incorporated
359 Clay Road, Mesquite TX 75182-9710. 972/226-0110.

Henderson Brick Company
PO Box 2110, Henderson TX 75653-2110. 903/657-3505.

Huntington/Pacific Ceramics
PO Box 7292, Fort Worth TX 76111-0292. 817/838-2323.

Interceramic
PO Box 472479, Garland TX 75047-2479. 214/503-5500.

Texas Clay Industries
PO Box 469, Malakoff TX 75148-0469. 903/489-1331.

For more information on career opportunities in stone, clay, glass, and concrete products:

<u>Associations</u>

THE AMERICAN CERAMIC SOCIETY
P.O. Box 6136, Westerville OH 43086-6136. 614/890-4700. World Wide Web address: http://www.acers.org. Offers a variety of publications, meetings, information, and educational services. Also operates Ceramic Futures, an employment service with a resume database.

NATIONAL GLASS ASSOCIATION
8200 Greensboro Drive, Suite 302, McLean VA

22102. 703/442-4890. World Wide Web address: http://www.glass.org.

<u>Magazines</u>

GLASS MAGAZINE
National Glass Association, 8200 Greensboro Drive, McLean VA 22102. 703/442-4890.

ROCK PRODUCTS
MacLean Hunter Publishing Company, 29 North Wacker Drive, Chicago IL 60606. 312/726-2805.

TRANSPORTATION/TRAVEL

All sectors of the transportation industry appear stable, particularly the domestic airline sector, which boasted record profits in 1997 that are expected to be topped in 1998. According to Brian D. Harris of Lehman Brothers Inc., the 11 largest airlines could post a 5 percent increase in profits and revenues. Despite an increase in labor costs and high fuel prices, air carriers have maintained high profits due to strong consumer demand coupled with high ticket prices.

Both Congress and the Transportation Department are proposing bills that would potentially spark more competition among airlines by seizing some of the takeoff and landing rights from larger airlines and granting them to smaller airlines, reports Business Week. *As safety and security issues have loomed larger in recent years, government demands for security upgrades on existing aircraft will be a growing priority for the next few years.*

A locomotive shortage may hinder some railroads in 1998, but mergers between companies such as Union Pacific Corporation and Southern Pacific Rail Corporation should benefit the industry, according to industry analyst James J. Valentine.

Rising labor costs and deregulation have forced the trucking industry to lower operating costs, but the U.S. Department of Commerce forecasts that industrial and commercial shipments should increase by about 17 percent annually until 2005.

AMR CORPORATION
AMERICAN AIRLINES
P.O. Box 619616, Mail Drop 5106, DFW Airport TX 76155. 817/963-1234. **Contact:** Human Resources Department. **World Wide Web address:** http://www.americanair.com. **Description:** AMR Corporation is an airline holding company whose principal subsidiary is American Airlines. American Airlines provides service to 106 domestic cities and 66 other cities worldwide. Domestic hubs are located in Dallas-Fort Worth, Chicago, Nashville, San Juan, Raleigh-Durham, and Miami. AMR Corporation's fleet consists of approximately 665 aircraft. **NOTE:** For positions other than flight attendants and pilots, request an application from American Airlines, Inc., P.O. Box 619040, Mail Drop 4146, DFW Airport TX 75261-9040. Send a self-addressed 9-by-12 inch envelope containing 52 cents postage. **Common positions include:** Accountant/Auditor; Customer Service Representative; Electrical/Electronics Engineer; Marketing Specialist; Sales Representative. **Educational backgrounds include:** Aviation. **Corporate headquarters location:** This Location. **Subsidiaries include:** SABRE Group conducts computer reservation operations and provides electronic data processing, information management, and computer services to clients in several industries; American Eagle is an airline that serves 170 cities in the U.S., Bahamas, and Caribbean; AMR Management Services, which leases aircraft, offers financial services, conducts training operations, and provides ground and cabin services. **Listed on:** New York Stock Exchange. **Number of employees at this location:** 27,000. **Number of employees nationwide:** 100,000.

ABILENE AERO INC.
2850 Airport Boulevard, Abilene TX 79602. 915/677-2601. **Fax:** 915/671-8018. **Contact:** Ron Clark, General Manager. **World Wide Web address:** http://www.abileneaero.com. **Description:** Operates a small airport offering flight instruction, charter and pilot service, aircraft fueling, parts, and maintenance. Abilene Aero Inc. is a fixed base operator. Founded in 1968. **Common positions include:** Accountant; Aircraft Mechanic/Engine Specialist; Customer Service Representative; General Manager; Sales Manager; Secretary. **Benefits:** 401(k); Medical Insurance; Profit Sharing.

Corporate headquarters location: This Location. **Subsidiaries include:** Lubbock Aero (Lubbock TX). **Annual sales/revenues:** $5 - $10 million. **Number of employees at this location:** 35.

ALFORD REFRIGERATED WAREHOUSES
318 Cadiz Street, Dallas TX 75207. 214/426-5151. **Contact:** Personnel. **Description:** A warehousing company engaged in the storage of frozen, cold, and dry food bought in grocery stores.

AMERICAN TRANSFER AND STORAGE
dba AMERICAN MAYFLOWER
4204 Lindberg Drive, Dallas TX 75244. 972/490-4444. **Contact:** Human Resources. **Description:** A moving van/truck line.

ASSOCIATED GLOBAL SYSTEMS
755 Port America Place, Suite 345, Grapevine TX 76051. 817/481-8302. **Contact:** Human Resources. **Description:** An air transportation company.

BALDWIN DISTRIBUTION SERVICES
7702 Broadway, Amarillo TX 79108. 806/383-7650. **Contact:** Rick Davis, Human Resources. **Description:** Provides long-haul trucking services. **Common positions include:** Truck Driver. **Benefits:** Disability Coverage; Life Insurance; Medical Insurance; Savings Plan.

BENCHMARK FOODS
2901 South Cravens Road, Fort Worth TX 76119-1857. 817/451-5599. **Contact:** Human Resources. **Description:** Transports food to penitentiaries.

BILBO TRANSPORTS INC.
2722 Singleton Boulevard, Dallas TX 75212. 214/637-1910. **Contact:** Human Resources. **Description:** A trucking company.

BOWDEN TRAVEL
410 West Chambers, Cleburne TX 76031. 817/925-6660. **Contact:** Human Resources. **Description:** A travel agency.

BUDGET RENT-A-CAR
P.O. Box 111520, Carrollton TX 75011. 972/404-7600. **Physical address:** 3350 Boyington Drive, Carrollton TX 75006. **Contact:** Human Resources. **Description:** A car rental service.

BURLINGTON NORTHERN AND SANTA FE RAILWAY COMPANY
2650 Lou Menk Drive, Fort Worth TX 76131. 817/333-2000. **Contact:** Human Resources. **Description:** A railroad transportation company operating on 24,500 miles of track in 25 western states and two Canadian provinces. The company is one of the largest haulers of western low-sulfur coal and grain in North America. **Corporate headquarters location:** This Location. **Listed on:** New York Stock Exchange.

CENTRAL FREIGHT INC.
P.O. Box 540277, Dallas TX 75354-0277. 972/579-4111. **Contact:** Human Resources. **World Wide Web address:** http://www.centralfreight.com. **Description:** A motor freight transportation company.

CITY MACHINE & WELDING INC.
9701 Interchange 552, Amarillo TX 79124-2333. 806/358-7293. **Contact:** Personnel Department. **Description:** Manufactures transport trailers and performs welding services.

CON-WAY TRUCKLOAD SERVICES, INC.
2322 Gravel Drive, Fort Worth TX 76118. 817/284-7800. **Contact:** Rick Fenske, Director of Personnel. **Description:** Con-Way Truckload Services (CWT), as a successor to Con-Way Intermodal, provides expanded services for over-the-road truckload transportation. As a full-service, multimodal truckload logistics company, its capabilities include expedited regional and

transcontinental highway operations with CWT drivers and company-owned trucks and trailers. CWT also retains the flexibility to offer its domestic intermodal operations. This service, marketed as the Con-Quest Premium Truckload Service, utilizes CWT's national long-haul alliances to provide time-definite intermodal truckload transportation. In addition, the company continues to offer basic intermodal marketing services, local and interstate container drayage, and international LCL shipping with its GlobalRate program. **Common positions include:** Accountant/Auditor; Brokerage Clerk; Clerical Supervisor; Customer Service Representative; Operations/Production Manager; Services Sales Representative. **Educational backgrounds include:** Accounting; Business Administration; Marketing. **Benefits:** 401(k); Dental Insurance; Disability Coverage; Life Insurance; Medical Insurance; Pension Plan; Profit Sharing; Savings Plan; Tuition Assistance. **Corporate headquarters location:** This Location. **Parent company:** Con-Way Transportation Services. **Operations at this facility include:** Administration; Regional Headquarters; Sales; Service. **Listed on:** New York Stock Exchange. **Number of employees at this location:** 140. **Number of employees nationwide:** 300.

CONCORDIA INTERNATIONAL FORWARDING CORPORATION
753 Port America Place, Suite 101, Grapevine TX 76051. 817/481-4560. **Contact:** Human Resources. **Description:** Engaged in the transportation of freight and cargo.

DALLAS AREA RAPID TRANSIT (DART)
P.O. Box 660163, Dallas TX 75266-7240. 214/749-3259. **Fax:** 214/749-3636. **Recorded jobline:** 214/749-3690. **Contact:** Human Resources. **Description:** A nonprofit, rapid transit system serving the Dallas metropolitan area. **Common positions include:** Administrative Assistant; Driver; Electrical/Electronics Engineer; Electrician. **Benefits:** 401(k); Dental Insurance; Disability Coverage; Life Insurance; Mass Transit Available; Medical Insurance; Tuition Assistance. **Special programs:** Internships.

DALLAS-FORT WORTH INTERNATIONAL AIRPORT
P.O. Drawer 619428, DFW Airport TX 75261-9428. 972/574-6032. **Recorded jobline:** 972/574-8024. **Contact:** Human Resources/Employment Office. **World Wide Web address:** http://www.dfwairport.com. **Description:** An airport.

DELTA AIR LINES, INC.
8700 North Stemmons Freeway, Suite 212, Dallas TX 75206. 214/630-3200. **Contact:** Personnel. **World Wide Web address:** http://www.delta-air.com. **Description:** One of the largest airlines in the United States. The company provides scheduled air transportation for passengers, freight, and mail on an extensive route that covers most of the country and extends to 32 foreign nations. The route covers 153 domestic cities in 43 states, the District of Columbia, Puerto Rico, the U.S. Virgin Islands, and 57 cities abroad. Major domestic hubs of Delta include the Atlanta, Dallas-Fort Worth, Salt Lake City, and Cincinnati ports with minor hubs in Los Angeles and Orlando. Delta has 550 aircraft in its fleet with 125 planes on order and 233 on option. Founded in 1929. **NOTE:** All hiring is done at the following location: Delta Air Lines Inc., Employment Office, P.O. Box 20530, Hartsfield International Airport, Atlanta GA 30320. 404/715-2600. **Corporate headquarters location:** Atlanta GA.

DUNCAN-ALEXANDER
1010 East Dallas Drive, Grapevine TX 76051. 817/329-6130. **Contact:** Human Resources Department. **Description:** Duncan-Alexander specializes in the transportation of all types of freight and cargo.

DYNAMEX
601 West Mockingbird Lane, Dallas TX 75247. 214/637-4000. **Contact:** Human Resources. **Description:** Offers customized warehousing and local outsourced delivery services for companies with no trucks or delivery vehicles. Founded in 1985.

EL CONEJO BUS LINES
627 North Westmoreland, Dallas TX 75211. 214/330-5930. **Contact:** Human Resources. **Description:** A bus line.

FFE TRANSPORTATION SERVICES, INC.
P.O. Box 655888, Dallas TX 75265-5888. 214/630-8090. **Contact:** Personnel. **World Wide Web address:** http://www.ffeinc.com. **Description:** A nationwide trucking transportation company.

FM INDUSTRIES, INC.
8600 Will Rogers Boulevard, Fort Worth TX 76140. 817/293-4220. **Contact:** Personnel Manager. **Description:** Produces hydraulic cushioning systems for railroad freight cars.

FEDERAL EXPRESS CORPORATION
109 North Chandler Road, Fort Worth TX 76111. 817/831-2383. **Contact:** Human Resources. **Description:** Federal Express Corporation offers delivery services in the United States and 187 other countries. The company's fleet consists of approximately 462 aircraft and over 30,000 delivery vehicles. The company also operates a business logistics service. Hubs and major sorting centers are in Alaska, Illinois, Indiana, California, New Jersey, and Tennessee. **Number of employees worldwide:** 70,500.

FORT WORTH JET CENTER
4201 North Main Street, Fort Worth TX 76106. 817/625-2366. **Contact:** Human Resources. **Description:** Refuels private corporate aircraft.

FRITZ COMPANIES
660 Fritz Drive, Coppell TX 75019. 972/471-7171. **Contact:** Human Resources Department. **World Wide Web address:** http://www.fritz.com. **Description:** Fritz Companies is a freight transportation company.

GOLDEN CAB
3131 Halifax, Dallas TX 75247. 214/630-8151. **Contact:** Human Resources. **Description:** A taxi service.

GREYHOUND LINES INC.
P.O. Box 660606, Dallas TX 75266-0606. 972/789-7000. **Contact:** Manager of Human Resources. **World Wide Web address:** http://www.greyhound.com. **Description:** Greyhound Lines is one of the country's largest, private transportation networks. Greyhound Lines conducts regular route, package express, charter, and food service operations. The fleet consists of over 1,600 buses that travel to over 2,600 destinations. **Other U.S. locations:** Nationwide. **Listed on:** American Stock Exchange.

INTERNATIONAL TOTAL SERVICES
8413 Sterling Street, Suite A, Irving TX 75063. 972/621-0255. **Contact:** Human Resources. **Description:** Engaged in aircraft cleaning services.

INTERSTATE TRAILERS, INC.
1102 Interstate 20 West, Arlington TX 76017. 817/465-5441. **Contact:** Human Resources. **Description:** A supplier of transportation equipment.

J.B. HUNT TRANSPORT INC.
5701 West Kiest Boulevard, Dallas TX 75236. 214/333-9768. **Contact:** Human Resources Department. **Description:** A freight transportation company. **Corporate headquarters location:** Lowell AR.

KITTY HAWK, INC.
P.O. Box 612787, DFW Airport TX 75261. 972/456-6000. **Contact:** Human Resources. **World Wide Web address:** http://www.kha.com. **Description:** Provides charter management and cargo services.

MARTINAIRE INC.
8030 Aviation Place, Suite 2000, Dallas TX 75235. 214/358-5858. **Contact:** Human Resources. **Description:** A freight carrier.

MESQUITE METRO AIRPORT
1130 Airport Boulevard, Suite 100, Mesquite TX 75181. 972/222-8536. **Contact:** Human Resources. **Description:** An airport.

N.T.S.
P.O. Box 921002, Fort Worth TX 76121. 817/731-8721. **Contact:** Human Resources. **Description:** Provides businesses with vehicle leasing services. **Parent company:** First Data Inc.

NIPPON EXPRESS USA INC.
P.O. Box 610548, Irving TX 75261. 972/621-1911. **Physical address:** 8065 Tristar Drive, Irving TX 75063. **Contact:** Human Resources. **Description:** Engaged in the transportation of freight and cargo.

NORTH TEXAS AIRCRAFT SERVICES
4480 Glenn Curtiss Drive, Dallas TX 75248. 972/713-6163. **Contact:** Human Resources. **Description:** Offers air transportation services.

OGDEN AVIATION SERVICES
P.O. Box 610031, DFW Airport, Dallas TX 75261. 972/621-2002. **Contact:** Human Resources Department. **Description:** Ogden Aviation Services provides airport ground handling and transportation services. **Corporate headquarters location:** New York NY. **Parent company:** Ogden Services Corporation.

SINGAPORE AIRLINES
8500 North Stemmons Freeway, Suite 1060, Dallas TX 75247. 214/631-6613. **Contact:** Human Resources. **Description:** An air transportation company.

SKEETER PRODUCTS INC.
P.O. Box 230, Kilgore TX 75663. 903/984-0541. **Contact:** Human Resources. **Description:** Manufactures boats.

SKY HELICOPTERS
2559 South Jupiter Road, Garland TX 75041-6011. 214/349-7000. **Contact:** Human Resources Department. **Description:** Sky Helicopters is engaged in helicopter transportation for both public and private use.

SOUTHWEST AIRLINES COMPANY
P.O. Box 36644, Dallas TX 75235-1644. 214/792-4213. **Fax:** 214/792-7015. **Contact:** SWA People Department. **World Wide Web address:** http://www.iflyswa.com. **Description:** One of the U.S.'s only major shorthaul, low-fare, high-frequency, point-to-point carriers. Southwest currently flies to 45 cities in 22 states and offers over 1,900 flights daily. **Common positions include:** Accountant/Auditor; Administrator; Aircraft Mechanic/Engine Specialist; Computer Programmer; Customer Service Representative; Flight Attendant; Human Resources Manager; Marketing Manager; Public Relations Specialist; Receptionist; Sales Representative; Secretary; Systems Analyst. **Educational backgrounds include:** Accounting; Computer Science; Liberal Arts; Marketing. **Benefits:** 401(k); Dental Insurance; Disability Coverage; Employee Discounts; Life Insurance; Medical Insurance; Profit Sharing; Savings Plan. **Special programs:** Internships. **Corporate headquarters location:** This Location. **Other U.S. locations:** Nationwide. **Listed on:** New York Stock Exchange. **Number of employees at this location:** 3,600. **Number of employees nationwide:** 17,000.

SPECTRO INC.
P.O. Box 1227, Arlington TX 76004-1227. 817/861-3367. **Contact:** Rex Havis, Owner. **Description:** Spectro Inc. conducts oil and wear-wheel oil analysis on aircraft.

STANLEY TRANSPORTATION
P.O. Box 35489, Dallas TX 75235. 214/631-8420. **Contact:** Human Resources. **Description:** A trucking company that hauls produce.

STEERE TANK LINES INC.
8700 King George Drive, Suite 124, Dallas TX 75235. 214/637-2400. **Contact:** Human Resources. **Description:** A commodity transporter. **Corporate headquarters location:** This Location.

SUPERIOR AVIATION SERVICES INC.
P.O. Box 780364, Dallas TX 75378. 214/350-2749. **Contact:** Human Resources. **Description:** Offers air transportation services.

TEXAS NORTHERN RAILWAY
P.O. Box 300, Lone Star TX 75668. 903/656-3761. **Contact:** Personnel Representative. **Description:** A regional rail system.

THAI AIRWAYS INTERNATIONAL LTD.
8700 North Stemmons Freeway, Suite 133, Dallas TX 75247. 214/631-8424. **Contact:** Human Resources. **Description:** An airline.

TRINITY INDUSTRIES, INC.
Route 13, Box 175, Longview TX 75602. 903/758-0761. **Contact:** Human Resources. **Description:** Manufactures an assortment of railroad and construction equipment and replacement parts. Trinity Industries also offers related services for the transportation, construction, aerospace, commercial, and industrial markets. Products include railcars, gas processing systems, petroleum transportation systems, guard rails, bridge girders and beams, airport boarding bridges, barges, tug boats, military marine vessels, and precision welding products. Trinity Industries also manufactures concrete and aggregates in Texas and produces metal components for the petrochemical, industrial, processing, and power markets.

TRINITY INDUSTRIES, INC.
P.O. Box 7596, Fort Worth TX 76111. 817/625-4161. **Contact:** Human Resources. **Description:** Manufactures an assortment of railroad and construction equipment and replacement parts. Trinity Industries also offers related services for the transportation, construction, aerospace, commercial, and industrial markets. Products include railcars, gas processing systems, petroleum transportation systems, guard rails, bridge girders and beams, airport boarding bridges, barges, tug boats, military marine vessels, and precision welding products. Trinity Industries also manufactures concrete and aggregates in Texas and produces metal components for the petrochemical, industrial, processing, and power markets.

TURBO-JET SPARES, INC.
2722 Burbank Street, Dallas TX 75235. 214/358-1777. **Contact:** Human Resources. **World Wide Web address:** http://www.turbojet.com. **Description:** Offers aircraft maintenance services.

UNITED PARCEL SERVICE (UPS)
P.O. Box 2047, Grapevine TX 76099-2047. 972/456-4928. **Recorded jobline:** 888/877-0924. **Contact:** Human Resources. **World Wide Web address:** http://www.ups.com. **Description:** This location houses area administrative offices for the parcel pickup and delivery service organization. UPS provides service to all 50 states and to more than 185 countries and territories worldwide. The company delivers approximately 12 million packages daily. **NOTE:** The jobline lists mainly part-time positions. People in search of full-time positions should fax resumes to the attention of Tom Mullen at 214/353-6565. **Common positions include:** Data Entry Clerk. **Educational backgrounds include:** Computer Science. **Benefits:** Dental Insurance; Disability Coverage; Life Insurance; Medical Insurance; Pension Plan; Profit Sharing; Savings Plan; Tuition Assistance. **Operations at this facility include:** District Headquarters.

WESTERN CARRIERS TRANSPORT INTERNATIONAL, INC.
P.O. Box 270, Fort Worth TX 76101. 817/335-4821. **Contact:** Personnel Representative. **Description:** A non-local trucking company.

YELLOW FREIGHT SYSTEMS, INC.
4500 Irving Boulevard, Dallas TX 75247. 214/631-7400. **Contact:** Personnel Department. **World Wide Web address:** http://www.yellowfreight.com. **Description:** A freight transportation

company. Yellow Freight Systems is a national long-haul truckload carrier, with over 585 terminal locations in 50 states, Puerto Rico, and many Canadian provinces. **Corporate headquarters location:** Overland Park KS.

Note: Because addresses and telephone numbers of smaller companies can change rapidly, we recommend you call each company to verify the information below before inquiring about job opportunities. Mass mailings are not recommended.

Additional small employers:

AIR TRANSPORTATION AND SERVICES

AOG
PO Box 540423, Dallas TX 75354-0423. 214/350-5334.

Atlantic Southeast Airlines
PO Box 612386, Dallas TX 75261-2386. 972/574-3741.

Bax Global
3015 N Airfield Dr, Dallas TX 75261-4309. 972/453-0722.

Business Jetsolutions
14651 Dallas Parkway, Fl 6, Dallas TX 75240-7476. 972/720-2800.

Continental Airlines Inc.
PO Box 612429, Dallas TX 75261-2429. 972/263-0523.

Express One International
3890 W est Northwest Hwy, Dallas TX 75220-8108. 214/902-2500.

Greenwich Air Services Inc.
9311 Reeves St, Dallas TX 75235-2048. 214/956-5000.

Greenwich Air Services Inc.
15225 FAA Blvd, Fort Worth TX 76155-2223. 214/956-4900.

International Aviation Services
4601 N Main St, Hangar 39N, Fort Worth TX 76106-2417. 817/626-0700.

Leading Edge Aircraft Detailing
10801 Baker St, Amarillo TX 79111-1235. 806/335-2616.

Million Air
4300 Westgrove Dr, Dallas TX 75248-2447. 972/248-1600.

Omniflight Helicopters Inc.
4650 Airport Pkwy, Dallas TX 75248-3206. 972/776-0130.

COURIER SERVICES

Federal Express Corporation
PO Box 61205, Dallas TX 75261. 972/456-4440.

Federal Express Corporation
3408 S Southwest Loop 323, Tyler TX 75701-9239. 903/581-4175.

Federal Express Corporation
4901 Airport Parkway, Dallas TX 75248-3317. 214/358-5271.

Federal Express Corporation
2825 W Kingsley Rd, Garland TX 75041-2409. 972/840-0515.

United Parcel Service
515 E 44th St, Lubbock TX 79404-3421. 806/742-8327.

United Parcel Service
2925 Merrell Rd, Dallas TX 75229-4905. 214/902-1034.

United Parcel Service
1300 East Northside Dr, Fort Worth TX 76102-1201. 817/347-3158.

United Parcel Service
9441 Lyndon B. Johnson Fwy, Dallas TX 75243-4545. 972/301-6001.

LOCAL AND INTERURBAN PASSENGER TRANSIT

ATE Management & Service Co.
2130 Hightower Dr, Garland TX 75041-6104. 972/278-1812.

Citibus
PO Box 2000, Lubbock TX 79457-0001. 806/767-2383.

City Cab of Dallas
2616 W Mockingbird Lane, Dallas TX 75235-5631. 214/350-4433.

Discount Shuttle & Tours
PO Box 1042, Euless TX 76039-1042. 214/361-7637.

Durham Transportation Inc.
5501 Martin L. King Blvd, Lubbock TX 79404-5033. 806/763-4481.

Presidential Taxi
2910 Jacksboro Hwy, Wichita Falls TX 76302-1019. 940/696-5466.

Super Shuttle DFW
729 E Dallas Rd, Grapevine TX 76051-4121. 817/329-2001.

MAINTENANCE FACILITIES FOR MOTOR FREIGHT TRANSPORTATION

CF Motor Freight
3925 Singleton Blvd, Dallas TX 75212-3504. 214/637-0104.

Roadway Express Inc.
200 N Belt Line Rd, Irving TX 75061-6306. 972/790-3611.

Roadway Express Inc.
800 E Berry St, Fort Worth TX 76110-4413. 940/387-9577.

MARINE CARGO HANDLING

Stevedore McIntosh Group
PO Box 884, Fort Worth TX 76101-0884. 817/335-7724.

MISC. TRANSPORTATION SERVICES

Progress Rail Services Corp.
PO Box 706, Waskom TX 75692-0706. 903/687-3388.

PACKING AND CRATING

Adamco Inc.
1750 Westpark Dr, Grand Prairie TX 75050-1922. 817/640-6430.

PASSENGER TRANSPORTATION ARRANGEMENT SERVICES

America's Travel Connection
1629 West Morton Street, Denison TX 75020-1748. 903/463-6193.

Dallas Travel Services
5080 Spectrum Drive, Dallas TX 75248-4648. 972/991-8500.

Rosenbluth International Inc.
PO Box 569630, Dallas TX 75356-9630. 214/689-7400.

Sammons Travel
10726 Plano Rd, Dallas TX 75238-1318. 214/210-6100.

World Travel Partners LP
5420 LBJ Freeway, Dallas TX 75240-6222. 972/702-1000.

RAILROAD EQUIPMENT

Gunderson Southwest Inc.
101 Park St, Cleburne TX 76031-4038. 817/556-9191.

Trinity Industries
2850 Peden Rd, Saginaw TX 76179-5517. 817/236-7141.

RAILROAD TRANSPORTATION

Quality Terminal Services
2400 Westport Parkway West, Haslet TX 76052-2700. 817/224-7166.

Union Pacific Corporation
1717 Main Street, Ste 5900, Dallas TX 75201-7339. 214/743-5600.

Union Pacific Corporation
PO Drawer 4427, Waco TX 76705. 817/878-4540.

TRUCKING

AAA Cooper Transportation
6909 Harry Hines Blvd, Dallas TX 75235-4212. 214/350-2466.

Action Delivery Service Inc.
PO Box 3062, Corsicana TX 75151-3062. 903/872-8313.

American Freightways Inc.
3100 S Belt Line Rd, Irving TX 75060-7100. 972/262-8911.

Bradford Trucking Inc.
PO Box 129, Cactus TX 79013-0129. 806/966-5164.

Burnham Service Corporation
1430 Bradley Lane, Ste 196, Carrollton TX 75007-4855. 972/446-8600.

Caliber System Co.
4901 Martin St, Fort Worth TX 76119-5232. 817/561-3008.

Central Freight Lines Inc.
5601 W Waco Dr, Waco TX 76710-5753. 254/772-2120.

Chaney Trucking
PO Box 1665, Roanoke TX 76262-1665. 817/430-0923.

Con-Way Southern Express
14500 Trinity Boulevard, Fort Worth TX 76155-2542. 817/358-3840.

Dalworth Trucking Co.
1840 NW Loop 286, Paris TX 75460-1780. 903/785-0326.

Daryl Flood Inc.
2009 Country Club Drive, Carrollton TX 75006-5702. 972/416-3385.

EDC Moving Systems
1232 Crowley Dr, Ste B, Carrollton TX 75006-1315. 972/245-6799.

Electronic Transport Corp.
908 North Bowser Rd, Richardson TX 75081-2869. 972/234-0827.

Ennis Transportation Company Inc.
Drawer 798, Ennis TX 75120-0798. 972/878-5801.

Federal/Ahart Moving & Storage Co.
11480 Anaheim Dr, Dallas TX 75229-2208. 972/241-3515.

Gulf Coast Transport Inc.
PO Box 851307, Mesquite TX 75185-1307. 972/226-3536.

Home Delivery Network
3440 Sojourn Dr, Ste 280, Carrollton TX 75006-2371. 972/248-4006.

James Helwig & Son Inc.
PO Box 1390, Rockwall TX 75087-1390. 972/771-0927.

KLLM Nationwide Carriers
215 Neal St, Seagoville TX 75159-2834. 972/287-2193.

MDR Cartage Inc.
1459 E Loop 304, Tyler TX 75701. 903/595-0740.

Mega Freight Lines Inc.
1002 Fountain Pkwy, Grand Prairie TX 75050. 972/988-8088.

Middleton Transportation Co.
PO Box 4529, Fort Worth TX 76164-0529. 817/336-2900.

Move Solutions Inc.
1673 Terre Colony Ct, Dallas TX 75212-6222. 214/630-3607.

MS Carriers Inc.
310 E Ave, Dallas TX 75203-3559. 972/266-1554.

NW Transport Service Inc.
4356 Singleton Blvd, Dallas TX 75212-3435. 214/638-3535.

Old Dominion Freight Line
2805 Mican Dr, Dallas TX 75212-4602. 214/951-7766.

Overnite Transportation Co.
2300 Time St, Irving TX 75061-8810. 972/721-9958.

Plains Transportation Inc.
PO Box 32230, Amarillo TX 79120-2230. 806/372-9290.

Ploof Truck Lines Inc.
102 Spinks Rd, Abilene TX 79603-7904. 915/691-1900.

Robert Heath Trucking Inc.
PO Box 2501, Lubbock TX 79408-2501. 806/747-1651.

Ryder Distribution Resources
1101 Everman Pkwy, Fort Worth TX 76140-4907. 817/293-8352.

Skyway Freight Systems Inc.
2020 McDaniel Dr, Ste 100, Carrollton TX 75006-6837. 972/263-0020.

Southeastern Freight Lines
1415 S Loop 12, Irving TX 75060-6321. 972/579-9955.

Southwest Freight Distribution
8189 S Central Expy, Dallas TX
75241-7820. 214/371-1901.

Tandy Transportation Inc.
2560 East Long Avenue, Fort
Worth TX 76137-4801. 817/834-
0421.

Truck Load Express Inc.
901 KCK Way, Cedar Hill TX
75104-8019. 972/293-3760.

USF Bestway Inc.
11430 Newkirk St, Dallas TX
75229-2028. 972/247-2426.

Willis Shaw Express Inc.
2425 South University Parks,
Waco TX 76706-6427. 254/753-
6331.

**WAREHOUSING AND
STORAGE**

Dry Storage Corporation
PO Box 5563, Arlington TX
76005-5563. 817/640-5498.

**We Pack Warehousing &
Distribution**
2510 S Church St, Paris TX
75460-7659. 903/737-0522.

**WATER TRANSPORTATION
OF FREIGHT**

Sea-Land Service Inc.
13465 Midway Road, Dallas TX
75244-5106. 972/716-4900.

**WHOLESALE OF
TRANSPORTATION
EQUIPMENT AND SUPPLIES**

Aviall Services Inc.
PO Box 7199, Dallas TX 75209-
0199. 972/406-6500.

Precision Air Parts
14280 Gillis Rd, Dallas TX
75244-3715. 972/233-5121.

For more information on career opportunities in transportation and travel industries:

Associations

**AIR TRANSPORT ASSOCIATION OF
AMERICA**
1301 Pennsylvania Avenue NW, Suite 1100,
Washington DC 20004. 202/626-4000. World Wide
Web address: http://www.air-transport.org. A trade
association for the major U.S. airlines.

AMERICAN BUREAU OF SHIPPING
2 World Trade Center, 106th Floor, New York NY
10048. 212/839-5000. World Wide Web address:
http://www.eagle.org.

AMERICAN SOCIETY OF TRAVEL AGENTS
1101 King Street, Suite 200, Alexandria VA 22314.
703/739-2782. World Wide Web address:
http://www.astanet.com. For information, send a
SASE with $.75 postage to the attention of the
Fulfillment Department.

AMERICAN TRUCKING ASSOCIATIONS
2200 Mill Road, Alexandria VA 22314-4677.
703/838-1700. World Wide Web address:
http://www.truckline.com. A trade association for the
trucking industry.

ASSOCIATION OF AMERICAN RAILROADS
50 F Street NW, Washington DC 20001. 202/639-
2100. World Wide Web address: http://www.aar.com.

**INSTITUTE OF TRANSPORTATION
ENGINEERS**
525 School Street SW, Suite 410, Washington DC
20024-2797. 202/554-8050. World Wide Web
address: http://www.ite.org. Scientific and educational
association, providing for professional development of
members and others.

MARINE TECHNOLOGY SOCIETY
1828 L Street NW, Suite 906, Washington DC 20036.
202/775-5966.

NATIONAL TANK TRUCK CARRIERS
2200 Mill Road, Alexandria VA 22314. 703/838-
1700. A trade association representing and promoting

the interests of the highway bulk transportation
community.

Directories

MOODY'S TRANSPORTATION MANUAL
Moody's Investors Service, Inc., 99 Church Street,
New York NY 10007. 212/553-0300. $12.95 per year
with weekly updates.

OFFICIAL MOTOR FREIGHT GUIDE
CNC Publishing, 1700 West Courtland Street,
Chicago IL 60622. 773/278-2454.

Magazines

AMERICAN SHIPPER
Howard Publications, P.O. Box 4728, Jacksonville FL
32201. 904/355-2601. Monthly.

FLEET OWNER
Intertech Publishing, 707 Westchester Avenue, White
Plains NY 10604-3102. 914/949-8500.

HEAVY DUTY TRUCKING
Newport Communications, P.O. Box W, Newport
Beach CA 92658. 714/261-1636.

ITE JOURNAL
Institute of Transportation Engineers, 525 School
Street SW, Suite 410, Washington DC 20024-2797.
202/554-8050. World Wide Web address: http://www.
ite.org. One year subscription (12 issues): $50.00.

**MARINE DIGEST AND TRANSPORTATION
NEWS**
Marine Publishing, Inc., P.O. Box 3905, Seattle WA
98124. 206/682-3607.

SHIPPING DIGEST
Geyer-McAllister Publications, 51 Madison Avenue,
New York NY 10010. 212/689-4411.

TRAFFIC WORLD MAGAZINE
529 14th Street NW, Washington DC 20045-2200.
202/783-1101.

TRANSPORT TOPICS
National Tank Truck Carriers, 2200 Mill Road, Alexandria VA 22314. 703/838-1772. World Wide Web address: http://www.ttnews.com.

Newsletters

AIR JOBS DIGEST
World Air Data, Department 700, P.O. Box 42360, Washington DC 20015. World Wide Web address: http://www.tggh.net/wad/index.html. This monthly resource provides current job openings in aerospace, space, and aviation industries. Subscription rates: $96.00 annually, $69.00 for six months, and $49.00 for three months.

Online Services

THE AIRLINE EMPLOYMENT ASSISTANCE CORPS.
http://www.csn.net/aeac. Site for aviation jobseekers providing worldwide classified ads, resume assistance, publications, and over 350 links to aviation-related Websites and news groups. Certain resources are members-only access.

JOBNET: HOSPITALITY INDUSTRY
http://www.westga.edu/~coop/hospitality.html. Provides links to job openings and information for airlines and cruise ships.

1-800-DRIVERS
http://rwa.metronetworks.com/800drivers.html. Designed to help job hunters find employment as a driver. This site offers an online job application, job listings, and links to various trucking companies.

TRAVEL PROFESSIONALS FORUM
Go: Travpro. To join this CompuServe forum, you will need to send an e-mail to the sysop for permission.

UTILITIES: ELECTRIC/GAS/WATER

Deregulation has greatly increased competition throughout all segments of the utilities industry. For example, many states now permit independent power producers to build electric power generating plants. In an effort to lower prices and compete with the new entrants, many existing electric utilities have resorted to layoffs and other cost-cutting measures. Although the utilities industry as a whole is expected to continue to grow, the U.S. Department of Labor forecasted that job growth would be only 12 percent in the period from 1992 to 2005, a rate much slower than the average for all industries.

B-K ELECTRIC COOPERATIVE, INC.
P.O. Box 672, Seymour TX 76380-2138. 940/888-3441. **Contact:** Human Resources Department. **Description:** An electric utility cooperative.

CENTRAL AND SOUTH WEST SERVICES INC.
P.O. Box 660164, Dallas TX 75266-0164. 214/777-1000. **Contact:** Human Resources. **World Wide Web address:** http://www.csw.com. **Description:** A diversified electric utility holding company whose subsidiaries provide electric power. Central and South West Services (CSW) serves over 1.5 million customers in Texas, Oklahoma, Louisiana, and Arkansas. The company also controls companies that are involved in cogeneration projects, leveraged leasing, data processing, and marketing. **Corporate headquarters location:** This Location. **Subsidiaries include:** Central Power and Light and West Texas Utilities operate in portions of south and central west Texas respectively; Public Service of Oklahoma operates in portions of eastern and southwestern Oklahoma; and Southwestern Electric Power operates in portions of northeastern Texas, northwestern Louisiana, and western Arkansas; Transok, Inc. is an interstate natural gas gathering, transmission, processing, storage, and marketing company which transports for and sells natural gas to and for non-affiliated companies; CSW Credit purchases accounts receivable of the operating companies and unaffiliated electric and gas utilities; CSW Energy, Inc. and CSW International pursue cogeneration projects and other energy ventures within the U.S. and internationally; CSW Communications provides communications services to the operating companies and non-affiliates; CSW Leasing invests in leveraged leases.

LONE STAR GAS COMPANY
301 South Harwood Street, Dallas TX 75201. 214/741-3750. **Contact:** Personnel Department. **Description:** A distributor of natural gas to Texas and southern Oklahoma. **Common positions include:** Accountant/Auditor; Attorney; Customer Service Representative; Draftsperson; Marketing Specialist; Mechanical Engineer; Systems Analyst. **Educational backgrounds include:** Accounting; Business Administration; Computer Science; Engineering; Finance; Marketing. **Benefits:** Dental Insurance; Disability Coverage; Life Insurance; Medical Insurance; Pension Plan; Profit Sharing; Savings Plan; Tuition Assistance. **Corporate headquarters location:** This Location. **Listed on:** New York Stock Exchange.

SOUTHWESTERN PUBLIC SERVICE COMPANY
P.O. Box 1261, Amarillo TX 79170-0001. 806/378-2121. **Contact:** Dave Tyler, Manager of Employee Services. **Description:** This location of Southwestern Public Service Company provides the Amarillo area with electricity. **Corporate headquarters location:** This Location. **Other U.S. locations:** KS; NM; OK.

TNP ENTERPRISES INC.
TEXAS-NEW MEXICO POWER COMPANY
P.O. Box 2943, Fort Worth TX 76113. 817/731-0099. **Contact:** Dennis Cash, Human Resources Manager. **World Wide Web address:** http://www.tnpe.com. **Description:** A public utility engaged

in the purchase, transmission, distribution, and sale of electrical power in Texas and New Mexico. TNP furnishes electric service to 88 municipalities in these states, with almost 170,000 customers and 490,000 people in its service area. **Common positions include:** Accountant/Auditor; Computer Programmer; Customer Service Representative; Electrical/Electronics Engineer; Systems Analyst. **Educational backgrounds include:** Accounting; Business Administration; Computer Science; Engineering. **Benefits:** Disability Coverage; Life Insurance; Medical Insurance; Pension Plan; Savings Plan; Tuition Assistance. **Corporate headquarters location:** This Location. **Listed on:** New York Stock Exchange.

TEXAS UTILITIES COMPANIES/TU ELECTRIC

1601 Bryan Street, Dallas TX 75201-3411. 214/812-4600. **Fax:** 214/812-8419. **Recorded jobline:** 214/812-8633. **Contact:** Staffing and Placement Manager. **Description:** A large investor-owned electric utility, providing electric service to 2 million customers in north, central, and western Texas. **Common positions include:** Accountant/Auditor; Administrative Manager; Architect; Branch Manager; Budget Analyst; Buyer; Chemist; Civil Engineer; Claim Representative; Clerical Supervisor; Computer Programmer; Construction Contractor; Cost Estimator; Customer Service Representative; Designer; Draftsperson; Economist; Electrical/Electronics Engineer; Electrician; Financial Analyst; General Manager; Human Resources Manager; Mechanical Engineer; Mining Engineer; Nuclear Engineer; Public Relations Specialist; Purchasing Agent/Manager; Quality Control Supervisor; Software Engineer; Structural Engineer; Systems Analyst. **Educational backgrounds include:** Accounting; Business Administration; Computer Science; Engineering. **Benefits:** 401(k); Dental Insurance; Disability Coverage; Life Insurance; Medical Insurance; Pension Plan; Savings Plan; Tuition Assistance. **Special programs:** Internships. **Corporate headquarters location:** This Location. **Subsidiaries include:** BRI; Chaco; TU Electric; TU Fuel Company; TU Mini; TU Services. **Parent company:** Texas Utilities. **Operations at this facility include:** Administration; Divisional Headquarters; Regional Headquarters; Sales; Service. **Listed on:** New York Stock Exchange. **Number of employees at this location:** 2,000. **Number of employees nationwide:** 10,000.

WEST TEXAS UTILITIES COMPANY

P.O. Box 841, Abilene TX 79604. 915/674-7000. **Contact:** Human Resources. **World Wide Web address:** http://www.csw.com. **Description:** An electric utility. **Parent company:** Central and South West Corporation (CSW) is a diversified electric utility holding company which provides electric power through subsidiaries Central Power & Light, Public Service of Oklahoma, Southwestern Electric Power, and West Texas Utilities.Central Power and Light and West Texas Utilities operate in portions of south and central west Texas respectively. Public Service of Oklahoma operates in portions of eastern and southwestern Oklahoma, and Southwestern Electric Power operates in portions of northeastern Texas, northwestern Louisiana, and western Arkansas. Another subsidiary, Transok, Inc., is an interstate natural gas gathering, transmission, processing, storage, and marketing company which transports for and sells natural gas to and for non-affiliated companies. Central and South West Services Inc. performs accounting, engineering, tax, legal, financial, electronic data processing, centralized economic dispatching of electric power, and other services for the CSW System. CSW Credit purchases accounts receivable of the operating companies and unaffiliated electric and gas utilities. CSW Energy, Inc. and CSW International pursue cogeneration projects and other energy ventures within the U.S. and internationally. CSW Communications provides communications services to the operating companies and non-affiliates. CSW Leasing invests in leveraged leases.

Note: Because addresses and telephone numbers of smaller companies can change rapidly, we recommend you call each company to verify the information below before inquiring about job opportunities. Mass mailings are not recommended.

Additional small employers:

ELECTRIC SERVICES

Brazo's Electric
PO Box 2585, Waco TX 76702-2585. 254/750-6500.

Denton County Electric Coop
3501 FM 2181, Denton TX 76205-3741. 940/321-4640.

Industrial Generating Company
PO Box 800, Fairfield TX 75840-0800. 903/389-2625.

Limestone Power Plant
RR 1, Box 85, Jewett TX 75846-9721. 903/626-9500.

Oklaunion Power Plant
12567 FM 3430, Vernon TX 76384-8825. 940/886-2631.

Pirkey Power Plant
RR 2, Box 165, Hallsville TX 75650-9654. 903/935-2361.

Southwestern Public Service Co.
PO Box 631, Lubbock TX 79408-0631. 806/765-2800.

Texas Power & Light Co.
PO Box 2599, Waco TX 76702-2599. 254/750-5398.

Texas Utilities Electric Co.
FM Rd 56 N, Glen Rose TX 76043. 254/897-8500.

Texas Utilities Electric Co.
2947 Executive Blvd, Mesquite TX 75149-2801. 972/216-3100.

Texas Utilities Electric Co.
PO Box 970, Fort Worth TX 76101-0970. 817/882-6490.

Texas Utilities Electric Co.
PO Box 1359, Tatum TX 75691-1359. 903/836-6513.

Texas Utilities Electric Co.
PO Box 1266, Mount Pleasant TX 75456-1266. 903/572-7906.

Texas Utilities Electric Co.
200 W Carpenter Fwy, Irving TX 75039-2003. 972/791-2888.

Texas-New Mexico Power Co.
PO Box 37, Bremond TX 76629-0037. 254/746-7604.

Texas-New Mexico Power Co.
PO Box 896, Lewisville TX 75067-0896. 972/317-1273.

Welsh Power Plant
PO Box 221, Pittsburg TX 75686-0221. 903/856-6638.

GAS AND/OR WATER SUPPLY

Dallas Water Utilities
1500 Marilla St, Dallas TX 75201-6318. 214/670-3144.

Texarkana Water Utilities
PO Box 2008, Texarkana TX 75504-2008. 903/798-3800.

GAS UTILITY SERVICES

Brazo's Gas Compressing Co.
PO Box 790, Mineral Wells TX 76068-0790. 940/325-1321.

Energas Company
PO Box 40, Amarillo TX 79105-0040. 806/378-3363.

Energas Company
PO Box 1121, Lubbock TX 79408-1121. 806/798-4451.

Lone Star Gas Co.
1500 W Loop 340, Waco TX 76712-6837. 254/750-1917.

Lone Star Gas Co.
100 W Morningside Dr, Fort Worth TX 76110-2707. 817/927-6980.

Lone Star Gas Co.
1310 Highway 66, Garland TX 75040-6731. 214/573-3727.

For more information on career opportunities in the utilities industry:

Associations

AMERICAN PUBLIC GAS ASSOCIATION
11094-D Lee Highway, Suite 102, Fairfax VA 22030. 703/352-3890. World Wide Web address: http://www.apga.org. Publishes a weekly newsletter.

AMERICAN PUBLIC POWER ASSOCIATION (APPA)
2301 M Street NW, Suite 300, Washington DC 20037. 202/467-2900. World Wide Web address: http://www.appanet.org. Represents publicly-owned utilities. Provides many services including government relations, educational programs, and industry-related information publications.

AMERICAN WATER WORKS ASSOCIATION
6666 West Quincy Avenue, Denver CO 80235. 303/794-7711.

NATIONAL RURAL ELECTRIC COOPERATIVE ASSOCIATION
4301 Wilson Boulevard, Arlington VA 22203. 703/907-5500. World Wide Web address: http://www.nreca.org.

Directories

MOODY'S PUBLIC UTILITY MANUAL
Moody's Investors Service, Inc., 99 Church Street, New York NY 10007. 212/553-0300. World Wide Web address: http://www.moodys.com. Annually available at libraries.

Magazines

PUBLIC POWER
American Public Power Association, 2301 M Street NW, Washington DC 20037. 202/467-2900.

MISCELLANEOUS WHOLESALING

 According to the U.S. Department of Commerce, the need to cut costs is increasing as wholesaling and distributing businesses become more global and competitive, leading to changes in manufacturer-distributor working relationships. The most significant of these is an improved efficiency in inventory management, whereby the distributor manages inventory at the customer's site.

Wholesaling has evolved into an industry driven by customer needs, and while companies now prefer to do business with fewer suppliers, they still expect quality services. Smaller wholesaling companies, therefore, are concentrating on offering specialized services that address customers' specific needs.

L.D. BRINKMAN/HOLLYTEX
1655 Waters Ridge Drive, Louisville TX 75057. 972/353-3500. **Contact:** Human Resources Department. **Description:** Engaged in the wholsale distribution of a variety of carpet and flooring products.

CELEBRITY, INC.
P.O. Box 6666, Tyler TX 75711. 903/561-3981. **Contact:** Human Resources. **Description:** A supplier of artificial flowers, foliage, flowering bushes, and other decorative accessories to craft stores and other specialty retailers and to wholesale florists throughout North America and Europe. Celebrity imports over 7,000 home accent, decorative accessory and giftware items including artificial floral arrangements; floor planters and trees; a wide range of decorative brass and textile products; and a broad line of seasonal items such as Christmas trees, wreaths, garlands and other ornamental products.

CLEMONS TRACTOR COMPANY
P.O. Box 7707, Fort Worth TX 76111. 817/834-8131. **Contact:** General Manager. **Description:** A dealer of construction and mining equipment.

GOLDTHWAITES OF TEXAS INC.
1401 Foch Street, Fort Worth TX 76107. 817/332-1521. **Contact:** Human Resources Department. **Description:** A distributor of Toro lawn and garden equipment. **Common positions include:** General Manager; Material Control Specialist. **Educational backgrounds include:** Marketing. **Benefits:** Dental Insurance; Disability Coverage; Employee Discounts; Life Insurance; Medical Insurance; Pension Plan; Profit Sharing; Savings Plan. **Corporate headquarters location:** This Location. **Operations at this facility include:** Administration; Regional Headquarters; Sales; Service.

HI-LINE
2121 Valley View Lane, Dallas TX 75234. 972/247-6200. **Contact:** Cindy Grieser, Human Resources Manager. **World Wide Web address:** http://www.hi-line.com. **Description:** A distributor of electrical and mechanical specialty products. **NOTE:** U.S. and Canada sales territories are available for qualified applicants. **Common positions include:** Manufacturer's/Wholesaler's Sales Rep. **Educational backgrounds include:** High School Diploma/GED. **Benefits:** Disability Coverage; Life Insurance; Medical Insurance; Pension Plan; Profit Sharing; Savings Plan; Tuition Assistance. **Corporate headquarters location:** This Location. **Operations at this facility include:** Administration; Sales. **Number of employees at this location:** 65.

For more information on career opportunities in the wholesaling industry:

<u>Associations</u>

**NATIONAL ASSOCIATION OF
WHOLESALERS (NAW)**
1725 K Street NW, Washington DC 20006.
202/872-0885. Offers publications on industry
trends and how to operate a wholesaling business.

EMPLOYMENT SERVICES

Many people turn to temporary agencies, permanent employment agencies, or executive recruiters to assist them in their respective job searches. At their best, these resources can be a valuable friend -- it's comforting to know that someone is putting his or her wealth of experience and contacts to work for you. At their worst, however, they are more of a friend to the employer, or to more experienced recruits, than to you personally, and it is best not to rely on them exclusively.

That said, there are several types of employment services for jobseekers to check out as part of their job search efforts:

TEMPORARY AGENCIES

Temporary or "temp" agencies can be a viable option. Often these agencies specialize in clerical and support work, but it's becoming increasingly common to find temporary assignments in other areas like accounting or computer programming. Working on temporary assignments will provide you with additional income during your job search and will add experience to your resume. It may also provide valuable business contacts or lead to permanent job opportunities.

Temporary agencies are listed in your local telephone directory and in *The JobBank Guide to Employment Services* (Adams Media Corporation), found in your local public library. Send a resume and cover letter to the agency, and call to schedule an interview. Be prepared to take a number of tests at the interview.

PERMANENT EMPLOYMENT AGENCIES

Permanent employment agencies are commissioned by employers to find qualified candidates for job openings. The catch is that their main responsibility is to meet the employer's needs -- not necessarily to find a suitable job for the candidate.

This is not to say that permanent employment agencies should be ruled out altogether. There are permanent employment agencies specializing in specific industries that can be useful for experienced professionals. However, permanent employment agencies are not always a good choice for entry-level jobseekers. Some will try to steer inexperienced candidates in an unwanted direction or offer little more than clerical placements to experienced applicants. Others charge a fee for their services -- a condition that jobseekers should always ask about up front.

Some permanent employment agencies dispute the criticisms mentioned above. As one recruiter puts it, "Our responsibilities are to the applicant and the employer equally, because without one, we'll lose the other." She also maintains that entry-level people are desirable, saying that "as they grow, we grow, too, so we aim to move them up the ranks."

In short, as that recruiter states, "All services are not the same." If you decide to register with an agency, your best bet is to find one that is recommended by a friend or associate. Barring that, names of agencies across the country can be found in *The Adams Executive Recruiters Almanac* or *The JobBank Guide to Employment Services*. Or you can contact:

National Association of Personnel Services (NAPS)
3133 Mount Vernon Avenue
Alexandria VA 22305
703/684-0180

Be aware that there are an increasing number of bogus employment service firms, usually advertising in newspapers and magazines. These companies promise even inexperienced jobseekers top salaries in exciting careers -- all for a sizable fee. Others use expensive 900 numbers that jobseekers are encouraged to call. Unfortunately, most people find out too late that the jobs they have been promised do not exist.

As a general rule, most legitimate permanent employment agencies will never guarantee a job and will not seek payment until after the candidate has been placed. Even so, every agency you are interested in should be checked out with the local chapter of the Better Business Bureau (BBB). Find out if the agency is licensed and has been in business for a reasonable amount of time.

If everything checks out, call the firm to find out if it specializes in your area of expertise and how it will go about marketing your qualifications. After you have selected a few agencies (three to five is best), send each one a resume with a cover letter. Make a follow-up phone call a week or two later, and try to schedule an interview. Once again, be prepared to take a battery of tests at the interview.

Above all, do not expect too much. Only a small percentage of all professional, managerial, and executive jobs are listed with these agencies. Use them as an addition to your job search campaign, not a centerpiece.

EXECUTIVE SEARCH FIRMS

Also known as headhunters, these firms are somewhat similar to permanent employment agencies. They seek out and screen candidates for high-paying executive and managerial positions and are paid by the employer. Unlike permanent employment agencies, they typically approach viable candidates directly, rather than waiting for candidates to approach them. Many prefer to deal with already employed candidates and will not accept "blind" inquiries.

These organizations are frequently not licensed, so if you decide to go with an executive search firm, make sure it has a solid reputation. Names of search firms can be found in *The Adams Executive Recruiters Almanac* or *The JobBank Guide to Employment Services*, or by contacting:

American Management Association (AMA)
Management Services Department
135 West 50th Street
New York NY 10020
212/586-8100

Association of Executive Search Consultants (AESC)
500 Fifth Avenue
Suite 930
New York NY 10110
212/398-9556

Note: On the following pages, you will find employment services for this JobBank book's coverage area. Because contact names and addresses can change regularly, we recommend that you call each company to verify the information before inquiring about opportunities.

TEMPORARY EMPLOYMENT AGENCIES

ABC TEMPS INC.
3109 Carlisle Street, Suite 208, Dallas TX 75204. 214/754-7052. **Fax:** 214/954-1525. **Contact:** Patti Perry, Regional Manager. **Description:** A temporary agency. Company pays fee. **Specializes in the areas of:** Accounting/Auditing; Manufacturing; Personnel/Labor Relations; Secretarial. **Positions commonly filled include:** Blue-Collar Worker Supervisor; Credit Manager; Customer Service Representative; Human Resources Specialist; Typist/Word Processor. **Benefits available to temporary workers:** Credit Union; Paid Holidays; Paid Vacation. **Average salary range of placements:** Less than $20,000. **Number of placements per year:** 200 - 499.

ACCLAIM SERVICES, INC.
5445 La Sierra, Suite 317, Dallas TX 75231. 214/750-1818. **Fax:** 214/750-4403. **Contact:** Manager. **Description:** A temporary agency. Company pays fee. **Specializes in the areas of:** Network Administration; Software Development; Technical Writing. **Positions commonly filled include:** Management Analyst/Consultant; Software Engineer; Systems Analyst; Technical Writer/Editor; Telecommunications Manager. **Average salary range of placements:** More than $50,000. **Number of placements per year:** 50 - 99.

ALLIANCE LEGAL STAFFING
1845 Woodall Rogers, Suite 1200, Dallas TX 75201. 214/954-8096. **Fax:** 214/954-1290. **Contact:** Manager. **Description:** A temporary agency. Company pays fee. **Specializes in the areas of:** Legal. **Positions commonly filled include:** Attorney; Paralegal. **Benefits available to temporary workers:** Paid Holidays; Paid Vacation. **Number of placements per year:** 200 - 499.

ATTORNEY RESOURCES, INC.
750 North St. Paul, Suite 540, Dallas TX 75201. 214/922-8050. **Toll-free phone:** 800/324-4828. **Fax:** 214/871-3041. **Contact:** Jennifer Colby, Manager. **E-mail address:** ari@airmail.net. **World Wide Web address:** http://www.cpgs.com/attorney.resource. **Description:** A temporary agency that also provides permanent placements in law firms. Company pays fee. **Specializes in the areas of:** Administration; Legal; Secretarial. **Positions commonly filled include:** Attorney; Legal Secretary; Paralegal. **Benefits available to temporary workers:** Paid Holidays; Paid Vacation; Referral Bonus Plan. **Number of placements per year:** 100 - 199.

BDE TEMPORARIES
5601 Bridge Street, 3rd Floor, Fort Worth TX 76112. 817/446-1898. **Fax:** 817/446-1899. **Contact:** Donnie Harley-Hayes, Owner. **Description:** A temporary agency that also provides some permanent and contract placements. Founded in 1992. **Positions commonly filled include:** Accountant/Auditor; Administrative Manager; Advertising Clerk; Aerospace Engineer; Civil Engineer; Clerical Supervisor; Computer Programmer; Customer Service Representative; Design Engineer; Designer; Draftsperson; Financial Analyst; Human Resources Specialist; Mechanical Engineer; Paralegal; Social Worker; Software Engineer; Structural Engineer; Systems Analyst; Technical Writer/Editor. **Benefits available to temporary workers:** Paid Holidays; Paid Vacation. **Other area locations:** Dallas TX. **Average salary range of placements:** $20,000 - $29,999. **Number of placements per year:** 50 - 99.

BACKLOG TEMPORARIES INC.
dba STAFF FORCE
9550 Skillman Street, Suite 204, Dallas TX 75243. 214/340-2325. **Contact:** Buzz Busby, Vice President. **Description:** A temporary agency. **Positions commonly filled include:** Human

Resources Specialist; Services Sales Representative. **Corporate headquarters location:** Houston TX.

BACKLOG TEMPORARIES INC.
dba STAFF FORCE
2925 LBJ Freeway, Suite 165, Dallas TX 75234. 972/484-6535. **Fax:** 972/484-6079. **Contact:** Kathy Lockwood, Branch Manager. **Description:** A temporary agency that also provides permanent placements. **Specializes in the areas of:** Clerical; Light Industrial. **Positions commonly filled include:** Customer Service Representative; Typist/Word Processor; Warehouse/Distribution Worker; Welder. **Corporate headquarters location:** Houston TX. **Average salary range of placements:** Less than $20,000. **Number of placements per year:** 50 - 99.

CDI TELECOMMUNICATIONS
2425 North Central Expressway, Suite 101, Richardson TX 75080. 972/480-8333. **Contact:** Branch Manager. **World Wide Web address:** http://www.cdicorp.com. **Description:** A temporary agency. **Specializes in the areas of:** Telecommunications. **International locations:** Worldwide. **Number of placements per year:** 1000+.

CO-COUNSEL
600 North Pearl Street, Suite 430, Dallas TX 75201. 214/720-3939. **Fax:** 214/720-0555. **Contact:** Staffing Coordinator. **Description:** A temporary agency. **Specializes in the areas of:** Legal. **Positions commonly filled include:** Attorney; Paralegal. **Average salary range of placements:** $30,000 - $50,000.

COMPUTEMP INC.
12870 Hillcrest Road, Suite 226, Dallas TX 75230. 972/661-1064. **Fax:** 972/661-9143. **Contact:** Linda Farris, Manager. **E-mail address:** dallas@computemp.com. **World Wide Web address:** http://www.computemp.com. **Description:** A temporary agency. Founded in 1984. Company pays fee. **Specializes in the areas of:** Computer Science/Software; Data Processing; Information Technology; Personnel/Labor Relations; Technical. **Positions commonly filled include:** Computer Operator; Computer Programmer; Internet Services Manager; Library Technician; MIS Specialist; Multimedia Designer; Software Engineer; Systems Analyst; Technical Writer/Editor; Telecommunications Manager. **Benefits available to temporary workers:** 401(k); Medical Insurance; Paid Vacation. **Average salary range of placements:** $30,000 - $50,000. **Number of placements per year:** 200 - 499.

CONTRACT DESIGN PERSONNEL
2225 East Randol Mill Road, Suite 223, Arlington TX 76011. 817/640-6119. **Fax:** 817/640-6256. **Contact:** Stan Baker, Director of Recruiting Operations. **Description:** A temporary agency that also offers some permanent placements. Company pays fee. **Specializes in the areas of:** Engineering; High-Tech; Multimedia; Technical. **Positions commonly filled include:** Aerospace Engineer; Architect; Chemical Engineer; Civil Engineer; Computer Programmer; Design Engineer; Designer; Draftsperson; Electrical/Electronics Engineer; Environmental Engineer; Industrial Engineer; Mechanical Engineer; Metallurgical Engineer; Mining Engineer; Multimedia Designer; Nuclear Engineer; Petroleum Engineer; Software Engineer; Structural Engineer; Systems Analyst; Technical Writer/Editor. **Benefits available to temporary workers:** Paid Holidays. **Number of placements per year:** 100 - 199.

DEPENDABLE DENTAL STAFFING
18601 LBJ Freeway, Mesquite TX 75150-5600. **Fax:** 972/681-9657. **Contact:** Karen Houston, Vice President. **Description:** A temporary employment agency. **Specializes in the areas of:** Health/Medical. **Positions commonly filled include:** Dental Assistant/Dental Hygienist; Dentist. **Average salary range of placements:** $30,000 - $50,000. **Number of placements per year:** 200 - 499.

DETAR SERVICES
1500 Norwood Drive, B202, Hurst TX 76054. 817/282-6510. **Contact:** Manager. **Description:** A temporary agency that also provides temp-to-perm placements.

DIVERSIFIED TEMPS
12801 North Central Expressway, Suite 210, Dallas TX 75243. 972/980-4398. **Fax:** 972/934-0151. **Contact:** Manager. **E-mail address:** ew821@aol.com. **Description:** A temporary agency. Company pays fee. **Specializes in the areas of:** Accounting/Auditing; Administration; Computer Science/Software; Personnel/Labor Relations; Sales; Secretarial. **Positions commonly filled include:** Accountant/Auditor; Adjuster; Administrative Manager; Budget Analyst; Claim Representative; Clerical Supervisor; Computer Programmer; Customer Service Representative; Draftsperson; Financial Analyst; General Manager; Human Resources Specialist; Management Trainee; Medical Records Technician; MIS Specialist; Purchasing Agent/Manager; Quality Control Supervisor; Services Sales Representative; Social Worker; Software Engineer; Telecommunications Manager; Typist/Word Processor. **Benefits available to temporary workers:** Dental Insurance; Medical Insurance. **Average salary range of placements:** $20,000 - $29,999. **Number of placements per year:** 1000+.

DRIVING FORCE, INC.
2030 Las Vegas Trail, Fort Worth TX 76108. 817/246-7113. **Contact:** G. Wayne Brown, Sr., President. **Description:** A temporary agency. **Specializes in the areas of:** Transportation. **Positions commonly filled include:** Driver. **Benefits available to temporary workers:** Credit Union; Dental Insurance; Life Insurance; Medical Insurance. **Average salary range of placements:** $30,000 - $50,000. **Number of placements per year:** 1 - 49.

ESPRIT TEMPORARY SERVICES
P.O. Box 35443, Dallas TX 75235. 214/631-3832. **Fax:** 214/638-2908. **Contact:** John Wilson, Recruiter. **Description:** A temporary agency. **Specializes in the areas of:** Administration; Customer Service; General Labor; Secretarial. **Positions commonly filled include:** Administrative Assistant; Administrative Manager; Blue-Collar Worker Supervisor; Computer Operator; Electrician; Human Resources Manager; Industrial Production Manager; Paralegal; Typist/Word Processor. **Benefits available to temporary workers:** Dental Insurance; Medical Insurance; Paid Vacation. **Average salary range of placements:** $30,000 - $50,000. **Number of placements per year:** 200 - 499.

FIRSTWORD STAFFING SERVICES
10000 North Central Expressway, Suite 118, Dallas TX 75231. 214/360-0020. **Fax:** 214/360-9206. **Contact:** Mary Burke, Corporate Services Manager. **Description:** A temporary agency. Company pays fee. **Specializes in the areas of:** Computer Science/Software; Personnel/Labor Relations; Secretarial; Technical. **Positions commonly filled include:** Claim Representative; Clerical Supervisor; Computer Programmer; Cost Estimator; Customer Service Representative; Electronics Technician; Paralegal; Typist/Word Processor. **Benefits available to temporary workers:** Dental Insurance; Medical Insurance; Paid Holidays; Paid Vacation; Referral Bonus Plan. **Average salary range of placements:** $20,000 - $29,999.

IMPRIMIS STAFFING SOLUTIONS
5550 LBJ Freeway, Suite 150, Dallas TX 75240. 972/419-1631. **Fax:** 972/419-1970. **Contact:** Meg Graham, Recruiter. **World Wide Web address:** http://www.imprimis-group.com. **Description:** A temporary agency that also offers some permanent placements. **Specializes in the areas of:** Accounting/Auditing; Administration; Clerical; Computer Science/Software; Finance; Insurance; Legal; Nonprofit; Personnel/Labor Relations; Secretarial. **Positions commonly filled include:** Accountant/Auditor; Administrative Assistant; Auditor; Clerical Supervisor; Computer Operator; Customer Service Representative; Graphic Artist; Human Resources Specialist; MIS Specialist; Sales Representative; Software Engineer; Typist/Word Processor. **Benefits available to temporary workers:** 401(k); Medical Insurance; Paid Holidays; Paid Vacation. **Average salary range of placements:** $20,000 - $29,999. **Number of placements per year:** 1000+.

INSURANCE TEMPORARY SERVICES, INC.
2777 Stemmons Freeway, LB26, Dallas TX 75207. 214/638-7777. **Fax:** 214/634-8500. **Contact:** Susie Lowry, President. **Description:** A temporary agency. **Specializes in the areas of:** Insurance. **Positions commonly filled include:** Adjuster; Claim Representative; Customer Service Representative; Typist/Word Processor.

KELLY SCIENTIFIC RESOURCES
2323 North Central Expressway, Suite 155, Richardson TX 75080. 972/234-8175. **Fax:** 972/690-4825. **Contact:** Branch Manager. **World Wide Web address:** http://www.kellyscientific.com. **Description:** A temporary agency for scientific professionals. **Specializes in the areas of:** Biomedical; Biotechnology; Chemicals; Environmental; Food; Petrochemical; Pharmaceuticals.

KELLY SERVICES, INC.
1800 Teague Drive, Suite 100, Sherman TX 75090. 903/893-7777. **Contact:** Branch Manager. **Description:** A temporary agency. **Specializes in the areas of:** Accounting/Auditing; Banking; Clerical; Computer Hardware/Software; Engineering; Finance; Food; Health/Medical; Legal; Manufacturing; Secretarial; Technical; Transportation. **Other U.S. locations:** Nationwide.

KELLY SERVICES, INC.
1616 South Kentucky, Building D, Suite 110, Amarillo TX 79102. 806/355-9696. **Fax:** 806/359-0308. **Contact:** Branch Manager. **Description:** A temporary agency. Founded in 1946. Company pays fee. **Specializes in the areas of:** Accounting/Auditing; Administration; Finance; Insurance; Secretarial. **Positions commonly filled include:** Administrative Assistant; Marketing Specialist; Secretary; Typist/Word Processor. **Benefits available to temporary workers:** Medical Insurance; Paid Holidays; Paid Vacation. **Other U.S. locations:** Nationwide. **Average salary range of placements:** $20,000 - $29,999. **Number of placements per year:** 500 - 999.

MANPOWER, INC.
12225 Greenville Avenue, Suite 495, Dallas TX 75243. 972/699-9337. **Contact:** W.H. Wilson, Area Manager. **World Wide Web address:** http://www.manpower.com. **Description:** A temporary agency. Company pays fee. **Specializes in the areas of:** Data Processing; Light Industrial; Office Support; Technical; Travel. **Benefits available to temporary workers:** Life Insurance; Medical Insurance; Paid Holidays; Paid Vacation. **Number of placements per year:** 1000+.

CURTIS McINTOSH ASSOCIATES
P.O. Box 884, Fort Worth TX 76101. 817/335-7724. **Contact:** Manager. **Description:** A temporary agency. **Specializes in the areas of:** Transportation. **Positions commonly filled include:** Truck Driver.

NORRELL SERVICES
511 John Carpenter Freeway, Suite 160, Irving TX 75062. 972/263-5045. **Fax:** 972/432-9359. **Contact:** Tina Power, On-Site Supervisor. **Description:** A temporary agency. **Specializes in the areas of:** Secretarial. **Positions commonly filled include:** Customer Service Representative; Typist/Word Processor.

NURSES TODAY, INC.
4230 LBJ Freeway, Suite 110, Dallas TX 75244. 972/233-9966. **Fax:** 972/233-5354. **Contact:** Anita Porco, CEO. **Description:** A temporary agency. Nurses Today is also a home health care agency and provider of case management services. **Specializes in the areas of:** Health/Medical; Industrial. **Positions commonly filled include:** Certified Nurses Aide; Licensed Practical Nurse; Registered Nurse. **Average salary range of placements:** $30,000 - $50,000.

OLSTEN STAFFING SERVICES
1445 MacArthur Drive, Suite 236, Carrollton TX 75007. 972/245-5700. **Fax:** 972/446-1020. **Contact:** Branch Manager. **Description:** A temporary agency. **Specializes in the areas of:** Accounting/Auditing; Administration; Banking; Computer Science/Software; Engineering; Finance; General Management; Health/Medical; Industrial; Insurance; Legal; Manufacturing; Personnel/Labor Relations; Secretarial; Technical. **Positions commonly filled include:** Accountant/Auditor; Administrative Manager; Blue-Collar Worker Supervisor; Chemical Engineer; Clerical Supervisor; Clinical Lab Technician; Computer Programmer; Credit Manager; Customer Service Representative; Human Resources Specialist; Mechanical Engineer; Medical Records Technician; Paralegal; Quality Control Supervisor; Registered Nurse; Respiratory Therapist; Software Engineer; Technical Writer/Editor; Typist/Word Processor. **Benefits available to temporary workers:** Daycare Assistance; Medical Insurance; Paid Vacation. **International**

locations: United Kingdom. **Average salary range of placements:** $20,000 - $29,999. **Number of placements per year:** 1000+.

OLSTEN STAFFING SERVICES
9400 North Central Avenue, Suite 112, Dallas TX 75231. 214/373-7400. **Fax:** 214/739-4649. **Contact:** Sorya Doeung, Office Automation Specialist. **Description:** A temporary agency. **Specializes in the areas of:** Accounting/Auditing; Industrial; Light Industrial; Sales; Secretarial. **Positions commonly filled include:** Administrative Assistant; Secretary; Typist/Word Processor. **Benefits available to temporary workers:** Medical Insurance; Paid Vacation. **International locations:** United Kingdom. **Average salary range of placements:** $20,000 - $29,999. **Number of placements per year:** 1000+.

OLSTEN STAFFING SERVICES
275 West Campbell, Suite 117, Richardson TX 75080. 972/669-8900. **Fax:** 972/669-2254. **Contact:** Melissa Reisberg, Customer Service Manager. **E-mail address:** choff.olsten@intur.net. **Description:** A temporary agency. Company pays fee. **Specializes in the areas of:** Personnel/Labor Relations. **Positions commonly filled include:** Customer Service Representative; Typist/Word Processor. **International locations:** United Kingdom. **Average salary range of placements:** Less than $20,000.

PRO STAFF PERSONNEL SERVICES
14755 Preston Road, Dallas TX 75240. 972/239-8800. **Toll-free phone:** 800/938-9675. **Fax:** 972/239-4600. **Contact:** Katherine Tolsch, Branch Manager. **Description:** A temporary agency that also provides some permanent placements. Company pays fee. **Specializes in the areas of:** Accounting/Auditing; Advertising; Computer Science/Software; Engineering; Finance; Light Industrial; Manufacturing; Sales; Secretarial; Technical. **Positions commonly filled include:** Accountant/Auditor; Administrative Manager; Advertising Clerk; Bank Officer/Manager; Blue-Collar Worker Supervisor; Branch Manager; Brokerage Clerk; Budget Analyst; Claim Representative; Clerical Supervisor; Computer Programmer; Cost Estimator; Design Engineer; Electrical/Electronics Engineer; Financial Analyst; General Manager; Human Resources Specialist; Industrial Engineer; Industrial Production Manager; Management Analyst/Consultant; Management Trainee; Manufacturer's/Wholesaler's Sales Rep.; Market Research Analyst; Mechanical Engineer; MIS Specialist; Operations/Production Manager; Purchasing Agent/Manager; Quality Control Supervisor; Services Sales Representative; Software Engineer; Systems Analyst; Technical Writer/Editor; Typist/Word Processor; Underwriter/Assistant Underwriter. **Benefits available to temporary workers:** 401(k); Medical Insurance; Paid Holidays; Paid Vacation. **Average salary range of placements:** $20,000 - $29,999. **Number of placements per year:** 1000+.

PRO STAFF PERSONNEL SERVICES
122 West John Carpenter Freeway, Suite 515, Irving TX 75039. 972/650-1500. **Fax:** 972/650-0857. **Recorded jobline:** 972/712-6528. **Contact:** Manager. **Description:** A temporary agency. **Specializes in the areas of:** Accounting/Auditing; Administration; Art/Design; Secretarial; Technical. **Positions commonly filled include:** Customer Service Representative; Light Industrial Worker; Receptionist; Typist/Word Processor. **Benefits available to temporary workers:** 401(k); Medical Insurance. **Average salary range of placements:** Less than $20,000. **Number of placements per year:** 1000+.

RESPIRATORY STAFFING SPECIALIST INC.
310 East Interstate 30, Suite 290, Garland TX 75043. 972/226-5421. **Toll-free phone:** 800/758-3275. **Fax:** 972/226-0323. **Contact:** Carla DeWitt, President. **Description:** A temporary agency. **Specializes in the areas of:** Health/Medical. **Positions commonly filled include:** Respiratory Therapist. **Average salary range of placements:** $20,000 - $29,999. **Number of placements per year:** 1 - 49.

RESTAURANT SERVERS, INC.
10530 Shady Trail, Dallas TX 75220. 214/350-1166. **Fax:** 214/350-0454. **Contact:** Carol Fisher, Owner. **Description:** A temporary agency that also provides contract services in event management and food protection management, as well as training and consulting services. **Specializes in the**

areas of: Food. **Positions commonly filled include:** Blue-Collar Worker Supervisor; Education Administrator; Management Trainee; Registered Nurse; Restaurant/Food Service Manager; Teacher/Professor. **Average salary range of placements:** Less than $20,000. **Number of placements per year:** 200 - 499.

SOS STAFFING SERVICES
1327 Empire Central, Suite 130, Dallas TX 75247. 214/638-0766. **Contact:** Manager. **Description:** A temporary agency that also provides some permanent placements. Company pays fee. **Specializes in the areas of:** Administration; Industrial; Manufacturing; Personnel/Labor Relations; Secretarial. **Positions commonly filled include:** Accountant/Auditor; Automotive Mechanic; Blue-Collar Worker Supervisor; Buyer; Claim Representative; Clerical Supervisor; Computer Programmer; Cost Estimator; Credit Manager; Customer Service Representative; Design Engineer; Draftsperson; Hotel Manager; Human Service Worker; Landscape Architect; Mechanical Engineer; Operations/Production Manager; Purchasing Agent/Manager; Restaurant/Food Service Manager; Telecommunications Manager; Travel Agent; Typist/Word Processor. **Benefits available to temporary workers:** Paid Holidays; Paid Vacation. **Number of placements per year:** 100 - 199.

ANNE SADOVSKY & COMPANY
7557 Rambler Road, Suite 1454, Dallas TX 75231. 214/692-9300. **Fax:** 214/692-9823. **Contact:** Manager. **Description:** A temporary agency. Company pays fee. **Specializes in the areas of:** Housing; Sales. **Average salary range of placements:** $20,000 - $29,999. **Number of placements per year:** 1000+.

SPECIAL COUNSEL
AMICUS LEGAL STAFFING INC.
901 Main Street, Suite 2830, Dallas TX 75202. 972/934-9111. **Contact:** Manager. **Description:** A temporary agency that also provides some permanent placements and executive searches. **Specializes in the areas of:** Legal.

TRC STAFFING SERVICES INC.
1300 Summit Avenue, Suite 634, Fort Worth TX 76102. 817/335-1550. **Contact:** Amy Haines, Operations Manager. **E-mail address:** trc@onramp.net. **Description:** A temporary and temp-to-perm employment agency. Founded in 1990. Company pays fee. **Specializes in the areas of:** Clerical; Industrial; Manufacturing; Secretarial; Technical. **Positions commonly filled include:** Accountant/Auditor; Buyer; Chemist; Claim Representative; Computer Programmer; Customer Service Representative; Paralegal; Systems Analyst; Technical Writer/Editor. **Benefits available to temporary workers:** Medical Insurance; Paid Holidays; Paid Vacation. **Number of placements per year:** 1000+.

TEMP 2000 TEMPORARY SERVICES, INC.
14114 North Dallas Parkway, Suite 420, Dallas TX 75240. 972/385-0060. **Contact:** Elizabeth Taylor, Operations Manager. **Description:** A temporary agency. **Specializes in the areas of:** Accounting/Auditing; Legal; Personnel/Labor Relations; Secretarial; Technical. **Positions commonly filled include:** Accountant/Auditor; Clerical Supervisor; Computer Programmer; Customer Service Representative; Human Resources Specialist; MIS Specialist; Paralegal; Systems Analyst; Typist/Word Processor. **Benefits available to temporary workers:** Paid Vacation. **Average salary range of placements:** $20,000 - $29,999. **Number of placements per year:** 100 - 199.

TEMPORARIES, INC.
1555 West Mockingbird Lane, Suite 204, Dallas TX 75235. 214/630-0365. **Contact:** Art Thompson, District Manager. **Description:** A temporary agency. **Positions commonly filled include:** Accountant/Auditor; Administrative Assistant; Administrative Worker/Clerk; Bookkeeper; Clerk; Computer Operator; Computer Programmer; Construction Trade Worker; Customer Service Representative; Data Entry Clerk; Dietician/Nutritionist; Driver; Factory Worker; General Manager; Legal Secretary; Light Industrial Worker; Medical Secretary; Receptionist; Secretary; Stenographer; Typist/Word Processor. **Number of placements per year:** 1000+.

TEMPORARY HELP SERVICE INC.
P.O. Box 53021, Lubbock TX 79453. 806/799-3159. **Fax:** 806/799-0183. **Contact:** John Arland, President. **Description:** A temporary agency. **Specializes in the areas of:** Legal; Manufacturing. **Positions commonly filled include:** Clerical Supervisor.

TEXAS WORKFORCE COMMISSION
4309 Jacksboro Highway, Suite 300, Wichita Falls TX 76302-2740. 940/322-8220. **Fax:** 940/322-8411. **Contact:** Manager. **Description:** A temp-to-perm agency.

TODAYS TEMPORARY
8445 Freeport Parkway, Suite 310, Irving TX 75063. 972/915-0555. **Fax:** 972/915-0551. **Contact:** Operations Manager. **World Wide Web address:** http://www.todays.com. **Description:** A temporary agency. Company pays fee. **Specializes in the areas of:** Secretarial. **Positions commonly filled include:** Administrative Manager; Advertising Clerk; Branch Manager; Claim Representative; Clerical Supervisor; Customer Service Representative. **Corporate headquarters location:** Dallas TX. **Other U.S. locations:** Nationwide. **Average salary range of placements:** $20,000 - $29,999. **Number of placements per year:** 1000+.

TODAYS TEMPORARY
4100 Alpha Road, Suite 215, Dallas TX 75244-4332. 972/788-4435. **Contact:** Kristen Prather, Operations Manager. **World Wide Web address:** http://www.todays.com. **Description:** A temporary staffing agency. Company pays fee. **Specializes in the areas of:** Accounting/Auditing; Computer Science/Software; Legal; Personnel/Labor Relations; Sales. **Positions commonly filled include:** Clerical Supervisor; Financial Analyst; Human Resources Specialist; Human Service Worker. **Benefits available to temporary workers:** Paid Holidays; Paid Vacation. **Corporate headquarters location:** 18111 Preston Road, Suite 700, Dallas TX 75252. **Other U.S. locations:** Nationwide. **Number of placements per year:** 1000+.

TODAYS TEMPORARY
18111 Preston Road, Suite 700, Dallas TX 75252. 972/380-9380. **Fax:** 972/713-4196. **Contact:** Rhonda Page, Communications Manager. **World Wide Web address:** http://www.todays.com. **Description:** A temporary agency. **Specializes in the areas of:** Accounting/Auditing; Banking; Legal; Secretarial. **Positions commonly filled include:** Accountant/Auditor; Administrative Manager; Advertising Clerk; Attorney; Brokerage Clerk; Claim Representative; Computer Programmer; Customer Service Representative; Paralegal; Typist/Word Processor. **Benefits available to temporary workers:** 401(k); Paid Holidays; Paid Vacation. **Corporate headquarters location:** This Location. **Other U.S. locations:** Nationwide. **Average salary range of placements:** Less than $20,000. **Number of placements per year:** 1000+.

TRYOUT TEMPS, INC.
3320 Troup Highway, Suite 230, Tyler TX 75701. 903/526-2460. **Contact:** Manager. **Description:** A temporary agency. **Number of placements per year:** 500 - 999.

VOLT SERVICES GROUP OF DALLAS
9330 LBJ Freeway, Suite 1060, Dallas TX 75243-9946. 972/690-8358. **Contact:** Office Manager. **Description:** A temporary employment agency. **Specializes in the areas of:** Clerical; Computer Hardware/Software; Engineering; Manufacturing; Personnel/Labor Relations; Technical.

WESTERN TEMPORARY SERVICE
323 Las Colinas Boulevard East, Irving TX 75039-5556. 972/831-8833. **Fax:** 972/831-8856. **Contact:** Staffing Coordinator. **Description:** A temporary agency. **Specializes in the areas of:** Industrial; Personnel/Labor Relations; Sales; Secretarial; Technical. **Positions commonly filled include:** Blue-Collar Worker Supervisor; Customer Service Representative; Human Resources Specialist; Management Trainee; Services Sales Representative. **Benefits available to temporary workers:** 401(k); Medical Insurance; Paid Holidays; Paid Vacation. **Number of placements per year:** 1000+.

PERMANENT EMPLOYMENT AGENCIES

AARP SENIOR COMMUNITY SERVICE EMPLOYMENT PROGRAM
2301 North Akard Street, Suite 111, Dallas TX 75201. 214/954-0442. **Contact:** Arnold Parra, Project Director. **Description:** A permanent placement agency. **Positions commonly filled include:** Accountant/Auditor; Administrative Manager; Blue-Collar Worker Supervisor; Branch Manager; Clerical Supervisor; Credit Manager; General Manager; Human Service Worker; Petroleum Engineer; Restaurant/Food Service Manager; Teacher/Professor. **Number of placements per year:** 1 - 49.

ABILENE EMPLOYMENT SERVICE
1290 South Willis Street, Suite 111, Abilene TX 79605. 915/698-0451. **Fax:** 915/690-1242. **Contact:** Vi Ballard, Owner. **Description:** A permanent employment agency. **Specializes in the areas of:** Accounting/Auditing; Banking; Computer Science/Software; General Management; Health/Medical; Insurance; Legal; Manufacturing; Retail; Secretarial; Transportation. **Positions commonly filled include:** Accountant/Auditor; Administrative Manager; Advertising Clerk; Aircraft Mechanic/Engine Specialist; Automotive Mechanic; Bank Officer/Manager; Blue-Collar Worker Supervisor; Branch Manager; Buyer; Clerical Supervisor; Computer Programmer; Cost Estimator; Counselor; Customer Service Representative; Electrician; General Manager; Human Service Worker; Landscape Architect; Medical Records Technician; Operations/Production Manager; Physical Therapist; Property and Real Estate Manager; Quality Control Supervisor; Real Estate Agent; Restaurant/Food Service Manager; Securities Sales Representative; Software Engineer; Systems Analyst; Travel Agent; Typist/Word Processor. **Average salary range of placements:** $20,000 - $29,999. **Number of placements per year:** 1 - 49.

ACCOUNTING ACTION PERSONNEL
3010 LBJ Freeway, Suite 710, Dallas TX 75234. 972/241-1543. **Contact:** Cheryl Bieke, Office Manager. **Description:** A permanent employment agency. Company pays fee. **Specializes in the areas of:** Accounting/Auditing; Administration; Finance. **Positions commonly filled include:** Accountant/Auditor; Administrative Assistant; Bookkeeper; Clerk; Credit Manager; Data Entry Clerk; Receptionist; Secretary; Typist/Word Processor.

AUSTIN MEDICAL PERSONNEL
1010 West Rosedale Street, Fort Worth TX 76104. 817/335-2433. **Contact:** Manager. **Description:** A permanent placement agency. **Specializes in the areas of:** Health/Medical.

AWARE AFFILIATES PERSONNEL SERVICE
P.O. Box 470183, Fort Worth TX 76147. 817/870-2591. **Fax:** 817/870-2590. **Contact:** Mike Keeton, President. **Description:** A permanent employment agency. **Specializes in the areas of:** Accounting/Auditing; Administration; Advertising; Finance; General Management; Health/Medical; Insurance; Legal; Manufacturing; Nonprofit; Personnel/Labor Relations; Publishing; Retail; Sales; Secretarial; Technical; Transportation. **Positions commonly filled include:** Accountant/Auditor; Adjuster; Administrative Manager; Advertising Clerk; Blue-Collar Worker Supervisor; Branch Manager; Claim Representative; Clerical Supervisor; Computer Programmer; Cost Estimator; Counselor; Credit Manager; Customer Service Representative; Editor; Financial Analyst; General Manager; Health Services Manager; Hotel Manager; Human Resources Specialist; Insurance Agent/Broker; Library Technician; Management Trainee; Manufacturer's/Wholesaler's Sales Rep.; Operations/Production Manager; Paralegal; Property and Real Estate Manager; Purchasing Agent/Manager; Quality Control Supervisor; Securities Sales Representative; Services Sales Representative; Transportation/Traffic Specialist; Travel Agent; Typist/Word Processor; Underwriter/Assistant Underwriter. **Average salary range of placements:** $20,000 - $29,999. **Number of placements per year:** 200 - 499.

B.G. PERSONNEL SERVICES
P.O. Box 803026, Dallas TX 75380. 972/960-7741. **Contact:** Manager. **Description:** A permanent employment agency. **Specializes in the areas of:** Real Estate.

BABICH & ASSOCIATES, INC.
6060 North Central Expressway, Suite 544, Dallas TX 75206. 214/361-5735. **Contact:** Anthony Beshara, President. **Description:** A permanent employment agency. Company pays fee. **Specializes in the areas of:** Accounting/Auditing; Administration; Clerical; Computer Hardware/Software; Engineering; Finance; Manufacturing; Sales; Technical. **Positions commonly filled include:** Accountant/Auditor; Administrative Assistant; Agricultural Engineer; Bookkeeper; Ceramics Engineer; Civil Engineer; Computer Programmer; Customer Service Representative; Data Entry Clerk; EDP Specialist; Electrical/Electronics Engineer; Financial Analyst; General Manager; Human Resources Manager; Industrial Engineer; Mechanical Engineer; Medical Secretary; Metallurgical Engineer; Receptionist; Secretary; Systems Analyst; Typist/Word Processor. **Number of placements per year:** 500 - 999.

BABICH & ASSOCIATES, INC.
One Summit Avenue, Suite 602, Fort Worth TX 76102. 817/336-7261. **Contact:** Anthony Beshara, President. **Description:** A permanent employment agency. Company pays fee. **Specializes in the areas of:** Accounting/Auditing; Administration; Clerical; Computer Hardware/Software; Engineering; Manufacturing; Sales; Technical. **Positions commonly filled include:** Accountant/Auditor; Administrative Assistant; Agricultural Engineer; Bookkeeper; Ceramics Engineer; Civil Engineer; Computer Programmer; Customer Service Representative; Data Entry Clerk; EDP Specialist; Electrical/Electronics Engineer; Financial Analyst; General Manager; Human Resources Manager; Industrial Engineer; Mechanical Engineer; Medical Secretary; Metallurgical Engineer; Receptionist; Sales Representative; Secretary; Stenographer; Systems Analyst; Typist/Word Processor. **Number of placements per year:** 500 - 999.

BRAINPOWER PERSONNEL AGENCY
4210 50th Street, Suite A, Lubbock TX 79413-3810. 806/795-0644. **Fax:** 806/795-0645. **Contact:** Phil Crenshaw, CPC, Owner. **Description:** A permanent employment agency. **Specializes in the areas of:** Accounting/Auditing; Administration; Computer Science/Software; Data Processing; Engineering; Finance; Health/Medical; Sales; Secretarial. **Positions commonly filled include:** Accountant/Auditor; Computer Programmer; Customer Service Representative; Electrical/Electronics Engineer; MIS Specialist; Social Worker; Software Engineer. **Average salary range of placements:** $20,000 - $29,999. **Number of placements per year:** 1 - 49.

BROWN & KEENE PERSONNEL
14160 Dallas Parkway, Suite 450, Dallas TX 75240. 972/701-9292. **Contact:** Manager. **Description:** A permanent employment agency. **Specializes in the areas of:** Administration.

BURNETT'S STAFFING, INC.
1200 Walnut Hill Lane, Suite 1000, Irving TX 75038. 972/580-3333. **Fax:** 972/580-7711. **Contact:** Manager. **Description:** A permanent, temp-to-hire, and temporary employment agency. **Specializes in the areas of:** Administration; Clerical; Secretarial.

BURNETT'S STAFFING, INC.
Burnett Building, 2710 Avenue E East, Arlington TX 76011. 817/649-7000. **Contact:** Paul W. Burnett, President. **Description:** A permanent employment agency. Company pays fee. **Specializes in the areas of:** Administration; MIS/EDP; Secretarial. **Positions commonly filled include:** Accountant/Auditor; Administrative Assistant; Administrative Manager; Advertising Clerk; Bookkeeper; Claim Representative; Clerical Supervisor; Computer Operator; Controller; Credit Manager; Customer Service Representative; Data Entry Clerk; Human Resources Manager; Marketing Specialist; Receptionist; Secretary; Typist/Word Processor; Webmaster. **Benefits available to temporary workers:** Medical Insurance; Paid Holidays; Paid Vacation; Profit Sharing. **Average salary range of placements:** $20,000-$29,999.

COLVIN RESOURCES GROUP
4141 Blue Lake Center, Dallas TX 75244-5132. 972/788-5114. **Fax:** 972/490-5015. **Contact:** Sheila Bridges, Senior Account Executive. **Description:** A permanent employment agency that also provides temporary placements. Company pays fee. **Specializes in the areas of:** Accounting/Auditing; Architecture/Construction; Banking; Finance; General Management; Health/Medical; Personnel/Labor Relations; Secretarial. **Positions commonly filled include:**

Accountant/Auditor; Budget Analyst; Credit Manager; Financial Analyst; Human Resources Specialist; Property and Real Estate Manager; Typist/Word Processor. **Average salary range of placements:** $30,000 - $50,000. **Number of placements per year:** 200 - 499.

CONTINENTAL PERSONNEL SERVICE

8700 North Stemmons Freeway, Suite 109, Dallas TX 75247-3715. 214/630-8912. **Contact:** Charles K. Cash, Owner. **Description:** A full-service employment agency. **Specializes in the areas of:** Accounting/Auditing; Administration; Banking; Computer Science/Software; Engineering; Finance; General Management; Insurance; Personnel/Labor Relations; Sales; Secretarial. **Positions commonly filled include:** Accountant/Auditor; Administrative Manager; Aerospace Engineer; Agricultural Engineer; Bank Officer/Manager; Blue-Collar Worker Supervisor; Branch Manager; Brokerage Clerk; Ceramics Engineer; Chemical Engineer; Claim Representative; Clerical Supervisor; Computer Programmer; Construction Contractor; Credit Manager; Customer Service Representative; Design Engineer; Draftsperson; Electrical/Electronics Engineer; Financial Analyst; General Manager; Health Services Manager; Hotel Manager; Human Resources Specialist; Insurance Agent/Broker; Management Trainee; Manufacturer's/Wholesaler's Sales Rep.; Materials Engineer; Mechanical Engineer; Medical Records Technician; Metallurgical Engineer; Mining Engineer; MIS Specialist; Nuclear Engineer; Operations/Production Manager; Paralegal; Petroleum Engineer; Property and Real Estate Manager; Purchasing Agent/Manager; Quality Control Supervisor; Restaurant/Food Service Manager; Securities Sales Representative; Services Sales Representative; Software Engineer; Structural Engineer; Systems Analyst; Technical Writer/Editor; Telecommunications Manager; Transportation/Traffic Specialist; Typist/Word Processor; Underwriter/Assistant Underwriter. **Average salary range of placements:** $20,000 - $29,999. **Number of placements per year:** 200 - 499.

DALLAS EMPLOYMENT SERVICES, INC.

750 North St. Paul Street, Suite 1180, Dallas TX 75201-3230. 214/954-0700. **Toll-free phone:** 800/954-1666. **Fax:** 214/754-0148. **Contact:** Christina Orlando, System Administrator. **E-mail address:** des@des-inc.com. **World Wide Web address:** http://www.des-inc.com/des. **Description:** A permanent employment agency that also offers temporary placements. Company pays fee. **Specializes in the areas of:** Accounting; Administration; Banking; Fashion; Finance; General Management; Health/Medical; Industrial; Insurance; Legal; Marketing; Personnel/Labor Relations; Publishing; Retail; Sales; Secretarial. **Positions commonly filled include:** Accountant; Administrative Assistant; Administrative Manager; Advertising Clerk; Assistant Manager; Budget Analyst; Claim Representative; Clerical Supervisor; Customer Service Representative; Financial Analyst; General Manager; Graphic Artist; Human Resources Manager; Management Trainee; Market Research Analyst; Marketing Specialist; Operations Manager; Paralegal; Production Manager; Public Relations Specialist; Sales Representative; Secretary; Typist/Word Processor; Underwriter/Assistant Underwriter. **Average salary range of placements:** $20,000 - $50,000. **Number of placements per year:** 200 - 499.

DATAPRO PERSONNEL CONSULTANTS

13355 Noel Road, Suite 2001, Dallas TX 75240. 972/661-8600. **Fax:** 972/661-1309. **Contact:** Jack Kallison, Owner. **Description:** A permanent employment agency. Company pays fee. **Specializes in the areas of:** Computer Programming; Computer Science/Software. **Positions commonly filled include:** Computer Programmer; EDP Specialist; Project Manager; Software Engineer; Systems Analyst; Technical Writer/Editor.

DUNHILL OF ARLINGTON

1301 South Bowen Road, Suite 370, Arlington TX 76013. 817/265-2291. **Fax:** 817/265-2294. **Contact:** Jon Molkentine, Director. **Description:** A permanent employment agency. **Specializes in the areas of:** Accounting/Auditing; Health/Medical. **Positions commonly filled include:** Accountant/Auditor; Human Resources Manager; Physical Therapist. **Number of placements per year:** 50 - 99.

EVINS PERSONNEL CONSULTANTS

209 South Leggett, Abilene TX 79605. 915/677-9153. **Contact:** Manager. **Description:** A permanent employment agency that also provides some temporary placements.

EVINS PERSONNEL CONSULTANTS OF KILLEEN, INC.
206 West Avenue B, Killeen TX 76541. 254/526-4161. **Fax:** 254/634-6913. **Contact:** Michelle G. Sweeney, Owner. **Description:** A permanent employment agency that also provides temporary placements and contract services. Company pays fee. **Specializes in the areas of:** Banking; General Management; Legal; Personnel/Labor Relations; Retail; Secretarial. **Positions commonly filled include:** Accountant; Administrative Assistant; Administrative Manager; Auditor; Bank Officer/Manager; Certified Nurses Aide; Clerical Supervisor; Computer Operator; Credit Manager; Dietician/Nutritionist; Editorial Assistant; Education Administrator; General Manager; Graphic Designer; Human Resources Manager; Licensed Practical Nurse; Management Trainee; Paralegal; Pharmacist; Physician; Registered Nurse; Sales Executive; Sales Manager; Secretary; Systems Analyst; Technical Writer/Editor. **Benefits available to temporary workers:** Paid Holidays; Sick Days. **Average salary range of placements:** Up to $29,999. **Number of placements per year:** 1 - 49.

EXPRESS PERSONNEL SERVICES
3701 South Cooper Street, Suite 250, Arlington TX 76015. 817/468-9118. **Fax:** 817/468-9211. **Contact:** Gary Gibson, Owner/Manager. **Description:** A permanent employment agency operating on a contingency basis. Express Personnel Services also provides some temporary placements. Company pays fee. **Specializes in the areas of:** Accounting/Auditing; Banking; Computer Science/Software; Finance; General Management; Health/Medical; Industrial; Insurance; Personnel/Labor Relations; Publishing; Sales; Secretarial. **Positions commonly filled include:** Accountant/Auditor; Administrative Manager; Advertising Clerk; Bank Officer/Manager; Blue-Collar Worker Supervisor; Branch Manager; Clerical Supervisor; Cost Estimator; Customer Service Representative; General Manager; Human Resources Specialist; Industrial Production Manager; Management Trainee; Paralegal; Public Relations Specialist; Quality Control Supervisor; Technical Writer/Editor; Typist/Word Processor. **Benefits available to temporary workers:** Medical Insurance; Paid Holidays; Paid Vacation. **Average salary range of placements:** $30,000 - $50,000. **Number of placements per year:** 1 - 49.

EXPRESS PERSONNEL SERVICES
P.O. Box 8136, Waco TX 76714-8136. 254/776-3300. **Contact:** J.G. Scofield, Owner. **Description:** A permanent employment agency that also provides temporary placements. Company pays fee. **Specializes in the areas of:** Accounting/Auditing; Administration; Architecture/Construction; Banking; Clerical; Computer Hardware/Software; Engineering; Finance; Food; Health/Medical; Insurance; Legal; Manufacturing; Physician Executive; Sales; Secretarial.

FINANCIAL PROFESSIONALS
4100 Spring Valley Road, Suite 307, Dallas TX 75244. 972/991-8999. **Toll-free phone:** 800/856-5599. **Fax:** 972/702-0776. **Contact:** Kathleen Knight, Vice President of Operations. **E-mail address:** ffsw039@prodigy.com. **Description:** A permanent employment agency that also provides temporary placements. Company pays fee. **Specializes in the areas of:** Banking; Finance. **Positions commonly filled include:** Accountant; Administrative Assistant; Auditor; Bank Officer/Manager; Branch Manager; Chief Financial Officer; Controller; Credit Manager; Customer Service Representative; Finance Director; Financial Analyst; Human Resources Manager; Operations Manager. **Benefits available to temporary workers:** Medical Insurance; Paid Holidays; Paid Vacation. **Average salary range of placements:** $20,000 - $29,999. **Number of placements per year:** 1 - 49.

HEALTHCARE STAFF RESOURCES, INC.
1445 MacArthur Drive, Suite 100, Carrollton TX 75007. 972/323-3388. **Toll-free phone:** 800/284-0429. **Fax:** 972/446-1920. **Contact:** Barb Greene, Human Resources Manager. **Description:** A permanent employment agency that also provides temporary placements. Company pays fee. **Specializes in the areas of:** Health/Medical. **Positions commonly filled include:** Occupational Therapist; Physical Therapist. **Benefits available to temporary workers:** 401(k); Dental Insurance; Life Insurance; Medical Insurance; Vision Plan. **Average salary range of placements:** More than $50,000. **Number of placements per year:** 100 - 199.

INFO TEC INC.
14275 Midway Road, Suite 140, Dallas TX 75244-3620. 972/661-8400. **Fax:** 972/490-5964. **Contact:** Kim Pinney, Vice President. **E-mail address:** infotec95@aol.com. **Description:** A permanent employment agency and consulting company offering permanent, contract, and contract-to-hire placements in both hardware and software positions. Company pays fee. **Specializes in the areas of:** Computer Science/Software. **Positions commonly filled include:** Computer Programmer; Management Analyst/Consultant; MIS Specialist; Systems Analyst; Technical Writer/Editor. **Benefits available to temporary workers:** Dental Insurance; Medical Insurance. **Average salary range of placements:** $30,000 - $50,000. **Number of placements per year:** 50 - 99.

JOB MARKET PERSONNEL AGENCY
2806 34th Street, Lubbock TX 79410. 806/797-8383. **Contact:** Ginger Hale, Owner. **Description:** A permanent employment agency. **Specializes in the areas of:** Retail; Sales; Secretarial; Technical; Transportation. **Positions commonly filled include:** Accountant/Auditor; Adjuster; Administrative Manager; Advertising Clerk; Agricultural Engineer; Automotive Mechanic; Bank Officer/Manager; Civil Engineer; Computer Programmer; Customer Service Representative; Design Engineer; EKG Technician; Environmental Engineer; Financial Analyst; General Manager; Industrial Production Manager; Management Analyst/Consultant; Mechanical Engineer; MIS Specialist; Property and Real Estate Manager; Quality Control Supervisor; Registered Nurse; Services Sales Representative; Software Engineer; Telecommunications Manager; Transportation/Traffic Specialist; Typist/Word Processor. **Number of placements per year:** 1 - 49.

LRJ STAFFING SERVICES
301 West Central Drive, Suite 200, Temple TX 76501. 254/742-1981. **Toll-free phone:** 800/581-1850. **Fax:** 254/774-9675. **Contact:** David Kyle, Branch Manager. **Description:** A full-service employment agency. Company pays fee. **Specializes in the areas of:** Computer Science/Software; Engineering; Industrial; Light Industrial; Manufacturing; Personnel/Labor Relations; Publishing; Technical. **Positions commonly filled include:** Blue-Collar Worker Supervisor; Computer Programmer; Customer Service Representative; Industrial Engineer; Industrial Production Manager; Services Sales Representative; Systems Analyst; Typist/Word Processor. **Benefits available to temporary workers:** Paid Holidays; Sick Days. **Average salary range of placements:** $20,000 - $29,999. **Number of placements per year:** 50 - 99.

MARQUESS & ASSOCIATES
15441 Knoll Trail Drive, Suite 280, Dallas TX 75248. 972/490-5288. **Fax:** 972/490-5004. **Contact:** Terri Marquess, Owner. **Description:** A permanent employment agency. Company pays fee. **Specializes in the areas of:** Retail; Sales; Secretarial; Technical. **Positions commonly filled include:** Accountant/Auditor; Administrative Manager; Advertising Clerk; Buyer; Clerical Supervisor; Computer Programmer; Credit Manager; Customer Service Representative; Electrical/Electronics Engineer; Financial Analyst; General Manager; Human Service Worker; Industrial Engineer; Management Trainee; Mechanical Engineer; MIS Specialist; Services Sales Representative; Software Engineer; Systems Analyst; Technical Writer/Editor; Telecommunications Manager. **Average salary range of placements:** $20,000 - $29,999. **Number of placements per year:** 50 - 99.

MEDTEX STAFFING
2100 Highway 360, Suite 404, Grand Prairie TX 75050. 972/647-2047. **Fax:** 972/660-6870. **Contact:** Office Manager. **Description:** A permanent employment agency. **Specializes in the areas of:** Health/Medical. **Positions commonly filled include:** Nurse.

OFICINA DE EMPLEOS, INC.
5415 Maple Avenue, Suite 112A, Dallas TX 75235-7429. 214/634-0500. **Fax:** 214/634-1001. **Contact:** Robert Wingfield, Jr., Owner. **Description:** A permanent employment agency that places documented workers, primarily from Mexico, with companies that need laborers in construction and landscaping. Company pays fee. **Specializes in the areas of:** General Labor. **Number of placements per year:** 500 - 999.

P&P PERSONNEL SERVICE
604 North Gray, Killeen TX 76541-4847. 254/526-9962. **Contact:** Gordon Plumlee, Owner. **Description:** A permanent employment agency. **Specializes in the areas of:** Accounting; Banking; Computer Science; Finance; General Management; Insurance; Legal; Secretarial. **Positions commonly filled include:** Accountant; Claim Representative; Clerical Supervisor; Dental Assistant; Insurance Agent; Licensed Practical Nurse; Management Trainee; Medical Records Tech.; Paralegal; Registered Nurse; Social Worker. **Number of placements per year:** 50 - 99.

PARKER WORTHINGTON
The Madison Building, 15851 Dallas Parkway, Suite 500, Dallas TX 75248. 972/980-1744. **Contact:** Susan W. Parker, President. **Description:** A permanent employment agency.

THE PERSONNEL CONNECTION
16479 North Dallas Parkway, Suite 110, Dallas TX 75248. 972/713-9900. **Contact:** Placement Officer. **Description:** A permanent employment agency. **Specializes in the areas of:** Administration; Office Support. **Positions commonly filled include:** Clerk; Receptionist; Secretary; Typist/Word Processor.

PERSONNEL ONE, INC.
RESOURCE MFG
7520 North MacArthur Boulevard, Suite 120, Irving TX 75063. 972/831-1999. **Fax:** 972/831-8668. **Contact:** Terez Scribner, Direct Hire Manager. **E-mail address:** irvingp1@aol.com. **Description:** A permanent employment agency specializing in all types of administrative support positions. The company also offers some temp-to-hire and temporary assignments. Company pays fee. Resource MFG (also at this location) specializes in the placement of manufacturing and technical professionals. **Specializes in the areas of:** Administration/MIS/EDP; Administrative Support; Secretarial. **Positions commonly filled include:** Administrative Assistant; Administrative Manager; Clerical Supervisor; Customer Service Representative; Data Entry; Human Resources Manager; Receptionist; Secretary; Typist/Word Processor. **Corporate headquarters location:** This Location. **Other U.S. locations:** Nationwide. **Average salary range of placements:** $30,000 - $50,000. **Number of placements per year:** 100 - 199.

PERSONNEL ONE, INC.
5400 LBJ Freeway, Suite 120, Dallas TX 75240. 972/982-8500. **Fax:** 972/982-8505. **Recorded jobline:** 972/982-8510. **Contact:** Christine McNunn, Branch Manager. **Description:** A permanent employment agency that also provides direct hire services and temporary placements. Company pays fee. **Specializes in the areas of:** Accounting/Auditing; Administration; Computer Science/Software; Engineering; General Management; Personnel/Labor Relations; Secretarial. **Positions commonly filled include:** Administrative Manager; Claim Representative; Clerical Supervisor; Counselor; Credit Manager; Customer Service Representative; Electrical/Electronics Engineer; Financial Analyst. **Benefits available to temporary workers:** Paid Holidays; Paid Vacation. **Average salary range of placements:** $20,000 - $29,999. **Number of placements per year:** 1 - 49.

PLACEMENTS UNLIMITED
932 North Valley Mills Drive, Waco TX 76710. 254/741-0526. **Fax:** 254/741-0529. **Contact:** Ginger Sharp, President. **Description:** A permanent employment agency. Company pays fee. **Specializes in the areas of:** Banking; Industrial; Manufacturing; Secretarial. **Positions commonly filled include:** Accountant; Aircraft Mechanic/Engine Specialist; Automotive Mechanic; Blue-Collar Worker Supervisor; Buyer; Clerical Supervisor; Customer Service Representative; MIS Specialist; Purchasing Agent/Manager; Technical Writer/Editor; Typist/Word Processor. **Average salary range of placements:** Less than $20,000. **Number of placements per year:** 100 - 199.

PROFESSIONS TODAY
2811 South Loop 289, Suite 20, Lubbock TX 79423. 806/745-8595. **Fax:** 806/748-0571. **Contact:** Gebrell Ward, Owner. **Description:** A permanent employment agency. Company pays fee. **Specializes in the areas of:** Accounting/Auditing; Administration; Computer Hardware/Software; Engineering; General Management; Health/Medical; Industrial; Sales; Secretarial. **Positions commonly filled include:** Accountant/Auditor; Administrative Assistant; Bookkeeper; Clerk;

Computer Programmer; Customer Service Representative; Data Entry Clerk; Legal Secretary; Marketing Specialist; Medical Secretary; Receptionist; Sales Representative; Secretary; Typist/Word Processor. **Number of placements per year:** 100 - 199.

REMEDY INTELLIGENT STAFFING
4225 Wingren Drive, Suite 115, Irving TX 75062. 972/650-2005. **Fax:** 972/650-1521. **Contact:** Manager. **Description:** A permanent employment agency. Company pays fee. **Specializes in the areas of:** Secretarial. **Positions commonly filled include:** Accountant/Auditor; Clerical Supervisor; Customer Service Representative; Management Trainee. **Benefits available to temporary workers:** Medical Insurance; Paid Holidays. **Average salary range of placements:** $20,000 - $29,999. **Number of placements per year:** 100 - 199.

RESOURCE RECRUITERS INC.
4100 Spring Valley Road, Suite 800, Dallas TX 75244. 972/851-5408. **Contact:** Ms. Terez Scribner, President. **Description:** A permanent employment agency. Company pays fee. **Specializes in the areas of:** Accounting/Auditing; Finance; Food; Insurance; Legal; Manufacturing; Personnel/Labor Relations; Sales; Secretarial. **Positions commonly filled include:** Accountant/Auditor; Advertising Clerk; Clerical Supervisor; Collector; Credit Manager; Customer Service Representative; Human Resources Manager; Management Trainee; Manufacturer's/Wholesaler's Sales Rep.; Restaurant/Food Service Manager; Services Sales Representative; Typist/Word Processor; Underwriter/Assistant Underwriter. **Number of placements per year:** 50 - 99.

SAY AHHH MEDICAL OFFICE SERVICES
2203 Eighth Avenue, Fort Worth TX 76110. 817/927-2924. **Contact:** Manager. **Description:** A permanent employment agency that also offers temporary placements. **Specializes in the areas of:** Health/Medical.

SNELLING PERSONNEL SERVICES
1925 East Beltline, Suite 403, Carrollton TX 75006. 972/242-8575. **Fax:** 972/242-7186. **Contact:** Manager. **Description:** A permanent employment agency. Company pays fee. **Specializes in the areas of:** Accounting/Auditing; Administration; General Management; Industrial; Legal; Personnel/Labor Relations; Sales; Secretarial. **Positions commonly filled include:** Accountant/Auditor; Administrative Assistant; Bookkeeper; Claim Representative; Clerk; Credit Manager; Customer Service Representative; Data Entry Clerk; Executive Assistant; Factory Worker; Legal Secretary; Light Industrial Worker; Marketing Specialist; Medical Secretary; Receptionist; Sales Representative; Secretary; Typist/Word Processor. **Number of placements per year:** 50 - 99.

SNELLING PERSONNEL SERVICES OF LONGVIEW
1800 Northwest Loop 281, Suite 205, Longview TX 75604. 903/297-2223. **Contact:** Carmen Jones, Owner. **Description:** A permanent employment agency.

TSP PERSONNEL SERVICES, INC.
2246 Lamar Boulevard, Paris TX 75460. 903/785-0034. **Fax:** 903/784-0864. **Contact:** Kelley Ferguson, Owner/Manager. **Description:** A permanent employment agency that also provides temporary placements. Company pays fee. **Specializes in the areas of:** Accounting/Auditing; Industrial; Light Industrial; Retail; Sales; Secretarial. **Positions commonly filled include:** Bank Officer/Manager; Clerical Supervisor; Electrician; Secretary. **Average salary range of placements:** $20,000 - $29,999. **Number of placements per year:** 200 - 499.

TARRANT COUNTY EMPLOYMENT NETWORK
1400 Circle Drive, Suite 100, Fort Worth TX 76119. 817/531-5670. **Fax:** 817/531-5677. **Contact:** Betty Johnson, Program Coordinator. **Description:** A permanent employment agency that also provides career counseling services. **Specializes in the areas of:** Accounting/Auditing; Administration; Computer Science/Software; Education; Finance; Food; General Management; Health/Medical; Industrial; Manufacturing; Personnel/Labor Relations; Retail; Sales; Secretarial; Transportation. **Positions commonly filled include:** Accountant/Auditor; Administrative Manager; Automotive Mechanic; Biomedical Engineer; Blue-Collar Worker Supervisor; Budget Analyst;

Claim Representative; Clerical Supervisor; Clinical Lab Technician; Computer Programmer; Construction and Building Inspector; Counselor; Credit Manager; Customer Service Representative; Dental Assistant/Dental Hygienist; Draftsperson; Education Administrator; EEG Technologist; EKG Technician; Electrical/Electronics Engineer; Electrician; General Manager; Health Services Manager; Human Resources Specialist; Insurance Agent/Broker; Librarian; Medical Records Technician; MIS Specialist; Operations/Production Manager; Property and Real Estate Manager; Purchasing Agent/Manager; Radiological Technologist; Restaurant/Food Service Manager; Securities Sales Representative; Systems Analyst; Teacher/Professor; Travel Agent; Typist/Word Processor. **Average salary range of placements:** $20,000 - $29,999. **Number of placements per year:** 200 - 499.

THOMAS OFFICE PERSONNEL SERVICE (TOPS)
3909 Flintridge Drive, Irving TX 75038. 972/252-2660. **Contact:** Margaret Thomas, Co-Founder. **Description:** A permanent employment agency. Company pays fee. **Specializes in the areas of:** Accounting/Auditing; Administration; General Management; Insurance; Manufacturing; Personnel/Labor Relations; Publishing; Secretarial. **Positions commonly filled include:** Accountant/Auditor; Branch Manager; Clerical Supervisor; Customer Service Representative; General Manager; Human Resources Specialist; Paralegal; Secretary; Typist/Word Processor. **Average salary range of placements:** $20,000 - $35,000. **Number of placements per year:** 1 - 49.

TODAYS LEGAL STAFFING
700 Pearl Street, Suite 350, Dallas TX 75201. 214/754-0700. **Toll-free phone:** 800/693-1514. **Contact:** Karen Gilmore, Branch Manager. **World Wide Web address:** http://www.todays.com. **Description:** A permanent employment agency. Company pays fee. **Specializes in the areas of:** Legal; Secretarial. **Positions commonly filled include:** Attorney; Paralegal; Typist/Word Processor. **Other U.S. locations:** Nationwide. **Average salary range of placements:** $30,000 - $50,000. **Number of placements per year:** 200 - 499.

TRAVEL SEARCH NETWORK
12860 Hillcrest Road, Suite 112, Dallas TX 75230-1519. 972/458-1145. **Fax:** 972/490-4790. **Contact:** Gina Tedesco, Vice President of Operations. **Description:** A permanent employment agency that also provides temporary placements. Company pays fee. **Specializes in the areas of:** Travel. **Positions commonly filled include:** Travel Agent. **Other U.S. locations:** Houston TX. **Average salary range of placements:** $30,000 - $50,000. **Number of placements per year:** 200 - 499.

VINSON AND ASSOCIATES
4100 McEwen, Suite 180, Dallas TX 75244. 972/980-8800. **Contact:** Fred Vinson, Manager. **Description:** An employment agency that provides both permanent and temporary placements. **Specializes in the areas of:** Accounting/Auditing; Banking; Clerical; Finance; Insurance; Legal; Manufacturing; Sales.

EXECUTIVE SEARCH FIRMS

ABACUS MANAGEMENT SERVICE
5215 North O'Connor Boulevard, Suite 200, Irving TX 75039. 972/868-9169. **Contact:** Manager. **Description:** An executive search firm.

ACCOUNTANTS EXECUTIVE SEARCH
ACCOUNTANTS ON CALL
1200 Summit Avenue, Suite 306, Fort Worth TX 76102. 817/870-1800. **Fax:** 817/870-1890. **Contact:** Mark Wegesin, Branch Manager. **Description:** An executive search firm operating on a contingency basis. Accountants On Call (also at this location) is a temporary agency. Founded in 1979. Company pays fee. **Specializes in the areas of:** Accounting/Auditing; Finance. **Positions**

commonly filled include: Accountant/Auditor; Credit Manager; Financial Analyst. **International locations:** Worldwide. **Number of placements per year:** 1000+.

ACCOUNTANTS EXECUTIVE SEARCH
ACCOUNTANTS ON CALL
2828 Routh, Suite 690, Dallas TX 75201. 214/979-9001. **Fax:** 214/969-0046. **Contact:** Branch Manager. **Description:** An executive search firm operating on a contingency basis. Accountants On Call (also at this location) is a temporary agency. Company pays fee. **Specializes in the areas of:** Accounting/Auditing; Finance. **Positions commonly filled include:** Accountant; Chief Financial Officer; Controller; Credit Manager; Finance Director; Financial Analyst. **Average salary range of placements:** $30,000 - $50,000.

ACCOUNTANTS EXECUTIVE SEARCH
ACCOUNTANTS ON CALL
5550 LBJ Freeway, Suite 310, Dallas TX 75240. 972/980-4184. **Fax:** 972/980-2359. **Contact:** Branch Manager. **Description:** An executive search firm. Accountants On Call (also at this location) is a temporary agency. **Specializes in the areas of:** Accounting/Auditing; Finance. **International locations:** Worldwide.

ACCOUNTING CONTRACTORS INC.
1100 Centennial Boulevard, Richardson TX 75231. 972/889-3321. **Contact:** Manager. **Description:** An executive search firm that also provides contract placements. **Specializes in the areas of:** Accounting/Auditing.

AGRI-LC
131 Degan Street, Lewisville TX 75057. 972/221-7568. **Fax:** 972/221-1409. **Contact:** Lawrence W. Keeley, Owner/Manager. **Description:** An executive search firm focusing on the recruitment of personnel in all segments of agriculture. Founded in 1969. Company pays fee. **Specializes in the areas of:** Accounting/Auditing; Administration; Advertising; Biology; Engineering; Finance; Food; General Management; Manufacturing; Personnel/Labor Relations; Sales. **Positions commonly filled include:** Accountant/Auditor; Administrative Manager; Agricultural Engineer; Bank Officer/Manager; Biochemist; Biological Scientist; Blue-Collar Worker Supervisor; Branch Manager; Budget Analyst; Buyer; Chemical Engineer; Chemist; Civil Engineer; Computer Programmer; Construction Contractor; Credit Manager; Customer Service Representative; Design Engineer; Editor; Environmental Engineer; Financial Analyst; Food Scientist/Technologist; Forester/Conservation Scientist; General Manager; Human Resources Specialist; Industrial Engineer; Landscape Architect; Licensed Practical Nurse; Management Trainee; Mechanical Engineer; MIS Specialist; Purchasing Agent/Manager; Quality Control Supervisor; Restaurant/Food Service Manager; Systems Analyst; Transportation/Traffic Specialist; Underwriter/Assistant Underwriter; Veterinarian. **Average salary range of placements:** $30,000 - $50,000. **Number of placements per year:** 1 - 49.

ALPHA RESOURCES GROUP
1916 Brabent Drive, Plano TX 75025. 214/692-1616. **Contact:** Manager. **Description:** An executive search firm. **Specializes in the areas of:** Hotel/Restaurant.

PETER W. AMBLER COMPANY
14651 Dallas Parkway, Suite 402, Dallas TX 75240. 972/404-8712. **Contact:** Research Department. **Description:** A generalist executive search firm operating on a retainer basis.

AMERI SEARCH
P.O. Box 427, Rockwall TX 75087. 972/722-8033. **Toll-free phone:** 800/226-0534. **Fax:** 972/722-0633. **Contact:** John Scott, Owner. **Description:** An executive search firm. Company pays fee. **Specializes in the areas of:** Food. **Positions commonly filled include:** Agricultural Engineer; Biochemist; Biological Scientist; Design Engineer; Electrical/Electronics Engineer; Environmental Engineer; Food Scientist/Technologist; General Manager; Human Resources Specialist; Industrial Engineer; Industrial Production Manager; Mechanical Engineer; Operations/Production Manager; Public Relations Manager; Purchasing Agent/Manager; Quality Control Supervisor; Stationary

Engineer; Transportation/Traffic Specialist; Veterinarian. **Average salary range of placements:** $30,000 - $50,000. **Number of placements per year:** 1 - 49.

ANDREWS-CARTER PERSONNEL SERVICE
P.O. Box 835956, Richardson TX 75083. 972/239-9484. **Fax:** 972/239-3753. **Contact:** Leann Andrews, Owner. **Description:** An executive search firm operating on both retainer and contingency bases. Company pays fee. **Specializes in the areas of:** Food; Health/Medical; Sales. **Positions commonly filled include:** Loan Officer; Restaurant/Food Service Manager; Sales Representative. **Number of placements per year:** 1 - 49.

APEX COMPUTER PLACEMENTS INC.
616 North Bell Avenue, Denton TX 76201. 940/565-0658. **Contact:** Manager. **Description:** Apex Computer Placements is an executive search firm. **Specializes in the areas of:** Computer Hardware/Software.

AUDIT PROFESSIONALS INTERNATIONAL
3312 Woodford Drive, Suite 400, Arlington TX 76013. 817/277-0888. **Contact:** Keith Malcolm, CPA, Vice President. **E-mail address:** hedman@onramp.net. **Description:** An executive search firm that also provides contract services. Founded in 1987. Company pays fee. **Specializes in the areas of:** Accounting/Auditing; Administration; Finance; Information Systems. **Positions commonly filled include:** Accountant/Auditor; Actuary; Internet Services Manager; Telecommunications Manager. **Average salary range of placements:** More than $50,000. **Number of placements per year:** 50 - 99.

R. GAINES BATY ASSOCIATES, INC.
12750 Merritt Drive, Suite 990, Lockbox 199, Dallas TX 75251. 972/386-7900. **Fax:** 972/387-2224. **Contact:** R. Gaines Baty, President. **E-mail address:** rgba@rgba.com. **Description:** A worldwide executive search firm for MIS management and information technology consulting positions, as well as bilingual accounting and auditing positions. Company pays fee. **Specializes in the areas of:** Computer Science/Software; Finance; MIS/EDP. **Positions commonly filled include:** Accountant/Auditor; Management Analyst/Consultant; MIS Specialist; Systems Analyst; Telecommunications Manager. **Average salary range of placements:** More than $50,000. **Number of placements per year:** 1 - 49.

BEST/WORLD ASSOCIATES
505 West Abram Street, 3rd Floor, Arlington TX 76010. 817/861-0000. **Toll-free phone:** 800/749-2846. **Fax:** 817/459-2378. **Contact:** G. Tim Best, President. **Description:** An executive search firm operating on a retainer basis. Company pays fee. **Specializes in the areas of:** Banking; Computer Science/Software; Engineering; Finance; Food; Manufacturing; Personnel/Labor Relations; Sales. **Positions commonly filled include:** Accountant/Auditor; Chemical Engineer; Economist; Electrical/Electronics Engineer; Environmental Engineer; Financial Analyst; Food Scientist/Technologist; Human Resources Specialist; Management Analyst/Consultant; Market Research Analyst; Mechanical Engineer; MIS Specialist; Quality Control Supervisor; Software Engineer; Statistician; Systems Analyst. **Average salary range of placements:** More than $50,000. **Number of placements per year:** 50 - 99.

BILSON & HAZEN INTERNATIONAL
1231 Greenway Drive, Suite 390, Irving TX 75034. 972/753-1193. **Fax:** 972/753-0969. **Contact:** Frederick Sagoe, President. **Description:** An executive search firm that also offers temporary and contract services. Company pays fee. **Specializes in the areas of:** Computer Science/Software; Personnel/Labor Relations; Sales. **Positions commonly filled include:** Administrative Manager; Branch Manager; Claim Representative; Computer Programmer; Design Engineer; Electrical/Electronics Engineer; Human Resources Specialist; Manufacturer's/Wholesaler's Sales Rep.; Market Research Analyst; MIS Specialist; Software Engineer; Technical Writer/Editor; Telecommunications Manager. **Benefits available to temporary workers:** Dental Insurance; Medical Insurance. **Average salary range of placements:** More than $50,000. **Number of placements per year:** 50 - 99.

BIOSOURCE INTERNATIONAL
1878 Hilltop Drive, Suite 100, Lewisville TX 75067-2114. 972/317-7060. **Fax:** 972/317-0500. **Contact:** Ric J. Favors, Principal. **E-mail address:** biosource@why.net. **World Wide Web address:** http://www.why.net/users/biosource/index.html. **Description:** An executive search firm. Company pays fee. **Specializes in the areas of:** Biotechnology; Health/Medical; Pharmaceuticals; Scientific; Technical. **Positions commonly filled include:** Biochemist; Biological Scientist; Biomedical Engineer; Chemical Engineer; Chemist; Chief Executive Officer; Compliance Analyst; Computer Programmer; Electrical/Electronics Engineer; General Manager; Management Analyst/Consultant; Mechanical Engineer; MIS Specialist; Multimedia Designer; Physician; President; Production Manager; Quality Assurance Engineer; Quality Control Supervisor; Science Technologist; Software Engineer; Statistician; Systems Analyst; Technical Writer/Editor. **Average salary range of placements:** More than $50,000. **Number of placements per year:** 1 - 49.

MARTIN BIRNBACH & ASSOCIATES
15150 Preston Road, Suite 300, Dallas TX 75248. 972/490-5627. **Contact:** Manager. **Description:** An executive search firm. **Specializes in the areas of:** Sales.

HOWARD C. BLOOM EXECUTIVE SEARCH
INTERIM LEGAL PROFESSIONALS
5000 Quorum Drive, Suite 770, Dallas TX 75240. 972/385-6455. **Fax:** 972/385-1006. **Contact:** Howard Bloom, President. **Description:** An executive search firm. Interim Legal Professionals (also at this location) provides permanent placements. Company pays fee. **Specializes in the areas of:** Legal. **Positions commonly filled include:** Attorney. **Number of placements per year:** 1 - 49.

BOLES & ASSOCIATES
1750 North Collins Boulevard, Suite 200, Richardson TX 75080. **Fax:** 972/480-9886. **Contact:** Terry C. Boles, Managing Partner. **E-mail address:** bolesassoc@aol.com. **Description:** An executive search firm operating on a retainer basis. Founded in 1989. **Specializes in the areas of:** Administration; Engineering; General Management; Human Resources; Sales. **Positions commonly filled include:** Telecommunications Manager. **Average salary range of placements:** More than $50,000. **Number of placements per year:** 1 - 49.

BOND & ASSOCIATES
8509 Fair Haven Court, Fort Worth TX 76176. 817/236-3549. **Contact:** Manager. **Description:** An executive search firm. **Specializes in the areas of:** Engineering; Health/Medical; Information Technology.

BRIDGE PERSONNEL
8350 North Central Expressway, Suite M1226, Dallas TX 75206. 214/692-8273. **Fax:** 214/369-6070. **Contact:** Jim Peeler, CPA/Owner. **Description:** An executive search firm. Company pays fee. **Specializes in the areas of:** Accounting/Auditing; Administration; Computer Science/Software; Finance; Information Systems. **Positions commonly filled include:** Accountant/Auditor; Computer Programmer; Financial Analyst; Software Engineer; Systems Analyst; Telecommunications Manager.

BROOKLEA & ASSOCIATES, INC.
12200 Ford Road, Suite 108, Farmers Branch TX 75234. 972/484-9400. **Fax:** 972/484-9400. **Contact:** Recruiter. **Description:** An executive search firm operating on a contingency basis. Company pays fee. **Specializes in the areas of:** Accounting/Auditing; Architecture/Construction; Art/Design; Finance; Health/Medical; Sales; Secretarial. **Positions commonly filled include:** Accountant/Auditor; Architect; Draftsperson; Emergency Medical Technician; Health Services Manager; Landscape Architect; Licensed Practical Nurse; Medical Records Technician; Occupational Therapist; Physical Therapist; Physician; Recreational Therapist; Registered Nurse; Respiratory Therapist; Services Sales Representative; Surgical Technician; Surveyor; Veterinarian. **Number of placements per year:** 100 - 199.

BUCKLEY GROUP
15851 Dallas Parkway, Dallas TX 75248. 972/490-1722. **Contact:** Manager. **Description:** An executive search firm. **Specializes in the areas of:** Marketing; Sales.

BUNDY-STEWART ASSOCIATES, INC.
13601 Preston Road, Suite 107W, Dallas TX 75240. 972/458-0626. **Fax:** 972/661-2670. **Contact:** Carolyn Stewart, Owner. **Description:** An executive search firm operating on a contingency basis. **Specializes in the areas of:** Accounting/Auditing; Administration; Computer Science/Software; Engineering; Industrial; Insurance; Manufacturing; Personnel/Labor Relations; Real Estate; Sales; Telecommunications. **Positions commonly filled include:** Accountant/Auditor; Aircraft Mechanic/Engine Specialist; Attorney; Buyer; Computer Programmer; Credit Manager; Customer Service Representative; Design Engineer; Draftsperson; Electrical/Electronics Engineer; Human Resources Specialist; Industrial Engineer; Industrial Production Manager; Market Research Analyst; Mechanical Engineer; MIS Specialist; Operations/Production Manager; Purchasing Agent/Manager; Quality Control Supervisor; Securities Sales Representative; Software Engineer; Systems Analyst; Telecommunications Manager.

CARPENTER & ASSOCIATES
8333 Douglas Avenue, Suite 875, Dallas TX 75225. 214/691-6585. **Fax:** 214/691-6838. **Contact:** Elsie Carpenter, President. **Description:** An executive search firm. Founded in 1981. Company pays fee. **Specializes in the areas of:** Advertising; Fashion; Personnel/Labor Relations; Retail. **Positions commonly filled include:** Buyer; Retail Manager; Retail Merchandiser. **Number of placements per year:** 1 - 49.

COMPUTER MANAGEMENT SEARCH
12801 North Central Expressway, Suite 1170, Dallas TX 75243. 972/458-0090. **Contact:** Manager. **Description:** An executive search firm. **Specializes in the areas of:** Computer Hardware/Software; Computer Programming; Computer Science/Software.

COMPUTER PROFESSIONALS UNLIMITED
13612 Midway Road, Suite 333, Dallas TX 75244. 972/233-1773. **Fax:** 972/233-9619. **Contact:** V.J. Zapotocky, Owner/President. **E-mail address:** zipzap@onramp.net. **Description:** An executive search firm that also provides contract services. Founded in 1978. Company pays fee. **Specializes in the areas of:** Computer Science/Software; Engineering; Information Technology. **Positions commonly filled include:** Computer Programmer; Electrical/Electronics Engineer; Internet Services Manager; MIS Specialist; Software Engineer; Systems Analyst; Technical Writer/Editor; Telecommunications Manager. **Average salary range of placements:** More than $50,000. **Number of placements per year:** 50 - 99.

CORPORATE SEARCH INC.
3028 Lubbock Avenue, Fort Worth TX 76109. 817/926-0320. **Toll-free phone:** 800/429-1763. **Fax:** 817/926-1610. **Contact:** John S. Gramentine, President. **Description:** An executive search firm. Company pays fee. **Specializes in the areas of:** Computer Science/Software; Food; Personnel/Labor Relations; Retail; Sales. **Positions commonly filled include:** Branch Manager; General Manager; Human Resources Specialist; Management Trainee; Public Relations Specialist; Services Sales Representative; Software Engineer; Systems Analyst; Telecommunications Manager. **Average salary range of placements:** More than $50,000. **Number of placements per year:** 200 - 499.

CRAIG AFFILIATES, INC.
901 Waterfall Way, Suite 107, Richardson TX 75080. 972/644-3264. **Fax:** 972/644-4065. **Contact:** Edward C. Nemec, President. **Description:** An executive search firm. **Specializes in the areas of:** Food. **Positions commonly filled include:** Branch Manager; Buyer; General Manager. **Number of placements per year:** 50 - 99.

DDR, INC.
8111 LBJ Freeway, Suite 1155, Dallas TX 75251. 972/783-9981. **Contact:** Account Executive. **E-mail address:** ddrdal@gte.net. **Description:** An executive search firm. **Specializes in the areas of:** Technical. **Positions commonly filled include:** Computer Animator; Computer Operator; Computer Programmer; Database Manager; Financial Analyst; Hardware Engineer; Operations Manager; Project Manager; Software Engineer; Systems Analyst; Technical Writer/Editor. **Benefits available to temporary workers:** Dental Insurance; Life Insurance; Medical Insurance.

DFM & ASSOCIATES
4201 Spring Valley Road, Suite 1400, Dallas TX 75244. 972/776-3536. **Contact:** Denise M. Frost, President. **Description:** An executive search firm. Company pays fee. **Specializes in the areas of:** Legal. **Positions commonly filled include:** Attorney; Legal Secretary; Paralegal. **Number of placements per year:** 100 - 199.

DAMON & ASSOCIATES, INC.
7515 Greenville Avenue, Suite 900, Dallas TX 75231. 214/696-6990. **Fax:** 214/696-6993. **Contact:** Dick Damon, President. **Description:** An executive search firm. As a member of the First Interview Recruiting Network, the company provides the opportunity to interview in over 100 major markets in the United States and Canada. Founded in 1978. Company pays fee. **Specializes in the areas of:** Sales. **Average salary range of placements:** $30,000 - $50,000. **Number of placements per year:** 50 - 99.

THE DANBROOK GROUP
4100 Spring Valley Road, Suite 700-LB #2, Dallas TX 75244. 972/392-0057. **Contact:** Anne Kennedy, Senior Partner. **Description:** An executive search firm operating on a contingency basis. Company pays fee. **Specializes in the areas of:** Accounting/Auditing; Banking; Finance; General Management; Insurance. **Positions commonly filled include:** Accountant/Auditor; Adjuster; Bookkeeper; Chief Financial Officer; Claim Representative; Credit Manager; Customer Service Representative; Finance Director; Financial Analyst; Insurance Agent/Broker; Sales Representative; Underwriter/Assistant Underwriter. **Average salary range of placements:** More than $50,000. **Number of placements per year:** 100 - 199.

JOHN DAVIDSON & ASSOCIATES
3198 Royal Lane, Suite 100, Dallas TX 75229. 214/352-7800. **Contact:** Manager. **Description:** A generalist executive search firm.

DENTON-LEWIS ASSOCIATES
4242 Lively Lane, Suite 100, Dallas TX 75220. 214/358-5597. **Fax:** 214/358-5684. **Contact:** Hank Denton, Principal Consultant. **Description:** An executive search firm. Founded in 1980. Company pays fee. **Specializes in the areas of:** Banking; Finance; Insurance; Personnel/Labor Relations. **Positions commonly filled include:** Marketing Specialist.

C. MICHAEL DIXON ASSOCIATES, INC.
P.O. Box 293371, Lewisville TX 75029. 972/317-0608. **Fax:** 972/317-0349. **Contact:** Mike Dixon, President. **E-mail address:** cmdixon@flash.net. **Description:** An executive search firm. Founded in 1988. Company pays fee. **Specializes in the areas of:** Chemicals; Engineering; Manufacturing; Petrochemical; Technical. **Positions commonly filled include:** Chemical Engineer; Electrical/Electronics Engineer; Industrial Engineer; Mechanical Engineer; Systems Analyst. **Average salary range of placements:** More than $50,000. **Number of placements per year:** 1 - 49.

EXECUTIVE RESTAURANT SEARCH
PINNACLE SEARCH GROUP
2925 LBJ Freeway, Suite 253, Dallas TX 75234. 972/484-8600. **Contact:** Manager. **Description:** An executive search firm specializing in all levels of restaurant management. Pinnacle Search Group (also at this location) is the agency's food sales division. **Specializes in the areas of:** Restaurant.

EXECUTIVE SEARCH CONSULTANTS
3030 North Josey Lane, Suite 101-117, Carrollton TX 75007. 972/394-4131. **Contact:** Manager. **Description:** An executive search firm. **Specializes in the areas of:** Accounting/Auditing; Sales.

EXECUTIVE SEARCH INTERNATIONAL
1700 Alma Drive, Suite 370, Plano TX 75075. 972/424-4714. **Contact:** Manager. **Description:** An executive search firm.

EXECUTIVE SEARCH PERSONNEL
14999 Preston Road, Box D212-308, Dallas TX 75230. 972/386-6633. **Fax:** 972/386-9933. **Contact:** Manager. **Description:** An executive search firm. Company pays fee. **Specializes in the areas of:** Accounting/Auditing; Administration; Banking; Finance; Food; General Management; Health/Medical; Industrial; Insurance; Manufacturing; Nonprofit; Personnel/Labor Relations; Retail; Sales; Technical. **Positions commonly filled include:** Accountant/Auditor; Attorney; Buyer; Financial Analyst; General Manager; Human Resources Manager; Management Analyst/Consultant; Manufacturer's/Wholesaler's Sales Rep.; Securities Sales Representative; Services Sales Representative; Underwriter/Assistant Underwriter. **Number of placements per year:** 1 - 49.

OTIS FAULKNER & ASSOCIATES INC.
2628 Windsor Place, Plano TX 75075. 972/423-1712. **Contact:** Manager. **Description:** An executive search firm. **Specializes in the areas of:** Medical Sales and Marketing.

FOX-MORRIS ASSOCIATES
5400 LBJ Freeway, Suite 1445, Dallas TX 75240. 972/404-8044. **Contact:** Manager. **Description:** An executive search firm that places upper-level managers. **Specializes in the areas of:** Human Resources; Sales.

GILLHAM & ASSOCIATES
3400 Carlisle Street, Suite 100, Dallas TX 75204. **Contact:** Rick Gillham, President. **Description:** An executive search firm operating on a retainer basis. Founded in 1982. **Specializes in the areas of:** Real Estate. **Positions commonly filled include:** Accountant/Auditor; Construction and Building Inspector; Construction Contractor; Financial Analyst; Hotel Manager; Management Analyst/Consultant; Market Research Analyst; Property and Real Estate Manager. **Average salary range of placements:** More than $50,000. **Number of placements per year:** 50 - 99.

GRIFFIN ANDERSON & ASSOCIATES
1631 Dorchester Drive, Suite 104-A, Plano TX 75075. 972/612-0188. **Contact:** Manager. **Description:** An executive search firm. **Specializes in the areas of:** Sales.

H+M RECRUITERS
P.O. Box 121747, Arlington TX 76012. 817/261-6565. **Fax:** 817/461-6565. **Contact:** Bruce Powers, Ph.D., Partner. **Description:** An executive search firm operating on a contingency basis. Founded in 1986. Company pays fee. **Specializes in the areas of:** Chemicals; Engineering; Industrial; Manufacturing; Plastics; Rubber; Technical. **Positions commonly filled include:** Biochemist; Chemical Engineer; Chemist; Design Engineer; Industrial Engineer; Mechanical Engineer. **Average salary range of placements:** More than $50,000. **Number of placements per year:** 1 - 49.

H.P.R. HEALTH STAFF
2201 North Collins Street, Suite 260, Arlington TX 76011. 817/261-3355. **Fax:** 817/543-3155. **Contact:** Vera E. Harris, CPC, Owner. **E-mail address:** vharris@1america.net. **Description:** An executive search firm operating on a contingency basis. Company pays fee. **Specializes in the areas of:** Health/Medical. **Positions commonly filled include:** Chief Financial Officer; Clinical Lab Technician; Controller; Dental Assistant/Dental Hygienist; Dentist; Dietician/Nutritionist; EEG Technologist; EKG Technician; Environmental Engineer; Health Services Manager; Human Resources Manager; Licensed Practical Nurse; Medical Records Technician; Nuclear Medicine Technologist; Occupational Therapist; Pharmacist; Physical Therapist; Physician; Psychologist; Radiological Technologist; Registered Nurse; Respiratory Therapist; Speech-Language Pathologist; Surgical Technician. **Average salary range of placements:** $30,000 - $50,000.

HARAGAN ASSOCIATES
8350 Meadow Road, Suite 262, Dallas TX 75231. 214/363-3634. **Fax:** 214/363-3652. **Contact:** Mr. Pat W. Haragan, Principal/Owner. **Description:** An executive search firm operating on a retainer basis. Haragan Associates focuses exclusively on the health care industry including pharmaceuticals, medical devices, biotechnology, diagnostics, medical equipment, and services. **Specializes in the areas of:** Biology; General Management; Health/Medical; Manufacturing;

Sales; Technical. **Positions commonly filled include:** Biochemist; Biological Scientist; Biomedical Engineer; Chemist; Clinical Lab Technician; Food Scientist/Technologist; General Manager; Health Services Manager; Human Resources Specialist; Nuclear Medicine Technologist; Occupational Therapist; Pharmacist; Physical Therapist; Physician; Quality Control Supervisor; Registered Nurse; Veterinarian. **Average salary range of placements:** More than $50,000. **Number of placements per year:** 1 - 49.

HEALTH NETWORK USA
13154 Coit Road, Suite 202, Dallas TX 75240. **Toll-free phone:** 800/872-0212. **Fax:** 972/918-9997. **Contact:** David J. Elliott, President. **E-mail address:** hninfo@hnusa.com. **Description:** An executive search firm. **Specializes in the areas of:** Health/Medical. **Positions commonly filled include:** Clinical Lab Technician; Dental Assistant/Dental Hygienist; Dental Lab Technician; Dentist; Dietician/Nutritionist; EEG Technologist; EKG Technician; Health Services Manager; Human Resources Manager; Licensed Practical Nurse; Medical Records Technician; Nuclear Medicine Technologist; Occupational Therapist; Pharmacist; Physical Therapist; Physician; Psychologist; Public Relations Specialist; Purchasing Agent/Manager; Radiological Technologist; Recreational Therapist; Registered Nurse; Respiratory Therapist; Social Worker; Speech-Language Pathologist; Surgical Technician. **Number of placements per year:** 50 - 99.

HEALTHCARE RECRUITERS INTERNATIONAL
4100 Spring Valley Road, Suite 800, Dallas TX 75244. 972/851-5470. **Contact:** Jim Wimberly, President. **Description:** An executive search firm. Company pays fee. **Specializes in the areas of:** Health/Medical; Sales; Technical. **Positions commonly filled include:** Biomedical Engineer; General Manager; Marketing Specialist; Sales Representative; Technician. **Number of placements per year:** 1 - 49.

HEDMAN & ASSOCIATES
3312 Woodford, Suite 200-400, Arlington TX 76013. 817/277-0888. **Contact:** Kent R. Hedman, Owner. **Description:** An executive search firm operating two divisions. One specializes in finance, and the other provides general placements. **Specializes in the areas of:** Accounting/Auditing; Finance.

HEIDRICK & STRUGGLES INC.
2200 Ross Avenue, Suite 4700-E, Dallas TX 75201. 214/220-2130. **Contact:** Manager. **Description:** An executive search firm that places personnel in a wide range of industries.

HORN & ASSOCIATES
P.O. Box 151944, Arlington TX 76015. 817/465-3463. **Contact:** Brian Horn, Owner. **Description:** An executive search firm. **Specializes in the areas of:** Health/Medical.

HUNTER & MICHAELS
7502 Greenville Avenue, Suite 500, Dallas TX 75231. 214/750-4666. **Contact:** Manager. **Description:** An executive search firm. **Specializes in the areas of:** Sales.

INSIDE TRACK
504 Hilltop Drive, Weatherford TX 76086. 817/599-7094. **Fax:** 817/596-0807. **Contact:** Matthew DiLorenzo, Senior Technical Recruiter. **Description:** An executive search firm. Founded in 1989. Company pays fee. **Specializes in the areas of:** Administration; Computer Science/Software; Engineering; High-Tech; Industrial; Manufacturing; Sales; Telecommunications. **Positions commonly filled include:** Computer Programmer; Design Engineer; Electrical/Electronics Engineer; General Manager; Marketing Manager; Materials Engineer; Mechanical Engineer; MIS Specialist; Operations Manager; Quality Control Supervisor; Sales Manager; Software Engineer; Systems Analyst; Telecommunications Manager. **Average salary range of placements:** More than $50,000. **Number of placements per year:** 1 - 49.

J.D. & ASSOCIATES
700 Highlander Boulevard, Suite 110, Arlington TX 76015. 817/467-7714. **Contact:** Manager. **Description:** An executive search firm that places personnel in a variety of industries.

JP & ASSOCIATES
4144 North Central Expressway, Suite 680, Dallas TX 75204. 214/827-4585. **Contact:** Manager. **Description:** An executive search firm. **Specializes in the areas of:** Computer Hardware/Software; High-Tech.

KAWA STIEWIG & EDWARDS INC. (KS&E)
12800 Hillcrest Road, Suite 232, Dallas TX 75230. 972/385-7757. **Contact:** Manager. **Description:** An executive search firm. Kawa Stiewig & Edwards Inc. also operates a temporary employment agency that places personnel in a variety of industries. **Specializes in the areas of:** Automotive.

A.T. KEARNEY EXECUTIVE SEARCH
500 North Akard, Suite 4170, Dallas TX 75201. 214/969-0010. **Contact:** Manager. **Description:** An executive search firm.

KENZER CORPORATION
3030 LBJ Freeway, Suite 1430, Dallas TX 75234. 972/620-7776. **Fax:** 972/243-7570. **Contact:** Melinda Sumurdy, Vice President. **Description:** An executive search firm operating on a retainer basis. Founded in 1973. Company pays fee. **Specializes in the areas of:** Fashion; Food; General Management; Retail; Sales. **Positions commonly filled include:** Accountant/Auditor; Branch Manager; Financial Analyst; Hotel Manager; Human Resources Specialist; Management Trainee; Manufacturer's/Wholesaler's Sales Rep.; Operations/Production Manager; Public Relations Specialist; Restaurant/Food Service Manager; Services Sales Representative. **Average salary range of placements:** More than $50,000. **Number of placements per year:** 200 - 499.

KEY PEOPLE INC.
P.O. Box 24773, Forth Worth TX 76124-1773. 817/457-6108. **Contact:** Don (Petro) Petrusaitis, President. **Description:** An executive search firm operating on a contingency basis. Company pays fee. **Specializes in the areas of:** Graphic Arts; Publishing. **Positions commonly filled include:** Administrative Manager; Blue-Collar Worker Supervisor; Buyer; Chemist; Clerical Supervisor; Computer Programmer; Customer Service Representative; Electrical/Electronics Engineer; General Manager; Human Resources Specialist; Industrial Engineer; Industrial Production Manager; Management Trainee; Mechanical Engineer; MIS Specialist; Operations/Production Manager; Quality Control Supervisor; Transportation/Traffic Specialist. **Average salary range of placements:** More than $50,000.

KORN/FERRY INTERNATIONAL
500 North Akard Street, 3232 Lincoln Plaza, Dallas TX 75201. 214/954-1834. **Contact:** Manager. **Description:** An executive search firm that places upper-level managers in a variety of industries. **International locations:** Worldwide. **Average salary range of placements:** More than $50,000.

EVIE KREISLER & ASSOCIATES
2720 Stemmons Freeway, Suite 812, Dallas TX 75207. 214/631-8994. **Contact:** Manager. **Description:** An executive search firm. **Specializes in the areas of:** Distribution; Manufacturing; Retail.

KRESSENBERG ASSOCIATES
8111 LBJ Freeway, Suite 665, Dallas TX 75251. 972/234-1491. **Contact:** Manager. **Description:** Kressenberg Associates is an executive search firm that places personnel in a wide variety of industries.

LAMALIE AMROP INTERNATIONAL
1601 Elm Street, Suite 4150, Dallas TX 75201. 214/754-0019. **Contact:** Manager. **Description:** A generalist executive search firm.

LEA RANDOLPH & ASSOCIATES
10210 North Central Expressway, Suite 216, Dallas TX 75231. 214/987-4415. **Fax:** 214/369-9548. **Contact:** Manager. **Description:** An executive search firm. **Specializes in the areas of:** Health/Medical.

LEGAL NETWORK
600 North Pearl Street, Dallas TX 75201. 214/777-6400. **Contact:** Manager. **Description:** An executive search firm. **Specializes in the areas of:** Legal.

M.H. LOGAN & ASSOCIATES
5641 Yale Boulevard, Suite 102, Dallas TX 75206. 214/706-0558. **Contact:** Manager. **Description:** An executive search firm that places most levels of professionals within the restaurant management industry. **Specializes in the areas of:** Restaurant.

LUCAS FINANCIAL STAFFING
12655 North Central Expressway, Suite 730, Dallas TX 75243. 972/490-0011. **Fax:** 972/991-4144. **Contact:** Andrea Jennings, Regional Manager. **E-mail address:** lucaslfs@aol.com. **Description:** An executive search firm operating on both retainer and contingency bases. Lucas Financial Staffing also provides some contract placements. Company pays fee. **Specializes in the areas of:** Accounting/Auditing; Finance. **Positions commonly filled include:** Accountant/Auditor; Budget Analyst; Chief Financial Officer; Controller; Credit Manager; EDP Specialist; Finance Director; Financial Analyst; Systems Analyst. **Benefits available to temporary workers:** 401(k); Medical Insurance; Paid Vacation. **Average salary range of placements:** $30,000 - $50,000. **Number of placements per year:** 200 - 499.

LUSK & ASSOCIATES PERSONNEL SERVICE INC.
P.O. Box 7500-331, Dallas TX 75209-0500. 214/528-9966. **Fax:** 214/528-2002. **Contact:** B.J. Alessio, President. **E-mail address:** dallasjob@aol.com. **Description:** An executive search firm operating on both retainer and contingency bases. Company pays fee. **Specializes in the areas of:** Accounting/Auditing; Administration; Finance; General Management; Personnel/Labor Relations; Sales; Secretarial. **Positions commonly filled include:** Accountant; Administrative Assistant; Administrative Manager; Chief Financial Officer; Controller; Customer Service Representative; Finance Director; Human Resources Manager; Marketing Manager; Marketing Specialist; Multimedia Designer; Purchasing Agent/Manager; Secretary. **Average salary range of placements:** $30,000 - $50,000. **Number of placements per year:** 1 - 49.

MH EXECUTIVE SEARCH GROUP
P.O. Box 868068, Plano TX 75086. 972/578-1511. **Contact:** Manager. **Description:** An executive search firm. **Specializes in the areas of:** Packaging.

MANAGEMENT RECRUITERS INTERNATIONAL
1660 South Stemmons, Suite 460, Lewisville TX 75067. 972/434-9612. **Contact:** Manager. **Description:** An executive search firm. **Specializes in the areas of:** Plastics; Sales. **Corporate headquarters location:** Cleveland OH. **Other U.S. locations:** Nationwide.

MANAGEMENT RECRUITERS INTERNATIONAL
4703 81st Place, Lubbock TX 79424. 806/749-2345. **Contact:** Manager. **Description:** An executive search firm. **Specializes in the areas of:** Engineering; Health/Medical; Marketing. **Corporate headquarters location:** Cleveland OH. **Other U.S. locations:** Nationwide.

MANAGEMENT RECRUITERS INTERNATIONAL
15150 Preston Road, Dallas TX 75248. 972/991-4500. **Contact:** George Buntrock, General Manager. **Description:** An executive search firm. Company pays fee. **Specializes in the areas of:** Accounting/Auditing; Administration; Computer Science/Software; Engineering; Food; General Management; Health/Medical; Paper; Retail; Technical. **Positions commonly filled include:** Ceramics Engineer; Chemical Engineer; Computer Programmer; Customer Service Representative; Electrical/Electronics Engineer; General Manager; Health Services Manager; Industrial Engineer; Industrial Production Manager; Materials Engineer; Mechanical Engineer; Metallurgical Engineer; Operations/Production Manager; Pharmacist; Physical Therapist; Purchasing Agent/Manager; Quality Control Supervisor; Registered Nurse; Software Engineer; Speech-Language Pathologist; Systems Analyst; Transportation/Traffic Specialist. **Corporate headquarters location:** Cleveland OH. **Number of placements per year:** 1 - 49.

MANAGEMENT RECRUITERS INTERNATIONAL

1009 West Randol Mill Road, Suite 209, Arlington TX 76012. 817/469-6161. **Contact:** Bob Stoessel, Manager. **Description:** An executive search firm. **Specializes in the areas of:** Accounting/Auditing; Administration; Advertising; Architecture/Construction; Banking; Communications; Computer Hardware/Software; Design; Electrical; Engineering; Finance; Food; General Management; Health/Medical; Insurance; Legal; Manufacturing; Operations Management; Personnel/Labor Relations; Procurement; Publishing; Retail; Sales; Technical; Textiles; Transportation. **Corporate headquarters location:** Cleveland OH. **Other U.S. locations:** Nationwide.

MANAGEMENT RECRUITERS OF DALLAS

13101 Preston Road, Suite 560, Dallas TX 75240. 972/788-1515. **Fax:** 972/701-8242. **Contact:** Robert S. Lineback, General Manager. **Description:** An executive search firm operating on both retainer and contingency bases. Company pays fee. **Specializes in the areas of:** Accounting/Auditing; Administration; Advertising; Architecture/Construction; Banking; Communications; Computer Hardware/Software; Design; Electrical; Engineering; Finance; Food; General Management; Health/Medical; Insurance; Legal; Manufacturing; Operations Management; Personnel/Labor Relations; Procurement; Publishing; Retail; Sales; Technical; Transportation. **Positions commonly filled include:** Accountant/Auditor; Actuary; Administrative Manager; Aerospace Engineer; Agricultural Engineer; Bank Officer/Manager; Biochemist; Biological Scientist; Biomedical Engineer; Branch Manager; Chemical Engineer; Chemist; Civil Engineer; Clinical Lab Technician; Computer Programmer; Design Engineer; Designer; Dietician/Nutritionist; EEG Technologist; EKG Technician; Electrical/Electronics Engineer; Emergency Medical Technician; Environmental Engineer; Financial Analyst; Food Scientist/Technologist; General Manager; Health Services Manager; Human Resources Specialist; Industrial Engineer; Licensed Practical Nurse; Management Analyst/Consultant; Management Trainee; Manufacturer's/Wholesaler's Sales Rep.; Mechanical Engineer; Medical Records Technician; Metallurgical Engineer; Mining Engineer; MIS Specialist; Multimedia Designer; Nuclear Engineer; Nuclear Medicine Technologist; Occupational Therapist; Operations/Production Manager; Petroleum Engineer; Pharmacist; Physical Therapist; Physician; Physicist; Purchasing Agent/Manager; Quality Control Supervisor; Radiological Technologist; Registered Nurse; Respiratory Therapist; Restaurant/Food Service Manager; Science Technologist; Securities Sales Representative; Services Sales Representative; Software Engineer; Structural Engineer; Surgical Technician; Systems Analyst; Telecommunications Manager; Transportation/Traffic Specialist; Underwriter/Assistant Underwriter. **Corporate headquarters location:** Cleveland OH. **Other U.S. locations:** Nationwide. **Average salary range of placements:** More than $50,000. **Number of placements per year:** 200 - 499.

MANAGEMENT RECRUITERS OF LBJ PARK/DALLAS

3003 LBJ Freeway, Suite 220E, Dallas TX 75234. 972/488-1133. **Fax:** 972/488-1099. **Contact:** Ray Vlasek, General Manager. **E-mail address:** mrdfw@airmail.net. **Description:** An executive search firm. Founded in 1960. Company pays fee. **Specializes in the areas of:** Engineering; Manufacturing; Software Engineering; Telecommunications. **Positions commonly filled include:** Computer Programmer; Electrical/Electronics Engineer; Mechanical Engineer; MIS Specialist; Software Engineer. **Number of placements per year:** 50 - 99.

McDUFFY-EDWARDS

3117 Medina Drive, Garland TX 75041. 972/864-1174. **Fax:** 972/864-8559. **Contact:** Tom Edwards, Partner. **E-mail address:** tom@mcduffy-edwards.com. **World Wide Web address:** http://www.mcduffy-edwards.com. **Description:** An executive search firm that also provides consulting services and seminars. Founded in 1980. Company pays fee. **Specializes in the areas of:** Computer Science/Software; Marketing; Sales; Scientific; Technical. **Positions commonly filled include:** Account Manager; Account Representative; Customer Service Representative; General Manager; Internet Services Manager; Management Analyst/Consultant; Market Research Analyst; Marketing Manager; Marketing Specialist; Operations Manager; Project Manager; Sales Engineer; Sales Executive; Sales Manager; Sales Representative; Software Engineer; Systems Analyst; Systems Manager; Telecommunications Manager; Vice President of Marketing and Sales. **Average salary range of placements:** More than $50,000. **Number of placements per year:** 50 - 99.

MEDICAL SEARCH SOLUTIONS
15905 Bent Tree Forest Circle, Suite 1065, Dallas TX 75248. 972/490-3778. **Fax:** 972/934-2246. **Contact:** Penny Peters, CPC, Medical Recruiting Specialist. **Description:** An executive search firm. Company pays fee. **Specializes in the areas of:** Health/Medical. **Positions commonly filled include:** Administrative Assistant; Administrative Manager; Assistant Manager; Clinical Lab Technician; Controller; Dietician/Nutritionist; EEG Technologist; EKG Technician; Emergency Medical Technician; Finance Director; Financial Analyst; Health Services Manager; Licensed Practical Nurse; Medical Assistant; Medical Records Technician; Nurse Practitioner; Occupational Therapist; Office Manager; Operations Manager; Pharmacist; Physical Therapist; Physician; Physician Assistant; Radiological Technologist; Recreational Therapist; Registered Nurse; Respiratory Therapist; Speech-Language Pathologist; Surgical Technician. **Average salary range of placements:** $30,000 - $50,000. **Number of placements per year:** 50 - 99.

MICHAEL JAMES & ASSOCIATES
191-A West Main Street, Lewisville TX 75057. 972/221-2400. **Contact:** Manager. **Description:** An executive search firm for the semiconductor industry. **Specializes in the areas of:** Electronics.

MOORE & MOORE ASSOCIATES
P.O. Box 797772, Dallas TX 75379. 972/248-4441. **Contact:** Manager. **Description:** An executive search firm. **Specializes in the areas of:** Medical Sales and Marketing. **Positions commonly filled include:** Sales Manager.

NOLL HUMAN RESOURCE SERVICES
5720 LBJ Freeway, Suite 610, Dallas TX 75240. 972/392-2900. **Toll-free phone:** 800/536-7600. **Fax:** 972/934-3600. **Contact:** Perry Smith, Manager. **E-mail address:** 103266.2233@compuserve.com. **World Wide Web address:** http://www.aol.nollinc.com. **Description:** An executive search firm operating on both retainer and contingency bases. Company pays fee. **Specializes in the areas of:** Logistics; Sales; Transportation. **Positions commonly filled include:** Database Manager; Environmental Engineer; Industrial Engineer; Manufacturing Engineer; Marketing Manager; MIS Specialist; Physician; Registered Nurse; Sales Engineer; Sales Executive; Sales Manager; Sales Representative; Software Engineer; Systems Analyst; Systems Manager; Telecommunications Manager; Transportation/Traffic Specialist. **Corporate headquarters location:** Omaha NE. **Average salary range of placements:** More than $50,000. **Number of placements per year:** 50 - 99.

ODELL & ASSOCIATES INC.
12700 Park Central Place, Suite 1404, Dallas TX 75251. 972/458-7900. **Fax:** 972/233-1215. **Contact:** Bob Dralle, Executive Vice President. **Description:** An executive search firm. Company pays fee. **Specializes in the areas of:** Accounting/Auditing; Data Processing; Engineering; Finance; Health/Medical; Legal. **Positions commonly filled include:** Accountant/Auditor; Actuary; Attorney; Computer Programmer; Financial Analyst; Medical Records Technician; Occupational Therapist; Registered Nurse; Respiratory Therapist; Systems Analyst. **Number of placements per year:** 100 - 199.

OPPORTUNITY UNLIMITED PERSONNEL CONSULTANTS
2720 West Mockingbird Lane, Dallas TX 75235. 214/357-9196. **Toll-free phone:** 800/969-0888. **Fax:** 214/357-0140. **Contact:** John T. Kearley, President. **E-mail address:** oui@onramp.net. **Description:** An executive search firm operating nationwide on a contingency basis. Founded in 1959. Company pays fee. **Specializes in the areas of:** Aerospace; Computer Science/Software; Data Processing; Engineering; Scientific; Technical; Telecommunications. **Positions commonly filled include:** Aerospace Engineer; Biomedical Engineer; Computer Programmer; Design Engineer; Electrical/Electronics Engineer; Mechanical Engineer; Multimedia Designer; Software Engineer; Systems Analyst; Telecommunications Manager. **Number of placements per year:** 200 - 499.

MERLE W. OWENS & ASSOCIATES
301 Commerce Street, Suite 1205, Fort Worth TX 76102. 817/335-1776. **Contact:** Manager. **Description:** A generalist executive search firm with clients in most major industries.

THE PAILIN GROUP

8500 North Stemmons Freeway, Suite 6070, LB #55, Dallas TX 75247-3832. 214/630-1703. **Fax:** 214/630-1704. **Contact:** David L. Pailin, Sr., Senior Partner. **E-mail address:** pailingrouppsc@compuserve.com. **Description:** An executive search firm operating on a retainer basis. Founded in 1989. Company pays fee. **Specializes in the areas of:** Accounting/Auditing; Administration; Advertising; Banking; Computer Science/Software; Economics; Engineering; Environmental; Finance; Food; General Management; Health/Medical; Industrial; Insurance; Legal; Manufacturing; Nonprofit; Personnel/Labor Relations; Retail; Sales; Transportation. **Positions commonly filled include:** Accountant/Auditor; Administrative Manager; Aerospace Engineer; Architect; Attorney; Bank Officer/Manager; Budget Analyst; Ceramics Engineer; Civil Engineer; Computer Programmer; Construction Contractor; Cost Estimator; Credit Manager; Customer Service Representative; Design Engineer; Environmental Engineer; Financial Analyst; General Manager; Health Services Manager; Human Service Worker; Industrial Engineer; Materials Engineer; Mechanical Engineer; Metallurgical Engineer; Mining Engineer; MIS Specialist; Nuclear Engineer; Petroleum Engineer; Pharmacist; Physician; Quality Control Supervisor; Securities Sales Representative; Services Sales Representative; Software Engineer; Statistician; Systems Analyst; Technical Writer/Editor; Telecommunications Manager. **Corporate headquarters location:** This Location. **Other U.S. locations:** Philadelphia PA. **Average salary range of placements:** More than $50,000. **Number of placements per year:** 100 - 199.

PATTERSON & ASSOCIATES

3109 Knox Street, Suite 535, Dallas TX 75205. 214/749-1935. **Contact:** Joel Patterson, President. **Description:** An executive search firm. Company pays fee. **Specializes in the areas of:** Sales. **Positions commonly filled include:** Management Trainee; Manufacturer's/Wholesaler's Sales Rep.; Sales Representative. **Number of placements per year:** 100 - 199.

PREMIER HEALTH STAFF

1905 Central Drive, Suite 200, Bedford TX 76021. 817/540-4067. **Toll-free phone:** 800/224-4488. **Fax:** 817/540-0680. **Contact:** Mike Mayeux, Vice President of Rehab Search. **E-mail address:** shiloh@onramp.net. **Description:** An executive search firm that also provides temporary and contract services. Company pays fee. **Specializes in the areas of:** Health/Medical. **Positions commonly filled include:** Physical Therapist; Speech-Language Pathologist. **Average salary range of placements:** More than $50,000. **Number of placements per year:** 50 - 99.

PROFESSIONAL EXECUTIVE RECRUITERS

1701 Gateway Boulevard, Suite 419, Richardson TX 75080. 972/235-3984. **Contact:** Manager. **Description:** An executive search firm. **Specializes in the areas of:** Construction.

PROTHERO & ASSOCIATES INC.

555 Republic Drive, Suite 200, Plano TX 75074. 972/516-4266. **Contact:** Manager. **Description:** An executive search firm.

PROVIDENT RESOURCES GROUP

13355 Noel Road, Richardson TX 75080. 972/702-7980. **Contact:** Vickie Thompson, Office Manager. **Description:** An executive search firm. Company pays fee. **Specializes in the areas of:** Construction; Real Estate. **Positions commonly filled include:** Construction Contractor; Construction Manager; Cost Estimator; Customer Service Representative; Operations/Production Manager; Purchasing Agent/Manager. **Average salary range of placements:** More than $50,000. **Number of placements per year:** 1 - 49.

QUALITY INFORMATION SERVICE (QIS)

P.O. Box 1559, Whitney TX 76692. 254/694-6319. **Fax:** 254/694-6434. **Contact:** Betty Schatz, Senior Account Manager. **Description:** Quality Information Service is an executive search firm. Company pays fee. **Specializes in the areas of:** Computer Science/Software. **Positions commonly filled include:** Computer Programmer; Database Manager; Electrical/Electronics Engineer; MIS Specialist; Software Engineer; Systems Analyst; Technical Writer/Editor. **Number of placements per year:** 50 - 99.

R&R PERSONNEL SPECIALISTS
409 South White Oak Road, Suite A, White Oak TX 75693. 903/759-4299. **Toll-free phone:** 800/575-1608. **Fax:** 903/759-4496. **Contact:** Rodney Lemons, CEO. **Description:** An executive search firm operating on both retainer and contingency bases. Founded in 1994. Company pays fee. **Specializes in the areas of:** Personnel/Labor Relations; Retail; Secretarial. **Positions commonly filled include:** Accountant/Auditor; Administrative Manager; Advertising Clerk; Agricultural Engineer; Aircraft Mechanic/Engine Specialist; Attorney; Automotive Mechanic; Blue-Collar Worker Supervisor; Branch Manager; Buyer; Claim Representative; Clerical Supervisor; Computer Programmer; Construction Contractor; Cost Estimator; Counselor; Credit Manager; Customer Service Representative; Dental Assistant/Dental Hygienist; Designer; Draftsperson; Education Administrator; EEG Technologist; EKG Technician; Electrical/Electronics Engineer; Electrician; Emergency Medical Technician; Financial Analyst; General Manager; Hotel Manager; Human Resources Specialist; Human Service Worker; Industrial Engineer; Industrial Production Manager; Insurance Agent/Broker; Licensed Practical Nurse; Management Trainee; Manufacturer's/ Wholesaler's Sales Rep.; Mechanical Engineer; Medical Records Technician; Mining Engineer; Operations/Production Manager; Paralegal; Pharmacist; Physical Therapist; Physician; Physicist; Psychologist; Public Relations Specialist; Purchasing Agent/Manager; Quality Control Supervisor; Registered Nurse; Respiratory Therapist; Restaurant/Food Service Manager; Securities Sales Representative; Services Sales Representative; Surgical Technician; Systems Analyst; Teacher/Professor; Technical Writer/Editor; Telecommunications Manager; Travel Agent; Typist/Word Processor.

RECRUITING ASSOCIATES
P.O. Box 8473, Amarillo TX 79114. 806/353-9548. **Fax:** 806/353-9540. **Contact:** Mike Rokey, CPC, Owner/Manager. **E-mail address:** mikedr@arn.net. **Description:** An executive search firm operating on a contingency basis. Founded in 1978. Company pays fee. **Specializes in the areas of:** Computer Science/Software; Engineering. **Positions commonly filled include:** Accountant/Auditor; Applications Engineer; Computer Operator; Computer Programmer; Database Manager; Design Engineer; Electrical/Electronics Engineer; Mechanical Engineer; MIS Specialist; Software Engineer; Systems Analyst; Technical Writer/Editor. **Benefits available to temporary workers:** 401(k); Medical Insurance. **Average salary range of placements:** $30,000 - $50,000. **Number of placements per year:** 1 - 49.

RICCIONE & ASSOCIATES INC.
16415 Addison Road, Suite 404, Dallas TX 75248. 972/380-6432. **Fax:** 972/407-0659. **Contact:** Nick Riccione, President. **E-mail address:** hitec@riccione.com. **World Wide Web address:** http://www.riccione.com. **Description:** An executive search firm operating on a contingency basis. The firm also provides some contract placements. Company pays fee. **Specializes in the areas of:** Computer Science/Software; Engineering; High-Tech. **Positions commonly filled include:** Computer Programmer; Electrical/Electronics Engineer; Software Engineer; Systems Analyst; Telecommunications Manager. **Average salary range of placements:** More than $50,000. **Number of placements per year:** 50 - 99.

ROMAC INTERNATIONAL
12770 Coit Road, Suite 128, Dallas TX 75251. 972/934-2111. **Contact:** Manager. **Description:** An executive search firm. **Specializes in the areas of:** Accounting/Auditing; Finance; Information Technology.

ROTH YOUNG PERSONNEL SERVICES/DALLAS
5344 Alpha Road, Dallas TX 75240. 972/233-5000. **Fax:** 972/233-8213. **Contact:** Ben Dickerson, Recruiter. **Description:** An executive search firm operating on both retainer and contingency bases. Company pays fee. **Specializes in the areas of:** Engineering; Food; General Management; Industrial; Light Industrial; Personnel/Labor Relations; Sales; Transportation. **Positions commonly filled include:** Account Manager; Account Representative; Applications Engineer; Biological Scientist; Buyer; Chemical Engineer; Chief Financial Officer; Controller; Design Engineer; Electrical/Electronics Engineer; Food Scientist/Technologist; General Manager; Human Resources Manager; Industrial Engineer; Industrial Production Manager; Manufacturing Engineer; Market Research Analyst; Marketing Manager; Mechanical Engineer; Operations Manager; Production Manager; Project Manager; Purchasing Agent/Manager; Quality Control Supervisor; Sales

Executive; Sales Manager; Sales Representative. **Corporate headquarters location:** New York NY. **Other U.S. locations:** Nationwide. **Average salary range of placements:** $30,000 - $50,000. **Number of placements per year:** 1 - 49.

ROTTMAN GROUP INC.
1425 Greenway Drive, Suite 565, Irving TX 75038. 972/518-1330. **Contact:** Manager. **Description:** An executive search firm that places professionals in the health care industry. **Specializes in the areas of:** Health/Medical.

RUSSELL REYNOLDS ASSOCIATES, INC.
2001 Ross Avenue, Suite 1900, Dallas TX 75201. 214/220-2033. **Contact:** Manager. **Description:** An executive search firm. **Specializes in the areas of:** Banking; Chemicals; Health/Medical; Technical.

SALINAS & ASSOCIATES PERSONNEL SERVICE
1700 Commerce Street, Suite 1660, Dallas TX 75201. 214/747-7878. **Fax:** 214/747-7877. **Contact:** Gerry Salinas, Owner/Recruiter. **E-mail address:** ger@flash.net. **Description:** An executive search firm operating on both retainer and contingency bases. Salinas & Associates also offers contract services and career/outplacement counseling. Company pays fee. **Specializes in the areas of:** Accounting/Auditing; Advertising; Banking; Computer Hardware/Software; Fashion; Finance; Personnel/Labor Relations; Sales. **Positions commonly filled include:** Account Manager; Account Representative; Accountant; Administrative Assistant; Administrative Manager; Advertising Account Executive; Advertising Clerk; Auditor; Bank Officer/Manager; Budget Analyst; Buyer; Chemist; Claim Representative; Controller; Counselor; Credit Manager; Customer Service Representative; Database Manager; Human Resources Manager; Market Research Analyst; Marketing Manager; Marketing Specialist; Sales Engineer; Sales Executive; Sales Manager; Secretary. **Average salary range of placements:** Less than $20,000. **Number of placements per year:** 50 - 99.

R.L. SCOTT ASSOCIATES
307 West Seventh Street, Suite 1800, Fort Worth TX 76102. 817/877-3622. **Fax:** 817/332-3947. **Contact:** Randall Scott, President. **Description:** An executive search firm operating on both retainer and contingency bases. Founded in 1988. Company pays fee. **Specializes in the areas of:** Health/Medical. **Positions commonly filled include:** Accountant/Auditor; Administrator; Chief Executive Officer; Chief Financial Officer; Controller; Counselor; Marketing Manager; Medical Records Technician; Recreational Therapist; Registered Nurse; Respiratory Therapist; Social Worker; Vice President of Finance; Vice President of Operations. **Average salary range of placements:** More than $50,000. **Number of placements per year:** 50 - 99.

SEARCH COM, INC.
12680 Hillcrest Road, Dallas TX 75230. 972/490-0300. **Contact:** Susan Abrahamson, President. **Description:** An executive search firm. Founded in 1986. Company pays fee. **Specializes in the areas of:** Advertising; Art/Design; Publishing; Sales. **Positions commonly filled include:** Designer; Editor; Market Research Analyst; Multimedia Designer; Public Relations Specialist; Technical Writer/Editor. **Average salary range of placements:** More than $50,000. **Number of placements per year:** 1 - 49.

SEARCH NETWORK INTERNATIONAL
12801 North Central Expressway, Suite 115, Dallas TX 75243. 972/980-4991. **Fax:** 972/980-8917. **Contact:** Manager. **E-mail address:** resumes@snint.com. **World Wide Web address:** http://www.snint.com. **Description:** An executive search firm operating on a contingency basis. Founded in 1976. Company pays fee. **Specializes in the areas of:** Accounting/Auditing; Computer Science/Software; Engineering; Food; Industrial; Manufacturing. **Positions commonly filled include:** Accountant/Auditor; Aerospace Engineer; Architect; Biochemist; Biomedical Engineer; Buyer; Chemical Engineer; Chemist; Civil Engineer; Computer Programmer; Cost Estimator; Design Engineer; Designer; Draftsperson; Environmental Engineer; Financial Analyst; Food Scientist/Technologist; Geologist/Geophysicist; Industrial Engineer; Industrial Production Manager; Internet Services Manager; Mathematician; Mechanical Engineer; Metallurgical Engineer; Mining Engineer; MIS Specialist; Multimedia Designer; Operations/Production

Manager; Petroleum Engineer; Public Relations Specialist; Purchasing Agent/Manager; Quality Control Supervisor; Software Engineer; Statistician; Structural Engineer; Systems Analyst; Telecommunications Manager. **Number of placements per year:** 500 - 999.

SEARCHAMERICA INC.
5908 Meadowcreek Drive, Dallas TX 75248. 972/233-3302. **Fax:** 972/233-1518. **Contact:** Harvey Weiner, President. **E-mail address:** searchamerica@aol.com. **Description:** An executive search firm focusing on the hospitality field. Industries covered include private country, city, and yacht club management, and corporate management for the hotel, restaurant, and club fields. SearchAmerica also provides consultation services to boards of directors. Founded in 1974. **Specializes in the areas of:** Consulting; General Management; Hotel/Restaurant; Personnel/Labor Relations. **Average salary range of placements:** More than $50,000. **Number of placements per year:** 50 - 99.

SELECT STAFF
8200 Nashville Avenue, Suite C109, Lubbock TX 79423. 806/794-5511. **Fax:** 806/794-5869. **Contact:** Manager. **Description:** An executive search firm operating on a contingency basis. Company pays fee. **Specializes in the areas of:** Accounting/Auditing; Administration; Food; General Management; Personnel/Labor Relations; Retail; Sales; Secretarial. **Positions commonly filled include:** Accountant/Auditor; Adjuster; Administrative Manager; Advertising Clerk; Architect; Attorney; Bank Officer/Manager; Blue-Collar Worker Supervisor; Branch Manager; Brokerage Clerk; Buyer; Chemical Engineer; Civil Engineer; Claim Representative; Clerical Supervisor; Counselor; Credit Manager; Customer Service Representative; Dental Assistant/Dental Hygienist; Draftsperson; Electrical/Electronics Engineer; Electrician; Environmental Engineer; General Manager; Health Services Manager; Hotel Manager; Human Resources Specialist; Human Service Worker; Industrial Engineer; Landscape Architect; Licensed Practical Nurse; Manufacturer's/Wholesaler's Sales Rep.; MIS Specialist; Operations/Production Manager; Paralegal; Pharmacist; Property and Real Estate Manager; Public Relations Specialist; Purchasing Agent/Manager; Quality Control Supervisor; Restaurant/Food Service Manager; Securities Sales Representative; Social Worker; Systems Analyst; Technical Writer/Editor; Telecommunications Manager; Transportation/Traffic Specialist; Underwriter/Assistant Underwriter. **Average salary range of placements:** $20,000 - $29,999. **Number of placements per year:** 500 - 999.

MARVIN L. SILCOTT & ASSOCIATES, INC.
7557 Rambler Road, Suite 1336, Dallas TX 75231. 214/369-7802. **Fax:** 214/369-7875. **Contact:** Marvin L. Silcott, President. **Description:** An executive search firm focusing on retained searches for general counsels, chief patent counsels, and other top legal positions. Founded in 1973. Company pays fee. **Specializes in the areas of:** Legal. **Positions commonly filled include:** Attorney. **Average salary range of placements:** More than $50,000. **Number of placements per year:** 50 - 99.

SNELLING PERSONNEL SERVICES
12770 Coit Road, Suite 250, Dallas TX 75251. 972/701-8080. **Contact:** Don Lummus, Owner. **Description:** An executive search firm. **Specializes in the areas of:** Accounting/Auditing; Engineering; Food; Health/Medical; Insurance; Legal; Manufacturing; Sales. **Other U.S. locations:** Nationwide. **Number of placements per year:** 200 - 499.

SNELLING PERSONNEL SERVICES
5151 Belt Line Road, Suite 365, Dallas TX 75240. 972/934-9030. **Fax:** 972/934-3639. **Contact:** Sam D. Bingham, CPC, Owner. **Description:** An executive search firm operating on a contingency basis. Company pays fee. **Specializes in the areas of:** Accounting/Auditing; Biology; Computer Science/Software; Engineering; Food; Industrial; Manufacturing; Sales; Secretarial; Technical. **Positions commonly filled include:** Accountant/Auditor; Chemical Engineer; Chemist; Computer Programmer; Credit Manager; Customer Service Representative; Electrical/Electronics Engineer; Environmental Engineer; Food Scientist/Technologist; Industrial Engineer; Industrial Production Manager; Mechanical Engineer; Metallurgical Engineer; Mining Engineer; Nuclear Engineer; Operations/Production Manager; Petroleum Engineer; Services Sales Representative; Software Engineer; Systems Analyst. **Other U.S. locations:** Nationwide. **Average salary range of placements:** $30,000 - $50,000. **Number of placements per year:** 100 - 199.

SOURCE SERVICES CORPORATION
5429 LBJ Freeway, Suite 275, Dallas TX 75240. 972/387-1600. **Contact:** Manager. **Description:** An executive search firm. Divisions at this location include Source EDP, Source Engineering, and Source Finance. **Specializes in the areas of:** Accounting/Auditing; Computer Hardware/Software; Engineering; Finance.

SPRADLEY LEGAL SEARCH
3131 McKinney Street, Suite 490, Dallas TX 75204. 214/969-5900. **Contact:** Manager. **Description:** An executive search firm. **Specializes in the areas of:** Legal.

STAFF EXTENSION INC.
13612 Midway, Suite 103, Dallas TX 75244. 972/991-4737. **Fax:** 972/991-5325. **Contact:** Jack R. Williams, President. **E-mail address:** staffing@staffext.com. **World Wide Web address:** http://www.staffext.com. **Description:** An executive search firm that also operates as a temporary agency and contract services firm. Founded in 1990. Company pays fee. **Specializes in the areas of:** Accounting/Auditing; Administration; Computer Science/Software; Engineering; Finance; General Management; Health/Medical; Manufacturing; Personnel/Labor Relations; Sales; Technical. **Number of placements per year:** 50 - 99.

R.A. STONE & ASSOCIATES
5495 Belt Line Road, Suite 153, Dallas TX 75240. 972/233-0483. **Contact:** Manager. **Description:** An executive search firm. **Specializes in the areas of:** Broadcasting; Health/Medical.

STRATEGIC OUTSOURCING CORPORATION
100 North Central Expressway, Suite 1000, Richardson TX 75080. 972/437-2220. **Fax:** 972/437-2310. **Contact:** Brandt Hamby, Recruiting Manager. **E-mail address:** 50C@why.net. **Description:** An executive search firm operating on a retainer basis. Company pays fee. **Specializes in the areas of:** Computer Science/Software; Engineering; General Management; Publishing; Sales; Technical. **Positions commonly filled include:** Branch Manager; Computer Programmer; General Manager; Software Engineer; Strategic Relations Manager; Systems Analyst. **Corporate headquarters location:** Dallas TX. **Average salary range of placements:** More than $50,000. **Number of placements per year:** 1 - 49.

TGA COMPANY
P.O. Box 331121, Fort Worth TX 76163. 817/370-0865. **Fax:** 817/292-6451. **Contact:** Tom Green, President. **Description:** An executive search firm. Company pays fee. **Specializes in the areas of:** Accounting/Auditing; Computer Science/Software; Finance; Information Systems; Technical. **Positions commonly filled include:** Accountant/Auditor; Chief Financial Officer; Controller; Credit Manager; Financial Analyst; MIS Specialist; Software Engineer; Systems Analyst. **Average salary range of placements:** More than $50,000. **Number of placements per year:** 50 - 99.

TNS PARTNERS, INC.
8140 Walnut Hill Lane, Suite 301, Dallas TX 75231. 972/991-3555. **Contact:** Manager. **Description:** A generalist executive search firm.

THE TALON GROUP
16801 Addison Road, Suite 255, Dallas TX 75248. 972/931-8223. **Fax:** 972/931-8063. **Contact:** Robert A. Piper, President. **E-mail address:** talongrp@gte.net. **Description:** An executive search firm operating on a retainer basis. Company pays fee. **Specializes in the areas of:** Construction; Housing; Manufacturing; Real Estate. **Positions commonly filled include:** Architect; Chief Financial Officer; Civil Engineer; Construction Superintendent; Controller; Cost Estimator; General Manager; Marketing Manager; MIS Specialist; Operations Manager; Production Manager; Project Manager; Purchasing Agent/Manager; Sales Manager; Vice President. **Average salary range of placements:** More than $50,000. **Number of placements per year:** 50 - 99.

TECH-NET
14785 Preston Road, Dallas TX 75240-7876. 972/934-3000. **Contact:** Chris Cole, Owner. **Description:** An executive search firm that focuses on the placement of engineers in sales

positions, particularly those positions which utilize UNIX-based design tools. Founded in 1989. Company pays fee. **Specializes in the areas of:** Computer Science/Software; Engineering; Sales; Technical. **Positions commonly filled include:** Aerospace Engineer; Design Engineer; Electrical/Electronics Engineer; Mechanical Engineer; MIS Specialist; Software Engineer; Technical Representative. **Average salary range of placements:** More than $50,000. **Number of placements per year:** 1 - 49.

TECHNICAL STAFFING SOLUTIONS

16775 Addison Road, Suite 240, Dallas TX 75248. 972/788-1771. **Fax:** 972/788-0661. **Contact:** Don Fink, Office Manager. **Description:** Technical Staffing Solutions is an executive search and contract services firm. Founded in 1989. Company pays fee. **Specializes in the areas of:** Accounting/Auditing; Chemicals; Engineering; Information Systems; Manufacturing; Oil and Gas; Technical. **Positions commonly filled include:** Accountant/Auditor; Administrative Worker/Clerk; Chemical Engineer; Chemist; Computer Programmer; Design Engineer; Electrical/Electronics Engineer; Environmental Engineer; Financial Analyst; Mechanical Engineer; Software Engineer. **Average salary range of placements:** More than $50,000. **Number of placements per year:** 100 - 199.

TOTAL PERSONNEL INC.

P.O. Box 28975, Dallas TX 75228. 214/327-1165. **Fax:** 214/328-3061. **Contact:** Sherry Phillips, President. **Description:** An executive search firm operating on both retainer and contingency bases. Company pays fee. **Specializes in the areas of:** Administration; Computer Science/Software; Data Processing. **Positions commonly filled include:** Computer Programmer; Education Administrator; Software Engineer; Systems Analyst; Teacher/Professor; Technical Writer/Editor; Telecommunications Manager. **Average salary range of placements:** More than $50,000. **Number of placements per year:** 1 - 49.

CRAIG TROTMAN & ASSOCIATES

3109 Carlisle Street, Suite 206A, Dallas TX 75204. 214/954-1919. **Contact:** Manager. **Description:** Craig Trotman & Associates is an executive search firm. **Specializes in the areas of:** Consumer Package Goods.

VICK & ASSOCIATES
RECRUITERS ONLINE NETWORK

3325 Landershire Lane, Suite 1001, Plano TX 75023-6218. 972/612-8425. **Fax:** 972/612-1924. **Contact:** Bill Vick, Owner. **World Wide Web address:** http://www.recruitersonline.com. **Description:** An executive search firm. Company pays fee. **Specializes in the areas of:** Computer Science/Software; General Management; Sales; Technical. **Positions commonly filled include:** Regional Manager; Sales Manager. **Number of placements per year:** 50 - 99.

WARD HOWELL INTERNATIONAL, INC.

7502 Greenville Avenue, Suite 500, Dallas TX 75231. 214/749-0099. **Contact:** Manager. **Description:** An executive search firm.

ROBERT WESSON & ASSOCIATES

14800 Quorum Drive, Suite 440, Dallas TX 75240. 972/239-8613. **Contact:** Bob McDermid, Partner. **Description:** An executive search firm. Company pays fee. **Specializes in the areas of:** Food; Sales. **Positions commonly filled include:** Accountant/Auditor; Architect; Human Resources Manager; Management Trainee; Purchasing Agent/Manager; Restaurant/Food Service Manager. **Number of placements per year:** 100 - 199.

WHEELER, MOORE & ELAM COMPANY

14800 Quorum Drive, Suite 200, Dallas TX 75240. 972/386-8806. **Contact:** Dr. Mark Moore, President. **Description:** An executive search firm operating on a retainer basis with clients nationwide. The company also provides career/outplacement counseling services. Founded in 1984. Company pays fee. **Specializes in the areas of:** Accounting/Auditing; Administration; Engineering; Finance; General Management; Legal; Manufacturing; Personnel/Labor Relations; Sales; Technical. **Average salary range of placements:** More than $50,000. **Number of placements per year:** 1 - 49.

WILLIAMS COMPANY
8080 North Central Expressway, Suite 100, Dallas TX 75206. 214/891-6340. **Contact:** Manager. **Description:** An executive search firm. **Specializes in the areas of:** Retail.

WITT/KIEFFER, FORD, HADELMAN & LLOYD
2 Lincoln Center, 5420 LBJ Freeway, Suite 460, Dallas TX 75240. 972/490-1370. **Contact:** Manager. **Description:** An executive search firm for upper-level professionals. **Specializes in the areas of:** Health/Medical.

THE WRIGHT GROUP
9217 Frenchman's Way, Dallas TX 75220. 214/351-1115. **Contact:** Jay J. Wright, President. **Description:** An executive search firm. Founded in 1985. Company pays fee. **Specializes in the areas of:** Advertising; Marketing. **Positions commonly filled include:** Market Research Analyst; Marketing Specialist. **Number of placements per year:** 1 - 49.

R.S. WYATT ASSOCIATES, INC.
501 Saint James Court, Southlake TX 76092. 817/421-8726. **Fax:** 817/421-1374. **Contact:** Robert S. Wyatt, Ph.D., Principal. **E-mail address:** rswassoc@aol.com. **Description:** An executive search and consulting firm operating on a retainer basis. The company provides services to the retail sector and to firms that support retail organizations. Company pays fee. **Specializes in the areas of:** Consulting; General Management; Personnel/Labor Relations; Retail. **Positions commonly filled include:** Accountant/Auditor; Branch Manager; Buyer; Computer Programmer; Credit Manager; Customer Service Representative; Design Engineer; General Manager; Human Resources Specialist; Industrial Engineer; Management Analyst/Consultant; Public Relations Specialist; Software Engineer; Systems Analyst; Transportation/Traffic Specialist. **Average salary range of placements:** More than $50,000. **Number of placements per year:** 1 - 49.

WYMAN & ASSOCIATES, INC.
P.O. Box 13253, Arlington TX 76094. 817/572-5212. **Fax:** 817/483-5550. **Contact:** David Wyman, President. **E-mail address:** wyman@arlington.net. **World Wide Web address:** http://www.1stpage.com/1/wyman. **Description:** An executive search firm operating on both retainer and contingency bases. Company pays fee. **Specializes in the areas of:** Advertising; Computer Science/Software; General Management; Health/Medical; Insurance; Personnel/Labor Relations; Restaurant; Sales. **Positions commonly filled include:** Administrative Assistant; Administrative Manager; Advertising Account Executive; Chief Financial Officer; Computer Programmer; Database Manager; Design Engineer; General Manager; Human Resources Manager; Internet Services Manager; Licensed Practical Nurse; Market Research Analyst; Marketing Specialist; Occupational Therapist; Physical Therapist; Public Relations Specialist; Purchasing Agent/Manager; Quality Control Supervisor; Registered Nurse; Sales Engineer; Sales Executive; Sales Representative; Software Engineer; Systems Analyst; Systems Manager; Telecommunications Manager; Transportation/Traffic Specialist. **Average salary range of placements:** $30,000 - $50,000. **Number of placements per year:** 1 - 49.

CONTRACT SERVICES FIRMS

ABACUS TECHNICAL SERVICE
1701 North Collins Boulevard, Richardson TX 75080. 972/644-4105. **Contact:** Manager. **Description:** A contract services firm. **Specializes in the areas of:** Technical. **Positions commonly filled include:** Computer Programmer.

ALTERNATIVE RESOURCES CORPORATION
15770 North Dallas Parkway, Suite 400, Dallas TX 75248. 972/934-0505. **Contact:** Manager. **World Wide Web address:** http://www.alrc.com. **Description:** Alternative Resources Corporation is a contract services firm.

B&M AIR & SPACE DIVISION
2925 LBJ Freeway, Suite 278, Dallas TX 75234. 972/241-8408. **Toll-free phone:** 800/745-9675. **Fax:** 972/241-4363. **Contact:** Miguel Zurita, Division Manager. **World Wide Web address:** http://www.bmanet.com. **Description:** A contract services firm. Company pays fee. **Specializes in the areas of:** Aerospace; Computer Science/Software; Engineering; Industrial; Personnel/Labor Relations; Scientific; Technical. **Positions commonly filled include:** Applications Engineer; Biochemist; Buyer; Civil Engineer; Computer Operator; Computer Programmer; Design Engineer; Draftsperson; Electrician; Environmental Engineer; Graphic Artist; Graphic Designer; Internet Services Manager; Manufacturing Engineer; Mechanical Engineer; Metallurgical Engineer; MIS Specialist; Multimedia Designer; Operations Manager; Project Manager; Purchasing Agent/Manager; Quality Control Supervisor; Software Engineer; Systems Analyst; Systems Manager; Technical Writer/Editor; Telecommunications Manager; Webmaster. **Benefits available to temporary workers:** 401(k); Medical Insurance; Paid Holidays; Paid Vacation. **Average salary range of placements:** More than $50,000. **Number of placements per year:** 1000+.

BELCAN TECHNICAL SERVICES
11482 Luna Road, Suite 100, Dallas TX 75234. 972/401-3636. **Toll-free phone:** 800/288-8418. **Fax:** 972/401-3388. **Contact:** Steven Roth, Team Leader. **E-mail address:** sroth@tech.belcan.com. **World Wide Web address:** http://www.belcan.com. **Description:** A contract services firm. Company pays fee. **Specializes in the areas of:** Administration; Engineering. **Positions commonly filled include:** Aerospace Engineer; Applications Engineer; Buyer; Chemical Engineer; Civil Engineer; Computer Animator; Computer Operator; Computer Programmer; Cost Estimator; Database Manager; Design Engineer; Designer; Draftsperson; Electrical/Electronics Engineer; Environmental Engineer; Graphic Artist; Graphic Designer; Human Resources Specialist; Industrial Engineer; Mechanical Engineer; MIS Specialist; Multimedia Designer; Project Manager; Quality Control Supervisor; Software Engineer; Structural Engineer; Systems Analyst; Systems Manager; Technical Writer/Editor; Telecommunications Manager. **Benefits available to temporary workers:** 401(k); Medical Insurance; Paid Holidays; Paid Vacation. **Average salary range of placements:** More than $50,000. **Number of placements per year:** 200 - 499.

BUTLER INTERNATIONAL
914 Royal Lane, Irving TX 76039. 817/355-9655. **Contact:** Manager. **Description:** A contract services firm. Company pays fee. **Specializes in the areas of:** Aerospace; Computer Science/Software; Engineering; Food; Industrial; Manufacturing; Personnel/Labor Relations; Technical. **Positions commonly filled include:** Aircraft Mechanic/Engine Specialist; Budget Analyst; Buyer; Chemical Engineer; Chemist; Civil Engineer; Clinical Lab Technician; Computer Programmer; Cost Estimator; Customer Service Representative; Design Engineer; Designer; Draftsperson; Editor; Electrician; Environmental Engineer; Industrial Engineer; Mechanical Engineer; MIS Specialist; Petroleum Engineer; Software Engineer; Structural Engineer; Systems Analyst; Technical Writer/Editor; Telecommunications Manager. **Benefits available to temporary workers:** Paid Holidays; Paid Vacation. **Corporate headquarters location:** Montvale NJ. **Number of placements per year:** 200 - 499.

CAREER PARTNERS
P.O. Box 167101, Irving TX 75016-7101. 972/518-0104. **Fax:** 972/518-0287. **Contact:** Cliff Taylor, Owner/Manager. **Description:** A contract services firm. **Specializes in the areas of:** Information Systems. **Positions commonly filled include:** Computer Programmer; MIS Specialist; Software Engineer; Systems Analyst; Telecommunications Manager. **Average salary range of placements:** More than $50,000. **Number of placements per year:** 50 - 99.

COMFORCE INFORMATION TECHNOLOGIES, INC.
5055 Keller Springs, Suite 550, Dallas TX 75248. 972/248-8555. **Fax:** 972/248-3181. **Contact:** Manager. **Description:** A contract services firm. **Specializes in the areas of:** Computer Science/Software.

DESIGN QUEST INC.
P.O. Box 6555, Tyler TX 75711. 903/561-6241. **Fax:** 903/534-9170. **Contact:** Louis Adams, Recruiter. **Description:** A contract services firm that provides technical engineering support to

companies. **Specializes in the areas of:** Engineering; Personnel/Labor Relations. **Positions commonly filled include:** Chemical Engineer; Civil Engineer; Design Engineer; Designer; Draftsperson; Electrical/Electronics Engineer; Industrial Engineer; Mechanical Engineer; Petroleum Engineer; Structural Engineer. **Average salary range of placements:** More than $50,000. **Number of placements per year:** 100 - 199.

EDP STAFFING SERVICES
4500 Fuller Drive, Suite 405, Irving TX 75038. 972/650-8384. **Contact:** Manager. **Description:** A contract services firm. **Specializes in the areas of:** Computer Hardware/Software; Technical.

PROVISION TECHNOLOGIES
5930 LBJ Freeway, Suite 301, Dallas TX 75240. 972/503-8500. **Toll-free fax:** 800/277-2037. **Contact:** Manager. **E-mail address:** information@provisiondallas.com. **World Wide Web address:** http://www.provisiondallas.com. **Description:** A contract services and consulting firm that also provides some permanent placements. **Specializes in the areas of:** Computer Science/Software; Information Technology.

REHABWORKS
9535 Forest Lane, Suite 114, Dallas TX 75243. 972/480-8034. **Contact:** Manager. **Description:** RehabWorks is one of two contract rehabilitation companies owned by Horizon Healthcare Corporation. Together, Community Rehabilitation Center and RehabWorks provide occupational, speech, and physical therapy services to patients in nursing homes and geriatric units at hospitals through 276 contracts, covering approximately 31,000 beds. **Specializes in the areas of:** Health/Medical.

TAD TECHNICAL SERVICES
4160 SW H.K. Dodgen Loop, Temple TX 76504. 254/773-3366. **Fax:** 254/773-4555. **Contact:** Branch Manager. **Description:** A contract services firm. **Specializes in the areas of:** Accounting/Auditing; Computer Science/Software; Engineering; Health/Medical; Industrial; Manufacturing; Personnel/Labor Relations; Secretarial. **Positions commonly filled include:** Accountant/Auditor; Aerospace Engineer; Architect; Blue-Collar Worker Supervisor; Budget Analyst; Chemical Engineer; Chemist; Civil Engineer; Clerical Supervisor; Clinical Lab Technician; Computer Programmer; Customer Service Representative; Design Engineer; Designer; Draftsperson; Editor; Electrical/Electronics Engineer; Electrician; Environmental Engineer; Financial Analyst; Human Resources Specialist; Industrial Engineer; Industrial Production Manager; Internet Services Manager; Licensed Practical Nurse; Manufacturer's/Wholesaler's Sales Rep.; Market Research Analyst; Mathematician; Mechanical Engineer; Medical Records Technician; Metallurgical Engineer; MIS Specialist; Multimedia Designer; Occupational Therapist; Operations/Production Manager; Public Relations Specialist; Purchasing Agent/Manager; Quality Control Supervisor; Registered Nurse; Services Sales Representative; Software Engineer; Structural Engineer; Systems Analyst; Technical Writer/Editor; Telecommunications Manager. **Benefits available to temporary workers:** 401(k); Medical Insurance; Paid Holidays. **Other U.S. locations:** Nationwide. **Average salary range of placements:** $20,000 - $29,999. **Number of placements per year:** 200 - 499.

TAD TECHNICAL SERVICES
901 North McDonald Street, Suite 405, McKinney TX 75069. 972/542-6175. **Fax:** 972/758-2116. **Contact:** K. Carter, Recruiter. **E-mail address:** clawson1@airmail.net. **World Wide Web address:** http://www.webz.airmail.net/tadtech1. **Description:** A contract services firm. **Specializes in the areas of:** Accounting/Auditing; Administration; Art/Design; Computer Science/Software; Engineering; General Management; Industrial; Light Industrial; Sales; Secretarial; Technical. **Positions commonly filled include:** Administrative Assistant; Applications Engineer; Blue-Collar Worker Supervisor; Chemical Engineer; Civil Engineer; Clerical Supervisor; Computer Operator; Computer Programmer; Cost Estimator; Counselor; Customer Service Representative; Database Manager; Design Engineer; Draftsperson; Economist; Electrical/Electronics Engineer; Environmental Engineer; Finance Director; Financial Analyst; Human Resources Manager; Industrial Engineer; Industrial Production Manager; Manufacturing Engineer; Mechanical Engineer; Medical Records Technician; MIS Specialist; Production Manager; Project Manager;

Purchasing Agent/Manager; Quality Control Supervisor; Sales Engineer; Sales Executive; Sales Manager; Sales Representative; Secretary; Software Engineer; Systems Analyst; Technical Writer/Editor; Typist/Word Processor. **Benefits available to temporary workers:** 401(k); Dental Insurance; Medical Insurance; Paid Holidays; Paid Vacation; Vision Insurance. **International locations:** Canada; England. **Average salary range of placements:** More than $50,000. **Number of placements per year:** 1000+.

TAD TECHNICAL SERVICES
4300 Alpha Road, Suite 100, Dallas TX 75244. 972/980-0510. **Contact:** Manager. **Description:** A contract services firm. **Specializes in the areas of:** Administration; Aerospace; Clerical; Computer Hardware/Software; Engineering; Manufacturing; Technical. **International locations:** Canada; England.

TECHNICAL CAREERS
12750 Merit Drive, Suite 1430, Dallas TX 75251. 972/991-9424. **Fax:** 972/851-0651. **Contact:** Cary Tobolka, President. **E-mail address:** rng@connect.net. **World Wide Web address:** http://www.technicalcareers.com. **Description:** A contract services firm operating on both retainer and contingency bases. Founded in 1978. **Specializes in the areas of:** Computer Science/Software; Engineering; Industrial; Manufacturing; Personnel/Labor Relations; Technical. **Positions commonly filled include:** Aerospace Engineer; Agricultural Engineer; Chemical Engineer; Civil Engineer; Computer Programmer; Design Engineer; Designer; Electrical/Electronics Engineer; Environmental Engineer; Human Resources Specialist; Industrial Engineer; Industrial Production Manager; Internet Services Manager; Management Analyst/Consultant; Manufacturer's/ Wholesaler's Sales Rep.; Mechanical Engineer; Metallurgical Engineer; MIS Specialist; Multimedia Designer; Nuclear Engineer; Purchasing Agent/Manager; Quality Control Supervisor; Science Technologist; Software Engineer; Structural Engineer; Systems Analyst; Telecommunications Manager. **Benefits available to temporary workers:** Dental Insurance; Life Insurance; Medical Insurance; Retirement Plan. **Corporate headquarters location:** This Location. **Other area locations:** 15851 Dallas Parkway, Suite 960, Dallas TX 75248. **Other U.S. locations:** San Diego CA; Addison TX. **Average salary range of placements:** More than $50,000. **Number of placements per year:** 100 - 199.

TECHNICAL CAREERS
15851 Dallas Parkway, Suite 960, Dallas TX 75248. 972/789-5313. **Contact:** Manager. **World Wide Web address:** http://www.technicalcareers.com. **Description:** A contract services firm. Founded in 1978. **Corporate headquarters location:** 12750 Merit Drive, Suite 1430, Dallas TX 75251.

VOLT TECHNICAL SERVICES
275 West Campbell Road, Suite 211, Richardson TX 75080. 972/669-0458. **Toll-free phone:** 800/531-7426. **Fax:** 972/669-9749. **Contact:** Katherine Lockwood, Regional Manager. **E-mail address:** lockwood@gte.net. **Description:** Volt Technical Services is a contract services firm. **Specializes in the areas of:** Computer Science/Software; Engineering; Technical. **Positions commonly filled include:** Administrative Manager; Aerospace Engineer; Aircraft Mechanic/Engine Specialist; Biochemist; Biomedical Engineer; Budget Analyst; Buyer; Chemical Engineer; Chemist; Civil Engineer; Computer Programmer; Design Engineer; Designer; Draftsperson; Electrical/Electronics Engineer; Electrician; Environmental Engineer; Human Resources Specialist; Industrial Engineer; Industrial Production Manager; Software Engineer; Statistician; Strategic Relations Manager; Systems Analyst; Technical Writer/Editor; Telecommunications Manager. **Average salary range of placements:** $30,000 - $50,000. **Number of placements per year:** 500 - 999.

H.L. YOH COMPANY
13601 Preston Road, Suite 1020E, Dallas TX 75240. 972/239-9875. **Contact:** Manager. **Description:** A contract services firm. **Specializes in the areas of:** Architecture/Construction; Computer Hardware/Software; Engineering; Manufacturing; Technical. **Other U.S. locations:** Nationwide.

RESUME/CAREER COUNSELING SERVICES

ALLEN & ASSOCIATES
4099 McEwen, Suite 150, Dallas TX 75244. 972/385-7112. **Toll-free phone:** 800/562-7214. **Fax:** 972/788-2131. **Contact:** Manager. **World Wide Web address:** http://www. allenandassociates.com. **Description:** A career/outplacement counseling firm. **Corporate headquarters location:** Maitland FL. **Other U.S. locations:** Nationwide.

FAIRCHILD BARKLEY & ASSOCIATES
15770 Dallas Parkway, Dallas TX 75248. 972/387-4800. **Fax:** 972/386-5210. **Contact:** R.J. Porter, President. **Description:** A career/outplacement counseling service. Company pays fee. **Positions commonly filled include:** Accountant/Auditor; Administrative Manager; Aerospace Engineer; Agricultural Engineer; Architect; Bank Officer/Manager; Biochemist; Biomedical Engineer; Branch Manager; Budget Analyst; Chemical Engineer; Civil Engineer; Claim Representative; Clerical Supervisor; Computer Programmer; Cost Estimator; Credit Manager; Customer Service Representative; Design Engineer; Economist; Environmental Engineer; Industrial Engineer; Management Analyst/Consultant; MIS Specialist; Operations/Production Manager; Petroleum Engineer; Public Relations Specialist; Restaurant/Food Service Manager; Services Sales Representative; Structural Engineer; Systems Analyst; Telecommunications Manager. **Average salary range of placements:** More than $50,000. **Number of placements per year:** 100 - 199.

INDEX OF PRIMARY EMPLOYERS

NOTE: *Below is an alphabetical index of primary employer listings included in this book. Those employers in each industry that fall under the headings "Additional employers" are not indexed here.*

X, Y, Z

Your Job Hunt
Your Feedback

Comments, questions, or suggestions? We want to hear from you. Please complete this questionnaire and mail it to:

The JobBank Staff
Adams Media Corporation
260 Center Street
Holbrook, MA 02343

Did this book provide helpful advice and valuable information which you used in your job search? Was the information easy to access?

Recommendations for improvements. How could we improve this book to help in your job search? No suggestion is too small or too large.

Would you recommend this book to a friend beginning a job hunt?

Name: _____

Occupation: _____

Which JobBank did you use? _____

Address: _____

Daytime phone: _____

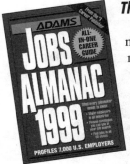

From the publishers of the Jobbank & Knock'em Dead Books

Visit our Web Site:
www.careercity.com

...free access to tens of thousands of current job openings plus the most comprehensive career info on the web today!

- Current job listings at top employers in all professions
- Descriptions and hot links to 27,000 major US employers
- Free resume posting gets noticed by top hiring companies
- Access to thousands of executive search firms and agencies
- Comprehensive salary surveys cover all fields
- Directories of associations and other industry resources
- Hundreds of articles on getting started, changing careers, job interviews, resumes, cover letters and more

CareerCity®
CUTTING EDGE CAREERS

www.careercity.com